DEVELOPMENTAL NEUROPSYCHOLOGY

Brain Damage, Behaviour and Cognition:
Developments in Clinical Neuropsychology
Titles in series

Developmental neuropsychology

A clinical approach

Vicki Anderson
*University of Melbourne and Royal Children's Hospital,
Melbourne, Australia*

Elisabeth Northam
Royal Children's Hospital, Melbourne, Australia

Julie Hendy
CBT Clinical Psychology Centre, Sydney, Australia

Jacquie Wrennall
Royal Children's Hospital, Melbourne, Australia

First published 2001 by Psychology Press Ltd
27 Church Road, Hove, East Sussex, BN3 2FA

www.psypress.co.uk

Simultaneously published in the USA and Canada
by Taylor & Francis Inc
325 Chestnut Street, Suite 800, Philadelphia, PA 19106

Psychology Press is part of the Taylor & Francis Group

British Library Cataloguing in Publication Data
A catalogue record for this book is available from the British Library

Library of Congress Cataloging-in-Publication Data
Developmental neuropsychology : a clinical approach / Vicki Anderson . . . [et al.].
    p. ; cm.—(Brain damage, behaviour, and cognition series, ISSN 0967-9944)
    Includes bibliographical references and index.
    ISBN 0-86377-704-X
    1. Pediatric neuropsychology. 2. Developmental disabilities. 3. Brain—
Diseases. I. Anderson, Vicki, 1958– II. Brain damage, behaviour, and cognition.
    [DNLM: 1. Brain Diseases—Child. 2. Brain Diseases—Infant. 3. Central
Nervous System—embryology. 4. Central Nervous System—growth &
development. 5. Mental Processes—Child. 6. Mental Processes—Infant.
7. Neuropsychology—Child. 8. Neuropsychology—Infant. WS 340 D489 2001]
    RJ486.5 .D48   2001
    618.92′8—dc21

                                                                    00–042547

ISBN 0-86377-704-X (Hb)
ISBN 0-86377-705-8 (Pb)

ISSN 0967-9944

Cover design by Joyce Chester
Typeset in Times by RefineCatch Limited, Bungay, Suffolk
Printed and bound in the UK by Biddles Ltd, www.biddles.co.uk

Contents

Series preface

From being an area primarily on the periphery of mainstream behavioural and cognitive science, neuropsychology has developed in recent years into an area of central concern for a range of disciplines. We are witnessing not only a revolution in the way in which brain–behaviour–cognition relationships are viewed, but a widening of interest concerning developments in neuro-psychology on the part of a range of workers in a variety of fields. Major advances in brain-imaging techniques and the cognitive modelling of the impairments following brain damage promise a wider understanding of the nature of the representation of cognition and behaviour in the damaged and undamaged brain.

Neuropsychology is now centrally important for those working with brain-damaged people, but the very rate of expansion in the area makes it difficult to keep up with findings from current research. The aim of the *Brain Damage, Behaviour and Cognition* series is to publish a wide range of books that present comprehensive and up-to-date overviews of current developments in specific areas of interest.

These books will be of particular interest to those working with the brain-damaged. It is the editors' intention that undergraduates, postgradu-ates, clinicians and researchers in psychology, speech pathology, and medi-cine will find this series a useful source of information on important current developments. The authors and editors of the books in this series are experts in their respective fields, working at the forefront of contemporary research. They have produced texts that are accessible and scholarly. We thank them for their contribution and their hard work in fulfilling the aims of the series.

CC and GH
Exeter and Birmingham, UK
Series Editors

Preface

The emergence of child neuropsychology as an identifiable sub-specialty of neuropsychology dates back almost 20 years and may be attributed, in large part, to the first theoretical conceptualisations of the brain–behaviour relationship within the developing brain. Prior to that time, research and clinical practice with children suffering from central nervous system (CNS) disorders was conducted within an adult neuropsychology paradigm, with methodological approaches and theoretical interpretations limited by these models, and with little understanding of the unique contribution of the developing brain to both the nature and outcome of CNS disorders.

With increasing knowledge of the process of CNS maturation, and the introduction of a small number of specifically "developmental" theories (e.g., Source's non-verbal learning disability syndrome, Dennis's critical period model), the relative complexities of the field of child neuropsychology have begun to be appreciated. Today clinicians and researchers acknowledge that it is inappropriate to interpret children's abilities on the basis of adult models alone. Rather, the state of CNS development, level of cognitive ability, and psychosocial context of the child must each be considered and integrated to gain an understanding of a child's neuropsychological profile and likely recovery and outcome. For children, the pattern of neurological and cognitive impairment may not be stable, but rather vulnerable to the influences of recovery, ongoing development, and the emergence of new skills. Some skills may be delayed, others deficient, or abnormal. This picture of change and variability provides significant challenges for the neuropsychologist working within a developmental context.

Although current developmental models have broadened the focus of child neuropsychology, none has incorporated all aspects of importance: nature and severity of insult, age (developmental stage) at insult, time since insult, and social context. The challenge for the future is to develop such theories, which, of necessity, require longitudinal studies of the natural history of various forms of childhood brain damage and dysfunction. To this end, such research is being conducted for a number of diseases and disorders common to childhood, including traumatic brain injury, epilepsy, cerebral infections and tumours, and various toxicities. These studies are likely to confirm that some of the tenets of adult neuropsychology are also true for child populations. For example, it is already established that, as for adults, children sustaining more severe CNS insult suffer greater neuropsychological impairment, but that with time from insult recovery can be documented. The more complex issues related to the impact of developmental stage, both neurological and cognitive, the effect of injury and insult on ongoing developmental processes, and the role of the environment remain unclear.

Although there has been an escalation in research and theory development, advances in the practice of child neuropsychology have been more difficult to achieve, both in research and clinical contexts. At the most basic level, the tools available have been limited, and often inappropriate. Most assessment procedures have been designed for use with adult populations primarily, and are not particularly attractive or motivating for children. Normative data, when available, is frequently poorly constructed and based on small samples, making detection of deviant performances unreliable. Additionally, there are few tests available which span a wide age band, resulting in the need to administer different measures with different age groups, further limiting the reliability of comparisons of ability profiles over time. The limitations of the tools employed, in combination with the relatively immature state of knowledge in the field, make diagnosis and prediction of outcome problematic. With increasing interest and enthusiasm in the field, these deficiencies are being acknowledged. New tests, developed specifically for children and reflecting age-appropriate themes and content, are gradually emerging. Many of these tests reflect a combination of traditional adult neuropsychology techniques and theoretical perspectives as well as an understanding of cognitive-developmental issues.

The purpose of this book is to address some of the core issues in child neuropsychology, with particular relevance for clinical practice. In order to do this we have chosen to focus on a number of areas. First, we are interested in the natural history of childhood CNS insult, and thus will concentrate our discussions to some extent on studies (research and single case) where children have been followed over time, to determine the impact of injury on ongoing development. It is our premise that, for the young child, whose daily activities focus around learning and developing new cognitive and social skills, the effects of CNS insult may be particularly detrimental, reducing his or her capacity to acquire and consolidate knowledge.

Second, the issue of brain plasticity and the impact of early CNS insult is a common theme throughout each chapter, with the aim being to provide a better understanding of the development of the CNS, its relative flexibility, and the conditions where cerebral plasticity may and may not occur. In addition, we will discuss the process of normal maturation, both neurological and cognitive, and offer a model of assessment for evaluating the functional correlates of development. It will be argued that a clear understanding of the normal process of development is required, if one is to be able to interpret the impact of any interruption to the process.

Finally, we aim to address the complex interactions of these biological and cognitive processes with the child's environment. The child suffering from brain dysfunction is heavily reliant on his or her psychosocial context to recover and mature, and there is increasing evidence that, over time, the relative importance of the quality of the psychosocial context outweighs that of the initial biological insult. Our model of child neuropsychology is founded on the belief that good practice requires not simply the collection of test data and observations, but the interpretation of this data in the context of age, developmental stage, injury/insult severity, and psychosocial context. On the basis of such multidimensional information realistic interventions, appropriately tailored to the child's neuropsychological profile and psychosocial environment, can be developed and implemented to achieve optimal outcome.

We hope to illustrate our clinical approach with reference to research and clinical data from several CNS disorders of childhood. We have opted not to provide an exhaustive review of developmental and acquired CNS diseases. Rather, we have chosen to focus on a small number of acquired and developmental CNS disorders common to childhood, each of which represents differing mechanisms of insult, including structural abnormality, trauma, infection, and metabolic dysfunction. We aim to provide readers with an understanding of the neurological and neuropsychological characteristics associated with each of these conditions. Further, we will reflect upon the consequences common to all disorders, which may reflect the "timing" or developmental aspects of the disorder primarily, and contrast those to the more "disorder-specific" features which reflect the organic nature and mechanisms associated with each disorder. Each condition will be illustrated with case examples to emphasise the interaction of multiple influences on the child's ultimate outcome, and the interventions possible.

As illustrated in Figure P.1 and in keeping with adult models, we suggest that any significant CNS insult or dysfunction will impact in at least three

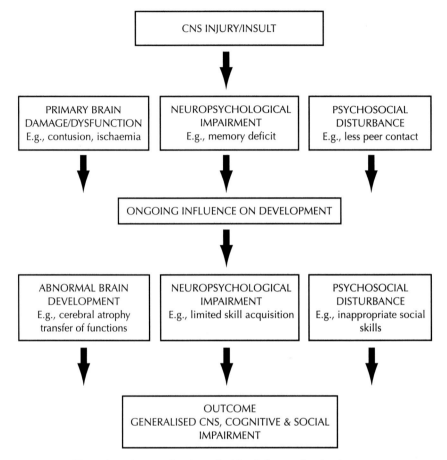

Figure P.1.   Impact of early cerebral insult for ongoing development.

domains—the biological, the neurobehavioural, and the psychosocial—resulting in initial changes to the CNS, as well as to the child's neurobehavioural abilities and social environment. Initial CNS insult may result in disruptions to cerebral circulation, changes in intracranial pressure, loss of tissue, or epilepsy. Such CNS damage will then be associated with neurobehavioural deficits including motor impairment, language deficits, attentional problems, and memory dysfunction. Behavioural and social difficulties commonly follow, due to the direct effects of CNS pathology, and as a secondary consequence. Over time, and in the context of ongoing development, cumulative problems may emerge. For instance, within the CNS, insult may lead to an interruption or deviation to the normal developmental process. Transfer of cognitive functions may occur within the brain, causing "crowding effects" within healthy brain tissue, resulting in aberrant functional localisation or impaired levels of cognitive ability. At the same time, psychosocial function may become increasingly problematic, due to failure of the child to acquire appropriate social skills, increasing social isolation, and associated family stresses. The long-term consequences of these multiple and interacting factors may result in a picture of global dys-function. However, appropriate and timely intervention and follow-up, based on knowledge of the disorder, its symptomatology, and likely outcome, may prevent such poor prognosis and enable the child and family to understand and manage these problems successfully.

Acknowledgements

This text reflects the nature and scope of neuropsychology practice, both clinical and experimental, within the Department of Psychology at the Royal Children's Hospital, Melbourne, and the New Children's Hospital, Sydney, Australia, which has now been translated to other contexts within Australia. Our model of child neuropsychology relies on close links with both neurosciences and mental health within the paediatric context, and the influence of these dual perspectives is emphasised in our approach to understanding and treating children with central nervous system disorders. It was the vision of Dr Patricia Leaper that identified a need for child neuropsychology services, and her support has facilitated ongoing expansion and development of the discipline, both within our hospitals and in the wider community.

A large team of clinicians, researchers, and students have contributed to our endeavours over the past 10 years, assessing and caring for children and families, conducting research programmes, contributing ideas and discussion, liaising with hospital and community workers, and increasing the profile and recognition of child neuropsychology. In particular, we would like to note our appreciation for the ongoing contributions of our creative and productive team of research staff and students over the last decade: Cathy Catroppa, Tim Godber, Peter Anderson, Rani Jacobs, Matthew Hughes, Linda Pentland, Genevieve Lajoie, Flora Haritou, and Dianne Anderson, and our colleagues and collaborators within our hospitals whose enthusiasm and respect have continually enriched our efforts: Simon Harvey, Geoffrey Klug, Jeff

Rosenfeld, Robyn Stargatt, Bob Adler, Sue Morse, George Werther, Gary Warne, Carolyn West, Margot Prior, and Terry Nolan.

For the opportunity to develop and conduct research to help us better understand the needs of children with brain disorders, we recognise the generous support of the Royal Children's Hospital Research Institute, which has funded a great deal of the research that we will describe in the coming pages.

Central to the development and formulation of our ideas and philosophy of child neuropsychology are the children and families who have contributed to our understanding of the impact of brain disease on child development. We appreciate their optimism and persistence, and acknowledge the burden that such illness places on child and family.

The authors and publishers would like to thank all the copyright holders of material reproduced in this volume for granting permission to include it. Every effort has been made to contact authors and copyright holders, but if proper acknowledgement has not been made, the copyright holder should contact the publishers.

Finally, we acknowledge the support and patience of our own families, who have "endured" this project with us, and provided ongoing encouragement and distraction!

Vicki Anderson
Elisabeth Northam
Julie Hendy
Jacquie Wrennall

PART ONE

Defining the neurodevelopmental context

CHAPTER ONE

Child neuropsychology: Dimensions of theory and practice

INTRODUCTION

Child neuropsychology is the study of brain–behaviour relationships, within the dynamic context of a developing brain. The central focus for the field is the understanding that, for childhood brain insult, the pathology occurs within a rapidly evolving system, and may result in alteration of the normal developmental process, both at a neurological and a cognitive level. Researchers and clinicians agree that this continually changing tapestry has both advantages and disadvantages for the child sustaining central nervous system (CNS) insult. On the one hand, the young brain may be more flexible and capable of transferring functions from damaged to undamaged tissue, resulting in minimal loss of function (Lenneberg, 1967; Teuber, 1962). Alternatively, the young damaged brain may be less able to support efficient attention, memory, and learning skills necessary for the acquisition of new knowledge. As a result, there may be an ever increasing gap between the child with CNS impairment and his or her age-matched peers (V. Anderson, 1988; V. Anderson & Moore, 1995; Dennis, 1989; Ewing-Cobbs, Miner, Fletcher, & Levin, 1989; St James-Roberts, 1979; Taylor & Alden, 1997; Wrightson, McGinn, & Gronwall, 1995).

This chapter aims to explore the domain of child neuropsychology, taking a developmental approach, and describing a field where simple assessment and diagnosis of brain dysfunction are insufficient. We will argue that, to fully understand the long-term consequences of brain dysfunction in children, it is necessary to address the "totality" of the child—the physical, cognitive, and psychosocial experiences that interact to influence recovery and development. Further, the importance of viewing children as more than just "little adults" will be canvassed, with emphasis on the dynamic path of maturation and development and the potential for disruption to this process. Finally, we will review a number of influential theoretical perspectives that have emerged in the last decade of the 20th century, and evaluate their contributions and current standing.

DIMENSIONS OF CHILD NEUROPSYCHOLOGY

Child neuropsychology takes its foundations largely from adult neuro-psychological models, utilising pre-existing understanding of cerebral localisation and integrated brain systems, to develop an appreciation of the functioning of the young brain. Although such adult models form the basis of our knowledge of neurological disorders in children, they relate to a more "static", mature system, and are unable to easily accommodate the dynamic nature of early cerebral pathology. It is well established that such perspectives are insufficient to understand the complex neurological, cognitive, and psychosocial consequences of cerebral insult for the child (Dennis & Barnes, 1994b; Fletcher & Taylor, 1984; Holmes-Bernstein & Waber, 1990; Rourke, Bakker, Fisk, & Strang, 1983; Taylor & Fletcher, 1990; Taylor & Schatsneider, 1992).

In an attempt to extend these adult-based models, child neuropsychologists have drawn from a range of associated fields to establish a knowledge base from which to understand the unique consequences of early CNS dysfunction. In particular, developmental neurology and cognitive psychology are crucial elements for mapping the expected changes that occur within the CNS throughout infancy and childhood, until the brain reaches relative stability and maturity during adolescence. Of specific relevance are recent research findings that support parallels between growth spurts within the CNS and increments in cognitive abilities (Anderson, 1998; Hudspeth & Pribram, 1990; Huttenlocher, 1990; Johnson, 1997; Levin et al., 1991; Luciana & Nelson, 1998; Thatcher, 1991, 1997; Welsh & Pennington, 1988; Yakovlev & Lecours, 1967). Although not surprising, these convergent findings support the close relationship between brain and behaviour. Such knowledge is especially important where the normal developmental process is disrupted by insult or injury, as it provides a template for gauging the impact of this interruption, both neurological and cognitive, not just at the time of insult, but in the longer-term post-insult. The likelihood that ongoing development may be influenced by a cerebral insult in childhood is not novel or unreasonable, and it is the challenge of the child neuropsychologist to grapple with the interactions among organic, cognitive, social, and developmental factors to reach an understanding of how these factors effect the child, and lead to observed outcomes.

The "neuro" dimension

The CNS can be identified quite early in gestation, with development ongoing through infancy and childhood. In the prenatal period development is largely concerned with structural formation, establishing the basic "hardware" of the CNS. Interruptions to CNS development during this period have been shown to result primarily in structural abnormalities (e.g., dysplasias, spina bifida, Dandy–Walker syndrome, agenesis of the corpus callosum). In contrast, postnatal development is largely directed towards elaboration of the CNS, establishing the connectivity vital for the system. This process of elaboration continues into early adolescence, and includes dendritic arborisation and myelination as well as biochemical changes, with the greatest maturation evident in anterior cerebral areas. It is generally thought that development occurs in a hierarchical manner, with anterior regions the last to reach maturity, in early puberty. Further, although some controversy remains (Lidow & Goldman-Rakic, 1991; Rakic et al., 1986), there is substantial support for a stepwise model of development, rather than a gradual progression, with convergent evidence that growth spurts occur in early infancy, again around age 7–10 years of age, with a final spurt during early adolescence (Fuster, 1993; Jernigan & Tallal, 1990; Klinberg et al., 1999; Kolb & Fantie, 1989; Risser & Edgell, 1988; Sowell & Jernigan, 1998; Stuss, 1992; Thatcher, 1991, 1992, 1997; Yakovlev & Lecours, 1967). A number of influences can impact on these developmental processes, including direct CNS injury or insult, infection or a variety of environmental factors such as malnutrition, severe sensory deprivation, or environmental toxins (e.g., lead, radiation).

There is growing evidence that disruption to early CNS development may have irreversible consequences. As is true for adults, the nature and severity of cerebral insult are of primary importance in determining outcome from CNS insult in childhood. Certainly, paediatric research consistently supports the dose–response relationships documented in adult populations, with more severe cerebral pathology leading to greater neuropsychological impairment (Ewing-Cobbs et al., 1989; Fay et al., 1993; Grimwood et al., 1995; Smibert, Anderson, Godber, & Ekert, 1996; Taylor et al., 1990). However, in contrast to the often localised cerebral pathologies of adulthood, CNS disorders acquired during childhood are more likely to be of a generalised nature, impacting on the brain as a whole (e.g., traumatic brain injury, hydrocephalus, cerebral infection, metabolic disorder). Focal disorders such as tumour or stroke are relatively rare. As a result, specific impairments such as aphasias and apraxias are less common in children, with generalised disturbances of information processing (attention, memory, psychomotor skills) and executive function more frequently reported (Dennis, 1989; Eslinger, Biddle, Pennington, & Page, 1999; Garth, Anderson, & Wrennall, 1997; Satz & Bullard-Bates, 1981).

Further discrepancies between adult and child CNS disorders are noted with respect to recovery profiles. Paediatric research indicates that, whereas acute recovery from cerebral insult may be similar irrespective of age, long-term recovery patterns differ, in favour of the more mature brain (V. Anderson, Morse, et al., 1997; Anderson & Moore, 1995; Ewing-Cobbs et al., 1989). Plasticity theorists (Kennard, 1936; Lenneberg, 1967; Rasmussen & Milner, 1977) have argued strongly that damage to the immature brain yields less significant disability than equivalent insults in adults; however, recent research indicates that such theories may have been excessively optimistic, with the true picture more likely to be one of increased "vulnerability". Certainly current conceptualisations of neural recovery suggest little advantage for the immature CNS (Duchowny et al., 1998; Finger & Stein, 1982; Johnson, 1997; Kolb & Gibb, 1999). In addition, the traditional notion of transfer of function, which argues that cognitive functions subsumed by damaged brain tissue have the capacity to transfer to healthy tissue with minimal functional implications, is also under debate. At best, the mechanisms associated with such transfer of function are likely to be far more complicated than previously thought, varying with respect to both timing (i.e., pre-, postnatal) and nature (i.e., focal, generalised) of insult (Anderson, 1988, 1997b; Duchowny et al., 1996; Mogford & Bishop, 1993; Woods, 1980). Recent research, employing structural imaging and cortical mapping techniques, indicates that prenatal CNS injury may not result in functional transfer, but that skills may be maintained ineffectually in damaged tissue, leading to developmental delays (Duchowny et al., 1996; Leventer et al., 1999). Even postnatally where transfer has been shown to take place (e.g., hemispherectomies, strokes), outcome remains less than optimal, with indications that "crowding" of skills occurs, leading to a generalised depression of neuropsychological functions (Aram, 1988; Dennis, 1980; Milner, 1967; Mogford & Bishop, 1993; Woods, 1980).

The developmental stage and nature of insult are of primary importance in young children, and the complex interactions between these variables are still to be researched. A further issue for consideration is the possible effect that cerebral insult may have on the process of ongoing development. For example, in children sustaining severe traumatic brain injury, serial computed tomography (CT) scans have detected increasing cerebral atrophy with time (Anderson & Pentland, 1998; Kolb, 1995; Stein & Spettell, 1995). Children contracting meningitis or suffering from febrile convulsions have been noted to develop hippocampal sclerosis leading to epilepsy (Ounstead, Lindsey, & Norman, 1966). Similarly, studies of children treated with cranial irradiation for cerebral tumour or leukaemia document development of delayed cerebral pathology, specifically cerebral calcifications and other white matter pathology (Matsumoto et al., 1995; Paakko et al., 1992). Such findings suggest that childhood CNS insult may not be static, but may interrupt ongoing maturation in a variety of ways detrimental to long-term outcome.

Many of the advances in neurological and neuropsychological theories of development may be linked to advances in electrophysiological and radiological techniques. Today, researchers can image increases in myelination during childhood using magnetic resonance imaging (MRI) techniques, providing evidence of both the rate and localisation of development over time (Giedd et al., 1996; Klinberg et al., 1999). Functional imaging methods, such as cerebral blood flow studies, single-photon emission tomography (SPECT), or positron emission tomography (PET), enable researchers to map cerebral activation in quite young children, thus directly describing brain correlates of specific behaviours. Possible function transfers can be investigated using non-invasive measures such as functional magnetic resonance imaging (fMRI) as opposed to the more invasive procedures used in the past, such as sodium amytal ablation and cortical mapping. Figure 1.1 provides examples of such techniques including MRI, SPECT, and fMRI data for a 9-year-old child with a tumour in the left frontal cortex, in the region corresponding to Broca's area (D. Anderson et al., 2000). This young girl presented with intractable partial seizures characterised by speech arrest, and deteriorating language function. The structural characteristics of the tumour are clearly illustrated using MRI (a). In the second image (b), ictal SPECT images demonstrate hyperperfusion in the location of the tumour during seizure activity. The final image (c) represents results from an fMRI study showing cerebral activation occurring during a language generation task. Scan results show cerebral activation in the area posterior to Broca's area, and in the corresponding area in the non-dominant hemisphere, suggesting that there is some co-dominance or transfer of function from damaged to healthy tissue for this child. The future utilisation of such precise data on localisation of cerebral function may be helpful in formulating further developmental theories. With respect to clinical implications, such information may be considered prior to surgical resection of the tumour, in an attempt to minimise removal of functional tissue important for expressive language, while also ensuring appropriate tumour resection, thus minimising the likelihood of tumour regrowth.

Electroencephalograms (EEGs) and event-related potentials (ERPs) have also been employed for measuring temporal aspects of cerebral function, via electrical activity. EEGs are traditionally employed in the diagnosis of epileptic disorders and sleep disturbance, whereas ERPs focus on dysfunction within sensory or information-processing systems (Gordon, 1994). Each of these measures provides useful information both clinically and for the endeavour of correlating more accurately the brain–behaviour relationships

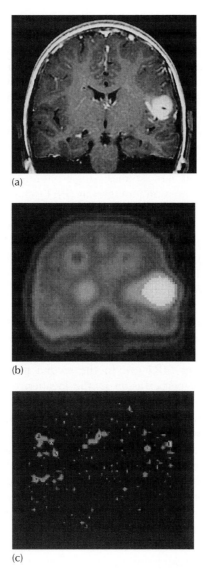

(a)

(b)

(c)

Figure 1.1. Coronal brain images of a 9-year-old child, KG, with tumour in left hemisphere, and intractable partial seizures, characterised by speech arrest. (a) The gadolinium anatomical MR image shows the tumour in the left inferior frontal sulcus, displacing the lateral sulcus inferiorly. (b) The ictal SPECT image shows focal hyperperfusion in the location of the tumour during a typical seizure, and (c) functional MRI scan, during a language production activation study, showing activation in the inferior frontal regions bilaterally, suggesting co-dominance or transfer of language function away from the damaged area.

seen following early brain insult. Research has shown that the features of such techniques vary considerably with age, suggesting maturation of function over time, and the importance of interpretation of these measures against age-appropriate norms. Further, such methods have been found to be helpful in mapping age changes through childhood. Thatcher's (1992, 1997) EEG coherence studies have suggested cyclical growth spurts within the CNS which begin at about 12–18 months of age, last for about 2–4 years, and involve an expansion from the posterior to anterior cerebral regions, as well as a lateralised sequence.

The "cognitive" dimension

Cognitive development is also rapid during childhood. Early conceptual models of cognitive development, originating with Piagetian theories (Piaget, 1963), emphasised a hierarchical or stage-like process, with children required to pass through a preset series of developmental stages, not unlike the preset genetic code underpinning cerebral development (Rourke et al., 1983). Although some individual variation is considered to occur with respect to the timing of these stages, the actual stages and the need to pass through each in order are argued to be invariant.

An analysis of the content of these cognitive stages suggests the quality and level of thinking are the key characteristics to change and progress. For example, classical Piagetian models, as well as those of more contemporary developmental psychologists, describe a number of stages of development, each characterised by increasing symbolic thought and the ability to deal with increasingly complex information (Bjorklund, 1989; Flavell, 1992; Piaget, 1963). The first of these stages (birth to 2 years) is usually defined primarily in terms of simple motor and sensory activities with little evidence of any abstract thought, with a gradual emergence of object permanence, which has been argued to provide the earliest indicators of working memory (Goldman-Rakic, 1986, 1987). The development of symbolic thought, around 2 years of age, is evidenced by the development of early language, communication, and mental imagery. However, higher-level skills remain limited, with children restricted to "unidimensional" approaches to problem solving and egocentric responses, indicating an inability to see the world from others' perspective. The transition to rudimentary levels of "operational" thought, at approximately 7 years of age, is reflected in increased reasoning and problem-solving ability, and the capacity to think in multiple dimensions and to perform mental transformations. From the neuropsychological perspective, this stage heralds the emergence of executive skills including reasoning, problem solving, organisation, and mental flexibility. These executive functions, which represent mature cognitive processes, then become fully established in the transition to the formal operational stage, which is thought to occur early in adolescence. A number of research groups have recently demonstrated that these cognitive transitions are evident on standard neuropsychological test measures (P. Anderson, Anderson, & Lajoie, 1996; V. Anderson, Lajoie, & Bell, 1995; Levin et al., 1991; McKay, Halperin, Schwartz, & Sharma, 1994; Welsh & Pennington, 1988).

There is some controversy regarding the exact ages at which these transitions occur. Most cognitive-developmentalists agree that children undergo extensive cognitive growth from birth to adulthood, and that this maturation occurs via a regular, stage-like process (Case, 1992; Fischer, 1987; Flavell, 1992; Pascual-Leone, 1987). This stage-like cognitive development is not unlike that described for cerebral development, with the timing of growth spurts in myelination, and metabolic and electrical activity roughly consistent with cognitive progressions (V. Anderson & Lajoie, 1996; Hudspeth & Pribram, 1990; Jernigan, Trauner, Hesselink, & Tallal, 1991; Kinney, Brody, Kloman, & Gilles, 1988; Levin et al., 1991; Luciana & Nelson, 1998; McKay et al., 1994; Piaget, 1963; Welsh & Pennington, 1988; Yakovlev & Lecours, 1967).

Traditionally, cognitive theories focus on particular skills or modules (Temple, 1997). In contrast, cognitive-developmental theories are not specific to isolated cognitive domains, but argue for a generalised progression of cognitive abilities through childhood (Flavell, 1992). In support of this position, recent evidence suggests that, as well as individual variations in the timing of transitions between developmental stages, there may also be different rates and progressions within specific cognitive domains. For example, motor skills may mature earlier than language skills or memory capacities. However, it is likely that the development of individual cognitive modalities is not an independent process. Rather, it appears that domain-specific development occurs in cooperation with similar maturation occurring within other systems. An example of this hypothesis may be seen within the domain of memory function. Children's basic capacity to store and retain information has been found to increase progressively through childhood (Anderson & Lajoie, 1996; Goswami, 1998; Halperin et al., 1989; Henry & Millar, 1993; Hulme, Thomson, Muir, & Lawrence, 1984). Authors argue that this improved "memory" capacity is due to more efficient information processing, or increasing ability to develop and implement strategies for recall (e.g., rehearsal, chunking), suggesting that a multidimensional relationship between memory and processing speed and executive functions is responsible for age-related progress (Bjorklund, 1989; Howard & Polich, 1985; Kail, 1986; Simon, 1974). Similarly for executive functions, research has shown that developmental increases in speed of information processing may enhance executive function (P. Anderson et al., 1996; V. Anderson et al., in press; Dempster, 1991; Goswami, 1998; Kirk, 1985). Once again this pattern of hierarchical functioning and interaction across skill areas is entirely consistent with our knowledge of maturational processes within the CNS.

What is the relevance of such developmental theories to neuropsychology? First and foremost, the presence of neuropsychological impairment in children must be measured against age-appropriate expectations. The major tasks for the child neuropsychologist are to plot the development of cognitive skills through childhood, to identify deviations from expected patterns of development, and to formulate a diagnosis and treatment plan based on this information. To do this it is necessary to have an understanding of the process of normal child development and access to appropriate test procedures that include normative data, describing not simply age expectations but also the range of individual variation for the normal child population. A further consideration for the child neuropsychologist is the use of adult-based tests for the evaluation of developing cognitive skills. Fletcher and Taylor (1984) note the unfounded assumption that tests designed for adults measure the same skills in children. To fully appreciate this statement it is useful to consider the multidimensional nature of most neuropsychological measures, where test performances are dependent on the relative contributions of various skill domains. Thus children may achieve similar endpoint scores by utilising a range of cognitive skills, or alternatively, they may perform poorly due to a range of cognitive deficits. For example, a commonly administered clinical test such as the Rey Complex Figure (Rey, 1941) is frequently employed in adult neuropsychology as a measure of higher-order cognitive skills including organisational and planning ability, where other lower-level skills required for task completion (e.g., motor skills, visual perception) are usually intact. Interpretation of test performance, as indicative of impairments in higher-order skills, is problematic in children. Poor performance on the task may equally reflect expected developmental progress, or impairment of lower-order skills such as visual perception, motor control, and visuomotor coordination, as well as the age-appropriate immaturity of higher-order executive skills.

To illustrate this point, Figure 1.2 shows the Rey Complex Figure productions of three healthy children, with no history of neurological or developmental disorder. These children were each evaluated as part of a normative project conducted to develop age-standardised data for school-aged children (V. Anderson, Lajoie, & Bell, 1995). The first production is from a 6-year-old boy, whose intellectual ability is within the superior range. It is evident that he shows little organisational skill and motor control is immature; however, his copy scores are within the average range for his age, suggesting that this level of skill development is age appropriate and not indicative of any impairment. The second figure, drawn by an 8-year-old child of high average abilities, is also age appropriate. In this example motor skills are more developed, but organisational capacity remains immature, reflecting normal developmental progression of these skills. The last figure, generated by a 12-year-old boy of high average intelligence, is more in line with adult expectations, showing good motor skills and evidence of emerging planning ability. These wide variations across the age span emphasise the importance of evaluating children's performances within an age-appropriate context. Where such information is not available, the clinician has no bench-mark to interpret level of performance and the possibility of a "clinically significant" impairment.

A corollary of this "development" is a need to acknowledge the limitations of evaluating immature skills when seeking evidence of deficits. We know from cognitive-developmental theory that executive skills, although developing from infancy, may not be measurable until late childhood. It follows that the identification of deficits in this domain cannot reliably occur until a stage at which they should be present and accessible in the child. For example, when assessing a 5-year-old child diagnosed to have a frontal lobe tumour, no executive dysfunction may be elicited in the child's initial test results. This may be because normal test expectations for young children do not require mature executive abilities. By age 12 the same child may be showing such deficits, with these impairments having emerged as the developmental expectations for the child extend to include functional independence and a capacity to plan, problem solve, and think flexibly. Banich, Cohen-Levine, Kim, and Huttenlocher (1990) illustrate this principle by comparing a sample of children with congenital cerebral injuries to age-matched controls using the Vocabulary and Block Design subtests of the Wechsler Intelligence Scale for Children. When children were aged 6 years there were no differences across the groups on these measures, but as the children progressed through childhood significant discrepancies emerged. As illustrated in Figure 1.3, by late childhood children sustaining congenital cerebral injuries were failing to exhibit expected developmental progress, with this pattern of impairment continuing into adolescence. In terms of test results, the child may appear to "grow into" his/her cognitive deficits as the brain matures. This picture of progressively emerging deficits does not necessarily reflect a deterioration in cognitive skills or an underlying progressive neurological condition. Rather it may be interpreted as a feature of early cerebral insult, suggestive of inefficient skill acquisition and associated slowing of cognitive development.

The "psychosocial" dimension

The child exists within a tight social system, the family unit, with that system responsible for the quality of the environment, access to resources, and provision of an appropriate context for learning and the acceptance of disability. Research addressing the psychosocial aspects of chronic illness and disability provides convincing evidence of the impact of disability on a child's quality of life, and on parental and family adjustment (Daniels, Miller, Billings, & Moos, 1986; Kazak, 1987; McKinney & Peterson, 1987; Wallender & Thompson, 1995). It is equally likely that acquired CNS conditions will have

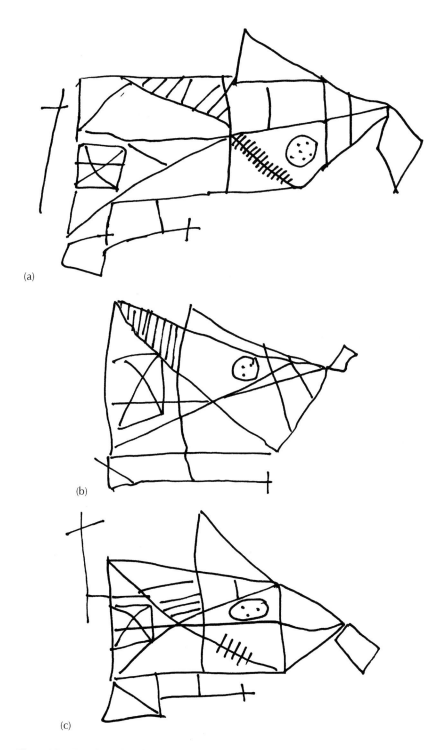

(a)

(b)

(c)

Figure 1.2. Rey Complex Figure productions from three healthy children with normal neurological and developmental histories. (a) 6-year-old boy, superior intelligence. (b) 8-year-old boy, high average intelligence. (c) 12-year-old boy, high average intelligence. All productions fall within age expectations, based on normative data for accuracy and organisational level.

13

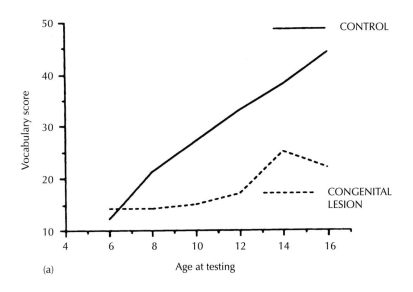

(a)

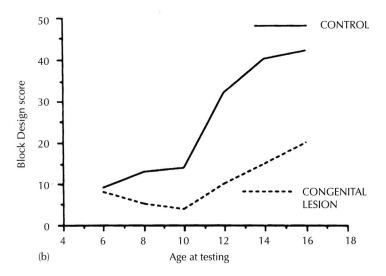

(b)

Figure 1.3. Developmental changes in performance on (a) Vocabulary and (b) Block Design subtests of the Wechsler Intelligence Scale for Children in children with congenital brain lesions and matched controls. Reprinted from Banich et al. Copyright 1990, with permission from Elsevier Science.

14

a similar influence, on the family unit and its efficient functioning, as has been shown in the limited literature addressing this issue (Curley, 1992; Fletcher et al., 1990; Max et al., 1997a; Northam et al., 1996; Perrott, Taylor, & Montes, 1991; Rivara et al., 1994; Rutter, Graham, & Yule, 1970; Wade et al., 1996).

Within the normal context, it may be argued that social skills develop over time. Children pass through a range of stages in their psychosocial development, not inconsistent with those described for neurological and cognitive development. In infancy, children are largely dependent on the family, with their social interactions supported and structured. The child learns social behaviours and rules within this context. As he or she begins to move into the outside world, to preschool and further, there is a need for the child to develop independence. Egocentricity recedes and children become more able to cooperate with those around them and make rational judgements. With the advent of adolescence the search for independence is paramount, and the need to develop an identity, via peer groups and broader social context, becomes vitally important.

Most children pass through these stages without crisis; however, where some disruption or impairment is present each transition may be more problematic. Theorists (Breslau, 1990; Sameroff, 1983; Taylor et al., 1995) stress the importance of the biological characteristics of the individual, the immediate home environment, and the broader social context as playing crucial roles in social development. Figure 1.4 illustrates the possible range of associations among these various dimensions, emphasising that no single factor can be adequately understood in isolation. The child adapts to the features and demands of the environment, which in turn are modified by the characteristics of the child. This results in a dynamic interplay in which both the child and the environment are influenced. If adaptive and positive, these interactions may promote healthy, social development. Alternatively, when problems exist, they may lead to a distortion in both the child and the environment.

In the case of the child with CNS insult, the impairments of the child may interact with the environment in this distorted way, with the consequence of disruption both at the child level and at the family level (Gruneberg & Pond, 1957; Ritchie, 1981). For example, children with an early onset of CNS disorder may have problems acquiring social knowledge and comprehending social rules, due to intellectual impairments, social stigma, and limited interaction with the environment (Curley, 1992; Rourke, 1995). As the child grows, and less social support is available, social interactions may become more problematic, eventually resulting in social withdrawal. On reaching adolescence there is a greater awareness of the severity of residual deficits, and their functional implications as young people seek peer acceptance. Physical disabilities, such as motor or speech impairments, are often present. These may restrict the child's capacity to participate in a full range of normal

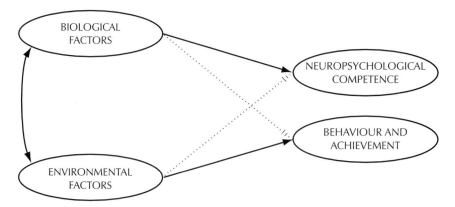

Figure 1.4. Model of interactions among neurological, cognitive, and psychosocial factors in children sustaining cerebral insult. From *Traumatic Head Injury in Children*, edited by Sarah Broman and Mary Ellen Michel, copyright © 1995 by Oxford University Press, Inc. Used by permission of Oxford University Press, Inc.

activities and emphasise the cognitive limitations that may be causing extra pressure in coping with academic and social expectations. Such a developmental pattern of increasing social problems has been identified in association with many childhood CNS disorders including non-verbal learning disability (Rourke, 1989), hydrocephalus (Fletcher et al., 1995a), traumatic brain injury (Brown et al., 1981), and epilepsy (Curley, 1992).

For children sustaining cerebral insult/disease it may be argued that there are two distinct aetiologies that influence outcome: the direct effects of brain injury, and secondary psychosocial factors. It is likely that these mechanisms interact to produce the picture of increased behavioural disturbance commonly documented following cerebral insult (Brown et al., 1981; Curley, 1992; Fletcher et al., 1990, 1995c; Perrott et al., 1991; Rutter et al., 1970).

Neurological correlates

The notion that behavioural changes post-insult are specifically related to brain dysfunction was initially addressed by Rutter and colleagues (Rutter et al., 1970). They found that psychiatric disorder occurred five times more frequently in brain-damaged children than in children with physical disorders not involving the CNS, with presence of epilepsy an additional risk factor (see Table 1.1). These findings have been supported in a number of subsequent studies, using larger samples, and including children with chronic physical illness (Breslau, 1985; Seidel, Chadwick, & Rutter, 1975; Weiland, Pless, & Roghmann, 1992). Results show that there is a direct contribution of brain dysfunction to behaviour and psychosocial functioning. Depending on the nature and localisation of cerebral pathology, children may also present

TABLE 1.1
Psychiatric disorder and physical illness in a
population-based sample

General population	6.7%
Chronic non-CNS illness	12.0%
Peripheral sensory deficits (deaf/blind)	18.0%
Idiopathic epilepsy	28.0%
Structural brain damage	35.0%
Structural brain damage with epilepsy	54.0%

Reproduced from Rutter et al. (1970) *A Neuropsychiatric Study in Childhood* © Lippincott-Raven Publishers.

as impulsive, hyperactive, aggressive, lacking in insight, depressed, and anxious (Curley, 1992; Perrott et al., 1991).

To further investigate this issue, and to evaluate the role of specific cerebral regions in behavioural disturbance, Anderson and Buffery (1982) studied a group of children who had sustained a traumatic brain injury in the acute recovery stage. They compared children with right/left and anterior/posterior lesions to healthy children, on a range of behavioural domains previously identified as disturbed in brain-injured samples (Black et al., 1969; Lishman, 1978; Pond, 1974; Roberts, 1969). These included depression, anxiety, aggression, hyperactivity/impulsivity, and the ability to express and perceive emotion.

Their findings indicated that more severe injury was associated with greater emotional and behavioural disturbance, as has been noted by other authors (Bolter, 1986; Brown et al., 1981; Camfield et al., 1984; Curley, 1992; Fletcher et al., 1990). They also identified right-sided lesions and anterior pathology as predictive of greater behavioural dysfunction, with children sustaining right anterior damage exhibiting generalised emotional and behavioural difficulties. In addition, they distinguished between characteristics that were primarily injury related, and those more clearly related to the secondary psychological trauma. Specifically, anxiety and depression were evident in all children regardless of injury site, indicating that such behavioural features may occur as a result of psychological factors including hospitalisation, family separation, adjustments to injury, and related impairments. In contrast, aggressive, hyperactive, and impulsive behaviours were specific to children with right anterior pathology, as were difficulties in expressing and perceiving emotions, and these latter characteristics were interpreted by the authors as directly related to underlying brain pathology.

Psychosocial correlates

There is little doubt that social factors influence the behavioural development of children with CNS disorders (Taylor, Schatsneider, & Rich, 1992).

The more critical question is whether such factors are more potent in this population. Following CNS insult, children must deal with a range of difficulties related to acceptance of, and adjustment to, illness and possible disability, as well as specific behavioural deficits directly associated with the nature and severity of brain insult. As is the case with children with medical and physical disabilities not involving the CNS, they will experience anxiety and uncertainty relating to their illness. They may miss substantial time at school, leading to reduced experience and confidence both socially and cognitively. Residual impairments may restrict ability to interact normally with peers, and lead to social stigma. The disruptions and adjustments required are multiple for the child. For the family, similar changes may occur: anxiety associated with illness/injury, separation within the family due to hospitalisation, difficulties coping with the new, and different demands of the child. If the condition is life threatening, a whole range of other "trauma"-related factors come into play.

Much of the research addressing such issues has taken a unidimensional view of the problem, evaluating the impact of psychosocial factors in isolation. Such approaches consistently identify low socioeconomic status (SES), presence of multiple family stresses, previous psychological disturbance, and low levels of maternal education as predictive of poorer long-term outcome (Coster, Haley, & Baryza, 1994; Fletcher et al., 1995c; Perrott et al., 1991; Taylor et al., 1995; Wade et al., 1996). Further, research has shown that children from previously disturbed families or low-SES families show more problems, and where parents are depressed or distressed the cognitive and social development of the child is reported to be poorer (Rickards, 1993). Conversely, better outcomes are found where there is family cohesion and supportive social networks (Rivara et al., 1993). These results are consistent with the "double-hazard hypothesis" (Breslau, 1990; Escalona, 1982; Taylor et al., 1992), which postulates that brain insults may have greater consequences in children from socially disadvantaged backgrounds. Contradicting such a theory, there is some evidence that disease effects are less marked in children with greater social disadvantage (Bendersky & Lewis, 1994). It may be that, for children who are already compromised by their social disadvantage, biological risks make less of a difference to recovery and outcome.

Research examining the long-term implications of brain insult on behaviour provides substantial support for the role of psychosocial factors. A prospective study conducted by Brown and his colleagues (Brown et al., 1981) aimed to address long-term outcome, specifically with respect to behavioural functioning. They found that, whereas children with mild traumatic brain injury presented with more pre-injury problems, those with severe injuries exhibited an increasing frequency of psychiatric disturbance with time since injury, as illustrated in Table 1.2. By $2\frac{1}{2}$ years post-injury 60% of severely injured children exhibited psychological disturbance, in contrast to only 29%

TABLE 1.2
Psychiatric disorder (percentages) following traumatic brain injury in childhood,
based on parent report

	Orthopaedic controls (n = 28)	Mild TBI (n = 29)	Severe TBI (n = 28)
Initial	10.7	31.0	14.3
4 months	14.3	20.7	53.6
1 year	22.2	17.2	50.0
2.5 years	24.0	24.1	60.7

Reproduced from Brown et al. (1981) with permission from Cambridge University Press.

of the mildly injured group. In more recent studies there is evidence that marital relationships fail over time post-insult, and that family isolation increases as parents are required to stay at home to care for their impaired child, and are less likely to socialise because of the behavioural difficulties exhibited by the child (Friedman et al., 1986; Hermann et al., 1988; Perrott et al., 1991; Ritchie, 1981; Taylor et al., 1995).

Recent research has also reported that the relative importance of risk factors may change with time since onset of disorder. For example, results from a prospective, longitudinal study of children with a history of bacterial meningitis show that early outcome is predicted primarily from disease sever-ity, whereas long-term outcome is more closely linked to psychosocial factors (V. Anderson & Taylor, 1999). Such findings argue that it may be too simplistic to treat biological and social issues in a linear manner. Rather, evaluation of the relative impact of these factors may be best conducted using a multi-dimensional approach (Hermann et al., 1988; Taylor et al., 1995), where a series of likely predictors of outcome can be assessed simultaneously, and at different time intervals.

Once again, such findings argue for the dynamic nature of functioning in the child with CNS dysfunction, and the importance of longitudinal research to fully understand the consequences of early cerebral insult. As with neuro-logical and cognitive dimensions, insult occurs in an ever-changing context with respect to behavioural and psychosocial development and may restrict the ongoing acquisition of appropriate skills, perhaps with a cumulative effect. Whereas group-based studies suggest increasing behavioural disturb-ance over time following cerebral insult, at an individual level recovery pat-terns vary widely, with no one factor able to predict outcome reliably. One way of conceptualising such variations may be to see the child in terms of relative vulnerability, on the basis of a number of possible risk factors, including premorbid characteristics of child and family, severity of insult and related impairment, age/developmental stage at insult, and socioeconomic factors.

Following is a case study that illustrates some of these complexities and tracks the interactions that occur among injury, social, developmental, and premorbid factors for the child with cerebral insult. This case describes a child with a severe cerebral insult, with reported normal development prior to her injury. Similarly, the family unit appeared to be previously well functioning and resourceful. Despite these various advantages, long-term follow-up shows continuing deterioration in neurological, cognitive, and behavioural function for the child, and ongoing stress and social difficulties for the family.

Case illustration: Jessica

Jessica was originally seen as an inpatient at a tertiary paediatric hospital where she had been admitted with a severe traumatic brain injury. She and her family were then followed for a period of 10 years, mapping her recovery and early childhood development, transition from rehabilitation to primary school and special school, and the social changes experienced by Jessica and her family over that time.

Background

Jessica was aged 3 years 11 months at the time of her injury. Prior to that, Jessica was described as a healthy, active toddler. She had no previous significant medical history, and had achieved age-appropriate developmental milestones, including advanced language skills. At the time of Jessica's accident her family lived in a rural community. Her father ran a successful but time-consuming dairy farm and her mother was involved in home duties. There were no significant family, social, or marital difficulties described by the family prior to Jessica's accident, and the family had a wide social network.

On an afternoon in March 1985, Jessica's mother put her to bed for an afternoon nap. Some time later Jessica left her room, and wandered onto the highway nearby. She was hit by a truck and as a result, sustained severe head injuries. She was unconscious at the scene of the accident and was taken to the local hospital by ambulance.

Acute presentation and early recovery

"Neuro" dimension.   On admission to hospital Jessica was diagnosed as suffering from a severe head injury, being deeply unconscious. CT scan detected frontal lobe contusions and haemorrhage. She underwent neuro-surgery to suture frontal lacerations and drain a large frontal hygroma. Repeat CT scan 4 days post-injury (see Figure 1.5) noted focal frontal contusions as well as more generalised cortical and subcortical damage.

Jessica remained unconscious for 4 weeks. She received intensive rehabilitation during her hospital stay, with her greatest impairments evident in speech, mobility, and coordination. On discharge, 9 weeks post-injury, Jessica

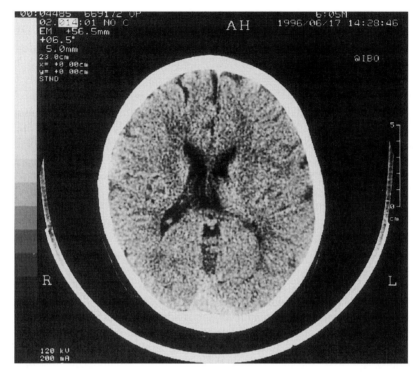

Figure 1.5.   CT scan in the acute period post severe TBI, depicting frontal contusions and diffuse cerebral damage.

had no functional expressive speech, with receptive language also reduced, and a very poor capacity to maintain attention. Jessica also displayed a severe truncal ataxia, broad-based gait, and mild intention tremor.

"Cognitive" dimension. Neuropsychological evaluation was first attempted approximately 8 weeks post-injury. At that time Jessica was unable to cooperate with test procedures. She had severely reduced attention, limited motor coordination (i.e., unable to pick up large wooden blocks to complete jigsaw puzzles), and no expressive speech. Her mother described her as "like a baby again", and noted that Jessica was totally dependent for daily living skills.

"Psychosocial" dimension.   During Jessica's hospitalisation her mother remained at the hospital, sleeping by her bed. Jessica's sister was sent to stay with her grandparents, and her father remained at home, maintaining the family farm and income. Such family fragmentation commonly occurs

following an acute CNS illness, resulting in an inability of the family to communicate adequately at a time of severe stress. Thus each family member may have a different experience of the acute illness period. In Jessica's case, her mother was consumed with the day-to-day survival of her child, while her father was more involved with regular day-to-day routines, and with the financial pressures caused by the accident. The long-term repercussions of such separation are often significant, changing the family dynamics irreversibly, perhaps in preparation for the changes that may occur once the family is reunited.

Chronic recovery and ongoing development

"Neuro" dimension.   Once recovered from neurosurgery, Jessica's health progressed well. She continued to receive rehabilitation intervention for several years after her illness, with specific emphasis on speech and motor coordination. Since her injury, Jessica has experienced a number of secondary medical problems including epilepsy and precocious puberty. Her speech is still slow and laboured, restricting her capacity for normal communication. Her difficulties with mobility and coordination have persisted, and she is unable to participate in sporting activities and tends to respond slowly in most situations. A recent MRI scan shows evidence of the previous pathology, with abnormalities in frontal, cerebellar, and brain stem regions. Additionally, she exhibits significant cerebral atrophy, particularly in anterior areas, perhaps indicating lack of expected development of these areas through childhood.

"Cognitive" dimension.   Jessica was first comprehensively assessed almost 7 months post-injury, and then on a number of subsequent occasions until the age of 12, almost 8 years post-injury. On each occasion, qualitative features of presentation included high levels of distractibility and impulsivity. These behavioural characteristics often impeded her test performance. Figure 1.6 plots her performance at each assessment on standardised measures of IQ, receptive language, memory, and visuomotor coordination. The scores are presented as age equivalents to enable direct comparison across tests. As these results suggest, Jessica exhibited age-expected progress in the first 18 months to 2 years post-injury, probably reflecting some recovery of function plus slightly slowed developmental progression. After this time her progress reduced, with little improvement evident in the following years. By 8 years post-injury, aged 12, Jessica's best results on neuropsychological test measures were at the level expected for a $7\frac{1}{2}$-year-old child.

This lack of developmental progress is consistent with her school history. Jessica commenced her education at age 6 years, and attended a mainstream school, with full-time support and a modified educational curriculum. After

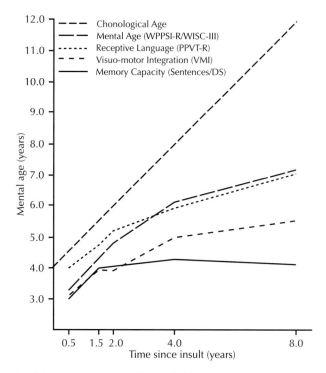

Figure 1.6. Cognitive recovery profile for "Jessica", following severe traumatic brain injury at age 3 years 11 months. Results illustrate the increasing discrepancy with time since injury between chronological age and developmental levels for mental ability, receptive language, visuomotor integration, and memory capacity.

several years, Jessica's reduced abilities became difficult to manage within the classroom, and she was transferred to a special school for children with intellectual impairment. Even in this environment Jessica experienced ongoing difficulties, both social and academic. In a recent review, aimed at looking at her future vocational options, it was evident that Jessica is unlikely to live independently or to attain employment. Although she is able to manage basic daily living skills including bathing, washing, dressing, and feeding, she is unable to perform more complex activities without supervision, for example cooking or shopping.

"Psychosocial" dimension. The long-term psychosocial repercussions for Jessica and her family are also substantive. Jessica's family tended to follow a pattern commonly observed following acquired CNS conditions of childhood. Within the family unit, Jessica's mother was required to spend large amounts of time travelling to multiple therapy sessions, and then carrying out

rehabilitation activities at home, organising appropriate community/ educational resources, and taking care of Jessica's daily needs, leaving her with little time for her husband, her other daughter, or for herself. The family wish was for their life to be "back to normal". Eventually, they were able to accept that Jessica would always be disabled, and set about providing appropriate resources for her. The parents moved from their farm, employed an attendant carer for Jessica, and opened a small business. However, they describe the continuing burden of needing to maintain and access resources for Jessica, to manage her physical, intellectual, and behavioural difficulties, and accept them.

Several crises have occurred over the years, reflecting the severity of Jessica's injury, the importance of the ongoing developmental process, and the relevance of the family unit. Jessica's parents separated after several years, the balance of their relationship having changed dramatically in the years post-injury. Such family disruption is commonly noted following acquired CNS insult in children. Jessica, her mother, and sister continue to be socially isolated, maintaining few old friendships, and with little capacity or motivation to establish new networks. Jessica herself initially displayed limited insight regarding her problems. She progressed through her early school years quite happily. As she moves through adolescence, she has developed some degree of insight, inventing a special friend who had also had a brain injury. Through her friend she was able to express some of her feelings of sadness and anger about being different from her peers. One of the major problems for Jessica and for many other children with CNS disorder is that she appears superficially to be quite normal, leading to unrealistic expectations and resultant disappointments from teachers, peers, and family.

Following Jessica from the time of her insult, through childhood to early adolescence, highlights the complex interaction among neurological, cognitive, and psychosocial influences. At the outset, Jessica may have been predicted to have a good prognosis. Although her cerebral insult was severe, her previous development had been good, her family unit cohesive and well functioning. She had access to appropriate early treatment and later rehabilitation, and adequate academic support. The observation of significant and increasing difficulties over time, for both Jessica and her family, emphasises the stress produced by CNS disease and the ongoing needs of such children and their families.

Summary

The dimensions of knowledge important to child neuropsychology— neurological, cognitive, psychosocial—must each be incorporated into future theoretical conceptualisations, with a great deal of energy being focused on such endeavours at present. Current theoretical perspectives represent a significant progression over the past 20 years, where understanding was based primarily on adult models of brain lesions. Today, developmental perspectives extend our breadth of knowledge, but continue to fall short of explaining the complexities of interruption to a system that is in a rapid state of development. There exists in our patient populations an unacceptably high degree of unexplained variation in outcome following early childhood CNS disorder. The challenge is to improve prediction of outcome by measuring the interacting influences of neural, cognitive, and psychosocial parameters, and their ever-changing matrix through childhood.

DEVELOPMENT OF A THEORETICAL FRAMEWORK FOR CHILD NEUROPSYCHOLOGY

Whereas child-based models have emerged over recent years, theories from adult neuropsychology models had a major impact on the field in the early days. The fundamental principles of adult neuropsychology also apply to childhood cerebral dysfunction. Adult clinical neuropsychology has been largely based on research of brain-injured populations, where documented brain lesions are correlated with observed cognitive dysfunction. One of the earliest examples of such an endeavour is provided by the work of Paul Broca (1861), who described symptoms of expressive language impairment in a patient with a lesion to the third frontal convolution of the left hemisphere. His observations led to this cerebral region being designated "Broca's area", and identified as the area subsuming expressive language. More recently, the concept of functional systems has emerged, based on the premise that cognitive abilities are not simply dependent on a single, isolated cerebral location, but are subsumed by integrated systems, with damage to any component of the system having repercussions for a range of behaviours incorporated within that system (e.g., Mirsky et al., 1991). Such progress has been essential for understanding the basic tenets of brain–behaviour relations within the mature CNS, but also has implications for childhood CNS disorders.

At a conceptual level, child neuropsychology assumes similar patterns of localisation of function and functional systems to those described in the adult literature. Acute responses to CNS insult also appear consistent across the lifespan, with similar dose–response relationships noted with respect to severity of insult for both child and adult samples. Further, child-based assessment and diagnostic principles are founded firmly in adult practice models. However, the unique characteristics provided by an immature CNS and developing cognitive skills cannot be easily accommodated within such paradigms. Additional "development-specific" principles must be generated to provide an appropriate knowledge base for child neuropsychology.

As adult neuropsychological models have evolved, they have perhaps become more relevant to child-based practice. Rourke, Fisk, and Strang

(1986) argue this point, emphasising three stages in the development of neuropsychological assessment practices to date. They describe the first, the detection and localisation of brain lesions, as largely irrelevant to child neuropsychologists. Within the developing brain the event of a cerebral insult may result in anomalous cerebral organisation, so that the ongoing development within the child's brain may be inconsistent with assumptions of localisation of function from adult models (Dennis, 1989; Finger & Stein, 1982; Fletcher & Taylor, 1984). The second phase of development reflected an increased awareness of functional implications of assessment data, with models focusing on identifying patterns of deficit, severity of deficit, and underlying components of impairments in performance. The third, and most useful advance was to emphasise the detection of cognitive strengths and weaknesses in relation to environmental demands. Such an approach can be generalised across the lifespan, so long as the dynamic, ever-changing nature of the child and his or her environment is acknowledged. Since Rourke and colleagues' views were published in 1986, a further advance has occurred, stemming from a need to relate test results to day-to-day performance more closely. The emergence of assessment techniques aimed at functional evaluation and fine-grained task analysis, and the effort to correlate such test performances to daily activities, shows promise and enables neuropsychologists to evaluate effectiveness of parallel treatment interventions. Such practices may have particular significance for child neuropsychology, where there is a need to utilise knowledge of an individual child's cognitive strengths and weaknesses when developing rehabilitation strategies or remediating functional impairments in educational and social skills following cerebral insult.

Developmental neurology: Plasticity and critical periods

A perusal of the field of child neuropsychology in recent times, since it has emerged as a distinct entity, yields only a handful of attempts to formulate brain–behaviour paradigms of a truly developmental nature. The earliest theoretical contributions to child neuropsychology can be traced to descriptions of plasticity and recovery of function following childhood brain damage. Researchers such as Kennard (1936, 1940) and Teuber (1962) are well known for their seminal works describing relative sparing of function following early cerebral insult, with the Kennard principle, interpreted by Teuber to suggest that if you're going to have brain damage, have it early. These workers and various others more recently (Lenneberg, 1967; Woods, 1980) have documented relatively good recovery following early insult. In particular, studies following recovery from aphasia note that, where injury severity is equivalent, there is evidence of greater improvement in children than is observed in adults (Alajouanine & Lhermitte, 1965; Hecaen, 1976;

Lenneberg, 1967). Similar findings are reported in follow-up studies of children undergoing hemispherectomy (Broca, 1865; Dennis, 1980, 1985; Krynauw, 1950; Rankur, Aram, & Horowitz, 1980; Rasmussen & Milner, 1977). Such results are interpreted according to a theory of recovery of function where the young child's brain is seen to be less differentiated than that of the mature adult, and more capable of transferring functions from damaged cerebral tissue to healthy tissue. Although there continues to be considerable debate regarding the conclusions drawn from this early research, the resultant theories represent an important contribution to the field of child neuropsychology, not least because they acknowledge the unique processes that may be acting in the developing brain following cerebral insult.

Notions of critical periods of development, although not constituting specific neuropsychological theory, have also added breadth to our conceptualisation of the mechanisms acting for the child sustaining early brain insult. Mogford and Bishop (1993) define a critical period as "the time window during which external influences have a significant effect" (p. 252). Hebb's (1942, 1949) work may be seen in this context. He argues that brain insult will have different consequences at different times throughout development. He goes further to conclude that, in some instances, brain insult early in life may be more detrimental than later injury, because some aspects of cognitive development are critically dependent on the integrity of particular cerebral structures at certain stages of development. Thus, if a cerebral region is damaged or dysfunctional at a critical stage of cognitive development it may be that the cognitive skill subsumed by that region is irreversibly impaired (Kolb, 1995). Further, research suggests that although there may be some functional plasticity early in life the time frame may be quite restricted, and not necessarily related to age in a linear manner. For example, children with prenatal lesions, or those sustaining insults during the first year of life, appear to exhibit particularly severe impairment (V. Anderson, Bond, et al., 1997; Duchowny et al., 1996; Riva & Cassaniga, 1986).

Much of the experimental research addressing the notion of critical periods of development is based on environmental deprivation or enrichment models. Studies of the visual system in various animal models have confirmed that development of cells is dependent upon the type of stimulation available early in life. Blakemore (1974) identified a sensitive period during which appropriate experience must occur if the functional characteristics of the visual system are to be normal. He noted that similar deprivation during "non-critical" periods did not lead to such irreversible consequences. As Kolb and Whishaw (1996) state, it appears that the visual system is pre-programmed to make normal connections and normal responses, but it can lose much of its capacity if it is not exercised during the early months of life (Atkinson, Barlow, & Braddick, 1982).

Less research is available with respect to critical periods for other aspects of cognitive development. Lenneberg (1967) has noted a period of rapid language development between the ages of 2 and 5 years, with slower development continuing through puberty. He suggests that, if brain damage is sustained during this "critical" period, it might be that language functions could shift from one hemisphere to the other, with minimal consequences. Lenneberg believed that, although some plasticity was present throughout childhood, major transfer could only happen during the critical period, that is, up to 5 years of age. Consistent with this suggestion, research following children who have been isolated from linguistic experience from birth shows that subsequent capacity to acquire language skills is best if intervention occurs within the preschool period, and then declines markedly to age 10 (Curtiss, 1981).

Neuropsychological theories

Rourke (1989) outlines the essential requirements of a "complete, unified developmental neuropsychological model" (p. 294). He argues that such models should explain (1) the spectrum of children's neurobehavioural abilities and disabilities, and (2) the progressive development and interaction of the three principal axes of relevance in brain–behaviour relationships: left–right, up–down, anterior–posterior. Further elements for incorporation in such models might include explanations of interactions among biological, cognitive, and psychosocial factors from a dynamic, developmental framework.

During the late 1980s two contrasting, but not inconsistent models were described, incorporating multiple dimensions and qualifying as "child neuropsychology" theories. The first, the theory of non-verbal learning disabilities, was defined by Byron Rourke (1987, 1988, 1989). Rourke described a syndrome of neuropsychological impairments resulting from CNS insult occurring during the perinatal period or in infancy. His model incorporates knowledge of changing cerebral development with specific cognitive profiles, in a truly brain–behaviour model. Rourke and colleagues have continued to build on this model, providing further descriptions of social and cognitive characteristics and their relevance across disorders, arguing that the timing of the insult is of primary importance. The second influential theory has been proposed by Maureen Dennis, with her "heuristic" focusing on cognitive development and changes with time. This model focuses primarily on the issues of age/developmental stage at time of insult and progression in cognitive skills with time since insult. Dennis does not propose a specific neurological mechanism for her theory, although other researchers have offered possible biological explanations. Contrary to early plasticity theorists, her approach argues for the increased vulnerability of the immature CNS, suggesting that the earlier the disruption to the brain, the fewer established cognitive skills, and the greater the impact on developing abilities.

These crucial developments are central to the position taken in this text, and so will be discussed in some detail to provide a theoretical fabric for coming discussions of specific disorders.

Non-verbal learning disability

The syndrome of non-verbal learning disability (NVLD) was originally described by Rourke in the late 1980s (Rourke 1987, 1989), to account for a consistent pattern of neurobehavioural deficits observed in children with a history of early, generalised cerebral dysfunction. The central characteristics of the syndrome include (1) bilateral tactile–perceptual deficits, more marked on the left side of the body; (2) impaired visual recognition and discrimination and visuospatial organisational deficiencies; (3) bilateral psychomotor coordination problems, more marked on the left side of the body; (4) difficulties managing novel information. However, deficits are not global, and children with NVLD present with a range of intact skills or cognitive assets, primarily within the auditory/verbal domain. Rourke lists these as: (1) simple motor skills; (2) auditory perception; (3) rote learning; (4) selective and sustained attention for auditory–verbal information; (5) basic expressive and receptive language (6) word reading and spelling. The essential elements of NVLD are illustrated in Figure 1.7.

Rourke suggests that a number of associated secondary and tertiary deficits evolve from the primary deficits that characterise NVLD. These include reduced exploratory behaviour, poor visual attention and memory, and difficulties learning complex or novel information, as well as problems of higher-order cognitive capacities, particularly concept formation, problem solving, strategy generation, hypothesis testing, and self-monitoring. In addition, Rourke identifies subtle language problems, specifically abnormal prosody and abnormal pragmatic skills. Secondary functional impairments are also common. Academic profiles indicate intact word recognition and spelling, with early but resolving writing difficulties. In contrast, poor concept formation and problem-solving skills impact on mathematical ability and other academic areas for which such skills are essential. Socioemotional problems are marked and reflect difficulty adapting to social situations, poor social perception and judgement, and problems with social interactions. Emotional disturbances are predominantly internalising in nature, with anxiety and depression frequently present.

In his more recent publications (Casey, Rourke, & Picard, 1991; Rourke, 1995), Rourke describes the developmental aspects of the syndrome, noting the dynamic interplay of cognitive and environmental factors. He argues that these children experience impairments in the very skills essential for learning.

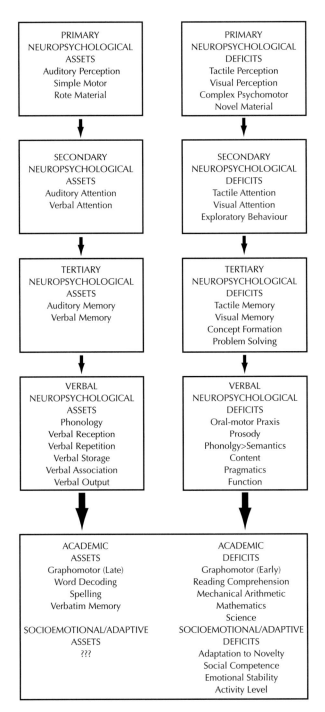

Figure 1.7. Elements and dynamics of the non-verbal learning disability syndrome. Reproduced from Rourke (1995) with permission from The Guilford Press.

Exploratory behaviours are restricted due to deficits in visual, psychomotor, and tactile abilities, impacting on new learning and understanding of the cause–effect relationships that occur constantly within the child's environment. These impairments reduce the child's confidence in exploring the environment, and thus limit exposure and experience. As the infant moves through childhood these problems manifest as difficulties in dealing with novel and complex non-verbal situations in a flexible manner, with the child relying heavily on routine auditory input. With respect to academic development, simple rote learning of information is intact (e.g., word recognition, times tables), but more conceptual material (e.g., maths concepts, comprehension skills) is grasped poorly. Social skills fail to develop with time and children with NVLD have been observed to become increasingly isolated as they move through childhood into adulthood (Rourke & Fuerst, 1991).

One of the greatest contributions of the NVLD model is to link cognitive-developmental characteristics to a possible underlying neurological explanation, "the white matter hypothesis". Rourke's neurological explanation for NVLD is derived from the adult model postulated by Goldberg and Costa (1981), in which the emphasis is on progressive left hemisphere lateralisation of function throughout the lifespan. The white matter hypothesis extends this theory to encompass early developmental phenomena. Rourke notes that the degree of white matter damage, the nature of the lesion, and the developmental stage at time of cerebral insult are important factors in determining the severity of symptoms. However, the essential element of the theory is his emphasis on the importance of intact white matter function within the CNS for normal development through childhood. Such a position is consistent with current knowledge that white matter develops through childhood, with the necessary process of axonal myelination beginning prenatally, but continuing into adolescence. Throughout this prolonged developmental period the cerebral white matter is thought to be particularly vulnerable to disruption. In support of this explanation, there is good evidence of white matter pathology in many of the disorder groups that Rourke suggests present with symptoms of NVLD, including traumatic brain injury (Adams, Mitchell, Graham, & Doyle, 1977; Levin et al., 1992), hydrocephalus (Del Bigio, 1993; Fletcher et al., 1995a; Volpe, 1989), and cranial irradiation (Matsumoto et al., 1995; Paakko et al., 1992).

White matter consists of axons connecting the grey matter of the cerebral cortex with other centres of the brain and spinal cord. Myelin, which comprises the bulk of this cerebral white matter, and progressively coats the axons within the CNS, provides insulation and facilitation of efficient neural transmission. The three principal classes of cerebral white matter are commissural fibres, which join the right and left hemispheres (corpus callosum, anterior, posterior, and habencular commissures, and the hippocampal commissure); association fibres, interconnecting cortical regions within each hemisphere (e.g., arcuate fasciculus); and projection fibres, which link cortical and subcortical regions. During development these fibres are progressively myelinated. Disruption of this ongoing myelination process, via injury, demyelinating diseases, or various toxicities (e.g., cranial radiation, head injury, hydrocephalus, metabolic disorders), may interfere with this developmental process.

To support his suggestion that visuospatial and other non-verbal abilities are specifically impaired, Rourke differentiates between development and function in right and left white matter. He argues that right hemisphere white matter is important for development and maintenance of functions (e.g., intermodal integration), whereas left hemisphere white matter is important for development but not necessarily maintenance of skills. The right hemisphere then is dependent upon the functional integrity of the brain as a whole, whereas left hemisphere functions are more encapsulated, and may be maintained in the absence of right hemisphere input. Thus Rourke suggests that a significant insult to the right hemisphere would be "sufficient" to produce an NVLD. However, the "necessary" condition for NVLD is destruction of the white matter, which subsumes intermodal integration functions.

Rourke's NVLD model has had a major influence in child neuro-psychology over the past decade. It meets many of the previously defined criteria necessary for child neuropsychology theories, with the exception that such models must encompass the "entire spectrum" of child-based neuro-psychological disorders. Evidence from other researchers suggests that child-hood CNS disorder does not always lead to symptoms consistent with NVLD (V. Anderson, Bond, et al., 1997; V. Anderson, Godber, Smibert, & Ekert, 1997; Dennis, Wilkinson, Koski, & Humphreys, 1995; Taylor et al., 1990; Temple, 1997). Further, it is unclear from the model at which develop-mental stages insult to the CNS may lead to NVLD. Do we expect to see such symptoms wherever a child sustains CNS insult/disease, or are they most likely with early lesions in the perinatal and infancy periods? The latter appears to be most likely, with NVLD symptoms occurring more commonly following early lesions, and neurobehavioural profiles moving more towards adult expectations in children sustaining CNS insults in later childhood and adolescence.

Although Rourke conceptualises his model along three axes—right–left, up–down, back–front—his dominant emphasis is on the role of the right–left axis, both neurologically and cognitively. An alternative neurological explan-ation, also consistent with developmental principles, is to consider the pos-sible contribution of the anterior–posterior axis. The relative immaturity of anterior cerebral regions through childhood may render them particularly vulnerable to the early insult/disease processes that Rourke describes. The nature of the resultant symptoms may not be greatly different from those described for NVLD, except that the emphasis is on "anterior" or "executive" functions, such as organisation, problem solving, concept formation, and mental flexibility, all previously identified as subsumed by anterior cerebral regions (Fuster, 1993; Stuss & Benson, 1987; Walsh, 1978). Rourke's primary sensory and psychomotor deficits may be less in evidence. The potential role of the up–down axis also needs to be examined. Myelination, as Rourke notes, continues through childhood, and may also be vulnerable to insult, leading to primary deficits in information processing and attentional capacity, and secondary or tertiary executive dysfunction.

Such a hypothesis does not argue against the presence of a syndrome of NVLD, but rather suggests that different axes may be of primary importance to the deficit pattern at different developmental stages. Thus the left–right dimension, causing NVLD, may be most important very early in development, with the cortical–subcortical and anterior–posterior axes coming into play in later years. Indirect evidence for this notion may be taken from studies of children treated with cranial irradiation, a prophylactic CNS treatment known to have an effect on white matter development (Anderson, Godber, et al., 1997; Waber et al., 1995). Findings from this population suggest that children treated between the ages of 2 and 5 years appear to have poorer outcome than those treated after age 5 with greatest dysfunction for information-processing skills, subsumed by subcortical white matter. Similarly, Garth et al. (1997) report that children sustaining closed head injury, with evidence of white matter shearing type lesions, prior to age 5 years are slower in processing information, but do not have poorer executive skills than those injured later in childhood. Although little research has been done, the logical progression would be to suggest that the earliest lesions will affect all axes, and result in global deficits, whereas later lesions will have a more specific impact, similar to the consequences of adult-based lesions. Thus, it may be that for very early insults there is an accumulation of deficits, reflecting dysfunction on all three cerebral axes, resulting in the typically generalised nature of early childhood syndromes. For older children, the profile of neuropsychological impairment may be more differentiated, reflecting intact early cerebral development, with deficiencies relating to the remaining immature structures.

Implications of developmental stage at insult for cognitive outcome

Maureen Dennis (1989) has also postulated a heuristic that has contributed to our understanding of the impact of childhood CNS disorders. Her model does not claim to meet some of the described criteria. For example, Dennis confines her model to language development following childhood brain damage; however, it could be argued that the model is easily extended to other cognitive domains. Also, Dennis does not attempt to provide a neuro-logical explanation to underpin her theory, although she does observe that current understanding of brain pathology in children is not inconsistent with her model.

Dennis argues the importance of viewing language disorders in children from a dynamic perspective. She develops her model within a framework where adult aphasia is not the "gold standard" for defining impairment to the language cortex for children. She suggests that, because language develop-ment may be incomplete at the time of insult, resultant impairments should be viewed in the context of age-appropriate linguistic expectations. Thus measurement of recovery and ultimate outcome needs to made via comparison with age-matched peers.

She defines three crucial age-related variables in her research: age at time of lesion, age at testing, and age of lesion (or time since insult). Age at lesion, she argues, determines the nature of the cognitive dysfunction, with similar insult generating different effects on language at different developmental stages. For example, congenital and perinatal lesions are most likely to affect the onset and rate of language development, whereas later lesions may be associated with a specific symptom pattern, such as high-level language dys-function. Age of insult refers to the time since injury. Research suggests that with time since injury there may be a relative deterioration in age-related performance (Anderson & Moore, 1995; Anderson, Morse, et al., 1997; Banich et al., 1990; Dennis et al., 1995; Ewing-Cobbs, Thompson, Miner, & Fletcher, 1994: Taylor & Alden, 1997). Dennis suggests further that there may be a detour or deviation in the normal pattern of behaviour. An interesting finding from a prospective, longitudinal study from our laboratory looked at this issue in infants sustaining bacterial meningitis. The study tracked language development in the postmeningitic sample in comparison to an age-matched healthy control sample. We found an initial delay in the onset of expressive language skills at 12 months post-illness. By 5 years post-meningitis, basic expressive abilities were age appropriate, but poor language comprehension and verbal generation skills were observed, along with associated literacy problems. Recent follow-up at early adolescence showed intact basic language skills and age-appropriate literacy skills, with deficits in high-level abilities such as making inferences and understanding abstract linguistic concepts (P. Anderson, Anderson, et al., 1997; V. Anderson, Bond, et al., 1997; V. Anderson, Leaper, & Judd, 1987; Grimwood et al., 1995; Pentland, Anderson, & Wrennall, 1997). These studies stress changes in the pattern of language deficits with time, with developing skills appearing to emerge at a delayed rate. Such a picture of changing outcomes is also relevant to Dennis's third age-based factor: age at testing. Clearly age at testing is a crucial variable, as even healthy children vary in their ability to perform cognitive tasks at different developmental stages. In this context, Dennis also emphasises one of the less well-known features of Kennard's work (1936, 1940), that whereas lesions in infancy appear to cause relatively few immediate problems, with ongoing development young organisms appear to "grow into" or "fail to acquire" expected skills.

Based on these factors, Dennis has proposed a heuristic to describe the impact of brain damage on language development, where these skills are in a process of ongoing maturation. She divides skill development into several levels: (1) *emerging*, where an ability is in the early stages of acquisition, but not yet functional: For example, the expressive language skills of the infant who can smile, babble and mimic others may be defined as at an emerging level; (2) *developing*, where a capacity is partially acquired but not fully functional. Using language as an example again, "developing" language may refer to the toddler who has a capacity to use single words and short sentences meaningfully, whereas more complex verbal skills remain immature; and (3) *established*, where abilities are fully matured. As illustrated in Figure 1.8, Dennis suggests that when brain dysfunction occurs in the context of an emerging skill the onset of that skill may be delayed and/or the order of acquisition may be garbled and out of normal sequence. For the developing skill, the rate of acquisition or the speed at which it emerges may be lagging behind age expectations, the cognitive processes used to implement the skill may represent a detour in strategy, and there may be a shortfall in the final level of skill competence. Established skills, of which there are few in early childhood, are less vulnerable to the impact of insult. The control of the skill may be deficient, resulting in a temporary loss of function, or the maintenance or upkeep of the skill may be affected.

If it is the case that the younger the child, the fewer the established skills, Dennis's model is in direct opposition to traditional plasticity theories, which propose greater plasticity of function, and thus greater recovery, following early cerebral insult. Rather, she suggests that the earlier the insult, the greater the impact on the ongoing development of language skill. The model implies that the full impact of childhood brain injury is not clear until cognitive skills are completely developed. There is a range of research that supports the general thrust of Dennis's model. Many studies note the greater impact of younger age at insult (Anderson, Bond, et al., 1997; Cousens, Ungerer, Crawford, & Stevens, 1991; Ewing-Cobbs et al., 1989, 1994, 1997; Fletcher et al., 1995b; Kriel, Krach, & Panser, 1989; Smibert et al., 1996), and others describe a pattern of increasing functional impairment with time since injury (Anderson & Moore, 1995; Banich et al., 1990; Rubenstein, Varni, & Katz, 1990; Wrightson et al., 1995).

Validation of the specific principles of Dennis's theory remains problematic for a number of reasons: (1) Most research employs chronological age as an arbitrary indicator of developmental stage. While this is generally acceptable, to test Dennis's model it is necessary to establish the

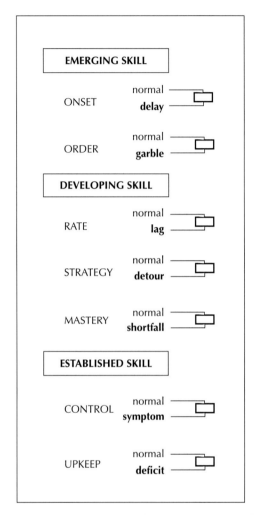

Figure 1.8. Heuristic framework for conceptualising the impact of brain insult on developing skills. From Dennis (1989). Copyright © 1988 by the American Psychological Association. Reprinted with permission.

child's developmental level with respect to the cognitive domain of interest at time of insult. To date, no studies have utilised such an approach. (2) The operationalisation of the core concepts of onset, order, rate, mastery, strategy, control, and upkeep has not yet been attempted, and may be difficult using traditional psychological tests or even experimental paradigms. Such fine-grained analysis is best suited to single-case design, within a longitudinal framework, rather than group-based research.

Clinical and research contributions to child neuropsychology theory

The theories of Rourke and Dennis have been central to progress in child neuropsychology. To adequately test their validity, carefully designed, methodologically sound research is required, which takes into account the complexities of child CNS disorder, using a developmental framework. Fletcher and Taylor (1984) have been influential in shaping this endeavour. They describe several unfounded assumptions that exist in the field: (1) that symptoms of adult brain-related disorders are similar for children; (2) that assessment techniques designed for adults measure equivalent skills in children; (3) that specific behavioural impairments are direct consequences of brain dysfunction. They emphasise the importance of not overstating the biological contribution to outcome following childhood CNS insult, but rather seeing it in the dynamic context of development and thus recognising the possible influence of moderator variables, for example, family and social factors. Further contributions have been made by a number of research groups working with a broad spectrum of disease/disorder groups, and employing these as models for understanding brain insult in childhood. Ongoing research is focused on developing appropriate and realistic research design for use in paediatric settings (e.g., prospective, longitudinal, subgrouping according to risk factors), development of well-normed, child-based assessment techniques, adaptation of adult techniques for child populations, and generating appropriate statistical analysis models for accurately tapping deficits and change over time in the context of imperfect measures. Examples of such research will be discussed in the coming chapters.

CHAPTER TWO

Cerebral development

INTRODUCTION

The development of the human central nervous system (CNS) is a protracted process that commences early in gestation and continues into adulthood, following a series of precise and genetically predetermined stages. It involves a sequence of complicated and overlapping processes, the outcome of which is partially determined by the outcome of each of the previous stages of development. Knowledge of CNS maturation and related cognitive development is continually increasing, in line with methodological and technical advances. Much early research and associated theory were dependent upon animal models and data obtained from brain-damaged subjects, each with their inherent problems and limited applicability to the healthy human CNS. Today's technology enables researchers to directly observe and even manipulate both pre- and postnatal development, using methods such as electron microscopy, insertion of chemical markers, and neuronal and tissue transplantation (Levitt, 1995), thus providing valuable information regarding timing and sequence of events occurring within the developing CNS, and the impact of any disruption to this process.

A number of aspects of CNS development are of relevance to professionals interested in both normal and aberrant patterns of cognitive development. First, knowledge of the biological processes and timing of CNS maturation may lead to the identification of parallels between specific stages of CNS development and associated cognitive progress (Anderson, 1998;

Welsh & Pennington, 1988). Second, an understanding of the sequence of events occurring within the CNS and their timing may enhance current knowledge of the nature and possible recovery of cognitive deficits exhibited by children sustaining pre- and postnatal CNS insult. Already research describing defined periods of neuronal redundancy within the CNS has led to hypotheses linking these periods with increased cerebral plasticity. At a more general level, increasing awareness of the interplay between genetically predetermined factors and experiential/environmental influences in both normal and aberrant development has emphasised the potential for optimising development and improving recovery following CNS insult via enriched environmental experiences and more traditional rehabilitation methods. Conversely, the possible negative consequences of disadvantaged environments, environmental toxins, and nutritional deficits have also been documented.

The aim of this chapter is to highlight the ongoing and dynamic interplay between biological, cognitive, and psychosocial factors in the process of development and its ultimate outcome. Superficially it may be argued that this interplay is least relevant in the early stages of CNS development, which are often described by terms such as "genetically predetermined" or "hardwired". However, a perusal of the recent literature in this field indicates that, even during the initial stages of development, there is a continuous dialogue between biological and environmental/experiential influences. In this chapter our aim is to review current knowledge of pre- and postnatal CNS development, and to explore the impact of interruptions to development, employing examples of both developmental and acquired cerebral insults. For a more detailed discussion of current perspectives of CNS development readers are directed to Gazzaniga (1995) and Johnson (1996, 1997).

BRAIN DEVELOPMENT: GENERAL PRINCIPLES

It is now well established that cerebral development is ongoing throughout gestation and childhood. The fastest rate of brain growth occurs prenatally, when it is estimated that every minute 250,000 brain cells are formed through continuous rapid cell division (Papalia & Olds, 1992). Although the structural morphology of the brain is mature by birth, growth continues during the postnatal period. Between birth and adulthood the human brain quadruples in size, increasing from around 400 g at birth to 1500 g at maturity in early adulthood, peaking between 18 and 30 years and then commencing a gradual decline (Caeser, 1993; Dekaban & Sadowsky, 1978). The postnatal increase in brain weight is largely due to differentiation, growth, and maturation of existing neurons, including elaboration of dendrites and synapses, and ongoing myelination.

Two qualitatively distinct stages of CNS development are apparent, with birth providing a rough marker for the transition. Prenatal development is primarily concerned with the structural formation of the CNS, and is thought to be largely genetically determined. Interruptions to development during this period, via genetic mechanisms or interuterine trauma or infection, is likely to have a significant impact on cerebral structure, so that the brain's morphology appears abnormal even at a macroscopic level. In contrast, postnatal development is associated with elaboration of the CNS, in particular, dendritic arborisation, myelination, and synaptogenesis. Although still largely genetically regulated, these processes are thought to be more susceptible to the impact of neuronal activity and thus to environmental and experiential influences (Nowakowski, 1996; Orzhekhovskaya, 1981; Rakic, 1995; Yakovlev, 1962). Brain damage sustained postnatally will have less impact on gross brain morphology, but may interfere with ongoing CNS elaboration, and the development of interconnections and functional systems within the CNS.

The CNS begins to develop early in gestation, around day 40 of embryonic life, commencing a process of lifelong change. The brain is recognisable in its mature form at around 100 days gestation, as illustrated in Figure 2.1, but not mature until early adolescence. Such a protracted developmental time frame is unique to the human species. During this prolonged period of maturation, a range of developmental mechanisms are acting, reflecting the complexity of the process. Suffice to say, cerebral development is not a simple, linear progression throughout the brain. Rather, there are a range of developmental phenomena that have been observed to occur simultaneously, reflecting differential developmental timing throughout various areas of the brain, and varying developmental models for specific elements of the cerebral system. A basic understanding of these maturational processes is central to a discussion of CNS development.

Within the immature CNS two major developmental processes have been described. The first, and most readily understood, is simple additive development, where there is an ongoing accumulation or growth process. It is generally agreed that several neuronal processes develop in this way. Myelination of the nervous system is one such process, with development progressing in a stage-like manner throughout the CNS during childhood and early adolescence. Similarly, there is a continuous increase in the formation and elaboration of dendritic connections throughout the CNS. Other neuronal elements display a different style of maturation, exhibiting periods of regression, characterised by an initial overproduction, and followed by an elimination of redundant elements (Blatter et al., 1995; Cowan, Fawcett, O'Leary, & Stanfield, 1984; Pfefferbaum et al., 1994; Reiss et al., 1996). For example, prenatally, the number of neurons generated is in excess of what is required in the mature CNS. During the differentiation stage of development, a number of these redundant neurons die off. A similar elimination of redundant

INFLUENCES ON BRAIN DEVELOPMENT

Brain development appears to follow a fairly fixed, genetically specified pattern. A number of factors can interfere with this process, leading to abnormal developmental consequences. The most common causes of prenatal pathology identified to date include biological agents such as genetic factors and intrauterine trauma (infections, toxins, injury). These factors, if acting while structural development is in progress, may lead to dramatic structural malformations and cerebral reorganisation. For example, contraction of rubella during the first trimester of pregnancy has been shown to have a significant impact on the structure and function of the CNS. Similarly, a range of environmental agents can influence development prenatally. Maternal nutrition, maternal alcohol intake, and drug addiction and even stress have also been implicated in anomalous development of the CNS.

Postnatal development, although susceptible to the effects of biological risks such as infection, is also subject to disruption due to external trauma, exposure to toxins, and environmental deprivation. Research from our laboratory has provided evidence that such agents have greatest impact on younger children, when the CNS is developing most rapidly. For example, traumatic brain injury in preschool children will lead to more severe and persistent intellectual disability than similar injuries in older children (Anderson & Moore, 1995). Whole-brain cranial irradiation for the treatment of leukaemia leads to significant neurobehavioural sequelae in children treated prior to age 5, whereas older children exhibit no such impairment (Smibert et al., 1996). Such results are supported by other research groups (Ewing-Cobbs et al., 1997; Rubenstein et al., 1990; Taylor & Alden, 1997; Wrightson et al., 1995). Table 2.1 provides a list of factors that may be responsible for disruption of CNS development.

Psychosocial factors also need to be considered in the developmental

TABLE 2.1
Risk factors for anomalies in CNS development

Prenatal factors
Maternal stress and age
Maternal health, e.g., history of infection, rubella, cytomegalovirus, AIDS, herpes simplex
Nutrition: diet, malnutrition
Maternal drug and alcohol addiction: smoking, alcohol, marijuana, cocaine, heroin
Environmental toxins: lead, radiation, trauma

Postnatal factors
Birth complications
Nutrition
Environmental toxins: lead, radiation, trauma
Cerebral infection
Environment/experience

---

equation. Quality of the mother–child relationship, level of stimulation available to the child, social support structures, and access to resources may all impact on development, with children from disadvantaged environments more highly represented in special education classes, and at the lower end of the IQ distribution (Aylward, 1997). When such factors are linked to biological vulnerabilities, authors have argued for a double hazard (Escalona, 1982; Taylor et al., 1992). Thus, children with severe CNS lesions or insults who come from disadvantaged environments will show particularly poor development, whereas children with less severe insults from well-resourced families show best outcome. The possibility of an active role for the environment in enhancing development and maximising recovery in children with CNS dysfunction argues for the importance of appropriate intervention and management.

PRENATAL CNS DEVELOPMENT

Structural features of CNS development

The earliest stages of human CNS development—dorsal and ventral induction—are not dissimilar to those observed in other vertebrates. The fertilised cell experiences rapid cell division, resulting in the formation of a cluster of cells which quickly becomes the embryonic disc. The embryonic disc comprises three layers which later form specific organic systems within the human body. The nervous system emerges via a process of *neurolation*, from the outer layer, or ectoderm, of the embryonic disc, which folds in on itself and forms a tube. The initial stages of neurolation are thought to commence during the second week of gestation (Johnson, 1997). In the third week of gestation, the *neural plate* becomes visible as a thickened area of the ectoderm. Gradually a longitudinal *neural groove* begins to form, and is flanked by two edges or *neural folds*. These neural folds deepen and fold until they fuse, creating a hollow cylindrical structure, the *neural tube*, by week 4 of gestation (Hynd & Willis, 1988). This developmental process is illustrated in Figure 2.2. Disruptions to development in this very early stage of CNS maturation may result in serious structural anomalies, in particular disorders of neural tube closure such as myelomeningocele (incomplete closure of the spinal cord, resulting in spina bifida), anencephaly (incomplete closure of the neural tube, leading to an absent skull vault, and usually incompatible with life) and Arnold–Chiari malformation (structural abnormality of the CNS often associated with hydrocephalus).

Johnson (1997) observes that the neural tube develops along three different dimensions—length, circumference, and radius—with each dimension having relevance for specific features of the CNS. The length dimension of the neural tube is important for the major structural aspects of the CNS: the

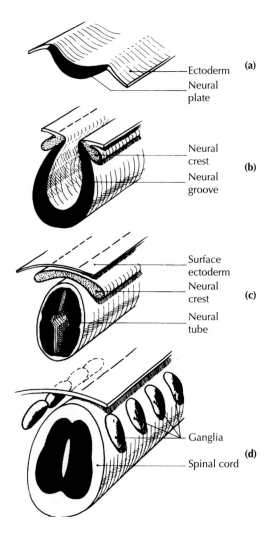

Ectoderm **(a)**

Neural plate

Neural crest **(b)**

Neural groove

Surface ectoderm

Neural crest **(c)**

Neural tube

Ganglia **(d)**

Spinal cord

Figure 2.2. Development of neural tube during the third and fourth weeks of gestation, illustrating the rapid development from neural plate to neural tube. Adapted from Tuchmann-Duplessis, Auroux, and Hagel (1975), with permission.

forebrain, midbrain, and spinal cord. As cell proliferation occurs within the neural tube, a number of bulges or *vesicles* emerge within the anterior portion. These vesicles are recognisable as mature CNS features by the fifth week of gestation and include the telencephalon, which later becomes the cortex, the diencephalon (thalamus and hypothalamus), the mesencephalon (midbrain), the metencephalon (pons, cerebellum), and the myelencephalon (medulla oblongata). The remaining areas of the neural tube form the spinal cord. These structures then grow, with further divisions emerging in each vesicle, forming the basic subdivisions, or cleavages, of the CNS (Capone, 1996) (see Figure 2.3). Disruption to development during this phase leads to a failure in the formations of these structural divisions, for example, holopros-encephaly (failure to form two cerebral hemispheres) and craniosynostosis (incomplete fusion of the skull).

The circumference dimension is responsible for differentiation between sensory and motor systems, with dorsal corresponding to sensory cortex, and ventral to motor cortex. The various association areas are arranged between these extremes. Radial differentiation leads to the layers and cell types observed within the brain. Across the radial aspect vesicles form, and it is within these vesicles that cells generate and are differentiated into specific cerebral systems.

Cellular basis of development

The process of neurolation progresses via the rapid generation of cells within the system. The nervous system consists of two main classes of cells: neurons and glial cells. These are produced by division of neuroblasts and glioblasts, each of which may be responsible for the formation of large numbers of cells. The structural maturation of the nervous system is largely dependent on the developmental processes related to the cellular bases of these entities.

The neuron, illustrated in Figure 2.4, is the basic functional unit of the CNS, and transmits impulses within a complex network of interconnecting brain cells. Although there are an enormous variety of neurons existing within the nervous system, their basic structure is similar and comprises four primary components: (1) the cell body, which serves the purpose of metabolic functions of the neuron and holds RNA and DNA; (2) the axon, a long projection from the cell body that conducts nerve impulses away from the cell body. The mature axon is covered by a coating of myelin allowing more rapid neural transmission; (3) the dendrites branch off the cell body and receive impulses from other neurons, conducting them towards the cell body. Dendritic spines are the locus of the synapse, where information is transmitted from one neuron to another; and (4) the presynaptic terminals, where neuro-transmitters are stored and released, cross the synaptic cleft and activate the neurons at the postsynapse.

The axon is responsible for conducting neural impulses from the cell body to the presynaptic terminal, from where it is transmitted to the connecting neuron via a synapse, to the dendrites of the connecting neuron. Depending on the location of the neuron, the characteristics of the axon and dendrites can vary, with long axons and large dendritic trees forming the basis of the

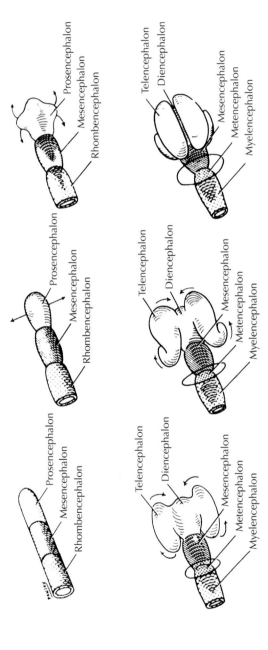

Figure 2.3. Development of the human brain, from neural plate to neural tube, during the first month of gestation. Adapted from House, Pansky, and Seigel (1979), with permission from The McGraw-Hill Companies.

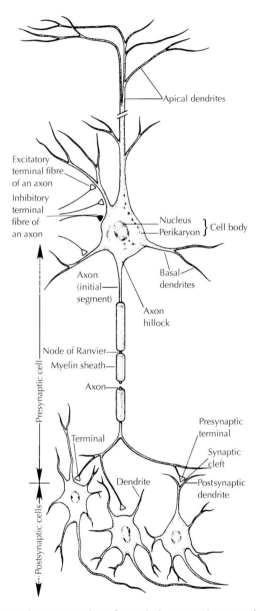

Figure 2.4. Diagrammatic representation of a typical neuron, demonstrating areas that are rapidly developing pre- and postnatally, including the axon, dendrites, and synapses. From *Fundamentals of Human Neuropsychology* by Bryan Kolb and Ian Q. Whishaw © 1996 by W. H. Freeman and Company. Used with permission.

49

major connections of the nervous system, and cells with smaller axons and dendritic connections associated with higher cortical function and found within the cortex.

In contrast to the active role of the neuron, glial cells play a more supportive and nutrient role within the nervous system, supporting the neurons, enabling regeneration of damaged neurons, producing scar tissue to occupy damage sites and transporting nutrients from nerve cells. There are nine times as many glial cells within the nervous system as there are neurons. Glial cells are differentiated from neurons by a lack of axons. There are several subtypes of these cells, for example: (1) astrocytes, which form the blood–brain barrier, support the cellular structure of brain, direct migration of neurons, and clean up and plug injury sites; (2) oligodendrocytes are responsible for speeding up the transmission of neural impulses throughout the nervous system, by coating axons with a substance called myelin. This process of progressive myelination continues throughout the CNS postnatally and well into childhood (Hynd & Willis, 1988; Klinberg et al., 1999); and (3) microglia clean up tissue around injury sites, primarily in the grey matter. Glial cells are relatively immature in the early stages of development and continue to generate with the increased maturity of the CNS.

Neurons and glial cells develop from neuroblasts and glioblasts respectively, with the process of development occurring in a predetermined sequence. Three major mechanisms underpin this process: (1) proliferation; (2) migration; and (3) differentiation. Each of these developmental stages occurs in sequence, with each successive stage commencing before the completion of the previous one, as illustrated in Figure 2.5.

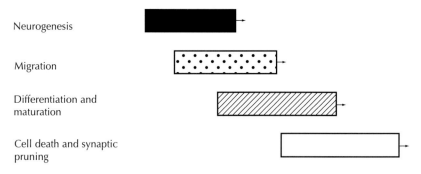

Neurogenesis

Migration

Differentiation and
maturation

Cell death and synaptic
pruning

Figure 2.5.   Schematic representation of the chronology of the major developmental processes occurring during prenatal development. Each successive process commences prior to the completion of the previous one. Modified from Kolb (1995).

Cell proliferation

Following fertilisation, rapid cell division occurs, leading to clusters of proliferating cells which then differentiate in a matter of days, into a three-layered structure known as the embryonic disc. Each of the three layers of this disc is destined to form a major organic system. The inner layer (endoderm) will form the internal organs, including the digestive and respiratory systems, whereas the skeletal and muscular structures will develop from the middle layer, or mesoderm. The outer layer, or ectoderm, eventually forms the nervous system and the skin surface (Johnson, 1997).

Cell generation, or cortical neurogenesis, via mitosis or division occurs within the neural tube. It begins early in gestation, around day 40, and is virtually complete by 6 months gestation, with the exception of a small number of cerebellar and hippocampal cells that continue to divide even after birth (Altman & Bayer, 1993; Baron, Fennell, & Voeller, 1996). Cell proliferation occurs within the neural tube in the germinal matrix, in the ventricular proliferative zone (Rakic, 1975), and cells then migrate from there to predetermined locations within the nervous system. The process appears to be precisely regulated so that appropriate numbers of cells are formed at predetermined times and in well-defined regions. These cell populations reside in particular regions of the expanding neural tube and are destined to develop into specific formations and structures within the CNS (Hynd & Willis, 1988; Johnson, 1997).

Migration

At the completion of the cell proliferation stage, but not before 6 weeks gestation, the neuroblasts formed within the neural tube begin to move, or migrate, to their permanent locations. Young neurons migrate in sheets of similar cells, created at similar times, towards particular areas of the outer layer of the neural tube, where they will eventually form the cortex and subcortical nuclei. Axons that connect this layer of the CNS to synapses form the white matter of the brain. The major migrational activity occurs from fetal week 8 to 16, with lesser activity continued to week 25 (Kuzniecky, 1994).

Two forms of migration have been identified. Passive migration, or cell displacement, occurs when cells are simply pushed away from where they originated by other cells that were generated more recently. In consequence these older cells are moved gradually towards the surface of the brain, whereas newer cells take up more internal positions. Passive migration is thought to lead to midline structures such as the thalamus, dentate gyrus, and regions of the brain stem. The second form, active migration, occurs when younger cells "overtake" the migrational activity of older cells, moving past them to external regions including the cerebral cortex. In this way, the laminar structure of the cortex develops, with different layers containing neurons that have differing migrational timetables (Johnson, 1997).

The mechanism by which neurons "know" where to move remains controversial. The most widely accepted theory suggests that radiating glial fibres direct neuronal migration from the ventricular proliferative area to the cerebral cortex. Cells migrate along these glial fibres to genetically predetermined regions of the brain (Shepherd, 1994). These radial glial fibres vary in length, with those guiding neuroblasts to occipital regions necessarily quite long. Once migration is completed, early in the postnatal period, these radial glia are transformed into astrocytes (Schmechel & Rakic, 1979). The migration process occurs quite rapidly and several cortical layers are visible during the fifth month of fetal development (Kolb & Fantie, 1989). The cortex shows signs of thickening and sulci begin to develop during this period.

Disorders of cell migration can lead to distribution of cells to wrong locations or inappropriate synaptic connections (Rayport, 1992). The resulting "heterotopias" may be widespread, characterised by abnormal laminar organisation within the cortex or in subcortical layers. Alternatively, they may be more localised, leading to large tightly clustered nodules of grey matter frequently located close to ventricles (Barkovich et al., 1996; Kuzniecky, 1994; Leventer et al., 1999). These heterotopic phenomena have been implicated in developmental disorders such as dyslexia (Geschwind & Galaburda, 1985), where abnormalities on the surface of the language cortex have been associated with deficits in language and reading acquisition. Similarly, Weinberger (1987) suggests that schizophrenia is the result of abnormal migration, where normal neuronal connections fail to be made between the dopaminergic and frontal systems. Migrational abnormalities are also implicated in disorders such as polymicrogyria (thin, highly folded cortex), lissencephaly (smooth cortex, normal thickness), and double cortex (presence of heterotopic layer beneath the cortex), with these malformations occurring during migration, specifically during the formation of the columnar structure of the cortex (Capone, 1996; Hallett & Proctor, 1996; Jacobs, Anderson, & Harvey, in press; Kuzniecky, 1994; Rakic, 1995). Such disorders are frequently associated with intellectual disability and epilepsy (Leventer et al., 1999).

Differentiation

This is a complex process, responsible for the diversity that eventually exists within the mature CNS. Once neurons have migrated they begin the process of differentiation, which occurs as four simultaneous processes: (1) development of cell bodies; (2) selective cell death; (3) dendritic and axonal growth; and (4) formation of synaptic connections. Simultaneously glial cells are differentiating, with oligodendrocytes forming myelin and astrocytes providing supportive functions within the CNS. During the differentiation stage cells become committed members of specialised systems, as relevant connections among neurons become established, and they begin to function. Activity may remain immature or poorly integrated for some time, and this is especially true for neurons whose axons have not yet myelinated and for systems that continue to evolve in infancy and early childhood.

Once the process of neuronal proliferation has ceased neurons are irreplaceable and, as they differentiate, their structure and function become quite unique. Thus while alternate neuronal systems may have the capacity to subsume impaired functions, destroyed neurons are not replaced. The number of cells generated during proliferation exceeds that required within the mature CNS. During differentiation this redundancy decreases, via a process of selective cell death, with authors suggesting up to 50% cell death in some areas of the nervous system (Brodal, 1992; Goldman-Rakic, Bourgeois, & Rakic, 1997; Kandel, 1985). It is thought that neurons that do not make appropriate connections become redundant and will be eliminated. This process of differentiation continues postnatally.

Once they reach their destination, neurons continue to develop or differentiate. It appears that axonal development may progress via "pioneer" axons. These axons are thought to contain high-concentration chemical markers that trace a developmental path that other axons recognise. It has been argued that such chemical markers are present only at selective periods during gestation, to ensure selective contact between specific neurons and systems. Within the peripheral nervous system, nerve growth factor stimulates the outward movement of axons, so that axons grow specifically into these areas. Brodal (1992) argues for a similar process within the CNS. Although axon growth appears to occur primarily during gestation, continued development has been observed, for example, within the corpus callosum, at least into early childhood. Nowakowski (1996) notes that axons do not necessarily grow directly to their target destination. He cites recent research that suggests there is an initial period of axonal growth to a range of sites, with a later elimination of redundant connections. There is some controversy as to the final destination of these axons, with some researchers arguing for a "preformist" explanation, determined solely by genetic factors. An alternative "empiricist" position is hypothesised by others, who suggest that environmental/experiential factors influence which connections are eliminated (Johnson, 1997).

Several additional developmental processes commence prenatally and continue into childhood and early adolescence. Each of these will be discussed in detail in the following discussion of postnatal development; they are simply alluded to at this time. Dendritic growth begins after the completion of the migration phase, and continues at a relatively slow rate into early childhood. Dendritic growth may be significantly affected by environmental agents. Synaptic development begins around the fifth month gestation

(Goldman-Rakic et al., 1997; Kolb & Fantie, 1989; Kolb & Gibb, 1999) and becomes more elaborate postnatally, along with the increased complexity of dendritic arborisation. Researchers have identified significant synaptic redundancy early in development, but gradually synaptic elimination occurs, to allow for more precise synaptic connections. Myelination commences later, with some cerebral regions showing evidence of this process at birth.

Disruptions to prenatal development

As previously noted, Figure 2.5 summarises the stages of prenatal development, and the timing of each relative to the other. Interruptions to these processes may have devastating effects for ongoing development. Genetic mutations, trauma, and infection are the most common biological causes of such disruptions. However, environmental factors, such as lead or radiation exposure, or poor maternal nutrition, alcohol or drug dependence, have also been shown to affect prenatal development. The timing of the insult may be more important to outcome than its nature and severity during this period. The earlier the disruption, the more likely it is to have a visible impact on gross cerebral morphology. Later in gestation, the consequences will be more likely to impact on migrational activity and neuronal differentiation. Further, specific structures in the process of development will be more vulnerable to the impact of insult. Table 2.2 lists the more common disorders and malformations observed following interruption to prenatal processes, giving an indication of the likely timing of insult, the pathogenesis, and observed clinical manifestations.

A recent study by Leventer and colleagues (1999) has described MR findings in a large group of children, identified as having malformations of cortical development. These authors noted that 70% of their sample displayed generalised hemispheric or multifocal pathology, with 60% of cases involving both cortical and subcortical abnormalities, illustrating the global implications of disruptions to development during the prenatal period. Several examples of such cerebral disruption are presented in Figure 2.6. Frontal lobe involvement was particularly common, possibly due to the late development of this cerebral region, and associated increased vulnerability to tetragenic or genetic influences. They identified a large spectrum of clinical problems in the group, including epilepsy, neurological deficits, intellectual retardation, and developmental delay. However, they were unable to establish a clear link between these symptoms and pathology on magnetic resonance imaging (MRI), emphasising the lack of knowledge regarding specific cognitive consequences of such drastic brain pathology.

TABLE 2.2

Impact of prenatal CNS dysfunction

Timing of insults	Description	Aetiology	Clinical manifestations
A. *Dorsal induction (weeks 3–4)*			
Myelomeningocele/spina bifida	Failure of closure of spinal cord	Genetic or nutritional factors	Motor, perceptual deficits
Anencephaly	Failure of neural tube to close, creating an absent vault of skull	Severe trauma, day 18 to week 4	Incompatible with life
B. *Ventral induction (weeks 5–6)*			
Holoprosencephaly	Defective division of forebrain, failure to form two hemispheres	Often genetic, e.g., anomalies in chromosomes 13 or 18	Generally incompatible with life
C. *Proliferation (2–5 months)*			
Microencephaly	Early cessation of cell division causing abnormally small head	Genetic or trauma factors, e.g., infection, fetal alcohol syndrome	Low intellectual abilities
Megalencephaly	Overproduction/poor elimination of neurons, abnormally large brain	Familial/genetic	No typical picture
Hydranencephaly	Cystic sacs containing cerebrospinal fluid replacing cerebral hemispheres	Possibly vascular aetiology, umbilical cord strangulation	Incompatible with life
D. *Migration (2–5 months)*			
Lissencephaly (agyria)	Smooth cortex, absence of sulci and gyri, but normal cortical thickness, neurons in abnormal locations	Disorder of migration 11–13 weeks	Severe mental retardation, seizures, neuromotor disorders
Schizencephaly	Agenesis of part of cerebral wall, cortical layers not evident	Disorder of migration 8 weeks	Mental retardation, seizures, neuromotor disorders
Polymicrogyria	Multiple small, shallow convolutions on brain surface, neurons in abnormal locations	Migrational disorder, 16–20 weeks Genetic/infectious mechanisms	May be asymptomatic, or associated with epilepsy, learning, behaviour problems

continued overleaf

Table 2.2 continued

Timing of insults	Description	Aetiology	Clinical manifestations
Agenesis of the corpus callosum	Absence or malformation of fibres crossing between the cerebral hemispheres	Genetic, weeks 12–22 gestation	May be asymptomatic, but has been associated with other disorders, e.g., spina bifida
Focal dysplasias (heterotopias)	Abnormalities of laminar structure or abnormally positioned cells	Migrational disorder, multiple origins	Epilepsy, learning disability, schizophrenia
Double cortex	Diffuse cortical dysplasia with a band of heterotropic matter between cortex and ventricles Cerebral surface may look normal	Migrational disorder, late in migration, once some waves of migration are complete	Often asymptomatic Epilepsy sometimes detected
E. Differentiation Porencephaly	Presence of large cystic lesions, usually bilaterally	5–7 months gestation, traumatic cause/vascular/infection	Sometimes asymptomatic, but also with retardation and epilepsy

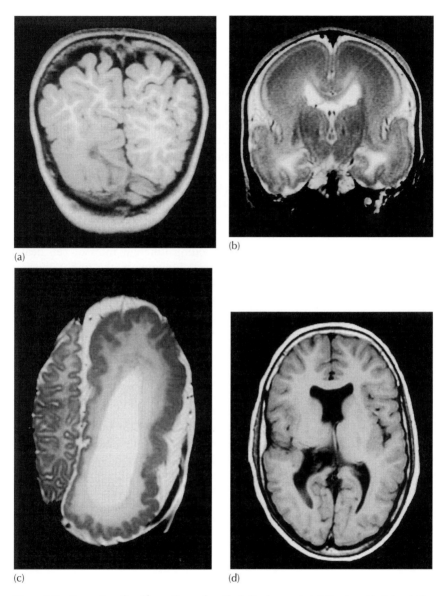

(a)

(b)

(c)   (d)

Figure 2.6. Examples of malformations of cortical development. (a) Focal cortical dysplasia, with evidence of poor grey–white matter differentiation and low white matter signal in the right hemisphere; (b) agyria–pachygyria (classical lissencephaly), characterised by smooth gyral pattern and thickened cortex; (c) hemimegencephaly, including markedly abnormal left hemisphere with a thickened, irregular cortex, excessive white matter, heterotopic grey matter, and a dilated, dysmorphic lateral ventricle; and (d) unilateral schizencephaly, with grey matter-lined cleft in right posterior frontal lobe communicating with right lateral ventricle.

POSTNATAL DEVELOPMENT

Human postnatal development is very much an extended process compared to that which occurs in other primates, continuing through childhood and into adolescence. This observation questions the use of primates as models for understanding postnatal cerebral development. Brain growth quadruples in size from birth to adulthood; this increase is not due to a proliferation of neurons, the full complement of which is established prenatally (Rakic, 1995). Rather, the increase reflects ongoing elaboration within the system, primarily due to three processes: dendritic arborisation, myelination, and synaptogenesis (Reiss et al., 1996).

Historically, most research investigating postnatal development has been limited to either animal research or autopsy studies. Huttenlocher (1994) has questioned the value of much animal research. He suggests that animal models are unable to provide data with respect to developmental processes and their trajectories, citing different rates of cell death in mice (30%), monkeys (15%) and less in humans, in the fine-tuning of the CNS. Huttenlocher (1994) notes that the presence of the prefrontal cortices in humans, and their rich projections with all other areas of the brain, necessarily implies a fundamental difference between human and other systems that cannot be ignored. Similar criticisms are directed to conclusions from autopsy data. Such studies are generally limited by small sample size, with samples contaminated by the possibility of undetected disease. As is the case for the study of prenatal development, recent technological advances have enabled expansion of knowledge regarding postnatal CNS development. In particular, radiological techniques, including structural imaging (e.g., MRI, computed tomography [CT] scans) and functional measures (e.g., position emission tomography [PET], functional magnetic resonance imaging [fMRI]), provide non-invasive methods for the investigation of CNS developmental processes such as myelination, and brain metabolism.

CNS elaboration

Dendritic arborisation

This aspect of development is thought to be additive in nature, with no evidence of regression or pruning of dendrites within the CNS (Becker, Armstrong, Chan, & Wood, 1984; Huttenlocher, 1996; Reiss et al., 1996). Dendritic growth is usually investigated by using staining techniques with neural tissue. Most of the data addressing dendritic development has derived from studies of the visual cortex, primarily in rats, but more recently in humans. Such investigations show that dendritic branching begins to occur as early as 25–30 weeks gestation, with continued branching occurring to birth.

However, the major changes occur postnatally, including increased length and branching, as shown in Figure 2.7. Becker and colleagues (Becker et al., 1984) describe the most dramatic development occurring between 5 and 21 weeks postnatally, with adult levels of development evident by 5–6 months. More recently, Huttenlocher (1996) has identified regional differences in dendritic development. He studied two regions: visual cortex and middle frontal gyrus. His results suggest that whereas dendritic changes within the visual cortex are consistent with previous findings, development within frontal areas continues at least to age 7.

There is evidence that environmental stimulation can increase dendritic development, and conversely that lack of stimulation can interfere with the process (Greenough, Juraska, & Volkmar, 1979; Kolb, 1995; Spinelli, Jensen, & Di Prisco, 1980). Kolb (Kolb, 1995; Kolb et al., 1998; Kolb & Gibb, 1999) has reported increases in dendritic growth in enriched environments, as well as a decrease in spine density, which he interprets as a capacity to develop more experience-specific branches, at the cost of less non-specific dendritic growth. He argues that this process may possibly explain observations of quicker, more efficient learning in such contexts. In contrast, stunted dendritic growth or abnormal dendritic morphology has been demonstrated in the brains of individuals with intellectual disability (Huttenlocher, 1974; Purpura, 1975).

Synaptogenesis

Synapses are the point of transmission between neurons, and their development is usually investigated via electron microscopy, using post-mortem tissue. Synaptic connections increase from birth, with bursts of rapid growth occurring at varying stages within different cerebral regions, and ultimate maturation achieved variably as well. The process begins in the second trimester of gestation, close to the end of the migrational phase (Molliver, Kostovic, & Van der Loos, 1973), although most development is postnatal. Synapses appear to develop randomly initially, with these early connections unspecified with respect to function (Huttenlocher, 1994). There is an overproduction and redundancy of synapses in the postnatal developmental phase. Gradually neural circuits emerge, and synaptic contacts are utilised within these systems. Those that remain unspecified regress (S. Anderson, Classey, et al., 1995; Goldman-Rakic et al., 1997; Huttenlocher & de Courten, 1987; Rakic, 1995) with this synaptic elimination commencing after 1 year, and progressing at different rates in different systems. Research suggests that, in contrast to the vulnerability of myelination and dentritic development to environmental influences, synaptic processes appear relatively immune to the effects of environmental stimulation or deprivation (Goldman-Rakic et al., 1997).

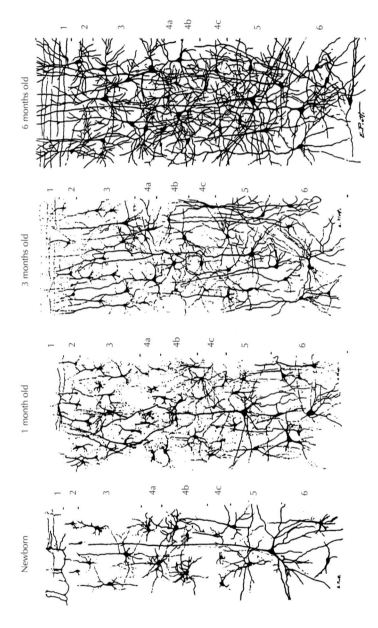

Figure 2.7. Cellular structure and development of human visual cortex from birth to 6 months. These illustrations indicate the increase in connectivity occurring in the brain during this period. From Johnson (1997), with permission.

60

Similar developmental time courses have been identified within the-auditory and visual cortex, with bursts at 3–4 months, and relative maturity achieved between 4–12 months. Within the prefrontal cortex development begins at the same time, but is slower, not reaching its peak until after 12 months of age (Huttenlocher, 1990, 1994; Huttenlocher & Dabholkar, 1997; Huttenlocher, de Courten, Garey, & Van der Loos, 1982; Johnson, 1997). Huttenlocher (1994) notes that this process is complete in the visual system at about age 7, but continues into early adolescence in the frontal cortex. He goes on to comment on the parallels between synaptogenesis, elimination of synapses, and functional plasticity, noting that although there is redundancy in the system there is more likelihood of functional plasticity, with redundant synapses being enlisted into damaged systems. He argues further that this plasticity and its temporal limits may be different in different systems, in keeping with the chronology of synaptic elimination.

Not surprisingly, similar developmental patterns have been observed with respect to neurotransmitter levels within the CNS, which show a "rise and fall" style of developmental progression. Huttenlocher argues that this is also consistent with the process of synaptogenesis. A parallel pattern of decrease in glucose metabolism has been observed by Chugani, Phelps, and Mazziotta (1987) and may also reflect synaptic density reduction.

Myelination

Nerve conduction velocity increases from 2 to 50 m s^{-1} once an axon has been myelinated, indicating the importance of this aspect of CNS development to efficient neurobehavioural functioning (Caeser, 1993). The advent of structural imaging technology has enabled researchers to apply non-invasive approaches to the study of myelination. In particular, MRI techniques are able to capture the dramatic increase in myelination in the first year of life, via changes in signal density evident on scans. The subtle increments occurring after this period are more difficult to image (Valk & Van der Knapp, 1992). A collation of findings from such studies has provided an approximate myelination schedule, showing that most myelination occurs postnatally, with rapid development in the first 3 years of life, and slower progress continuing into the second decade (Holland, Haas, Brant-Zawadski, & Newton, 1986; Jernigan et al., 1991; Kinney et al., 1988; Klinberg et al., 1999; Pfefferbaum et al., 1994; Sowell & Jernigan, 1998; Yakovlev & Lecours, 1967). Recent research has identified further significant change in the peri-pubertal stage, possibly associated with hormonal changes within the brain (Benes, Turtle, Khan, & Farol, 1994; Giedd et al., 1996; Sowell & Jernigan, 1998).

A number of general rules of myelination have also been established, suggesting that, within the CNS, proximal pathways become myelinated before distal, sensory before motor, projection before association, central areas before poles, and posterior zones before anterior (Fuster, 1993; Hudspeth & Pribram, 1990; Staudt et al., 1993). Specifically, vestibular and spinal tracts, related to basic postural control, are myelinated as early as 40 weeks gestation, with the cerebellum, internal capsule, thalamus, and basal ganglia also showing evidence of myelination prenatally. Midbrain cortical–visual pathways show evidence of myelination by 2–3 months of age and descending lateral cortical spinal tracts by the end of first year of life, when fine motor control appears (Caeser & Lagae, 1991). Cerebellar–cerebral connections are not myelinated until the second year of life, with hippocampal and other limbic structures and the reticular tracts still maturing at school age and tracts connecting specific and associative cortical areas showing ongoing development into adulthood (Benes et al., 1994; Klinberg et al., 1999; Sowell & Jernigan, 1998; Yakovlev and Lecours, 1967). The prefrontal region is one of the last areas to be fully myelinated, with considerable myelination continuing during late childhood and early adolescence (Cummings, 1993; Klinberg et al., 1999; Paus, Zijdenbos, & Worsley, 1999; Reiss et al., 1996; Steen, Ogg, & Reddick, 1997). This sequence of development is consistent with the previously discussed hierarchical models of CNS development, and with the documented emergence of cognitive and information-processing abilities through childhood.

Myelination is not an all-or-none process. Rather there is a gradual increase in the thickness of the myelin sheaths surrounding the axon. The process is not complete until early adulthood. The rate of myelination varies across cerebral regions, with the process occurring more quickly and reaching maturity sooner in some areas. It is generally agreed that the frontal lobes are the last cerebral region to become myelinated, with the process particularly protracted in these areas. Disruption to the process of myelination has been noted to occur due to cerebral trauma (e.g., traumatic brain injury) or environmental toxicity (e.g., radiation therapy). Neurobehavioural correlates of interruptions to normal myelination have been reported to include slowed speed of response, reduced attention, and generally impaired information-processing capacity. Other researchers have linked such problems to more severe conditions such as intellectual disability or developmental delays (van der Knapp et al., 1991). Where such events occur during critical stages of myelination, abnormal ongoing cerebral development has also been noted (Fernandez-Bouzas et al., 1992; Paakko et al., 1992). Kinney and colleagues (Kinney et al., 1988) suggest that the most vulnerable period for myelination occurs during the first 8 months of life, when myelination initiation and completion are most active.

Indirect evidence of cerebral development

In addition to research that focuses on direct measures of dendritic arbor-isation, synaptogenesis, and myelination, a range of studies that have investi-gated other aspects of cerebral functioning provide corroborative evidence for the processes described above. Studies of cerebral metabolism have described the pattern of overdevelopment similar to that demonstrated for synaptogenesis. Chugani et al. (1987), using functional imaging techniques, identified a rise in brain metabolism (i.e., glucose uptake) during the first 12 months, with different metabolic patterns evident in subcortical, posterior, and frontal regions. They observed a peak level of activity (higher than adult levels) from 4 to 5 years of age, which was maintained until around 9 years. After that time there was a gradual decline to adult levels into the second decade of life. Similarly, Chiron et al. (1992) monitored regional cerebral blood flow, which they found to be low and variable at birth, with a rapid increase to adult levels by age 2, continued rise until age 9, and then a decline back to adult levels in the second decade of life. Findings from these studies suggest developmental trends consistent with those documented for synaptic development and elimination.

Electroencephalogram (EEG) patterning and evoked potentials have also been employed to map cerebral development (Parmalee & Sigman, 1983; Thatcher, 1992, 1997). These approaches have identified changes in EEG patterns through childhood, which appear relatively independent of environmental influences. They show that the immature brain has relatively long latencies, which they suggest may be associated with longer transmission time across immature synapses and along unmyelinated axons. Thatcher (1991, 1997) has described a number of growth periods, the first between birth and 2 years, another from 7 to 9 years, with a final spurt in late ado-lescence (16–19 years). These growth spurts are thought to be associated with increases in either the number or strength of cortical synaptic connections. Consistent with Thatcher's findings, Hudspeth and Pribram (1990) document EEG data that indicate maturational peaks and plateaux continuing through childhood and into adolescence. They report a differential pattern of regional cerebral development, with simultaneous completion of maturation throughout the CNS. In frontal regions, they describe accelerated develop-ment from 7 to 10 years which then terminates synchronously with develop-ment of other brain regions. Rourke et al. (1986) comment that initially electrical activity is fairly non-specific, but becomes more localised and function specific with maturity. They note that the parietal area shows regular activity first, with the prefrontal regions last.

Age-related prefrontal RNA development, through to approximately 9 years of age (Uemura & Hartmann, 1978), and changes in patterns of meta-bolic activity and levels of various enzymes (Kennedy, Sakurada, Shinohara,

& Miyaoka, 1982), are also consistent with an additive model of CNS development.

Frontal lobe development

The frontal regions of the brain have particular significance in the developmental process. These cerebral regions are relatively immature during childhood, with development thought to be a protracted process that continues into early adolescence (Cummings, 1993; Rabinowicz, 1976; Reiss et al., 1996; Yakovlev & Lecours, 1967). In particular, processes such as dendritic arborisation, myelination, and synaptogenesis have all been reported to reach maturity last in these anterior regions (Fuster, 1993; Huttenlocher, 1997, 1979; Jernigan & Tallal, 1990; Klinberg et al., 1999; Kolb & Fantie, 1989; Risser & Edgell, 1988). This is not surprising, given that the frontal lobes are dependent upon input from posterior and subcortical cerebral regions for their function. In particular the prefrontal cortex, thought to be the primary mediator of executive functions, receives input from all areas of the frontal and posterior neocortex (Barbas, 1992; Fuster, 1993). Thus sensory and perceptual data are processed by the frontal lobes where actions are organised and executed, with efficient functioning reliant upon the quality of information received from other cerebral regions. This pattern of connectivity suggests that although prefrontal regions may "orchestrate" behaviour, they are also dependent on all other cerebral areas for input, with efficient functioning reliant upon the quality of information received from other cerebral regions.

Initially studies of frontal lobe development were influenced by a view that these regions were "functionally silent" in infancy and early childhood (Golden, 1981). A number of neurophysiological studies now refute this view, documenting clear evidence of frontal lobe activity even in infancy. One of the first studies to refute this view was conducted by Chugani and colleagues (Chugani et al., 1987). They measured local cerebral metabolic rates of glucose in infants and young children, and found evidence of frontal activation in infants as young as 6 months of age. Similarly Bell and Fox (1992) have documented changes in scalp-recorded EEG in frontal regions during the first year of life, relating these to improvements in behavioural performance. Such findings are now commonplace, particularly in the functional imaging literature, where a number of research groups have documented frontal lobe activation in both normal children and in groups with cerebral pathology (Gaillard et al., 2000; Hertz-Pannier et al., 1997; Muller et al., 1998).

It is generally agreed that the frontal lobes are hierarchically organised, with processes such as myelination progressing through a number of stages, from primary and sensory areas to association areas and finally frontal regions (Fuster, 1993; Hudspeth & Pribram, 1990; Staudt et al., 1993).

There is a growing body of developmental research that argues that a number of discrete growth spurts occur in frontal lobe development specifically (Bell & Fox, 1992; Cummings, 1993; Klinberg et al., 1999; Reiss et al., 1996; Thatcher, 1991, 1997), the first commencing around age 6, a second about age 10, with a final spurt in early adolescence. This data is supported by behavioural research that has documented a series of improvements in executive skills, through childhood, with evidence of a plateau in mid-adolescence. Further, the timing of these developmental increments consistent with those described by neurophysiological researchers (P. Anderson, Anderson, & Lajoie, 1996; V. Anderson, Anderson, Northam, Jacobs, & Catroppa, in press; Diamond, 1988, 1990; Levin et al., 1991; Stauder, Molenaar, & van der Molen, 1999; Welsh, Pennington, & Groisser, 1991).

SPECIALISATION OF THE CEREBRAL CORTEX

Neuropsychological models generally presume a "localisationist" approach (Luria, 1973; Walsh, 1985), which ascribes particular behavioural functions to specific cortical regions. Such theories are largely based on lesion studies of adult patients who show similar deficits following similarly located lesions. While such functional specialisation may be the case for the mature CNS, it remains unclear whether this is true from early in gestation, when the CNS begins to emerge, or if such a localisation of function occurs gradually during the developmental process. Current understanding of prenatal development provides some support for prespecified functional organisation, at least at a relatively gross level. In particular, the processes of neuronal proliferation and migration suggest that neurons are preprogrammed to form particular cerebral structures, which then subsume specific behavioural functions. However, the functional aspects of later development, the possible flexibility of the CNS with respect to behaviour, and the role of environment/ experiential factors in this process are less clearly understood.

Johnson (1997) argues that at least some aspects of the CNS are "hard-wired" and primarily determined by cellular and molecular interactions (e.g., the laminar structure of the brain), with little chance for any environmental/ experiential influence. However, he concedes that such observations may not be readily applied to cortical function. He goes on to describe two contrasting views of cortical specialisation, the first supporting innate specialisation and the second supporting a "tabula rosa" view, where cortical specialisation is dependent upon external input. The innate specialisation or "protomap" model states that differentiation begins prenatally, at the time of proliferation and migration, where neurons follow radial glial fibres to predetermined destinations and then become components of particular cerebral regions. In this theory cortical structure and function are determined prior to postnatal experience (Rakic, 1988). Studies addressing structural cerebral asymmetries support this view. For example, a number of researchers (Gal-aburda, LeMay, Kemper, & Geschwind, 1978; Geschwind & Levitsky, 1968; Witelson & Pallie, 1973) have demonstrated that the planum temporale, argued to be important for aspects of language function, is larger in the left hemisphere, supporting prenatal lateralisation of at least some components of language function.

This view is not consistent with early plasticity notions, which argue that there is the opportunity for transfer of language functions within the CNS following cerebral insult. However, recent research has demonstrated that such perspectives may be too simplistic. Rather than function "transfer" there may be a process of "recruitment" where additional skills (subsumed by healthy brain regions) are engaged to compensate for those disrupted as a result of cerebral pathology (D. Anderson et al., 2000; Heiss et al., 1999; Thulborn, 1998). Such a view is more in keeping with Johnson's "hard-wired" perspective of cerebral specialisation.

The alternative view, which better accommodates plasticity notions, argues that the cortex is initially undifferentiated with respect to function, but gradually becomes specialised during the postnatal period, in response to input from the thalamus (Killackey, 1990; O'Leary, 1989). This perspective allows for an impact of postnatal experience, via sensory and motor input to the thalamus and suggests that cortical regions could subsume a variety of functions depending on the early input they receive. A review of the relevant literature indicates that there is surprisingly little evidence for the innate spe-cialisation theories, suggesting that it is more likely that regions of the cortex are relatively unspecified intrinsically, and that specificity gradually develops via external input, the processes of which remain unclear (Johnson, 1997). Such a position has important implications for early cerebral insult, suggesting that cerebral damage occurring during childhood, before special-isation is complete, may permanently alter functional localisation within the CNS.

GENDER DIFFERENCES IN CEREBRAL DEVELOPMENT

There is growing evidence that gender differences exist with respect to brain development. Autopsy studies consistently document such differences in overall brain size, with adult males having 10% greater brain volume (Blatter et al., 1995; Pfefferbaum et al., 1994; Reiss et al., 1996). Recent research has indicated that these differences are present early in cerebral development (Reiss et al., 1996). Morphological studies, investigating the nature of these gender differences, show that the male brain has increased cortical grey mat-ter, suggesting greater cortical neuronal density, with this pattern consistent across most cerebral structures (Giedd et al., 1996; Jernigan et al., 1991;

Pfefferbaum et al., 1994). Witelson, Glezen, and Kigar (1995) have qualified these findings, documenting greater cortical density for women in specific layers of the cortex within posterior temporal regions of the brain. In contrast, animal studies have been employed to study brain connectivity, which has also been argued to differ for males and females. A number of studies have found that, although there is some variation throughout the brain, overall the female brain has more dendritic material in pyramidal neurons (Jacobs & Scheibel, 1993; Kolb, 1995; Kolb & Stewart, 1991; Seymoure & Juraska, 1992; Stewart & Kolb, 1994). Such a finding raises the possibility of a greater number of synapses as well, despite fewer neurons. Interestingly, no gender differences have been identified with respect to brain asymmetry (Reiss et al., 1996).

In addition to these basic structural differences, neuroanatomical studies, mainly on non-human species, suggest that cortical development follows a differential path in males and females, possibly associated with hormonal factors. There is evidence for differences in growth patterns of grey and white matter in girls and boys 4–18 years (Caviness et al., 1996; Giedd et al., 1997). In particular, females have been found to exhibit more rapid left hemisphere development during early childhood (Hanlon, Thatcher, & Cline, 1999; Kolb, 1995), with males showing faster right hemisphere development. Hanlon and colleagues (1999) also note that this pattern of brain maturation is reversed in later childhood.

CONCLUSIONS

The specific details of normal CNS development remain poorly understood, with new technologies only now enabling researchers to study the immature brain more directly. As a result, a number of developmental principles are beginning to emerge, which demonstrate that maturation is not a simple, linear progression. Rather there is a gradual "fine-tuning" of the cerebral system, characterised by initial neural growth, later specification, and ultimate connectivity within and between functional systems, until optimal efficiency is achieved. This process is highly complex and tightly defined with respect to timing. Any interruption may divert the expected developmental course, and ultimate outcome. Research indicates that prenatal development occurs largely according to a biologically predetermined template, with neurons generated, transported, and aggregated into set neural systems, via a complex and sophisticated series of developmental stages. Disruptions, either biological or environmental, occurring during this period may lead to alterations in the structural formation of the CNS. Postnatal development may also be prespecified, although perhaps to a lesser extent. The CNS continues to be vulnerable to the influence of environmental and experiential factors during postnatal growth, with the immature CNS susceptible to disruption through childhood and into early adolescence. The consequences of this disruption may be qualitatively different, depending upon the timing, with dysfunction of the elaboration and connectivity of the CNS more likely postnatally.

CHAPTER THREE

Cognitive development

From birth to adulthood children undergo dramatic changes in cognitive skills. This is an extremely rich and complex process, with interactions occurring across and between different cognitive domains. Current models see the child as an active participant, seeking out knowledge and using past experience to understand and integrate information, thus developing more sophisticated repertoires. Not surprisingly, attempts to increase our understanding of cognitive development have flourished, with cognitive scientists, developmentalists, linguists, and neuroscientists, to name but a subset, all participating in the endeavour. In this chapter we do not attempt to address this vast literature, but rather to draw out some aspects specifically relevant in the context of central nervous system (CNS) dysfunction. The focus of discussion will be on the development of information processing and executive skills—abilities that are frequently observed to be impaired as a consequence of cerebral insult during childhood (Anderson & Pentland, 1998; Ewing-Cobbs et al., 1998; Kaufmann et al., 1993; Levin et al., 1997; Loss, Yeates, & Enrile, 1998: Taylor, Hack, & Klein, 1998; Todd, Anderson, & Lawrence, 1996; Yeates, Blumstein, Patterson, & Delis, 1995). Our discussion attempts to explore the links between observable increments/progress in cognition and associated parallels in underlying neural growth and maturation, and also to explore the possible impact of cerebral insult on the development and consolidation of cognitive processes.

PARALLELS BETWEEN COGNITIVE AND CEREBRAL DEVELOPMENT

By and large, the investigation of cognitive development has progressed with minimal reference to the underlying processes of cerebral maturation. It is surprising to review even recent accounts of cognitive development, and note the limited role allocated to the CNS in the development of cognitive functions (e.g., Flavell, 1992). Some researchers do suggest that the progression observed in cognitive capacity may be related to the underlying maturation of the CNS. At the most general level, the observation that cognitive and cerebral development are each rapid during childhood, plateauing in early to mid-adolescence, warrants further consideration. A number of researchers have drawn attention to parallels between traditional cognitive-developmental models and neurological evidence (e.g., Piaget, 1963; Welsh & Pennington, 1988; Welsh et al., 1991). In fact, the parallels are difficult to ignore. Numerous studies have reported that executive functions, in particular, progress in a stage-like manner, consistent with growth spurts identified within the CNS (V. Anderson, 1998; P. Anderson et al., 1996; Kirk, 1985; Levin et al., 1991; Stuss, 1992; Welsh & Pennington, 1988; Welsh et al., 1991).

Historically, cognitive models have strongly supported a hierarchical view of development. In particular, Piaget's theory of cognitive development (Piaget, 1963), although providing no specific reference to possible neural substrates, is highly compatible with hierarchical theories of cerebral development. Piaget describes four sequential cognitive stages: Sensorimotor (birth to 2 years), Preoperational (2–7 years), Concrete Operational (7–9 years), and Formal Operational (early adolescence). Such models suggest a fixed progression, across all cognitive domains simultaneously, where all processes are subject to the same level of cognitive competence. Although more contemporary developmental psychologists now dispute the specific principles of Piagetian theory (Flavell, 1992), it is worthy of note that the hypothesised timing of transitions between Piaget's cognitive stages coincide quite closely with growth spurts identified within the CNS (Hudspeth & Pribram, 1990; Klinberg et al., 1999; Thatcher, 1991, 1992, 1997).

Contemporary models of development have moved somewhat from these simplistic, stage-based explanations, arguing for a less global process of development. As previously discussed, although neural maturation does appear to be continuous, phase-like developments are observed to occur in different systems at different times, with individual cerebral systems maturing at different times as well. The notion of critical or sensitive periods attached to specific domains (e.g., language, visual processing) provides support for this contemporary, more "domain-specific" perspective, arguing that various functional systems have discrete but different developmental time frames, where uninterrupted progress is crucial. Although there may be interplay between systems, each system is maturing separately, probably due to underlying processes, such as progressive myelination and synaptogenesis. Such independent development across systems is not consistent with the traditional more global, systemic stepwise model of developmental progression.

The move away from restrictive, stage-like models of development has a number of implications for developmental neuropsychology. First, it provides the possibility that the child may utilise parallel or alternative routes to those employed in the normal acquisition of a particular skill. This is particularly relevant for understanding the child with CNS dysfunction, where the traditional steps to development may be blocked. Similarly, it broadens a conceptualisation of abnormal development to include the possibility of displaying a "deficit" rather than simply a "delay" in achieving the next stage in development. In addition, it enables the inclusion of the notion of individual differences in the developmental process, where the child may employ a variety of alternative routes or pathways to achieve the same developmental endpoint. Depending on the nature of these varying developmental processes, skills may be established at different times and rates for individual children (Temple, 1997).

Cognitive theorists, too, are moving in this direction. Flavell (1992), in his review of theoretical advances in cognitive development, states that developmental cognitive theorists no longer view cognitive development as a series of fixed steps as Piagetian theory suggested. They do, however, recognise that some aspects of development, although specific in themselves—for example, information-processing capacity—may underpin the development of other specific skill domains (Case, 1992; Pascual-Leone, 1987; Temple, 1997). Many Neo-Piagetian theorists see the development of cognition as largely based on advances in information processing—both speed and capacity. Siegler (1991, p. 354) goes so far as to suggest that the mechanism of cognitive development may be defined as "any mental process that improves children's ability to process information". Others argue that such development is likely based on underlying CNS maturational processes (Diamond, 1995). From the neuropsychologist's perspective, it is the interruption to development of these very "CNS" processes that is so often associated with damage and thus deficit in childhood brain dysfunction (e.g., traumatic brain injury, hydrocephalus, cranial irradiation). For this reason, the following discussion of cognitive development will focus primarily on the development of these information-processing skills. Table 3.1, however, provides readers with a summary of major developmental progressions in a number of cognitive domains, and the reader is referred to the following texts for further information on development of specific domains including language and visual abilities: Bjorklund (1989); Goswami (1998); Mogford and Bishop (1993); Siegler (1991).

TABLE 3.1

Development of motor and perceptual skills through early childhood

Age	Motor function	Visual function	Communication/social function
Birth–6 weeks	Reflex sucking, rooting, swallowing Infantile grasping	Turns head, blinks to light Follows dangling ball briefly Fixes on mother's face from 3 weeks	Eye-to-eye contact Turns head to speaker
6 weeks–3 months	Increasing neck control, extends and turns neck when prone Unable to take weight on legs Finger play	Preoccupation with human face Follows dangling ball attentively Defensive blink Converges eyes for finger play	Smiles when played with
3–6 months	Grasps objects with both hands Extends arms to be lifted Takes weight on legs Rolls and sits with support	Visually alert for near and far Turns to objects in visual field Regards small object Reaches and grasps toys	Localises sounds Loud vocalisations to others Primitive articulated sounds Noisy cries/protests when distressed Laughs aloud and shows pleasure
6–12 months	Sits independently Crawls Thumb–forefinger grasp Pulls to stand Reaches for toys without falling	Follows dangling ball all directions Looks for fallen or hidden toys Anticipates rotating ball Increased attention span for visual stimuli	Babbles using strings of syllables Smiles at self in mirror Responds to name and familiar sounds Imitates sounds and gestures Increased reserve with strangers Demonstrates affection Seeks attention via gestures and vocalisation
1–2 years	Walks independently Crawls upstairs Kneels without support Able to release objects from grasp	Full adult visual acuity Picks up threads and small pellets	Expresses 2–4 words with meaning Understands several nouns Conversation like jargon

72

Age	Motor / Physical	Cognitive	Language / Social
2–3 years	Runs safely Climbs on furniture Walks up and down stairs Bends and picks up objects Turns knobs Able to partially dress	Can match objects and pictures	Two- to three-word sentences Uses pronouns accurately Points to body parts Obeys simple commands Plays simple games Symbolic play emerges
3–5 years	Peddles tricycle Runs on tip-toe Climbs ladders, trees Drawing skills emerge	Recognises letters and numbers	Speech fully intelligible Extensive vocabulary Asks questions Recites nursery rhymes Plays with others
5 years +	Dresses and undresses independently Skips and hops Ties shoelaces		Repeats digits Names colours Gives personal details (e.g., name) Narrates/retells stories Correct grammatical usage

DEVELOPMENT OF
INFORMATION-PROCESSING ABILITIES

Cognitive scientists are limited by the indirect markers available to map development. Although chronological age is frequently employed as the indicator of developmental levels, individual differences in maturation mean that this is not a precise benchmark. For example, as indicated in Table 3.1, the emergence of most functional abilities cannot be accurately determined, with considerable variation in the timing of skill acquisition across the normal population. Where some interruption occurs to this developmental process, this variability is increased, so that developmental predictions become even less reliable. Similarly, measures employed to examine developmental processes are usually multidimensional, tapping into a range of skills and complicating the ability of the scientist to address isolated cognitive abilities. For many cognitive abilities our understanding of mature cognitive processes is incomplete, and descriptions of development of these skills are in their infancy (e.g., Baddeley, 1990; Cowan, 1988, 1997; Posner, 1978; Posner & Petersen, 1990). These problems are particularly evident in the field of information processing, where even adult models remain controversial.

The information-processing system may be divided into a number of processes or structures, depending on the theoretical perspective taken. For the purpose of the following discussion, we will employ a model described by Cowan (1988, 1995) that is primarily structural and incorporates components of attention, memory, output, and central executive. Cowan's model is an integrative, systemic model, in keeping with our view of both neural and neurobehavioural function (see Figure 3.1), providing some comment on the processes that may relate to the specific structures he describes. He suggests that the individual must first attend to information, register and encode it, and then store it in memory. Finally the information needs to be retrieved and outputted. There are links among each of these steps, but directing the focus of attention and formulating strategies for efficient performance is the role of the "central executive", which has links with all aspects of the system. Development in each one of these components has flow-on effects to other parts of the system. Conversely, developmental limitations in any of these components will affect the efficiency of the system as a whole.

Attention

It is generally agreed that attention is represented cerebrally by an integrated neural system, involving contributions from a range of structures, including the brain stem and reticular activating system, posterior and anterior cerebral regions (Borchgrevik, 1989). One of the earliest neuropsychological models of attention was postulated by Alexander Luria (1973). He suggested that

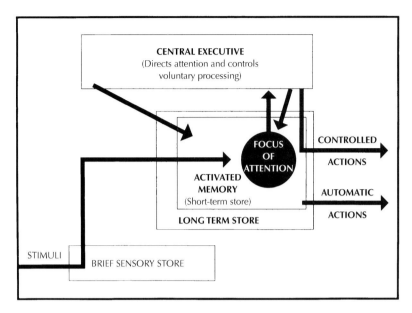

Figure 3.1.   Cowan's model of information processing. From Cowan (1988). Copyright © 1988 by the American Psychological Association. Adapted with permission.

two attentional systems operated within the brain. The first he described as a reflexive or environmentally triggered system that responded primarily to novel, biologically meaningful stimuli. Luria (1973) observed that this system was characterised by rapid habituation, with higher-order cognition largely unnecessary to its efficient functioning. The second unit, responsible for "volitional attention", he identified as a system involving a person's interpretation of environmental stimuli. He suggested that this system was mediated by more sophisticated cognitive processes. Luria's model postulated that these two systems work in parallel in the mature brain, allowing the individual to monitor the environment for events that might require a response, while pursuing various goals guided by intentional behaviours. Luria's model did not address possible developmental aspects of these two systems, except to suggest that the more primitive attentional system emerges first, soon after birth, with the second, more sophisticated system developing along with increasing experience and maturation.

Posner (1978; Posner & Peterson, 1990) also supports a dual-system model of attention, and has been a particularly influential figure in the development of neuropsychological models of attention, based on cognitive approaches. Consistent with Luria's earlier model (1973), Posner has suggested two components to attentional processing, derived from findings from his extensive empirical research. First, he describes a system predominantly located in the posterior cerebral cortex, in particular the parietal lobes, and parts of the thalamus and midbrain. This system is primarily directed towards selective attention, and directs shifts in spatial attention. Posner suggests that there is evidence that this system is functional very early in life, as young as 4 months of age, in keeping with positron emission tomography (PET) studies showing mature metabolism within the parietal lobes around this stage of development (Chugani et al., 1987). A second, anterior system, he argues is a higher-order system, with substantial neural links to the posterior system. This system is more associated with enhancing the intensity of the attention directed towards particular cognitive tasks. Posner and colleagues (1978, 1990) argue, from both PET studies and behavioural data, that the anterior cingulate gyrus and areas of the prefrontal cortex are important in the mediation of this aspect of attention, with development more protracted, due to the immaturity of the areas subsuming these skills.

Other theorists have argued for a specific role for the right hemisphere in mediating attention (Heilman, Voeller, & Nadeau, 1991; Mesulam, 1985; Robertson, 1999). Heilman and his associates (1991) employ evidence from adult brain-damaged patients and functional imaging research to propose that the symptoms exhibited by children with attention deficit hyperactivity disorder may reflect unilateral dysfunction within a neural network underlying attentional abilities. They argue that right hemisphere dysfunction is associated with deficits in attention, arousal, and motor activation.

More recently, attempts have been made to compartmentalise attention into a number of separate but interacting components, each subsumed by particular cerebral regions and forming an integrated cerebral system. Any disruption to this system has been argued to result in deficits in one or more aspects of attentional skills (Mirsky, 1996; Mirsky et al., 1991; Stuss, Shallice, Alexander, & Picton, 1995). Mirsky and his colleagues (Mirsky, 1996; Mirsky et al., 1991) have taken such an approach. The first element in their multicomponent model of attention is the *sustain* element, which refers to vigilance or the ability to maintain attention over time. Where this component is inefficient, the specific characteristic of performance is a quicker than expected deterioration in the ability to maintain attention. Using data from his own research, as well as that from a variety of animal studies, to support his hypothesis, Mirsky postulates that this element of attention is mediated to a large extent by the reticular formation, other brain stem structures, and the medial thalamus (Bakay Pragay et al., 1975; Bakay Pragay, Mirsky, & Nakamura, 1987; Ray, Mirsky, & Bakay Pragay, 1982). Others (e.g., Heilman et al., 1991; Mesulam, 1985; Stuss et al., 1995) argue that anterior cerebral structures also play a role in this aspect of attention. *Focused attention* refers to the ability to "concentrate attentional resources on a specific task, and to be able to screen out distracting peripheral stimuli" or to identify salient stimuli and perform motor responses in the presence of background distraction. Mirsky and colleagues (1991) suggest that focused attention is associated with the superior temporal, inferior parietal, and striatal regions. There is also evidence that this aspect of attention may be represented throughout the attentional system. The ability to *shift attentional focus* relates to mental flexibility or the capacity to shift attention from one aspect of a stimulus to another in a flexible, efficient manner. The model argues that this component reflects higher-order skills, consistent with more "executive" processes, and as such is subsumed by the prefrontal cortex, including the anterior cingulate gyrus. In his most recent publications Mirsky (1996) includes a fifth attentional component, *stability of attentional effort*, which he suggests is mediated by brain stem and midline thalamic structures. This model is illustrated in Figure 3.2.

Although not included in Mirsky et al.'s (1991) approach, other components of attention have also been described. Of particular relevance in the developmental context are *divided attention* and *inhibition/impulsivity*. Divided attention refers to the capacity to simultaneously attend to two tasks/ stimuli, and is generally argued to be a function of the frontal regions of the brain (Stuss et al., 1995). The ability to inhibit prepotent responses, or to suppress impulsive responses, has also been linked with frontal lobe function (Barkley, 1990). Deficits in these processes are commonly described as a characteristic of both developmental and acquired disorders (V. Anderson, Fenwick, Manly, & Robertson, 1998; Barkley, 1990; Pennington, 1997).

Developmental research demonstrates that the young child has a limited attentional capacity, possibly reflecting the immaturity of underlying neural substrates, for example, unmyelinated axons and developing frontal lobes (McKay et al., 1994; Ruff & Rothbart, 1996). Kinsbourne (1996) argues that the development of attention is characterised by a systematic increase in the child's ability to override innate response tendencies, and replace them with more appropriate ones, in situations where it is advantageous to do so. He suggests that these increases in attentional capacity depend on the ability to transmit information both within the cortex and via subcortical–cortical connections. It is argued (Hudspeth & Pribram, 1990; Klinberg et al., 1999; Schwartz, 1997; Thatcher, 1991) that the development of these tracts occurs in a set order, and within a set time frame, with anterior–posterior connections not fully developed until late childhood. Consistent with such a perspective are observations from the developmental psychology literature that attentional skills improve with age (Cooley & Morris, 1990; Lane & Pearson, 1982; McKay et al., 1994; Shepp, Barrett, & Kolbet, 1987), with different developmental trajectories identified for the separate elements of attention.

Ruff and Rothbart (1996) track attentional development through infancy and childhood, describing a variety of experimental approaches to measurement. They argue that the development of attention is closely linked with

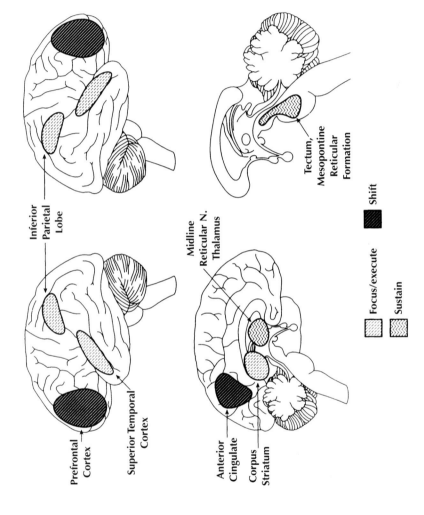

Figure 3.2. Mirsky's model of attention, indicating the cerebral regions subsuming the major components of attention: focus, sustain, and shift. Adapted from Mirsky et al. (1991) with permission from Plenum Publishing Corporation.

progress in other cognitive domains, as well as to social development. They support an interactional process, whereby underlying neural substrates dictate potential development, with environmental input determining the extent to which development approximates this potential. In their view, specific components of attention are separable even very early in development, with more automatic, reflex aspects on line initially in early infancy, and volitional attention emerging in later childhood. Their model is consistent with current thinking in the neurosciences, and with neuropsychological theories put forward by Luria and more recently by Posner and Petersen (1990).

Not surprisingly, attentional abilities are difficult to measure accurately in infants and young children, and the bulk of the literature on attentional developmental has focused on the school-aged population. For example, McKay et al. (1994) have plotted the development of sustained and selective attention skills and response speed in a normative sample of children aged between 6 and 13 years, and compared their performance to that of an adult sample. They report relatively early maturation of selective attention, with adult-level performance achieved in their youngest children on tasks tapping these skills. For sustained attention, abilities appeared relatively stable through childhood, with a developmental spurt around age 11. Tests of response speed showed more gradual progress, with increments in performance observed up until 11 years of age.

Research from our group, obtained while developing normative data for the Test of Everyday Attention for children (TEA-ch: Manly, Robertson, Anderson, & Nimmo-Smith, 1999), shows similar developmental patterns. From 6 to 15 years children show advances in their performance on a range of attentional components and across modalities. The TEA-ch includes a number of subtests, and has been designed to measure various aspects of attention including sustained, focused, divided, and shifting attention skills across both auditory/verbal and visual/spatial modalities. To examine auditory selective attention skills the "Score" paradigm has been utilised. On these tasks children are asked to listen and count a series of tones, which are presented to them auditorily at irregular intervals. The baseline task, "Score" includes 10 items where only the tones are presented. A second task, "Score—Digital Distraction", presents numbers simultaneously with tones, with the task still to count only the tones, ignoring background noise. The third measure includes a divided attention component where the child needs to count the tones as well as identify an animal name embedded in a news broadcast presented simultaneously with tones. Figure 3.3 shows the performance of the different age groups on these three measures. Results show a gradual increment in auditory selective attention skills through childhood, with older children achieving consistently higher scores. In addition, although interference reduces overall level of performance, the age effects are similar. For the divided attention task ("Score—Dual"), children 9 years and older are less

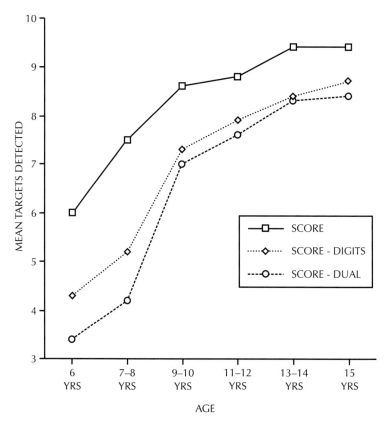

Figure 3.3. Development of auditory attention skills through childhood. Age-related performances of children 6–15 years on the "Score" paradigm of the TEA-ch, showing a continuing increase in auditory attention skills through childhood.

disadvantaged by task complexity, suggesting a possible developmental spurt in these divided attention skills around age 9. This possibly reflects the frontal underpinnings of these aspects of attention, and the relative immaturity of these cerebral regions in early to middle childhood.

A second paradigm employed in the TEA-ch examines visual attention. On the "Sky Search" tasks, children are required to circle target stimuli, in this case spaceships, on a coloured sheet. The measures recorded include number of targets detected (visual selective attention) and time to completion (response speed). A variation of this task, "Sky Search Dual Task" (divided attention), requires the child to continue this basic task while counting a series of tones presented to them via audiotape. Figures 3.4(a) and 3.4(b) illustrate age-related trends on these measures, showing relatively little change in visual selective attention (number of targets identified), with a gradual improvement

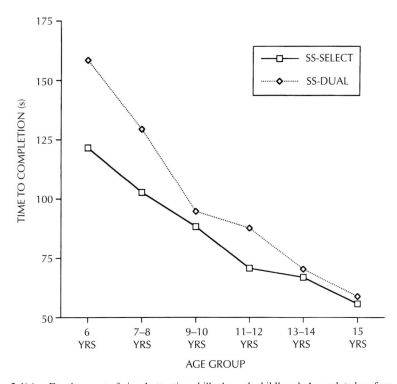

Figure 3.4(a).   Development of visual attention skills through childhood. Age-related performance of children 6–15 years on the "Sky Search" (SS) paradigm of the TEA-ch. (a) Completion
time on these tasks, an indicator of speed of processing, shows a continuous decrease with age.
(Continued overleaf.)

in response speed (time to completion). Similar to findings in the auditory
modality, where the attentional demands are greater (Sky Search Dual
Task), younger children perform significantly more poorly, taking longer to
complete tasks. This discrepancy is less evident in the older age groups.

Abnormalities in attentional development are seen in a range of developmental and acquired disorders, for example, autism (Casey, Gordon, Mannheim, & Rumsey, 1993; Wainwright-Sharp & Bryson, 1993), attention deficit
hyperactivity disorder (August & Garfinkel, 1990), Asperger's syndrome
(Klin et al., 1995), traumatic brain injury (Anderson et al., 1998; Anderson
& Pentland, 1998; Catroppa et al., 1999; Ewing-Cobbs, Prasad, et al., 1998;
Kaufmann et al., 1993), insulin-dependent diabetes myelitis (Northam, et al.,
1998), cranial irradiation (V. Anderson, Godber, Smibert, Weiskop, & Ekert,
2000; Brouwers, Riccardi, Poplack, & Fedio, 1984), and Tourette's syndrome
(Harris et al., 1995; Lang, Athanasopoulous, & Anderson, 1998; Yeates &
Bornstein, 1994). The nature of attention deficits appears to vary across these

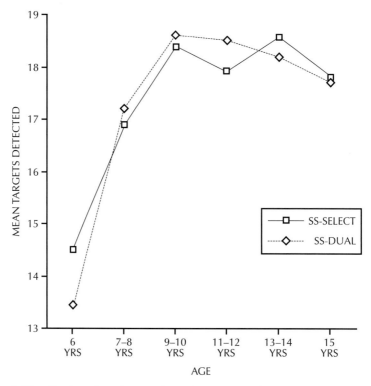

Figure 3.4(b). Total number of targets detected suggests a different developmental trajectory for visual selective attention, with a significant improvement in detection from 6 to 10 years, followed by stable performance, suggesting maturation of these skills around age 10.

groups, perhaps due to different underlying cerebral pathology, or perhaps due to timing of onset of the condition. The influence of such factors is well illustrated in the case of traumatic brain injury (Ponsford & Kinsella, 1992). Within the adult literature, many researchers now argue that attentional skills are intact, but speed of processing is reduced post-traumatic brain injury. When injury is sustained during childhood, the pattern of deficits appears to be more global. Although children do exhibit slowed processing speed, they also display deficits in other aspects of attention, including sustained attention and shifting attention in particular (Anderson & Pentland, 1998; Catroppa, Anderson, & Stargatt, 1999; Ewing-Cobbs, Prasad, et al., 1998; Kaufmann et al., 1993). Further, deficits vary according to injury severity, with minimal evidence of attentional deficits following mild traumatic brain injury, but significant impairment in moderate and severe traumatic brain injury (Catroppa & Anderson, 1999; Catroppa et al., 1999; Ponsford, Sloan, & Snow, 1995; Willmott, Anderson, & Anderson, 2000).

Although the investigation and description of attention deficits following brain insult during infancy and childhood may add to our theoretical knowledge, of equal importance is the impact of such deficits for ongoing development. If a child is unable to attend efficiently to the environment, learning of new skills and knowledge may be limited, resulting in cumulative deficits as is evidenced in the gradual deterioration in IQ scores in a number of CNS conditions where children exhibit attention deficits (Anderson & Moore, 1995; Anderson, Smibert, Ekert, & Godber, 1994; Ewing-Cobbs et al., 1997; Gronwall, Wrightson, & McGinn, 1997). Thus, a thorough understanding of the nature of attention and its development across childhood, together with appropriate methods of assessment, are vital for the paediatric neuropsychologist.

Memory

Many models have been proposed to explain the process by which information is registered, encoded, stored, and, retrieved. Some authors focus on defining modality-specific systems (McCarthy & Warrington, 1990; Milner, 1971; Zangwill, 1946), whereas others postulate more interactive approaches (Atkinson & Shiffrin, 1968; Baddeley, 1986, 1990; Broadbent, 1958; Cowan, 1988; Sternberg, 1975). There is some consistency, however, with respect to the major components described in these models. For example, the notion of a *sensory store*, where information enters the system via the sense organs and is held, for a brief duration, in a "literal" form, has been maintained over time (Baddeley, 1990; Broadbent, 1958; Cowan, 1988). Models defining relationships between other memory components such as *short-term memory, long-term memory, and working memory* or processes such as encoding, storage, and retrieval are less consistent, but generally incorporate notions of encoding and analysis, which involve active processes such as rehearsal and chunking. A *central executive* is also commonly described as taking a managerial role in directing voluntary attention and enabling voluntary retrieval and activation of stored information (Baddeley, 1990; Cowan, 1988, 1995).

Another approach to understanding memory function differentiates a number of types of memory, for example, declarative versus procedural, or implicit versus explicit. Although there are some differences in terminology, declarative and or explicit memory usually refers to a memory for which the individual has conscious awareness, with recall commonly in the form of a proposition or a visual image. Procedural or implicit memory, in contrast, refers to memory for a skilled activity, such as playing the piano, for which the individual does not have conscious recall (Nelson, 1995).

A number of neural structures have been proposed to subsume these memory processes. There is some evidence to suggest that maturation of these cerebral areas, including myelination of nerve fibres, may parallel memory development. At a process level, the younger child may transmit new information more slowly, due to the relative inefficiency of unmyelinated nerve tracts (Case, 1992; Thatcher, 1991, 1992; Uemura & Hartmann, 1978; Yakovlev & Lecours, 1967). In addition, incomplete development of frontal lobes during childhood implies limited ability to organise information and utilise strategies to optimise information-processing capacity. Thus, where models such as those suggested by Baddeley (1990) and Cowan (1995) are concerned, regardless of possible capacity differences, the central executive may be a less effective information processor in children than in adults.

At the level of memory structure, the basal ganglia and brain stem structures, which mature relatively early in infancy and early childhood, have been linked to procedural memory skills and acquisition of conditioned responses, which are also noted to emerge in early infancy (Barkovich, Kjos, Jackson, & Norman, 1988; Chugani, 1994; Kandel, Schwartz, & Jessell, 1991; Nelson, 1995). The temporal lobes, and in particular the hippocampus, are implicated in the encoding and storage of information (Columbo & Gross, 1994; McCarthy & Warrington, 1990; Mishkin, Malamut, & Bachevalier, 1984) and thus in more declarative aspects of memory. Consistent with the later maturation of these cerebral regions (Eckenhoff & Rakic, 1991), these skills are slower to develop (Bachevalier & Mishkin, 1984; Diamond, 1995; Nelson, 1995; Overmann et al., 1993). The frontal lobes may subserve the functions of selective attention, voluntary action, and management generally attributed to the central executive (Baddeley, 1990; Cowan, 1995). Although these structural components may be the same regardless of age, developmental differences in memory capacity and strategies are well documented (Baddeley, 1986; Diamond, 1985; Dirks & Neisser, 1977; Goswami, 1998; Henry & Millar, 1993; Hulme et al., 1984; Paris & Lindauer, 1976).

Memory and learning begin at birth, although these processes are more difficult to elicit in infants and young children. A number of traditional research paradigms have been employed with very young children, providing evidence of a capacity for retention. Research utilising object permanence tasks and delayed matching to sample have reported development of memory skills in the first year of life, particularly from 6 to 12 months, with infants able to demonstrate memory for objects following longer and longer delay periods (Bjorklund, 1989; Diamond, 1985). Methods based on preference for novelty, where infants show reducing attention with repeated presentation, have documented that even newborns exhibit the expected habituation to familiar stimuli, i.e., memory for the familiar stimulus, with the duration of retention increasing over the first year of life (Fagan, 1973; Friedman, 1972; Rovee-Collier & Gerhardstein, 1997). Similarly, efficient recognition memory has been observed in very young children (Bjorklund, 1989).

Advances in memory function are clearly documented throughout childhood, although there is some variation seen in the developmental trajectories of particular aspects of memory function. Recognition skills are argued to mature relatively early in childhood, with adult abilities achieved around 4 years of age (Brown & Scott, 1971; Siegler, 1991). Immediate memory capacity, as measured by the number of digits or letters a child can hold at a time, increases steadily with age. Whereas preschool children can hold three or four "chunks" of information, this capacity will extend to five or six items by age 9, and seven or more by early adolescence (Dempster, 1981; Luciana & Nelson, 1998). Recall and repetition show gradual development through childhood, with a different pattern of recall from adults. In young children there is little evidence of the expected primacy effect, and this emerges with age; however, a recency effect has been demonstrated (Bjorklund, 1989; Cole, Frankel, & Sharp, 1971).

Cognitive psychologists attribute such developmental gains to increases in the capacity to acquire information (Simon, 1974), expanded storage capacity (Pascual-Leone, 1970), faster speed of information processing (Howard & Polich, 1985), greater resistance to interference (Diamond, 1995; Kinsbourne, 1996), and the ability to selectively retrieve information in response to environmental demands (Ruff & Rothbart, 1996). Others hypothesise that improvements may be due to the development of memory strategies, which are used more frequently and more efficiently by older children (Bjorklund, 1989; Ceci & Liker, 1986). The role of metacognition—knowledge about one's individual cognitive preferences—is also argued to be an important source of memory development. That is, older children may have greater insight into the workings of their own memory systems and may use this understanding to allocate memory resources appropriately and choose relevant strategies to generate best retention (Bjorklund, 1989). A further suggestion proposes that, as children mature, they are better equipped to predict what is most important for them to retain in a set of information. This greater content knowledge may explain their superior memory and retention (Siegler, 1991).

The continued change and maturation of memory and information-processing skills through childhood represent a significant challenge for neuropsychologists who are frequently required to evaluate aspects of memory capacity in young children. The accurate assessment and interpretation of memory function are crucial to appropriate intervention and management of children suffering neuropsychological disorders. To attain valid diagnostic information the practitioner requires: (1) a model of memory function that provides a framework from which to assess and interpret various components of the memory process; (2) well-standardised tests with reliable norms that may be used as references for "normal" memory performance across a range of ages; and (3) an understanding of the way in which memory deficits may impinge on daily functioning in young children.

In neuropsychological practice, memory functions are often difficult to evaluate in infants and young children, where it is often impossible to gain sufficient response, and thus differentiate components of memory function on traditional memory tasks such as story recall or sentence repetition. In addition, there is a scarcity of reliable measures of memory in this age group. As a result, neuropsychological assessment of memory function is often omitted in this age group, both in clinical and research contexts. For the school-aged child a great deal of emphasis is placed on examining memory functions, with a number of test batteries recently developed for this purpose (Children's Memory Scale, Test of Memory and Learning, Wide Range Assessment of Memory and Learning). Developmental norms are also available for a number of adult memory tests in recent times (Anderson, Lajoie, & Bell, 1995; Kolb & Whishaw, 1996; Spreen & Strauss, 1991).

Recently, in our lab, we have collected data that provides evidence of memory development as measured by traditional clinical neuropsychological tests (see Anderson & Lajoie, 1996). Our sample consisted of 376 children, aged from 7 to 13 years. Subjects were divided into seven groups, according to age. We administered a range of memory tasks tapping (1) immediate memory capacity (Digit Span, Block Span); (2) verbal memory and learning (Story Recall, Rey Auditory–Verbal Learning Test); (3) visual/spatial learning (Spatial Learning Test, Rey Complex Figure—recall); and (4) delayed recall, utilising 30-minute recall of verbal and visual/spatial measures. The results for each test and each age group are provided in Table 3.2 and Figures 3.5 and 3.6.

Our findings indicate that the capacity to register new information increases with age for both verbal and spatial material, supporting previous research that has described such improvements (Baddeley, 1986; Simon, 1974). Comparing memory spans for verbal and visuospatial material at each age level, mean scores were generally similar, with a tendency for older children to exhibit slightly longer verbal memory spans. The data suggested two developmental "spurts" in registration (or immediate memory) capacity, the first around age 8 and a second around age 12. Similar patterns were evident for measures of memory and learning, with increases in encoding and storage detected across age groups for recall of stories, word lists and visuospatial material. Figures 3.5 and 3.6 illustrate data from the Rey Auditory–Verbal Learning Test and the Spatial Learning Test. Each of these tasks involves multi-trial learning situations, where information is presented to children over a number of trials. Results demonstrate different levels of performance across age groups for both verbal and spatial learning, but the learning curves themselves are relatively similar. It has been argued that such age-related changes in memory and learning skills are simply a reflection of the already identified increments in registration capacity (Simon, 1974). Although the ability to register new material did have a significant effect on our results, memory and learning performance could not be fully accounted for by

TABLE 3.2
Memory skills across age groups

		_7_ (n = 51) M (SD)	_8_ (n = 51) M (SD)	Age group _9_ (n = 59) M (SD)	_10_ (n = 59) M (SD)	_11_ (n = 51) M (SD)	_12_ (n = 54) M (SD)	_13_ (n = 51) M (SD)
Registration	Digit Span (no. corr.)	4.9 (0.9)	5.1 (1.1)	5.3 (1.0)	5.6 (0.9)	5.9 (0.9)	6.1 (1.2)	6.4 (1.2)
	Block Span (no. corr.)	4.7 (0.8)	5.2 (0.9)	5.2 (0.7)	5.4 (0.8)	5.6 (0.8)	5.7 (1.0)	5.8 (1.0)
Verbal memory	Story Recall: A (no. items)	10.4 (3.0)	12.0 (3.5)	12.3 (3.2)	13.5 (3.1)	14.0 (2.9)	12.8 (3.2)	13.9 (3.3)
	Story Recall: B (no. items)	12.11 (4.5)	13.8 (4.8)	14.7 (4.6)	16.4 (4.0)	17.7 (2.9)	16.3 (3.3)	17.4 (3.4)
	RAVLT (total words)	40.2 (9.8)	43.9 (10.0)	48.1 (9.3)	49.2 (9.2)	50.1 (7.5)	52.0 (6.7)	53.3 (8.5)
Visual memory	Rey Figure (recall score)	11.0 (5.1)	11.5 (6.0)	13.7 (5.0)	16.2 (5.7)	17.7 (4.9)	17.9 (6.6)	19.7 (6.1)
	Spatial Learn. (no. trials)	2.8 (1.9)	2.9 (1.6)	2.9 (1.7)	2.6 (1.3)	2.4 (1.6)	3.0 (1.6)	2.5 (1.1)
Delayed recall	Story Recall: A (no. items)	8.9 (3.6)	10.3 (3.8)	11.4 (3.3)	12.6 (3.0)	12.6 (3.4)	11.9 (3.6)	13.5 (3.4)
	Story Recall: B (no. items)	11.3 (5.3)	12.8 (5.0)	15.0 (5.0)	16.0 (3.9)	17.3 (3.5)	16.2 (3.4)	17.6 (3.4)
	RAVLT (total words)	8.8 (2.9)	10.6 (2.4)	11.6 (2.3)	11.5 (2.4)	11.2 (2.0)	11.5 (2.0)	12.0 (2.4)
	Rey Figure (recall score)	11.0 (4.6)	11.3 (5.5)	14.1 (4.6)	16.4 (5.4)	16.7 (5.0)	17.6 (6.5)	19.3 (6.9)
	Spatial Learn. (no. trials)	7.5 (1.7)	7.9 (1.1)	8.0 (1.2)	8.0 (1.0)	8.0 (1.1)	7.9 (1.2)	8.1 (1.2)

RAVLT, Rey Auditory–Verbal Learning Test.

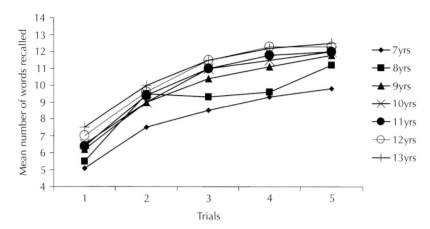

Figure 3.5. Learning curves across age groups on the Rey Auditory–Verbal Learning Test. Results show a learning curve for all age groups, but a flatter curve for children aged 7–8. There is little difference in performance associated with age for older age groups.

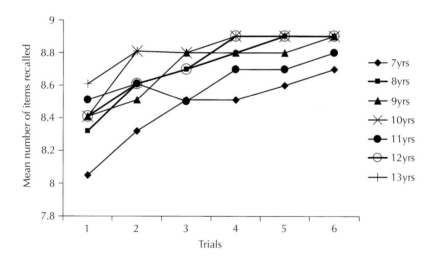

Figure 3.6. Learning curves across age groups on the Spatial Learning Test. Results indicate relatively rapid learning of spatial material, with minimal age effects.

differences in registration capacity, arguing for developmental gains for both components of memory.

Alternatively, increases in performance on memory tests may reflect the implementation of memory strategies or better capacity to organise information, as has been suggested by cognitive psychologists (Bjorklund,

1989; Siegler, 1991). There is some evidence to support this interpretation from our data. First, results showed that older children benefit from familiarity with stimulus material, suggesting that they may utilise their prior knowledge of the task to improve performance. Further, the trend for a reduction in the discrepancy between spontaneous recall and recognition scores with age on multi-trial learning tasks may indicate that better organisational skills allow efficient retrieval in older children.

Developmental progress was also found on delayed recall components of the memory measures. However, when the confounding effects of initial registration, memory, and learning skills were statistically controlled, a less compelling trend was demonstrated, suggesting that the ability to recall information after delay or interference is largely dependent on efficient processing through earlier components of the system. These results argue that, in contrast to documented maturation of registration and memory skills, the capacity of the child to retain information over time (i.e., long-term memory) does not change greatly with age.

Many groups of children with documented or suspected CNS dysfunction have been found to demonstrate memory deficits. As with attentional impairments, these deficits may vary considerably due to a range of insult/injury-related and developmental factors. A number of children will experience memory deficits due to focal damage or dysfunction to areas of the brain directly involved in the memory system. Children with epileptic disorders, particularly those involving the temporal lobes, survivors of cerebral infections including some forms of encephalitis and meningitis, or those experiencing an episode of hypoxic brain damage, may be at significant risk for specific memory impairments, due to the involvement of midline structures including the hippocampus. For example, a child with left-sided hippocampal sclerosis may exhibit material-specific impairment for both recall and recognition on neuropsychological measures tapping verbal memory skills, such as word list learning, or paired-associate paradigms. Children with focal frontal lesions, in contrast, may show deficits in retrieval across modalities, although performing adequately on recognition tasks, more consistent with the notion of frontal amnesia (Walsh, 1978, 1985). Memory problems are also observed in children sustaining more generalised developmental and acquired conditions such as traumatic brain injury (Catroppa & Anderson, 2001; Kinsella et al., 1995; Levin et al., 1988; Yeates, Blumstein, et al., 1995, 1997), attention deficit hyperactivity disorder, and learning disabilities (Anderson & Stanley, 1992; Swanson, Cooney, & Brock, 1993). Memory impairments associated with such conditions are often less specific, and may be related to other information-processing difficulties in attention and processing speed.

The implications of memory and learning difficulties are particularly significant during childhood. The young child has a relatively small store of well-learned knowledge and skills. Using Dennis's model of cognitive development, emerging memory processes may be particularly vulnerable to interference following early cerebral insult. The earlier the insult occurs, the greater the degree and generalisation of the problem. A memory impairment occurring during childhood will interfere with the efficient acquisition and accumulation of knowledge and skills, limiting the child's potential development. In functional terms, such problems are commonly reflected by poor educational progress and difficulties learning social rules. The neuropsychologist's task may be to identify and detail the memory profile of the child, in the context of other neurobehavioural abilities, and to provide support and advice for treatment and management. There are many useful strategies that may be implemented to manage memory difficulties, both within rehabilitation and educational contexts. The appropriate intervention may be based on the nature of the identified memory difficulty. For example, a problem with immediate memory capacity may require a substantially different approach from a deficit in retrieval skills. Similarly a child with a material-specific memory impairment may be able to utilise different strategies from a child with global memory difficulties.

Speed of processing

The rate at which information is transmitted throughout the information-processing system is a reflection of the efficiency of the overall system. At a simple level, faster processing speed allows a task to be completed more quickly, thus minimising chances of exceeding attentional capacity, and enabling the child to progress to the next requirement. Faster processing also ensures minimal loss or "decay" of material, so that a task can be completed while the necessary information or instructions are still available to the child.

Young children take more time to execute cognitive processes than do older children. Age-related increases in speed of processing have been described over a range of activities including motor tasks, requiring both verbal and visuomotor responses, immediate processing of information, processing of information from within working memory, and retrieval of information from long-term memory (Hale, 1989; Hoving, Spencer, Robb, & Schulte, 1978; Kail, 1988; Siegler, 1991). Figures 3.7 and 3.8 provide normative data from two common clinical measures—the Trail Making Test (Reitan, 1969) and the Contingency Naming Test (Taylor et al., 1990)—both of which incorporate speeded components. The Trail Making Test is a dot-to-dot task, where the child is required to join dots with numbers inside (TRAILS A) and then to join dots together using an alternating number–letter sequence (TRAILS B). The resultant score reflects the time taken to complete the task. Figure 3.7 demonstrates the faster completion time recorded as children get older. Similarly, for the Contingency Naming Test, the task is to rapidly name colours and shapes of stimuli (CNT: 1+2), and

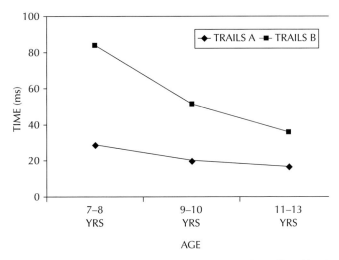

Figure 3.7. Age-related performance for time to completion on the Trail Making Test, indicating increasing speed of processing through childhood. From P. Anderson, Lajoie, & Bell (1995).

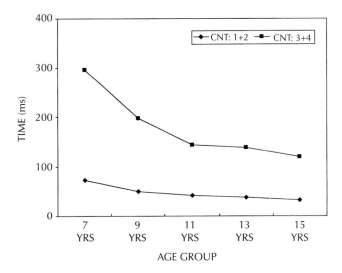

Figure 3.8. Age-related performance for time to completion on the Contingency Naming Test (CNT), indicating increasing speed of processing through childhood. CNT: 1+2 = total time to completion for subtests 1 and 2; CNT: 3+4 = total time to completion for subtests 3 and 4.

then to name the same stimuli according to increasingly complex rules (CNT: 3+4). Figure 3.8 shows the decrease in completion time across age groups both for simple naming and for more complex tasks. There is some debate as to the cause of this increase, with researchers suggesting improved implementation of strategies and familiarity with tasks. Current theorists argue that, although these features may enhance rate of processing, there is evidence that increases in speed of processing do occur, independent of higher-order processes, and our data (Figures 3.7 and 3.8) would support such a stance.

From a physiological perspective, increasing rate of processing is related to the ongoing maturation of the CNS. In particular, the gradual myelination of axons is thought to speed up neural transmission and allow for more rapid processing. In support of this premise, both adults and children sustaining axonal damage that serves to interrupt the ongoing process of myelination, or disturb established myelination, have been reported to exhibit slowed rate of processing. This finding is well established in samples of individuals sustaining traumatic brain injury, with the hallmark of such patients being slowed processing (Ponsford et al., 1995, 1997; van Zomeren & Brouwer, 1994). Similar characteristics are noted in children with hydrocephalus and in children treated with cranial irradiation for various forms of cancers, where cerebral white matter is compromised (Anderson, Smibert, et al., 1994; Anderson, Godber, Smibert, & Ekert, 1997; Fletcher et al., 1995b).

Such impairments may have wide-reaching implications for children who may be unable to keep up with peers in a variety of circumstances. Where speech output speed is affected, the child may appear dysfluent and experience difficulties conversing adequately in general conversation. Slowed motor output will restrict the child within the classroom environment, where work may fail to be completed within time limits. Slowed responses may limit the child's capacity to participate in sporting and other leisure activities.

DEVELOPMENT OF EXECUTIVE FUNCTIONS

Executive functions may be depicted as the *central executive* component of the information-processing system—the component that directs attention, monitors activity, and coordinates and integrates information and activity. In a recent comprehensive review of neuropsychological assessment procedures, Lezak states that executive functions are "capacities that enable a person to engage successfully in independent, purposeful, self-serving behaviors" (Lezak, 1995, p. 42). She suggests that they may be conceptualised as having four components: (1) volition; (2) planning; (3) purposeful behaviour; and (4) effective performance; with each involving a discrete set of activity-related behaviours. Lezak distinguishes between cognitive abilities, which may be seen as domain specific, and executive skills, which act more globally and impact upon all aspects of behaviour. She argues that the integrity of these functions is necessary for appropriate, socially responsible conduct. Stuss (1992) provides an integrated model of executive function, including a set of associated skills that allow the individual to develop goals, hold them in active memory, monitor performance, and control for interference in order to achieve those goals. Other authors include focused and sustained attention, generation and implementation strategies, monitoring, and utilisation of feedback under the umbrella term "executive functions" (Glosser & Good-glass, 1990; Levin et al., 1991; Mateer & Williams, 1991; Stuss & Benson, 1987). Walsh (1978) and Shallice (1990) fine-tune the concept further, arguing that executive functions are not required for the execution of routine, well-learned behaviours, but are specifically activated in novel or unfamiliar circumstances, where no previously established routines for responding exist.

Such definitions may be operationalised to include three separable, but integrated components: (1) attentional control: selective attention and sustained attention; (2) cognitive flexibility: working memory, attentional shift, self-monitoring, and conceptual transfer; and (3) goal setting: initiating, planning, problem solving, and strategic behaviour (V. Anderson, Anderson, Northam, et al., in press; Duncan, 1986; Lezak, 1995; Luria, 1973; Neisser, 1967; Shallice, 1990). Thus "executive dysfunction" may be reflected by poor planning and organisation, difficulties generating and implementing strategies for problem solving, perseveration, inability to correct errors or use feedback, and rigid or concrete thought processes (Stuss & Benson, 1987; Walsh, 1978). Qualitative features of executive dysfunction may include poor self-control, impulsivity, erratic careless responses, poor initiation, and inflexibility (Lezak, 1995). Although these behaviours are commonly considered to be "deviant" in adults, a similar interpretation may not always be warranted for children. Before determining whether such behaviours are indicative of executive dysfunction in children, developmental expectations need to be considered.

There is a growing body of developmental research that describes sequential improvement of executive functions through childhood, coinciding with growth spurts in frontal lobe development (Anderson, Anderson, Northam, et al., in press; Bell & Fox, 1992; Levin et al., 1991; Luciana & Nelson, 1998; Thatcher, 1991, 1992; Welsh & Pennington, 1988). Such findings have been interpreted as support for the mediation of executive functions via anterior cerebral regions, and the prefrontal cortex specifically. Although this may be the case, these cerebral regions are dependent upon other cerebral areas for input, making it difficult to isolate frontal functions from those of other developing cerebral areas. It may be that the gradual maturation of executive function observed through childhood reflects the integrity of cerebral development throughout the brain. Further, the development of executive functions may be inextricably associated with the gradual emergence of other cognitive capacities, with ample evidence for associated gradual increments in skills such as language (Gaddes & Crockett, 1975; Halperin et al., 1989;

Luria, 1973), attention (McKay et al., 1994; Miller & Weiss, 1981), speed of processing (Anderson, Lajoie, & Bell, 1995; Howard & Polich, 1985), and memory capacity (Baddeley, 1986; Case, 1985; Hale, Bronik, & Fry, 1997; Henry & Millar, 1993; Paris & Lindauer, 1976; Simon, 1974).

Knowledge of CNS maturation and related cognitive development is gradually increasing with advances in technical methodologies. Initially developmental neuropsychology was influenced by a view that the frontal lobes were "functionally silent" in infancy and early childhood, with executive skills not measurable until the second decade of life (Golden, 1981). Recent research strongly refutes this position. Diamond and Doar (1989), among others (Chelune & Baer, 1986; Levin et al., 1991; Passler, Isaac, & Hynd, 1985; Welsh & Pennington, 1988; Welsh, Pennington, & Groisser, 1991), argue that the cognitive skills necessary for executive function (mental flexibility, concept formation, impulse control, problem solving) are readily demonstrated even in young children. A number of neurophysiological studies also refute this position, documenting frontal lobe activity even in infancy. For example, Chugani et al. (1987) measured local cerebral metabolic rates of glucose in infants and young children, and found evidence of frontal activation in infants as young as 6 months of age. Similarly Bell and Fox (1992) have documented changes in scalp-recorded electroencephalograms (EEGs) in frontal regions during the first year of life, relating these to improvements in behavioural performance. Many workers now support the notion that these biological growth markers may explain some of the age-related variation in "non-biological" development such as cognition (Caeser, 1993; Thatcher, 1991, 1992).

It is generally agreed that the frontal lobes are hierarchically organised, with processes such as myelination progressing through a number of stages, from primary and sensory areas to association areas and finally frontal regions. Results from a variety of methodological approaches (EEG, functional and structural imaging, metabolic analyses) have demonstrated a number of growth periods within the frontal regions, the first between birth and 2 years, another from 7 to 9 years, with a final spurt in late adolescence (16–19 years) (Fuster, 1993; Hudspeth & Pribram, 1990; Kennedy et al., 1982; Klinberg et al., 1999; Staudt et al., 1993; Thatcher, 1991, 1997; Uemura & Hartmann, 1978). A number of behavioural researchers have extended these findings to examine possible links between early cognitive development and frontal lobe development. In a series of investigations, Diamond and Goldman-Rakic (Diamond, 1988; Diamond & Goldman-Rakic, 1985, 1989; Goldman-Rakic, 1987) employed the classic Piagetian object permanence paradigm, as well as an object retrieval task, to investigate goal-directed behaviours in infants. To establish links with possible cerebral substrates, they compared performance of human infants to those of both adult and infant rhesus monkeys with focal lesions. They found that infants as young as 12 months were able to exhibit object permanence, as were monkeys with parietal lesions. In contrast, older rhesus monkeys with frontal lesions were unable to successfully complete these tasks. For object retrieval tasks, human infants also showed age-related improvements in planning and self-control, mirroring those of normal infant monkeys. Monkeys with frontal lesions were unable to master this task. These results have been interpreted as evidence that frontally mediated, goal-directed, planful behaviour is present as early as 12 months of age in human infants.

Other studies have attempted to map developmental trajectories for aspects of executive function in older children. Passler et al. (1985) report one of the earliest studies employing this methodology. Using measures of executive functioning adapted from adult neuropsychology, they demonstrated that children as young as 6 were able to exhibit strategic and planful behaviour. Their results suggest a stage-like progression of executive skills, with mastery still incomplete in early adolescence. In a follow-up study, Becker, Isaac, and Hynd (1987) report a similar pattern of results, once again noting a failure to achieve adult levels on all executive measures by age 12. In contrast, using the Wisconsin Card Sorting Test as their measure of executive function, Chelune and Baer (1986) documented improvements in performance between 6 and 10 years, with adult performance achieved by 12 years. Further, they observed that 6-year-old children demonstrated difficulties similar to those seen in adults with focal frontal lesions.

More recently, a number of researchers have employed a "battery model", administering a range of tests purported to measure executive function. Levin et al. (1991) evaluated normal children and adolescents in three age bands: 7–8 years, 9–12 years, and 13–15 years. They administered a range of "executive" measures and identified developmental gains across all tasks, reflecting progress in concept formation, mental flexibility, planning, and problem solving through childhood. Although their sample size was relatively small ($n = 52$), they performed principal components analysis on their data, identifying three factors that they argued were associated with specific aspects of executive function, as well as unique developmental patterns. Factor 1 tapped semantic association/concept formation and Factor 3 was primarily concerned with problem solving. Each of these abilities showed a gradual progression over the three age ranges. Factor 2 was related to impulse control and mental flexibility, and these behaviours were noted to reach adult levels by age 12.

Welsh et al. (1991) also studied a sample of normal children, aged from 3 to 12 years, using a series of measures of executive function. Consistent with previous findings, their results provide evidence for stage-like development, with some components of executive function maturing earlier than others, thus supporting a multidimensional notion of executive function. They argue for three distinct developmental stages, the first commencing around age 6, a second about age 10, and a final spurt in early adolescence. They suggest that the ability to resist distraction is the first skill to mature, at around age 6. Organised search, hypothesis testing, and impulse control reach adult levels at around age 10, with verbal fluency, motor sequencing, and planning skills still not at adult levels at age 12.

Using a similar methodology and with the primary aim of providing normative data for a number of commonly used clinical tests, purported to measure executive functions, we have also examined age trends in this domain (Anderson, Lajoie, & Bell, 1995; Anderson et al., 1996, in press). Our sample included 376 children aged 7–13 years, selected to be representative of the general population with respect to social factors and gender. A number of executive function tests were administered to children including the Tower of London, Controlled Oral Word Association Test, and the Rey Complex Figure (Anderson, Lajoie, & Bell 1995). Clear age trends were evident on all measures, as is illustrated in Figure 3.9. For the Tower of London, younger children achieved fewer correct responses and made more errors than older children. Findings suggested greatest development of the planning skills tapped by this measure between the ages of 9 and 13 years, with relatively stable performance in later adolescence. Similar developmental trajectories are evident for the Controlled Oral Word Association Test and the Rey Complex Figure, with rapid development in middle childhood, and more gradual progress in later childhood and adolescence.

More recently, we have investigated a series of further executive measures (Jacobs, Anderson, & Harvey, 1997) including the Twenty Questions Test,

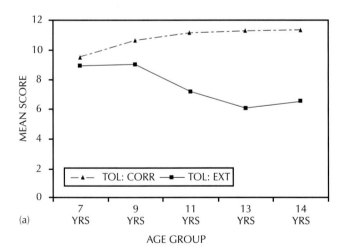

Figure 3.9(a). Developmental gains in executive function through childhood, as illustrated by performance on (a) Tower of London (TOL). TOL: CORR = number correct, TOL: EXT = extra attempts.

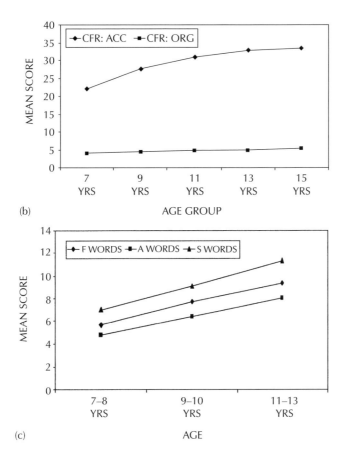

Figure 3.9(b) and (c).   (b) Complex Figure of Rey (CFR); (c) Controlled Oral Word Association Test (COWAT). TOL: CORR = number of items correct; TOL: EXT = number of extra attempts required; CFR: ACC = copy score; CFR: ORG = organisation score; F words, A words, S words = number of words generated beginning with these letters.

Contingency Naming Test, Judgement of Time, and the Concept Generation Test. In line with the work of Levin et al. (1991) and Welsh et al. (1991), results from this study also confirm significant development of executive skills through middle childhood, with some differentiation within the range of executive skills. A further observation was made on the basis of observed patterns of performance across age groups. Consistent with the work of Ursula Kirk (1985) and comments by Kinsbourne (1996), findings suggested that developmental spurts may not be clean cut. Rather, around the time of a developmental spurt, children's performance on standard test measures may actually decline. For example, our data on children's performance on the

Tower of London Test (Anderson et al., 1996) supports this suggestion. Comparison of performance between 10- and 12-year-old groups demonstrated a clear and consistent improvement on all measures, including summary or standard score, solution time, number correct, and number of failed attempts. In contrast, for the 11-year-old group there was an observed decline in summary scores, explained by an increase in number of failed attempts, along with relatively stable solution time. Although such findings may indicate a more impulsive approach in 11-year-olds, the greater frequency of failed attempts may also reflect greater mental flexibility and an increase in the ability to formulate and implement strategies, added to a capacity to work through various possible solutions more quickly.

The parallels between the developmental trajectories described in these studies and those reported in neurophysiological research are difficult to ignore. Although all measures employed in these studies provide evidence for progressive development through childhood, it appears that executive functions, rather than being a unitary concept, may be divided into a number of specific components, exhibiting different developmental trajectories, and maturing at different rates. These varying patterns may reflect mediation by specific areas within the frontal lobes, which are also maturing at different rates. From a biological perspective, the possible influence of ongoing development of other cerebral areas also needs to be considered. For example, the quality of neural transmission from posterior and subcortical regions may impact upon the functioning of the frontal and prefrontal cortices, which have rich connections with all cerebral areas. Maturation of these posterior regions may then enhance the functioning of anterior cerebral areas. From a cognitive viewpoint, similar considerations are important. The gradual emergence of greater memory capacity, more advanced language skills, and faster speed of processing will all enhance the child's capacity to perform on measures of executive functioning. Although tentative links have been established, there is still a way to go to define relationships between the development of executive skills and frontal structures, and isolate cognitive gains specific to executive functions, divorced from lower-order cognitive capacities. Regardless, this convergence of evidence emphasises the importance of close communication among disciplines involved in improving our understanding of brain–behaviour relationships in the developing child.

The impact of executive functions on long-term development is as yet unknown, with few studies addressing this complex issue. A handful of case studies of adults sustaining damage in childhood have revealed the expected pattern of poor problem solving, reduced planning, and inappropriate social skills (Ackerly & Benton, 1948; Eslinger et al., 1999; Eslinger, Grattan, Damasio, & Damasio, 1992). Mateer (1990) has followed a small group of children who had sustained an early cerebral insult, documenting perseveration, reduced attention, rigidity, lability, and social difficulties. These reports suggest intact or mildly depressed intellectual ability, despite presence of frontal pathology. In contrast, early data from our longitudinal study on children with focal frontal lesions suggests that even discrete lesions, sustained prenatally and in early childhood, may have devastating effects on ongoing development. In contrast, focal frontal lesions in later childhood tend to have more specific consequences, paralleling those seen following similar pathology in adults (Jacobs, Anderson, & Harvey, 1998). Such contrasts support the premise that for the normal development of cognitive skills in general the child requires at least some period of access to healthy frontal lobe function and associated intact executive skills.

Clinicians frequently identify executive dysfunction in their patients. Research studies have identified such impairments in children with learning and attentional difficulties (Barkley, 1990; Wansart, 1990), autistic children (Prior & Hoffman, 1990), as well is in those with acquired lesions such as traumatic brain injury (Garth et al., 1997; Pentland, Todd, & Anderson, 1998). However, a number of cautions must be considered in the diagnosis of such impairments. While the identification and documentation of executive skills are possible, it is more difficult to determine aetiology. Further, much of the research claiming executive dysfunction, and thus frontal lobe dysfunction, is fraught with difficulties. Bearing in mind that executive functions are reliant on lower-order skills, it is important to identify any deficits in these abilities before attributing the cause to pure executive impairment. Condor, Anderson, and Saling (1996), in their study of learning-disabled children, found that, although learning-disabled children performed more poorly on an executive function task, difficulties were eliminated if the child was provided with additional time to process the task. On the basis of this "microanalysis" of task performance, these authors suggest that their sample demonstrated a primary deficit in speed of processing, which then compromised performance on measures of executive function. From a different perspective, when working within the developmental context, the issue of appropriate developmental expectations is also relevant. A recent study conducted by Todd et al. (1996) illustrates this point. These researchers investigated planning ability in a sample of mildly head-injured adolescents and compared performances to those of healthy age- and gender-matched controls. Their results suggested that adolescents with a history of mild head injury did exhibit planning problems. However, their results were indistinguishable from those recorded for the matched controls, arguing for an interpretation related to a general developmental process, where all adolescents are immature on such tasks, rather than an explanation based on injury factors. These findings emphasise the importance of employing a developmental context when interpreting performance below adult levels in children and adolescents as "impairments".

CONCLUSIONS

The process of normal cognitive maturation is complex and multidimensional. Although knowledge in this field remains imperfectly understood, some understanding of normal developmental expectations is critical if deviations from these levels are to be accurately identified and interpreted. Recent evidence linking CNS maturation and cognitive development provides a framework for understanding brain–behaviour relationships through childhood. In addition, these parallels may be usefully employed in instances of deviant development. Where the normal developmental process is interrupted due to cerebral insult, the consequences for ongoing cognitive maturation may be devastating, with the outcome bearing little resemblance to the effects observed following equivalent insult in adulthood. Developmental neuropsychologists argue that the timing of insult, the stage of skill development, and the context of the child interact to determine the eventual outcome for the child. The earlier the insult, the smaller the store of well-learned knowledge and skills, and the greater the likelihood of global impairment. Where specific skills are at a critical period of development they may be irreversibly impaired. Given the dynamics of the developing system, such impairments provide the potential for "downstream" effects on the acquisition of other skills (Dennis, 1989; Temple, 1997), with a deficit in one cognitive domain leading to problems in other, related domains. The eventual accumulation of primary and secondary impairments may explain the commonly encountered "global impairment profile" following childhood CNS damage.

PART TWO

Common CNS disorders of childhood:
Neurological, developmental, and
psychosocial dimensions

Recovery from early brain insult: Plasticity, early vulnerability, and their neural bases

INTRODUCTION

The consequences of brain insult sustained early in life have long been regarded as both qualitatively and quantitatively distinct from the sequelae of insults occurring in adulthood. Pathological conditions that would almost certainly lead to severe cognitive dysfunction in an adult, such as severe unilateral brain disease or localised cerebrovascular accidents, can have quite different consequences for children. Children with early left hemisphere disease, for example, may go on to acquire many age-appropriate language abilities, free from obvious symptoms of aphasia observed following similar lesions in adulthood (Heywood & Canavan, 1987; Taylor & Alden, 1997). Similarly early vascular accidents need not preclude normal or higher intellectual and academic achievements (Smith & Sugar, 1975). Even if an entire cerebral hemisphere is removed, a child can develop relatively normal cognitive function. In contrast, children sustaining generalised cerebral insult, for example, traumatic brain injury or cerebral infection, have been shown to have slower recovery and poorer outcome than adults with similar insults (Anderson & Moore, 1995; Anderson & Taylor, 1999; Gronwall et al., 1997; Taylor & Alden, 1997). This chapter aims to explore the range of outcomes associated with early cerebral damage, in an attempt to develop an understanding of the variability that occurs. To do this it is important to address what is known about the biological mechanisms that underpin recovery, and any advantages that may exist for the immature brain. The competing theoretical perspectives of plasticity versus early vulnerability will also be examined, in the context of current empirical evidence, with a view to identifying factors that may contribute to the child's level of recovery.

The possibility of grossly normal cognitive development, in spite of significant early brain insult, is consistent with early "plasticity" theories. Such observations, taken at face value, suggest a significant degree of redundancy or plasticity in the developing central nervous system (CNS) (Dennis & Whitaker, 1976; Neville, 1993; Smith, 1981). As was evident in Chapter 2, the timing of the CNS insult is particularly important within the immature brain. The consequences of trauma are dependent upon what is happening in the developing CNS at time of insult. It is generally accepted that early trauma has greater potential influence, impacting on the basic structure of the brain. Further, if insult occurs at a sensitive or critical developmental period specific structures or functions may be disrupted. As the child moves through later childhood and adolescence, the nature of impairments comes to resemble the adult picture more closely, reflecting the near-mature CNS, and the reduction in plasticity/flexibility for recovery and reorganisation.

Despite a lively and continuing interest in this area, recovery from early brain damage remains imperfectly understood, and a number of controversies continue to attract attention. One of the major debates is provided by the "plasticity versus early vulnerability" theorists. Here the focus is on the degree to which the immature brain has a greater capacity for recovery than the adult brain. This debate is argued at both biological and cognitive levels. A further and somewhat related argument centres on whether specific cerebral functions (e.g., speech, memory) are innately localised to a particular brain region, with limited potential for transfer, with the contrasting view arguing that the immature brain is equipotential, with localisation of function developing progressively during early childhood, thus explaining why early injury may not lead to the specific neurobehavioural consequences seen following similar adult pathology (Aram, 1988; Oddy, 1993). These two debates will be taken up in the following discussion.

PLASTICITY VERSUS EARLY VULNERABILITY: WHAT IS THE EVIDENCE?

For many years there has been debate between plasticity theorists and those who argue for an early vulnerability model. Plasticity theories hypothesise that the child's brain is immature and thus less susceptible to the impact of cerebral damage. Huttenlocher and Dabholkar (1997) define plasticity as "the capacity of a system for molding in response to environmental influences" (p. 80), and argue that this process will be most effective when CNS development is active, and when there are synapses and dendritic connections that are yet to be specified. This "plasticity" position has been supported by a number of researchers, employing both animal models and human subjects. The underlying premise states that within the immature brain functional organisation is less committed than it is for the mature adult, and has a greater capacity for transferring functions from damaged cerebral tissue to healthy tissue. Thus an early injury can result in the reorganisation of functions, either within the damaged hemisphere (intra-hemispheric reorganisation) or in the opposite hemisphere (inter-hemispheric reorganisation). This plasticity is thought to explain instances where lesions to the CNS in early childhood result in less severe consequences than would be seen in adults sustaining equivalent lesions.

The classic disease populations employed in early research addressing outcome from early brain insult include children with focal unilateral lesions of prenatal origin, such as congenital hemiplegias, usually due to antenatal or perinatal insults, children undergoing hemispherectomy for treatment of intractable epilepsy, and children with acquired focal lesions to language cortex who do not exhibit the expected aphasic symptoms exhibited by adults (Alajouanine & Lhermitte, 1965; Aram & Enkelman, 1986; Basser, 1962; Riva & Cassaniga, 1986; Vargha-Khadem, O'Gorman, & Watters, 1985; Woods & Carey, 1979). Much of this research was conducted pre-CT/MRI (computed tomography/magnetic resonance imaging) technology. Localisation of pathology was generally assumed from clinical signs, rather than radiological evidence. It is argued that such methodologies may have been less than optimal, and many patients participating in these early studies may have sustained more generalised cerebral pathology, thus clouding accurate interpretation. Interestingly, more recent, better-controlled, longitudinal research restricted to samples of children sustaining focal vascular insults indicates similar patterns of recovery (Aram & Eisele, 1994; Dall'Oglio et al., 1994), supporting earlier findings.

Researchers such as Kennard (1936, 1940) and Teuber (1962) are well known for their seminal works describing relative sparing of function following early cerebral insult—the Kennard principle being interpreted by Teuber to suggest that "if you're going to have brain damage, have it early" (Schneider, 1979). These workers, and various others more recently (Lenneberg, 1967; Vargha-Khadem et al., 1992; Woods, 1980) have documented relatively good recovery following early insult. In particular, studies following recovery from aphasia note that, where injury severity is equivalent, there is evidence of greater improvement in children than is observed in adults (Alajouanine & Lhermitte, 1965; Hecaen, 1976; Lenneberg, 1967). Similar findings are reported in follow-up studies following hemispherectomy (Broca, 1865; Dennis, 1980; Krynauw, 1950; Rankur, Aram, & Horowitz, 1980; Rasmussen & Milner, 1977).

Although plasticity theory may provide a model for understanding the impact of localised cerebral insult to the developing brain, it is not universally applicable. It is unable to accommodate observations that some children with early cerebral insults do exhibit significant residual functional deficits. In particular, where damage is more diffuse, the pattern of sequelae appears to be quite different. Longitudinal research investigating outcomes from generalised cerebral insults such as traumatic brain injury, cerebral infection, and cranial irradiation for treatment of childhood cancers indicates that children sustaining insults in early childhood experience greatest deficits, with sequelae reducing as the age at insult, and thus the maturity of the brain, increases (Anderson, Bond, et al., 1997; Anderson & Moore, 1995; Anderson, Morse, et al., 1997; Dennis, 1989; Ewing-Cobbs et al., 1997; Jannoun & Chessels, 1987; Kaufmann et al., 1993; Smibert et al., 1996; Taylor & Alden, 1997).

Many of the studies that argue for early plasticity have a range of methodological flaws. The majority are based on selected case studies or small samples. These samples are commonly heterogeneous with respect to critical variables including nature, timing, and localisation of lesions. Outcome measures are often insensitive, and intelligence quotient (IQ) is used almost universally in such studies. Many have employed simplistic interpretations, assuming that verbal IQ (VIQ) represents left hemisphere and language functions, and performance IQ (PIQ) reflects right hemisphere and non-verbal skills. The common finding of reduced PIQ, regardless of laterality of lesion, is interpreted as representing right hemisphere vulnerability specifically. Rather, it may be that PIQ reductions reflect the dependence of these measures on intact higher-level skills (e.g., memory, executive function), which are still developing at the time of insult in these children and may be permanently disrupted. Finally, follow-up periods are frequently too short to rule out the emergence of later significant functional deficits. Review of larger-scale investigations of conditions affecting the CNS, for example, infantile hemiplegia and hydrocephalus, shows that group means within these populations on more sensitive cognitive and academic measures are uniformly depressed. A critical evaluation of the literature suggests that plasticity theories may represent an oversimplification of the range of possible effects of early brain insult (St James-Roberts, 1979; Taylor & Alden, 1997).

In contrast, early vulnerability proponents postulate that brain insults occurring during childhood are particularly detrimental to development. One of the earliest supporters of this position was Hebb (1949), who argued that plasticity theories ignore the possibility that brain insult will have different consequences at different times throughout development. He went further to conclude that, in some instances, brain insult early in life may be more detrimental than later injury, because some aspects of cognitive development are critically dependent on the integrity of particular cerebral structures at certain stages of development. Thus, if a cerebral region is damaged and dysfunctional at a critical stage of cognitive development it may be that the cognitive skill is irreversibly impaired (Kolb, 1995, p. 76).

Other researchers postulate that, although there may be some plasticity early in life, the time frame may be quite restricted and not necessarily related to age in a linear manner. For example, studies of children with prenatal lesions, or those sustaining insults during the first year of life appear to report greatest impairment (Anderson, 1988; Anderson, Bond, et al., 1997; Duchowny et al., 1996; Leventer et al., 1999; Riva & Cassaniga, 1986). In addition, there remains some controversy as to the implications of plasticity processes. Even if reorganisation of function does occur, it may lead to a "crowding effect" where the functions normally subsumed by two healthy hemispheres are crowded into one, with a general depression of all abilities. Many studies that provide evidence for the vulnerability model document impairments in abilities important to the acquisition of knowledge and skills (e.g., learning, executive function) (Anderson, Godber, et al., 1997; Ewing-Cobbs et al., 1997; Wrightson et al., 1995). Deficits in these domains may have a cumulative effect on ongoing development, with increasing deficits emerging through childhood as more functions are expected to mature and need to be subsumed within the undamaged tissue. Milner (1974, p. 87) was one of the first workers to articulate such a possibility, by describing the process of crowding and its implications as follows: "there is always a price to pay for such plasticity . . . verbal skills tend to develop at the expense of non-verbal ones in this kind of hemispheric competition, but the fact remains. Both are low."

BIOLOGICAL MECHANISMS OF RECOVERY: ADVANTAGES FOR THE DEVELOPING BRAIN

One method of furthering the plasticity debate is to determine whether there may be biological advantages for the young brain during the recovery process. There has been much research directed to establishing a fuller understanding of the recovery process, both in children and adults. Today, we are aware of many of the physiological consequences of brain insult and the underlying aspects of recovery. There is some dispute regarding the relative efficiency of these processes in the immature child's brain versus the fully developed adult brain, with some evidence for greater recovery following early brain insult. In the following discussion, we will review theories of recovery of function in general and go on to discuss whether these processes may be particularly efficacious for children.

Brain damage results in a number of changes in brain tissue, depending on the type of damage incurred. Once the lesion occurs, be it vascular, traumatic, or aplastic, a number of degenerative events follow, as are described in Table 4.1. These events involve the death and shrinkage of axons and associated neural structures, and the consequent actions of glial cells in repairing the

TABLE 4.1
Degenerative events following brain damage

Pathology	Description
Anterograde degeneration	Degeneration of an axon after it is cut from the cell body
Calcification	Deposits of calcium build-up in areas of neural degeneration
Gliosis	Replacement of cell bodies by glial cells in areas of degeneration
Necrosis	Death of individual cells or cell groups in localised areas
Phagocytosis	Mitochondria and astrocytes remove dead cells from damaged areas
Neural degeneration	Death or shrinkage of damaged axon and connected cell bodies, axon terminals, and dendrites after axon is cut

Adapted from Kolb and Whishaw (1996), with permission.

damage as much as possible. Although these degenerative processes may occur primarily in the acute phases post-injury, there is some evidence for ongoing degeneration and cumulative pathology in children following cerebral insult, such as traumatic brain injury or cranial irradiation (Anderson & Pentland, 1998; Fernandez-Bouzas et al., 1992; Paakko et al., 1992; Stein & Spettell, 1995). These mechanisms are well demonstrated in the case of "Jamie", a toddler who sustained a severe traumatic brain injury, with focal frontal damage at age 3 years, as a result of a tractor accident. The brain scans illustrated in Figure 4.1 were obtained immediately post-injury, and 7 years later. The initial CT scan (a) shows the extent of the damage, particularly within the right frontal lobe. MR scans taken 7 years later clearly display the original frontal lobe injury, and subcortical pathology (b), but, in addition, the right hemisphere now shows dramatic evidence of generalised atrophy (c).

Despite these various pathological processes, some recovery of function is evident, both biologically and functionally. The proposed mechanisms of recovery can be grouped into two general classes: restitution theories and substitution theories (Kolb & Gibb, 1999; Laurence & Stein, 1978; Rothi & Horner, 1983). Restitution of function suggests that spontaneous physiological recovery occurs after brain damage. As damaged brain tissue heals, neural pathways are reactivated and so functions are restored. In contrast, substitution theories refer to restoration via transfer of functions from damaged brain tissue to healthy sites.

Restitution of function

One of the best-known and accepted restitution theories is that of *diaschisis* (von Monokow, 1914), which describes a period of rapid recovery immediately following brain insult, and explains the generalised nature of

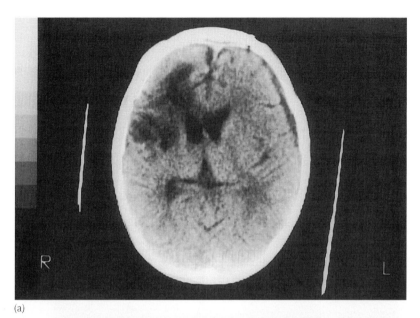

(a)

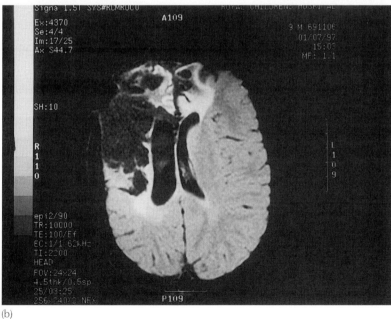

(b)

Figure 4.1(a) and (b). Brain scans depicting pathology following severe traumatic brain injury in a 3-year-old child. (a) Acute CT scan demonstrating extent of initial injury, which includes extensive right frontal damage. (b) MRI scan 7 years post-injury, illustrating the initial pathology. (Continued overleaf.)

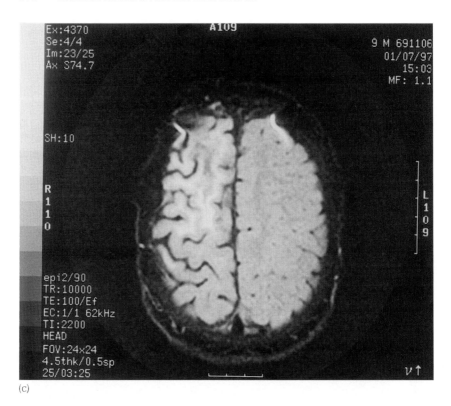

(c)

Figure 4.1(c). MRI scan 7 years post-injury, illustrating the generalised right hemisphere atrophy.

impairment in the early stages post-insult. In the first days and weeks after injury the patient's rapid improvement in conscious state and neurological function is said to reflect the physiological recovery of spared neural tissue, the function of which has been interrupted but not destroyed. Von Monokow used his theory of diaschisis to distinguish between transient central nervous system (CNS) disorders due to suppression of brain activity and the deficits that result from damaged tissue that will not recover. Diaschisis may be viewed as a kind of general inertia that temporarily suppresses cerebral activity in cerebral regions far from the injury site, because of widespread effects on processes such as blood flow, intracranial pressure, and neurotransmitter release. As these transient effects subside, the patient's condition improves. Except in so far as any young system will recuperate more effectively than the old, this process does not prescribe any age-related advantages in recovery for early insults.

Following this initial period of diaschisis, a number of additional recovery processes have been described. *Regeneration*, the process by which damaged neurons, axons, and terminals regrow and establish previous neuronal connections, is the best documented, and has been demonstrated to be functionally advantageous in the peripheral nervous system, as well as in the CNS in animal studies (Kolb & Gibb, 1999). The possibilities for such regrowth in the CNS are less clear (Bjorkland & Stenevi, 1971; Finger & Stein, 1982; Rothi & Horner, 1983), although it has been demonstrated, at least in primates, that the hippocampus and the olfactory bulb can produce new neurons during adulthood (Altman & Bayer, 1993; Lois & Alvarez-Buylla, 1994). In reality, such regeneration is often hindered by scar tissue and blood clots. Although axons may start to regrow, only a subset will reach their destination, resulting in incomplete or even maladaptive recovery. A second recovery process is that of *sprouting*, where remaining nerve fibres develop branches that occupy sites left empty by damaged neurons, thus reinnervating unoccupied areas. Sprouting is reported to occur quite early post-insult, being complete in a matter of weeks, with some evidence that it leads to associated behavioural improvement (Kolb & Whishaw, 1996). *Denervation supersensitivity* (Cannon & Rosenbleuth, 1949; Ungerstedt, 1971) provides another possible mechanism for restoration of function, suggesting that, in areas of damage, postsynaptic processes may become supersensitive to neurotransmitter substance leaking from pre-lesion neurons, thus allowing activation of post-lesion pathways and restitution of normal functioning. Currently much research effort is focused on application of pharmacological treatments that may enhance these physiological recovery processes.

The underlying mechanisms described in restitution theories may be argued to be equally efficacious in the mature and the developing brain, with no clear neurophysiological evidence to support a notion of better recovery in the developing brain. Finger and Stein (1982), in their work on age and recovery, argue that anomalous neural growth following CNS insult, via restitution mechanisms, is more likely in the immature brain, due to the less rigid organisation present. One of the possible mechanisms acting in the recovery process, that of neural competition, provides a basis for this vulnerability position. This competition hypothesis suggests that, following cerebral insult in early stages of development, there occurs a relocation of function, resulting in a decrease in synaptic sites available for mediating behaviours. The number of available synaptic sites is reduced, due to neuronal damage, and functional systems must work with a smaller number of synaptic connections, leading to reduced levels of functioning and the "crowding" phenomenon. In the longer term, there remain fewer synaptic sites available to be taken up by new, emerging, skills, leading to a picture of cumulative deficits and increasing problems with developmental progressions (Aram & Eisele, 1994; Vargha-Khadem et al., 1992).

Substitution of function

Substitution theories, arguing for either anatomical reorganisation or functional adaptation, provide some evidence for plasticity, arguing that the relatively unspecialised state of the immature CNS allows for transfer or re-routing of behavioural functions, with little evidence of impairment. The first group of substitution theories, those supporting *anatomical reorganisation*, have a long history, having been developed many years ago. Theorists such as Munk (1881), Lashley (1929), and Luria (1963) put forward arguments that there are large areas of the brain that are "unoccupied" or equipotential, and have the capacity to subsume functions previously the responsibility of damaged tissue. The advantages of such mechanisms are generally thought to diminish with age, with young children having more "uncommitted" brain tissue, and are thus more able to reorganise function. Recent research showing that the most dramatic effect of cerebral insult may be as a result of prenatal pathology is not consistent with these theories (e.g., Duchowny et al., 1996).

Behavioural compensation (Kolb & Whishaw, 1996; Rothi & Horner, 1983) is a second possible mechanism for substitution of function. This model suggests that the patient develops new strategies or routes for cognitive functions that were previously dependent on damaged tissue. For example, a child with right parietal damage, resulting in visual analytical impairments, may develop a range of verbal mediation strategies to implement when faced with visually based tasks. Alternatively, external strategies may be employed to minimise residual deficits. A child with memory deficits may employ a diary or note system to compensate for poor learning. This perspective underpins the philosophy for rehabilitation intervention following CNS insult, aiming to maximise behavioural compensation by suggesting strategies and modifying the individual's environment to their needs. As with restitution theories, although this model suggests that it may be beneficial for children following brain insult, there is no indication that children will benefit more than do adults (Anderson, 1988).

PLASTICITY AND EARLY VULNERABILITY: A CONTINUUM?

Both plasticity and early vulnerability theories have their inherent problems, with contemporary theorists suggesting that perhaps the two positions represent opposite extremes along a continuum (Lesser & Kaplan, 1994). The outcome for the child is then determined by the interaction of a range of factors including lesion variables, developmental parameters, gender, and environmental factors, as summarised in Table 4.2.

TABLE 4.2
Injury characteristics and recovery from early brain insult

	Plasticity	*Vulnerability*
Severity of lesion	Bimodal effect: small lesions and very large lesions may cause interhemispheric reorganisation	More severe insults result in greater vulnerability
Nature of lesion	Focal lesions, e.g., stroke, tumour	Generalised trauma, e.g., traumatic brain injury, infections
Age at onset	Greatest in initial 12 months and decreasing through childhood	Greatest for prenatal insults and decreasing through childhood
Gender	More common in females, especially for left hemisphere	More common in males, greater for right hemisphere
Psychosocial context	High SES, access to rehabilitation, early intervention	Low SES, limited access to resources

SES, socioeconomic status.

Nature and severity of insult

Research suggests differential outcomes associated with specific types of cerebral insult. Findings supporting good outcome from early cerebral insult are primarily based on focal lesion patients (Aram & Eisele, 1994; Kolb & Whishaw, 1996; Mogford & Bishop, 1993; Seidenberg et al., 1997; Stark & McGregor, 1997). With respect to size and severity of focal lesions, it appears that there may be a non-linear relationship. As expected, small lesions appear to be associated with good recovery. Interestingly, a similar result has been argued for large, unilateral lesions, with the proposition being that, in these conditions, interhemispheric transfer of function may occur, with minimal impact on functional abilities. However, there is evidence to suggest that there may be a "crowding effect" in these cases. Thus, where one hemisphere needs to take on functions usually subsumed by the whole brain, there is a general depression of neurobehavioural function. For moderate and/or bilateral lesions, functional plasticity is generally not evident, and outcome is argued to be particularly poor (V. Anderson et al., 1997; Kolb, 1995).

In contrast, when insult is generalised, for example, in traumatic brain injury or cerebral infection, results are generally poorer and indicative of global dysfunction (Anderson & Moore, 1995; Taylor & Alden, 1997). Further, research consistently documents a clear dose–response relationship between severity and outcome in these conditions, where greater severity is associated with greater behavioural impairment. Such trends have been reported in several studies conducted in our lab (e.g., Catroppa, Anderson, &

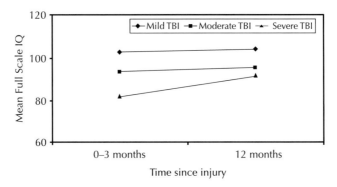

Figure 4.2. Impact of severity of traumatic brain injury (TBI) on intellectual function in school-aged children.

Stargatt, 1999; Pentland et al., 1998). Figure 4.2 provides an example of these findings, showing IQ scores for school-aged children sustaining traumatic brain injury, with results plotted at the acute phase and 12 months post-injury. Although children with more severe injuries show some recovery in the 12 months post-injury, they do not achieve pre-injury levels. There is a highly significant difference in IQ across severity groups at both time points, with children sustaining more severe injuries showing lower IQ scores (V. Anderson, Catroppa, et al., 2000). We have identified similar "severity" effects on IQ measures for preschool children sustaining traumatic brain injury (V. Anderson et al., 1997), for children with complicated versus uncomplicated meningitis (Grimwood et al., 1995), and for children treated with varying doses of cranial irradiation for the treatment of leukaemia (V. Anderson, Smibert, Ekert, & Godber, 1994).

Age/developmental level at time of insult

Chronological age is generally employed as an estimate of both cerebral and cognitive development. Younger age at insult reflects a less mature CNS and less developed cognitive functions. Research suggests that a complicated relationship exists between age at insult and plasticity of function. Recent studies have shown that prenatal injury may have the poorest outcome, with no evidence of transfer of function from the lesion site to undamaged tissue, resulting in significant developmental disability (Duchowny et al., 1996; Leventer et al., 1999). In contrast, the impact of early acquired insult may be more consistent with plasticity theories, resulting in abnormal cortical organisation and a greater sparing of cognitive function (Devinsky et al., 1993). It has been argued that the time frame for "functional plasticity" may not be constant, but rather may be functionally specific (Dennis, 1989; Lenneberg,

1967), in keeping with previously discussed notions of critical or sensitive periods. It may be that cerebral structures and associated cognitive functions in the process of most rapid development at the time of insult are most vulnerable to interference.

In addition, the interval between insult and evaluation of outcome, and the age at evaluation are also particularly important in paediatric research (Taylor & Alden, 1997). Although children may appear relatively functionally intact immediately post-insult, over time they may fail to make age-appropriate developmental gains (Dennis, 1999, 1989). As a result, the gap between children with brain dysfunction and their peers will widen with time. As new skills are expected to come "on line" during later childhood, add-itional deficits may emerge for the injured child, giving the impression that they "grow into" their deficits (Anderson & Moore, 1995; Dennis, 1989; Eslinger et al., 1999; Taylor & Alden, 1997; Wrightson et al., 1995).

Gender

The evidence that supports a gender-specific effect following early brain insult remains controversial. Neuroanatomical studies suggest that cortical development follows a differential path in males and females, largely due to hormonal factors, with the female brain developing more rapidly, during early childhood (Kolb, 1995). Similarly functional imaging research has iden-tified gender-specific patterns of cerebral activation in males and females, with males showing greater lateralisation of function, and females exhibiting more bilateral activation (Shaywitz et al., 1995). Such findings are not uni-versal, however, with more recent research unable to detect any gender differ-ences in language lateralisation (Frost et al., 1999). Others have noted greater dendritic volume in females (Jacobs & Scheibel, 1993; Kolb & Stewart, 1991). There is some suggestion that these structural differences may be important for recovery of function following brain injury. If female brains are more diffusely organised, there may be greater potential for plasticity and reorgan-isation of function. There is some evidence that females show a greater cap-acity for functional transfer (Strauss, Wada, & Hunter, 1992). Kolb (1995) reviews a number of studies that demonstrate earlier left hemisphere matur-ation in females. He suggests that this rapid development leaves fewer synap-ses free in the language cortex, and therefore there is a greater likelihood of transfer of function to the less specific right cortex. Thus, the female brain may be better able to cope with the impact of early lesions than the more lateralised male brain.

Such mechanisms may have been argued to provide some insight into the high prevalence of males with developmental disorders such as autism, specific learning disability, and attention deficit hyperactivity disorder (Kolb, 1995).

Psychosocial context

Family function, socioeconomic status, access to rehabilitation, and response to disability will also play a role in recovery following cerebral insult (Breslau, 1990; Perrott, Taylor, & Montes, 1991). Studies evaluating the impact of such factors in the context of insult severity suggest that psychosocial factors become more important with time (Anderson & Taylor, 1999). Thus although severity is of primary importance immediately post-insult, environmental factors become more relevant in the long term. With time since injury, children with severe cerebral insults, from disadvantaged social backgrounds, and with limited access to support resources, exhibit significantly greater impairment and slower recovery than children with adequate social resources (Breslau, 1990; Taylor & Alden, 1997; Taylor et al., 1992)

Animal research also argues for the importance of environmental variables. Studies of laboratory animals show that early experience affects brain structure and organisation and that manipulation of post-injury environment influences subsequent learning capacities (Greenough, Black, & Wallace, 1987; Fischer & Rose, 1994; Kolb, 1995; Kolb & Fantie, 1989; Neville, 1993; Taylor & Alden, 1997).

LANGUAGE LATERALISATION AND EARLY BRAIN INSULT

Equipotentiality versus innate specialisation

Within the context of cerebral development and plasticity, language functions have been studied most thoroughly, perhaps due to the observation that children sustaining cerebral insult to the left hemisphere rarely develop the aphasic symptoms typically observed in association with adult pathology. Within this field of study the "plasticity versus early vulnerability" positions are restated with the parallel theories of cerebral equipotentiality (Lenneberg, 1967) and early specialisation (Witelson, 1976).

Equipotentiality theories

Equipotentiality theories suggest that, at birth, the two cerebral hemispheres are equally able to subsume language functions, but that during childhood the left hemisphere takes on a progressively more important role, until middle childhood, when language functions are fixed within the dominant hemisphere. To support this model, Lenneberg (1967) employed findings from a study that described the outcome of a group of children who had undergone hemispherectomy for the treatment of intractable epilepsy (Basser, 1962). In contrast to reports of severe language disturbance following similar surgery in adults, the study detected no impairment of speech function following surgery regardless of lateralisation of initial injury or subsequent cortical removal. Lenneberg interpreted these results as evidence that both hemispheres are equally able to mediate speech functions early in development.

Although he argued strongly for an initial equipotentiality for language processing, Lenneberg recognised that this was only the case in infancy. He went on to propose a period of rapid language development between the ages of 2 and 5 years, with slower development until puberty. If brain damage was sustained during this rapid or "critical" period of development, he believed that there continued to be some potential for language functions to shift from one hemisphere to the other, with minimal consequences in terms of functional language skills. Lenneberg's theory claimed that, although some plasticity was present throughout childhood, major transfer could occur only during the critical period, that is, up to 5 years of age. Consistent with this suggestion, research following children who have been isolated from linguistic experience from birth shows that subsequent capacity to acquire language skills is best if intervention occurs within the preschool period, and then declines markedly to age 10 (Curtiss, 1981). Further, early onset of left hemisphere seizure foci has been associated with altered language lateralisation (Devinsky et al., 1993), with greater than expected language representation observed within the right hemisphere.

Innate specialisation

In keeping with the localisationist approach described in Chapter 1, the innate specialisation position argues that language is somehow "biologically special", and that there are predetermined areas of the cortex that are critical for language acquisition, having innate representations for language. It follows then, at a neuronal level, that this innate specialisation must be represented by predetermined neural circuitry and synaptic connectivity (Johnson, 1997). If these areas prespecified for language function are damaged, impairment of language function will result. It is this premise that has provided the basis of research in this field.

One of the greatest problems in evaluating the potential of these innate specialisation models has been the lack of direct evidence of lateralisation of language function. It is only more recently, with the use of procedures such as sodium amytal ablation, cortical activation, positron emission tomography (PET), and functional magnetic resonance imaging (fMRI) techniques, that researchers have been able to obtain a direct measure of lateralisation of language function, thus providing "hard" evidence to either support or reject these theoretical positions. A number of such studies have failed to support notions of equipotentiality, rather suggesting that the left hemisphere is innately specialised for language, and that even early lesions result in language impairments (Dall'Oglio et al., 1994; Riva & Cassaniga, 1986; Vargha-Khadem et al., 1985, 1991; Woods & Carey, 1979). The observation that language impairments resulting from early insult do not mirror those demonstrated in adult patients does not suggest that they are any less detrimental.

Most of the early literature in the field can be categorised into three groups: (1) studies investigating IQ differences associated with unilateral lesions; (2) studies of patients with intractable epilepsy who undergo unilateral chemical ablation procedures prior to temporal lobectomy; and (3) studies employing normal infants and children, and employing various experimental lateralisation paradigms.

IQ as a measure of lateralisation: Evidence from unilateral lesion studies

These studies have been based on samples of children who have sustained unilateral, focal vascular lesions, or hemispherectomy for treatment of intractable epilepsy. Such research commonly reports that IQ performance is related to age of onset of lesion, with lower IQs reported as age increases (Aram & Eisele, 1994; Cohen-Levine, 1993). However, the major focus of these research programmes has been to examine discrepancies in verbal and performance scores. Early studies were based on the assumption that VIQ is indicative of left hemisphere function, and thus linguistic abilities, whereas PIQ measures right hemisphere function, with the neurobehavioural correlate being non-verbal ability.

Despite methodological differences and heterogeneity of samples, a review of these studies identifies some consistent trends across samples. It appears that intellectual outcome can be categorised according to timing of lesion and laterality of lesion as follows:

(1) *Early left-sided lesions (<1 year)*: VIQ and PIQ are both depressed, suggesting a global reduction in intellectual ability, not consistent with adult literature (Aram & Ekelman, 1986; Ballantyne, Scarvie, & Trauner, 1992; Riva & Cassaniga, 1986; Vargha Khadem et al., 1985).

(2) *Early right lesions (<1 year)*: VIQ and PIQ are both lowered (Aram & Ekelman, 1986; Vargha-Khadem et al., 1985; Woods, 1980) or alternatively PIQ is differentially poor, again not consistent with adult patterns (Ballantyne et al., 1992; Riva & Cassaniga, 1986).

(3) *Later left-sided lesions (>1 year)*: VIQ and PIQ are both intact (Riva & Cassaniga, 1986), in comparison to the typical pattern of intact PIQ and reduced VIQ described following left-sided lesions in adults (Aram & Ekelman, 1986).

(4) *Later right lesions (>1 year)*: VIQ is intact, but PIQ is substantially

reduced, in keeping with reports following right hemisphere insult in adults (Aram & Ekelman, 1986; Riva & Cassaniga, 1986; Woods, 1980).

Despite the traditionally held view that the first 12 months of life is the optimal period for neural plasticity and functional reorganisation, these studies suggest that even if plasticity and reorganisation occur, such processes may not be related to improvements in functional abilities. Clearly cerebral insult during this time may be particularly detrimental to outcome, leading to global cognitive deficits. After the first year, left hemisphere lesions are associated with little observable impairment on IQ testing, whereas right hemisphere lesions result in specific impairments for non-verbal skills. It should be noted that, although IQ has been the accepted indicator of "outcome" in these studies, more subtle neurobehavioural deficits may also be present, but currently remain incompletely understood.

Aram and Ekelman (1986) have employed a more sophisticated approach to the use of IQ measures, employing the Kaufmann factor model (Kaufmann, 1975), which identifies three factors within the Wechsler tests: Verbal Comprehension, Perceptual Organisation, and Freedom from Distractibility. These factors, derived from statistical procedures, may be argued to provide a more "pure" representation of specific cognitive skills. Aram and Ekelman found that all children sustaining brain insult, regardless of age at lesion onset, or localisation of lesion, exhibited impaired performance on the Freedom from Distractibility factor, suggesting that brain damage sustained in childhood may have a general affect on attention and processing ability.

The data indicating a global deficit in IQ might be argued to support the equipotentiality theory, with both hemispheres able to take up functions subsumed by the either damaged dominant or non-dominant hemisphere. However, if this is the case, then it is clearly at a cost, and consistent with "crowding theories" which suggest that while functions may transfer they are then crowded into one hemisphere with a consequence of depression of all abilities. Findings with respect to later lesions indicate that there may be some sparing of language functions, as there is no evidence for a deficit in VIQ, regardless of laterality of lesion. This "sparing of function" provides support for the plasticity of language functions, with the interpretation being that language functions, rather than being differentially impaired, are reorganised to another location, and continue to function normally.

These studies suggest that functional plasticity is more apparent after age 1 year, with greater vulnerability associated with injuries in the first year of life. However, it is important to be aware that results are not entirely consistent. Further studies have a number of inherent flaws that need to be considered. First, sample sizes are necessarily small, owing to the rare nature of focal, lateralised cerebral insults in childhood. Second, samples are often quite heterogeneous, including children with a variety of aetiologies including pre-, peri-, and postnatal insults. Although many studies state that they include only focal lesions, the description of included insults argues against such claims, listing conditions known to cause generalised cerebral pathology, such as traumatic brain injury, cerebral infection, and anoxia. Inclusion of children with epilepsy may also cloud the results. Although there may be a localised epileptic focus, effects of ongoing seizures and medications may have their own consequences.

Of equal importance in these IQ-based studies is the assumption that VIQ represents left hemisphere function and PIQ reflects right hemisphere function. Such a simplistic dichotomy, although supported historically, is no longer tenable (Walsh, 1978). Evidence suggests that the two IQ scores, and each of the subtests within the scales they represent, are multidetermined, utilising both verbal and non-verbal skills. Thus simplistic lateralising statements based on these assumptions must be considered with some degree of caution. Further, it is now clear that IQ scores may not reflect the full extent of neurobehavioural impairment. Many studies now document average intellectual abilities in their patient groups, despite significant deficits in other skills including attention, memory, and higher-order language and executive skills. Future research examining these additional domains may help clarify long-term outcomes.

Functional measures of lateralisation of language

Sodium amytal ablation studies

More compelling research findings come from the work on language lateralisation, using techniques such as unilateral hemisphere ablation (WADA), usually employed in children and adults being considered for surgery for relief of intractable epilepsy. It is from these procedures that Rasmussen and Milner (1977) first made the observation that some of their patients did not exhibit the expected pattern of language localisation. Following ablation of the left, language-dominant hemisphere they observed a subgroup of patients to have no signs of aphasia. Further analysis of their sample showed that, although patients with seizure (lesion) onset prior to age 6 years were slightly more likely than expected to have atypical speech representation (left-sided speech = 81%, right-sided speech = 12%, bilateral speech = 7%), the figures were substantially different if left-handers only were considered (i.e., cases where lesion severity was sufficient to cause a change in handedness). In these patients, 28% demonstrated left-sided speech, 53% right-sided speech, and 19% had bilateral representation, indicating a dramatic reorganisation of speech dominance associated with a change in hand dominance. Rasmussen and Milner argued that several factors influenced functional reorganisation, including age of lesion onset, severity of lesion, and focus of lesion. Their results showed that language transfer only occurred when the language cortex was damaged. When areas other than language cortex, within the left hemisphere, were damaged, language functions tended to remain within the left hemisphere.

Functional imaging research

Many techniques used to examine cerebral function, for example, PET or cortical activation procedures, are inappropriate for children due to the invasive procedures involved. However, with the advent of fMRI, it is now possible to investigate cerebral activation patterns even in quite young children. Researchers utilising these methodologies argue that by using language-based activation paradigms it is possible to accurately localise language function and thus explore issues of functional reorganisation more directly. Initial findings have provided evidence that in cases of early childhood insult there is the potential for relocation of language skills to the non-dominant hemisphere (Muller et al., 1999). However, such findings are not universal, with other researchers hypothesising a less dramatic effect, where undamaged areas are recruited to support, rather than take over, language function (D. Anderson et al., 2000; Heiss et al., 1999; Thulborn, 1998).

With a view to unravelling these issues, our research group has recently conducted a study employing fMRI with a sample of 12 children who had sustained left hemisphere lesions either prenatally or during early childhood (D. Anderson et al., 2000). All children completed a language-based activation task, purported to involve left frontal regions, where they were asked to think of words beginning with a certain letter. Despite evidence of early left hemisphere pathology in 10 of the children, no child recorded specifically right-sided language, and only one child recorded bilateral cerebral activation. These findings would suggest that if language transfer does occur it is not universal.

This work has stimulated much research, with the issues not just of theoretical interest, but critical in the treatment of disorders which might be likely to lead to some functional reorganisation. This is particularly relevant in instances where surgical interventions are required, where it is important for professionals to accurately characterise the functional organisation of specific functions, and the risks of resecting tissue in areas such as language cortex.

Experimental studies with normal infants and children

Innate specialisation proponents argue that the brain is pre-programmed for language development. A number of lines of research support this hypothesis. In particular, the work on anatomical asymmetries within the cerebral cortex provides compelling evidence for lateralised language function. Post-mortem studies of infants and fetuses indicate that areas of the left hemisphere known to be associated with language function are larger in the left hemisphere. Specifically the planum temporale, within the Sylvian fissure, has been found to be more commonly larger in the left hemisphere regardless of age or developmental status (Geschwind & Levitsky, 1968; Wada, Clark, & Hamm, 1975; Witelson & Pallie, 1973).

Electrophysiological research also supports these anatomical asymmetries, showing that in general infants exhibit greater amplitude responses to speech sounds within the left hemisphere, suggesting a greater involvement of the left hemisphere in processing speech stimuli (Molfese & Molfese, 1980). Additionally, a range of behavioural paradigms have indicated a left hemisphere preference for language in neonates and infants, including techniques tapping head turning behaviour, dichotic listening, and sucking responses to speech stimuli (Lesser & Kaplan, 1994).

It appears that there may be some innate specialisation for language, observable in normal infants and young children, but that when catastrophe strikes, in the form of early brain insult, the brain has some capacity to transfer language functions to alternate cerebral regions. It may be that there is a primary system that mediates language in unexceptional circumstances, but there is also a back-up mechanism that comes into play when something goes wrong, once again displaying the flexibility or redundancy inherent in the developing CNS. The consistent observation that the possibility for transfer of language function diminishes with time into adulthood reflects the ongoing specification of function within the system.

MECHANISMS FOR CEREBRAL REORGANISATION: A SUMMARY OF FINDINGS

New techniques may facilitate progress in understanding the process of functional transfer, enabling the extension and verification of findings from earlier research and clinical case material which has identified a range of options available for functional reorganisation. Three clear possibilities emerge: intrahemispheric maintenance, intrahemispheric reorganisation, and interhemispheric reorganisation. An analysis of the available literature suggests that specific outcome is dependent upon a number of factors, as detailed in Table 4.3.

Intrahemispheric maintenance refers to an absence of transfer, where skills subsumed by damaged tissue are maintained within that tissue, resulting in maximum dysfunction. This is the model usually described for adult cerebral insult, where little plasticity is assumed to occur within the mature brain. For infants and young children this mechanism appears most likely to occur in association with pre- and perinatal lesions. Following an early lesion, functions are thought to remain located within damaged tissue, resulting in

TABLE 4.3
Factors affecting cerebral organisation of language following early CNS insult

	Age at onset	Lesion characteristics
Intrahemispheric maintenance	Prenatal/ perinatal	Unilateral, small/medium generalised
Interhemispheric transfer	0–2 years	Unilateral, small, but including language cortex
		Generalised, e.g., hemispherectomy
Intrahemispheric transfer	2–6 years	Unilateral, focal, in language cortex

severe impairments, operationalised as we see them clinically, as developmental disorders or mental retardation. Unilateral pre- or perinatal lesions may lead to specific speech and language delay, whereas more generalised lesions may result in global developmental delay (Anderson, 1997a; Aram & Ekelman, 1986; Devinsky et al., 1993; DeVos et al., 1995; Duchowny et al., 1996; Riva & Cassaniga, 1986). Such a pattern may also be observed for adolescents, where the brain is fully matured and recovery mirrors that seen in adults. Intrahemispheric maintenance has also been reported with very small, focal lesions with little consequence, or, alternatively, with generalised cerebral insult sustained in early childhood (e.g., traumatic brain injury, infection, hypoxia) where there is minimal healthy tissue to take up skills normally subsumed by damaged tissue (Anderson & Moore, 1995; Dennis, 1989; Taylor & Alden, 1997).

Interhemispheric transfer is thought to result from either very small lesions, based on reports of such pathology in language cortex or in hippocampal structures (Rasmussen & Milner, 1977; Vargha-Khadem et al., 1985; Woods & Carey, 1979), or very large unilateral lesions causing dysfunction involving most of one hemisphere (e.g., hemidecortication). Under these circumstances it is argued that language functions and possibly some non-language functions (e.g., memory) may transfer to the analogous site in the non-damaged hemisphere. An alternative explanation suggests that, rather than total reorganisation, other cerebral regions may be recruited when necessary to perform functions normally subsumed by damaged tissue. Regardless of the mechanism, it appears that there is an age limit to this process, reflecting critical periods for language development. Consistent with Lenneberg's (1967) premise of increasing language specialisation through childhood, interhemispheric transfer appears most likely in the first 2 years of life. As is the case in various instances of functional plasticity, this process may not be greatly advantageous in children, leading to "crowding effects" and generally depressed cognitive functions, in contrast to the more function-specific impairments observed following similar pathology in adults (Milner, 1974; St James-Roberts, 1979).

Intrahemispheric transfer, or reorganisation of functions within the damaged hemisphere, is less well researched, possibly because this mechanism has been more difficult to detect using available technologies and procedures, for example, laterality indicators, sodium amytal ablation, and PET. Transfer of function within hemispheres has been noted to occur where unilateral and focal pathology is present. Limited research argues that this process is most likely to occur in older children, and is usually reported for patients between 2 and 8 years of age, but techniques such as fMRI will enable fuller investigation of this possible transfer condition in the future. Research from our laboratory has provided some initial support for such a process. Serial scanning of an 8-year-old child with focal left frontal tumour, corresponding to Broca's area, has demonstrated some intrahemispheric transfer of cortical activation. Using a language generation task soon after the diagnosis of her tumour, the child showed minimal activation on fMRI and associated deficits in language function on standard clinical testing. Several months later, the child was rescanned using the identical language paradigm, with fMRI showing activation in the region posterior to the tumour, suggesting that this area had taken up these language functions, although language impairments remained evident on clinical measures (D. Anderson et al., 2000).

CONCLUSIONS

Review of the complex and often contradictory findings achieved from research investigating outcome from early cerebral insult suggests that neither plasticity nor early vulnerability is able to explain the range of consequences observed. Rather, it may be that these two models describe extremes along a recovery continuum, with factors such as nature, size and timing of lesion, developmental stage, gender, and psychosocial factors all influencing outcome. Both biological and environmental agents may interact to determine the nature and degree of any plasticity, and its functional significance. There is a need for further research to explain the range of recovery patterns observed following early brain insult. It may be that recent radiological advances, such as the emergence of functional imaging appropriate for use with children, will facilitate these endeavours. Already, researchers have been able to demonstrate some evidence for transfer of function using these methods with a small group of children.

CHAPTER FIVE

Traumatic brain injury in children

INTRODUCTION

Traumatic brain injury (TBI) is one of the most common causes of acquired disability during childhood. While the majority of such injuries are mild and result in few, if any, functional sequelae, children sustaining more significant insults may experience ongoing cognitive and behavioural deficits. Clinical reports indicate residual impairments in a range of skills, particularly information processing, attention, memory, and learning. These deficits may impact on a child's capacity to interact with the environment effectively, resulting in lags in skill acquisition, and increasing gaps between injured children and their age peers. Secondary deficits may also emerge, relating to family stress and adjustment difficulties. Long-term follow-up of these patients and their families indicates that, even with access to excellent rehabilitation resources, these problems persist, although the nature of stressors changes with time since injury and with the developmental level of the child. Treatment and management of the head-injured child and family requires long-term involvement, where the role of the neuropsychologist is more than simply one of monitoring neurobehavioural recovery. Rather the task is to understand the child's difficulties, to inform parents and the wider community of the cognitive and behavioural implications of the child's injuries, to liaise with teachers and rehabilitation workers, to design academic interventions and behaviour management programmes, and to provide counselling with respect to adjustment issues for the child and family. This chapter aims to address each of these areas, plotting recovery from TBI, beginning with acute phases and medical issues, and then considering current knowledge of subacute and long-term outcome, with respect to physical, cognitive, and psychosocial factors.

Although research in the area of adult TBI has been extensive, studies conducted in the paediatric population are more limited, and many unanswered questions remain. Despite the large numbers of children sustaining TBI, our knowledge of recovery processes, functional sequelae, and efficacy of interventions remains incomplete. What we do know is that there is wide variation in outcomes seen following paediatric TBI (Fletcher et al. 1995c) and that, as yet, we have failed to identify the range of important predictors of long-term outcome. Many factors identified as predictive of outcome in adults are also significant in paediatric patients (e.g., injury severity, duration of coma, premorbid characteristics, socioeconomic status). However, a number of parameters specific to children also require consideration (e.g., age at injury, time since injury, family environment). To fully investigate these issues it is necessary to conduct large-scale, longitudinal research within a developmental framework, acknowledging the possible interactions between injury and ongoing maturation. To date, only a handful of studies have employed such designs (e.g., Chadwick et al., 1981a; Fay et al., 1993; Fletcher, Miner, & Ewing-Cobbs, 1987; Kinsella et al., 1997; Klonoff, Low, & Clark, 1977; Prigatano, O'Brien, & Klonoff, 1993; Taylor et al., 1995).

EPIDEMIOLOGY

It is estimated that as many as 250:100,000 children experience TBI in any one year. Of these, half will not seek any medical care, between 5% and 10% will experience temporary and/or permanent neuropsychological sequelae, and 5–10% will receive fatal injuries (Goldstein & Levin, 1987). One in every 30 newborn children will sustain a TBI before age 16 (Annegers, 1983). Based on their research, Kraus et al. (1986) have reported that 85% of the head injuries are classified as mild, with 44% having no documented loss of consciousness. Examination of data relating specifically to children admitted to hospital with a severe TBI shows that the mortality rate is approximately one third, with another third of children making a good recovery, and the last third exhibiting residual disability (Michaud, Rivara, Grady, & Reay, 1992). Such incidence levels establish childhood TBI as a significant problem for the community.

The causes of childhood TBI are diverse and, as for adults, the majority of injuries are related to some form of road traffic accident (Goldstein & Levin, 1987). There is, however, a higher incidence of injuries due to falls, pedestrian accidents, and non-accidental injury than is observed in adult populations.

Incidence, cause, and nature of paediatric TBI have been reported to vary with respect to age, gender, and psychosocial context of the child.

Age

Circumstances leading to TBI within the paediatric population are partially dependent upon age, or developmental level, with children younger than 3 years having the highest incidence of head injury. Nature of injury also varies with age. Infants are more likely to experience trauma associated with falls or child abuse. Holloway, Bye, and Moran (1994) note that, for non-accidental injuries (i.e., child abuse), 61% of such injuries occur in children less than 12 months old and commonly result in more severe injury and higher mortality and morbidity than accidental injuries. The preschool stage is a high-risk period, with the majority of injuries due to falls. There is also a relatively high incidence of pedestrian accidents, in keeping with the greater mobility of this age group and their lack of awareness of danger (Lehr, 1990). School-aged children and adolescents are more frequently victims of sporting, cycling, or pedestrian accidents. To illustrate these age trends, Table 5.1 provides data showing the cause of injury in a sample of 1123 children admitted to the Comprehensive CNS Trauma Centers in Texas over a 3-year period (Brooks, 1985). In this cohort, falls were the mechanism of injury in more than half of children aged less than 4 years, with the proportion of children injured as a result of motor car accidents increasing progressively through childhood and into adolescence. The range of causal mechanisms for childhood TBI is likely to lead to variations in the resultant pathophysiology. These differences need to be considered in any age-based comparisons of outcome (Goldstein & Levin, 1987).

TABLE 5.1
Causes of head injury in children (*n* = 1123) admitted to the Comprehensive CNS Trauma Centers in Houston and Galveston, 1980–1982 (in percentages)

Cause of injury	<1 yr (n = 68)	1–4 yrs (n = 221)	5–9 yrs (n = 183)	10–14 yrs (n = 134)	15–19 yrs (n = 517)
MCA: passenger	26.0	17.2	25.7	37.3	51.8
MCA: cyclist	–	1.4	10.9	9.7	10.6
MCA: pedestrian	1.5	20.4	39.3	15.7	6.0
Falls	61.8	50.7	18.6	20.1	9.7
Gunshot wounds	1.5	2.3	–	4.5	7.9
Assault	5.9	2.7	0.5	3.0	8.5
Other	3.3	5.3	5.0	9.7	5.5

MCA, Motor car accident.
Reproduced from Brooks (1985) with permission from University of Texas Press.

There is also evidence that patient fatality rates increase as age decreases. Michaud et al. (1992) report that, in their study, 14% of children injured over the age of 14 years died from their injury, whereas the fatality rate for children under 2 years was 50%. In addition, they found better recovery with increasing age. Death was the most common outcome for the under 2 age group, while the majority of children injured over 14 years were classified as showing good recovery. This data argues for greater vulnerability associated with younger age at injury.

Gender

As is commonly reported, boys and girls are not equally at risk of sustaining TBI. A comparison of gender ratios shows that, in preschool children, the male:female ratio is approximately 1.5:1 (Hayes & Jackson, 1989; Horowitz et al., 1983). In contrast, school-aged males are more than twice as likely than age-matched females to suffer TBI (Kraus, 1995). Girls are more likely to sustain TBI associated with falls or as passengers in cars (Berney, Favier, & Froidevaux, 1994a). Males tend to sustain more severe trauma, with the mortality rate for male over female children estimated to be around 4:1 (Annegers, 1983). Further, Kraus et al. (1986) note that the incidence of TBI increases in males through childhood and adolescence, with a relative decline for females through childhood. This sex-related trend is illustrated in Figure 5.1, which represents data from children admitted to the Comprehensive CNS Trauma Centers in Texas (Brooks, 1985). Lehr (1990) suggests that such gender differences, which have been consistently identified, may reflect higher levels of activity and exploratory behaviour in boys.

Psychosocial factors

Epidemiological research demonstrates that childhood TBI occurs most frequently on weekends, holidays, and afternoons, when children are more likely to be involved in leisure activities. Such trends have been interpreted as an indication that many such injuries result from reckless behaviour in poorly supervised environments (Chadwick et al., 1981a; Dalby & Obrzut, 1991). Further, it is often stated that TBI is more common in families where parents are socially disadvantaged, unemployed, or emotionally disturbed (Anderson, Morse, et al., 1997; Brown et al., 1981; Klonoff, 1971; Rivara et al., 1993; Taylor et al., 1995), where parental neglect and poor supervision are evident (Moyes, 1980), and in children with pre-existing learning and behavioural deficits (Asarnow et al., 1991; Brown et al., 1981; Craft, Shaw, & Cartlidge, 1972). Some researchers have gone so far as to suggest that many post-injury sequelae may merely be a reflection of premorbid cognitive, behavioural, and social disturbances. Although this view has become well accepted in the paediatric TBI literature, a number of recent studies have failed to support

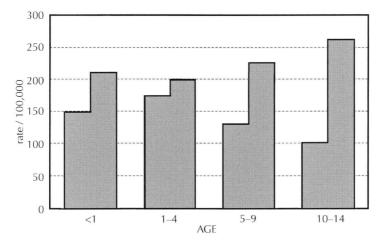

Figure 5.1. Incidence of paediatric traumatic brain injury, by age and gender (females represented on the left in each age range). From *Traumatic Head Injury in Children*, edited by Sarah Broman and Mary Ellen Michel, copyright © 1995 by Oxford University Press, Inc. Used by permission of Oxford University Press, Inc.

such findings, arguing that children who sustain injury cannot be differentiated from the general population with respect to pre-injury characteristics (Perrot et al., 1991; Prior et al., 1994).

PATHOPHYSIOLOGY

TBI refers to a traumatic insult to the brain, capable of producing brain damage and associated with functional impairment. These traumatic insults are usually caused by a physical blow or wound to the head that is sufficient to result in altered consciousness and may lead to neurological or neurobehavioural sequelae (Begali, 1992). It is this alteration of conscious state that is often used to distinguish between true TBI and more minor insults. In children, the causes of TBI are various and include falls, blows, missile wounds, and child abuse, as well as the more common motor vehicle accidents. Although TBI is frequently depicted as a unitary entity, the mechanics and underlying pathophysiology associated with these injuries are substantially different, resulting in a range of possible outcomes. The consequences of TBI are also dependent upon a number of other risk factors including (1) the magnitude of the force of impact; (2) the intracranial vectors of transmitted force (linear, rotational); (3) the thickness of the scalp and skull; (4) the site of impact; and (5) presence or absence of skull fracture (Amacher, 1988). The greater the force applied, the more severe the associated damage.

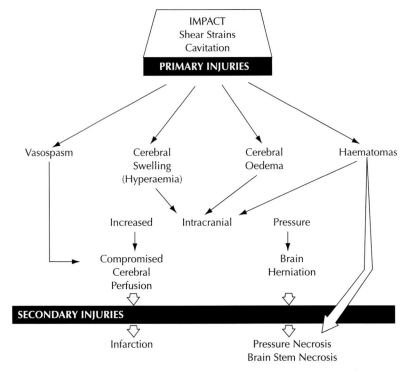

Figure 5.2. Mechanics and pathology associated with traumatic brain injury. Primary injuries cause haematoma, oedema, cerebral swelling, and vasospasm, resulting in increased intracranial pressure and brain herniation. Secondary consequences include cerebral infarction and necrosis. Adapted from Ylivasaker (1985).

As illustrated in Figure 5.2, the typical pathophysiology of TBI may be classified based on the relationship to the initial insult: (1) *primary impact injuries* occur as a direct result of the application of force to the brain and include fractures, contusions and lacerations, and diffuse axonal damage. Such injuries are generally permanent, and show little response to early treatment; (2) *secondary injuries* occur as a consequence of the primary injury and may include vascular disruption, which may lead to extradural, subdural, and intracerebral haemorrhage. Raised intracranial pressure, brain swelling, hypoxia, and infection, as well as metabolic changes including hypothermia, electrolyte imbalance, and respiratory difficulties, may also occur (Begali, 1992; North, 1984; Pang, 1985). Secondary injuries are more responsive to appropriate and timely medical interventions. For children who die as a result of TBI, common findings at autopsy include raised intracranial pressure, brain swelling, contusions, ischaemia, cerebral herniation, diffuse white matter damage, and subarachnoid haemorrhage (Bruce et al., 1979;

Graham et al., 1989; Michaud et al., 1992; Sharples, Stuart, Matthews, & Eyre, 1995).

There are two major classes of TBI: penetrating (or open) head injury and closed head injury. The characteristics of each of these are quite different with respect to the associated mechanics and pathophysiology, incidence, and neurobehavioural outcomes.

Penetrating head injury

The hallmark of penetrating injuries, as the term suggests, is penetration of the skull by some form of "missile", usually a bullet, rock, or knife. This type of injury accounts for approximately 10% of all childhood TBI. In penetrating head injury cerebral pathology tends to be localised around the path of the missile, with tissue destroyed in these areas, as illustrated in Figure 5.3. Additionally, damage may result from penetrating skull fragments or

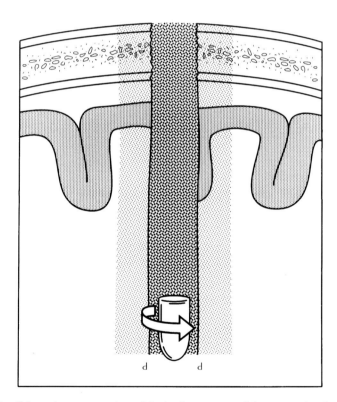

Figure 5.3. Schematic representation of brain damage caused by penetrating head injury, where a bullet has penetrated the skull, tearing a track that has filled with blood and debris. There are additional zones of tissue damage (d) surrounding the bullet track.

shattered fragments from the missile itself. Secondary damage may occur due to cerebral infection (from the alien object entering the brain), swelling, bleeding, and raised intracranial pressure. Although loss of consciousness is relatively uncommon following penetrating head injury, neurological deficits and post-traumatic epilepsy are frequently observed, and are much more prevalent following penetrating head injury than in closed head injury.

Neurobehavioural sequelae from penetrating head injury tend to reflect the focal nature of the lesion sustained. Children usually exhibit quite specific deficits consistent with the localisation of the lesion, with other skills relatively intact. Although these specific impairments are likely to persist, there is an opportunity to use intact abilities to develop compensatory strategies, or "alternative routes" for coping with cognitive demands.

Closed head injury

Closed head injury accounts for the majority of paediatric TBI. In closed head injury, the skull is not penetrated, but rather the brain is shaken around within the skull cavity, resulting in multiple injury sites, as well as diffuse axonal damage. The most common cause of such injuries is motor vehicle accident, associated with high-velocity deceleration forces. Damage results from compression and deformation of the skull at the point of impact, and the primary pathology includes contusion, or bruising, at the point of impact of the blow and at other cerebral sites. Research suggests that there are specific areas of the brain that are particularly vulnerable to such injury-related contusions, including basal frontal regions and temporal lobes, where severe surface damage may occur to blood vessels and cortical tissue (Courville, 1945). Additionally, in response to the impact, the brain is shaken backwards and forwards and rotated, with the extent of this process dependent on the force of the blow. The associated injuries caused by this shaking include damage to cerebral areas opposite the site of damage and shearing injuries to white matter, as these nerve tracts are bent and torn (Amacher, 1988). Figure 5.4 illustrates the mechanisms that may occur in such a closed head injury.

Whereas more focal lesions occur as a result of translational (linear) trauma, diffuse axonal injury is associated with rotational forces. Rotational forces cause the brain to "swirl and glide" within the skull, stretching and tearing the long white nerve fibres that connect the brain stem to cortical areas, and causing neural tearing throughout deep cerebral structures, particularly at the junctions between grey and white matter, including the area around the basal ganglia, hypothalamus, cerebellum and brain stem, corpus callosum, and frontal and temporal poles (Amacher, 1988; Gale, Johnson, Bigler, & Blatter, 1995; Pang, 1985). These angular or rotational forces are commonly seen in motor vehicle accidents and sporting accidents associated with blows that rotate the head on impact (Ponsford, Sloan, & Snow, 1995).

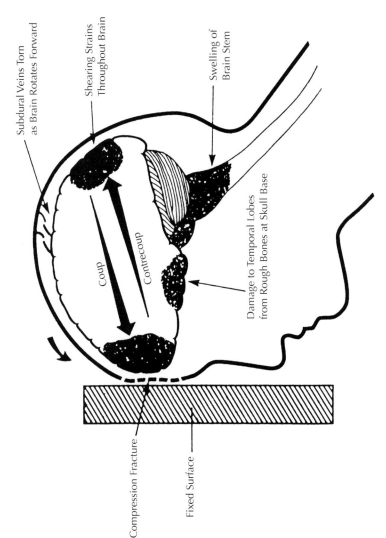

Figure 5.4. Brain damage caused by closed head injury, showing the impact of coup and contrecoup insults at the site of impact, and directly opposite, as well as shearing and vascular damage. Reproduced from Begali (1992). *Head Injury in Children and Adolescents: A Resource and Review for School and Allied Professionals.* Copyright © 1992 John Wiley & Sons, Inc. Reprinted by permission of John Wiley & Sons, Inc.

Evidence of these rotational forces and axonal injuries is seen even in quite trivial head injuries and concussions, contrary to theories that suggest that such injuries result only in reversible, non-structural changes specific to the brain stem (Pang, 1985).

Recent research has suggested that further secondary damage may be due to neurochemical processes. Elevated levels of excitatory amino acids, such as glutamate and aspartate, have been measured in cerebrospinal fluid immediately post-TBI and found to persist for several days. Such high levels have been reported to disrupt cell function and lead to cell death (Yeates, 1999). Further, these high levels have been correlated with degree of anatomical pathology demonstrated on computed tomography (CT) scan (Baker, Moulton, MacMillan, & Sheddon, 1993). Animal research suggests that pharmacological interventions may be successful in reducing brain injury due to such mechanisms (Novack, Dillon, & Jackson, 1996).

Secondary injuries, including haematoma, cerebral oedema, and raised intracranial pressure, may also occur following closed head injury, and have been found to be predictive of poor outcome (Quattrocchi, Prasad, Willits, & Wagner, 1991). The movements within the brain at the time of impact may lead to disruption and tearing of blood vessels. As a result of this vascular disruption, the formation of haematomas is quite common. These bleeds may be more or less serious depending on their size and location, and may be indicated by a deterioration in conscious state in the hours following TBI. Resultant mass effects lead to increased cerebral volume and raised intracranial pressure. If not treated quickly, usually via surgical evacuation, these secondary complications may cause cerebral herniation and ultimately death. The major types of haematoma include epidural, subdural, and intracranial, with the labels defining the site of blood collection. Epidural and subdural haematoma are situated within the meningeal coverings of the brain. *Epidural haematomas* refer to bleeds above the dura, just below the surface of the skull, and not directly involving brain tissue. They are usually related to a skull fracture, where vessels in the meninges have been damaged. When treated promptly outcome is good (Michaud et al., 1992). However, if left untreated, blood mass increase may cause cerebral shift and herniation (see Figure 5.5). *Subdural haematomas* present as a collection between the dura and the arachnoid mater, resulting from injury to the blood vessels in the cortex, or to the venous sinuses. These are more common and serious than epidural collections, mostly occurring as a consequence of massive cortical disruption and lacerations to blood vessels within the brain, where the underlying damaged brain may undergo rapid oedema formation leading to mass effect, and requiring surgical evacuation. *Intracerebral haematomas* involve an accumulation of blood within the brain. These are relatively uncommon following closed head injury, and more frequently observed in penetrating head injury or in association with

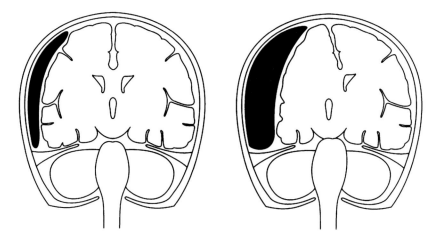

Figure 5.5.   Evolution of subdural haematoma in the period post-trauma associated with mid-line shift and disruption to the ventricular system.

depressed skull fractures. Prognosis depends on the site and extent of related damage.

Cerebral oedema, or brain swelling, refers to an increase in fluid volume within the skull. It may develop due to a failure of the autoregulatory mech-anism of cerebral blood flow, due to hypoxia, hypercapnia, or obstruction to cerebral circulation. Alternatively, brain swelling can occur as a result of increased fluid within the brain, associated with a range of possible causal factors, including obstruction of cerebrospinal fluid flow, accumulation of fluid within cells, increased intravascular pressure, or damage to blood ves-sels. Brain swelling may be either regionalised or diffuse, and related to brain shift and raised intracranial pressure (Pang, 1985; Ponsford et al., 1995). Any increase in the content of the brain (i.e., brain, cerebrospinal fluid, cerebral blood volume, extracellular fluid) will cause increased intracranial pressure. In the case of TBI, the presence of brain swelling or haematoma will be the primary cause of raised intracranial pressure, with the possible consequences including brain shift and reduction in cerebral blood flow, leading to diffuse ischaemic brain damage and cerebral herniation. Intracranial pressure is routinely monitored following TBI, and surgical treatment may be required to reduce pressure in some patients.

Although relatively uncommon following closed head injury, a number of delayed complications may develop in the subacute stages post-injury. Com-municating hydrocephalus may occur when there is an obstruction of the flow of cerebrospinal fluid, often due to vascular disruption. Cerebral infections may arise in association with skull fractures. These infections usually take the form of meningitis or cerebral abscess. Each of these complications may be detected on the basis of increased intracranial pressure and associated late deterioration in function. Following closed head injury patients also have increased risk of epilepsy. Early seizures occur quite frequently post-injury, but later post-traumatic epilepsy is less common, with risk factors including more severe injury, presence of focal pathology, and younger age at insult (Jennett, 1979; Pang, 1985; Ponsford et al., 1995; Raimondi & Hirschauer, 1984).

Case illustrations

The following case descriptions provide a comparison between recovery and outcome from penetrating head injury and closed head injury, where the injuries have been severe, resulting in permanent cerebral pathology, neurological deficit and neuropsychological impairment. The two children described were of similar age and developmental levels when they sustained severe TBI. Each had normal medical, developmental, and educational histories prior to their injuries. Adam sustained a penetrating head injury, resulting in quite focal damage and specific cognitive deficits. In contrast, Michael's injury resulted in more generalised insult, characteristic of closed head injury, with more global functional impairment and poorer recovery.

Adam

The typical features of penetrating head injury are well illustrated in the neurobehavioural deficits and recovery pattern exhibited by Adam. Adam was 11 years old when he sustained a severe penetrating head injury when struck on the head by a motor-boat propeller while swimming at a local beach. He was unconscious at the scene of the accident and noted to have a fixed, dilated right pupil. CT scan on admission to hospital revealed a right-sided parieto-occipital fracture, right parietal contusion, and haematoma extending to the lateral ventricle. There was no oedema or midline shift noted, and no evidence of generalised cerebral damage. CT scan results are presented in Figure 5.6. Following admission, Adam underwent neurosurgery to clean the wound and elevate the skull fracture. He was irritable and disoriented for about 10 days post-injury, but made good physical progress. He participated in physiotherapy and occupational therapy while an inpatient, but was not involved in further rehabilitation after discharge.

Interview with his family indicated that, prior to his injury Adam had been a healthy, well-functioning child. He had no history of medical problems, had shown normal to advanced development, and was described by his parents as an above average student. No pre-injury social or behavioural difficulties were reported. His family unit was intact and he was the elder of two children.

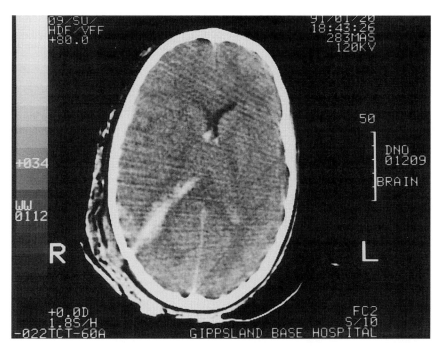

Figure 5.6. CT scan showing penetrating injury sustained by 11-year-old boy struck by motor-boat propeller. Damage involves penetrating injury to right parieto-occipital regions extending to the lateral ventricle.

Adam was seen for neuropsychological evaluation on several occasions during the acute recovery phase. Initially he presented with left-sided weakness, sensory loss, right lower quadrant visual field impairment, and some left-sided spatial neglect. His presentation was quite flat, lacking in animation and initiative, and his conversation was minimal. He improved rapidly in the days post-injury, both with respect to neurological functioning and mental state.

First assessment was performed on emergence from post-traumatic amnesia, 12 days post-injury, and then again several days later. At that stage Adam was administered some drawing tests, including the Rey Complex Figure, a task which requires a child to copy a complex geometric design. As illustrated in Figure 5.7, in the acute stages of recovery Adam exhibited significant difficulties on the Rey Complex Figure. Qualitatively he showed signs of visuomotor incoordination, poor constructional abilities, and visuospatial problems. Left-sided neglect was also evident in his failure to reproduce much of the left side of the figure. By 9 months post-injury Adam's deficits appeared to have largely resolved, with his Rey Complex Figure copy at age-appropriate level. Qualitative observations suggest that, in addition to

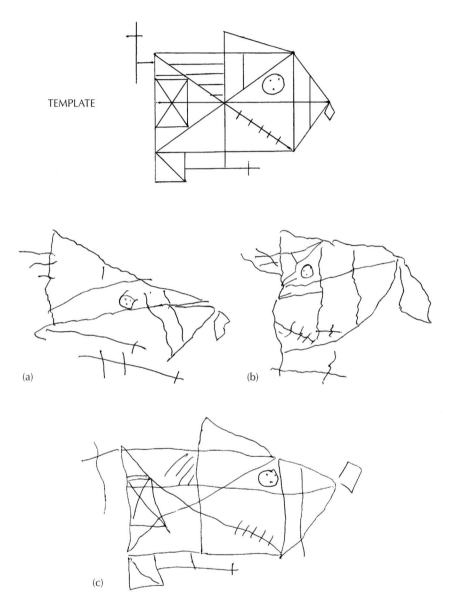

TEMPLATE

(a)

(b)

(c)

Figure 5.7. Adam's neuropsychological test results. Copy of Rey Complex Figure at (a) 12 days, (b) 17 days, and (c) 9 months post-injury, showing some resolution of visuospatial and visuomotor deficits.

improved performance associated with recovery, Adam's good production was due to his capacity to recode complex visual material into a series of verbally mediated strategies. When questioned, Adam described this process clearly, noting that he verbally labelled each component of the figure (e.g., rectangle triangle) and its spatial relationship to other components (e.g., below, to the right) before attempting to reproduce it. As a result of this strategy Adam was able to produce appropriate detail, but at quite a slow rate.

Intellectual evaluation, at 2 months and 10 months post-injury, using the Wechsler Intelligence Scale for Children—Revised (Wechsler, 1974), showed that, consistent with the focal nature of his injury, Adam had intact (high average) verbal skills, which were maintained, with some slight improvement over time (Figure 5.8). In keeping with his difficulties on the Rey Complex Figure at acute assessment, Adam exhibited significant problems on visually based subtests at 2 months post-injury, with poorest performances on measures requiring motor coordination. Executive function, memory, and

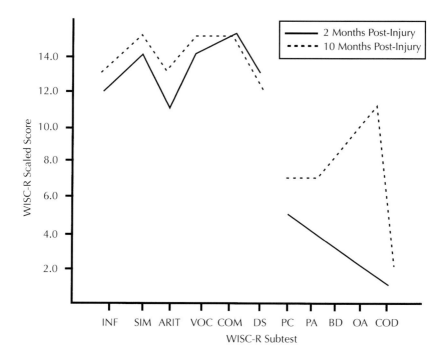

Figure 5.8. Adam's IQ (WISC-R) profiles at 2 months and 10 months post-injury, showing a pattern of stable verbal skills and improving non-verbal abilities.

learning skills were assessed as age appropriate to advanced, and educational skills were intact. Over time many of Adam's weaknesses improved to within the average range. However, as with the Rey Complex Figure, performances were very slow, suggesting that Adam was formulating intervening verbal strategies to compensate for primary visual processing problems.

This pattern of specific deficits in the context of otherwise intact adaptive, intellectual, and memory skills is common following penetrating head injury, where cerebral damage is quite focal. In such instances neuropsychological impairments reflect the underlying localised brain pathology, in Adam's case in the parieto-occipital area. The "recovery" of test scores over time may reflect both underlying physiological recovery and a "re-routing" of affected skills via the development of compensatory strategies, in keeping with behavioural compensation theories described in Chapter 4. As Adam's executive, verbal, and memory skills were intact he was able to utilise these to compensate for his visual difficulties in many situations. While he continues to experience difficulties with these functions, as evidenced by subtle deficits with complex mathematical concepts and visual tasks in day-to-day life, he is functioning well in most other areas. He is achieving average grades at school, although he requires extra tuition in mathematics. He has recently successfully completed high school, and is a popular and social boy. His sporting abilities continue to be limited due to mild persisting motor problems, but he is involved in a range of other activities.

Michael

Michael was 13 years old when he sustained a severe closed head injury when hit by a train while riding his bike across a railway crossing. His injuries included similar focal pathology to that described for Adam, but with the addition of more extensive focal damage, and the hallmark diffuse axonal injury. CT scan on admission showed mass effect due to haematoma, associated midline shift, and raised intracranial pressure (see Figure 5.9). Specific pathology included right parietal skull fracture, right parietal contusion, and left frontal contusion and haematoma. Michael underwent surgery to treat these problems, and later developed a cerebral abscess in the right parietal region, which slowed his recovery significantly. He remained in a coma for 2 months, and was confused and disoriented for several weeks after that. On regaining consciousness he exhibited a dense left-sided hemiplegia and slow, dysarthric speech. These symptoms have persisted to the present time. Michael was involved in intensive rehabilitation in the first 12 months post-injury, and continued to have regular input from physical therapists for many years. He also required ongoing educational and psychological interventions.

Michael's previous history was largely unremarkable. He had experienced no medical or behavioural problems and development was reported to be

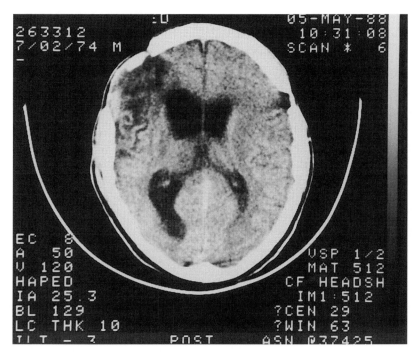

Figure 5.9.   CT scan showing effects of severe closed head injury sustained by 13-year-old boy hit by a train. The injury involves right skull fracture and contusion, and left frontal contusion and haematoma.

normal. Michael was described as an average student with special skills in art and design. Michael is the youngest child in an intact family unit, and was said to be an affectionate and happy child, with many friends and leisure interests.

Michael has been seen for neuropsychological evaluation on numerous occasions following his injury, and thus his recovery profile may be plotted in some detail. Initial evaluation occurred on emergence from post-traumatic amnesia, approximately 4 months post-injury. He was reviewed at 12 months, 18 months, 2 years, and 3 years post-injury, with intermittent contact since then. Initially he presented as lacking in responsiveness with slow and slurred speech, extreme psychomotor slowness, and poor concentration. Michael's neuropsychological profile in the acute recovery phase was not dissimilar to that presented by Adam. He showed marked difficulties on tasks tapping visuomotor, visuospatial, and constructional abilities, as evidenced by his production of the Rey Complex Figure and his intellectual profile (Figures 5.10 and 5.11). Michael also exhibited severe attention difficulties, reduced memory function, and poor planning and reasoning skills. This pattern of

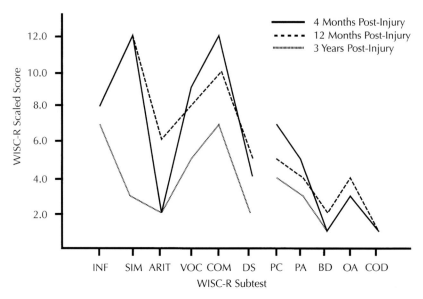

Figure 5.10. Michael's IQ profiles at 4 months, 1 year, and 3 years post-injury, showing evidence of persisting deficit, for both verbal and non-verbal skills.

specific deficits in the context of more generalised cognitive dysfunction is common following severe closed head injury, reflecting a picture of multiple focal lesions and diffuse axonal injury.

Whereas Adam exhibited significant recovery and compensation over time since injury, Michael's deficits persisted. As Michael's intellectual profile suggests, by 3 years post-injury he was performing more poorly than in the acute recovery stages post-TBI, indicating little or no recovery, and reduced development. Qualitatively, he continued to respond very slowly, and exhibited poor memory and executive function. These problems are illustrated by his attempt to complete the Rey Complex Figure at 12 months post-injury. When confronted with the design, Michael noted that he had been trained to draw the figure at his frequent therapy sessions. He then proceeded to produce a well-organised copy, although time to completion was 25 minutes, much slower than expected. To determine whether these training skills had generalised to other planning tasks Michael was asked to copy the Taylor Figure, an alternative version of the Rey Complex Figure. His attempt is shown in Figure 5.11, and is of similar quality to his earlier productions, suggesting minimal generalisation across these similar tasks.

Michael's long-term outcome is typical of children who sustain very severe closed head injury. He initially returned to school with the support of an integration aide, and a modified curriculum. He experienced problems with mobility and socialisation, as well as with academic requirements. He

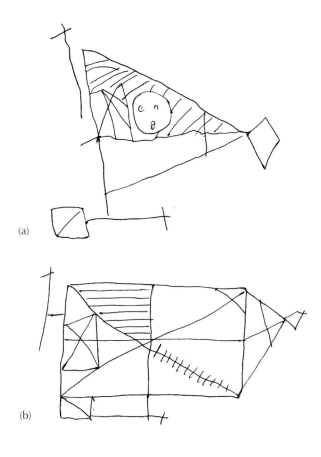

(a)

(b)

Taylor Figure   Michael's copy

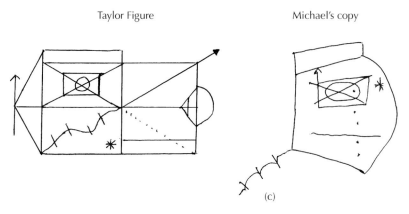

(c)

Figure 5.11. Michael's Complex Figure of Rey production at (a) 4 months, (b) 12 months (with intervening occupational therapy training with the figure), and (c) 12 months, using alternative Taylor Figure. These productions show limited resolution of visuospatial and visuomotor deficits, and poor generalisation of training.

eventually transferred to a special school for intellectually disabled children. This placement was more successful, and Michael coped better both academically and socially in this sheltered context. Despite numerous attempts at supported employment since leaving school, Michael remains unemployed, and lives with his family, assisted by a full-time attendant carer. He is very isolated socially, rarely going out of the house and having no friends. He has recently experienced an episode of depression requiring medication. Michael's pattern of persisting impairment and increasing psychosocial dysfunction is characteristic following severe closed head injury during childhood, where there is a failure to meet expected developmental gains, and an increasing social isolation.

Age at insult, mechanics of injury, and resultant pathophysiology

A range of age-specific injury mechanisms may be acting at different stages of development, depending upon the maturity of the CNS at the time of injury. First, as noted in Table 4.1, the aetiology of TBI changes during childhood, with infants and toddlers more likely to be injured due to falls and older children more commonly involved in accidents associated with recreational activities or motor car accidents (Kraus, 1995), thus leading to varying injury processes. In addition, the skull and brain develop throughout childhood, resulting in different injury consequences at different stages. For example, the infant has relatively weak neck muscles that do not adequately support a proportionately large head, leading to less resistance to force of impact. Further, the infant and toddler possess a relatively thin skull, easily deformed by a direct blow, and resulting in more frequent skull fractures. Studies show that more than one-third of children in this age bracket who sustain TBI will have skull fractures. In contrast, contusions, lacerations, and subdural haematomas are extremely rare in infancy (Berney et al., 1994a; Choux, 1986; Sharma & Sharma, 1994). This may be due to the flexibility and open sutures present in the infant skull. For older children and adolescents, intracranial mass lesions (haematomas, contusions) are more common, although not as common as in adult samples (Berger et al., 1985; Bruce et al., 1978). Contrecoup lesions are relatively rare in all age groups, but least for young children, with a gradual increase through childhood (Berney, Froidevaux, & Favier, 1994b).

The relative lack of myelination present in the CNS during infancy and early childhood also leads to different consequences in response to TBI. Immature myelination causes the cerebral hemispheres to be relatively soft and pliable, enabling them to absorb the force of impact better than in an older child or adult. However, unmyelinated fibres are particularly vulnerable to shearing effects, rendering the younger child more vulnerable to diffuse axonal injury (Zimmerman & Bilaniuk, 1994). Bruce et al. (1978) report that TBI in children is more likely to result in diffuse cerebral swelling associated with vascular disruptions, and this finding is supported by those of Jennett et al. (1977), who identified such pathology in one-third of the children in their sample. Outcomes are also different. Babies and toddlers lose consciousness less frequently than other age groups; however, post-traumatic epilepsy is more common following early TBI (Berney et al., 1994b; Raimondi & Hirschauer, 1984). The implications of these age-related differences are important, and argue that pathophysiology, sequelae, recovery, and outcome from childhood TBI cannot easily be extrapolated from adult findings.

DIAGNOSIS AND RECOVERY

Evaluation and treatment of the traumatised patient begins at the scene of the injury, where conscious state and neurological status are evaluated. On admission a range of data are collected to determine the nature and severity of the injury and the extent of primary and secondary pathology. By the time the TBI patient reaches hospital they will have sustained permanent primary impact-related brain injury, which is thought to be relatively insensitive to medical treatment. Secondary effects of insult will also be developing, and these have been shown to be more amenable to medical intervention. Early treatment is very much directed towards the accurate identification of these secondary complications and their rapid treatment (Miller, 1991). A number of parameters are particularly informative for determining injury severity at this early stage: level of consciousness, clinical evidence of skull fracture or cerebral pathology, and neurological and mental status.

Measuring injury severity

Most emergency departments routinely evaluate severity using a number of specific measures. The Glasgow Coma Scale (Teasdale & Jennett, 1974) measures degree of impairment of consciousness, and post-traumatic amnesia scales provide information on the child's alertness and level of confusion once they regain consciousness. In addition to assessing consciousness, cerebral pathology is investigated, usually via CT scan initially, and then magnetic resonance imaging (MRI) where further complications are suspected. These techniques provide the neurosurgical team with information regarding the need for surgical intervention, for example where a bleed is present causing mass effect, and brain shift, or where raised intracranial pressure is evident, requiring drainage. Neurological examination is also performed to identify any neurological anomalies that may help in localising cerebral damage.

TABLE 5.3
Injury severity and duration of post-traumatic amnesia

Duration	Injury severity
Less than 5 minutes	Very mild
5 minutes to 1 hour	Mild
1 to 24 hours	Moderate
1 to 7 days	Severe
More than 1 week	Very severe
More than 4 weeks	Extremely severe

Reproduced with permission from Jennett (1976).

TABLE 5.4
The Children's Orientation and Amnesia Test (COAT)

General orientation
1. What is your name (first, last)?
2. How old are you? When is your birthday (month, year)?
3. Where do you live (city, state)?
4. What is your father's name? What is your mother's name?
5. What school do you go to? What grade are you in?
6. Where are you now?
7. Is it daytime or night-time?

Temporal orientation
8. What time is it now?
9. What day of the week is it?
10. What day of the month is it?
11. What is the month?
12. What is the year?

Memory
13. Say these numbers after me in the same order?
    (strings of numbers of increasing length are presented to the child for recall)
14. How many fingers am I holding up?
15. Who is on *Sesame Street* (or substitute other TV show)?
16. What is my name?

Adapted from Ewing-Cobbs et al. (1990).

the patient reaches a criterion level of functioning. When defined using such standardised protocols it has been argued that duration of post-traumatic amnesia is a more reliable indicator of functional outcome than other severity measures (Ewing-Cobbs et al., 1990; Shores, 1989).

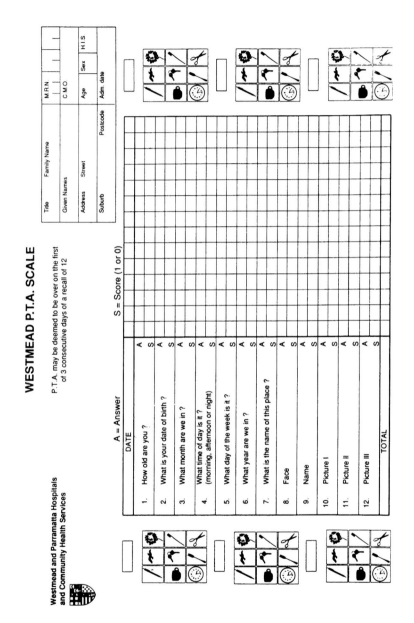

Figure 5.12. Westmead Post-Traumatic Amnesia Scale. Reproduced with permission from Shores (1989).

149

A particularly crucial transition for the child with a TBI is the transition from home to school. The preschool child, spending the majority of time within the family unit, tends to be sheltered from the demands of the world. School entry may emphasise the child's limitations; for example, motor incoordination may be apparent in poor sporting ability or writing and drawing difficulties. Communication and attentional difficulties may limit the child's capacity to participate fully in many academic and social activities. Children experiencing these problems may require support additional to that provided within regular school resources. In such situations parents may need to play a major role in accessing, financing and securing such resources, as well as in informing teachers of their child's needs and supporting their child's adjustment within the school environment and the wider community. Perhaps the most stressful transition of all is into adolescence, where peer pressure and issues of identity are paramount. Adolescents may refuse to accept extra therapy or intervention that identifies them as different. They may become depressed as they begin to fully appreciate the impact that their deficits will have on their future.

Paralleling these child-based issues, family variables may also be acting. Although there is little systematic research on long-term family functioning when a child has sustained a serious TBI, adult literature suggests increasing family burden and stress with time. Family members, particularly mothers, report increase in depression, anger, and feeling trapped (Mauss-Clum & Ryan, 1981). These stresses are primarily related to behavioural and emotional problems in the child, rather than to physical disabilities.

This pattern of recovery, with its developmental implications, argues that children sustaining moderate and severe TBI require ongoing professional support into adulthood, particularly as the children and their families gradually adjust to residual physical, cognitive, and behavioural sequelae, and then at critical developmental transitions.

NEUROPSYCHOLOGICAL FINDINGS

Early research into childhood TBI was largely directed at determining whether there were any long-term sequelae from such injuries. The prevailing view was that, as children's brains were more plastic and better able to accommodate the effects of the brain insult, they would experience fewer deficits than adults. Despite some inconsistent results in this initial research, it was quickly apparent that TBI in childhood did have measurable consequences in terms of functional impairment. Studies then moved on to investigate the importance of injury severity as a predictor of outcome. This endeavour was thwarted by the previously noted problems of measuring injury severity in children, particularly young children, with traditional adult measures of Glasgow Coma Score and post-traumatic amnesia inappropriate for use with children. The development of child-specific measures has facilitated the ability to investigate severity accurately. Results from such research have been less than ideal, showing that, although severity may account for a proportion of the variance in post-injury performance, there is still much left unexplained. Such findings have led researchers to examine a wide variety of additional factors that may be important in influencing recovery and outcome. Some have argued that many of the deficits observed reflect premorbid behavioural or learning deficits, or other psychosocial factors such as family dysfunction or low socioeconomic status. Others have investigated age at injury and time since injury, predicting that developmental processes may be largely responsible for variations in outcome. Historically, these variables have been studied separately, and it is only recently that researchers have attempted large-scale studies that incorporate measures of pre-injury child and family characteristics, age at injury, and recovery over time in a multidimensional model, in an attempt to begin to tease out the complex interactions and the relative contributions of these various factors to outcome.

The following discussion aims to review the key findings from the major studies conducted in the field of paediatric TBI, with an emphasis on research that has made a major contribution to current understanding of the consequences of TBI in children.

Early studies

Klonoff studies

The studies of Klonoff and his associates represent the first systematic attempts to evaluate the effects of TBI in children. This programme of research commenced in the 1960s with the collation of a prospective sample of 231 children, representing consecutive hospital admissions with a diagnosis of closed head injury over a 15-month period. Mean age of the sample at injury was 8.3 years. Researchers were interested in examining (1) antecedent factor—age, sex, premorbid functioning; (2) injury factors—severity, nature of insult; and (3) outcome—education, social skills, neurological and neuropsychological outcome. Each head-injured child was matched for sex and age with a healthy control subject. Klonoff and colleagues have reported on outcomes at discharge, 1 year ($n = 196$), 2 years ($n = 163$), 5 years post-injury ($n = 117$), and more recently a description of the sample in adulthood ($n = 159$) has been published (Klonoff, 1971; Klonoff, Clark, & Klonoff, 1995; Klonoff et al., 1977; Klonoff & Paris, 1974).

At 1 year post-injury 40% of children were suffering some form of residual sequelae, including neurological abnormalities, neuropsychological deficits, or subjective complaints, with this figure decreasing to 39% at 2 years group performed similarly to orthopaedic controls on measures of verbal and visual learning and memory.

Taken together, these findings suggest that, despite some initial recovery, persisting memory and learning problems may be expected following severe TBI, with outcome more variable in less serious injuries. The broader impact of such memory deficits has been described in a number of recent longitudinal studies. For example, Kinsella et al. (1997) note that verbal learning skills are predictive of educational progress at 2 years post-injury, demonstrating that children with learning deficits post-TBI are more likely to be in a special school environment or in need of individual remedial intervention. Yeates et al. (1997) also comment on the importance of verbal learning skills in the context of family burden and perceived family stressors.

Attention skills

Deficits in attention and information-processing skills may also impede learning and accumulation of new knowledge, possibly resulting in the global cognitive dysfunction commonly reported in the long term following childhood TBI (Anderson & Moore, 1995; Dennis et al., 1995; Fletcher et al., 1987). Within the adult literature research findings suggest quite specific attentional problems, with sustained and focused attentional skills largely intact, and psychomotor slowness underpinning many observed "attention" deficits (Ponsford & Kinsella 1992; Shum, McFarland, Bain, & Humphreys, 1990; Stuss et al., 1989). Although clinical reports of attention deficits in children with TBI are similar to those described for adults, only a handful of studies have formally investigated these skills, with the majority assessing children within the first year post-injury (Chadwick et al., 1981b; Gulbrandsen, 1984; Levin & Eisenberg, 1979; Timmermans & Christensen, 1991).

Kaufmann et al. (1993) describe attentional problems in their study, demonstrating that younger, severely injured children exhibited greatest difficulties. Although these findings support the presence of attentional impairment following TBI in children, their significance with respect to specific components of attention remains unclear. Murray, Shum, and McFarland (1992), using a task that enabled identification of specific stages of information processing, found that TBI children exhibited difficulty with rate of motor execution and with response selection, with other aspects of processing intact, suggesting a wider range of deficits than has been identified following adult TBI (Ponsford & Kinsella, 1992; Shum et al., 1990; Stuss et al., 1989).

Anderson and Pentland (1998) also examined residual attentional abilities in adolescents with moderate to severe TBI. Results showed no evidence for deficits in sustained attention or focused attention. In contrast, severe deficits were identified on measures incorporating a speeded component, and on tasks requiring complex processing or higher-order attentional skills. Performances were noted to be highly variable within the TBI group, suggesting fluctuating attention, which may be difficult to detect on traditional attention measures. To address the relationship of these problems to injury severity, a subsequent study from our group (Willmott et al., in press) examined attentional performance in a mild TBI group using similar measures. No deficits were detected on any formal test measures in this group, despite parent and teacher reports of some mild behaviourally based attentional problems. This lack of evidence of deficit following mild TBI is supported by Ponsford et al. (1997), who report that children sustaining mild TBI perform similarly to controls, even in the weeks post-injury. Similar severity-related attentional impairments have also been described in a number of recent studies (Anderson, Fenwick, Manly, & Robertson, 1998; Dennis et al., 1995; Ewing-Cobbs et al., 1998; Fenwick & Anderson, 1999). These authors report both age at injury and severity-based deficits in sustained and focused attention, as well as in divided attention and shifting attention.

Few studies have evaluated the recovery of attention skills post-TBI. Two studies in our laboratory have attempted to address this issue. Bakker et al. (2000) compared recovery of attention in preschool children with mild and moderate/severe TBI, using videotapes from a test session and a free play session. They analysed behaviour using indicators of focused attention, arousal, hyperactivity, and impulsivity. Results showed that children sustaining severe TBI were more inattentive, both at acute and 6-month assessments. Although some recovery was apparent at 6 months, severely injured children continued to exhibit significant attentional problems. Catroppa (Catroppa & Anderson, 1999; Catroppa, Anderson, & Stargatt, 1999) evaluated attention in a school-aged sample, acutely and at 6 months post-injury, excluding children with evidence of pre-existing attentional deficits. All children showed improved attention from acute to 6-month follow-up, regardless of injury severity, suggesting some initial impairment of attentional skills even for mild TBI. Children with severe TBI exhibited global deficits initially, most marked on tasks of psychomotor speed. This group showed recovery on simple attention tasks, with ongoing deficits evident on more complex attentional measures, and where a speeded component was required.

Summarising these various studies, it appears that, in contrast to the specific psychomotor slowing seen following moderate to severe adult TBI, children present with more global attention deficits, with many of these problems persisting beyond the acute recovery stage. These more generalised problems may reflect the relatively immature state of attention development at the time of injury. The injury, and its associated pathology, may interrupt ongoing development, so that components of attention that usually emerge and differentiate post-injury will fail to do so, leading to delayed or deficient performance. Thus, the implications of attention deficits following childhood TBI may be twofold: In addition to the initial injury and associated cognitive impairment, there may be an ongoing impact on cerebral development as well as an inability to acquire new skills. This may lead to increasing lags in knowledge and skills, and a failure in the development and differentiation of cognitive and attentional abilities.

Executive functions

Deficits in executive functions are commonly reported in children who have suffered TBI, in keeping with the vulnerability of the prefrontal regions in head trauma (Courville, 1945; Walsh, 1978). Despite these observations, there have been few formal studies of executive abilities, although some case descriptions do exist (Dennis et al., 1996; Mateer & Williams, 1991; Passler et al., 1985, Williams & Mateer, 1992). Neuropsychological studies by Levin et al. (1994, 1997) have examined performance on a range of traditional executive function tests including the Tower of London, Wisconsin Card Sorting Test, and Twenty Questions Test showing that performance on these measures is related to injury severity. These authors note a trend for younger age at injury to be related to poorer performance on tests of executive function. Garth et al. (1997) described a similar pattern of deficient executive functioning following moderate to severe TBI, with children exhibiting poor planning and problem solving, reduced capacity for abstract thought, and slowed speed of response. Again, younger age at injury was associated with poorer executive function, and in particular slower speed of response.

For milder injuries findings are less clear. A recent study by Todd et al. (1996) investigated planning skills in a group of adolescents following mild TBI in comparison to controls. Adolescents were required to provide a plan for hosting a party, including details such as when to send out invitations or pick up food, as well as delegating tasks to family members, and fitting these tasks within a specified time frame. The test measured the adolescents' ability to plan as well as hold a number of dimensions in mind simultaneously. Results showed no significant group differences on this task, although there was a trend for planning ability to decrease with increasing injury severity, indicating that planning deficits may be observed in a more severe sample. Pentland et al. (1998) extended this study, employing the same test protocol with a group of adolescents who had sustained severe TBI, As might be expected they found that severely injured adolescents made more errors and used less efficient strategies, and provided ineffective or unworkable planning strategies as a result.

Functional outcome following TBI in childhood

Children who suffer TBI frequently make a good physical recovery, and appear outwardly normal. The expectations of their abilities and behaviours are frequently determined by this relatively healthy presentation, despite ongoing significant cognitive and behavioural difficulties (Johnson, 1992). In instances of mild TBI, children may perform adequately on neuropsychological testing, but continue to experience problems when faced with the complexities of everyday life, in particular learning and skill acquisition and psychosocial functioning (Asarnow et al., 1991, 1995; Willmott et al., 2000)

Educational and behavioural development and adaptive functions are dependent upon the intact capacities of learning, attention, and executive function. As previously discussed, many of these skills are impaired as a result of TBI, even while intellectual functioning, as measured by traditional psychometric tests, may appear intact.

Educational abilities

Even the early studies of childhood TBI were interested in educational outcome. Klonoff et al. (1977) originally documented a relationship between injury severity and educational achievement. In their study 26% of children 9 years or younger at injury had been placed in remedial classes by 5 years post-injury. Authors since then have argued that academic failure may be one of the most serious consequences of paediatric TBI (Catroppa & Anderson, 2000; Goldstein & Levin, 1985; Greenspan & MacKenzie, 1994; Levin, Grafman, & Eisenberg, 1987). However, it is sometimes difficult to access the degree of educational deficit, with limited tests available to tap the subtleties of these skills and teachers frequently hesitant to document the negative functioning of their students (Kinsella et al., 1997). Further, researchers have argued that the incidence of academic problems may be higher in this group premorbidly, raising issues of overestimation of the effects of TBI on educational outcome.

Studies generally measure educational performance via standardised tests, but it may be that information on school placement provides a better indicator. Recently a number of authors have employed this parameter to investigate severity of educational deficit. Kinsella et al. (1995, 1997) have followed a group of TBI children screened for premorbid educational difficulties over 2 years post-injury. They found that at 1 year post-TBI children with moderate to severe TBI were more likely to experience school difficulties requiring special assistance. At 2 years post-injury all children had returned to school, with 7 out of 10 children with severe injuries receiving special education, in contrast to 2 of 5 in the moderate group and none of mild TBI. Need for specialist education was directly related to injury severity and neuropsychological performance, with verbal learning being a particularly strong indicator of educational outcome. Stalings, Ewing-Cobbs, Francis, and Fletcher (1996) also note greater educational difficulties in the first 2 years post-TBI for children with more severe injuries. These authors identify low socioeconomic status, male gender, maladaptive behaviours, and reduced psychomotor processing as predictors of poorer academic achievement post-injury. These findings are similar to those of Donders (1994), who found that 48% of children with TBI required formal special education intervention during the first year after their return to school.

Qualitative analysis of data from these studies suggests that reading skills appear to be relatively resilient following TBI in school-aged children, with arithmetic and comprehension more vulnerable (Catroppa & Anderson, 2000; Barnes, Dennis, & Wilkinson, 1999; Berger-Gross & Shackelford, 1985; Kinsella et al., 1997).

A further variable of relevance to educational outcome is age at injury. Children who have acquired basic literacy skills prior to injury appear to maintain these skills relatively well. In contrast, preschool TBI, even of mild degree, has been noted to be associated with school failure. Gronwall and colleagues (Gronwall et al., 1997; Wrightson et al., 1995) have followed a group of children sustaining mild TBI prior to school entry. They report that, despite appearing to be fully recovered immediately post-injury, these children were more likely to have reading difficulties and require special education input. Barnes et al. (1999) have also addressed the issue of age at injury in association with educational impairment. They compared reading abilities in children sustaining TBI before age 6.5 years, from 6.5 to 9 years, and older than 9 years and found a different pattern of deficit, depending on age at injury. For reading decoding skills children in the youngest age at injury group achieved poorest results, with the other two groups performing similarly. Reading comprehension was reduced for children sustaining injuries before age 9 but intact for the older group. These findings suggest that the age at injury may interact with the level and complexity of skills previously acquired to determine the outcome.

Behaviour and adaptive abilities

Over the years there has been considerable debate regarding the aetiology of behavioural and adaptive problems following TBI. As previously noted, some authors argue that these problems reflect premorbid behavioural and family problems, whereas others support an important impact of brain injury (Donders, 1992; Farmer et al., 1996; Max, Castillo, et al., 1997; Max, Smith, et al. 1997; Prior et al., 1994; Wade et al., 1996). These inconsistent interpretations may be due to the methodological problems inherent in measuring behaviour. The absence of objective pre-injury measures, the use of subjective tools such as parent report, the lack of appropriate or sensitive objective measures, all hinder our understanding in this area.

Clinical reports frequently document behavioural changes post-TBI. These range from initial problems of irritability and fatigue, to more persistent difficulties such as hyperactivity, aggression, poor impulse control, distractibility, lack of motivation, depression, anxiety, and sleep disturbance (Black et al., 1969). Frequently reduced self-esteem and social difficulties accompany these problems. These features are most likely explained by a variety of factors including the direct effects of injury, secondary adjustment problems, premorbid behavioural functioning, and family supports. For many children, behavioural problems represent the most disabling aspect of their injury, and may increase rather than diminish with time, as has been shown in studies that have followed children sustaining TBI into adulthood (Cattelani, Lombardi, Brianti, & Mazzuchi, 1998; Klonoff et al., 1995).

Evidence supporting impairments in behaviour and adaptive function has been provided from several studies. Adaptive functioning may be defined as the successful negotiation of day-to-day functional activities and requires considerable integration of information, flexibility of thought, and organisational capacity. Research by Fletcher et al. (1990) found that children who had sustained severe TBI displayed poor adaptive living skills and ineffective problem-solving behaviour even in cases where there were few or no noted problems on intellectual, academic, and neuropsychological tests. Papero, Prigatano, Snyder, and Johnson (1993) report that these problems appear to be more severe in boys following TBI, regardless of injury severity.

Behavioural and psychiatric problems following TBI have been reported by a number of authors (Asarnow et al., 1991; Bohnert, Parker, & Warschausky, 1997; Brink, Imbus, & Woo-Sam, 1980; Brown et al., 1981; Butler, Rourke, Fuerst, & Fisk, 1997; Klonoff et al., 1995; Max, Smith, et al., 1997), with the pattern of impairment paralleling that described in cognitive domains. Children sustaining mild TBI are least likely to exhibit post-injury behavioural difficulties, whereas those with severe injuries show a marked increase in psychiatric disturbance, both acutely and in long term post-injury. Brink et al. (1980) report that although only 10% of their sample of severely head-injured children had any persisting neurological impairment, 46% had severe emotional/behavioural disturbances requiring professional counselling. Brown et al. (1981) noted that the rate of new psychiatric disorder was more than doubled in the severely injured group in comparison to controls. Within this severely injured group, history of pre-injury behavioural deficits was predictive of later psychiatric disturbance, with over half of these children developing a disturbance in the 12 months post-injury, in contrast to a figure of 29% for children with no premorbid problems.

More recently, Perrott et al. (1991) compared children with TBI and sibling controls on neuropsychological, academic, and behavioural measures, and in addition collected data from parents looking at the child's adaptive behaviours, family stress, and family functioning. Despite the fact that a number of the children in the study had sustained severe TBI, there were surprisingly few differences between the groups on neuropsychological measures, with differences evident only on psychomotor speed and abstract reasoning tasks. In contrast, both parents and teachers rated TBI children as having more behavioural difficulties, less social competence, and poorer academic performance than controls. Further, parents noted that for the child with TBI the parent–child relationship was more stressful than that with the healthy sibling.

A number of studies report increasing problems in behaviour, and increased incidence of psychiatric disturbance post-TBI (Brink et al., 1980; Brown et al., 1981; Cattelani et al., 1998; Perrott et al., 1991). This pattern may be due to the direct effects of TBI—e.g., increased impulsivity, hyperactivity associated with right frontal damage—or may be related to depression or other adjustment factors, coming to terms with disabilities and long-term implications of injury. Bohnert et al. (1997) comment on the negative consequences of these behavioural problems in the context of social interactions and peer relationships. They report that children sustaining TBI are less socially competent and have difficulty developing intimacy in their friendships, with these problems more debilitating for children with a history of severe injury.

In summary, children sustaining severe TBI are at significant risk of developing serious psychiatric, behavioural, and social disturbances. This risk is increased where such problems were present premorbidly. The pattern of recovery in this area indicates ongoing or even increasing difficulties over time, with an interaction among premorbid functioning, injury factors, and secondary adjustment issues.

INJURY-RELATED PREDICTORS OF OUTCOME

Since the initial work of Klonoff and Rutter, there has been less emphasis on documenting recovery patterns following childhood TBI. The prevailing view has been that, despite documented cognitive and functional impairments acutely, children recover better, probably back to pre-injury levels. However, the data presented in the previous discussion of neuropsychological and functional sequelae of childhood TBI clearly shows that this is not the case, particularly following serious injury. In this section we provide a description of the current knowledge of recovery processes following childhood TBI and predictors of long-term recovery.

Recovery following TBI is variable and difficult to predict. For example, as shown in the schematic depicted in Figure 5.18, neurological recovery probably stabilises earliest, with the majority of transient neurological symptoms

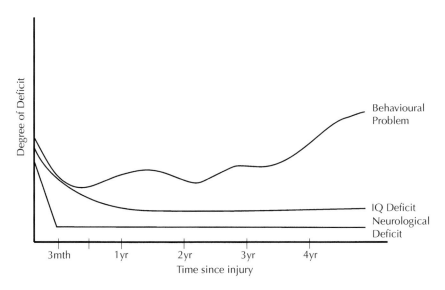

Figure 5.18. Schematic representation of differential recovery of neurological, behavioural, and intellectual functions following traumatic brain injury in children.

abating by about 3 months post-injury. In more severe injuries, neurological symptoms persist, and may indicate permanent impairment. Behavioural recovery is not so clear cut. It appears that there is an initial reduction in symptoms, perhaps indicating a decrease in the global effects of cerebral injury, and reductions in fatigue and irritability. Over time, most researchers describe an increase in psychological problems and psychiatric disturbance. It is likely that, rather than resulting from physiological factors, these emerging symptoms reflect the secondary adjustment problems that the child may experience in response to physiological and cognitive disability.

Intellectual "recovery" has also been documented by a number of authors (Chadwick et al., 1981a; Jaffe et al., 1995; Prior et al., 1994), however, there are a range of factors that may impact on recovery of cognitive function. For example, younger age at injury has been noted to be associated with poorer recovery initially, and a failure to maintain developmental progress in the years post-injury (Anderson, 1988; Anderson & Moore, 1995; Anderson, Catroppa, et al., 2000; Ewing-Cobbs et al., 1997; Gronwall et al., 1997). Additionally, reduced access to services, special education, and significant psychiatric problems may all impact on future recovery. Nature and degree of injury are also paramount. Recovery has been shown to be more complete in mild injuries (Ponsford et al., 1997), and more compensation for disabilities may be possible in focal injuries, where much brain remains intact. Also, psychosocial factors such as tendency for marriage breakup and the consequent family difficulties must also be considered. Recovery is a complex and individualised process, with current knowledge providing only a rough indicator of likely outcome for these children. Long-term follow-up of paediatric TBI patients is essential to gain a better understanding of the significant factors and their pattern of interaction and association.

It may be that different variables are predictive of impairment at different times post-TBI. For example, it appears that injury severity is a crucial predictor of function in the acute stages of recovery, but may become less important as other factors also come into play. Yeates et al. (1997) suggest that premorbid factors may influence outcome, and additionally Rivara et al. (1994) report that better outcome is associated with better family functioning. Other factors such as the degree of family burden—e.g., financial, time stress, degree of child disability—may also play a role in determining the functional outcome of the child in the long term post-TBI. Although numerous longitudinal studies are underway (Anderson et al., 1997; Ewing-Cobbs et al., 1997; Jaffe et al., 1995; Kinsella et al, 1997; Taylor et al., 1995) that build on the knowledge of functional impairment already gained from two decades of active research, there remains little information regarding outcome at greater than 2 years post-injury. It may be that the ensuing years may provide additional insights and identify other parameters that help predict degree of recovery more accurately.

Injury severity

Injury severity is well established as an important predictor of outcome from TBI, with clear impairments in a range of neuropsychological and functional areas identified for children sustaining severe TBI. These findings will not be reiterated; however, it is important to acknowledge that much of this previous research has been cross-sectional in design. Thus, it has not been possible to plot the nature and degree of recovery of these skills. A recent prospective, longitudinal study by Jaffe et al. (1995) has addressed some of these gaps in knowledge, investigating the relationship between injury severity, recovery, and outcome by following a cohort of children sustaining TBI, following children for up to 3 years post-injury.

Jaffe et al. (1995) describe recovery patterns from the acute phase to 3 years post-TBI. They have examined a wide variety of cognitive domains including IQ, academic performance, memory, problem solving, motor performance, and daily living skills. As with previous research they note that severity exerts a significant influence on recovery patterns in the period post-injury. Both severe and moderate groups showed significant deficits across the range of domains assessed, whereas children with mild injuries exhibited age-appropriate performance. Figure 5.19 summarises the findings of this study, showing that at initial evaluation there was a consistent dose–response

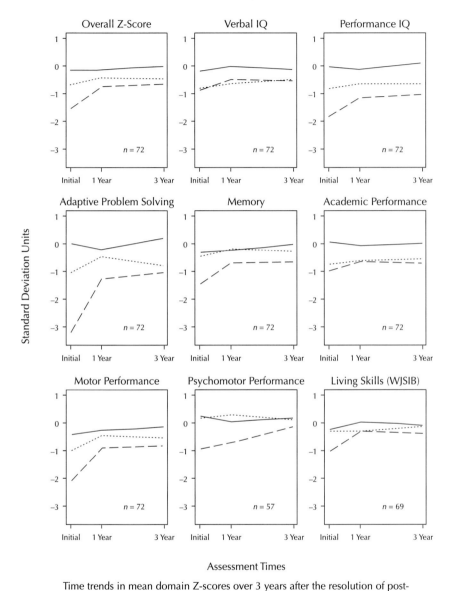

Figure 5.19. Cognitive recovery trajectories in the 3 years post-injury. Reproduced with permission from Jaffe et al. (1995).

relationship, with severely injured children exhibiting most impaired performance in all areas, and the moderate TBI group exhibiting less severe deficits. Significant recovery was observed in these groups in the 12 months post-injury, but performance then plateaued, remaining stable over the following 2 years. For the mild TBI group, the recovery curve was consistently flat across domains, with performance levels age appropriate, suggesting minimal initial impact of injury on cognitive skills.

Jaffa's findings (Jaffe et al., 1995) for the initial period post-TBI are consistent with those described by other researchers. It appears that, although degree of residual deficit may be at least similar for children and adults, the observation of a relatively short "recovery" period in children, as opposed to the more extensive 2 year recovery phase commonly quoted for adult TBI, merits some consideration. This brief recovery phase may suggest differing pathophysiological processes, perhaps a quicker neuronal recovery reflecting a younger CNS. Alternatively, it may be that this plateauing of test scores represents the additive effects of underlying physiological recovery, plus the negative impact of cognitive sequelae on ongoing development. Thus although at a superficial level the recovery process for adults and children may appear similar, such an interpretation does not account for the ongoing development expected in children. More extended longitudinal research is needed to tease out the affects of recovery and development following childhood TBI.

The nature of injury is also relevant to recovery and long-term outcome. Researchers have documented a range of injury characteristics that are related to poorer prognosis in children, including depth of lesion (Ommaya & Gennarelli, 1974), presence of secondary damage due to intracranial haematomas (Berger et al., 1985; Walker, Mayer, Storrs, & Hylton, 1985), diffuse axonal injury (Filley, Cranberg, Alexander, & Hart, 1987), oedema, hypoxia, haemorrhage, and herniation (Gentry, Godersky, & Thompson, 1988). Severity of total injuries has also been identified as a predictive factor (Michaud et al., 1992).

Age at injury

The persisting effects of brain damage in infancy and early childhood have been reported recently, with some evidence that young children sustaining generalised brain insult are at great risk for long-term cognitive deficits (Anderson, Bond, et al., 1997; Anderson, Smibert, Ekert, & Godber, 1994; Anderson & Taylor, in press; Cousens et al., 1991; Ewing-Cobbs et al., 1989; Gronwall et al., 1997; Taylor & Alden, 1997), perhaps due to the vulnerability of the immature brain. Interestingly, the areas of function commonly documented as deficient following TBI, such as information processing, memory, and executive function, implicate involvement of neural substrates particularly vulnerable to the impact of TBI. Further, these regions are in a rapid state of development in early childhood. Deficiencies in these skills are particularly significant for children as they reduce the ability to interact with and learn from the surrounding environment, potentially affecting not only cognitive ability but also social and emotional development (Anderson, 1988).

A handful of studies have addressed the relationship between age at injury and neuropsychological performance, including very young children in their samples. The majority of these studies have detected no relationship between age at injury and neurobehavioural outcome (Chadwick et al., 1981a; Klonoff et al., 1977; Tompkins et al., 1990). However, a small number of studies have identified differences between children sustaining TBI during the preschool years and those injured in later childhood (Ewing-Cobbs et al., 1989; Kriel et al., 1989; Lange-Cosack et al., 1979). Each of these studies has reported that children sustaining early injuries have poorer outcomes in terms of both cognitive and motor abilities. A study conducted in our laboratory (Anderson & Moore, 1995), evaluating children with moderate and severe TBI at 4 and 24 months post-injury, found that whereas children injured after age 7 years showed recovery profiles similar to those seen in adults, children injured prior to age 7 showed minimal recovery. In contrast to the generally reported trends for IQ, younger age at injury was related to deterioration in verbal IQ scores over time, perhaps indicating a failure to acquire verbal knowledge from the environment. For performance IQ, a small increase in scores was evident for both age groups, but this was greater for children injured after age 7, suggesting "recovery" of performance skills is not so evident for younger injuries. These results are illustrated in Figure 5.20, which depicts these declines in cognitive ability in terms of the chronological age–mental age discrepancy.

Other researchers have also shown a shorter recovery period for children injured in the preschool years (Ewing-Cobbs et al., 1997), with recovery curves plateauing as early as 6 months post-injury, rather than within the second year post-injury, as has been documented for adults.

Premorbid and psychosocial factors

It is not surprising that pre-injury levels of functioning predict outcome from brain insult. Based on clinical data, Rourke et al. (1983) have argued that a child who possesses a range of neuropsychological strengths will show a better outcome post-insult than where pre-existing difficulties or low skill levels are present. Their position is supported by a number of recent longitudinal studies that identify pre-morbid levels of functioning as strong predictors of outcome (Anderson, Morse, et al., 1997; Yeates et al., 1997). This relationship may be more robust for behavioural and psychiatric outcome.

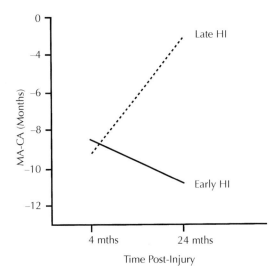

Figure 5.20. Comparison of recovery trajectories for children injured before and after 7 years, represented by mental age – chronological age (MA – CA) at 4 months and 24 months post-injury. These findings suggest that earlier age at injury is related to poorer recovery post-injury.

The early work by Rutter and associates (Brown et al., 1981; Rutter et al., 1983) was the first to describe this relationship, arguing that children sustaining TBI were at greater risk for developing psychiatric and cognitive sequelae if they had demonstrated such problems premorbidly. They noted that over half of the children with some evidence of pre-injury behavioural or psychiatric disorder developed a clinically significant disorder by 12 months post-injury, and none were without symptoms. For those children with no pre-existing problems, more than half were symptom free 12 months post-injury. It appears that where pre-injury problems are present, TBI may exacerbate them.

One of the problems with these early studies was the crude measurement of pre-injury functioning. Although authors agree that accurate measurement of premorbid levels of functioning is problematic, clearly such variables are relevant to long-term outcome. Many studies employ gross measures of premorbid functioning (e.g., presence of developmental disorder, intellectual deficit, learning disability) as exclusion criteria. Others attempt to quantify premorbid functioning by obtaining pre-injury indicators from families. This latter approach may be influenced by the "halo" effect, where the injured child is idealised by the parents and teachers. It is generally considered that such pre-injury measures should be obtained as early as possible, preferably while the injured child remains in coma, so that current levels of functioning do not influence family perceptions.

Premorbid levels of family function have also been found to be predictive of outcome, both for the child and family, within the behavioural domain. Wade et al. (1996) found that degree of perceived family burden and parental problems post-injury was greater in families who reported chronic life stress and maladaptive coping styles. These families reported primary concerns about their child's injuries, interpersonal stresses with other family members, and disruption of family routines and school and work schedules. Within the TBI sample 45% of families reported clinically significant symptoms of stress and family dysfunction, but few sought any intervention. Yeates et al. (1997) extended these results, identifying a relationship between injury severity and family/psychosocial factors. They noted that premorbid psychosocial functioning was an important determinant of rate of recovery. Further, they found that for specific cognitive domains, including memory and adaptive functioning, the impact of severe TBI was buffered by above-average social resources and exacerbated by below-average resources. Similarly, Rivara et al. (1993, 1994) note that family measures account for a significant percentage of variance in a child's behaviour, as well as being associated with academic performance. Further, pre-injury family functioning and coping, along with ratings of child behaviour pre-injury, predicted which families within the severely injured group would be most affected.

These multidimensional research programmes reinforce the complexity of childhood TBI, and the need to follow children over the years post-injury to determine the relevance of the various factors impacting on the injured child and their role in ultimate outcome. Future research extending these findings is important to further our knowledge.

MANAGEMENT AND INTERVENTION

The previous discussion has described likely outcomes and recovery following TBI. Although this literature was slow emerging, we now have an understanding of the importance of injury severity, age at injury, and pre-injury factors with respect to outcome. We also know more about the most likely deficits to occur post-TBI, and are developing knowledge regarding the impact on the ongoing developmental process during childhood. Unfortunately, we are slower to develop and implement paediatric rehabilitation and intervention for children, with limited availability of paediatric-specific rehabilitation programmes. This may be due to the tendency to aim to get children back home to a familiar environment, in the care of their parents as quickly as possible. In addition, the need for school reintegration is seen as paramount, and even inpatient rehabilitation programmes for children tend to focus on providing school exposure and reintegrating children as soon as possible to their school and friends.

Principles of rehabilitation

Paediatric rehabilitation is a multidisciplinary endeavour, usually including rehabilitation physicians, physiotherapists, occupational therapists, speech therapists, play therapists, special educators, and social workers as well as neuropsychologists. Parents are often an integral part of the process, with therapists training them to implement rehabilitation procedures with their child. The rehabilitation process is designed to promote recovery and help the child compensate for residual deficits. The major goals of rehabilitation for children include maximising physical recovery and communication skills, understanding and treating cognitive and behavioural impairments, and monitoring family and other social factors (Rourke et al., 1983; Ylvisaker, 1985).

Approaches to rehabilitation tend to vary depending on a therapist's particular philosophy, but three general principles are commonly employed: (1) restoration of function, which has as its aim the re-establishment of impaired functions, and tends to be the focus of physical and speech therapy in the early stages of recovery; (2) functional adaptation, where intact abilities are utilised to "re-route" skills that have been disrupted via behavioural training— for example, training a child in visual imagery strategies to compensate for a verbal memory deficit; and (3) environmental modification, altering the child's environment to meet his or her new needs, which is particularly relevant once the child has returned home to family and school, in the post-acute phase. Typically such strategies could include utilisation of a word processor for motor coordination difficulties, or use of a diary for memory impairments (Ponsford et al., 1995). In many centres a combination of these approaches is employed. There is little research available on the relative efficacy of each of these approaches. Such evaluative research is important to provide guidance for rehabilitation staff in maximising patient recovery.

The neuropsychologist's role

In the early stages of recovery, during hospitalisation and emergence from coma and post-traumatic amnesia, the clinical role of the neuropsychologist may be minimal. Input may be sought regarding issues such as emergence from post-traumatic amnesia or appropriate environment for optimal recovery, but by-and-large these tasks are incorporated into other therapists' roles. The neuropsychologist becomes more central once the child is able to cope with assessment procedures, and an initial evaluation may be conducted to determine early impairment. Neuropsychological findings may then be fed back to other therapists and consultants and parents to guide rehabilitation. The neuropsychologist also has an important role in the school reintegration process, providing appropriate assessment data that explains the child's cognitive strengths and weaknesses and their implications within the school context, and indicates the nature of any specific rehabilitation/remediation required. Close liaison with teachers and parents during this phase is important. The neuropsychologist may provide guidance with respect to the amount of time spent at school, initially including time for socialisation and familiarisation with the environment and children. Later, as problems of fatigue and physical symptoms reduce, the child will begin attending classes—half-days and later full-days. This process may extend over several months depending on the needs and recovery of the child.

Once full reintegration has occurred and the child is required to cope with the tasks of a normal day, the need for extra educational support may become evident. Special aides to provide individual instruction or tailoring of educational programmes are frequently used to maximise recovery. The child may continue to receive therapies during this period, either at a rehabilitation facility or via the school. These professionals too need to liaise with school staff regarding the child's progress. Regular, though not necessarily frequent, meetings need to be established among school staff, parents, and involved professionals, to ensure that programmes are being implemented appropriately, that they are having the desired impact, and to help maintain an understanding of the specific needs associated with the sequelae of TBI.

The need for continued regular intervention will vary depending on the resources of the child, the family, and the school. Many families and schools take on initial information, and work productively together to provide the optimal learning environment for the child. In such instances input may be required only at times of transition, or where specific problems arise. However, in other situations, frequent input and support may be needed to provide an appropriate environment. This may be particularly the case for the child who exhibits severe cognitive and behavioural problems, where family resources are limited, and the neuropsychologist needs to act as an advocate for the child, or where the school is unable to cope with the demands of the child within their resources.

Once the initial phase of recovery is complete, many therapists may discharge the child from regular therapy. It is at this time that the long-term commitment of the neuropsychologist becomes particularly apparent. Ongoing assessment of recovery and current levels of functioning is important in order to inform the neuropsychologist of the child's current needs. Material from these reviews will inform parents and teachers about any recovery that may have occurred, or of plateaus in recovery. It may provide much needed motivation, or help determine why the child is not progressing despite enthusiastic input. It is crucial for the support system that goals of rehabilitation and education are realistic and provide the opportunity to measure improvement. In addition such reviews may alert the neuropsychologist to the need for extra therapeutic intervention. For example, the child with a significant memory deficit may be considered for a memory group, or the child experiencing social difficulties may use a social group of similarly injured children to work through social problems.

Family support and intervention

A number of researchers have reported on the importance of the family to the recovery process. Well-functioning and resourceful families may optimise recovery, whereas a disruptive family environment may inhibit a child's progress. We know that families who exhibited difficulties pre-injury are at particular risk, and may benefit from counselling and support. The added demands of the child's injury, in terms of emotional, financial, and physical resources, may be great. Issues of blame, loss, and grief may need to be addressed. Feelings of hopelessness, being trapped, and ambivalence to the child may also emerge. Even in families that cope well, behavioural difficulties exhibited by the TBI child are often difficult to understand and manage. Treatment of these problems may be best done by the neuropsychologist, perhaps in consultation with a family therapist or individual counsellor. Clearly, the well-being of the child is dependent upon the level of functioning of the family, and so the family too needs nurturing.

CONCLUSIONS

Many principles that have been developed in the context of adult TBI may be extended to paediatric populations. Clearly, a relationship exists between injury severity and outcome, although it is an imperfect one, with many authors commenting on the great variability in outcome following TBI in childhood. Summarising findings to date, it appears that mild TBI may result in few, if any, residual impairments for the normal child. In contrast, children with premorbid vulnerabilities, for example, behavioural or learning problems, are more likely to demonstrate continued or increased problems. For moderate-to-severe injuries residual deficits are common. Crystallised skills (e.g., well-learned skills and knowledge) appear less vulnerable than fluid skills (e.g., planning, reasoning, problem solving), with greatest deficits in attention, memory speed of processing, and high-level language and non-verbal abilities. However the consequences of childhood TBI also appear to be qualitatively different from those observed following similar damage to the mature CNS. Whereas adult injury may lead to immediate consequences in terms of brain injury, cognitive disability, and behavioural impairment, in the child there is an ongoing interaction among these domains, resulting in cumulative and often global dysfunction. Thus, recovery is less complete, with additional deficits often "emerging" as the child passes through each developmental stage.

Recent longitudinal research has shown that recovery and ultimate outcome are dependent on a number of biological, developmental, and psychosocial factors, including nature and severity of injury, premorbid abilities, developmental level at time of injury, time since injury, stability of family unit, and access to resources. The relative importance of each of these parameters, the possibility that their impact may be greatest at different stages in the recovery process, and their mechanisms of interaction, are still to be determined. Although significant gains in knowledge and understanding of childhood TBI have been achieved in recent years, future research needs to address these complexities, in the context of longitudinal, multidimensional research, to plot the natural history of these injuries.

CHAPTER SIX

Hydrocephalus and spina bifida

INTRODUCTION

Hydrocephalus occurs when there is an imbalance between the production and absorption of cerebrospinal fluid (CSF), secondary to some other pathological event or structural brain anomaly. This condition can impact on the structure and function of the brain, with recent research describing characteristic pathophysiological changes within the central nervous system (CNS), corresponding to a range of neuropsychological sequelae. This chapter will examine the consequences of hydrocephalus for the developing brain and for cognitive development, in the context of both clinical and research findings.

Under normal circumstances, CSF is formed by the choroid plexus located in the lateral ventricles, and flows through the paired foramina of Monro into the third ventricle, before passing through the cerebral aqueduct to the fourth ventricle. From there, it flows through the foramina of Luschka and the foramen of Magendie into the subarachnoid spaces surrounding the brain and spinal cord. Finally the fluid is reabsorbed into the venous circulation by the arachnoid villi (see Figure 6.1). CSF protects the brain from the impact of blows, provides a barrier between brain and blood, and may also play a role in the removal of waste products from the CNS (Menkes, 1990).

When normal CSF circulation pathways are disrupted, fluid accumulates within the system and pressure is exerted on the brain. This situation is called hydrocephalus (HYD). HYD can be classified according to type (obstructive, communicating), aetiology (congenital, acquired), and/or the presence of

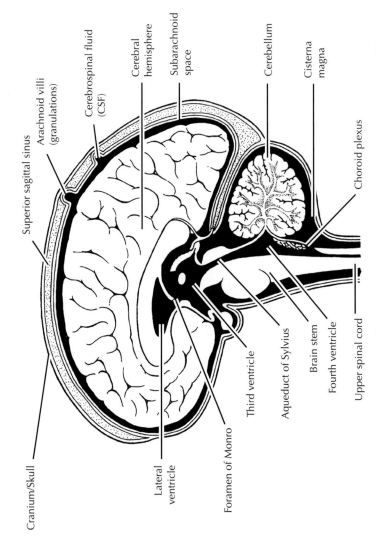

Figure 6.1. Cross-section of the brain, illustrating cerebrospinal fluid circulation. Adapted from "Hydrocephalus", Madeline Foundation (1995).

186

co-morbidities (Fletcher et al., 1995a). Obstructive HYD occurs when there is obstruction to CSF flow, either within the ventricles or cerebral acqueduct or at the outlet of the fourth ventricle, preventing free flow of CSF between the ventricles and the subarachnoid space. In communicating HYD there is free flow of CSF within the ventricular system but the absorption of CSF is disrupted within the subarachnoid spaces. More rarely, a communicating HYD may result from excess formation of CSF, secondary to a choroid plexus papilloma, where the arachnoid villi are unable to absorb the volume of fluid present within the system.

In response to diagnostic difficulties, Raimondi (1994) has proposed an alternative way of defining and classifying HYD based on the degree of excess CSF in the system. In this view, HYD is classified as (1) intraparen-chymal, in which there is a pathological increase in CSF inside the par-enchyma of the brain; or (2) extraparenchymal, reflecting increased fluid within the subarachnoid spaces, cisterns, or ventricles. Raimondi (1994) pro-poses a gradation of effects from cerebral oedema (accumulation of fluid within the parenchyma) to fluid accumulation in the subarachnoid spaces (the initial stages of communicating HYD), through to increased fluid in the cisterns and ultimately within the ventricles, leading to significant ventricular dilation and pressure effects on brain tissue.

In cases of diffuse cerebral atrophy, HYD is compensatory and, of itself, not of clinical concern. In general though, enlarging ventricles result in raised intracranial pressure and a variety of neurological symptoms. In the infant, before the cranial sutures have fused, the head enlarges at an abnormal rate and the child may present with a bulging anterior fontanelle and downward deviation of the eyes, the so-called "sunset gaze" (Klug, 1994). Irritability, lethargy, and poor feeding may be noted although some infants are surpris-ingly asymptomatic. Headaches, vomiting, motor incoordination and incontinence are common presenting symptoms in the older child. HYD is treated by inserting a shunt or piece of silastic tubing, usually in the right parietal region of the brain, to drain excess CSF from the ventricles into another body cavity, most commonly the stomach, as illustrated in Figure 6.2. Shunts may block periodically, requiring surgical revision, and each procedure is associated with a risk of haemorrhage and infection.

AETIOLOGY AND EPIDEMIOLOGY

Congenital forms of HYD occur in disorders of embryogenesis, such as spina bifida, aqueduct stenosis, and the Dandy–Walker syndrome, and are usually of the obstructive type (Fletcher et al., 1995a). Spina bifida is a defect of neural tube closure in early embryogenesis, occurring around the end of the first month of gestation, during the primary neurulation phase. It manifests as a malformation along the spinal cord, occurring at any point from the

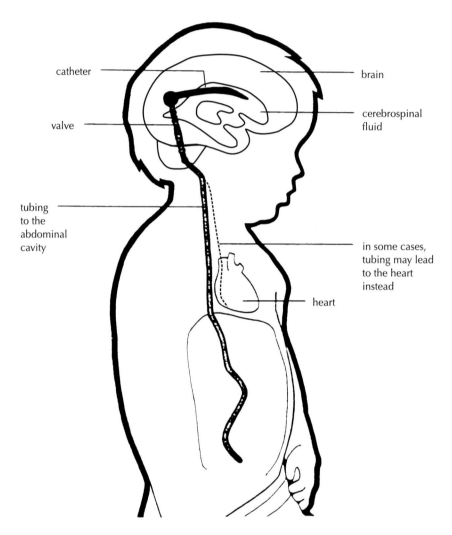

Figure 6.2. This schematic diagram illustrates the typical shunt system used to treat hydro-cephalus, with the shunt running from the ventricular system to the abdominal cavity. Adapted from *Children with spina bifida and/or hydrocephalus at school*, with permission from the Association for Spina Bifida and Hydrocephalus.

cervical to lower sacral regions. There are three forms of graded severity. Spina bifida occulta is asymptomatic and occurs when the vertebral arches are incomplete but the spinal cord itself, and the CNS, develop normally. It has been reported to be present in approximately 5% of the general popula-tion, and may be evidenced by abnormalities in the skin and overlying tissue

	Spinal cord (close up)	**Location of spina bifida**
Occulta Outer layer of vertebrae not completely joined. Spinal cord and covering (meninges) undamaged. Hair often at site of defect.	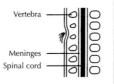	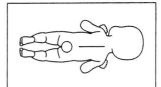
Meningocele Outer part of vertebrae split. Spinal cord normal. Meninges damaged and pushed out through opening.	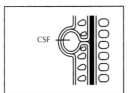	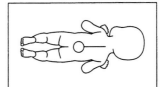
Myelomeningocele Outer part of vertebrae split. Spinal cord normal. Meninges damaged and pushed out through opening. Possible hydrocephalus.	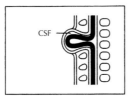	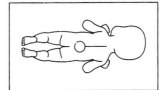
Encephalocele Part of brain pushed out through a defect in the skull.	Spinal cord unaffected	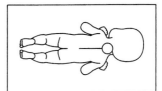
Anencephaly Absence of brain and sometimes defect of the skull. These babies cannot live long.	Spinal cord unaffected	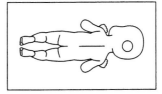

CSF = cerebrospinal fluid

Figure 6.3. Types of spina bifida. From *Children with spina bifida and/or hydrocephalus at school*, with permission from the Association for Spina Bifida and Hydrocephalus.

in the region of the malformation. Spina bifida cystica occurs in two forms, meningocele and myelomeningocele, as shown in Figure 6.3. Meningoceles are usually found in the lumbosacral region and involve a protrusion of the meninges and CSF through abnormal vertebral arches to form a skin-covered sac. The spinal cord and CNS are usually intact, although there is a slightly increased risk of HYD. The most severe, and the most common, form of spina bifida, myelomeningocele, occurs when the spinal cord itself protrudes through the midline defect. Children with myelomeningocele often have associated neurodevelopmental disorders such as polymycrogyria, callosal dysgenesis, and the Arnold–Chiari II malformation, in which the brain stem and cerebellum are deformed and herniate through the foramen magnum, creating a barrier to CSF outflow from the ventricular to the subarachnoid spaces. A progressive form of HYD, requiring shunting, occurs in 80–90% of cases of myelomeningocele (Bryan, 1994). Callosal dysgenesis is also found in children with aqueduct stenosis, a condition in which there is blockage of CSF flow at the aqueduct of Sylvius. The Dandy–Walker syndrome is characterised by the failure of the cerebellar midline to develop normally, leading to obstruction of CSF flow within the fourth ventricle. Cortical dysplasias and agenesis of the corpus callosum may also be present (Welch & Lorenzo, 1991).

Communicating HYD most often occurs as a result of perinatal or post-natal insults to a brain that has otherwise developed normally and is therefore classified as acquired (Fletcher et al., 1995a). The most common cause of acquired HYD is intraventricular haemorrhage in very low-birthweight premature infants, but it can also occur secondary to cerebral trauma, malignancies, or infections such as meningitis or encephalitis (Del Bigio, 1993; Fletcher et al., 1995a, 1997; Welch & Lorenzo, 1991). Premature infants who suffer intraventricular haemorrhage bleed into the germinal matrix and parenchyma, ultimately clogging the arachnoid villi responsible for reabsorbing CSF. Periventricular leukomalacia and porencephalic cysts are common long-term sequelae of intraventricular haemorrhage. The differential diagnosis of obstructive versus communicating HYD is often difficult because aqueduct blocks may develop as a secondary effect of communicating HYD and subarchnoid blocks may complicate obstructive HYD (Welch & Lorenzo, 1991).

It is difficult to find reliable estimates of the overall incidence of HYD because prevalence rates are usually cited for the individual aetiologies. Fletcher et al. (1995a) suggest that approximately 70% of cases of HYD are of the obstructive, congenital form with acquired, usually communicating, forms making up the remaining 30%. Spina bifida cystica (meningocele and myelomeningocele) is the second most common birth defect after cerebral palsy and the most common congenital cause of HYD, occurring in 1–4 per 1000 live births (Bryan, 1994; Charney, 1992). Regional variations in incidence have been described, with the highest incidence in Ireland and England, and the lowest in Japan. Increased availability of antenatal diagnosis and subsequent termination of affected pregnancies, in addition to maternal folic acid supplement as a prophylactic measure against neural tube defects, is likely to result in decreasing numbers of children born with spina bifida and associated HYD in the future (Bryan, 1994). A definitive aetiology is yet to be determined but is likely to be multifactorial (Welch & Lorenzo, 1991). Folic acid deficiencies, environmental toxins, maternal diabetes, elevation of maternal core temperature in early pregnancy and heredity have each been implicated as causative factors (Charney, 1992; Hynd & Willis, 1988; Welch & Lorenzo, 1991).

Acqueduct stenosis accounts for 20% of all cases of HYD, while the Dandy–Walker syndrome is relatively rare (Menkes, 1990). Intraventricular haemorrhage occurs in up to 50% of premature infants with a birthweight less than 1800 g (Fletcher et al., 1997; Landry, Chapieski, Fletcher, & Denson, 1988). Estimates of progressive HYD requiring shunting in premature infants range from 0.7% in North America (McCallum & Turbeville, 1994) to 1% in Sweden (Fernell, Hagberg, & Hagberg, 1993). Girls slightly outnumber boys with spina bifida, whereas the percentage of boys is higher in children with other aetiologies of HYD (Fletcher et al., 1995a; Wills, 1993). Prior to the development of a surgical procedure to treat HYD, only 25% of children affected by a progressive form of the condition survived to adulthood and most were mentally retarded (Shurtleff, Foltz, & Loeser, 1973; Wills, 1993).

PATHOPHYSIOLOGY

Hydrocephalus has major consequences for the developing brain. White matter is more affected than cortex, although both may be compromised in severe cases (Del Bigio, 1993; Fletcher et al., 1995a; Welch & Lorenzo, 1991). Rubin et al. (1975) describe a series of events consisting of ventriculomegaly, disruption of the periventricular ependyma, periventricular oedema, axonal destruction, secondary myelin disintegration, and finally a reactive astrocytosis. As the ventricles enlarge, usually in a posterior to anterior direction, the fibres of the corpus callosum are stretched or thinned, projection fibres are compromised, optic and olfactory tracts may be damaged, and myelination disrupted (Del Bigio, 1993; Fletcher et al., 1996b). Injury to nerve cells is a late phenomenon, but if the HYD persists there is a reduction in the cortical mantle and overall brain mass. There may be reduced cerebral blood flow and ischaemia following damage to the anterior cerebral artery during ventricular enlargement (Baron & Goldberger, 1993). Functionally, the frontal lobes may be affected because the pathways between the prefrontal cortex and the posterior brain regions and limbic subcortical system are disrupted. When HYD is associated with early gestational disorders, there may be additional brain abnormalities including cortical dysplasias (heterotopias and polygyria), where cells lodge in abnormal locations and make atypical connections. The periventricular leukomalacia and porencephalitic cysts associated with intraventricular haemorrhage are an additional source of damage to brain cells.

edit speech for completeness, semantics, and form) rather than at the level of words and sentences, and conclude that children with HYD exhibit a disorder of language usage rather than of language content.

One aspect of the language of hydrocephalic children that has received a lot of attention is the so-called "cocktail party" syndrome, a term first used by Hagberg (1962) to describe a form of language marked by superficial content and a tendency to "talk too much". Tew and his co-workers (Tew, 1979; Tew & Laurence, 1979) operationalised this phenomenon and studied it in a cohort of children with spina bifida, using a longitudinal research design. They identified the syndrome in 48% of girls and 32% of boys in their sample. They noted that vocabulary and syntactical skills were generally intact, but observed that the spontaneous speech of hydrocephalic children was marked by instances of perseveration, excessive use of overlearned social phrases, overfamiliarity of manner, tangential comments, and poor-shared topic maintenance. They also suggested that the syndrome became less evident with age.

Several other studies have found evidence of hyperverbal and over-familiar behaviour (E. Anderson & Spain, 1977; Culatta & Egolf, 1980; Hurley et al., 1990), but it is also clear that the syndrome is not universal in children with HYD. In fact, Dennis et al. (1987) argue that the "cocktail party" phenomenon is not a true syndrome, pointing out that only a minority of children with HYD exhibit this pattern of superficial, perseverative language, and that the term describes, but does not explain, the atypical language of some affected children. They contend that "cocktail party" language is more strongly associated with depressed IQ and impaired mobility than with HYD itself—an observation that has some empirical support (E. Anderson & Spain, 1977; Byrne, Abbeduto, & Brooks, 1990; Hurley et al., 1990; Spain, 1974, Tew, 1979; Tew & Laurence, 1979). "Cocktail party" language has also been associated with visuoperceptual deficits and poor abstraction skills (Hurley et al., 1990) and with increased distractibility and a lack of task persistence (Culatta & Egolf, 1980). It is listed by Rourke (1989) as one of the features of non-verbal learning syndrome, providing further support for it being a symptom of a broader pattern of cognitive impairment.

A number of explanations have been proposed to explain the pragmatic language difficulties clinically apparent in children with HYD. Dennis et al. (1987) speculated that the "cocktail party" phenomenon might be better con-ceptualised as a reflection of word-finding and sequencing deficits. Difficul-ties with the rapid serial ordering of speech and word-finding problems will reduce fluency, and may lead to reliance on stereotypic and overlearned phrases and a tendency to use language not well understood. Empirical sup-port for this interpretation is provided by two recent reports (Brookshire et al., 1995a; Fletcher et al., 1995a), each of which compared children with HYD associated with acqueduct stenosis, spina bifida, and prematurity, to control groups of children with similar conditions but no hydrocephalus. They found that the HYD group performed more poorly than controls on measures of verbal fluency, rapid naming, timed word retrieval or automaticity, and word finding. It is noteworthy though, that fluency, word finding, and confrontation naming are all timed tasks. Poor performance on such tasks might reflect slowed processing speed—a deficit to be expected in a population known to suffer significant white matter compromise—rather than deficient language skills. Assessment on the same task under timed and untimed conditions would help clarify the component processes contributing to fluency and word-finding deficits. Visual problems, commonly associated with HYD, may also contribute to poor results on naming and sequencing tasks. For example, children with visual defects may require more time to focus on pictorial information and to visually track stimuli on a serial order task.

An alternative view was put by Horn et al. (1985) who found that children with HYD had greater difficulty than matched controls focusing on the salient aspects of tasks and ignoring less relevant distractors. They suggested that the "off topic" and hyperverbal behaviour evident in some children with HYD might reflect a deficit in selective attention, rather than impoverished language. Yet another interpretation, proposed by Baron and Goldberger (1993), is that excessive or irrelevant chattiness results from a failure of executive control, rather than a fluency/word retrieval problem. These authors suggest that children with HYD have difficulty initiating, inhibiting, and monitoring their speech output for logic and salience.

Dennis et al. (1987) found that the language development of children with HYD varied with illness variables. Extraventricular (communicating) HYD preserved higher-order language functions but disrupted fluent speech production, suggesting that subtentorial brain regions are important for verbal fluency. In contrast, fluency was preserved in intraventricular (obstructive) HYD but lexical access, sequencing, and grammatical comprehension were impaired. These deficits were particularly apparent in children with spina bifida. In general, prenatal aetiologies of HYD were associated with greater compromise of language skills than were peri- or postnatal causes.

Similar but not identical results were obtained by Fletcher and his associates (Brookshire et al., 1995a; Fletcher et al., 1995a). In these studies, children with spina bifida performed more poorly than those with a history of prematurity, whereas the performance of children with aqueduct stenosis most closely approximated that of normal children. Children with aqueduct stenosis demonstrated an isolated difficulty on an automatised naming task—a timed, cross-modal task in which children were asked to provide verbal labels for pictured objects. The investigators interpreted this finding as reflecting the specificity of CNS damage in this group, which is limited to callosal defects. This pathology would be expected to compromise performance on tasks requiring rapid interhemispheric transfer of information from posterior cortex to the anterior left hemisphere.

The emerging language profile associated with HYD has a number of functional implications. Dennis et al. (1987) argue that HYD language is neither globally preserved nor globally impaired and this variability in itself may be problematic. A discrepancy between their apparent facility with language and the actual communicative content of what children with HYD say may lead others to overestimate their true capacity. Furthermore, language difficulties may increase with age as children are expected to process increasingly complex linguistic material. Dennis et al. (1987) found age-related increments in language abilities although there was a tendency for children with HYD to improve at a slower rate across development than did controls, placing them at cumulative disadvantage in both academic and social settings. This slowed skill acquisition may reduce the prognostic value of early language assessments, which may overestimate likely language outcome. Deficient metalinguistic awareness, poor understanding of inferential language, together with slowed comprehension of complex grammatical structures, may increasingly limit the ability of children with HYD to access linguistic information conveyed at the age-expected level of complexity and speed of presentation.

Perceptual motor abilities

There is consistent evidence of visuomotor and visuoperceptual deficits in children with HYD (Billard et al., 1985; Brookshire et al., 1995b; Dennis et al., 1981; Donders et al., 1991; Fennell et al., 1987; Fletcher et al., 1992b, 1995a, 1997; Friedrich et al., 1991; Prigatano et al., 1983; Snow et al., 1994; Tew & Laurence, 1975; Thompson et al., 1991; Wills et al., 1990). Wills (1993) provides three explanations for selective deficits in these areas. First, motor and visual difficulties, including oculomotor deficits, are common in children with HYD. Second, verbal scores may overestimate true ability, leading to verbal/non-verbal discrepancies, suggestive of particular weaknesses in the latter. Third, executive deficits in planning, organisation, attentional control, self-monitoring, and impulsivity will impair results on perceptuomotor tests more than on verbal ones. To this list might be added the possible impact of restricted opportunities for experiential learning through play in children with motor deficits in association with HYD.

Baron and Goldberger (1993) point out that the neuroanatomical changes associated with HYD make motor and visual impairments almost inevitable in affected children. As the ventricles enlarge, optic nerves and motor pathways are likely to be damaged. The cerebellum is critically involved in the fine control of voluntary movement, and the cerebellar dysgenesis associated with many forms of HYD may result in problems with balance and both upper and lower limb dysfunction (Landry et al., 1994). The incidence of left-handedness and mixed-handedness is elevated in hydrocephalic populations (Anderson & Spain, 1977; Baron & Goldberger, 1993; Dennis et al., 1981; Lonton, 1976; Shaffer et al., 1986). Children with spina bifida have additional sensory and motor deficits, dependent upon lesion level and degree of spinal cord involvement (Wills, 1993). A slowed speed of motor response on visuo-perceptual tasks that require manipulation of test materials and visual tracking skills will lead to depressed scores on timed tasks. For example, Coding, a subtest from the Wechsler Intelligence Scales for Children, which draws heavily on visual tracking and eye–hand coordination skills, is often the lowest of the WISC subtest scores in this population (Donders et al., 1990; Fletcher et al., 1992b; Hurley et al., 1990; Lonton, 1977; Wills et al., 1990).

A number of investigators have attempted to dissociate performances impaired by deficient motor dexterity and/or visual deficits from those reflecting higher-order deficits in motor planning, perceptual analysis, or spatial reasoning skills. Poor performances on embedded figures, pattern matching, and visual recognition/discrimination tasks has been reported by a number of investigators (Anderson & Spain, 1977; Shaffer et al., 1986; Willoughby & Hoffman, 1979; Zeiner & Prigatano, 1982). These tasks place minimal or no demand on motor skills, although all depend upon intact visual functions. Fletcher et al. (1992b) used both visuomotor and motor-free tasks and found deficient performance on both, more pronounced on tasks with a motor component. These results were replicated in a follow-up of this cohort (Brookshire et al., 1995b; Fletcher et al., 1995a). Fletcher et al. (1995a) also noted that children with shunted HYD performed more poorly than the arrested and no-HYD groups on all visuoperceptual tasks, but group differences were larger for complex tasks involving form consistency, figure–ground relationships, and spatial memory, and least on simple matching to sample tasks, a complexity effect also found by Thomspon et al. (1991). In contrast, Donders et al. (1991) documented essentially normal performance on both visuoperceptual and visuomotor tasks, in an uncontrolled study from which all low-functioning subjects had been excluded. Attempts to distinguish the relative contribution of primary visual or motor deficits from that reflecting compromise of higher-order perceptual, analytic, and spatial reasoning skills to poor performance remains an ongoing assessment challenge, but it is probably important not to accept a simple motor explanation too readily.

The neuropathological correlates of the condition provide a coherent explanation for non-verbal deficits in HYD. Fletcher et al. (1992a, 1995a, 1996c) have conducted concurrent neuropsychological evaluation and neuroimaging in samples of children with HYD associated with spina bifida, aqueduct stenosis, and prematurity. In the first of their reports, Fletcher et al. (1992a) found that visuoperceptual deficits correlated with right lateral ventricle size, and with both right and left internal capsule size, suggesting that the development of non-verbal cognitive skills is dependent upon the integrity of CNS white matter in both hemispheres. When corpus callosal anomalies were present they always involved the posterior body and splenium (Fletcher et al., 1996a). The posterior body joins association areas in the parietal lobes involved in spatial processing and sensorimotor integration, whereas the splenium connects the occipital lobes responsible for visual processes. These findings are consistent with Rourke's hypothesis (Rourke, 1995) that visuoperceptual and visuomotor deficits in children with white matter disease reflect reduced input–output and cross-modal integration of sensory and motor information due to disturbance of the corpus callosum and projection pathways. Drawing on the ideas of Goldberg and Costa (1981), Rourke (1995) points out that the white: grey matter ratio is increased in the right hemisphere—the hemisphere specialised for processing novel, complex stimuli and integrating cross-modal information—whereas the left hemisphere is specialised for processing unimodal and overlearned codes such as language.

Memory and learning

Intuitively, one would expect to find memory deficits in children with HYD. An enlarging ventricular system is likely to damage hippocampal structures important for the acquisition of novel information, whereas subcortical white matter damage has been associated with compromised retrieval of information from long-term memory (Delis, Kramer, Kaplan, & Ober, 1991). Empirical attempts to evaluate memory processes in children with HYD have been marked by methodological difficulties. The use of small and heterogeneous patient groups, variable test protocols across studies, poorly standardised or insensitive measures, and a failure to control for IQ, severity of HYD, and the presence of co-morbid conditions complicate interpretation of early findings (Baron & Goldberger, 1993; Wills, 1993).

Recent studies have addressed many of these methodological inadequacies and reveal a number of specific verbal memory deficits in children with HYD. Immediate recall of meaningful material (sentences, prose) appears relatively unaffected by HYD (Cull & Wyke, 1984; Donders et al., 1991; Fletcher et al., 1992b; Scott et al., 1998), although there have been isolated reports of compromised performance, particularly evident in the spina bifida and premature subgroups (Dennis et al., 1987; Fletcher et al., 1995a). Scott et al. (1998) found compromised delayed recall of stories in the context of intact immediate recall, and argue that verbal memory deficits cannot be explained on the basis of language problems as these should also affect immediate recall. There is consistent evidence of compromised word list, paired associate, and new fact learning in the HYD population (Cull & Wyke, 1984; Donders et al.,

1991; Fletcher et al., 1992b, 1997; Holler et al., 1995; Prigatano et al., 1983; Scott et al., 1998; Yeates et al., 1995). Deficits in initial encoding (Prigatano et al., 1983; Scott et al., 1998), rate of learning (Fletcher et al., 1992b; Prigatano et al., 1983; Scott et al., 1998; Yeates et al., 1995), and delayed recall and spontaneous retrieval of information (Cull & Wyke, 1984; Yeates et al., 1995) have been reported, suggesting difficulties across all stages of the memory process. Recognition memory and cued recall appear much less affected. Yeates et al. (1995) found that performance did not vary with age at testing and concluded that children with HYD exhibit a stable pattern of impaired learning. In contrast, Holler et al. (1995) found relatively greater impairment on a long-term verbal memory task in older children, suggesting that the discrepancy between age-expected and actual performance may increase as tasks become more complex.

This pattern of performance, with relatively intact immediate recall of meaningful prose, but impaired spontaneous retrieval of information and word list learning, suggests difficulties in two areas. First, children with HYD exhibit an over-reliance on rote recall as well as impaired development of the higher-level organisational strategies necessary for efficient storage and retrieval of information over time. The strong recency effect noted in the Yeates study (Yeates et al., 1995) is consistent with this hypothesis. Second, children with HYD have trouble retrieving information from memory store unless they are cued in some form. Yeates et al. (1995) found that children with shunted HYD showed greater improvement on recognition tasks than unshunted and normal children—a pattern that is consistent with the suggestion of Delis et al. (1991) that retrieval problems are directly related to severity of subcortical white matter damage. Prigatano et al. (1983) speculated that word-finding problems, that is, an inability to retrieve the exact word, might also account for deficient recall of unrelated words in the context of appropriate recall of contextually meaningful stories.

Interpretation of empirical findings regarding visual memory in HYD is complicated by the need to disassociate a pure memory deficit from a performance-impaired one because of fine-motor or visual problems. Donders et al. (1991) found no deficits in visual memory using a face recognition (motor free) paradigm, whereas Prigatano et al. (1983) reported impaired immediate memory for designs (a copying task)—a pattern of findings suggesting that motor difficulties may explain poor performance on visual memory tasks. However, Scott et al. (1998) demonstrated pervasive memory deficits on both immediate and delayed recall of designs and on a motor-free spatial learning task. This group noted both encoding and retrieval difficulties on the learning task and felt that deficits could not be explained by motor difficulties. Fletcher et al. (1992b) found poorer performance on a non-verbal selective reminding test in children with shunted HYD, but cautioned that these results may have been influenced by task difficulty, as a number of the younger children in their sample were unable to perform the test. Counter-intuitively, there is limited evidence for more impaired visual than verbal memory in children with HYD. Fletcher et al. (1992b) found a trend towards poorer non-verbal than verbal memory scores, but on repeated assessment of the same cohort 1 year later there was no discrepancy and this finding was replicated in a later study of premature children with shunted HYD. Consistent with these findings, there was no evidence for material specific (verbal versus spatial) effects on a serial learning task in the children studied by Scott et al. (1998).

In two recent studies conducted by Yeates and colleagues (Kiefel et al., 1997; Yeates, Enrile, & Loss, 1998), an attempt was made to distinguish memory impairments from executive dysfunction. These researchers asked children to recall complex stories and to draw and recall a complex geometric design. In each instance their findings suggested that, when compared to sibling controls, children with myelomeningocele and shunted hydrocephalus exhibited poorer recall of information. However, further analysis indicated that the organisational difficulties exhibited by these children on each of the tasks hindered efficient encoding and retrieval of information, resulting in poor performance. Such results once again emphasise the importance of considering a range of possible explanations for poor performance on multidetermined neuropsychological test measures.

On the basis of current findings, it is difficult to quantify the contribution that motor difficulties make to impaired performance on design-copying tasks in children with HYD, but it is clear that deficits are also apparent on memory and learning tasks that involve no motor demand. In addition, the absence of any conclusive evidence for a material-specific memory deficit in HYD suggests that visual difficulties alone do not explain impaired performance on non-verbal memory tasks. The negative correlation between severity of HYD and memory and learning deficits apparent in several studies (Fletcher et al., 1992b; Scott et al. 1998; Yeates et al., 1995) supports the view that specific disease processes such as ventriculomegaly lead to compression of the hippocampus and other medial temporal and diencephalic structures are important in human memory and learning (Zola-Morgan & Squire, 1993).

Attention

Arousal and alertness are impaired during the acute stages of HYD (Menkes, 1990) and anecdotal reports of poor concentration and distractibility in treated, asymptomatic children are common. Although empirical studies focusing directly on attentional processes have been limited, deficits are often inferred from performance on other tasks. For example, Horn et al. (1985) interpreted the vocabulary deficits found in their sample as reflecting a problem with selective attention, that is, an inability to focus on the salient aspects of the task, while ignoring distractors. Distractibility and attentional deficits were commented upon by Culatta and Egolf (1980) in their analysis of perceptual and linguistic skills in children with spina bifida and HYD. Dennis and Barnes (1994b) attempted to dissociate attentional difficulties secondary to prematurity from those associated with HYD. They compared same-sex twins concordant for prematurity but discordant for HYD and found impaired attention in the HYD twin.

Deficits in vigilance and sustained visual attention have been reported in children with HYD using a Continuous Performance Test paradigm (Fennell et al., 1987; Tew, Laurence, & Richards, 1980), although Lollar (1990), using the same methodology, found performance to be within normal limits. Fennell et al. (1987) conducted a qualitative analysis of their data and found that children with HYD make both omission and commission errors on a computerised vigilance task, suggesting both inattention and impulsivity. Willoughby and Hoffman (1979) found poorer performance in spina bifida children on an embedded figures task but not on an auditory discrimination test, and suggested that there may be greater compromise of visual attentional systems in HYD, at least in this subgroup. The most systematic evaluation of attentional processes in children with HYD has been conducted by Fletcher et al. (1996b). This group noted deficits in selective and focused attention and concluded that poor performance on executive tasks in their sample could be explained in terms of impaired attention, specifically involving the arousal–activation systems, mediated by posterior white matter regions of the brain. The findings of Fletcher et al. (1996b), which suggest compromise of posterior, subcortical attentional systems, are at variance with the conclusion reached by Wills (1993). She suggested that simple focused attention was intact in children with HYD, in the context of deficits on selective, divided, or shifting attention tasks, and those that involve planning, mental tracking, or the inhibition of overlearned responses—a pattern consistent with damage to anterior brain regions.

Executive functions

Empirical attempts to delineate executive skills have only recently been undertaken, despite a strong clinical perception that children with HYD struggle to acquire higher-level organisational skills and the capacity to integrate novel or complex information into previously overlearned schemas. In an elegant study, Landry et al. (1994) compared executive skills of young children with spina bifida and HYD and IQ-matched controls and found that the clinical group spent more time on simple manipulation of toys and less time in goal-directed behaviour. The groups did not differ on the number of play activities or social interactions initiated, or in the time spent off task.

These researchers suggested that children with HYD in association with spina bifida exhibit a specific impairment in their ability to sustain a behaviour to reach a goal, despite intact capacity to alert to tasks and initiate activity. On the basis of their findings, Landry et al. (1994) felt unable to distinguish between competing explanations for impaired performance, such as problems in sequencing, attentional control, planning, or some combination of these or other aspects of executive dysfunction. It is also possible that an apparent lack of goal directedness in this subgroup of children with HYD has an experiential, rather than an organic, basis. Landry et al. (1994) point out that developmental theories emphasise the importance of early exploratory play and interactions with the physical environment for the development of curiosity, goal directedness, and mastery motivation. Such opportunities may be limited in children with impaired mobility.

Fletcher et al. (1996b) examined attentional and executive skills in children with shunted, arrested (unshunted), and no hydrocephalus and felt that the pattern of findings was suggestive of posterior, rather than anterior cerebral impairment. They found that children with shunted HYD solved fewer problems on the Tower of London Test (TOL), particularly on the first trial, achieved fewer categories on the Wisconsin Card Sort Test (WCST), and performed more poorly on tests of focused and selective attention. There were no significant differences on planning time or number of broken rules on the TOL, perseverative errors on the WCST, or on the degree of interference on the Stroop Test—variables on which one might have expected group differences if children with HYD exhibit specific executive dysfunction. Children with arrested HYD did not differ on a qualitative basis from children with shunts; rather they formed a less affected group, their performance falling between that of the shunted HYD group and controls.

Fletcher et al. (1996b) argue that their findings do not support an executive dysfunction explanation and suggest a number of alternative possibilities. Noting that executive tasks did not differentiate HYD from non-HYD as robustly as measures of spatial cognition, this group argue for a generalised spatial problem-solving deficit, consistent with Rourke's (1995) suggestion that children with white matter disease have difficulty on complex integrative tasks and novel problem-solving activities, dependent upon the integrity of right posterior systems. This interpretation is also consistent with the earlier findings of Donders et al. (1991), who reported that by 8 years of age children with HYD were impaired when processing complex or novel stimuli—difficulties that were particularly apparent on visuospatial tasks. In further comment on their data set, Fletcher et al. (1996b) speculated that the core difficulty might be a problem of arousal/activation, implicating impairment of subcortical brain structures in the posterior right hemisphere. As an alternative or additional explanation they suggest that there may be a failure to commit fully to a task—a possibility that is consistent with the findings of Landry et al. (1994), who postulated deficits in goal-directed behaviour.

Two recent investigations reach conclusions somewhat discrepant from those of Fletcher et al. (1996b). Snow et et al. (1994) identified a pervasive difficulty with abstraction skills evident across different subgroups of children with spina bifida and concluded that anterior cortical damage was a common underlying feature in this population. Dise and Lohr (1998) also studied subjects with spina bifida. Despite IQ within average limits, deficits in a range of higher-order mental functions were apparent, including conceptual reasoning, problem solving, mental flexibility, and mental efficiency. Hendy and Anderson (1994) offer a unifying developmental theory that may be helpful in defining links between brain pathology and functional difficulties in children with HYD. They suggest that disturbed cerebral development of subcortical pathways will compromise frontal/executive functions over time because of the mutual dependence between these regions at the functional level. Taking such a systemic approach, they argue that pathology within subcortical regions will compromise the quality and efficiency with which information is transmitted to anterior cerebral regions, regardless of the structural integrity of these areas. As a result, executive functions may be impaired, not due to frontal dysfunction *per se*, but because these regions do not receive information of sufficient quality for further processing.

Processing speed

It is surprising that few investigators have specifically examined processing speed in children with HYD, given the white matter abnormalities associated with the condition. However, there have been a number of incidental observations of slowed processing speed on tasks measuring other cognitive skills and more can be inferred. As described earlier, there is abundant evidence that children with HYD obtain low scores on timed tasks that require visual tracking, eye–hand coordination skills and the physical manipulation of test stimuli. There is also evidence of slowed processing on tasks that do not impose a motor or visual demand. Dennis et al. (1981) noted depressed response speed on word-finding tasks and slowed comprehension of complex grammatical forms in their sample of children with HYD. The HYD subgroups were slower on all three trials of the Stroop test in the study by Fletcher et al. (1996b), suggestive of some generalised slowing for automatic responses. This task also requires transfer of visual information from posterior brain areas to naming centres in the left frontal regions—a crossmodal task on which impairments might be predicted in a population with a high incidence of corpus callosal abnormalities.

Academic skills

Intact word recognition with poor comprehension of contextual information has been a consistent finding in studies of children with HYD (Anderson & Spain, 1977; Barnes & Dennis, 1992; Friedrich et al., 1991; Wills et al., 1990; Zeiner et al., 1985), although there is a recent report (Fletcher et al., 1997) of depressed scores across both domains. Barnes and Dennis (1992) observed that children with spina bifida/HYD depend more heavily on word knowledge and less on contextual integration of information based on meaning. Visual scanning deficits and slowed processing speed may also contribute to impaired passage comprehension because information is "lost" from working memory because of the time taken to process it. Spelling abilities are compromised in HYD, and are often below the level predicted on the basis of reading age (Barnes & Dennis, 1992; Fletcher & Levin, 1988; Fletcher et al., 1997; Friedrich et al., 1991; Shaffer et al., 1985; Tew & Laurence, 1975; Wills et al., 1990). It is possible that visuospatial, visual memory, and sequencing deficits contribute to poor spelling in this population, but contributing factors have yet to be defined in empirical studies.

There is an increased incidence (estimates range from 20 % to 40 %) of left- and mixed-handedness in children with HYD (Anderson & Spain, 1977; Baron & Goldberger, 1993; Fletcher et al., 1996b; Shaffer et al., 1985). A lack of right dominance has been associated with poorer performance on academic measures (Lonton, 1976) and, in particular, left or mixed dominance may contribute to the deficient handwriting and copying skills evident in children with HYD. In an early study, Anderson and Spain (1977) noted that letter formation was adequate but the alignment and spacing of letters and words were poor, resulting in output that was difficult to read. In addition, children with HYD perform written tasks at a slower rate than expected for age (Anderson & Spain, 1977; Fletcher et al., 1997; Wills et al., 1990).

Arithmetic skills are depressed in children with HYD (Barnes & Dennis, 1992; Fletcher & Levin, 1988; Fletcher et al., 1997; Friedrich et al., 1991; Shaffer et al., 1985; Tew & Laurence, 1975; Wills et al., 1990). Difficulties with mathematical problem solving are evident early in life (Thompson et al., 1991) and may increase with age (Wills et al., 1990). Rourke (1995) has suggested that visuospatial deficits explain difficulties with mathematical problem solving in children with HYD as in other conditions involving white matter pathology. Working memory deficits, yet to be evaluated in children with HYD, may contribute to computational problems. It is also unclear what role depressed processing speed, attentional and executive deficits, such as difficulty shifting mental set, may play in the mathematical difficulties exhibited by children with HYD, nor to what extent hospitalisation and school absence may compromise sequential learning of mathematical concepts.

Subgroups of children with HYD may be at particular risk for academic difficulties. Left- or mixed-handedness has been linked to compromised attainment of educational skills (Anderson & Spain, 1977; Baron & Goldberger, 1993; Shaffer et al., 1985). Hurley et al. (1990) found that children who exhibited the "cocktail party syndrome" performed more poorly on academic measures than IQ-matched peers. Fletcher et al. (1995a) suggest that children with HYD secondary to aqueduct stenosis may be less "at risk" academically than other aetiological groups. They found that the aqueduct stenosis subgroup had intact decoding and reading comprehension scores, whereas the spina bifida and premature groups had pervasive difficulties across all academic parameters.

Case example

Although there is significant variation in neuropsychological presentation for children with HYD, the following case study illustrates some of the clinical features commonly described in empirical studies, in particular the unusual discrepancy between PIQ and VIQ scores, and the qualitative aspects of HYD.

Background information

Neville was referred for neuropsychological evaluation at age 15 years 6 months by his paediatrician. He had seen an educational psychologist for psychometric assessment and educational counselling 4 years prior to this assessment, and the IQ results from that evaluation are included in Table 6.1, which also provides current test data.

Neville's early medical history was uneventful, with no evidence of trauma during pregnancy and birth. At the age of 8 months Neville was referred to a neurosurgeon because of concerns regarding his large head size and some developmental delay, particularly in motor skills. Investigations at that time detected a large posterior fossa arachnoid cyst, impacting on the cerebellum, and causing significant hydrocephalus. The cyst was drained but quickly refilled, with Neville experiencing signs of left-sided weakness in the few weeks post-surgery. Investigations revealed a recurrence of the hydrocephalus and a ventricular–peritoneal shunt was inserted in the right parietal region. This was effective, and Neville was generally well after that time, with the exception of two episodes associated with a blocked shunt at ages 4 and $5\frac{1}{2}$ years. Successful shunt revision was performed on both occasions.

Neville received ongoing rehabilitation, including physiotherapy and occupational therapy, throughout his preschool years, and attended a kindergarten for children with special needs at age 5. His parents reported that Neville showed age-appropriate language skills and socialised well with other children. However, he was cautious physically, and tended to sit quietly rather than explore his environment. He progressed very well during his kindergarten year and it was recommended that he attend a regular school. Neville's early school progress was noted to be good. Consistent with empirical findings, Neville acquired reading skills quickly and was a reasonable speller. Although he was able to learn his "times" tables, he experienced difficulties in other areas of mathematics. His writing was observed to be slow and laboured.

When seen for assessment Neville was in year 10 at a regular secondary school. His parents reported that he was struggling with the curriculum, most particularly with mathematics and information technology. They were eager to find a more appropriate school environment—one that could take advantage of his cognitive strengths, which they perceived to be in language skills, music, and art. They did report that Neville experienced great difficulties socially, being unable to interact and keep up with his peers. This was interpreted as due to motor incoordination and general slowness.

Assessment

Neville presented as a very talkative, sociable adolescent. However, after some time with him it was apparent that his social interactions consisted of a number of stereotyped phrases and responses, which he used indiscriminately. Neville also had difficulty interpreting social cues, and often acted inappropriately within the test situation (e.g., misinterpreting gestures encouraging him to sit down, moving to sit behind the desk in the clinician's chair, asking personal questions irrelevant to the situation). In addition, his response speed was very slow in all contexts. He took a long time to respond verbally in an informal interview, and his test responses were particularly laboured.

Test results are presented in Table 6.1. Neville's scores on intellectual measures clearly indicate his relative difficulties in non-verbal areas with a PIQ/VIQ discrepancy of 46 points. Neville's average VIQ of 97 reflects generally age-appropriate well-learned verbal knowledge, although there is some suggestion of fall-off from initial assessment 4 years earlier. On many verbal subtests Neville was able to supply a simple verbal response within the structure of the test situation. Of interest was Neville's relatively poor performance on the Comprehension subtest of the WISC-III, which requires some understanding and application of social rules. He had great difficulty generating responses on this test, and his answers were often tangential or inappropriate. Similarly, Neville's verbal fluency and abstract thinking were well below age expecations. Qualitatively, Neville's use of language was in keeping with the descriptions of Dennis and Barnes (1993, 1994b), who

TABLE 6.1
Neuropsychological assessment data for Neville, aged 15 years 6 months

A.   General intelligence (WISC-III)

	'98	'94		'98	'94
Information	10	(10)	Picture Completion	3	(3)
Similarities	12	(13)	Coding	2	(2)
Arithmetic	9	(10)	Picture Arrangement	5	(2)
Vocabulary	11	(12)	Block Design	1	(2)
Comprehension	6	–	Object Assembly	2	(1)
Digit Span	13	(14)	Symbol Search	3	(2)
Verbal IQ	97	(107)			
Performance IQ	51	(49)			

B.   Educational skills

Neale Analysis of Reading	Accuracy	Age appropriate
	Comprehension	6.0 years
Wide Range Achievement Test	Reading	14.0 years
	Spelling	12.0 years
	Arithmetic	8.6 years

C.   Psychomotor skills

Developmental Test of Visuomotor Integration (age equivalent)	5.11 years

D.   Memory (Wide Range Assessment of Memory and Learning)

Verbal Scale (scaled scores):	Story Memory	2
	Sentence Memory	6
Visual Scale (scaled scores):	Picture Memory	2
	Design Memory	2
	Finger Windows	2
Learning Scale (scaled scores):	Verbal Learning	1
	Visual Learning	1

E.   Executive skills

(i) COWAT	Total Words	9 (standard score = 3)
(ii) Trail Making Test	Part A	38 s, 0 errors (st. score = 3)
	Part B	72 s, 0 errors (st. score = 5)
(iii) CFR	Copy/Recall	<1st centile (see Figure 6.6)

suggest HYD is associated with an impairment of language usage rather than of language content.

Non-verbal abilities were globally and severely impaired, with Neville's PIQ falling within the "intellectually disabled" range. His poor performance was characterised by deficits in a number of domains including motor skills, speed of processing, spatial abilities, and executive functions. Specifically, Neville demonstrated poor attention to visual detail, difficulties analysing spatial relationships, slowed speed of response, poor self-monitoring, impaired planning, and an inability to move flexibly from one solution approach to another. Wherever possible Neville attempted to use verbal mediation strategies on non-verbal tasks, but his approach was often inefficient and unhelpful. Neville's difficulties in dealing with non-verbal information are well illustrated in his attempt to copy the Complex Figure of Rey, as illustrated in Figure 6.6. His attempt is piecemeal and shows no evidence of planning strategies. It scores poorly in terms of accuracy and process. Not surprisingly, his capacity to recall the figure was also severely impaired.

Neville exhibited reduced memory and learning capacity. Although his immediate memory for auditory–verbal material was a relative strength, he was unable to register or retain new visuospatial information of any kind. Repetition of information was not beneficial, and Neville was unable to demonstrate a learning curve on tasks where multiple trials were administered.

Somewhat surprisingly, Neville's literacy skills were relatively intact, and may explain his ability to cope adequately during his early school years. Word recognition and decoding skills were noted to be age appropriate, and spelling skills were at a functional level. In contrast, Neville exhibited poor reading comprehension, and this is reflected in his current difficulties in the areas of English and literature. Mathematical abilities are also reduced, and Neville struggles to produce written work both at school and at home. Although the use of word-processing facilities has helped his work output, these problems continue to be of concern. Neville's pattern of educational abilities mirrors that described within the HYD population (Anderson & Spain, 1977; Barnes & Dennis, 1992; Fletcher & Levin, 1988).

Conclusions

Neville's neuropsychological profile is consistent with much of the empirical literature described for children with HYD, although his particular difficulties are more severe than is commonly seen, possibly due to delays in initial treatment. The pattern of intact basic literacy and verbal knowledge, but poorer language application, globally impaired non-verbal abilities, poor memory and learning, and difficulties on measures of executive function underlie significant functional problems. These functional difficulties in academic progress and social interaction appear to have been increasing over time, despite access to appropriate educational resources, as evidenced by his parents' perception that he is no longer able to cope within the normal school environment. Neville's developmental progress mimics that described by Rourke (1989) in his depiction of non-verbal learning difficulty, and suggests a complex interaction between early cerebral pathology and associated cognitive impairments, leading to increasing difficulties coping with developmental demands.

COPY

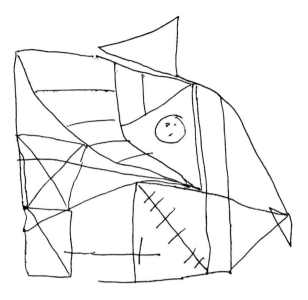

RECALL

Figure 6.6. Neville's reproductions of the Rey Complex Figure. His copy is characterised by poor organisation and overdrawing. Not surprisingly, given his poor copy, recall is severely impoverished.

213

ILLNESS-RELATED PREDICTORS OF OUTCOME

Aetiology and severity of HYD as well as the timing of treatment in response to raised intracranial pressure (both initially and subsequently in the context of shunt blockage), shunt complications, and co-morbid conditions, have all been identified as possible predictors of subsequent development in children with HYD. Congenital, obstructive HYD is associated with a "snowballing" effect on all subsequent brain development, commonly seen in disorders occuring early in gestation. Communicating HYD most often occurs as a result of peri- or postnatal insults to a brain that has developed normally. This led Raimondi and Soare (1974) to suggest that morbidity will be less in children with communicating forms of HYD. However, empirical findings in support of this contention are mixed. Several studies have shown that site of obstruction (intraventricular, extraventricular) does not predict intellectual outcome in any systematic way (Dennis et al., 1981; Fletcher et al., 1992b, 1995a; Riva et al., 1994; Thompson et al., 1991). There is evidence that uncomplicated congenital HYD (as in aqueduct stenosis) is associated with higher intelligence than when other major CNS supratentorial malformations (as in spina bifida) are present (Dennis et al., 1981; Fletcher et al., 1992b, 1995a; Riva et al., 1994; Shurtleff et al., 1973) or when HYD occurs secondary to cerebral infections (Dennis et al., 1981). Fletcher et al. (1992a) noted that children with an intact corpus callosum had the highest IQ scores in their sample. Correlations between the corpus callosum and cognitive performance were significant for both verbal and non-verbal measures, but more strongly for the latter. They concluded that the corpus callosum plays an important role in the development of cognitive skills, particularly visuospatial processing capacities.

The relationship between lesion level in children with spina bifida and IQ has been studied by a number of investigators, with most finding that higher lesions are associated with lower IQ scores (Bier et al., 1997; Donders et al., 1991; Hunt & Holmes, 1976; Soare & Raimondi, 1977). A threshold effect for thoracic lesions (associated with lower IQ) was found by Wills et al. (1990) but there were no systematic differences between IQ scores of children with lumbar and sacral lesions. Friedrich et al. (1991) suggested that VIQ was more sensitive to lesion level whereas other investigators report the opposite, that is, higher lesion level predicted lower PIQ scores but there was no association between lesion level and VIQ (Hoffman, 1981; Shaffer et al., 1985). Shaffer et al. (1985) speculated that restricted opportunities for exploratory play, together with greater motor impairments in children with higher lesions, might explain the differential impact on performance skills.

In general, children with shunts perform more poorly on intellectual and neuropsychological measures than children with arrested HYD not requiring shunting (Friedrich et al., 1991; Fletcher et al., 1992b, 1995a, 1996b, 1997;

Wills et al., 1990). This is not an unexpected finding given that children requiring shunts would have experienced more severe forms of HYD, which did not arrest spontaneously. In the spina bifida subgroup, there may be an interaction between lesion level and presence of shunt. Friedrich et al. (1991) found that children with higher-level lesions had better outcomes if they were shunted, whereas for lower lesion levels unshunted patients performed better. In the series studied by Wills et al. (1990) the effect of shunt/no shunt was most marked at the thoracic level.

A history of shunt infections or bleeding has been consistently associated with poorer developmental outcomes (Hunt & Holmes, 1976; Mapstone et al., 1984; McLone et al., 1982; Selzer, Lindgren, & Blackman, 1992; Shaffer et al., 1985; Shurtleff et al., 1973; Wills et al., 1990) but empirical attempts to document associations between number of shunt revisions and neuro-psychological status have produced inconsistent findings. Some studies have found no correlation between test scores and number of shunt revisions (Dennis et al., 1981; Fletcher et al., 1996b; Jensen, 1987; McLone et al., 1982; Raimondi & Soare, 1974; Riva et al., 1994), whereas others have shown a progressive decline in IQ scores with increasing numbers of surgical interventions (Bier et al., 1997; Holler et al., 1995; Menkes 1990), particularly if these occur after age 2 (Hunt & Holmes, 1976). These discrepant findings may reflect the fact that there are both positive and negative effects of shunt revisions, and these may be difficult to disentangle. Prompt revision suggests a well-maintained shunt but with an increased risk of infection and haemor-rhage. There is some evidence that IQ scores drop at times of shunt blockage when compared with baseline testing at a time when the shunt was well functioning and improve again following surgical intervention, although there is considerable individual variation (Wills, 1993).

Side of shunt placement may also be an important determinant of neuro-psychological outcome but is difficult to study as shunts are overwhelmingly placed in the right parietal region in the first instance, with children receiving left-sided shunts only in the event of initial shunt failure. Fletcher et al. (1995a) among others have argued that placement in the right parietal region may impose another dimension of risk to the development of visuospatial skills, in addition to the risks associated with the underlying brain pathology. Furthermore, the opportunity for transfer of functions across cerebral hemi-pheres is unlikely in these children due to damage to the corpus callosum. Prompt treatment of progressive HYD is important, with a number of stud-ies finding that poorer neurodevelopmental outcome is associated with longer duration of untreated HYD (Billard et al., 1985; Dennis et al., 1981; Lorber, 1968; Raimondi & Soare, 1974; Young, Nulsen, Weiss, & Thomas, 1973).

The presence of co-morbid conditions is an additional risk factor for adverse outcomes. Lower IQ scores, particularly PIQ, have been found in children with cerebral palsy, significant visual impairments, or seizures in addition to HYD (Dennis et al., 1981; Laurence, 1969; McCullough & Balzer-Martin, 1982; McLone et al., 1982). In the premature subgroup, severity of haemorrhage was associated with lower IQ scores (Krishnamoorthy et al., 1979; Landry et al., 1984, 1988) but neonatal complications (jaundice, anoxia, maternal antepartum haemorrhage) did not exert a significant effect (Dennis et al., 1981).

Ventricular size or the ventricular–brain ratio before shunting appear to be poorly predictive of post-operative IQ (Hunt & Holmes, 1976; Raimondi & Soare, 1974). Relationships between the size of the ventricles post-shunting, cortical mantle, and developmental status have been found in a number of studies (Dennis et al., 1981; Fletcher et al., 1992a, 1995a, 1996c; Lonton, 1979; Thompson, Fletcher, & Levin 1982), with both very enlarged or slit-like ventricles associated with poorer outcomes. Others (Shurtleff et al., 1973; Young et al., 1973) suggest a threshold effect with a relationship between ventricular enlargement and IQ scores only apparent when cortical mantle was reduced by more than 22% or below 2.8 cm. PIQ appears more sensitive to the disruptive effects of enlarged ventricles than does VIQ (Dennis et al., 1981; Fletcher et al., 1992a; Lonton, 1979; Selzer et al., 1992). Dennis et al. (1981) concluded, on the basis of their findings, that the pure effect of uncomplicated HYD appeared to be on visuospatial and visuomotor skills, with other cognitive deficits explained by trauma, infection, or associated brain anomalies.

PSYCHOSOCIAL ISSUES

Hydrocephalus, particularly in its milder forms, may provide a useful model for understanding the impact of neuropsychological deficits on psychosocial functioning. Unlike many forms of CNS disorder, children with successfully treated HYD may have no evidence of physical disability, no permanent neurological signs or symptoms, and require no regular treatment or medication. However, there is evidence that the significant cognitive sequelae of HYD may affect the child's emotional function and social interactions, and alter parental expectations and family roles. Lowered IQ is likely to affect self-esteem and growth towards independence, as well as compromise academic success. Within the family system, a handicapping condition may influence parental expectations, alter family roles, demand sibling acceptance of the greater attention directed to the affected child, and impose financial and practical stresses, all of which may be exacerbated during developmental transitions in the affected child (Baron & Goldberger, 1993). In addition, the child with visible motor handicaps may experience restricted opportunities for play and peer interaction, as well as psychological feelings of being damaged or at least different.

The neuropsychological profile associated with HYD will have implications for the socioemotional functioning of children. A tendency to verbose, tangential, and overfamiliar verbal output observed in some children with HYD is likely to be offputting to others and to actually impede communication. Rourke (1995) suggests that children with non-verbal learning deficits are at high risk for behaviour problems and social skill deficits because of their failure to appreciate cause-and-effect relationships, their over-reliance on verbal forms of communication and their relative inability to interpret non-verbal cues and gesture. Interpersonal relatedness and mastery of adaptive living skills demand an ability to initiate, self-direct, monitor, and sequence goal-directed behaviour. Landry et al. (1994), among others, has drawn attention to the lack of goal directness and deficient self-regulation of behaviour apparent in children with HYD.

Clinically, affective symptoms such as anxiety and depression are often noted in older children with HYD and they have been described in empirical reports as socially inappropriate and immature (Horn et al., 1985) with poor socioemotional judgement (Wills et al., 1990). Younger children may exhibit a tendency to indiscriminate friendliness and overfamiliarity, whereas social withdrawal is often observed in adolescents. Early estimates of the prevalence of emotional disorder in children with HYD range from 24% to 44% (Connell & McConnel, 1981) with a similar prevalence of psychological distress in parents (Dorner, 1975). In their own study, Connell and McConnel (1981) noted a mixture of internalising and externalising symptoms and found that 19 of 45 children met interview-based criteria for a psychiatric disorder. A number of other investigators have studied children with HYD, sometimes in mixed samples of children with handicapping or chronic conditions and report clinically significant behavioural problems, predominantly of the internalising type (Fennell et al., 1987; Lavigne, Nolan, & McLone, 1988; Murch & Cohen, 1989; Thompson, Kronenberger, Johnson, & Whiting, 1989; Wallander et al., 1989). None of these investigators collected self-reports.

In contrast to these reports of greatly elevated risk for psychosocial disturbance, several recent studies suggest a more positive outcome. Donders, Rourke, and Canady (1992) used a psychiatric inventory, the Personality Inventory for Children—Revised (PIC-R), to assess psychological symptoms in children with shunt-treated HYD. They found no evidence for a specific "hydrocephalic personality" and suggested that parent-reported symptoms in their children were largely confined to concerns about development, achievement, and cognitive functioning. Donders et al. (1992) interpreted the elevated score on the Psychoticism scale as reflecting greater dependency and immaturity rather than a true psychoticism. It is important to note that this was an uncontrolled study of very young children and the possibility that more difficulties may emerge as children experience greater demands cannot be discounted.

In another recent study, Fletcher et al. (1995b) found that HYD group mean scores on the Child Behavior Checklist (CBCL) were not significantly different from controls although twice as many children with HYD scored above the clinical cut-off, T-score 64. Symptomatic children were more likely to be boys and to have problems within the internalising spectrum. Deficits in adaptive functioning were apparent only for the children with spina bifida and only on the daily living skills domain (Fletcher et al., 1995b) whereas negative self-percepts were confined to the physical competence subscale of the Harter Scale of Perceived Competence. This study is important because it clearly demonstrates that psychosocial adjustment problems in children with HYD are not confined to the spina bifida subgroup. In their most recent investigation of premature children, Fletcher et al. (1997), found that children with shunted HYD had lower social competence scores than those who had not required surgical intervention, but did not differ on behaviour problems. Parents of children with shunts expressed heightened levels of concern about the cognitive development of their offspring and rated both arrested and shunted subgroups of children as having lower adaptive skills and more attentional and achievement difficulties.

Some investigators have examined relationships between severity or degree of disability, family and demographic variables, and risk for behaviour problems with mixed findings. Family cohesion and organisation, low conflict, and high socioeconomic status (SES) were protective in the mixed sample of chronic and handicapping conditions studied by Wallander et al. (1989), but medical variables and degree of disability did not affect outcome—a similar finding to that reported by Connell and McConnel (1981). Donders et al. (1992) found no relationships between symptoms in the child and any of the medical, family, or demographic factors they examined. In contrast, Fletcher et al. (1995b) noted that children with shunts, particularly if these had required revision, were more likely to have behaviour problems, whereas aetiology and SES variables did not affect risk. Lower lesions and younger age were associated with higher adaptive scores, and later shunt placements with poorer socialisation skills in children with spina bifida in another recent report (Holler et al., 1995). The wide variety of variables examined and the lack of consistency across studies of the instruments chosen to measure them probably account for these discrepant findings.

High levels of parent distress have been described (Connell & McConnel, 1981; Dorner, 1975; Wallander et al., 1989), with feelings of guilt, social isolation, and depression commonly reported. Almost half the parents in the sample studied by Donders et al. (1992) were "cases" on the Symptom Checklist 90 R, although this group were not able to establish any direct relationship between parental distress and level of child disability.

CONCLUSIONS

With improved neuroimaging it will be possible in the future to distinguish damage related to the direct effects of HYD (e.g., disruption of white matter fibres and loss of cortical mantle by ventricular distension, effect of the shunt placement) from early brain anomalies (neuronal migration problems, prenatal callosal dysgenesis, cerebellar malformations), thus enabling a better understanding of the functional implications of both aspects of cerebral pathology. Variations in both prenatal aetiology and specific characteristics of the HYD itself indicate that, although there may be some characteristic features of HYD (e.g., disruption of white matter fibres), HYD cannot be seen as a unitary disorder, defined by a single pattern of pathology or a unique profile of neuropsychological strengths and weak-nesses (Baron & Goldberger, 1993). In consequence, it is unlikely that a single syndrome, such as non-verbal learning disability, will provide a model to fit all instances of HYD.

Rather than attempting to establish a single neuropsychological des-cription of HYD it may be more fruitful to focus on developing qualitative methods to distinguish aspects of impairment still confounded in the literature, for example, speed of processing, motor skills, and executive function. From a broader perspective, no research to date has examined the natural history of HYD across childhood into adulthood in any systematic manner. Longitudinal studies that incorporate medical, cognitive, and psy-chosocial dimensions are needed to better understand and predict outcome and the interactions that may occur across these dimensions. Multi-site, collaborative studies will help to increase statistical power and decrease sampling bias and cohort effects, thus enabling more useful comparisons of different forms of HYD.

CHAPTER SEVEN

Cerebral infections

INTRODUCTION

A number of viruses and pathogens have the capacity to invade the central nervous system (CNS). Intrauterine infections such as toxoplasmosis and rubella may affect the developing fetus, and more recently cases involving the HIV virus have been reported. The most common cerebral infections affecting children after birth are meningitis and encephalitis. Meningitis involves infection and inflammation of the meningeal membranes surrounding the brain and spinal cord, whereas encephalitis occurs when a virus invades the brain tissue itself. Common presenting symptoms across both illnesses include fever, headache, neck stiffness, vomiting, confusion, and lethargy, progressing to depressed conscious state and seizures unless early and aggressive treatment is instituted. Such infections may result in a range of physical and neurobehavioural sequelae, from severe disability to subtle problems or complete recovery. This chapter will examine neuropsychological impairments occurring following such cerebral infections, in the context of the nature and degree of underlying cerebral involvement, and with a view to identifying predictors of outcome.

BACTERIAL MENINGITIS

Aetiology and epidemiology

Meningitis is a relatively common childhood disorder, characterised by inflammation of the meningeal membranes surrounding the brain. It can occur as a result of either bacterial or viral infection. Although viral infection is more common, it is difficult to diagnose and, as a result, has attracted relatively little behavioural outcome research. In contrast, pathogens causing bacterial meningitis are readily identified, and there have been a number of research programmes conducted to investigate the sequelae of the disease. Findings indicate that bacterial disease is associated with higher morbidity and mortality (Cherry, 1992; Davies & Rudd, 1994). Although the present chapter will focus on bacterial meningitis, it is worthy of note that the limited research available on child survivors of viral meningitis suggests a similar pattern of neuropsychological sequelae for both infective processes (Anderson & Taylor, 1999; Baker et al., 1996; Bergman et al., 1987; Farmer, MacArthur, & Clay, 1975; Rorabaugh et al., 1993).

In the pre-vaccine era, annual incidence rates for bacterial meningitis were reported to be around 30–70 per 100,000 children aged under 5 years (Feigin, 1992; Sell, 1987). An immature immune system appears to constitute the strongest risk factor for bacterial meningitis, with some evidence that psycho-social disadvantage (overcrowded housing, group childcare, smoking, limited access to health care) may also be important (Feigin, 1992; Takala & Clements, 1992). Some cultural groups have been found to be at high risk, with the incidence of bacterial meningitis in indigenous populations from America, Australia, and New Zealand 10 times greater than that for the general population (D'Angio et al., 1995; Hanna, 1990; Takala & Clements, 1992; Ward et al., 1981). Psychosocial factors also appear to be particularly important for neonatal meningitis, contracted in the first few weeks of life, where poor maternal nutrition, hygiene, and health have been directly linked to the disease. Further, neonatal meningitis has been found to have particularly poor outcome, with physical and psychological sequelae common (Davies & Rudd, 1994).

Prior to the advent of antibiotics in the 1950s, mortality rates in bacterial meningitis exceeded 90% and there was little interest in the neuro-psychological sequelae of the disease. Survival rates have increased dramatically since then, with a recent report (Davies & Rudd, 1994) citing a mortality rate of around 10% overall (3.5% for meningococcal meningitis, 7.7% for *Haemophilus influenzae* type b meningitis, and 30% for infections involving the pneumococcal pathogen). A meta-analysis of 19 prospective studies reported a 4.5% mortality rate and at least one major adverse outcome (e.g., severe intellectual disability, spasticity, seizures, or deafness) in 16% of survivors (Baraff, Lee, & Schriger, 1993). A vaccine for *Haemophilus influenzae* type b meningitis was developed in the mid-1980s and is now widely available, at least in developed countries. This has resulted in significant reductions in prevalence rates and a dramatic change in the distribution of causative pathogens (Adams et al., 1993; Peltola, Kilpi, & Antilla, 1992). Schuchat et al. (1997) found a 55% reduction in *Haemophilus influenzae* type b cases following the introduction of vaccination programmes and noted that Group B streptococcus had become the predominant pathogen in newborns, *Neisseria meningitidis* in children 2–18 years, and *Streptococcus pneumoniae* among adults. Median age of meningitis sufferers increased from 15 months in 1985 to 25 years in 1995, reflecting the fact that the now less common *Haemophilus influenzae* type b meningitis has its peak incidence in the first 2 years of life.

Treatment of bacterial meningitis involves isolation and identification of the specific pathogen involved and institution of appropriate antibiotic treatment, together with fluid restriction and anticonvulsant therapy when required. Diagnosis is often delayed because presenting symptoms are non-specific (e.g., high temperature, irritability) and the child has often had a preceding febrile illness, such as upper respiratory tract infection or otitis media. In a rarer presentation, known as fulminating meningitis, the child becomes ill suddenly and deteriorates rapidly. Outcome is said to be poorer in this form of bacterial meningitis (Klein, Feigin, & McCracken, 1986). Diagnosis is usually confirmed by identifying bacteria in the cerebrospinal fluid (CSF) in association with elevated levels of protein and decreased CSF glucose. Accurate identification of the causal pathogen is necessary to determine the appropriate antibiotic regime. Steroids are now often added to the treatment regime in an attempt to reduce CNS inflammation and minimise permanent brain damage, but the efficacy of this form of treatment is still the subject of debate (Feigin, 1992). The child is watched carefully during the initial days of recovery, with regular monitoring of conscious state, neurological function, electrolyte levels, fluid retention, and drug levels. Additional investigations, such as structural imaging, electroencephalography, or angiography are usually not performed unless there is a deterioration in function.

Pathophysiology

Bacterial meningitis survivors provide a useful population to investigate the impact of transient, generalised CNS trauma on cognitive development. In the acute phase, bacterial meningitis may be associated with disrupted cerebrovascular and cerebrospinal fluid dynamics, leading to a sequence of consequences including raised intracranial pressure, hydrocephalus, cerebral oedema, and subdural effusions, as depicted in Figure 7.1 (Anderson & Taylor, 1999; Horowitz, Boxerbaum, & O'Bell, 1980; McMenemin & Volpe,

Mucosal colonisation by bacteria

↓

Bacterial invasion of and survival within bloodstream

↓

Penetration of blood–brain barrier and into CSF

↓

Local release of inflammatory cytokines into CSF

↓

Adhesion of leukocytes to brain endothelium and diapedesis into CSF

↓

Exudation of albumin through opened intercellular junctions of meningeal venules

↓

Brain oedema, increased intracranial pressure, altered cerebral blood flow

↓

Cranial nerve injury, seizures, hypoxic–ischaemic brain damage, herniation

Figure 7.1. Pathogenesis and pathophysiology of bacterial meningitis. Adapted from Quadli-arello and Scheld (1992).

1984; Mertsola et al., 1991; Snyder et al., 1981; Stovring & Snyder, 1980; Thomas & Hopkins, 1984).

Hypoxic damage due to shock, breathing difficulties, and seizures may also occur. The loss of cerebrovascular autoregulation induced by bacterial meningitis may interfere with cerebral blood flow and lead to either hyperperfusion or hypoperfusion, which appears to affect the region of the middle cerebral artery in particular (Pomeroy, Holmes, Dodge, & Feigin, 1990; Quagliarello & Scheld, 1992). Disruption of blood flow in this region may compromise the integrity of the pre- and post-central gyri, the superior and inferior parietal lobules, and the superior and middle temporal gyri. Raised intracranial pressure will obstruct the flow of CSF in the ventricular system and may lead to herniation of the hindbrain and damage to cranial nerves (Feigin, McCracken, & Klein, 1992). Hence, vestibular disturbance and sensorineural hearing loss are relatively common sequelae, and whereas the former usually resolves over time, hearing impairment is often permanent (Grimwood et al., 1995). A communicating hydrocephalus may result from a build up of purulent exudate around the basal cisterns, cerebellum, ventricles, and spinal cord, particularly in very young patients. Figure 7.2 provides two examples of cerebral pathology occurring in association with bacterial meningitis. In the first scan, cerebrovascular changes, including left frontal empyema and bilateral capsular infarcts are present, whereas the second shows evidence of hydrocephalus requiring surgical treatment in the form of a ventricular shunt.

Biochemical changes are also found in the acute stages of the illness (Feigin, 1992). There is decreased concentration of glucose in CSF and cellular electrolyte imbalance may occur. Secretion of the antidiuretic hormone may be disrupted, resulting in cerebral oedema as water shifts into the intracellular compartment.

Acute-phase neurological complications have been reported in up to 55% of children with bacterial meningitis (Grimwood et al., 1995; McIntyre, Jepson, Leeder, & Irwig, 1993; Taylor et al., 1990). An example of the range and frequency of these complications is provided in our own research (Grimwood et al., 1995, 1996) and illustrated in Table 7.1. Although many of these problems resolve over time (Feigin, 1987; Pomeroy et al., 1990), a proportion of children are left with permanent changes in CNS function. A recent meta-analysis (Baraff et al., 1993) suggests that 16% of survivors exhibit major long-term neurological sequelae including total deafness (11%), bilateral severe or profound hearing loss (5%), mental retardation (6%), hemiparesis (4%), and seizure disorders (4%). Risks varied according to disease type. Although *Haemophilus influenzae* type b meningitis was associated with the lowest mortality rate, it resulted in greater morbidity than other strains. The neuropsychological and behavioural sequelae of bacterial meningitis are less clearly documented, in part because investigators prior to the mid-1980s

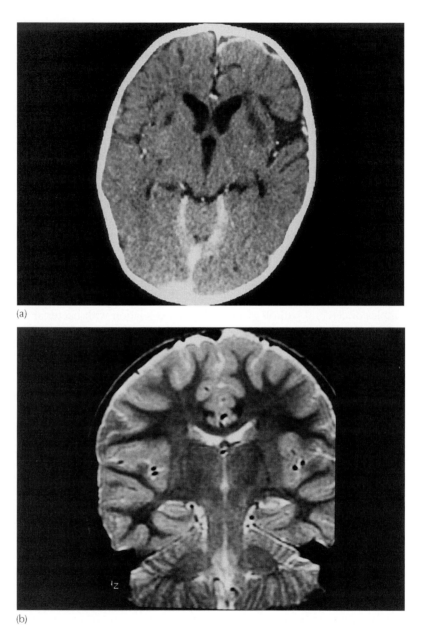

(a)

(b)

Figure 7.2. (a) One-year-old child suffering from pneumococcal meningitis. Contrast-enhanced axial CT scan illustrates left frontal empyema and bilateral internal capsule infarcts. (b) Two-year-old child with a history of *Haemophilus influenzae* meningitis in infancy who developed hydrocephalus in the acute stages of recovery, requiring insertion of ventricular shunt. Contrast-enhanced axial MRI scan illustrates evidence of hydrocephalus.

226

TABLE 7.1
Acute-phase neurological complications[a] associated
with bacterial meningitis

	Grimwood et al. (1995) (n = 130)
Seizures, n (%)	41 (31)
Obtundation/coma, n (%)	23 (18)
Sensorineural hearing loss, n (%)	8 (6)
Hemiparesis, n (%)	12 (9)
Ataxia, n (%)	9 (6)
Hydrocephalus, n (%)	3 (2)
Cortical blindness, n (%)	3 (2)

[a] Eight children (5%) of the original sample died during the acute phase of the illness.

relied almost exclusively on measures of general ability (IQ scores) to evaluate outcome. Such generalised measures have been shown to be relatively insensitive to specific neurobehavioural deficits.

Neuropsychological findings

Some early studies (e.g., Feigin et al., 1976; Feldman et al., 1982; Ferry et al., 1982), but not all (Emmett, Jeffery, Chandler, & Dugdale, 1980; Tejani, Dobias, & Sambursky, 1982; Wald et al., 1986), found mildly depressed IQ scores in survivors of bacterial meningitis. However, methodological difficulties, such as small and unrepresentative samples, absent or poorly matched controls, and retrospective designs, limit the conclusions that can be drawn from these reports. Sell, Webb, Pate, and Doyne, (1972) conducted one of the first prospective, controlled studies examining neuropsychological outcomes following childhood bacterial meningitis. They restricted their sample to children who were free of obvious disease sequelae and found that bacterial meningitis survivors obtained IQ scores that were within the low average range and significantly lower than either sibling or peer controls. Further, they observed that there was greater variability in scores in the clinical group, with 29% of the postmeningitic children scoring one full standard deviation below their sibling controls.

Taylor and his colleagues have conducted several studies investigating bacterial meningitis survivors, designed to minimise the methodological limitations of previous work in this area (Feldman & Michaels, 1988; Taylor et al.,1984, 1990, 1996; Taylor, Barry, & Schatschneider, 1993; Taylor, Schatschneider, & Rich, 1992. In an early report of a small sample followed up 6–8 years after their illness, the postmeningitic children obtained lower performance IQ (PIQ) and full-scale IQ scores than sibling controls, but there were no differences on verbal IQ (VIQ). PIQ/VIQ discrepancies were greater in the meningitic group (Taylor et al., 1984). In a subsequent, larger-scale, longitudinal study (Taylor et al., 1990, 1992, 1993, 1996), these findings were not replicated. In the later study Taylor and colleagues retrospectively identified a group of bacterial meningitis survivors ($n = 127$) from hospital records across three paediatric centres, and compared their abilities with a sibling control sample in a range of behavioural domains. They found no significant differences between postmeningitic children and controls on intellectual and neuropsychological measures and only small differences on educational measures, although the test scores of the clinical cases were noted to be consistently below those of their unaffected siblings. When postmeningitic children with acute-phase neurological complications (on theoretical grounds, an "at risk" subgroup) were compared to their respective siblings, a different picture emerged. This "complicated" subgroup obtained lower scores on both PIQ and full-scale IQ. None of the differences between index cases without acute-phase neurological complications and their siblings were significant. Taylor et al. (1993) subsequently demonstrated disease-related effects on VIQ as well as PIQ and full-scale IQ, when they reanalysed these data comparing postmeningitic children with acute-phase complications with a comparison group formed by combining index cases without complications and siblings. Follow-up of this cohort several years later showed stability of group differences on IQ measures (Taylor et al., 1996).

Findings from a large-scale prospective cohort study of bacterial meningitis survivors at a tertiary centre in Melbourne, Australia (P. Anderson et al., 1997; Grimwood et al., 1995, 1996, 2000) differ slightly from those of Taylor and his associates. Children in this study were recruited during initial hospitalisation, and illness parameters and recovery course were documented prospectively. Treatment protocol and clinical data for the cohort were standardised. Children with a premorbid history of CNS disease or trauma were excluded. At hospital discharge, children were neurologically evaluated and parents were interviewed to determine any changes in behavioural function post-illness. The cohort was later evaluated on IQ and other measures at 12 months, 7 years and 12 years post-illness. Fifty-six per cent of the original cohort experienced acute-phase neurological complications, including seizures, coma, hydrocephalus, hemiparesis, cranial nerve palsies, vision and hearing deficits, and ataxia (Grimwood et al., 1995). By 12 months, 15% showed persisting neurological sequelae and this figure had dropped to 8.5% at the 7-year follow-up, remaining stable at 12-year review (Anderson, Leaper, & Judd, 1987; Grimwood et al., 1995, 2000). In contrast, subtle neurodevelopmental anomalies increased with length of follow-up. At discharge, 25% of the children exhibited gross or fine motor impairments, language difficulties, sensory deficits, and/or behavioural problems. This number had

TABLE 7.2
Early and long-term outcome following bacterial meningitis (Melbourne cohort)

	1 year (n = 158)	*7 years* (n = 130)	*12 years* *Survivors* (n = 109)	*Controls* (n = 96)
	n	*n*	*n*	*n*
Major sequelae	24 (15%)	19 (8.5%)	19 (8.5%)	0
Spasticity	5	4	4	0
Blindness	3	3	3	0
Severe/profound deafness	8	7	10	0
Epilepsy/shunt	6	6	6	0
Intellectual impairment (IQ <70)	13	10	11	0
Minor sequelae	64 (40%)	38 (18.5%)	32 (29.5%)	11 (11.5%)
Fine motor problems	22	20	12	4
Mild/moderate deafness	8	7	16	0
Mild intellectual deficit (IQ 70–80)	13	8	9	3
Behaviour problems	27	20	20	3

increased at 12 months post-illness, with 40% of children exhibiting behavioural problems or deficits in fine motor skills, hearing, or language, and difficulties were still evident in 38% of the children 7 years later. The nature and frequency of residual major and minor sequelae for the sample are shown in Table 7.2. This pattern of early resolution of acute-phase neurological problems is in keeping with other research (Feigin, 1987; Pomeroy et al., 1990), but does suggest that subtle neurodevelopmental problems may only become evident over time, when skills fail to develop as expected.

Seven years post-illness, the postmeningitic group obtained significantly lower IQ scores than grade- and gender-matched controls, and these differences remained significant when children with persisting neurological sequelae (*n* = 14) were excluded from the analyses (Grimwood et al., 1995). Furthermore, when cases with acute-phase complications (*n* = 56) and those with uncomplicated episodes of meningitis (*n* = 74) were compared with controls (*n* = 130) on IQ measures, both postmeningitic groups obtained significantly lower scores than controls, although the difference was greater for the complicated group. These group differences have remained stable from 7- to 12-year follow-up (Grimwood et al., in press), and are in contrast to those of Taylor and his associates (1990, 1992, 1993), in that they suggest that disease effects on general intelligence can be demonstrated regardless of acute-phase neurological status, although children with complications will show greater impairments.

Methodological differences may explain the more significant disease sequelae demonstrated in the Melbourne study in comparison to the findings reported by Taylor et al. (1990, 1992, 1993). Although both groups conducted controlled studies involving large samples, followed over time with comprehensive test batteries, subject selection procedures and study designs differed. Taylor and his colleagues (1990) evaluated a subset of children selected from a much larger pool of survivors of *Haemophilus influenzae* type b meningitis and used sibling controls in a retrospective design, whereas Grimwood et al. (1995) recruited survivors of all forms of bacterial meningitis, together with socioeconomic status (SES) matched peer controls, and studied them prospectively from diagnosis. The latter procedure may have yielded a more representative sample and more accurate documentation of disease variables. Furthermore, the peer controls recruited by Grimwood et al. (1995) were more closely matched on age and had not experienced the possible adverse effects of a life-threatening illness within the family.

Language skills

Recent studies have incorporated measures of specific abilities into their test protocols, in addition to evaluating illness-related effects on general intelligence. Language skills have been a particular focus of interest in bacterial meningitis survivors because of the well-documented risk of hearing impairments. Hearing loss is likely to have particular significance for preverbal infants or very young children. Furthermore, language may be particularly vulnerable to disease effects as it is in a rapid and critical phase of development during the first 2 years of life, when the illness is most prevalent.

Empirical findings do suggest that language disorders or delays are more common in meningitis survivors (Anderson et al., 1997; Feldman et al., 1982; Pentland, Anderson, & Wrennal, 2000; Sell et al., 1972; Taylor et al., 1984), even when children with major and minor hearing problems are excluded. Sell (1983) found that 15% of survivors had receptive and/or expressive language delays, whereas Feldman and colleagues (1982) reported language difficulties in an even higher number (27%) of postmeningitic children. In their prospective study, Anderson et al. (1997) found that language-based abilities, including VIQ, comprehension of instructions, verbal fluency, memory for verbal material, and literacy competence were depressed in comparison to controls, although the postmeningitic children still obtained scores within the average range. The results from this study are summarised in Table 7.3. Deficits could not be attributed to hearing impairment, as children with obvious sensory deficits were excluded from the analyses and auditory acuity did not differ across cases and controls. However, the postmeningitic children were poorer at discriminating speech against background noise, suggesting a central auditory processing difficulty that might interfere with language acquisition and the development of reading skills within a noisy classroom environment. Of the deficits exhibited by the postmeningitic children, language difficulties showed the strongest relationship with illness parameters.

TABLE 7.3
Comparison of outcomes for children with bacterial meningitis with acute
complications, no complications, and controls

	Test/measure	Cases with complications (n = 56) M (SE)	Cases without complications (n = 74) M (SE)	Controls (n = 130) M (SE)
General intelligence	Verbal IQ[a]	94.2 (2.4)	99.9 (2.1)	101.6 (1.6)
	Performance IQ	97.4 (2.6)	101.3 (2.4)	105.5 (1.7)
	Full-scale IQ[b]	95.4 (1.9)	101.0 (1.7)	104.3 (1.5)
Language skills	Token Test: total[b,c]	49.2 (1.1)	50.5 (0.9)	51.9 (0.7)
Executive skills	COWAT: total[a,c]	18.0 (1.1)	19.0 (1.0)	21.1 (0.8)
	CFR: copy[a]	21.8 (1.0)	22.9 (0.9)	25.6 (0.8)
Memory and learning	CFR: recall[c]	9.7 (1.0)	10.3 (0.9)	12.6 (0.8)
	RAVLT: total words	37.3 (1.5)	36.2 (1.3)	38.6 (1.0)
	Story recall: total[a,c]	7.3 (0.5)	7.4 (0.5)	8.8 (0.4)
Reading ability	Accuracy (%)[a]	46.0 (4.2)	45.0 (3.7)	55.1 (3.3)
	Comprehension (%)[a]	41.6 (4.0)	48.9 (3.4)	56.9 (3.1)

[a] Significant differences between cases without complications and controls.
[b] Significant differences between cases with and cases without complications.
[c] Significant differences between cases with complications and controls only.
COWAT, Controlled Oral Word Association Test; CFR, Complex Figure of Rey; RAVLT, Rey Auditory–Verbal Learning Test.

Although children contracting bacterial meningitis before the age of 12 months (i.e., in a critical stage for language development) exhibited no greater incidence of acute complications, they did demonstrate significantly poorer linguistic abilities than those having the disease after 12 months of age. Although illness severity was also associated with language outcome, it was a less powerful predictor than younger age at illness.

In a more detailed analysis of the language skills in a subset of children from this cohort, Pentland et al. (2000) found that the meningitic survivors did not differ from population means on a measure of fundamental language skills—the Clinical Evaluation of Language Fundamentals—but performed more poorly on a test of language comprehension and reasoning—the Test of Language Competence—Expanded. The authors interpreted this pattern of results as suggestive of well-established primary language skills, but delayed or deficient acquisition of higher-level language skills, as illustrated in Figure 7.3. In keeping with previous findings, difficulties were particularly evident in children who were aged under 12 months of age at the time of illness and, to a lesser extent, those who had suffered acute-phase complications, suggesting an interaction between the timing and nature of the illness and subsequent sequelae. Pentland et al. (2000) speculated that the failure to develop age-expected higher-level language skills necessary to appreciate humour and

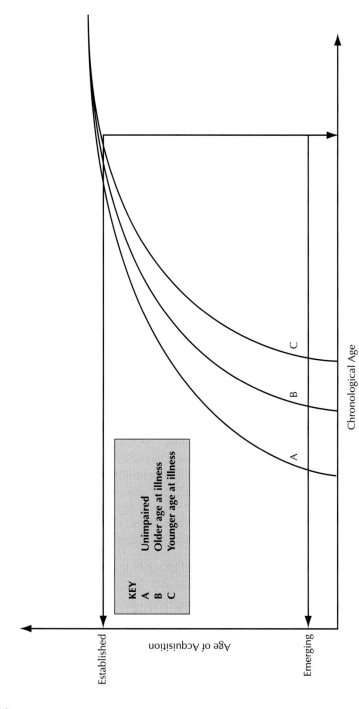

Figure 7.3. Diagrammatic representation of the impact of delayed development on the acquisition of cognitive skills.

infer meaning from complex utterances may contribute to social difficulties and exacerbate behaviour problems in survivors of bacterial meningitis. In contrast to these significant findings, Taylor and colleagues (1990, 1992, 1993) failed to find verbal deficits in their postmeningitic group as a whole, although "complicated" cases obtained lower scores on the verbal subtests of the WISC-R than cases without acute-phase complications or sibling controls.

Memory and learning

Only two groups have included specialised measures of learning and memory in the protocols used to examine neuropsychological sequelae of bacterial meningitis. In their earlier study, Taylor (1984) found that postmeningitic children performed more poorly than controls on a measure of long-term memory—the Verbal Selective Reminding Test—but in their most recent evaluation (Taylor et al., 1990, 1993), memory deficits were limited to non-verbal measures and evident only in those children who had suffered acute-phase complications. Immediate recall of simple information (Digit Span, Block Span) was intact in the cohort studied by Grimwood and colleagues (Anderson et al., 1997; Grimwood et al., 1995, in press). In contrast, the postmeningitic group performed more poorly than controls on complex learning and memory tasks, regardless of presentation modality, with the differences between clinical and control cases increasing from 7 to 12 years post-illness (see Table 7.3). Anderson et al. (1997) interpreted this as evidence for a deficit or a delay in the acquisition of the strategic and organisational skills necessary to perform more complex memory tasks.

Motor skills

Long-term neurological abnormalities such as hemiplegia, ataxia, and cerebral palsy, and visual and sensorineural disturbance have been reported in 3–7% of bacterial meningitis survivors and are likely to compromise performance on gross and fine-motor tasks. When children with obvious neurological sequelae are excluded from study samples, however, postmeningitic children still perform more poorly than controls on tasks dependent upon eye–hand coordination, particularly under timed conditions (Anderson et al., 1997; Taylor et al., 1984; Wald et al., 1986). Furthermore, perceptual deficits have been reported on tasks that place minimal demands upon motor control, suggesting that poor performance on visuomotor integration tasks cannot be explained fully by motor deficits.

Grimwood et al. (in press) suggest that there may be a developmental delay, rather than a persisting deficit, for more subtle motor skills in bacterial meningitis samples. In evidence they cite changing patterns of group differences across time in their cohort. They found significant group differences on neurodevelopmental, speed of processing, and psychomotor measures across their postmeningitic and control samples at 7 years post-illness (mean age of sample = 8.4 years). By 12 years post-illness (mean age of sample = 11.1 years), these group differences were no longer present, with the postmeningitis group improving to age-appropriate levels, suggesting a "catch-up" of these skills from earlier evaluation. If replicated, this finding is of particular interest, and in contrast to findings from other clinical groups with acquired brain insult (e.g., traumatic brain injury, cranial irradiation, epilepsy), where ongoing deterioration, rather than catch-up, occurs.

Executive functions

Executive dysfunction in bacterial meningitis survivors is suggested by the findings of Anderson et al. (1997), who initially identified verbal fluency deficits and a reduced ability to apply organisational strategies on complex learning and memory tasks in their clinical sample (Table 7.3). Later follow-up of these children (Grimwood et al., in press) has further supported these early findings, documenting impairments for the clinical sample on a wide range of measures of executive function. Taylor et al. (1993), found that children with acute-phase complications performed more poorly on measures of abstract reasoning, mental flexibility and working memory. A subsequent factor analysis of their data revealed lower scores on perceptual performance, response speed, and planning–sequencing composites among the "complicated" cases, in comparison to children without acute-phase complications or sibling controls. Furthermore, executive deficits were found to predict poorer learning and adaptive outcome (with a lesser effect on behaviour) even when primary language and perceptual skills were accounted for (Taylor et al., 1996).

Academic skills

Educational progress can be regarded as a measure of functional outcome following early brain disease. Academic deficits, particularly in reading, have been noted in survivors of bacterial meningitis and are not limited to those with known biomedical risk factors (Anderson et al., 1997; Grimwood et al., 1995, in press; Jadavji, Biggar, Gold, & Prober, 1986; Kresky, Buchbinder, & Greenberg, 1962; Sell, 1983; Sproles et al., 1969; Taylor et al., 1990). Both decoding (word recognition) and comprehension were poorer in postmeningitic children in the cohort studied by Anderson et al. (1997), leading them to suggest that literacy problems might reflect more general difficulties acquiring higher-order language skills. In contrast, Taylor and his group (1984, 1990, 1992) found that achievement scores were lower than controls only in those children who had experienced acute-phase complications, although they noted that the academic difficulties evident in their sample were greater than would be predicted on the basis of IQ scores. Taylor et al. (1990) also point out that the postmeningitic children in their studies had received more special educational assistance, both at school and at home, than their unaffected sibling controls, emphasising the importance of considering background environmental factors when interpreting findings.

Illness-related predictors of outcome

The nature of the infective pathogen, duration of symptoms, biochemical imbalances, acute-phase neurological complications, and age at illness have emerged as predictors of neuropsychological outcome following bacterial meningitis, with gender and family background playing a less clearly defined role (Anderson & Taylor, 1999). Acute-phase neurological complications (seizures, hemiparesis, coma, and bilateral hearing impairment) were the strongest predictor of outcome at the cognitive, behavioural, and educational levels in the study by Taylor et al. (1990, 1992, 1993). Furthermore, children with persisting neurological signs did more poorly than those whose signs resolved, although neuropsychological sequelae were still reported in some children with no residual neurosensory deficits at the time of testing (Taylor et al., 1993).

Grimwood et al. (1996) found that adverse outcomes were associated with age <12 months at the time of illness, symptom duration >24 h pre-treatment, seizures developing or persisting after 72 h of treatment, deteriorating conscious state in hospital, focal neurological signs, *streptococcus pneumoniae* as the causative pathogen, CSF leucocyte concentrations <1000 mm^{-1} and serum sodium concentration <130 mmol per litre. The association between symptom duration and adverse outcome remained significant after controlling for all other neurological risk factors. This finding is consistent with previous research suggesting significant links between high antigen (organisms) and low glucose concentrations in CSF at the time of diagnosis or persisting high levels of pathogens in CSF (surrogates for duration of symptoms) and adverse sequelae (Davies & Rudd, 1994; Feigin et al., 1976; Feldman et al., 1982; Lebel et al., 1989; Schaad et al., 1990). In contrast, others (e.g., Kilp et al., 1993; Radetsky, 1992; Wilson & Haltalin, 1975) have not found any association between symptom duration and adverse outcomes.

Differences in length of follow-up and outcome variables may account for these discrepant findings. Alternatively, it is possible that duration of symptoms is confounded by some other factor such as neurological complications or early age of illness. Feldman et al. (1982) point out that children with higher pre-treatment concentrations of bacteria in CSF and, probably, longer duration of symptoms were more likely to have acute-phase neurological complications such as subdural effusions or seizures and suggest that it may be these secondary factors that explain adverse sequelae. Kilp et al. (1993)

development, and may appear to be deficient, and so on. Such an interpretation of current data suggests that a transient impact to the CNS may have an equally transient impact on cognitive development, in direct contrast to findings where permanent, structural damage is present.

ENCEPHALITIS

Aetiology and epidemiology

Encephalitis occurs when the brain is invaded by a virus or another microorganism, resulting in acute inflammation of cerebral tissue with possible associated neuronal damage or death (Toltzis, 1995). A more delayed, postinfectious demyelination of white matter may also occur. Viruses that may cause acute illness include the common childhood infections such as rubella, varicella, Epstein–Barr, and cytomegalovirus, as well as herpes simplex virus, coxsackievirus, arbovirus, and the enteroviruses, with each having characteristic features and consequences (Krugman et al., 1992). The major pathogens associated with encephalitis are listed in Table 7.4.

Viruses may invade the CNS through the bloodstream, the nose, or the peripheral nervous system (Fennell, 1998; Whitley, 1990), and lead to one of four forms of encephalitis: acute viral encephalitis, postinfectious encephalomyelitis, chronic degenerative disease of the CNS, or slow viral CNS infection (Whitley, 1990; Whitley & Lakeman, 1995). Resultant cerebral pathology varies depending on both the type of virus and the form of the illness. Similar to meningitis, inflammatory changes, neuronal death, cerebrovascular pathology, and focal areas of infection are common.

Some pathogens are best known for their impact during gestation. For example, congenital rubella, resulting from maternal infection in the early stages of pregnancy, may result in abnormalities of the heart, eyes, and CNS. Sequelae include sensorineural deafness, congenital cataracts, spasticity and developmental delay (Shrier, Schopps, & Feigin, 1996; Weil & Levin, 1995).

TABLE 7.4
Common pathogens in childhood encephalitis

Pathogens	Percentage of cases
Measles, mumps, rubella	30.4
Herpes viruses	24.1
Respiratory viruses	18.3
Microplasmal pneumonia	13.1
Enteroviruses	9.7
Postvaccination encephalitis	1.0
Other	34.9

Adapted from Weil and Levin (1995).

Congenital forms of herpes simplex virus can result in microcephaly and cerebral calcifications (Whitley, 1990). Postnatally, the measles virus is associated with a progressive, and usually fatal, form of the disease: subacute sclerosing panencepalitis (Nester, 1996). Herpes simplex virus type 1 encephalitis involves focal inflammation, selectively affecting the temporal–limbic structures and, in severe cases, the posterior areas of the prefrontal cortex. Rasmussen's encephalitis, a chronic form of encephalitis, causes intractable epilepsy with progressive neurological degeneration, usually involving one hemisphere, at least initially (Honavar, Janota, & Polkey, 1992; McLachlan, Girvin, Blume, & Reichman, 1993; Rasmussen, 1978). Onset typically occurs in childhood although cases with similar clinical features have been reported in adults (McLachlan et al., 1993).

Early symptoms of encephalitis are often non-specific and may include fever, headache, vomiting, and lethargy, progressing to behavioural changes, motor, sensory, and speech disturbances and altered conscious state (Rantala et al., 1991). Electroencephologram (EEG) changes commonly include generalised slowing, although in some cases there may be spiking, usually confined to temporal regions. Computed tomography (CT) and magnetic resonance imaging (MRI) typically show symptoms of cerebral oedema and the related inflammatory process (Fennell, 1998). Coma and seizures may occur and death may result as a function of brain stem involvement (Sartori et al., 1993).

Some forms of encephalitis, such as herpes simplex virus type 1 encephalitis, can be treated with the antiviral drug acyclovir, and hemispherectomy appears to stop progressive neurological deterioration in Rasmussen's encephalitis. In other forms of encephalitis, careful management of clinical symptoms (e.g., seizure control, monitoring of intracranial pressure) remains the only treatment. Diagnosis is difficult, and in many children, although the disease is "suspected" it is not clearly established, even after careful investigation.

Toltzis (1995) cites a mortality rate of 5% for most forms of encephalitis, with around one-third of patients exhibiting neurological sequelae (paresis, ataxia, seizures) or cognitive impairment at the time of discharge. Herpes simplex virus type 1 encephalitis is one of the most common forms, accounting for 5–10% of the 20,000 cases of encephalitis per year in the USA (Gordon et al., 1990) and is also associated with the poorest outcome. Early treatment with acyclovir has reduced mortality from herpes simplex virus type 1 encephalitis from 70% to 20%, but significant morbidity remains, with full recovery occurring in only 13–14% of patients (Fennell, 1998; McKendall, 1989). At follow-up 2 years after an episode of mumps encephalitis, Koskiniemi, Donner, and Pettay (1983) reported neurological sequelae in one-quarter of their sample but only one death, whereas almost a third of children in another study had some neurological abnormality at follow-up

(Rantala et al., 1991). Varicella was the most common causal agent in the series studied by Rantala et al. (1991), but the aetiology was unknown in almost half the sample.

Pathophysiology

CNS changes have been documented most comprehensively in patients with herpes simplex virus type 1 encephalitis. Acutely, herpes simplex virus type 1 encephalitis causes necrosis, cerebral oedema, and haemorrhage, particularly involving the mesiotemporal areas, and extending, in severe cases, into the orbitofrontal regions of the brain (Sartori et al., 1993; Sellal et al., 1996; Yoneda, Mori, Yamashita, & Yamadori, 1994). Bilateral involvement is usual but in cases of unilateral, disease left-sided lesions may be more common (Barbarotto, Capitani, & Laiacona, 1996; Laurent et al., 1991; Yoneda et al., 1994). Kapur et al. (1994) used MRI to document anatomical changes in herpes simplex virus type 1 encephalitis survivors and found damage to hippocampal and adjacent medial temporal lobe structures, bilateral pathology in anterior and inferior temporal lobe gyri and, less consistently, damage to the mamillary bodies and fornix. CNS changes in paraneoplastic encephalitis involve more focal damage, restricted to the hippocampus and immediately adjacent structures, such as the parahippocampal gyrus and the amygdala (Kapur et al., 1994). Ataxia, dysarthria and impaired conscious state were common in the series studied by Koskiniemi et al. (1983), leading them to speculate that mumps encephalitis selectively involves the cerebellar, pontine and mesencephalic structures. Microglial nodules, astrocytosis, and neuronal degeneration in the affected hemisphere are regarded as the definitive features of Rasmussen's encephalopathy (McLachlan et al., 1993; Vining et al., 1993).

Neuropsychological findings

Herpes simplex virus type 1 encephalitis offers an important opportunity to study brain–behaviour relationships because of the relatively specific brain regions affected. It is surprising, then, that to date neuropsychological follow-up has been limited to single-case or small group studies of largely adult survivors. In these reports, sequelae range from severe dementia to mild impairments of memory and speech in the context of relatively preserved general cognitive capacities (Counsell, Taylor, & Whittle, 1994; Hokkanen et al., 1996; Kapur et al., 1994; Martin, Haut, Goeta-Kreisler, & Blumenthal, 1996; McCarthy, Evans, & Hodges, 1996; Pietrini et al., 1988; Varney, Campbell, & Roberts, 1994). Gordon et al. (1990) describe neuropsychological outcome in a small group of patients with herpes simplex virus type 1 encephalitis who were treated aggressively and prior to the loss of consciousness. Patients with left hemisphere involvement had significant dysnomia, reduced VIQ, and severely impaired verbal memory and new learning, whereas the patient with right-sided changes had deficits in PIQ, visual memory, and learning, together with alterations in mood. These findings suggest that there is significant morbidity associated with herpes simplex virus type 1 encephalitis even after early, aggressive treatment. The patients studied by Kapur et al. (1994) were also described as having received prompt and appropriate treatment and to have made good recoveries from moderately severe episodes of herpes simplex virus type 1 encephalitis. WAIS PIQ was normal and, with the exception of Information, verbal subtest scores were generally within average limits, suggesting relative sparing of general intellectual ability. More than half of the sample, though, exhibited a dense amnesia (delayed Memory Quotient <50 on the Wechsler Memory Scale—Revised) with the remainder experiencing less pervasive disruption of memory processes. MRI documented damage to the mesial limbic structures, particularly hippocampal damage, which correlated with the severity of memory impairment. These researchers (Kapur et al., 1994) concluded that by far the most disabling deficit following herpes simplex virus type 1 encephalitis was amnesia and noted that only 2 of the 10 subjects studied had been able to return to open employment.

A number of other reports describe amnesic syndromes following herpes simplex virus type 1 encephalitis (Barbarotto et al., 1996; Cermak & O'Connor, 1983; Damasio, Tranel, & Damasio., 1989; Laiacona, Capitani, & Barbarotto, 1993; McCarthy et al., 1996; Sartori et al., 1993; Wilson, Baddeley, & Kapur, 1995). Hokkanen et al. (1996) found that herpes simplex virus type 1 encephalitis survivors obtained IQ scores that did not differ from those of a group of patients with non-herpetic forms of encephalitis, but they were significantly more impaired on tests of memory and verbal semantic functions. Survivors typically presented with a pattern of relatively intact immediate recall, rapid forgetting, an inability to learn new information, and a variable degree of retrograde amnesia. Thus, encoding and consolidation in long-term memory appear more affected than initial acquisition of new information, although this may not be normal either. Deficits in episodic memory (recall of specific events) were often severe and pervasive, causing chronic disruption of daily living activities and preventing patients from resuming previous work commitments. As lateral temporal and basal forebrain structures become involved in the disease process, more extensive problems with semantic memory become evident (Damasio et al., 1989). When present, semantic deficits (recall of concepts) are often category specific, with research demonstrating selective impairment of the capacity to categorise living things in the context of relative sparing of the ability to process non-living things (Barbarotto et al., 1996; Laiacona et al., 1993; Sartori et al., 1993; Warrington & Shallice, 1984).

The paucity of empirical data documenting neuropsychological sequelae of encephalitis in children is puzzling, particularly as it is not a rare condition. Memory and learning deficits, in particular, are likely to have a relatively greater impact on children, as their previously acquired stores of overlearned memories will be more restricted and the demands for acquisition of new knowledge correspondingly greater. It is also possible that there may be more generalised disruption of cognitive development, affecting a greater range of specific skills, following childhood encephalitis, in line with current evidence that very early brain damage often results in more severe and more pervasive deficits than a similar insult in an adult brain (Anderson & Moore, 1995; Taylor & Alden, 1997).

The limited empirical evidence to date suggests that postencephalitic children generally function within the average range, but obtain lower scores than controls, on tests of general intelligence (Rantala et al., 1991; Sells, Carpenter, & Ray, 1975). Outcome is poorer in Rasmussen's encephalitis, with most sufferers exhibiting progressive deterioration leading to mild to moderate intellectual impairment (Honavar et al., 1992; Vargha–Khadem et al., 1991; Vining et al., 1993). Improved IQ scores post-hemispherectomy were reported by Vining et al. (1993) but not by others (Caplan, Curtis, Chugani, & Vinters, 1996; Honavar et al., 1992). Language skills were globally affected in the series studied by Sells et al. (1975) but this may reflect the specific skills sampled by the investigators, rather than a specific illness effect, as Rantala et al. (1991) did not find depressed VIQ in their study. Caplan et al. (1996) identified specific deficits in social communication (illogical thinking, loose associations) in children with Rasmussen's encephalitis, which were partly ameliorated following hemispherectomy.

A clinical audit of children with a diagnosis of encephalitis seen in our inpatient and outpatient clinics in recent years suggests a wide range of outcomes, with some evidence that more severe illness is associated with poorer outcome. In keeping with available literature, language impairment and memory deficits were demonstrated in this group, ranging from severe aphasias and amnesias to milder anomias and memory disturbance. Behavioural changes were also observed, with anxiety disorders being the most common presentation. Interestingly, one child had been seen in our clinic 12 months prior to the onset of encephalitis for evaluation of learning difficulties. He suffered a relatively severe episode of encephalitis and was assessed 1 month following diagnosis. Results showed that he was performing at premorbid levels in all areas including language and memory, providing no evidence for a deterioration in function associated with his illness.

Illness-related predictors of outcome

Younger age at illness, greater neurological compromise during the acute illness phase, and the herpes simplex virus as the causative pathogen have been associated with poorer outcome (Earnest et al., 1971; Hokkanen et al., 1996; Kennedy, Duffy, Smith, & Robinson, 1987; Sells et al., 1975; Toltzis, 1995). Unilateral disease may be associated with a more favourable outcome (Laurent et al., 1991; Yoneda et al., 1994). Sartori et al. (1993) concluded that bilaterality of damage was a more critical determinant of severity of amnesia than total amount of damage. Early onset and a prolonged uncontrolled seizure disorder are predictors of poor outcome in Rasmussen's encephalitis, whereas early hemispherectomy and improved seizure control are associated with a more favourable outcome (Caplan et al., 1996; Vining et al.,1993).

Psychosocial issues

Behavioural changes similar to those described in the classical Klüver–Bucy syndrome are also noted following encephalitis, consistent with disruption of the corticolimbic pathways responsible for emotional regulation (Gordon et al., 1990; Koskiniemi et al., 1983; Sellal et al., 1996). Behavioural sequelae have been more strongly associated with right-sided disease and include increased lability of mood, episodic rage, and depression (Gordon et al., 1990; Hokkanen et al., 1996). When damage extends to the prefrontal cortex, impulsivity, apathy, rigidity, and deficits in self-awareness and judgement are also apparent, which, when combined with memory deficits, have profound implications for daily functioning, work, and interpersonal relationships (Sellal et al., 1996).

Case study

The following case study illustrates some of the typical acute clinical features of childhood encephalitis, where a child may be confused and disoriented, representing generalised cerebral disruption. The opportunity for longer-term follow-up provides a useful comparison, demonstrating the resolution of some difficulties but residual impairments in other areas.

Andrew was admitted to hospital in July 1996, following a tonic–clonic seizure in the context of a 2-week history of headache, sporadic fevers, and symptoms of upper respiratory tract infection. CT scan of the brain was initially normal, but a repeat investigation 5 days later revealed cerebral oedema particularly involving the left temporal region. A lesion in the left globus pallidus and enhancement of the basal meninges was documented on MRI, leading to a diagnosis of meningoencephalitis, although the serology of the infection was never clarified. Andrew's MRI results are illustrated in

Figure 7.4. During a 5-week hospitalisation, Andrew's conscious state fluctuated and he developed a right hemiparesis. At discharge he exhibited signs of increased irritability and lethargy, lowered frustration tolerance, poor speech, impaired judgement and deficient behavioural regulation. His parents report that, premorbidly, Andrew had been an average student, an active sportsman, and a well-adjusted boy who made friends easily.

A brief neuropsychological assessment was attempted 1 week post-discharge. Although it was not difficult to elicit spontaneous conversation, Andrew exhibited very limited capacity to monitor his output for logic and

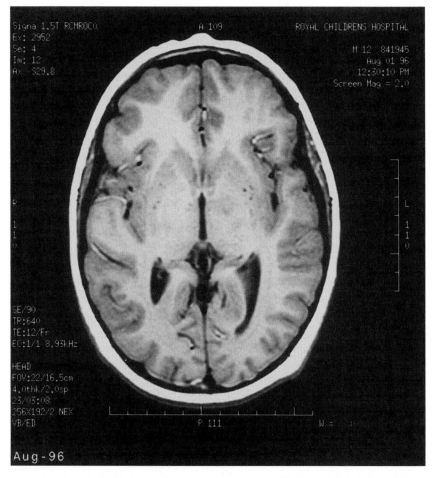

Figure 7.4. Andrew's MRI scan illustrating a meningeal inflammatory process, particularly along the midline and more prominent in the left hemisphere, specifically in the left globus pallidus and hypothalamus and the top of the fourth ventricle.

relevance. When asked to perform specific tasks or respond to actual questions, he became restless and agitated, protesting loudly that he "didn't know" although he would sometimes spontaneously produce the correct answer some minutes later. A very limited assessment of memory was attempted. Andrew performed within normal limits on Digit Span and sentence repetition tasks but had difficulty retaining more than a few isolated facts from a short prose passage. Minutes later, he was unable to retrieve any of the story at all; in fact he could not recall that he had listened to a story. This performance was consistent with his mother's report that he could repeat a brief instruction immediately after it had been given but seemed to forget what he had been asked to do before he had time to do it. Episodic memory deficits were suggested by his inability to recall the outcome of a football match the previous day (which his favourite team had won) or even that he had attended the game.

Neuropsychological reviews were conducted 6 and 18 months post-illness. On the first of these occasions, his parents reported that the extreme agitation and restlessness that Andrew had exhibited in the early stages of recovery had settled, but that he remained emotionally fragile and quick to anger. They also reported that he seemed unable to structure and organise his own activities and were very concerned about his insatiable appetite and associated weight gain, commenting that he appeared to eat and drink when he was bored but also "seemed to forget that he had already eaten". A gradual return to school had been achieved, with integration support, but there were serious concerns about his behaviour and he was doing little work. There was also great anxiety about the transition to secondary school, particularly in view of the imminent withdrawal of his integration support following a letter from his paediatrician stating that "he appears to have made an almost complete recovery".

Six months post-illness, Andrew presented as a friendly, very talkative boy, although much of his spontaneous conversation was tangential and marked by abrupt topic changes. He was generally willing to attempt tasks and showed some limited capacity to tolerate frustration, although there were still times when he became irritable and oppositional. Andrew's test scores at this assessment and a subsequent evaluation 18 months post-illness are presented in Table 7.5. On the first occasion, visual processing skills were within the average range, with weaker performance on measures of language, memory, learning, and executive skills. Qualitatively, Andrew exhibited reduced attentional control (particularly on linguistic tasks), impulsivity, poor self-monitoring of his performance, and a limited capacity to self-regulate his behaviour. Although in fact requiring more time to accurately process and output information, he was inclined to respond impulsively and rush his responses, thus sacrificing accuracy for speed.

At his most recent review, Andrew's ability to maintain a shared topic of

TABLE 7.5

Neuropsychological data for Andrew at 6 months and 18 months postencephalitis

	Test/measure	Test 1 (12 years)	Test 2 (13 years)
General intelligence	VIQ	70	82
(WPPSI-R/WISC-III)	PIQ	94	–
	Information	6	–
	Similarities	1	5
	Arithmetic	7	9
	Vocabulary	4	7
	Comprehension	5	5
	Digit Span	9	9
	Picture Completion	–	–
	Coding	6	5
	Picture Arrangement	9	11
	Block Design	7	8
	Object Assembly	14	–
Memory/attention	RAVLT (T1–T5)	5,5,6,8,5	2,5,3,5,8
	Total (stanine)	1	1
	Recognition (correct)	8	7
	WRAML: Vis. Learn. (ss)	–	2
	Stories (ss)	9	–
	Stories: delayed (ss)	1	–
	Design Memory (ss)	Refused	3
	CFR: recall (stanine)	Refused	1
Executive function	COWAT (stanine)	Unable to follow rules	1

conversation had improved although he still had difficulty extending or developing ideas in a linguistic form and in organising and articulating a lengthy response. His capacity to focus and sustain attention was very dependent upon high levels of external structure and close supervision, particularly when tasks required verbal processing. Receptive and expressive vocabulary were now within average limits but higher-order verbal fluency and conceptual and practical reasoning skills remained quite depressed. This pattern suggests some resolution of the semantic memory deficits observed in the immediate post-illness phase. However, Andrew's ability to utilise previously overlearned word knowledge in novel, dynamic, and conceptually demanding situations remained compromised. Memory and learning skills were very depressed. Although Andrew seemed able to register a small amount of information in immediate memory, he was unable to "hold" this long enough to "work" with it or to consolidate it in long-term memory. This problem is well illustrated in his attempt to recall the Complex Figure of Rey following a 5-minute delay, as shown in Figure 7.5. Thus Andrew

COPY

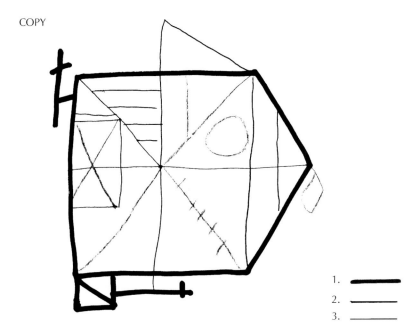

1. ▬▬▬
2. ───
3. ───

RECALL

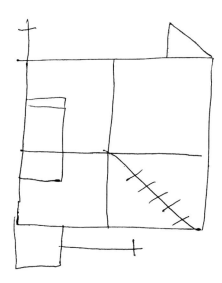

Figure 7.5. Andrew's performance on the Rey Complex Figure. Copy demonstrates intact accuracy, but impoverished recall is consistent with a pattern of significant memory impairment. (1., 2., 3. = order of copy.)

247

demonstrates the classic pattern of "rapid forgetting" that is consistently described as a core feature of a postencephalitic presentation.

Behavioural issues were also of concern to Andrew's parents. They felt that his ability to modulate his emotional responses, regulate his behaviour, and organise his leisure activities was still compromised. Socially, he had become isolated as he was reluctant to participate in activities outside the home or to interact with others with the exception of extended family members, predominantly his much younger cousins. Sleep disturbance and poor appetite control were still evident, suggestive of some disease-related disruption of the hypothalamus, although it is possible that a reactive depression may also be contributing.

Over time, Andrew's initial confusion and inattention have diminished, leaving a picture of impairments in memory and higher-order skills, which in turn impact on his daily life, and are especially evident in academic and social areas. As he moves through school, he is likely to require ongoing support and supervision, as well as a modified curriculum that takes into account significant memory problems, and the need for support in planning and problem-solving activities. Optimally, Andrew's ongoing recovery/ development should be monitored through adolescence to provide information and support to his family and those who are working with him in educational and vocational areas.

CONCLUSIONS

Bacterial meningitis and encephalitis commonly occur in the very young child, when the immature CNS may cause the child to be particularly vulnerable to insult and much development is still to occur. Disease effects have been documented on measures of general intelligence as well as for specific skill areas, such as language, perception, memory, information processing, and executive function. Developmental influences interact with organic factors to determine outcomes. Following cerebral infection, adverse neuropsychological sequelae are most evident in, but not limited to, those children who develop the illness prior to 12 months of age, experience a prolonged illness, and/or suffer acute-phase complications. Gender and socioeconomic factors appear to play a minimal role in disease outcomes. Long-term follow-up is essential for accurate determination of neuropsychological sequelae as deficits may not become fully apparent until skills fail to develop at the expected time.

CHAPTER EIGHT

Endocrine and metabolic disorders

INTRODUCTION

A number of endocrine and metabolic disorders impact on central nervous system (CNS) function. For example, the thyroid plays a critical role in growth and development and a deficiency of thyroid hormone in early life has a profound effect on many organ systems, including the developing brain (Werther, 1994). Inborn errors of metabolism such as phenylketonuria, glycogen storage disease, and galactasaemia result from autosomal, recessive enzyme defects (Thompson, 1994). When an enzyme is defective, the substrate normally metabolised by that enzyme may accumulate to levels that are toxic to the brain and other organ systems. Insulin-dependent diabetes mellitus is a disorder of glucose metabolism. Glucose is the major energy source for the brain and adequate supplies are essential for normal neuronal activity.

With advances in medical knowledge, many metabolic and endocrine disorders can now be treated effectively, and there are growing numbers of children suffering from such disorders who are coming to the attention of professionals. Early diagnosis and treatment adherence have become important goals, to minimise any unnecessary cognitive sequelae resulting from the effects of metabolic/endocrine imbalances. Not surprisingly, psychosocial problems commonly occur in these children, associated with adjustments typical of chronic illness in childhood, for example, difficulties maintaining medication/treatment regimes, missed schooling associated with periods of illness, child/parent interdependencies, and issues of feeling different to peers.

hydroxylase is transaminated to phenylpyruvic acid or phenylethylamine, and together these substances flood the CNS, interfering with neuronal function (Gillberg & Hagberg, 1998). Accumulation of Phe is particularly toxic to a developing brain and untreated, classical phenylketonuria is associated with reduced brain size and weight compared to normal developmental expectations. Abnormalities in myelination are also commonly described (Bauman & Kemper, 1982). At a functional level, mental retardation, seizures, and behavioural disturbance are features of untreated phenylketonuria (Brunner, Berch, & Berry, 1987), and a majority of affected children have pale complexions, blue eyes, and blond hair. They also have a characteristic musty odour, especially evident in their urine (Gillberg & Hagberg, 1998). The genetic basis for phenylketonuria has been investigated, and although not fully understood, it has been found that the gene for Phe maps on to chromosome 12q24.1 (Lidsky et al., 1985).

As for congenital hypothyroidism, the introduction of routine neonatal screening and early treatment of classical phenylketonuria with a Phe- and protein-restricted diet is associated with a much more positive outcome, even though treated individuals often have Phe levels well above normal (1–3 mg dl^{-1}), at times exceeding 30 mg dl^{-1} (Fishler, Azen, Friedman, & Koch, 1989). Screening is performed using the Guthrie test between 4 and 6 days after birth. Earlier testing may fail to detect the disease, as children will still be protected, to some degree, by maternal metabolism. The diet is instituted immediately upon diagnosis; however, the required duration of the protein-restricted diet is not universally agreed (Levy & Waisbren, 1994). Whereas some centres maintain children on diet into adulthood, others allow them to resume a normal diet around age 8, with the rationale being that the CNS is relatively mature, and less vulnerable to the effects of the disease by middle childhood. The beneficial effect of diet on late-treated children is much less evident. CNS damage already present cannot be reversed, although some studies have shown that adhering to the diet limits further deterioration (Lowe et al., 1980). Women with phenylketonuria are required to recommence diet prior to pregnancy, with failure to do so linked to microcephaly and mental retardation. Similar paternal effects have not been documented (Gillberg & Hagberg, 1998).

Pathophysiology

Classical phenylketonuria is associated with biochemical, structural, and electrophysiological changes within the CNS. High Phe levels inhibit neuronal uptake and metabolism of tyrosine and tryptophan, the amino acid precursors of dopamine, noradrenaline, and serotonin (Krause et al., 1985; Lou, 1994; McKean, 1972; Welsh, 1996). Magnetic resonance imaging (MRI) studies in phenylketonuria patients have demonstrated pathological changes in the periventricular cerebral white matter (Bick et al., 1993; Cleary, Walter, Wraith, & Jenkins 1995; Fishler et al., 1989; Pearson, Gean-Marton, Levy, & Davis, 1990; Thompson et al., 1990; Ullrich et al., 1994), similar to those observed in other metabolic disorders (Koopmans et al., 1989). Changes are most pronounced in the parieto-occipital region, with extension into frontal regions in severely affected patients (Bick et al., 1993).

The underlying mechanism of these documented white matter changes is still unclear. Initially it was thought that they represented permanent cerebral pathology. However, recent MRI studies have documented at least partial regression of these abnormalities in small groups of adults with phenylketonuria following substantive improvements in dietary control (Bick et al., 1993; Cleary et al., 1995). These findings suggest that altered metabolism within subcortical areas may underlie some of the observed changes, which then normalises as Phe levels reduce. Increased water content in myelin has been suggested as a possible explanation for these unexpected, short-term changes in white matter appearance (Cleary et al., 1995). The fact that abnormalities are more highly correlated with concurrent or recent Phe levels than with time of treatment inception or lifetime dietary control is further support that some changes may be transient. Bick et al. (1993) argue, though, that permanent demyelination may also occur, if the metabolic disturbance occurs during a vulnerable period during early brain development.

The functional significance of observed changes in cerebral structures is still unclear although a study presently underway in our laboratory is addressing possible relationships between white matter pathology and neurobehavioural function in a group of 40 children and adolescents with phenylketonuria. The study aims to correlate MRI results with dietary adherence data and neuropsychological performance to establish any links between these parameters. To date, findings indicate that a surprisingly large number of children, almost half, have evidence of white matter pathology on MRI. Preliminary data analyses, detailed in Table 8.1, suggest that these white matter abnormalities are associated with lower cognitive and information-processing skills, with specific deficits in verbal skills, auditory selective attention, verbal memory, and arithmetic noted in children with abnormal findings.

Figures 8.2 and 8.3 provide examples of MRI results and Phe levels from birth for two children participating in our study. Child A, Peter, aged 8, exhibits marked periventricular white matter abnormalities, most marked in inferior parietal and superior temporal regions, and less pronounced in frontal regions. The adjacent Phe chart shows regular periods of significantly increased Phe levels (that is, >400 μmol L^{-1}) throughout early childhood, particularly during the first 3 years of life, suggesting that metabolic state was often abnormal throughout this period. In keeping with these observations,

TABLE 8.1
Intellectual abilities of children with early treated phenylketonuria

	Normal MRI scan (n = 16)	White matter abnormalities (n = 26)
Verbal IQ M (SD)*	96.8 (7.8)	90.7 (9.5)
Performance IQ M (SD)	98.8 (12.8)	92.4 (9.6)
Full-scale IQ M (SD)*	97.4 (10.2)	90.9 (7.4)

*$p < .5$.

Peter's neuropsychological assessment reveals depressed intellectual ability, slowed processing speed, and poor attentional skills.

Child B, Andrew, aged 13 years, has a more normal MRI, with age-appropriate myelination, and generally normal cerebral structure. Some very mild white matter loss was identified in the parietal regions bilaterally. Andrew's Phe chart suggests better control, with periods of mildly increased Phe levels during the first year of life, and good control through the preschool period. Despite Andrew's consistently unacceptable high Phe levels from age 5 years, currently he is performing within the average range on neuropsychological testing. Such trends are common in the data set to date, and provide initial support for a relationship between dietary control and structural and functional impairment in phenylketonuria. Whether there is a critical period in which poor dietary control has a greater effect is not yet clear. Similarly, any detrimental effect of high Phe levels in the supposedly safe period after cessation of diet is still to be determined.

Other approaches to the investigation of cerebral function in phenylketonuria samples have employed eletroencephalography. Such studies report that electroencephalogram (EEG) changes are almost universal in patients with untreated phenylketonuria (Pietz et al., 1993) and the frequency of abnormalities remains high even in early treated phenylketonuria (Gross, Berlow, Schuett, & Fariello, 1981; Korinthenberg, Ullrich, & Fullenkemper, 1988; Pietz et al., 1988). Age-related changes in the nature of the abnormalities, for example, hypsarrhythmia during infancy, irregular, generalised slow waves and spikes during childhood, and general slowing, but less overt epileptiform activity, in older patients have been described (Lutcke, 1971), similar to the pattern observed in other conditions involving inborn errors of metabolism. Pietz et al. (1988) found that EEGs became increasingly abnormal until 10–11 years of age (44% of all patients), then abnormalities reduced, despite a continued rise in Phe levels. An increased incidence of EEG anomalies in children following diet cessation has also been reported by some (Cabalaska et al., 1977; Seashore, Friedman, Novelly, & Bapat, 1985), but others have found no correlation with age of treatment inception or quality of dietary control (Gross et al., 1981; Korinthenberg et al., 1988; Pietz et al., 1988).

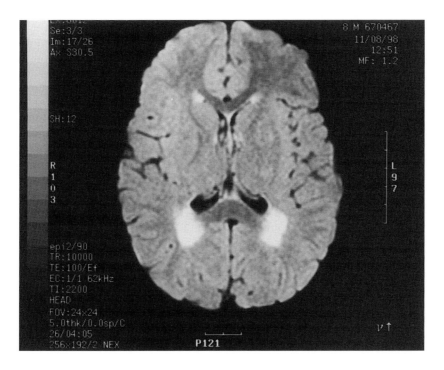

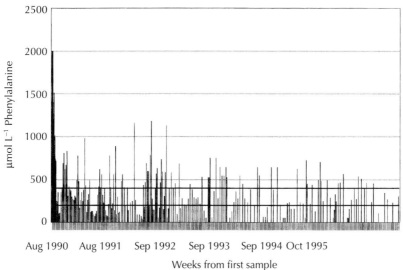

Aug 1990   Aug 1991   Sep 1992   Sep 1993   Sep 1994 Oct 1995

Weeks from first sample

Figure 8.2. (Top) Child A, aged 8 years, exhibits marked periventricular white matter abnormality, most marked in inferior parietal and superior temporal regions, and less pronounced in frontal regions. (Bottom) The Phe chart shows regular periods of significantly increased Phe levels throughout early childhood, particularly during the first 3 years of life, suggesting that metabolic factors may have been acting throughout this period.

259

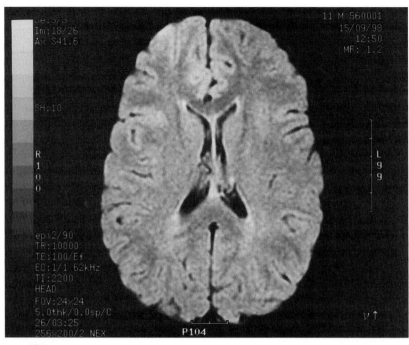

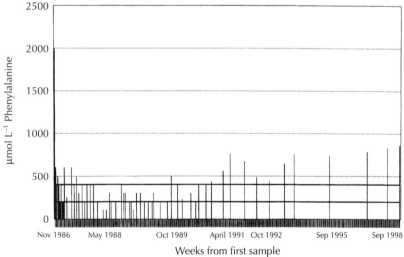

Figure 8.3. (Top) Child B, aged 12 years, has a more normal MRI, which shows age-appropriate myelination, and generally normal cerebral structure. There is some very mild white matter loss in the parietal regions bilaterally. (Bottom) The Phe chart suggests better control in "high-risk" periods, with some mildly increased Phe levels during the first year of life, and good control through the remainder of the preschool period. Consistently high Phe levels from age 5 years are associated with cessation of diet.

Neuropsychological findings

Children with early treated phenylketonuria generally function within the average range on measures of general intelligence, although most studies report small, but statistically significant, differences in intellectual quotients compared to unaffected siblings or unrelated controls (Azen et al., 1996; Brunner, Jordan, & Berry, 1983; Burgard et al., 1996; Holtzman et al., 1986; Koch, Azen, Friedman, & Williamson, 1984; Ris et al., 1994; Waisbren, Brown, de Sonneville, & Levy, 1994; Waisbren, Mahon, Schnell, & Levy, 1987; Williamson, Koch, Azen, & Chang, 1981). Despite normal intelligence, subtle perceptual and cognitive deficits are still evident. Research to date suggests that the skills most likely to be affected include selective and sustained attention (Ris et al., 1994; Ullrich et al., 1994; Welsh et al., 1990), and visuomotor integration, visual perception, complex problem solving, and conceptual reasoning (Brunner et al., 1983; Diamond, 1994; Faust, Libon, & Pueschel, 1986; Fishler et al., 1989; Griffiths, Paterson, & Harvie, 1995; Krause et al., 1985; Lou et al., 1985; Pennington, van Doornink, McCabe, & McCabe, 1985; Ris et al., 1994; Seashore et al., 1985; Welsh et al., 1990). Deficits cannot be explained on the basis of depressed intellectual skills (Clarke et al., 1987; Pennington et al., 1985; Welsh et al., 1990). Language and memory skills appear less affected. It should be noted, though, that these skills have been less rigorously evaluated in children with phenylketonuria. An increased prevalence of learning difficulties, particularly affecting mathematical skills, has been reported in children with early treated phenylketonuria (Berry, O'Grady, Perlmutter, & Bofinger, 1979; Brunner et al., 1983; Faust et al., 1986; Fishler et al., 1989).

Cognitive impairments in phenylketonuria are thought to result from altered availability of neurotransmitters, particularly dopamine, together with the effects of disrupted myelination at critical periods during early brain development. Brunner et al. (1987) noted that IQ best discriminated phenylketonuria children from their sibling controls, consistent with a mild generalised cerebral insult rather than a specific localised lesion. Others (Diamond, 1994; Diamond & Herzberg, 1996; Gourovitch et al., 1994; Pennington et al., 1985; Weglage et al., 1996; Welsh et al., 1990) conceptualise phenylketonuria as a disorder of dopamine depletion with a selective impact on brain function. They note the high dopamine turnover in the prefrontal cortex, and the tertiary association areas with strong connections to anterior regions of the brain, and argue that dopamine depletion associated with phenylketonuria is likely to have its greatest impact on these cortical regions. Furthermore, they claim that it is these areas of the brain which myelinate after birth, with maturation occurring well into adolescence, and hence they are likely to be more vulnerable to high Phe levels during childhood than are the thalamic and midbrain structures, which substantially develop prenatally while protected by maternal regulation of Phe. As a result, complex cognitive processes mediated by the prefrontal cortex and the tertiary association areas, such as executive functions and higher-order integrative skills, are argued to be depressed in phenylketonuria. Available MRI data is not consistent with such explanations, implicating cerebral white matter specifically, and noting that normalisation of cerebral white matter following improved dietary adherence may lead to functional improvements (Bick et al., 1993: Cleary et al., 1995; Fishler et al., 1989; Pearson et al., 1990; Thompson et al., 1990; Ullrich et al., 1994).

Although current neurodevelopmental research supports postnatal myelination of frontal regions, it also suggests ongoing myelination of other cerebral regions into early childhood. Thus an explanation incorporating abnormal myelination must imply more global cerebral and behavioural problems, including generalised processing and attentional difficulties, in addition to the specific features of prefrontal involvement. Research refining these competing explanations is yet to be conducted. Empirical findings to date fail to support one position over another, with test results not sufficiently specific to directly implicate prefrontal function as opposed to more generalised patterns of impairment. However, deficits in selective attention and visual search (Craft et al., 1992), higher-order reasoning (Brunner et al., 1983; Diamond, 1994; Faust et al., 1986), attentional control (Brunner et al., 1987; Weglage et al., 1996; Welsh et al., 1990), as well as "reduced channel capacity" or working memory (Diamond, 1994; Faust et al., 1986), and slowed choice reaction times (Clarke et al., 1987; Krause et al., 1985), have been described, suggesting possible compromise of a wide range of areas and functional systems within the brain.

Gourovitch et al. (1994) found that children with early treated phenylketonuria demonstrated slowed left to right interhemispheric transfer compared to normal controls and children with attention deficit hyperactivity disorder, consistent with delayed or deficient myelination. Welsh et al. (1990) tested the hypothesis that phenylketonuria is associated with deficits in executive functions, secondary to dopamine depletion in the prefrontal cortex, and found that their sample of preschool-aged children was impaired, relative to controls, on a composite "executive functions" measure, but not on a "nonexecutive" control test of visual recognition memory. In contrast, Mazzocco et al. (1994) examined executive functions in older school-aged children with phenylketonuria, some of whom had previously participated in the study by Welsh et al. (1990), and found no significant differences with intelligence-matched controls on executive tests, although the phenylketonuria children performed more poorly on a test of visual perception and visuomotor integration skills. They argued that these discrepant findings support a developmental delay in myelination, rather than a permanent deficit. Animal models of phenylketonuria (e.g., Reynolds, Burri, Mahal, & Herschkowitz, 1992), showing deficient myelination early in life which then normalises, provide some support for this interpretation.

Qualitative features of phenylketonuria children's performance also fit with compromise to the prefrontal and tertiary association regions of the brain. Tendencies to perseveration and higher-order deficits in goal directed-ness, maintenance of mental set and motor planning (Welsh et al., 1990), reduced mental flexibility and self-regulation (Griffiths et al., 1995) and poor strategy use and an inability to integrate information (Brunner et al., 1987) have been described. Diamond (1994) found that young children with early treated phenylketonuria followed longitudinally were indeed compromised, relative to controls, in their performance on tasks requiring inhibitory control and planning abilities, but not on "control" tasks assumed to be mediated by parietal or medial temporal cortex. However, little attention has been paid to other likely confounding abilities such as processing speed and attention. Future studies, fractionating executive aspects of task performance (e.g., strategy formation, organisational ability, mental flexibility) from lower-order task requirements (e.g., perception, information acquisition) may help to clarify the specific nature of deficits exhibited within phenylketonuria populations.

Illness-related predictors of outcome

Phe level at diagnosis and at the time of testing, age at treatment inception, long-term dietary control, and age at diet cessation may all be important determinants of neuropsychological performance in children with phenyl-ketonuria. In addition, the nature and timing of biochemical disturbances may interact with characteristics of brain maturation at the stage when disruption occurs, further complicating prediction of outcome.

There is evidence to suggest that brain development during the early post-natal period is particularly vulnerable to high Phe levels. Mildly affected children (i.e., those whose initial serum Phe level was <20 mg dl^{-1} at diagnosis), particularly if treated early, achieve higher scores on tests of general intelligence than severely affected children or those with later commencement of treatment (Barclay & Walton, 1988). Williamson et al. (1981) found that age at treatment inception was a stronger determinant of intellectual outcome than exposure to high Phe levels over the first 6 years of life, although both were important. Children treated early and maintained in good dietary control obtained intellectual quotients scores at 6 years that were no different from those of sibling controls or those predicted on the basis of maternal intellectual ability. Together, these findings underline the critical importance of early diagnosis and prompt treatment.

Correlations between cognitive deficit and higher Phe levels at the time of testing have been reported, suggesting that excess phenylalanine exerts both transient and permanent effects on cognitive function. Higher concurrent Phe levels have been associated with increased error rates, attentional deficits, and slowed responses in studies involving both adults and children (de Sonneville, Schmidt, Michel, & Batzler, 1990; Lou et al., 1985; Pietz et al., 1993; Schmidt et al., 1994). Clarke et al. (1987) and Krause et al. (1985) both showed a reversible prolongation of performance time on tests of higher integrative functions when Phe levels were elevated, but there was no effect on tests of simple reaction time, suggesting that task complexity may be a critical determinant of sensitivity to Phe. These findings highlight the importance of controlling for the effects of concurrent Phe level when interpreting performance on neuropsychological tests.

The relationship between lifetime biochemical control and cognitive deficit is less clear, possibly because of the difficulty obtaining reliable, retrospective estimates of dietary adherence (children can adjust their diet in anticipation of a forthcoming hospital visit, producing Phe levels that are poorly indicative of their usual dietary control). Some studies have found positive associations between high lifetime Phe levels and cognitive deficit (Koch et al., 1984; Krause et al., 1985; Pietz et al., 1993; Van Der Schot, Doesburg, & Sengers, 1994; Waisbren et al., 1987) whereas others have not (Barclay & Walton, 1988; Brunner et al., 1983; Fishler et al., 1987). Welsh et al. (1990) found that compromised executive functions were associated with both concurrent and mean lifetime Phe levels, but more strongly with the former. The relationship between Phe levels and intellectual abilities was not significant. These researchers (Welsh et al., 1990) interpret their results as support for the hypothesis that a biochemical anomaly such as dopamine depletion may exert both transient and permanent effects on cognition. Executive functions and dynamic information-processing capacities may be particularly sensitive to concurrent neurochemical state whereas IQ is less state dependent, but may be reduced because of early and irreversible brain damage. Support for this interpretation is provided by Ris et al. (1994), who found that early insult was the best predictor of intellectual outcome whereas performance on a novel problem-solving task was associated with current Phe level.

It was initially believed that a protein-restricted diet was unnecessary beyond 5–8 years of age as intellectual deterioration would not occur after this time because myelination was thought to be complete (Clarke et al., 1987). Early studies examining the effects of diet discontinuation in middle childhood produced little consensus, possibly because of methodological limitations, for example, small samples of children who discontinued the diet at different ages, uncontrolled designs, a failure to distinguish between actual loss of metabolic control and stated time of diet cessation, test batteries limited to measures of global intelligence, and variable duration of follow-up.

There is now growing evidence that the neurotoxicity of Phe may extend beyond early childhood, in line with current understanding about brain development continuing well into the second decade of life. The National Collaborative Study of Children Treated for Phenylketonuria has evaluated the effects of diet termination at various ages and produced serial reports (Azen et al., 1991, 1996; Fishler et al., 1987; Holtzman et al., 1986; Koch et al., 1984), suggesting that diet discontinuation, at least before 10 years of age, is associated with decline in intellectual and educational ability. A fall in measured intellectual ability following diet discontinuation, or lower scores relative to unaffected controls or phenylketonuria children remaining on diet, has also been reported in a number of single-centre studies (Legido et al., 1993; Naughten, Kiely, Saul, & Murphy, 1987; Pietz et al., 1993; Schmidt, Mahle, Michel, & Pietz, 1987; Seashore et al., 1985; Smith, Beasley, & Ades, 1991; Waisbren et al., 1987). Waisbren et al. (1987) found that good dietary control was the best predictor of intellectual ability, whereas diet discontinuation was the best predictor of intellectual loss. Holtzman et al. (1986) examined the influence of prediagnosis Phe level, age of treatment inception, and dietary control in early life, Phe at time of testing and age at which dietary control was actually lost on intellectual performance and behaviour. Age at which dietary control was lost was the best, and often the only, predictor of subject–sibling and subject–parent intellectual differences. IQ increased progressively the longer dietary control lasted. In a study that controlled for the effects of age of treatment inception and quality of metabolic control through the first 5 years of life, early treated patients off diet from 5 years showed an IQ drop of 5 points and an IQ significantly below a group of phenylketonuria children still on the diet at 11 years of age (Legido et al., 1993). There was no demonstrable benefit in remaining on diet in the subgroup whose initial treatment was delayed beyond 3 months of age, suggesting that they had suffered irreversible brain damage.

A similar picture emerges when the effects of diet cessation on specific cognitive processes are examined. Academic and conceptual reasoning difficulties (Seashore et al., 1985), increased reaction times (Krause et al., 1985; Lou et al., 1985), visuoperceptual problems (Faust et al., 1986; Welsh et al., 1990), and atypical sensory evoked potentials (Pueschel, Fogelson-Doyle, Kammerer, & Matsumiya, 1983) have been reported after diet cessation. Some of these deficits may be reversible with reinstitution of a strict diet. Giffin, Clarke, and d'Entremont (1980) found that visual attention improved, whereas others (Clarke et al., 1987; Krause et al., 1985) report gains in processing speed with improvements in dietary control, consistent with a reported normalisation of neurotransmitter metabolites following dietary therapy and a reduction in Phe (Villasana, Butler, Williams, & Roongta, 1989). It should be noted, though, that relationships between diet cessation and apparent cognitive worsening may be artefactual. Some difficulties may reflect early brain damage, which is not accessible to detailed testing in early childhood, and becomes apparent only when skills fail to emerge at the expected time.

INSULIN-DEPENDENT DIABETES MELLITUS

Aetiology and epidemiology

Insulin-dependent diabetes mellitus (IDDM) is a serious and life-long disorder of glucose metabolism. It is one of the most common paediatric illnesses and its incidence appears to be increasing worldwide (Dorman, O'Leary, & Koehler, 1995). Prevalence and incidence rates vary across countries and racial groups, with annual incidence rates ranging from 1 per 100,000 children under the age of 15 in Japan to 38 per 100,000 in Finland (Weber, 1989). The aetiology of IDDM is still not perfectly understood. Current evidence suggests that an autoimmune process triggered by some environmental event (toxin, infection, antigen) destroys the insulin-producing islet cells in the pancreas in genetically predisposed individuals (Weber, 1989). Disease onset may occur at any time from infancy to young adulthood, with a peak incidence between 11 and 14 years, suggesting that, in contrast to congenital hypothyroidism and phenylketonuria, most children with IDDM experience a period of normal cerebral and cognitive development prior to diagnosis. From disease onset, a complex daily treatment regimen of insulin by injection, balanced with diet and exercise, is required to approximate a normal metabolic state. Insulin requirements and food intake must be constantly adjusted to avoid hyperglycaemia (high blood sugar) and hypoglycaemia (low blood sugar).

Pathophysiology

The CNS is one of a number of organ systems affected by IDDM. Glucose accounts for more than 90% of the metabolic fuel of the brain (Mooradian, 1988). A constant supply of glucose is essential for normal cerebral metabolism as the capacity of the brain to store carbohydrate is limited. Under extreme conditions, the brain can oxidise ketones and other substrates as alternative energy sources but this is not optimal as ketones are used primarily by the lower centres and the midbrain (Bessman, 1985). Children are likely to be particularly sensitive to glucose disruption as they have a higher cerebral metabolic rate than adults because of energy requirements related to brain growth and development (Lester & Fishbein, 1989; McCall & Figlewicz, 1997). Even well-controlled IDDM is associated with wide fluctuations in blood glucose levels throughout the day because of the reduced efficiency of exogenous insulin. Acutely, glycaemic extremes cause impaired consciousness, coma, seizures, and focal neurological deficits (McCall & Figlewicz,

1997). There is also evidence of chronic CNS changes in IDDM at the functional, structural, and electrophysiological levels (Biessels et al., 1994; McCall & Figlewicz, 1997; Mooradian, 1988).

Reduced cerebral blood flow and altered cerebrovascular reactivity have been reported in IDDM (McCall & Figlewicz, 1997). These changes correlate inversely with duration of IDDM and presence of complications and positively with degree of chronic hyperglycaemia (Duckrow, Beard, & Brennan, 1987; Harik & LaManna, 1988). Transport of brain nutrients and metabolism of neurotransmitters are also altered in IDDM (McCall & Figlewicz, 1997; Mooradian, 1988). Hyperglycaemia suppresses dopaminergic and forebrain noradrenaline neurotransmission, whereas hypoglycaemia-related cerebral energy failure is associated with marked changes in amino acids and a significant rise in the concentration of tissue aspartate, a known neurotoxin (Choi, 1988; McCall & Figlewicz, 1997). The frontal and temporal regions of the brain appear to be particularly sensitive to abnormal blood glucose levels (Chalmers et al., 1991; McCall & Figlewicz, 1997; Tallroth, Ryding, & Agardh, 1992). The possibility that the brain may also be sensitive to abnormal levels of insulin because of the role insulin plays in neurotransmitter metabolism has recently been raised (McCall & Figlewicz, 1997). Evoked potential studies provide growing evidence that IDDM is associated with prolonged response latencies (Dejgaard et al., 1991; Pozzessere et al., 1991; Seidl et al., 1996). An increased incidence of EEG abnormalities has been noted in both paediatric and adult patients with IDDM, particularly in association with a history of severe hypoglycaemia (Haumont, Dorchy, & Pelc, 1979; Soltesz & Acsadi, 1989) or chronically elevated blood glucose levels (Hauser et al., 1995).

Neuropsychological findings

The first published report of a study examining cognitive functioning in a diabetic population appeared in 1922, when Miles and Root described attentional and memory deficits in a group of patients with IDDM. Since then a number of studies have documented mild neuropsychological dysfunction in adults with IDDM (see Holmes, 1990, for a comprehensive review), most evident in those with biomedical complications (Ryan, Williams, Orchard, & Finegold, 1993). Deficits have been noted across a range of cognitive processes, including speed of processing, attention, memory, new learning, abstract reasoning and problem solving, and psychomotor efficiency (Holmes, 1990). In general, effect sizes have been small, with IDDM subjects obtaining scores on standardised tests that are below those of controls, but still within the average range.

Somewhat surprisingly, early research failed to provide consistent evidence of cognitive impairment in paediatric and adolescent patients with IDDM.

Illness-related predictors of outcome

Current evidence suggests that neuropsychological dysfunction in IDDM is selective. Not all cognitive processes, nor all individuals with insulin dependent diabetes mellitus, are equally affected. History of metabolic control, age of onset, and duration of illness have been identified as specific risk factors for IDDM-related neuropsychological sequelae (Holmes, 1990; Ryan, 1990).

Clinically, patients report mental confusion, lethargy, and slowed speed of processing during hypoglycaemia. These anecdotal reports are supported by empirical findings documenting increased reaction times, impaired planning and decision making, and reduced mental flexibility when blood glucose falls below 2.5 mmol L^{-1} in both adults (Hoffman et al., 1989; Holmes, Koepke, & Thompson, 1986; McCrimmon et al., 1996; Pramming et al., 1986) and children (Reich et al., 1990; Ryan et al., 1990). Holmes et al. (1986) found a linear relationship between increasing task complexity and deteriorating performance, and concluded that the pattern of deficits observed during hypoglycaemia is consistent with transient bilateral frontal lobe compromise disrupting attentional and executive processes. Previously, it was thought that cognitive efficiency was fully restored with normoglycaemia. It is now clear that neurocognitive recovery lags well behind the resolution of physical symptoms (Reich et al., 1990; Ryan et al., 1990). There is also growing evidence from both adult and paediatric studies that recurrent severe hypoglycaemia may be associated with subtle permanent impairment (Bjorgaas, Gimse, Vik, & Sand, 1997; Deary et al., 1992; Golden et al., 1989; Hershey, Craft, Bhargava, & White, 1997; Hough, Wysocki, & Linscheid, 1994; Langan, Deary, Hepburn, & Frier, 1991; Northam et al., 1998; Rovet et al., 1987, 1988; Wredling, Levander, Adamson, & Lins, 1990) although not all studies report significant effects (Diabetes Control and Complications Trial, 1994).

Adults with a history of chronic hyperglycaemia, particularly those with evidence of diabetes complications, such as neuropathy or retinopathy, have been shown to perform more poorly on cognitive tasks (Lichty & Klachko, 1985; Ryan et al., 1990, 1993; Ryan, Williams, Orchard, & Finegold, 1992). As these complications are not found in prepubertal children, associations between chronic hyperglycaemia and cognitive deficits were thought unlikely in paediatric populations and null findings in several early studies (Golden et al., 1989; Rovet et al., 1987; Ryan et al., 1985) provided support for this belief. However, these studies used a single (concurrent) measure of glycosylated haemoglobin (HbA1C) as their index of hyperglycaemia. This provides no information about metabolic control history beyond the previous 2–3 months, hence relationships between significant periods of poor metabolic control in the past and current neuropsychological status were not actually tested. Several recent prospective studies have used multiple serial measurements of glycosylated HbA1C to examine the effects of longer-term metabolic control on cognitive status. There was no relationship between cognitive decline and metabolic control history over the first 6 years of IDDM in the study by Kovacs et al. (1992), but this conclusion was based on a very limited assessment of cognitive abilities. Using more comprehensive test batteries and serial measurement of glycosylated haemoglobin, Rovet et al. (1990) documented hyperglycaemia-related deficits in verbal abilities and visuomotor integration skills, whereas memory and learning were the skills most compromised by chronically elevated blood sugar levels in the study by Northam et al. (1999). Both studies found that slower acquisition of mathematical concepts was associated with higher glycosylated haemoglobin levels.

An association between early onset of IDDM (before 5 years) and poorer cognitive abilities was first reported by Ack, Miller, and Weil (1961). Diagnosis early in life has since emerged as one of the strongest risk factors for neuropsychological sequelae in children with IDDM (Hagen et al., 1990; Holmes & Richman, 1985; Northam et al., 1998; Rovet et al., 1987; Ryan et al., 1985). Holmes and Richman (1985) found lower performance IQ, mental slowing, and reading and memory impairment in long-duration and early onset subgroups of diabetic children. Correlational analyses suggested that early onset was exerting a stronger influence on scores than was duration of illness. Widespread cognitive deficits were found in children diagnosed before 5 years in a study of adolescents conducted by Ryan et al. (1985). The early onset group obtained lower scores than children diagnosed after 5, and a non-diabetic control group on measures of general intelligence, visuospatial ability, learning and memory, mental and motor speed, and attention and school achievement. There were no statistically significant differences between children with IDDM onset after 5 years and controls, although the former tended to obtain lower scores. IDDM onset before 5 years of age was associated with negative change on performance IQ within 2 years of diagnosis in the cohort study of Northam et al. (1998).

Ryan (1990) has suggested that the "early onset" effect is a surrogate for the impact of hypoglycaemia on an immature brain. He points out that very young children are more likely to experience serious hypoglycaemia as their food intake and activity levels are often unpredictable and they lack the capacity to perceive and communicate early symptoms. There is also evidence of a heightened sensitivity to insulin in the child under 5 (Ternard, Go, Gerich, & Haymond, 1982). Ryan suggests that the early onset effect will be most evident on measures of "fluid intelligence" such as those assessed on the Performance scale of the Wechsler tests, with "crystallised" or overlearned verbal abilities being more resilient to the effects of mild brain damage. Rovet et al. (1990) agree that there may be a critical period of increased cerebral sensitivity to the effects of IDDM. They suggest an alternative (but not mutually exclusive) hypothesis, that chronic hyperglycaemia disrupts myelin formation in very young children still experiencing brain development. They point out that animal studies have shown that IDDM affects myelination because of defective incorporation of acetate and glucose into nerve lipids (Vlassara, Brownlee, & Cerami, 1983). If defective myelination is the explanation, one would expect deficits in processing speed and in abilities dependent upon the integrity of the prefrontal cortex.

Some support for Ryan's hypothesis is provided by electrophysiological studies that report an association between a history of serious hypoglycaemia, early onset, and increased risk of EEG abnormalities (Haumont et al., 1979). Furthermore, deficits in early onset children have been most apparent on measures of "fluid intelligence" such as performance IQ, rapid visual scanning, and visuospatial problem solving (Golden et al., 1989; Holmes & Richman, 1985; Hough et al., 1994; Northam et al., 1998; Rovet et al., 1987, 1988; Ryan et al., 1985). However, tests tapping these skills are often timed and compromised processing speed, secondary to defective myelination, is an equally plausible explanation for such results. The alternative hypotheses of Rovet et al. (1990) and Ryan (1988) suggest a non-linear relationship between neuropsychological dysfunction and glycaemic control; that is, patients with low blood sugar levels (good metabolic control) but frequent hypoglycaemia and those with chronically high blood sugar levels (poor metabolic control) are both at risk for neuropsychological sequelae, although for different reasons. Northam et al. (1999) provide empirical support for this interpretation with both glycaemic extremes associated with performance decrements as early as 2 years after disease onset.

Psychosocial issues

The family both affects, and is affected by, the child with a chronic medical condition (Shapiro, 1983). The diagnosis itself is experienced as a significant psychological crisis in which the parents grieve the loss of the idealised child (Maddison & Raphael, 1971). Thereafter patterns of communication and interactions within the family will be altered as parents attempt to steer a middle course between "uninformed carelessness and frantic over-solicitude" (Kanner, 1960). Enjoyment of the parental role may be diminished as parents struggle to balance the psychological needs of the child with the restrictions and treatment requirements imposed by the illness. In addition, family adaptation to illness is not a static process, but must change to take account of the child's developing maturity and capacity for self-management of his/her condition.

The dietary restrictions necessary for good metabolic control of phenylketonuria and IDDM must be negotiated on a daily basis and are a constant reminder to the child that he/she is "different", a psychological burden that may well increase as the child develops cognitive maturity and more sophisticated ways of understanding the implications of a genetic disorder. Parental anxiety is likely to be particularly high in IDDM because of the possibility that hypoglycaemia may occur rapidly and with little warning, precipitating a potentially life-threatening metabolic crisis. The psychological challenges common to all chronic illnesses may be further complicated in metabolic disorders as there is evidence that abnormal metabolic states may contribute directly to alterations in behaviour and mood, such as increased restlessness and irritability (Rovet, Ehrlich, & Sorbara, 1989).

Meta-analytic reviews provide evidence for an elevated incidence of behavioural problems in children with chronic illness (Lavigne & Faier-Routman, 1992). Empirical studies of specific illness groups, however, have produced inconsistent findings. Mildly elevated levels of parent-reported psychological difficulties of a predominantly internalising kind have been reported in some studies of children with IDDM, but not in others (Johnson, 1995). Burgard, Armbruster, Schmidt, and Rupp (1994) found a doubled incidence of psychopathology in children with phenylketonuria, in contrast to the normal behavioural adjustment reported by Shulman et al. (1991) in children with the same condition. Another group (Weglage et al., 1996) found no evidence of increased behavioural maladjustment at 10 years but heightened levels of socioemotional disturbance during adolescence in phenylketonuria patients, suggesting an interaction between developmental stage and disease effects on psychological functioning. Hypothyroidism has been linked to more difficult temperament in infancy (Rovet et al., 1989) and more behaviour problems in middle childhood (Rovet, 1996), but a meta-analysis of controlled studies of children with congenital hypothyroidism failed to document any significant increase in behaviour problems (Derksen-Lubsen & Verkerk, 1996), possibly reflecting the less intrusive treatment requirements associated with this condition, in comparison with phenylketonuria and IDDM.

Empirical studies of family functioning in children with metabolic disorders have also produced inconsistent findings. There is some evidence that parenting stress levels are higher and that families of chronically ill children in general perceive themselves as less cohesive and more rigidly organised than control families (Hanson et al., 1989; Kazak, Reber, & Snitzer, 1988; Northam et al., 1996; Wysocki, Huxtable, Linscheid, & Wayne, 1989) while others report few differences (Shulman et al., 1991; Wertlieb, Hauser, & Jacobson, 1986).

Relationships between psychological factors (child adjustment, parental mental health, family functioning) and health outcome have been examined, particularly in families with a child with IDDM. Anecdotally, parents report greater mood lability and restlessness in children with high Phe or blood glucose levels and there are empirical reports of elevated levels of behavioural disturbance in children with poorly controlled phenylketonuria (Holtzman et al., 1986; McCombe et al., 1992; Smith & Beasley, 1989) and IDDM (Simonds, Goldstein, Walker, & Rawlings, 1981). Shulman et al. (1991) report a positive correlation between family cohesion and dietary adherence in their study of families with a phenylketonuria child. In contrast, some IDDM studies (e.g., Close, Davies, Price, & Goodyer, 1986; Fonagy et al., 1987; Rovet & Ehrlich, 1988; Weissberg-Benchell & Glasgow, 1997) report associations between poorer psychological adjustment, particularly symptoms of anxiety, depression, and negative mood, and better glycaemic control. Similarly, rigidly organised, inflexible families have been associated with both better (Klemp & La Greca, 1987) and poorer (Hanson, Henggeler, & Burghen, 1987) metabolic control in the child, whereas Evans and Hughes (1987) found that strict parental supervision was associated with better health outcomes but greater psychological dependency in the child. Together these findings suggest that health and psychological outcomes may not always coincide and that overzealous compliance with treatment regimes may have a psychological cost for some children. Further research is needed to clarify these complex relationships. It is likely that family factors interact with specific child variables such as developmental stage, temperament, and IQ and with specific characteristics of the illness to produce outcomes not tapped by simple linear models.

It has been suggested that the non-specific effects of chronic illness on emotional well-being, self-esteem, and motivation may explain the neuropsychological deficits found in children with metabolic disorders. If psychogenic explanations are valid, one would expect to find correlations between measures of psychosocial status and test performance. The few studies that have directly tested such relationships provide little empirical support for the claim that deficits can be so explained. Both parent-reported behaviour problems and self-rated affective symptoms are unrelated to test scores in studies of children with IDDM (Hagen et al., 1990; Kovacs, Goldston, & Iyengar, 1992; Northam et al., 1998; Ryan et al., 1985).

Academic and cognitive difficulties in children with metabolic disorders are also attributed to chronic illness-related school absence, but empirical support for this suggestion is also lacking. Fowler, Johnson, and Atkinson (1985) examined the relationship between health variables, school absenteeism, and academic achievement in a cohort of children with chronic health conditions. Children with IDDM had the second lowest rates of absenteeism, after children with congenital heart disease. Nevertheless, apart from children with CNS diseases, those with diabetes had the lowest levels of academic achievement. In another study, school grades declined with increasing duration of IDDM (Kovacs et al., 1992), but absenteeism was not higher than the community average. Together, these findings suggest that school absence does not explain educational and neuropsychological deficits in children with IDDM.

Positive relationships between illness variables and neuropsychological deficit and the failure to find such a relationship between psychosocial status and deficit argues for a neural, rather than a psychogenic, basis for cognitive and academic difficulties in children with metabolic disorders. However, both factors may interact to impact on development and functional outcome. Parents of children with IDDM and phenylketonuria may limit exploratory activities in their young child because of their concern about a dietary indiscretion. In IDDM, there is the additional fear that a very young child will be unable to recognise and communicate early symptoms of hypoglycaemia. Thus, opportunities for experiential learning may be reduced. It is possible that limited opportunities to test out cause-and-effect relationships and to learn through discovery may then contribute to the deficits in spatial reasoning and visuomotor skills that have been documented in children with phenylketonuria or early onset IDDM. In middle childhood, curtailed environmental experiences may be reflected in deficient strategy generation and poor problem-solving skills. Chronically ill children may feel less motivated to achieve, while parent and teacher expectations of a child with a medical disorder may be reduced, setting up an invitation to underachieve that some children will find irresistible. These hypotheses are speculative but warrant empirical investigation.

CASE STUDY

The following case illustrates some of the difficulties encountered by a child with a chronic metabolic disorder with possible effects on the CNS. In particular, the opportunity to follow Sophie and her family from diagnosis in early childhood to adolescence facilitates examination of the natural history of such illnesses, and the ongoing interplay of biological, developmental, cognitive, and psychosocial factors.

Sophie was well and developing normally until 14 months of age. Over a 4-week period, her behaviour changed and she became uncharacteristically irritable and lethargic. Her parents also noticed that she was drinking a lot and appeared to be losing weight but attributed this to heightened activity levels since she had started walking. Finally, Sophie became acutely unwell, her conscious state deteriorated and she was admitted to hospital in diabetic ketoacidosis.

Sophie's parents were shocked and distressed by the diagnosis of IDDM. Initially, their anxiety about their daughter's well-being was such that they were reluctant to leave her in the care of a baby-sitter or even extended family members. Their confidence in their ability to provide adequate care for Sophie was further undermined when she had several hypoglycaemic convulsions. Her mother recalls that battles to get a reluctant toddler to eat prescribed foods on schedule dominated the next few years. However, over time,

Classification systems

The first efforts to introduce an internationally accepted classification system focused on defining seizure type on the basis of seizure symptomatology and the EEG findings. The Commission on Classification and Terminology of the International League Against Epilepsy (ILAE) published its first classification system in 1964, and a revised system in 1981. This system has significant limitations, and the more recently developed classification system has adopted a syndrome approach. Because the process of diagnosing epilepsy syndromes encompasses information other than seizure symptomatology and EEG findings, it is a more powerful tool for prognosis and treatment than the classification system based on seizure type alone (Wyllie & Lüders, 1996b).

Classification of seizure type

The major subdivisions of the ILAE system (1981) for classifying seizure type are shown in Table 9.1. Seizures are separated into two main categories: partial and generalised. Partial seizures are those where the first clinical (i.e., behavioural) and/or EEG changes indicate the initial activation of a limited number of neurons in part of one hemisphere. Generalised seizures are those where the first clinical and/or EEG changes indicate initial activation of neurons throughout both hemispheres.

Partial seizures are further divided into simple partial—seizures during which consciousness in thought to be preserved—and complex partial—seizures during which consciousness is impaired. An additional category—partial seizures secondarily generalised—is included for seizures where activity begins focally, but subsequently spreads to involve both hemispheres. Seizures may begin as partial seizures, progress to a complex partial seizure, then become secondarily generalised. The simple partial component of a seizure is the stage recalled by the patient as an "aura". The term aura refers to the component of the seizure that can be recalled by the patient before "consciousness" (or later memory for the seizure) is impaired. This may be experienced by the patient in as many forms as there are simple partial seizure types. Automatisms are automatic behaviours associated with the seizure (during or following) and include behaviours such as chewing, expressions of fear, gestures, or repetition of a word or phrase.

Generalised seizures are also divided into a number of different seizure types. The term absence seizure replaces the older term "petit mal" for a seizure characterised by a sudden onset, interruption of ongoing activities, and a blank stare, possibly with a brief upward rotation of the eyes (Wyllie & Lüders, 1996a). Absences can be further subdivided according to additional behavioural changes observed during the seizure. The term tonic–clonic seizure replaces the older term "grand mal" to refer to a seizure where there is an initial sharp, tonic contraction of muscles, as a result of which the patient

TABLE 9.1
Classification of seizure type

I. Partial (focal, local) seizures
    A. Simple partial seizures (consciousness not impaired)
        1. With motor symptoms
        2. With somatosensory or special sensory symptoms
        3. With autonomic symptoms
        4. With psychic symptoms

    B. Complex partial seizures (with impairment of consciousness)
        1. Beginning as simple partial seizures and progressing to impairment of consciousness
            (a) With no other features
            (b) With features as in A.1–4
            (c) With automatisms
        2. With impairment of consciousness at outset
            (a) With no other features
            (b) With features as in A.1–4
            (c) With automatisms

    C. Partial seizures secondarily generalised

II. Generalised seizures (convulsive or non-convulsive)
    A. 1. Absence seizures
        2. Atypical absence seizures
    B. Myoclonic seizures
    C. Clonic seizures
    D. Tonic seizures
    E. Tonic–clonic seizures
    F. Atonic seizures

Adapted from the Commission on Classification and Terminology of the ILAE (1981), *Epilepsia, 22*, 489–501.

falls to the ground. The tonic stage then gives way to clonic convulsive movements lasting for a variable period of time. Additional generalised seizure types include: myoclonic seizures, referring to sudden, brief, shock-like contractions that may involve widespread, or specific, muscle groups; clonic seizures that are characterised by repetitive clonic jerks; tonic seizures, where there is a sudden muscular contraction, fixing the limbs in some strained position; and atonic seizures in which the person suddenly loses muscle tone, leading to a drop of a specific body part, such as a drop of the head or loss of all muscle tone leading to a fall to the ground. When atonic seizures are very brief they may be referred to as "drop attacks".

The category "unclassified epileptic seizures" includes all seizures that cannot be classified. Many seizures occurring in infancy currently fall into this category.

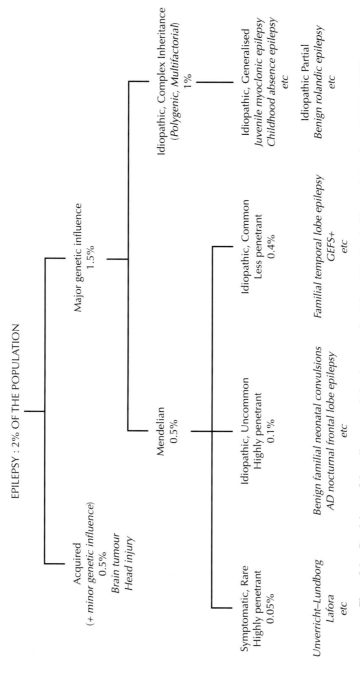

Figure 9.1. Breakdown of the epilepsy population in terms of aetiology. Reprinted with permission from Berkovic (1998).

O'Donohoe (1994) points out, age, growth, and development are not only of primary importance in determining whether or not epilepsy develops, but also influence the clinical and electrical manifestations of seizures and the type of epileptic syndromes encountered.

The interaction between age and aetiology is illustrated by the observation that epilepsy is more likely to result from an underlying neurological disorder in younger age groups. For example, in neonates and infants, epilepsy is more likely to be the first sign of a serious underlying abnormality, particularly in its more severe intractable forms. Causes of symptomatic epilepsy in the neonate include hypoxic–ischaemic encephalopathy, infection, haemorrhage, congenital brain abnormality, metabolic disorder such as hypoglycaemia, inborn errors of metabolism, and genetic disorders (Mizrahi, 1996). Epilepsy syndromes with onset at different stages during childhood could be regarded as age-related epileptic reactions to various non-specific exogenous brain insults acting at varying age-specific stages of development (Ohtahara & Ohtsuki, 1996).

The importance of congenital cerebral abnormalities in the epilepsies is becoming more evident as brain-imaging techniques improve. The mechanisms by which cortical malformations result, when the normal process of brain development is disrupted, have already been reviewed in Chapter 2. Many of these malformations are highly epileptogenic (Palmini et al., 1995). Genetic factors have been isolated in a number of conditions associated with cortical malformations. Tuberous sclerosis is the most common of these. Periventricular nodular heterotopia and subcortical band heterotopia have recently both been linked to the X chromosome (Harvey et al., 1998).

It is likely that families exhibiting more simple inheritance patterns hold the key to understanding the genetics of epilepsy and to future breakthroughs in this field. For example, recent studies have begun to consider genetic mechanisms by which febrile seizures are inherited, suggesting that inheritance is likely to be complex (polygenic or multifactorial), with rare families showing autosomal dominance. Linkage analysis in one such family in the USA has implicated a specific chromosome region (Wallace et al., 1996), although this locus has not as yet been implicated in other families. Familial partial epilepsy with variable foci (Scheffer et al., 1998) is an example of an inherited, partial epilepsy syndrome, identified in an Australian family, with a suggestion of linkage on chromosome 2q. In another family with generalised epilepsy with febrile seizures past the age of 6 years (GEFS+) a mutation in a gene that codes for a sodium channel subunit has been identified (Wallace et al., 1998). As other genes coding for ion channels have also been implicated in idiopathic epilepsies, these seizure disorders are being thought of increasingly as possible "channelopathies" (Berkovic, 1998).

DIAGNOSIS AND TREATMENT

Diagnosis

Careful and detailed history taking is the essential element in the diagnosis of epilepsy (O'Donohoe, 1994). A careful description of the suspected seizures will usually exclude non-epileptic events that may be misdiagnosed as seizures. These include syncope or fainting and breath holding, both of which may be associated with jerky movements towards the end of the episode, and in the case of breath holding even a brief stiffening of the body.

Electroencephalography, first developed for use in epilepsy in the 1930s, measures differences in electrical potential arising between different parts of the head resulting from the spontaneous activity of the underlying brain. EEGs are typically recorded for at least 20 min using scalp electrodes placed in a standardised array. The appearance of the EEG pattern changes considerably during infancy and childhood, reflecting the process of structural and neurophysiological maturation. The normal EEG pattern seen while the child is awake also changes in response to the different stages of sleep, and in response to hyperventilation and intermittent photic stimulation (flashing light). Sleep, hyperventilation, and photic stimulation may be utilised during an EEG recording to "activate" abnormalities in the EEG pattern that may be diagnostic of epilepsy. Abnormal epileptic activity may be apparent on the EEG as sudden changes in frequency, decreases in voltage, or increases in voltage, which commonly appear as "spikes". Figure 9.2 illustrates EEG changes associated with three different seizure types.

The EEG recording may confirm the diagnosis of epilepsy, particularly if an epileptic pattern is recorded at the onset of a suspected seizure (an ictal recording). A normal or abnormal interictal EEG recording, however, does not exclude or confirm a diagnosis of epilepsy. The EEG may also be used for accurate classification of seizure types, as characteristic abnormal patterns are associated with particular types of seizures. Occasionally the EEG may help determine the cause of seizures, as particular EEG patterns may also be associated with specific disorders causing CNS dysfunction such as cerebral infections and brain tumours and other space-occupying lesions. Simultaneous EEG recording and video monitoring may be necessary in certain children to exclude non-epileptic events, such as psychoseizures that closely mimic epileptic seizures, or to provide more precise characterisation of seizures in potential surgical candidates.

Neuroimaging studies may also be performed if an underlying structural lesion is suspected (computed tomography [CT], magnetic resonance imaging [MRI]), or to help in identifying the location of an underlying seizure focus (position emission tomography [PET], single-photon emission computed tomography [SPECT]).

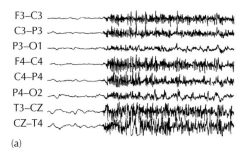

(a)

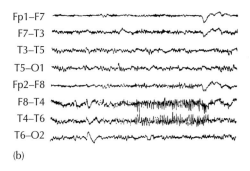

(b)

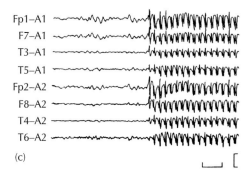

(c)

Figure 9.2. EEG change with onset of three different seizure types. (a) Beginning of a tonic seizure with repetitive sharp activity beginning simultaneously over both hemispheres. (b) Repetitive spikes occurring with sudden onset in the right temporal region during a seizure associated with transient alteration of arousal. (c) Generalised, bilateral synchronous 3 Hz spike-and-wave activity occurring during an absence attack. Reprinted from Aminoff (1996) with permission from McGraw-Hill Book Company.

Treatment with anti-epilepsy drugs

Anti-epileptic drugs (AEDs) are the standard form of treatment for epilepsy and are likely to remain so for some time to come. They effectively control seizures in the majority of people with epilepsy. The mechanism by which the individual AEDs control seizures varies. Their postulated mode(s) of action include the modulation of voltage-dependent neuronal ion channels, enhancement of the major inhibitory neurotransmitter (GABA) or suppression of excitatory amino acid (mainly glutamate) neurotransmission.

The action of an individual drug on the brain is determined by the concentration of free drug in brain tissue, specifically in the synaptic cleft. The serum concentration (amount of drug present in the blood) is used as an indication of this level. The therapeutic range refers to the upper and lower serum levels within which the drug is effective. If the serum level rises above the therapeutic range, toxic side effects may result. The duration of activity of AEDs is dependent on their rate of biotransformation in the body. Rates of biotransformation vary from drug to drug and also from individual to individual, depending on genetic influences, age, sex, diet, and interaction with other drugs, particularly other AEDs. The rate at which a particular AED is metabolised can be substantially decreased, and so increasing the risk of toxic side effects, or increased when it is taken with other AEDs, leading to difficulty in maintaining an effective therapeutic level.

Drug dosage is adjusted according to efficacy and tolerability for individual patients. The serum level of AEDs may be monitored to assist in maintaining this level within the therapeutic range at the lowest troughs between doses and to avoid peaks after administration that would take the serum level into the toxic range. Closer monitoring and adjustments of dosage may be necessary in young children (under 5 years) because of the more rapid rate at which AEDs are metabolised. Adjustments to dosage may not be needed during the middle childhood years, because the decrease in rate of biotransformation is balanced by an increase in body weight. Dosage is often increased with the onset of puberty, when children become more like adults in drug utilisation patterns. Most AEDs are administered twice a day, morning and night, but three or even four daily administration may be needed. Monotherapy (treatment with a single AED) is the treatment ideal, but polytherapy (combinations of more than one AED) may be necessary to bring the seizures under better control. Combining AEDs with different modes of action may in fact increase the efficacy and tolerability of AED therapy.

All the AEDs have known side effects, including adverse CNS effects. In particular, weight gain, excess hair growth, behavioural changes, and cognitive problems are commonly documented. AEDs may cause acute side effects associated with their use in the short term or more chronic side effects in the longer term. Much more is known of the acute side effects of AEDs, with the possible chronic side effects more difficult to ascertain. All AEDs may also produce idiosyncratic side effects associated with individual responses that are largely unpredictable. When seizures are difficult to control, the positive effects obtained through polytherapy, in terms of seizure control, need to be carefully balanced against the negative effects which can include adverse effects on cognition and behaviour.

Table 9.3 lists the AEDs that are most commonly used to treat epilepsy in childhood. Both the generic and trade names are given for each. Pheno-barbitone (PB) has been in use since 1912 and is still considered a major AED, although its sedative and behavioural side effects, particularly in children, are well recognised. Phenytoin (PHT) was introduced in 1938 and, along with carbamazepine (CBZ) and sodium valproate (VPA), is still considered one of the main AEDs for treatment of childhood epilepsy. The more recent approach to pharmacological treatment of epilepsy has been to try to develop AEDs that either enhance synaptic inhibition (GABA mediated) or reduce excitatory neurotransmission. Vigabatrin and Tiagabine are two of the newer AEDs that reflect this approach.

TABLE 9.3
Anti-epileptic drugs (AEDs) commonly used in
treatment with epilepsy

Generic names	Trade names
Frequently used	
Newer AEDs	
Vigabatrin	Sabril
Lamotrigine	Lamictal
Older AEDs	
Carbamazepine[a]	Tegretol
Sodium valproate[a]	Epilim, Depakene
Less frequently used	
Newer AEDs	
Topiramate	Topamax
Tiagabine	Gabitril
Gabapentin	Neurontin
Oxcarbazepine	Trileptil
Older AEDs	
Phenobarbitone[a]	Luminal, Garbenal
Phenytoin[a]	Dilantin, Epanutin
Ethosuximide[a]	
Benzodiazepines	
Clonazepam	Rivotril, Clonopin (Klonopin)
Clobazam	Frisium
Diazepam	Valium

[a] Serum-level monitoring recommended.

A detailed summary of the relevant information regarding the use of each AED in children is beyond the scope of this review. However, a brief review of a selection of the more commonly prescribed AEDs is presented to acquaint the reader with specific issues relevant to the use of these AEDs in children. For more information regarding the use of individual AEDs the reader is directed to reviews by Bourgeois (1996a), Richens (1996), and the relevant chapters in Wyllie (1996).

Carbamazepine

CBZ, available since the early 1960s in Europe, has become the drug of first choice for the treatment of partial seizures and generalised tonic–clonic seizures in children. It is well tolerated in comparison with the older drugs, has no cosmetic side effects, and is generally considered to have minimal impact, if any, on behaviour, mood, and cognitive function. It is viewed as an effective and safe drug for use in treating children. Acute toxicity from CBZ is unusual and is dose related. Dizziness, drowsiness, diplopia, and gastrointestinal symptoms can occur with higher doses or when introduced too rapidly. CBZ is usually administered twice daily, but in very young children may need to be administered up to four times daily because of the very rapid rate of biotransformation (O'Donohoe, 1994). However, the availability of controlled release formulations can overcome this difficulty, and help to smooth out the peaks and troughs in serum levels between doses. CBZ is ineffective in treating absence or myoclonic seizures so has a limited role in the idiopathic, generalised epilepsies (Richens, 1996). Children commenced on CBZ may, very occasionally, develop an allergic reaction comprising a skin rash or some other manifestation of hypersensitivity. There are also extremely rare but serious idiosyncratic bone marrow and liver side effects.

Sodium valproate or valproic acid

The anti-epileptic properties of VPA were discovered in the early 1960s and it was first marketed in the UK in 1974. The mechanisms by which it has an anti-epileptic effect are still largely undefined; however, it appears to enhance the activity of the neurotransmitter GABA (O'Donohoe, 1994).

VPA is particularly effective in the treatment of absence seizures, and reduces the frequency and duration of spike-and-wave discharges in patients with typical and atypical absences. It is one of the most effective drugs in the treatment of myoclonic seizures, and is comparable to other AEDs in the control of generalised tonic–clonic seizures. Epilepsy with photosensitivity responds well to VPA, and it is useful in the treatment of Lennox–Gastaut syndrome and related forms of epilepsy, including infantile spasms. VPA can also be effective in the treatment of simple and complex partial seizures (Bourgeois, 1996a).

VPA is generally well tolerated by children and it is regarded as non-sedative in usual doses. Changes in behaviour, including hyperactivity, aggressiveness, and irritability, are unusual but can occur in some children (O'Donohoe, 1994). A serious hepatotoxic reaction can occur, but an increased awareness of the associated risk factors has made this an extremely rare complication. Weight gain and hair loss may also occur—side effects which, if present for example in an adolescent girl, could represent a significant burden in addition to the diagnosis of epilepsy (O'Donohoe, 1994). Hyperammonaemia is frequently found in children treated with VPA but is argued to be symptomatic only rarely. Baron et al. (1996), however, suggest that even in milder cases this may result in subtle cognitive deficits.

Phenytoin

PHT is an effective treatment for a wide range of seizure types, with absence seizures being one notable exception. It is an essential drug in the treatment of status epilepticus, being used for prevention of recurrences once initial control has been established by administration of a benzodiazepine, commonly valium. Due to its difficult pharamacokinetics (i.e., it is difficult to establish and maintain a therapeutic level) and the frequency with which PHT causes adverse reactions, it is no longer a drug of first choice for maintenance therapy (Richens, 1996). PHT remains, however, a widely used AED particularly in adult patients. Cerebellar signs of intoxication, including nystagmus, ataxia, and dysarthria, occur almost universally if plasma levels rise high enough. Sedation may also occur. Gum hypertrophy is a common side effect, together with a tendency to develop excessive body hair. For these reasons, use of PHT is generally avoided in prepubertal children, especially girls.

Vigabatrin

VGB was the first new AED to be licensed in the UK (and elsewhere) since the introduction of VPA in the early to mid-1970s. It is a synthetic derivative of GABA and acts as an irreversible inhibitor of GABA transaminase, the enzyme responsible for the breakdown of GABA. This action leads to a prolonged increase in GABA-mediated inhibition at the synapse (Richens, 1996). VGB is used as an add-on AED in chronic and intractable epilepsy in adults and children. Interactions with other AEDs are not significant, with the exception of a small fall in plasma PHT levels (O'Donohoe, 1994). Partial seizures, with and without secondary generalisation, have shown the best response to VGB. In children, however, its efficacy is not limited to partial seizures, and it is emerging as a potential first-choice AED against infantile spasms (Bourgeois, 1998).

Identified side effects include drowsiness, fatigue, dizziness, and behavioural changes including the development of acute psychosis in adults.

Excitement, agitation, hyperactivity, and insomnia have been reported in children (Bourgeois, 1996a; O'Donohoe, 1994; Richens, 1996). VGB may at times exacerbate seizures (as do some other AEDs), an effect that has been found to be associated with particular epilepsy syndromes. Lortie et al. (1993) found exacerbation occurred in patients with non-progressive myoclonic epilepsy and Lennox–Gastaut syndrome. Of greater concern are recent reports of visual field constriction, bilateral optic disc pallor, and subtle peripheral retinal atrophy. These cases have prompted the recommendation of initial and periodic (3-monthly) ophthalmological examinations in patients treated with VGB (Bourgeois, 1998). Weight gain is very often associated with the introduction of VGB.

Lamotrigine

LTG was first utilised in clinical trials in the early 1990s. It is thought to have an inhibitory effect on sodium channels and on the release of the excitatory neurotransmitter, glutamate, at the synapse. In "add-on" trials in children it has been found to be useful in controlling a range of partial and generalised seizure types including typical and atypical absence, myoclonic, atonic, and tonic seizures.

LTG is similar to CBZ in terms of its effectiveness in treating partial seizures but evidence is emerging to suggest that it may be better tolerated. Meador and Baker (1997) recently reviewed the findings of several studies that have linked improved functioning in patients with their commencement on LTG. Two of these studies, using children and adolescents with significant pre-existing cognitive impairments, reported positive effects of LTG, including improvements in alertness, speech, mobility, and independence, and in those with autism a reduction in "autistic" symptoms. In one study these behavioural changes were also seen in children who did not have an improvement in seizure control. Pellock (1997) also reviewed the use of LTG, concluding that it would appear to have fewer sedative effects than CBZ or PHT. This author also noted reports that LTG is associated with a "brightening" or "alerting" effect in significant numbers of children, especially those with encephalopathic epilepsies such as the Lennox–Gastaut syndrome.

Agitation, ataxia, and drowsiness have been reported in children. Other AEDs may increase or decrease the rate of biotransformation of LTG but there are no other significant interactions. When added to CBZ, LTG may enhance its neurotoxic side effects, precipitating diplopia and dizziness. Some form of rash develops in 3–5% of children commenced on LTG, and there have been reports of more serious and life-threatening rashes occurring in a small number of adult patients. However, a very slow introduction of LTG appears to minimise the risk of any form of rash developing.

Topiramate

TPM is a recent addition to the AEDs, and may well prove to be very effective in treating childhood epilepsies. Clinical trials suggest it is particularly effective for intractable partial seizures. However, cognitive side effects have been commonly reported in adult patients, and further trials in children are needed to clarify the implications for the use of TPM in children.

Surgical treatment

Surgery has proven to be an effective treatment for medically intractable epilepsy, particularly symptomatic partial epilepsy in adults and adolescent patients, but also increasingly in young, and very young, children. Surgery for epilepsy may be either resective, involving removal of an area of brain that contains a structural abnormality, or functional, attempting to modify brain function to improve seizure control. Some interventions combine both techniques (Polkey, 1996). The most commonly performed surgical procedures in children with epilepsy are summarised next.

Resective surgery

Temporal lobe resections are the most common form of epilepsy surgery and may involve limited resection of temporal neocortex or mesial temporal structures (amygdala–hippocampectomy), but more often involve removal of both superficial and mesial temporal structures. Resection of frontal lobe cortex containing a structural abnormality linked to focal onset of seizures is the most commonly performed extratemporal resection. These extratemporal resections may be aided by electrocorticography, with recording of epileptic activity from the brain surface during the surgery guiding the extent of tissue removal. Hemispherectomy involves extensive removal of one cerebral hemisphere. The modern technique involves removal of large sections of the hemisphere with blocks of cortex left anteriorly and posteriorly, but isolated functionally by callosal section. This technique minimises some of the complications that resulted from the earlier, more extensive approaches. Hemispherectomy is performed when there is severe but unilateral disease, uncontrolled seizures, and evidence of hemiplegia. Earlier surgery may help to protect the unaffected hemisphere from possible damage as a result of severe, ongoing seizure activity from the affected hemisphere.

Functional surgery

Callosotomy and multiple supial transection are the most commonly performed types of functional surgery. Callosotomy involves division of the fibres of the corpus callosum to prevent the spread of seizure activity from one hemisphere to the other. Although complete freedom from seizures following callosotomy is unlikely, it can relieve certain kinds of disabling seizures, such as "drop attacks", and is viewed as a useful palliative intervention for some patients (Engel et al., 1993). Multiple supial transection (MST) involves making multiple supial cuts in the cortex to isolate blocks of cortical neurons, thus preventing horizontal spread of epileptic activity while preserving the vertical functional connections of these cortical neurons. Electrocorticography is used to monitor this process, which aims to extinguish "spiking". MST can be used in conjunction with resection when appropriate.

Selection for surgery

In general there are three criteria for selecting suitable candidates for epilepsy surgery: (1) disabling seizures resistant to high therapeutic levels of AEDs; (2) a well-defined region of seizure onset; and (3) an epileptogenic zone within functionally silent cortex (Duchowny, 1996). At times, however, the risk of a postoperative deficit is weighed against the potential benefits of the surgery in quality of life terms.

Localisation of seizure focus involves a staged process that moves from an initial use of least invasive techniques to more invasive techniques as required, as described in Table 9.4. Initial investigations include *video/EEG monitoring*, which enables analysis of EEG and behavioural changes associated with ictal events. This procedure is possible in children of any age, although it is demanding of children and parents, as the child is required to remain in front of the video camera for long periods of time. *Structural imaging*, using MRI, is also considered essential in identifying structural

TABLE 9.4
Selection process for temporal lobectomy

Stage 1	Medication
	Monotherapy, polytherapy
Stage 2	Investigation of epileptic focus
	Scalp EEG
	Video/EEG monitoring
	Brain imaging to detect structural lesion
	(Subdural and depth electrodes)
Stage 3	Assessment of neurobehavioural function
	Neuropsychological assessment
	(Sodium amytal ablation)
	(Functional brain imaging)
Stage 4	Temporal lobectomy
Stage 5	Follow-up
	Monitoring of seizure activity
	Neuropsychological review

NB. Bracketed stages are optional.

abnormalities corresponding to the epileptic focus. *Functional imaging techniques* such as SPECT and PET are regularly used in selecting children for surgery. SPECT is conducted during video/EEG monitoring to allow for precise localisation of ictal events. It involves the injection of intravenous photon-emitting tracers, which become fixed within minutes of injection and remain *in situ* for several hours, so that later brain images reflect activity at the time of injection. An area of brain suspected of involvement in seizure onset could be expected to be "hypometabolic" at rest (showing less uptake of the tracer on interictal SPECT), but "hypermetabolic", during a seizure (showing increased uptake of tracer on ictal SPECT). Establishing speech dominance is important in determining risk of an unacceptable postoperative deficit. Functional MRI (fMRI) techniques are currently being developed that visualise brain function, through the use of changes in local oxygenation of venous blood, and have been successfully used in children as young as 6 years (Harvey et al., 1998). In the future, fMRI may replace the more invasive procedures currently used to establish language dominance—techniques that are usually avoided in young children.

The limitation of scalp EEG in localising seizure onset may be overcome by placement of electrodes closer to the base of the brain. Sphenoidal or foramen ovule electrodes are used to lateralise and localise seizure onset. More precise localisation may need to be established by intracranial recording from electrodes inserted into the brain (*depth electrodes*) or from strips or grids of electrodes placed subdurally over the brain surface (subdural electrodes). Improved techniques for identifying hippocampal sclerosis on MRI have decreased the need for invasive monitoring in temporal lobe epilepsy (TLE); however, localisation of lateral temporal and extratemporal seizure foci is often more dependent on the use of subdural recording. Subdural electrodes can also enable functional mapping of language, motor and sensory cortex to be conducted prior to surgery in children to minimise the risk of postoperative deficit. These invasive monitoring techniques are not commonly used in very young children.

The *neuropsychological assessment* is important for establishing fulfilment of the second and third criteria for selection, and may identify areas of deficit consistent with suspected epileptic focus. Assessment may also alert the clinician to possible adverse consequences of surgery, in terms of its impact on postoperative functioning. The pattern of assessment results should be concordant with results from the neurological investigations. However, interpretation of neuropsychological data may be complicated by issues of functional reorganisation in children with very early brain pathology. Differences in the patterns of deficit identified in child and adult surgical samples are discussed in detail later in this chapter.

Intracarotid sodium amytal (Wada) testing is routinely used in evaluation for temporal lobe surgery, to mimic effects of surgery, to help lateralise language function, and assess risk of postoperative amnesia. It may also be used to predict degrees of memory decline (Trenerry et al., 1996). The procedure involves injection of sodium amytal, an anaesthetic agent, into either the left or right internal carotid through a catheter inserted into the femoral artery. This results in hemiparesis and speech arrest (if the language-dominant hemisphere is involved). Usually video EEG monitoring is conducted throughout the procedure to monitor electrical activity. Language testing and presentation of material for recall (memory items) are commenced once there is evidence of EEG slowing. Recall of the memory items is examined later, following return to normal function. While one hemisphere is functionally ablated in this way, the viability of the contralateral hippocampus to form new memories can be established.

The use of Wada techniques and the specific administration methods vary across centres. In our unit Wada testing is not routinely conducted, being used only when there is doubt regarding the ability of the contralateral hippocampus to support adequate memory function. Only a single injection is used, ipsilateral to suspected seizure focus. The procedure has been successfully conducted in children as young as 8, and in children with intellectual disability. It is a demanding procedure, requiring intensive familiarisation for successful outcome, and results can be difficult to interpret. Memory testing involves simple material, usually three pictured objects. A sentence chosen to have particular meaning to the child may be read out, for example, "Dr H. (child's neurologist) likes red jelly beans", to provide additional information about verbal recall. Recall (spontaneous or by recognition) of two of the three pictured objects represents a "technical pass". However, careful questioning of the child about their recall of events (what was said, what they did, how they felt) during the test often provides as much useful information as formal testing. Using this procedure the risk of a postoperative amnesia can usually be excluded; however, predictions about more subtle post-surgery memory impairments cannot be made.

Outcome in children

Surgery has proven to be a safe and effective method of treating medically intractable epilepsy in children. With careful selection, it is possible to maximise the effectiveness of surgery in terms of improved seizure control and to minimise the risk of an additional postoperative deficit. Aicardi (1994) has noted that outcome depends on the size and focal nature of the original lesion, as well as the surgical approach employed. For example, 70–85% of TLE patients with small easily resected lesions may achieve seizure freedom following surgery. Findings from our centre are consistent with this observation (Wrennall & Hopkins, 1989). However, patients with bigger lesions such as large, difficult-to-remove dysplasias, may have a less favourable outcome, with less than 50% achieving good seizure control. Early surgery may avoid cumulative adverse psychological (cognitive, behavioural, and social) difficulties that are associated with epilepsy. It may also avoid the potential detrimental impact of uncontrolled seizures on the brain.

Early resective surgery may avoid the poor developmental prognosis associated with catastrophic early epilepsy. The poor prognosis associated with severe congenital, acquired, or destructive lesions that result in epilepsy in infancy and early childhood has been well documented. There is some evidence that seizure activity itself is disruptive to ongoing development of new skills and may undermine skills already acquired, causing developmental regression, supporting the importance of early surgery. However, long-term outcomes of early versus delayed or no surgery are not known (Wyllie, 1996). There is evidence that early hemispherectomy results in less dramatic deficits in terms of language and motor function than such surgery performed at a later age, reflecting greater plasticity of the very young brain. Some studies evaluating the effect of temporal lobe resection in children and adolescents have shown decreases in memory functioning similar to those observed in adult patients (Oxbury, Creswell, Oxbury, & Adams, 1996; Westerveld et al., 1993; Zentner et al., 1995), although others have reported contradictory findings. In particular, Szabó et al. (1998) examined the effect of surgery on verbal memory in a group of 14 preadolescent children and found a greater mean decline in immediate verbal recall in the children with left-sided resection and a pre- to post-surgery decline in delayed recall in all children. Similarly, Beardsworth and Zaidel (1994) assessed memory for faces in children and adolescents with left and right TLE, before and after surgery. Pre-surgery, the right TLE group performed more poorly on each learning trial and on a delayed recall trial. Post-surgery they improved significantly on all trials except delayed recall. The left TLE group's performance was unchanged following surgery.

While these findings argue against severe deterioration post-surgery, even mild declines have the potential to impact on development. In adults a mild additional deficit in verbal memory following left temporal lobectomy may be well tolerated. The same change may represent significant impairment to a young child, who is still establishing skills. For an adolescent in the final years of school, where large amounts of verbal information must be learned, a mild verbal memory deficit may significantly limit academic progress. When a risk of an additional deficit is identified prior to surgery, counselling about the possible consequences is necessary. Delaying surgery may be the preferable option, perhaps until vocational training has been completed.

Successful epilepsy surgery during childhood can be associated with unexpected challenges to the child/adolescent and his/her family. Although seizures may be controlled, cognitive, learning, and behaviour difficulties often persist. For the adolescent, difficulties with social interaction with peers, a common source of distress, may also continue. Whereas seizures and medication may be blamed for such difficulties pre-surgery, the role of inherent strengths and weaknesses begins to be better understood post-surgery. These may be difficult to accept, particularly for the adolescent, indicating the importance of ongoing support from medical and allied health professionals who are informed regarding these issues.

Vagal nerve stimulation

Vagal nerve stimulation involves the implant of a small stimulator on the left vagal nerve. The mechanism of action remains unclear, but it is presumed to be through the activation of a variety of subcortical centres, leading to an inhibitory effect on seizures. In clinical trials, patients with chronic partial seizures show some decrease in seizure frequency but have not become seizure free (Sander, 1998). It may be that vagal nerve stimulation will become useful as an adjunctive therapy in some patients. To date there is little evidence of its effectiveness in child populations.

Diet

The ketogenic diet, which is a high-fat diet producing ketosis and acidosis, has been shown to be effective against all seizure types, but has been most successful in young children with Lennox–Gastaut syndrome and other difficult-to-treat childhood epilepsies. If the diet is strictly adhered to, complete seizure control can be achieved in up to 50% of previously refractory patients, with others deriving at least some benefit (Bourgeois, 1996c). Modifications to the diet have made it somewhat more palatable than the original form, although modified versions may be less effective. Kinsman et al. (1992) reported improved seizure control in 67% of young patients commenced on the diet, with a reduction in AED therapy being possible in 64%. Improvements in behaviour and alertness have also been observed in patients with good response to the diet.

Psychological interventions

It is generally recognised that external factors can lower the so-called "seizure threshold" and increase seizure frequency (Bourgeois, 1996b). Lowering of the seizure threshold can be caused by relatively non-specific and common life situations, such as stress, sleep deprivation, and intense emotional reactions, or it can be related to specific stimuli or activities, including strenuous physical exercise or certain types of light stimuli. An awareness of the possible influence of such factors can be helpful in developing strategies for management of epilepsy. For example, maintaining a good sleep routine may be helpful in managing juvenile myoclonic epilepsy, which is particularly sensitive to sleep deprivation or disruption. Absences are commonly precipitated by photic stimuli, particularly intermittent bright light. Wearing sunglasses may help reduce the risk of seizures where photic stimuli cannot be easily avoided. Classical conditioning paradigms, including habituation and presenting stimuli that are gradual approximations to the critical stimulus, have been used to treat rare reflex epilepsies where seizures are triggered by specific sensory stimuli.

Relaxation and other cognitive-behavioural techniques may be helpful when seizures have a mood-related prodrome or when interpersonal difficulties seem to triggers seizures (Goldstein, 1997). In relaxation training children are taught diaphragmatic breathing to counteract hyperventilation, which in itself may lower seizure thresholds and contribute to the occurrence of seizures. Approaches to seizure reduction that have involved EEG training using biofeedback may be effective. This technique involves the child, on recognition of pre-seizure signals, generating an "anticonvulsant" EEG rhythm that has been learned, so inhibiting the imminent seizure. After reviewing studies investigating the effectiveness of such techniques, Goldstein (1997) concluded that well-designed studies using larger groups are needed to determine the efficacy of these approaches to accurately evaluate their prognostic value.

Non-compliance with medication may be an important factor in increased seizures in as many as 50% of patients with epilepsy, and is noted to be a particular problem in adolescents (Caplan, 1998). Education, monitoring, and supportive counselling addressing issues such as AED therapy may help to reduce the impact of non-compliance.

SPECIFIC EPILEPSY SYNDROMES

The following descriptions of a selection of childhood-onset epilepsy syndromes are included to illustrate some of the diversity of these disorders in terms of their impact on children.

West syndrome is one of the epileptic encephalopathies of infancy. It presents during the first year of life, usually between 3 and 8 months. The syndrome includes three main features: infantile spasms, hypsarrhythmia, and psychomotor delay. Infantile spasms consist of clusters of sudden briefly sustained movements of the axial musculature (head, neck, and limbs). Hypsarrhythmia refers to the interictal EEG pattern of high-voltage slow waves, spikes, and sharp waves that seem to occur randomly from all cortical regions, giving the impression of chaotic disorganisation of cortical electrogenesis; Figure 9.3 illustrates an EEG recording for a child with typical hypsarrhythmia. Cryptogenic and symptomatic varieties of West syndrome are identified, and aetiology is diverse, including neurocutaneous disorders such as tuberous sclerosis, cerebral malformations, prenatal and perinatal brain

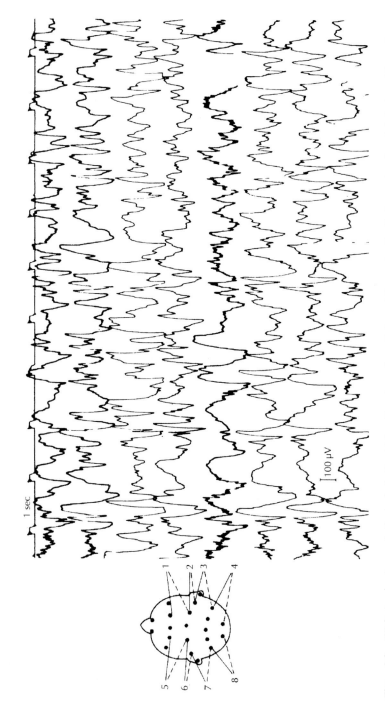

Figure 9.3. EEG showing hypsarrhythmia, including high-voltage irregular activity and frequent spike discharges in a female infant aged 6 months. Reprinted with permission from O'Donohoe (1994).

injury, and metabolic disorders. West syndrome is said to be cryptogenic in children who had previously been healthy, were developing normally, and in whom no cause is identified. The prognosis is generally poor, with mental retardation, hyperactivity, and autism commonly reported (Dulac, Plouin, & Jambaque, 1993). Normal development is reported in 12–25% of patients and is strongly influenced by the presence, and nature of a structural abnormality underlying the syndrome. Treatment includes AEDs, corticosteroids, and surgery if focal cerebral pathology is identified. Better outcome has been documented for children who respond to treatment, with behavioural regression observed where response to treatment is poor (Koo, Hwang, & Logan, 1993; Schlumberger & Dulac, 1994).

The rate of spontaneous remission of West syndrome is around 25% within 1 year of onset; however, if treatment does not control seizures children go on to develop other seizures as they get older, and 25% of children are later diagnosed with Lennox–Gastaut syndrome (Hrachovy, Glaze, & Frost, 1991; Ohtahara, Ohtsuka, & Yoshinaga, 1988; Yamatogi & Ohtahara, 1981).

Lennox–Gastaut syndrome is an early childhood-onset epileptic encephalopathy, characterised by multiple seizure types (atonic, atypical absence, tonic, and tonic–clonic seizures), mental retardation, and slow spike–wave discharges on EEG. Approximately 70–75% of cases result from demonstrable brain abnormality or occur in patients with previous developmental delay or epilepsy (Aicardi, 1996). Seizure onset occurs between the ages of 1 and 7 years, and up to 25% of patients have a premorbid history of West syndrome. The prognosis for Lennox–Gastaut syndrome is quite poor, and although the multiple seizure types evolve into a single predominant pattern by the second decade, mental impairment and psychosocial handicap are usually permanent. Early onset (before age 2) is associated with a higher incidence of poor outcome, and seizures are often difficult to control with AED therapy, although the newer AEDs are proving to be more successful (Dulac & Kaminska, 1997; Glauser, 1997; Timmings & Richens, 1992).

Temporal lobe epilepsies are characterised by simple partial, complex partial, and secondarily generalised seizures, or combinations of these. Frequently there is a history of febrile seizures and a family history of seizures (Wyllie & Lüders, 1996b). Onset is commonly in childhood or young adulthood. Two subtypes of TLE have been delineated: hippocampal (mesiobasal limbic or rhinocephalic) TLE, the most common form; and lateral TLE. The features of the seizures associated with each may be different, reflecting the origin of seizure onset. For example, hippocampal TLE may be associated with rising epigastric discomfort, nausea, and marked autonomic signs. In contrast, auras associated with lateral TLE include auditory hallucinations, illusions, or dreamy states. Surgical intervention for TLE, and the role of neuropsychology in this process, will be discussed in later sections of this chapter.

Frontal lobe epilepsies (FLE), as with TLE, are associated with a range of epilepsy types, including simple partial, complex partial, and secondarily generalised seizures, and are categorised according to the area of the frontal lobes involved in seizure activity (Quesney, Constain, & Rasmussen, 1992). Common features of seizures include bilateral movements, automatisms, short (less than 1 min) but frequent (25–100 per month) episodes, and minimal postictal confusion (Williamson, 1992). Frontal lobe epilepsy is relatively rare in childhood, although as this form of epilepsy becomes better defined more children are being identified. Caplan (1998) suggests that FLE is characterised by (1) brief periods of unresponsiveness, without loss of consciousness, and with intact language comprehension and (2) tonic or clonic motor phenomena, involving face and arms. Other features may include laughter, crying, screaming, or sexual behaviours. Patients frequently present with features typical of frontal dysfunction, including normal intelligence, executive dysfunction, and behavioural disturbance. FLE is generally considered difficult to control, with AEDs being the most common treatment option.

Childhood absence epilepsy is characterised by brief episodes of altered consciousness in which the child suddenly stops an activity and stares vacantly for a short time, and then continues the activity, with no evidence of postictal confusion (Lockman, 1989). Typical absence seizures occur in school-aged children, with an increased risk where there is a family history of epilepsy, or where the child has a history of febrile convulsions. Absences can occur frequently, many times during a single day, and are characterised by generalised spike-and-wave discharges at a rate of 3 Hz on EEG (Caplan, 1998). Absences are frequently detected by teachers who comment that the child is vague or has a tendency to daydream, and these episodes may impinge on developmental progress, particularly within the classroom environment, as the child may miss important instruction during seizures. Some researchers have noted that, although intellectual ability is generally intact, attentional skills may be specifically impaired (Duncan, 1988; Mirsky, 1989). Absence seizures are generally well controlled by AEDs, and where control is adequate over 2 years or more seizures frequently remit (Caplan, 1998).

Acquired epileptic aphasia (Landau–Kleffner syndrome) and epilepsy with continuous spike–waves during slow-wave sleep have been "discovered" and described only recently, and have been referred to as "epilepsies with cognitive symptomatology", because the main manifestation is a disturbance of cognition, language, and/or behaviour (Deonna, 1996). There are many clinical and EEG similarities between these two disorders, leading to arguments that they represent somewhat different manifestations of the same pathological process. Seizures are observed, but not always.

Acquired epileptic aphasia is associated with onset during the toddler/ preschool years, with regression of previously acquired language, both expressive and receptive, word deafness, and auditory agnosia (Aicardi, 1986; Deonna, 1996), and is often accompanied by other behavioural and cognitive dysfunction. The EEG is commonly abnormal, with epileptic activity evident during wake recordings and becoming more pronounced during sleep. Although there is no characteristic EEG pattern, paroxysmal sharp and spike–wave complexes are often encountered in the central temporal and parietal regions, usually in a bilateral distribution with the dominant hemisphere most involved (Duchowny & Harvey, 1996). Seizures, if present, usually remit before the age of 15 years, as do EEG abnormalities. Prognosis is variable, and many patients are left with significant language impairment. The pathogenesis of acquired epileptic aphasia has not been established. Results of neuroimaging have failed to demonstrate any morphological abnormalities. PET studies have shown asymmetric metabolic activity in the temporal lobes, which is not seen after remission. Investigations searching for a specific encephalopathy or subacute encephalitis, including cerebral biopsy, have yielded inconsistent findings and have not supported the presence of a structural lesion (Genton, Bureau, Dravet, & Roger, 1996).

The syndrome of *epilepsy with continuous spike–wave during slow-wave sleep* is generally defined as the coexistence of cognitive and behavioural disturbance, atypical absence, and other seizure types with EEG demonstrating almost complete spike–wave activity during slow-wave (non-REM) sleep (Duchowny & Harvey, 1996). Onset is typically between 4 and 6 years of age, and it is reported to occur in 0.5% of children (Morikawa et al., 1985), after either normal or abnormal previous development. Diagnosis is made on the basis of sleep EEG findings of general spike–wave discharge, onset of seizures following previously normal development, in conjunction with evidence of behavioural and intellectual deterioration (Perez et al., 1993). Language disturbance is often observed, although qualitatively different from that seen in acquired aphasia, in that expressive ability is intact, but language content is often disorganised, reflecting high-level dysfunction (Genton & Guerrini, 1993; Perez et al., 1993). Behavioural disturbances are also characteristic of higher-level disorders and may include disinhibition, lack of insight, reduced attention, and perseveration (Perez et al., 1993). As for acquired aphasia, epileptic symptoms often remit by age 15, and some researchers suggest reversibility of behavioural and cognitive impairments on remission or in association with seizure control (Bureau et al., 1990; Tassinari et al., 1982), although others have not replicated these findings (Perez et al., 1993).

Both these conditions are difficult to treat with AED therapy and treatment with corticosteroids may be beneficial. There are reports of successful surgical treatment of patients with acquired epileptic aphasia using a multiple supial transection technique. In the absence of clearly identified seizures, and in view of the finding of abnormal EEG in children free of seizures and cognitive symptoms, some clinicians remain sceptical about the concept of cognitive epilepsies and legitimately fear the risk of making an unprovable diagnosis with unwarranted practical implications (Deonna, 1996).

Benign epilepsy of childhood with centrotemporal spikes is the most common epilepsy syndrome with onset during childhood, accounting for 25% of all epileptic syndromes in children under age 12. Onset peaks between 7 and 9 years of age, and the condition usually remits by age 16. It is characterised by brief, simple, partial, hemifacial motor seizures, frequently having associated somatosensory symptoms that have a tendency to evolve into generalised tonic–clonic seizures (Watanabe, 1996). Seizures typically occur within hours of falling asleep, although most children have few seizures, with 15% reporting a single seizure, and 56% two seizures (Caplan, 1998). Centrotemporal spikes with a characteristic horizontal dipole are seen on EEG, indicating involvement of the perirolandic cortex. Clinical reports suggest patients show normal development and are neurologically asymptomatic; however, research indicates that such EEG abnormalities may impact on cognitive function, so further investigation is needed to further examine functional outcome in these children. There is a high incidence of a positive family history, suggesting that genetic factors are important in this disorder.

COGNITIVE AND BEHAVIOURAL ISSUES

Overview

Children with epilepsy have a higher incidence of intellectual, academic, and behaviour difficulties than their peers (Curley, 1992; Farwell, Dodrill, & Batzel, 1985; Hoare, 1984; Rutter et al., 1970; Seidenberg et al., 1986; Stores, 1978). They are at greater risk of academic and behaviour difficulties than children with other chronic illness conditions, such as asthma and diabetes (Austin, Huberty, Huster, & Dunn, 1998; Hoare, 1984). It is also true, however, that many children with epilepsy function "normally". Many studies have attempted to identify specific factors that may have the greatest influence on the psychological functioning of children with epilepsy. Most have concluded that there is a complex interdependence among a number of factors. Isolating their individual impact has proven to be extremely difficult (Austin et al., 1992; Curley 1992; Hermann, Whitman, & Dell, 1989).

Children with brain damage, or any kind of pathological (disease) process that impacts on brain function, are at risk of intellectual, academic, and learning difficulties, as a direct result of the impact of the brain dysfunction on their psychological functioning. The detrimental impact of brain dysfunction on development is a recurring theme in this volume. Within the field of childhood epilepsy, children with symptomatic epilepsy (with a documented brain abnormality) have generally been identified as having significantly higher rates of psychological difficulties than children with ideopathic epilepsy (Bourgeois et al., 1983; Rutter et al., 1970). The underlying disease or damage is considered by many to be the most important determinant of functioning of children with epilepsy. (Camfield, 1997; Kasteleijn-Nolst Trenité, 1996). Children with epilepsy that is not linked to brain damage are also at increased risk of cognitive and psychological difficulties (Rutter et al., 1970), and a wide range of factors have been identified as potentially important in determining functional outcome in this group, as listed in Table 9.5. These include seizure-related variables, such as age of onset of epilepsy, type of epilepsy, duration and severity of the seizures, presence and nature of neuropsychological impairments, and of course, the psychosocial burden that is associated with the disorder. Treatment with AEDs has been particularly implicated as having a detrimental effect on cognition and behaviour. Subclinical epileptic activity has also been identified as an important factor, potentially impacting on the day-to-day functioning of the child, between seizure episodes.

The following review will concentrate on the epilepsy-specific risk factors (listed in Table 9.5) that may impact on the cognitive and behavoural functioning of the child with epilepsy, with or without identified brain pathology. The important issue of stability of cognitive functioning over time is also addressed.

Stability of cognitive function

One of the major concerns for children with epilepsy is the possibility of deterioration in functioning, as a direct result of the seizure disorder. Clinical experience suggests that some children do perform more poorly over time.

TABLE 9.5
Factors associated with outcome in children with epilepsy

Seizure-related factors
  Presence of underlying brain pathology
  Age at seizure onset
  Type of epilepsy
  Duration and severity of seizures and seizure disorder
  Treatment with anti-epileptic drugs
  Subclinical epileptic activity

Other factors
  Nature and degree of cognitive impairment
  Perceived psychosocial burden
  Access to appropriate intervention

Identification of children at risk of developmental regression, and factors that contribute to this deterioration, is of particular importance to clinicians involved in the care of children with epilepsy. Research suggests that developmental regression is very often associated with certain epilepsy syndromes, particularly with the so-called "encephalopathic" epilepsies, such as West syndrome and Lennox–Gastaut syndrome. These syndromes, with onset in infancy and early childhood, may have a devastating impact on development. Often developmental regression in early childhood appears to coincide with the development or worsening of seizures, even in the presence of identified brain pathology. For example, Scott and Neville (1998) note that, in tuberous sclerosis, symptoms of cognitive impairment and autistic regression appear to be closely correlated to the onset of epilepsy in the first year of life. Surgical treatment is increasingly used in tuberous sclerosis, to achieve seizure control and relief of autistic symptomatology, and is also associated with significant developmental gains (Duchowny et al., 1998). Similarly, diagnosis of epileptic aphasia is dependent upon a deterioration in language functioning, but the extent to which these symptoms relate to epileptic activity is a subject of ongoing debate (Bishop, 1985).

In studies examining intellectual functioning of samples of adults and children with epilepsy, IQ is usually found to be within the normal range, but shifted downwards (Glosser et al., 1997; Rodin et al., 1986). Differences between studies reflect bias for selecting those towards the more severe end of the epilepsy spectrum. Samples of children with epilepsy, possibly selected with less bias, have been shown to have a mean IQ closer to population expectations (Bourgeois et al., 1983). Adult studies tend to document stability in IQ over time. For example, Selwa et al. (1994) conducted serial cognitive testing in 47 patients with temporal lobe epilepsy, 31 before and after temporal lobe resection. Slight overall gains in performance were in the direction and within the range expected for a normal population. Similarly, Holmes et al. (1998) followed a group of adults with intractable, complex partial seizures over a 10-year period and found no overall change in intelligence or neuropsychological functioning, although a few subtle losses were noted for speed of response and visuospatial skill. These changes did not seem to be related to a worsening of seizure disorder over time.

Most studies report group results, where individual deterioration may be masked by the overall group stability. Further, IQ is a relatively insensitive measure and normal IQ does not exclude other subtle, but significant cognitive deficits. Such subtle cognitive impairment may have greater significance during childhood because of the potential to impact on developing skills. However, results from child-based studies are variable. Bourgeois et al. (1983) prospectively studied 72 children with epilepsy, within 2 weeks of diagnosis and at yearly intervals thereafter for an average of 4 years. The mean IQ for the group (99.7, SD = 20.2) was not different from their non-epileptic siblings, and did not change significantly over time. There was a subgroup of children identified who did demonstrate decreasing IQ. These children were characterised by a high number of toxic AED levels, severity of seizure disorder, and younger age at onset. In contrast, children with symptomatic epilepsy showed stable intellectual performance over time. Rodin et al. (1986) conducted a retrospective analysis of IQ performance for 64 children with epilepsy over a mean follow-up period of 9.6 years (5–33 years). They found a non-significant mean decrease in IQ from 91.6 to 90.2. When individual predictors were examined, they found a trend towards a rise in IQ scores in children who had been seizure free for at least 2 years, and a significant decrease in performance IQ for the subgroup with persisting seizures. This pattern was the same regardless of aetiology of epilepsy. Similar results have been reported from a large population-based study (Ellenberg, Hirtz, & Nelson, 1986), where children who had their first, non-febrile seizure between 4 and 7 years of age were identified and IQ matched with controls at age 4 years. By age 7 there were no IQ differences between the groups. Further, seizure variables were not related to IQ.

Increasing academic difficulties have also been suggested by some researchers. Rodin et al. (1986) found that children with epilepsy failed to make expected academic progress over time, reflected in falling scores on the Wide Range Achievement Test, but these results are yet to be replicated. There has been little attention to behavioural functioning, but in a 2½- to 3-year follow-up of boys with epilepsy (Curley, 1992) initial high rates of behaviour problems were identified (30 of the original sample of 40 boys). Although the number and severity of problems tended to persist, behaviour had improved at follow-up.

These results appear to be reassuring; however, many of the studies have significant limitations. First, follow-up periods are relatively short, and it may be necessary to follow children throughout childhood into adulthood before the full impact of a seizure disorder on development is apparent. Second, many studies have a selection bias towards children with more severe epilepsy, and treat epilepsy as a unitary disorder. Third, results from different IQ measures at different ages are not directly comparable, and variability in children's performance is not considered, nor is the influence of AED serum levels at time of assessment. Prospective studies, particularly of children identified early in the course of their seizure disorder, have great potential to increase our understanding of the developmental implications of seizures during childhood. Selecting groups of children with specific epilepsy syndromes will also enable the unique impact of these syndromes to be evaluated.

One such study was commenced at the Royal Children's Hospital, Melbourne, in 1991. A group of children and adolescents with recent-onset TLE ($n = 63$) underwent psychological assessment as part of initial ascertainment for a longitudinal study of TLE during childhood. The demographic and neurological characteristics of the sample have been previously described by Harvey et al. (1997). A subset of the original sample ($n = 35$) has also been reassessed 5 years later (Wrennall et al., 1998). Initial IQ assessment involved the WPPSI-R/WISC-R, with follow-up using the WAIS-R/WISC-III. For this subgroup, mean full-scale IQ (FSIQ) at initial assessment was 99.7 (SD = 18.5). At follow-up, FSIQ had decreased to 87.8 (SD = 19.0), a fall of nearly 12 points. Some of this decrease can be explained by comparison of the WISC-III and WISC-R. FSIQ from the WISC-R is reported to be some 5 points higher than for the WISC-III (Wechsler, 1991). Even allowing for this difference IQ appears to be significantly lower at follow-up for this group, by 7or 8 points.

The sample was divided into three subgroups on the basis of aetiology, each group having a similar age of seizure onset (Harvey, Berkovic, Wrennall, & Hopkins, 1997): *developmental TLE*, children with evidence of cortical malformations, long standing non-progressive tumours and hamartomas; *TLE with HS/significant antecedents*, children with hippocampal sclerosis and/or a history of a significant antecedent; and *cryptogenic TLE*, children for whom no underlying cause had been identified at the time of enrolment. Initial and follow-up FSIQ for each group are listed in Table 9.6, and illustrate significant group differences.

The HS/antecedent group had lower FSIQ than the other groups initially, and fell further behind age expectations over time, functioning close to the intellectually impaired range. The developmental group, in comparison, remained stable, with difference in FSIQ accounted for by change from WISC-R to WISC-III. The poor progress of the cryptogenic group is surprising, and may reflect its heterogeneous nature. This group is likely to include children with as yet unidentified brain abnormalities and children with epilepsy of genetic origin. The impact of other variables, including severity of seizure disorder and AED therapy, is yet to be analysed. These findings are in

TABLE 9.6
FSIQ at initial and follow-up (>5 years) evaluations for children with temporal lobe epilepsy across subgroups

	TLE subgroup[a]		
	Cryptogenic	*HS/Antecedent*	*Developmental*
n	22	7	5
FSIQ: Initial M (SD)	103.6 (15.1)	81.9 (23.3)	107.6 (13.1)
FSIQ: Follow-up M (SD)	89.7 (18.1)	72.7 (17.7)	102.0 (13.2)

[a] One child was unclassified.
From Wrennall et al. (1998).

contrast to previous studies, suggesting that for TLE at least there is evidence of deterioration, with the presence and nature of an identified brain abnormality an important predictor.

The following three case examples provide further illustrations of fall-off in abilities over time for children with epilepsy. These children each display changes in performance on intellectual and neuropsychological measures over time, suggestive of a deterioration in functioning.

Nancy, now aged 15 years, was diagnosed with absence seizures, confirmed by EEG, at the age of 8 months. Over time she experienced a range of generalised seizure types that have never been completely controlled by AED therapy. No underlying brain abnormality has been identified on CT or MRI. Nancy was first seen for neuropsychological assessment at age 7 years, when she was found to be functioning solidly within the "low average" range of intellectual ability. She was, however, experiencing significant academic and social difficulties at that time. Over time a series of intellectual assessments have indicated a gradual fall in IQ, with Nancy now functioning within the "mildly intellectually retarded" range (i.e., FSIQ = 67). There was no history of developmental regression, rather the change in IQ reflected a failure to progress at the expected rate.

Tony, aged 15 years, has an early medical history that includes acute lymphoblastic leukaemia treated with cranial irradiation at the age of 17 months, and an episode of bacterial meningitis at the age of 5 years. At the age of 10 years Tony began having complex partial seizures, arising from the temporal lobe. His epilepsy remains uncontrolled despite a combination of three kinds of AEDs. When first seen for neuropsychological assessment, just after his diagnosis with temporal lobe epilepsy, he gained an FSIQ score of 98, an encouraging result in view of his earlier illnesses. However, seen some 5 years later, Tony's FSIQ is now well below this level, and falls within the "mildly intellectually retarded" range. As with Nancy, the fall in Tony's intellectual abilities appeared to reflect a "failure to progress".

Peter, aged 14 years, was diagnosed with gelastic epilepsy at the age of 7, although he may well have been experiencing gelastic seizures, characterised by laughing, since the age of 4. An MRI scan revealed a hypothalamic hamartoma, a common form of pathology underlying gelastic epilepsy. When seen for neuropsychological assessment at age 9 years, Peter's FSIQ was within the "average" range (FSIQ = 102). When seen again at 13 years, prior to his surgery, Peter was found to be functioning within the "mildly retarded" range. His mother reported developmental regression, with a loss of previously acquired skills. At this time Peter displayed a virtual "amnesic syndrome" in terms of his ability to recall day-to-day events. EEG recordings revealed continuous epileptic activity.

Seizure-related factors

A number of seizure-related variables have been implicated as influential in cognition, academic ability, and behaviour generally. These include age of onset of seizures, duration and severity of the seizure disorder, and seizure type. Laterality and location of the epileptic focus have also been investigated, with studies describing specific neuropsychological deficits associated with these parameters.

Age of seizure onset and seizure severity

Studies looking at the impact of early seizures on subsequent development are relatively scarce. Some information is available from the National Institutes of Health (NIH) Collaborative Perinatal Project, which recruited 55,000 babies at birth and monitored them to age 7 years. There were 431 sibling pairs discordant for febrile seizures in this cohort. The sibling pairs were identical in WISC and WRAT scores when assessed age 7 years, unless the child was known to be neurologically abnormal before their febrile seizure(s). Of the 14 children who had febrile status epilepticus (SE), lasting at least 1 h, none had lower IQ scores than their siblings (Ellenberg & Nelson, 1978). Although these results are positive, they do not exclude the possibility of more subtle cognitive deficits resulting from seizures, or the later emergence of problems as children are required to employ higher-order cognitive abilities. In a similar study, Maytal, Shinnar, Moshé, and Alvorez (1989) studied children with SE (defined as a seizure lasing >30 min) with no recognised acute or progressive cause. They found only two children had any serious sequelae. However, in the groups with acute symptomatic SE or SE associated with an underlying progressive encephalopathy, 27% had neurological sequelae. These children, who tended to be much younger, appeared more vulnerable to further deficit, possibly due to the presence of existing brain pathology.

In a study aimed to investigate the additional burden caused by epilepsy on children with documented brain damage, Vargha-Khadem et al. (1992) examined cognitive functioning of children with cerebral palsy and associated left or right hemisphere damage and the additional presence of a seizure disorder, resulting from prenatal or perinatal insults. They found that cognitive impairment was highly related to the presence of seizures and/or severe EEG abnormality. Children with hemiplegia and no seizures tended to have relatively mild cognitive deficits. Children with more severe damage, but no seizures, exhibited fewer deficits than did the children with seizures and mild damage. These results argue that the presence of seizure disorder (or anti-epilepsy medication) has an independent and deleterious impact on cognitive ability, regardless of the presence or degree of underlying brain damage.

Others have studied the relationship between seizure-related variables and cognitive, academic, and behavioural functioning. O'Leary et al. (1983) investigated age of onset (before or after 5 years) and seizure type (generalised/partial) on neuropsychological functioning in children referred to a specialised epilepsy centre. Four groups were compared: early onset/ partial seizures; early onset/generalised seizures; late onset/partial seizures; and late onset/generalised seizures. Irrespective of seizure type, children with early onset achieved poorer scores for verbal IQ, performance IQ, and Trail Making Test. Seizure type was not predictive of performance. Farwell et al. (1985) also examined the influence of seizure variables (seizure type, seizure frequency, age of onset, and duration of seizure disorder) on intellectual and neuropsychological functioning. They found a significant relationship between age of onset and duration of seizure disorder, with lower IQ scores associated with earlier seizure onset.

The contribution of seizure variables to academic performance is unclear. Although some researchers do not find seizure-based effects (e.g., Huberty, Austin, Risinger, & McNelis, 1992) others have identified a number of predictors of academic outcome. Seidenberg et al. (1986) reported a generally high incidence of academic problems in children with epilepsy, with greatest difficulties in arithmetic (33%), followed by spelling, reading comprehension, and word recognition (10%). Difficulties were more pronounced in older children. Additional risk factors included younger age at seizure onset, higher lifetime total seizure number, and multiple seizure types, although seizure-related variables provided only a modest amount of predictive value for academic functioning.

The relative contribution of seizure-related variables to behaviour difficulties in children has also been studied. Hermann and colleagues (Hermann et al., 1989; Hermann & Whitman, 1986) utilised a "multi-aetiologic" model, which identifies four types of variables (biological, psychosocial, medication related, demographic) as influential in the development of psychopathology in children with epilepsy. For the sample as a whole, gender and seizure control (biological) emerged as the strongest predictor variable of behaviour. Parental marital status (psychosocial) was also strongly predictive, particularly for boys, followed by polytherapy/monotherapy (medication). The predictors, however, were not independent, making interpretation difficult. Examining similar factors, Hoare and Kerley (1991) found increased psychiatric disturbance associated with early onset of seizures and higher seizure frequency. Curley (1992) also utilised a biopsychosocial model to account for the increased incidence of behavioural disturbance in boys with seizures, but normal IQ. The emphasis in this model was on biological (seizure-related) factors, psychological (neuropsychological/intellectual) factors, and social (family/marital) factors. The important seizure-related variables were total seizures experienced, severity of seizure disorder over the preceding year, and time since last seizure, with neurocognitive status, as reflected by IQ, accounting for the largest proportion of the variance. At a later follow-up, severity of seizure disorder in the year prior to study commencement was the most important predictor of behaviour. The relative contribution of biological and psychological factors to this variable remains unclear.

The detailed investigation of individuals with TLE provides an opportunity to study factors such as age at seizure onset and seizure severity within a somewhat more homogeneous population. Such studies have established the importance of age of seizure onset for later cognitive functioning (Glosser et al., 1997; Hermann, Seidenberg, Schoenfield, & Davies, 1997; Saykin et al., 1989; Strauss et al., 1995), with Glosser et al. (1997) identifying age at onset as more important than the timing of the neurological damage presumed to underlie the epilepsy. However, the relationship is complex. Although later age of onset is linked to better cognitive performance, it is also related to poorer cognitive outcome following surgery in adult samples, with greater risk of decline in postoperative memory function (Hermann, Seidenberg, Haltiner, & Wyler, 1995; Wolf et al., 1993).

Glosser et al. (1997) felt the results of their study were consistent with the hypothesis that ongoing seizures in childhood pose risks to cognitive development. Evidence for increased vulnerability of the young brain to the effects of seizures was also provided by Hermann et al. (1997), who looked at cognitive performance in two groups of adults, with and without significant mesial temporal sclerosis (MTS) who had undergone temporal lobectomy. Patients identified as having significant MTS were found to be more impaired on a range of cognitive measures than patients with no or mild MTS. The subjects with significant MTS had an earlier age of onset of seizures, once again implicating early onset/longer-duration disorder in poor outcome.

The nature of the observed association between early febrile seizures, MTS, and TLE is the subject of ongoing debate. It is useful to review this debate in the context of a possible increased vulnerability of the immature CNS to seizure-induced damage. In studies of patients with TLE, prolonged or focal febrile seizures are commonly reported and typically precede the onset of partial seizures by several years. In a community-based study of children with new-onset TLE, described earlier, complex partial seizures were antedated by idiopathic febrile seizures in 21% of the children (Harvey, Berkovic, et al., 1997). However, the findings of studies following up cohorts of children with febrile seizures have been variable in terms of indicating an association between early febrile seizures and later epilepsy, possibly due to difficulties identifying complex partial seizures in young children (Harvey, 1999), or because duration of included febrile seizures has been relatively short (Maher & McLachlan, 1995; Verity, Ross, & Golding, 1993). Regardless of any possible relationship, it is important to stress that TLE remains a relatively rare outcome of febrile seizures during early childhood.

MTS is the most common pathological finding in adults with TLE.

Evidence suggests that MTS is the cause, not the consequence, of TLE. Prolonged febrile seizures and SE have been implicated as major predisposing factors for MTS, although the mechanism for damage to the mesial temporal lobe structures and the hippocampus remains uncertain (Harvey, 1999). Animal models have been used to demonstrate a relationship between prolonged seizures and MTS. When kainic acid (KA), an excitatory amino acid, is administered in sufficient doses to experimental animals prolonged seizures ensue. In survivors, widespread cerebral lesions are found, similar to those observed in human TLE, with hippocampal structures sustaining most damage, although the effect is mainly seen in adult animals. Such age differences suggest a relative invulnerability of the immature brain to the effects of SE (Holmes, 1997). However, Wasterlain (1997) has developed animal models of SE in young animals, which they report uniformly produce brain damage. For example, Wasterlain observes that KA-induced seizures damage the hippocampus of 10-day-old rabbits, raising the possibility that KA resistance is species specific. Although the immature brain may be less vulnerable to damage caused by prolonged and recurrent seizures, it is not immune to such damage. There is also evidence that seizures retard brain growth even when they produce no histological lesions, although later "catch-up" growth is observed (Moshé et al., 1996).

Seizure type

The impact of different seizure types has received some attention in the literature, although less so in recent times, reflecting the move away from a seizure type to a seizure syndrome approach. Diagnosis of particular types of epilepsy, rather than seizure type, is linked with different expectations for development and outcome. Syndromes with similar clinical characteristics, but with onset at different stages during childhood, for example, complex partial seizures, can be associated with different outcomes.

A number of studies have found patients with partial seizures perform better on cognitive tasks than patients with generalised seizures (Fedio & Mirsky, 1969; Kløve & Matthews, 1974); however, differences between early studies in classification of seizure type and influence of other seizure-related variables, such as age of onset, make comparisons difficult. Giordani et al. (1985) controlled for a number of seizure-related and medication variables in a study that compared adults and children with seizures classified as partial (simple or complex), generalised, or partial secondarily generalised. Patients with different seizure types did not differ in terms of summary IQ scores; however, those with generalised seizures or partial seizures that were secondarily generalised performed more poorly on subtests particularly sensitive to attentional factors and speed of response. These "attributes" are argued to impact on the performance of children and adults with epilepsy, and will be addressed in detail in a later discussion. In a similar study, O'Leary et al. (1983) found that children with partial and generalised seizures performed similarly on the Halstead Neuropsychological Test Battery for Children, with only one group difference, in favour of the partial seizure group, on Tactual Performance Test—Time, again a test involving speed of response. The researchers later divided the partial seizure group into simple partial, complex partial, and secondarily generalised. These groups differed on only Tactual Performance Test— Location, but there was a trend for the secondarily generalised group to do more poorly, possibly indicating a more severe seizure disorder. There was no one pattern of cognitive dysfunction that was typical of children with particular seizure types.

Farwell et al. (1985) have also examined outcome according to seizure type, identifying group differences in both IQ and neuropsychological performance. Children with minor motor seizures and atypical absences exhibited lower IQ than other groups. In contrast, children with classic absence seizures had normal IQ, and children with partial and generalised tonic-clonic seizures demonstrated a similar IQ distribution. These authors noted that neuropsychological function was more sensitive in discriminating seizure subgroups, although they did not report the details of their findings. Jambaquè et al. (1993) also compared children according to seizure type, specifically idiopathic generalised seizures versus various forms of partial seizures. They found that, although children with idiopathic generalised seizures gained higher IQ scores, significant differences were found only between children with bitemporal lobe EEG abnormalities and the other seizure types, with the bilateral temporal lobe children performing more poorly. Further, children with generalised seizures displayed memory difficulties relative to controls, but performed better than those with partial seizures. Within the partial seizure subgroups, different memory profiles were observed. Generalisations from these studies are limited due to small and probably unrepresentative samples; however, findings point to functional differences for children associated with the nature of seizure disorders, which need to be further investigated.

Academic and behavioural function has also been related to seizure type. Holdsworth and Whitmore (1974) found that children with major motor seizures (atonic–clonic), as compared to absence seizures, were experiencing more educational difficulties. Seidenberg et al. (1986) found seizure type differentiated arithmetic abilities, with children with generalised seizures performing relatively more poorly than children with partial seizures. They also found that children with mixed seizures (absence and tonic–clonic) were significantly more impaired across all academic areas than children with a single generalised seizure type, although this result was confounded by seizure severity, earlier age of onset, and a higher average number of AEDs.

Studies addressing behavioural patterns and seizure type provide contradictory findings. Although a number of research groups have found no relationship between specific seizure types and psychopathology (Austin, Risinger, & Beckett, 1992; Hoare & Kerley, 1991; Whitman, Hermann, Black, & Chhabria, 1982), Rutter et al. (1970) reported greatest behavioural pathology in children with psychomotor seizures and Hoare (1984) documented increased psychopathology among children with complex partial seizures. In support of these latter findings, a more recent study (Camfield et al., 1993) identified a relationship between social outcome and seizure type, with best social outcome associated with simple partial seizures. Unfortunately, each of these studies is limited by a relatively unidimensional approach, and an inability to encompass important variables such as aetiology, age of onset, and the nature of the EEG abnormality. Looking to the future, the syndrome approach may be more fruitful in identifying factors that impact on functioning and development in the child with epilepsy.

Laterality and location of seizure focus

In many instances, it is possible to locate an epilepsy focus within the brain, from which epileptic activity originates. Such a focus is commonly seen as an indicator of localised brain pathology or dysfunction, and linked with specific patterns of neuropsychological impairment. Many studies have described differences in the effects of epileptic foci in the left versus right hemisphere, or within different regions of the same hemisphere. Much of this literature has been dominated by research on outcomes following epilepsy surgery, particularly temporal lobectomy. This tradition argues for an association between poorer verbal memory pre- and post-surgery with a left temporal seizure focus, and between poorer visual (non-verbal) memory and right temporal foci. However, although bilateral damage to the hippocampi is linked to the amnesic syndrome, verifying the important role of the mesial temporal lobe structures, particularly the hippocampus, in the acquisition of new information (Milner, 1958; Squire & Zola-Morgan, 1991), many studies have been unable to establish a clear-cut difference in memory function between right and left temporal lobes (Glosser et al., 1997; Hermann, Seidenberg, Haltiner, & Wyler, 1992; Oxbury & Oxbury, 1989; Selwa et al., 1994).

Many studies note generalised cognitive impairment in their samples, with particularly poor performance for left TLE patients, perhaps reflecting the presence of a significant verbal memory deficit from early in life that impacts on the acquisition of skills and knowledge during childhood, and results in lowered intellectual function. Further, studies using improved imaging and histopathological cell-counting techniques have linked degree of memory impairment to degree of damage and cell loss in the hippocampus, associated with MTS (Baxendale et al., 1998). But, although some reports have described verbal-specific memory deficits in left TLE patients (Hermann et al., 1997; Selwa et al., 1994), or in both left and right TLE patients (Saling et al., 1993), specific right TLE memory profiles remain elusive. Regardless of the radiological technique, it appears that the nature of the memory task is crucial to detection of memory deficits. For example, the Associate Learning paradigm from the Wechsler Memory Scale has been found to discriminate patients with left hippocampal pathology, with such individuals unable to learn the designated "hard pairs" (e.g., school—grocery) (Saling et al., 1993). Other verbal and spatial memory measures (e.g., story recall, visual reproduction) appear to detect more general memory deficits, perhaps due to the requirement for confounding cognitive skills.

With a very small number of exceptions, child-based studies have also failed to identify a neuropsychological measure that can reliably identify a specific right temporal memory deficit. In a much referred to study, Fedio and Mirsky (1969) found children with left TLE were impaired in verbal intelligence and delayed verbal memory, with intact immediate verbal memory, performance IQ and immediate as well as delayed non-verbal memory. In contrast, children with a right TLE displayed deficits in non-verbal intelligence and delayed memory for non-verbal material, but intact verbal intelligence and verbal memory. Jambaquè et al. (1993) also document this pattern of material-specific memory deficits, although group differences in IQ, specifically lower verbal IQ in children with left-sided lesions, make interpretation of these findings problematic.

Others have been unable to replicate these results (Camfield et al., 1984; Cohen, 1992; Mabbott & Smith, 1998; Stanford, Chelune, & Wyllie, 1998). Stanford et al. (1998) studied children with unilateral hippocampal sclerosis and found no difference between the left and right subgroups on measures of verbal and visual memory. Mabbott and Smith (1998) used verbal (story recall and list learning) and non-verbal (recall of a complex design and face recognition) measures of memory to assess a group of children and adolescents with left and right TLE, and a comparison group of children with an extratemporal seizure focus. Performance on the memory measures was below the expected level for all children. A material-specific effect was found for face recognition following surgery, with the performance of the right TLE being improved post-surgery but significantly below the other groups. No material-specific differences were observed before surgery. It could be concluded from these studies that early lesions to the temporal lobe structures cause more generalised impairments of memory, rather than the material-specific impairments found in adults with TLE. Using an experimental memory battery, Cohen (1992) found a significant difference between left and right TLE groups in their performance on one measure of verbal memory (a verbal selective reminding task), with the left TLE group performing more poorly, as expected. No group differences were identified for visual/spatial memory tasks. This may be because the right temporal lobe memory function does not parallel that seen in the left temporal lobe. However, it is also the case that non-verbal memory measures are more difficult to develop, and that present understanding of right temporal lobe memory function is limited by models that have been successful for the left hemisphere. Recent research suggests that measures of right temporal lobe memory function may need to be quite different in content from those presently in use (Maguire et al., 1996).

In working clinically with children with TLE material-specific memory deficits can certainly be observed. This is illustrated in the following case description.

Case illustration: Mark

Mark, aged 9 years 10 months, was referred for neuropsychological assessment prior to planned left temporal lobe resection for intractable complex partial seizures. Previous video/EEG monitoring had confirmed the left temporal onset of his seizures. MRI scans identified a large area of cortical dysplasia within the medial left temporal lobe. There was also some suggestion of an additional mass lesion, possibly a ganglioglioma, arising within the area of dysplasia, and concern about an apparent change in the appearance of this abnormality over time. The results of the neuropsychological assessment are presented in Table 9.7. Of interest to the present discussion is the severity and specificity of Mark's verbal memory impairment. Of particular note is the apparent sensitivity of the Paired Associate Learning subtest, from the WMS-R, to the presence of this deficit; Mark had great difficulty learning the "hard pairs", a pattern that mirrors the adult pattern associated with left (dominant) temporal lobe pathology involving the hippocampus. Mark's retention of visual (non-verbal) material is intact. This case reflects our clinical experience that verbal-specific memory deficits are observed in children with left (dominant) temporal lobe epilepsy. It is, however, somewhat unusual to find such a specific deficit in children with early developmental lesions such as Mark's. There is a possibility that the degree of Mark's memory deficit reflects some later acute exacerbation of his underlying pathology. Mark's neuropsychological profile is discussed in more detail later in this chapter.

Piccirilli and colleagues have attempted to further our understanding of the functional consequences of the specific laterality and localisation of seizure focus by examining cognitive function in children with benign epilepsy of childhood with rolandic paroxysmal discharges. They studied children with focal seizures and EEG discharges, but no identified brain damage. Although children with this form of epilepsy are generally observed to have normal intellectual function, subtle cognitive anomalies have also been observed by this research group (D'Alessandro et al., 1984, cited by Piccirilli et al., 1994;

TABLE 9.7
Neuropsychological data for Mark

A. General intelligence (WISC-III)

	9; 10 years	(8; 10 years)		9; 10 yrs	(8; 10 years)
Information	8	(5)	Picture Completion	11	(11)
Similarities	10	(7)	Coding	7	(5)
Arithmetic	6	(9)	Picture Arrangement	8	(6)
Vocabulary	7	(11)	Block Design	15	(12)
Comprehension	–	(8)	Object Assembly	–	(10)
Verbal IQ	92	(85)	Performance IQ	102	(93)

Full-scale IQ = 96 (87)

B. Memory skills
Verbal memory and learning profile

Story recall (raw scores)	Immediate	14 ($x = 26.95 \pm 7.2$)
	Delayed (30 min)	7 ($x = 26.32 \pm 7.4$)

Rey Auditory–Verbal Learning Test—learning profile

Trial	1	2	3	4	5	Delayed recall	Recognition
	2	3	5	5	5	2	1

Total words (raw score) 20 ($x = 48 \pm 9.1$)

WMS-R Paired Associate Learning—learning profile

Learning trial	Easy pairs (= 4)	Hard pairs (= 4)
1	1	0
2	2	2
3	3	0

Non-verbal (visual) memory and profile

WMS-R Visual Reproduction (raw scores)	Immediate	38 ($x = 29.3 \pm 4.3$)
	Delayed (30 min)	30 ($x = 23.8 \pm 6.1$)

CFR Recall (raw score) 24 ($x = 13.71 \pm 5$)
(see Figure 9.4)

D'Alessandro et al., 1990) including impairments on verbal tests in children with left-sided foci. Similarly, Piccirilli et al. (1994) also found that children with right-sided or bilateral EEG focus performed more poorly than children with left-sided EEG focus and controls when judging the visuospatial characteristics of the geometric stimuli. These authors conclude that laterality of epileptic focus, in the absence of underlying brain damage, is associated with different types of cognitive deficits.

Few studies have addressed laterality and location of seizure focus in relation to academic performance. Stores and Hart (1976) found that children with focal EEG abnormalities in the left hemisphere had poorer reading comprehension scores (but not reading accuracy scores) than children with a right hemisphere focus, and Camfield et al. (1984) found poorer arithmetic

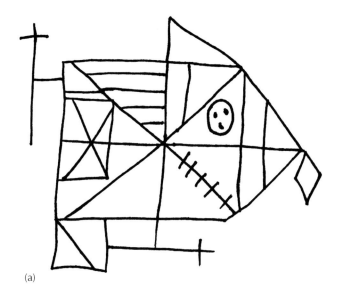

(a)

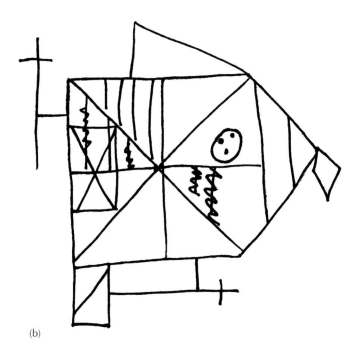

(b)

Figure 9.4. Mark's Rey Figure copy (a) and recall (b).

skills for children with left TLE, but both studies had methodological problems that restrict interpretation of their findings.

In the past an association between TLE and psychopathology in adults has been reported by some researchers (Bear & Fedio, 1977), although others have failed to find this association (Hermann & Whitman, 1984). An increased risk of behaviour disorders in children with complex partial seizures and/or temporal lobe epilepsy has also been cited, with some evidence that the presence of such problems is related to cognitive dysfunction (Camfield et al., 1984; Stores, 1978, 1980).

Laterality and age at onset

Some interesting interactions between laterality of seizure focus and age of onset, pertinent to child-based practice, have been reported in recent adult studies. Strauss et al. (1995) found verbal IQ to be lower in those with earlier age of seizure onset and in those with left-sided seizure focus. The risk of intellectual impairment associated with left-sided seizure focus was reduced as age of onset of seizures increased. Early age of seizure onset, focus outside the temporal lobe, and atypical speech lateralisation were associated with poor non-verbal reasoning, as measured by performance IQ, possibly reflecting reorganisation of cognitive functions that may occur following early lesions in the left hemisphere. Others have noted that adults with evidence of early insult to the left temporal lobe, although showing a greater initial impairment in verbal memory (and in intellectual function), tend to have a better outcome post-surgery, both in terms of seizure control and freedom from additional memory impairment (Baxendale et al., 1998; Glosser et al., 1997; Hermann et al., 1997; McMillan, Powell, Janota, & Polkey, 1987; Saykin et al., 1989), suggesting that earlier age of onset acts as a protective factor against further memory impairment.

Laterality/age-of-onset associations have also been reported in FLE. Upton and Thompson (1997) examined the effect of age of onset (0–6 years, 7–11 years, >12 years) and laterality of FLE. They found significant interactions between laterality of focus and age of onset for measures of executive function (Porteus Mazes Test: time taken; Modified Wisconsin Card Sorting Test: percentage perseverative errors) and primary motor skill. No consistent pattern emerged for the executive function tasks but, for the motor tasks, early onset of right-sided FLE did not impair performance compared with a later onset within the same hemisphere. This sparing of performance was not observed in the left hemisphere. The authors concluded that differences in age of onset and laterality of FLE result in different patterns of neuropsychological impairment. Despite some confounding factors, including older age of onset of the right FLE group and possible differences in aetiologies across groups, this study highlights the complex interrelationships between various seizure-related variables. Evaluating the specific impact of laterality and location of epileptic activity and age at onset on cognitive function provides significant methodological challenges. It is difficult to design satisfactory research models than can evaluate the effects of multiple epilepsy-related factors, or isolate single factors. Assessing the role played by the epilepsy itself independent of other variables is particularly difficult.

Subclinical epileptic activity

The brain is clearly dysfunctional during epileptic attacks. However, as Dodrill (1992a) has observed, the brain continues to be dysfunctional between seizures in many people, with interictal EEG recordings typically showing epileptiform abnormalities.

The term "subclinical" discharges is used to refer to epileptiform events (apparent on EEG recording as spikes or spike–wave activity) that are not accompanied by epileptic seizures, that is, by an easily recognisable behavioural manifestation (Binnie & Marston, 1992; Piccirilli et al., 1994). The influence of this subclinical activity on cognition has been of interest since the EEG came into clinical use in the early 1930s. The term "transitory cognitive impairment" (TCI) was first used by Aarts, Binnie, Smith, and Wilkins (1984) to refer to the momentary cognitive deficit associated with the occurrence of a subclinical discharge.

The distinction between clinical and subclinical discharges is somewhat blurred by the observation of TCI, which could be viewed as an ictal phenomenon, that is, a very brief seizure (Binnie & Marston, 1992). However, studies evaluating the impact of TCI on cognitive function have produced some valuable insights into the potential of subtle "epileptic" events to impact on people with epilepsy. Parents of children with intractable epilepsy often describe marked variability in their child's functioning from one day to the next, and even during the course of a single day. This fluctuation may be associated with observed seizure activity, but may also occur when the child has had no observed seizures. A possible increase in subclinical epileptic activity on "bad" days may explain this fluctuation. Raising the awareness of the parents and teachers to this aspect of their child's epilepsy can be very helpful in managing the child's ongoing difficulties. The influence of sub-clinical epileptic activity may also explain some of the observed variability in test results over time in individual children, and the variability frequently observed in studies evaluating cognitive functioning over time (Bourgeois et al., 1983; Farwell et al., 1985; Rodin et al., 1986).

A Dutch research group (Kasteleijn-Nolst Trenité et al., 1988, 1990a) has conducted an interesting set of studies in this area, illustrating the functional significance of subclinical epileptic activity in children. Using simultaneous continuous EEG and video monitoring, which allows for precise evaluation of the relationship between performance and epileptic discharges, these authors tested children with and without seizures with a standardised intelligence test. They observed that children with epileptiform discharges during testing performed poorly on a paired learning task, and that reading performance was significantly impaired during subclinical discharges, resulting in repetitions, corrections, hesitations, omissions, and additions (Kasteleijn-Nolst Trenité et al., 1988; Siebelink, Bakker, Binnie, & Kasteleijn-Nolst Trenité, 1988). In a later study they compared children with frequent focal subclinical discharges, and found that right-sided discharges impaired performance on visuospatial tasks to a greater degree and left-sided discharges impaired performance on verbal tasks (Kasteleijn-Nolst Trenité et al., 1990a). When they compared three subgroups—bilateral discharges, predominantly left- or right-sided discharges—they found lower reading scores for the group with left discharges in comparison with the right-sided group. Although all groups performed below year level on arithmetic, there were no group differences, which is not surprising as arithmetic is a complex task requiring left and right hemisphere skills (Kasteleijn-Nolst Trenité et al., 1990b).

These results are consistent with findings of others identifying specific difficulties associated with focal epileptic activity. Stores and Hart (1976) noted that children with mainly left-sided epileptic activity had poorer reading performance than children with right-sided epileptic activity. Piccirilli et al. (1994) found that an attentional task involving spatial material was completed poorly by children with benign focal epilepsy associated with right-sided epileptic discharges.

Recent research shows that AEDs may lead to suppression of subclinical discharges as well as seizures, with associated improvements in function. Kasteleijn-Nolst Trenité (1996) reports results of a trial of VPA in a small number of children with focal epileptic discharges in the context of a diagnosis of epilepsy, and suggests that, in children with subclinical epileptic activity, suppression of discharges can be associated with improvement in function but benefits need to be balanced against possible detrimental effects of AED therapy. Because spike-and-wave discharges occur in awake and sleep EEGs of children with no history of seizures or identified cognitive and behavioural difficulties, it is important to consider intervention with AEDs with this in mind.

Treatment with AEDs

Overview

The potential for adverse effects of AEDs on cognition and behaviour has long been recognised. In 1942, Lennox listed AEDs, along with brain damage, seizures, heredity, and psychosocial factors, as detrimental to "mental" function in people with epilepsy (Lennox, 1942). As the factors identified as impacting on the functioning of people with epilepsy are usually causally interrelated, extricating the specific effects of AEDs has proved to be a major methodological challenge (Bourgeois, 1998).

A number of studies published in late 1970s and early 1980s highlighted the detrimental impact of AEDs on cognitive function (Dodrill & Troupin, 1977; Thompson & Trimble, 1982; Trimble & Corbett, 1980). Findings from these studies prompted a shift in emphasis from control of seizures to prevention of harmful, cognitive side effects (Aldenkamp et al., 1993). In the late 1980s and into the 1990s, a number of better-controlled studies have failed to find any cognitive side effects from the more commonly used AEDs (CBZ, VPA, PHT), implicating a range of other factors as influential in earlier studies (Dodrill & Troupin 1991; Meador et al., 1991; Smith et al., 1987). Further, a number of recent reviews have been critical of early studies, and have highlighted their inherent methodological flaws (Bourgeois, 1998; Cochrane, Marson, Baker, & Chadwick, 1998; Devinsky, 1995; Vermeulan & Aldenkamp, 1995), including selection bias, study design, and statistical limitations. The difficulty in attributing cognitive difficulties to the effects of specific AEDs was illustrated by Dodrill and Troupin (1991), who compared the relative effects of PHT and CBZ on the performance of adults on a range of neuropsychological measures. In their initial published results (Dodrill & Troupin, 1977) they reported that subjects taking CBZ performed significantly better on a number of measures, but they failed to control for the effects of higher serum level in some subjects on PHT. When this difference was corrected, analyses failed to support the earlier interpretation. Monitoring serum levels at the time of the cognitive assessment is important to accurately evaluate the effects of AEDs.

The number of controlled or systematic studies of the cognitive effects of AEDs in children is relatively small (Bourgeois, 1998). Cochrane et al. (1998) reviewed randomised control trials (RCTs), published between 1966 and 1996, illustrating the range of problems limiting interpretation of these studies. He identified twelve studies, which included children only, and a further three, which included both children and adults. He notes that a large number of different neuropsychological measures were used in the studies they reviewed. Of the 80 or so measures used in the 40 RCTs published, 43 measures were used only once. At times the same test was referred to by different names, and administration and scoring procedures were rarely described. Devinsky (1995) includes "violations of common sense" in his list of methodological shortcomings of previous research, pointing out that most studies look at group means, not at individuals. He comments that "individual and group variability is apparent to all who practise but is rarely commented on in the discussion of many cognitive and behaviour studies." (p. S51). He also makes the point that there is clear evidence that seizure frequency, severity, and years of active seizures impact on cognitive and behavioural functioning, and that because AEDs control seizures, direct effects of AEDs on cognition and behaviour must be interpreted in light of their positive effects in reducing seizure frequency and severity.

More recent studies have attempted to address previous methodological pitfalls. The multicentre Holmfrid study, conducted in Sweden (Aldenkamp et al., 1993), examined the cognitive effects of withdrawal of AED treatment on 83 children who had been seizure free on monotherapy for at least a year prior to their withdrawal from medication. The majority of children were treated with CBZ and the remaining children with VPA and PHT. Children were included if they had been seizure free for the 3 months following drug withdrawal. A range of computerised neuropsychological measures, selected as potentially sensitive to AED effects, were administered before and after AED therapy was ceased. These included measures of speed, information processing, and attention and memory function. Performance of the epilepsy subjects was compared with a group of healthy controls matched for sex, age, and education level. A significant improvement attributable to drug withdrawal was found on only a single measure of motor speed, suggesting that the effects of AED monotherapy (CBZ, VPA, or PHT) on cognitive function in children are rather limited in magnitude.

The Holmfrid Study produced more positive findings when the subjective complaints of children and parents were analysed before and after AED discontinuation (Aldenkamp et al., 1998). Interestingly, children did not describe themselves differently from control children while on AED therapy. Following withdrawal they reported feeling "less tired". Mothers, however, reported significant improvements in alertness, concentration, tiredness, memory, and drowsiness. This seemed to indicate that mothers felt their children were underaroused during AED treatment. No differences were found for type of AED, duration of epilepsy, or the seizure-free period. It is important to note that, overall, the children in this study represented the more benign end of the epilepsy spectrum. Further, parents of children with epilepsy rated their children more positively than the parents of healthy controls, suggesting that the parents' relief about their children being cured of epilepsy may have impacted on their perceptions of their child's functioning.

In a more recent study, Williams et al. (1998a) investigated short-term effects of AEDs on cognition, using a group of newly diagnosed children with epilepsy. Children were assessed on the day of diagnosis of their epilepsy, prior to commencing AED therapy, and again 6 months later, on a range of measures of attention, concentration, memory, complex motor processing speed, and behaviour, and compared to matched controls with newly diagnosed diabetes mellitus to control for effect of diagnosis of a chronic illness, maturation, and practice. To further restrict the influence of confounding variables, all children were on monotherapy, and serum levels were monitored at the 6-month follow-up to ensure they were within the therapeutic range. Only children whose seizures were controlled remained in the study group. The authors found no group differences in performance on cognitive and behavioural measures, providing no evidence of adverse effects from AED monotherapy during the first 6 months of treatment.

Uncertainty about the effects of AEDs on cognitive function remains. Although more is known of the effects of the AEDs that have been in use over a longer time, information on the impact of AEDs in children is restricted, due to the small number of well-designed studies using children. There is consistent evidence that adverse cognitive and behaviour effects are associated with PB. For example, in children with pre-existing hyperactivity, PB can exacerbate hyperactivity and aggressive tendencies. PHT is also implicated but its effects appear to be milder. CBZ and VPA are widely regarded as being well tolerated, and at standard dosages cause little or no impairment on cognitive or behavioural functioning. Most of the negative effects of AEDs appear to be associated with higher plasma concentrations and with polytherapy. However, individual variability is considerable and some patients do not tolerate even low serum levels. Some children may have unexpected and almost paradoxical responses to specific AEDs. The slow introduction of a new AED can help to prevent some side effects. From the published studies it appears that there may be specific subgroups of children at greater risk of adverse cognitive and behavioural effects of AEDs. For example, children with pre-existing attentional difficulties and hyperactivity may be more vulnerable to intensification of baseline "behavioural" difficulties. Also, children with significant intellectual impairment may be more susceptible to cognitive loss as a result of AED therapy.

It is clear that AEDs can impair cognitive functions and can affect behaviour in children with epilepsy. There appears to be a common view among those treating children with epilepsy that, for the majority of children treated with AEDs, these effects are not clinically relevant and when they do occur are readily recognised (Bourgeois, 1998). However, milder and/or more chronic effects associated with AED treatment may be much more difficult for physicians to monitor in an individual child. Even very mild adverse effects of AED therapy may have a lasting impact on the psychological development of the child. Well-designed studies looking at both the short- and longer-term adverse effects of AED therapy are necessary to provide clear and reliable information to help guide treatment choices.

AEDs and the developing CNS

The treatment of women during pregnancy, infants, and very young children with AEDs is of particular concern, because of mounting evidence of the greater vulnerability of the developing CNS to exposure to AEDs. The use of AEDs during pregnancy by mothers with epilepsy has been linked with a higher incidence of birth defects, thought to reflect teratogenic effects of the AEDs, that is, a tendency to cause derangements of embryogenesis. These birth defects include both major malformations, such as neural tube defects and orofacial clefts, as well as more minor malformations, such as dysmorphic facial features and digital abnormalities. Animal studies suggest that older AEDs in particular are teratogenic, but the results of human studies are inconclusive and it remains uncertain which AEDs are less teratogenic (Meador, 1998). The role of other factors, including seizures during pregnancy, maternal age, and heredity also remains unclear. Ransom and Elmore (1991) reviewed a number of studies from the late 1970s through the 1980s that linked AED use during pregnancy with smaller head circumference at birth and poorer intellectual development. However, a large, prospective study reported by Hanson and Ellenberg (1982; cited by Ransom & Elmore, 1991) found that the presence of a maternal seizure disorder may be more predictive than use of AEDs during pregnancy.

A number of studies have demonstrated adverse effects of AEDs, PB in particular, on developing neurons in tissue culture (in vitro studies) and in animal models (in vivo studies). Holmes (1997) notes previous research findings of reduced neuronal number in rat pups born to dams that received PB during pregnancy, and reductions in brain weight in rat pups receiving injections of PB within a few days of birth. Chronic exposure of cultured spinal cord neurons to PB leads to decreased cell survival and decreases in length and number of dendrite branches. Similar findings in tissue culture studies have been found following exposure to a number of other AEDs (Ransom & Elmore, 1991). Mikati et al. (1994) treated rats (36–153 days old) with a KA-induced seizure disorder, with administration of PB. KA was administered at 35 days, the age thought to correspond to the human prepubescent stage of brain development. The animals' memory, learning, and activity levels were assessed following discontinuation. As expected, rats with KA seizures and no PB treatment did more poorly than controls; however, rats treated (but not controlled) with PB performed even more poorly, suggesting that PB treatment exacerbated the impact of the induced brain damage in these animals.

Studies looking at the possible adverse effects of AEDs on behaviour and cognition in patients with epilepsy have recognised the possibility of differences in the responses of adults and children. To date, studies have not looked for a difference in adverse effects on infants and very young children in comparison with the impact on older children and adolescents. It is possible that adverse effects, even when very mild, may have a much greater impact on the development of infants and very young children.

Studies that have followed up infants and young children treated with PB following febrile seizures have produced variable findings. Ellenberg and Nelson (1978) and Wolf et al. (1981) found no evidence of adverse effects on cognition. In contrast, Camfield et al. (1979) found no overall IQ effect, but some specific adverse effects on memory and comprehension. In a large-scale study, Farwell et al. (1990) studied AED treatment with PB after occurrence of febrile seizures. Children were randomised to prophylactic treatment with PB or placebo. IQ was tested after 2 years on treatment, and again 6 months after PB had been ceased. At the "on treatment" assessment, IQ was 8.4 points lower in the PB group. IQ scores improved somewhat in the PB group and the control group (but not the placebo group) at the 6-month follow-up assessment, with the PB group still performing 5 points lower overall. Importantly, this study failed to find any significant benefit associated with taking PB in terms of reducing the likelihood of recurrence of seizures. In that respect this study found no benefit against which to measure the possible deleterious and ongoing impact on intellectual development. The follow-up period in these studies was relatively short, from 1 to 3 years, and it is possible that cognitive deficits may emerge over a longer follow-up period, as the brain matures.

Just as there is continued debate about the impact of epileptic seizures on the immature CNS (Camfield, 1997; Wasterlain, 1997), there is also ongoing concern about the greater vulnerability of the immature CNS to the effects of AED therapy. Unfortunately, many of the epilepsy syndromes affecting children in infancy and the preschool period, when the CNS is likely to be most vulnerable, are particularly severe and often unresponsive to AED therapy, making investigation of these relationships especially difficult.

Issues for clinical practice

The complex interaction between factors likely to impact on the functioning of a child with epilepsy makes attributing any cognitive and behaviour difficulties specifically to AED therapy problematical. Parents are quick to attribute such problems to medication effects, and it is often necessary to reassure parents about the relative safety of AEDs. However, the observations of those who have most contact and knowledge of the child (parents, other family members, teachers) are crucial in assessing the impact of AEDs, both positive and negative. In difficult-to-control epilepsy, the balance between adequate seizure control and unacceptable side effects of AED therapy is a constant dilemma. Parents, in consultation with the physician, often have responsibility for maintaining this delicate balance. It is often evident when the introduction of a new AED is producing significant change in behaviour. However, more subtle and insidious effects are much harder to distinguish. It is important that the clinician is aware of the complex issues surrounding the use of AEDs in treating children with epilepsy. Such knowledge may assist the clinician to manage children and their families who experience complex problems associated with epilepsy.

Neuropsychological impairment

There is a large body of research evidence suggesting that degree of cognitive impairment may be the single most important factor influencing academic performance, behaviour, and social outcome in individuals with epilepsy (Camfield et al., 1984; Curley, 1992; Kokkonen, Kokkonon, Saukkonen, & Pennanen, 1997; Seidenberg, 1989). Cognitive functioning of children and adolescents with epilepsy is likely to reflect a complex interplay between diverse factors including the presence of underlying brain damage, the impact of seizure-related variables, such as focal epileptic abnormalities, and treatment with AEDs, together with environmental and genetic influences. Although there does not appear to be a specific profile of neuropsychological difficulties in children with epilepsy, there is considerable evidence that attentional difficulties are commonly associated with the presence of epilepsy even when other neurological findings are absent.

Results from studies of adults and children with epilepsy have suggested that general impairments in attention, reaction time, and motor speed may influence performance on cognitive tests, and so impact on the outcome of neuropsychological studies (Dodrill, 1992b; Hara, 1989; Piccirilli et al., 1994; Smith et al., 1986). Studies attempting to avoid selection bias towards the more severe end of spectrum of childhood epilepsy have suggested that epilepsy may be associated with specific deficits in attention, which are unrelated to other factors such as IQ and treatment. Mitchell, Zhou, Chavez, and Guzman (1992) studied reaction time, attention, and impulsivity in 112 children with epilepsy (4.5–13 years), using a computerised test formatted as a video game involving coloured shapes. Children with epilepsy were found to be significantly slower and made more omission errors than healthy controls. In addition, variability in the response patterns of the epilepsy group suggested fluctuations in attentional capacity. These differences persisted even when the comparison was restricted to children with at least average intelligence. Williams et al. (1996) also observed that children with epilepsy, without documented learning and behavioural disorders, have intact memory skills, but may exhibit subtle difficulties with attention. In a later study, this research group (Williams, Griebel, & Dykman, 1998b) administered a range of measures of intelligence, verbal and visual memory, achievement (reading and mathematical skills), visual motor integration, executive function, and motor speed, to a group of children with epilepsy. Their results indicated that, in general, neurocognitive skills were within expectations, given the overall low average level of intellectual function within the group. However, tasks utilising verbal and visual attention skills were performed relatively more poorly, suggesting a specific attentional impairment. This pattern of poor attention was also identified by parents who rated their children as having clinically elevated attentional problems on the Child Behaviour

Checklist. These findings persisted even when children diagnosed with attention deficit hyperactivity disorder were excluded from the analyses.

Academic function and cognitive ability

Academic underachievement is commonly observed in children with epilepsy (Seidenberg et al., 1986). It may be argued that problems with attention are a critical characteristic underlying the educational problems of these children (Holdsworth & Whitmore, 1974; Stores, 1978). Although there appears to be no clear evidence for specific types of learning impairment associated with epilepsy in schoolchildren, attentional difficulties have been described in a number of studies (Sturniolo & Galletti, 1994; Vermeulan et al., 1994; Williams et al., 1998b). One explanation for this common observation may be that these "attentional" difficulties reflect a general effect of anti-epilepsy medication. However, Bennet-Levy and Stores (1984) reported that children with epilepsy, matched with controls for educational attainment, were rated by teachers as less alert than their peers, which included children who were no longer taking AEDs. The authors concluded that impaired alertness may be an attentional disorder characteristic of children with epilepsy in general, and possibly unrelated to AED therapy.

Seidenberg et al. (1986) divided children with epilepsy into two groups, on the basis of academic achievement, to investigate the cognitive–neuropsychological correlates of academic functioning in children with epilepsy. One group was labelled as a "successful achiever" group and included children (n = 18) whose academic achievement was average or better, and the other was labelled an "unsuccessful achiever" group (n = 30), which included children who were achieving below expectations (in terms of age and IQ level). The test battery administered included the Halstead Neuropsychological Battery for Children, the WISC-R, and the Wechsler Memory Scale (WMS). Although IQ level was similar, the two groups differed in their performance on measures of verbal abilities, attention and concentration. Seidenberg noted the overlap between the difficulties experienced by the unsuccessful achiever group and those experienced by children with learning difficulties without epilepsy, namely difficulties with auditory–visual integration, verbal conceptualisation, verbal expression and word knowledge, and short-term verbal memory (e.g., digit span and story recall).

In contrast with this finding, Sturniolo and Galletti (1994) observed a quantitative rather than qualitative difference in neuropsychological functioning, associated with the varying levels of academic achievement in a group of primary school-aged children with epilepsy and normal IQ. These authors found that around two-thirds of their sample were achieving below the level expected on the basis of their level of intellectual functioning.

Children who were performing more poorly were noted to have relatively lower IQ scores and to have greater visuomotor impairment.

Social competence and cognitive ability

A number of studies have identified a significant relationship between cognitive functioning and the behavioural and emotional adjustment of children and adolescents with epilepsy. Camfield et al. (1984) identified a subgroup of children with TLE who were rated as "maladjusted" on the Personality Inventory for Children and who also showed significantly lower neuropsychological test functioning. Hermann (1982) used the Child Behavioural Checklist to compare the psychosocial functioning of two groups of children with epilepsy, defined on the basis of "poor" or "good" performance on a standardised battery of neuropsychological measures. Children with poor neuropsychological function manifested significantly more aggression and overall psychopathology, and less overall social competence, in comparison to children with relatively good neuropsychological function. Similar findings were reported by Curley (1992). She included measures of neuropsychological functioning when examining the relationship between a range of variables and behaviour problems in boys with epilepsy aged 6–12 years. She noted that the overall neurocognitive status of the boys accounted for the largest proportion of the variance on behavioural measures. All of the children had normal intellectual function, as children with an IQ of less than 80 were excluded.

Not all studies have supported the strength of this association. Hoare and Kerley (1991) found no relationship between psychosocial morbidity and lower cognitive function in a group of children with epilepsy. However, their sample was skewed towards the severe end of the epilepsy spectrum and included severely retarded and multiply handicapped children. The impact of cognitive functioning may well have been diluted by the level of impairment present in this group. Approximately half of the children in the study showed evidence of disturbance as rated by their parents or teachers, with this rate higher than reported in other studies. Mitchell, Scheier, and Baker (1994), using a longitudinal study design, investigated variables which influenced outcome of children with epilepsy 18–30 months after their enrolment in the study. A moderate and significant relationship was identified between IQ and behaviour problems at enrolment, but IQ did not appear to directly influence behaviour problems at follow-up. The authors did concede, however, that the effect of IQ in their study design may have been mediated through other baseline measures. In addition the follow-up period was relatively short.

Cognitive functioning during childhood has been identified as an important factor influencing psychosocial outcome in adults with epilepsy. Dodrill and Clemmons (1984) observed that measures of cognitive ability were significant predictors of adjustment and behavioural functioning in their study examining vocational adjustment and independent living of adolescents with epilepsy. In a population-based cohort of children (Camfield et al., 1993), selected as intellectually normal on the basis of available information (e.g., previous assessment), the presence of a learning disorder was found to be a crucial predictor of social outcome. Cognitive difficulties may well have contributed to the identified learning disorders in the study group, so that in fact the findings of this study may also reflect the important influence of cognitive function on social outcome.

Kokkonen et al. (1997) conducted a population-based study of psychosocial outcome in young adults with a previous diagnosis of epilepsy. They found that young adults with epilepsy during childhood had retarded social growth into adulthood more often than controls, characterised by a more parent-based living style and lack of gainful vocational education. The most significant risk factors identified were impaired intellectual capacity and learning disabilities. In this study group, the epilepsy itself and AED therapy did not have a significant impact on social development. Psychiatric morbidity was found to be similar for the epilepsy and control groups, perhaps reflecting the "unselected" nature of this population sample.

Case illustration: Mark

The research findings reviewed suggest that when any child with epilepsy is encountering difficulties, whether behavioural, social, or learning related, the influence of possible cognitive difficulties needs to be considered. The importance of careful neuropsychological assessment is well illustrated by the case of Mark, whose assessment results were introduced earlier in this chapter.

Mark was reported to exhibit academic and social difficulties within the school context. He was noted to have difficulty retaining instructions and in working independently, and did not appear to be learning from previous exposure to academic tasks. He was falling behind grade level in acquiring literacy skills. Other problems noted included poor recall of teachers' and classmates' names and trouble remembering the rules of games. A speech pathologist's assessment and two intellectual assessments conducted by the school's psychologist had failed to identify the cause of these difficulties. Mark's intellectual, and expressive and receptive language skills were well within the normal range.

It was the neuropsychological assessment, conducted in the context of planned surgery for left temporal lobe epilepsy, which identified the nature of Mark's underlying cognitive disorder. Although Mark continues to achieve scores within the "average" range on tests of intellectual ability (see Table 9.7), as already described he displays a severe, verbal-specific memory. An awareness of Mark's severe impairment of the acquisition of new verbal information is essential if the nature of his learning and social difficulties is to be fully understood.

In addition to his verbal memory impairment, Mark is quite slow to process auditory/verbal information. Spoken information, particularly when more complex or lengthy, needs to presented slowly to allow him time to successfully process its meaning. Mark seems to have adapted to this by simply "tuning out" of conversations that do not require him to take an active role. It takes some time for him to be re-engaged in a conversation, leading to an awkwardness in conversing with him if others are present. At times he seems surprised that a response is expected from him. Mark's apparent vagueness, and difficulty in following normal, verbal interactions and making appropriate responses, have led to questions about a possible "autistic-spectrum" disorder. Following a 6-month period of individual therapy, his therapist concluded that autism was an inappropriate diagnosis, and could not account for Mark's difficulties with social interaction. This very experienced worker was unable to explain his difficulties further within a psychiatric framework.

Mark's verbal memory deficit has a very significant impact on his interaction with others, particularly in the school context. Mark has difficulty learning the names of his teachers and classmates, an unusual difficulty for a boy of normal intellectual ability. The ability to remember people's names is important in normal social interchange. Similarly, Mark has difficulty joining in with games because he has difficulty recalling the rules. Fearful of making mistakes, Mark tends to withdraw from these opportunities for group interaction, further limiting his social experiences and skills. Mark has developed interests that he can pursue on his own and that utilise his strengths in non-verbal memory. For example, he is passionate about computers and how they work and has acquired quite a collection of obsolete machines, viewed by others including his mother as "junk". Mark's literacy skills are falling behind age-expected levels. It is likely that as a result of the verbal memory impairment Mark's sight-reading vocabulary is developing more slowly than his peers.

An awareness of Mark's verbal memory impairment has enabled his parents and teachers to implement strategies to manage the impact of this specific but very significant difficulty. One example is his teacher's efforts to help Mark learn the names of all of his classmates. The teacher organised a small group of Mark's classmates, five at a time, to wear name tags, giving Mark a visual cue to each child's name that allows for repeated exposure to this information. Over time, Mark is slowly learning the names of classmates, leading to an increase in his confidence in relating with his peers. The school has also been able to access a visiting specialist teacher who spends regular sessions with Mark and also provides support and direction to his teacher.

PSYCHOSOCIAL ISSUES

A number of factors have been identified as impacting on psychosocial development of children and adolescents with epilepsy (see Table 9.8). Many of these factors are associated with the impact of chronic illness and disability in general; however, research suggests that this impact may be particularly evident in the functioning of people with epilepsy. A considerable social stigma continues to be associated with epilepsy. Furthermore, the person's own perception of this stigma has been implicated as having a potentially greater impact than the stigma itself. Scambler and Hopkins (1990) observed that, whereas one-third of adults were able to cite an instance of discrimination against themselves, 90% of these adults reported feelings of being stigmatised. Parents' perceptions of stigma have also been implicated as being a potentially important influence on the child with epilepsy, contributing to the development of the child's own feelings of stigma (Carlton-Ford, Miller, Nealeigh, & Sanchez, 1997).

Social stigma associated with epilepsy may have its origins in fears related to a public loss of self-control. Heightened anxieties about this lack of control over the body and behaviour may hinder the child's development of a healthy self-image, particularly during adolescence. A study by Viberg, Blennow, and Polski (1987) examined these issues, using a sample of 16

TABLE 9.8

Psychosocial factors potentially influencing psychological functioning of children and adolescents with epilepsy

---

Social factors
Stigma
Discrimination
Social exclusion

Environmental factors
Family environment, parent perceptions/attitudes, parenting style
School environment, teacher perceptions/attitudes
Social support, peer perceptions
Employer perceptions/attitudes

Individual factors
Locus of control
Self-perceptions
Fear of seizures

Additional factors
Lifestyle restrictions
   Recreational activities
   Driving
   Vocational choice
Negative life events

---

adolescents with epilepsy (aged 11–16 years). They found that adolescents were influenced by their disease, irrespective of the type of epilepsy, their level of seizure control, or age at onset. These authors concluded that adolescents were distrustful of their bodies and themselves. The importance of the individual's perceptions of their situation and psychological "well-being" has also been highlighted in a study by Collings (1990), who investigated a large sample of adults in Great Britain and Ireland. They found that the discrepancy between subjects' current self-perception and anticipated self without epilepsy was by far the most important correlate of overall feelings of "well-being".

The literature suggests that children with chronic illness, and epilepsy in particular, may have an increased susceptibility to developing psychological problems in response to a less than optimal family environment. Mulder and Suurmeijer (1977), in a small-scale, descriptive study, reported an association between family stress and behavioural disturbance in a sample of children with epilepsy. These results have been replicated by a number of researchers. Hermann et al. (1989) found that divorced or separated parents were a significant predictor of behaviour problems, being related to depression in both boys and girls. Friedman et al. (1986) demonstrated that parental disharmony, based on parent and adolescent reports, was closely related to the adolescent's poor compliance with medication regimens. Highlighting the complex relationships between child and family function, Austin (1988) reported that families of children with behavioural problems had significantly poorer behavioural functioning, less intrafamily esteem and communication, less extended family support, and less financial security than families of children without such problems. Hoare and Curley (1991) describe the double hazard effect seen in other groups of children with CNS dysfunction, relating lower socioeconomic status, negative maternal attitudes, and more severe impairment in the child to psychological disturbance.

The effect of the presence of a child with epilepsy on family functioning has also received some attention, and it has been observed that poorly controlled seizures in children can be a major disruptive influence. Despite these observations, Ferrari (1989) reviews research findings that indicate that the severity of epilepsy alone is not a good predictor of family disruption. Rather, it seems that individual family members' perceptions of the degree of disruption and burden caused by the disorder may be more predictive than objective measures of the level of disruption. To address the assumption that families of children with epilepsy function differently from families with healthy children, an investigation of intrafamilial communication was conducted by Ritchie (1981), using videotaped, structured family problem-solving sessions. Comparisons of families with and without a child with epilepsy indicated that children with epilepsy played a more passive role in family interactions and demonstrated a reduced level of involvement in family decision making. Mothers of children with epilepsy were more likely than other "control" mothers to take a prominent role in family discussions, and to be strongly linked to the child. It may be argued that Ritchie's choice of control group was flawed, and that his results may be generalised to all chronic illness conditions, rather than specific to epilepsy. To overcome this weakness, Ferrari, Matthews, and Barabas (1983) investigated differences in reactions of families of children with epilepsy, those with a diabetic child, and those with healthy children. They found similar results to Ritchie (1981) and concluded that the presence of seizures in children places the family at greater risk for problems in communication, cohesion, and integration.

Children's perceptions of their illness and its effects may be directly influenced by parental reactions. Carlton-Ford et al. (1997) attempted to evaluate the impact of parental fears of their child being stigmatised, and associated tendencies to adopt more controlling parenting styles on the child's emotional and behavioural outcome, in a pilot study. Their results suggested that the characteristics of the epilepsy, types of medication, perceived stigma, perceived lifestyle limitations resulting from seizures, and parenting style form a web of interactions that predict children's behavioural problems. In this study parent reactions appeared to play a significant role in mediating between seizure and medication variables and behavioural and emotional outcomes.

These studies highlight the complex interrelationships between family and child characteristics and responses of the family to the child with epilepsy, reflecting, in part, social attitudes and parental anxiety of these social attitudes. To date, however, there has been little attempt to evaluate the relative contributions of psychosocial factors, together with biological, neuropsychological, and treatment parameters that have also been found to impact on children's functioning. Austin et al. (1992), adopting such a multi-aetiological approach, attempted to identify the contributions of demographic, seizure, and family variables for predicting behaviour problems. Using the Child Behaviour Checklist (Achenbach, 1991), and a sample of children with epilepsy aged between 8 and 12 years, they found that children who were experiencing behavioural problems tended to exhibit poorer seizure control and were more likely to be members of troubled families, in which mothers were receiving insufficient support from relatives and friends. Mitchell et al. (1994) adopted a longitudinal design and attempted to identify child and family characteristics that best predicted long-term psychosocial and medical outcome in children with epilepsy. They followed a group of children ($n = 88$) over a period of 18 months, and reported that sociocultural factors were the primary cause of ongoing parental anxiety and negative attitudes towards epilepsy. In spite of efforts to educate families over the duration of the study, inappropriate and exaggerated fears continued to be common in the study sample, particularly among the large group of less "acculturated" (i.e., fewer years residency in the USA), poorly educated parents. Forty-five per cent of the families in this study identified languages other than English as the primary language spoken at home.

Curley (1992) adopted a biosocial model of behaviour in her study with children with epilepsy. She examined a range of variables including parenting and marital harmony factors, and unlike many other studies also incorporated measures of child function. Biological factors (cognitive outcome and seizure-related variables) were found to be central to outcome, despite the omission of this area of functioning in many studies of family and child functioning. Further, disagreements about parenting children with epilepsy were found to be associated with the externalised behaviour problems of the children.

The relationship between psychosocial factors and academic performance has received little attention to date. Seidenberg (1989) has noted that chronic illness factors (both general and epilepsy-specific), teacher and parent behaviour and attitudes towards the child, and misconceptions about the disorder were all potentially important issues. Further, other researchers have suggested that parental overprotection and lowered parental and teacher expectations may also be influential for academic achievement. Ferrari (1989) studied 21 families of children with a child with epilepsy, and asked parents to predict future performance of the child in a range of personal, social, and academic areas, as well as that of a sibling. For eight of the ten areas covered, parents rated the child with epilepsy lower. Although these results did not specify which factors contributed to these lower expectations, Ferrari concluded that such attitudes may play a role in the underachievement and adjustment problems of children with epilepsy. Although these results are interesting, they are limited as there were no controls for the presence of cognitive and learning difficulties that would realistically influence parental attitudes.

The attitude of children themselves may also impact on academic performance. Matthews, Barabas, and Ferrari (1983) looked at school-related self-perceptions in matched samples of children with epilepsy and healthy controls, and found that children with epilepsy had poorer self-concepts related to intellectual ability, were more worried about tests and more nervous if called on by the teacher. The authors adopted a "learned helplessness" model to account for their findings.

Austin et al. (1998) recently conducted a study that aimed to identify differences in academic achievement and school adaptive functioning between children with epilepsy and children with asthma, excluding children with intellectual impairment. Significant group differences were found in each area of academic performance, with the epilepsy group achieving poorer results. Further, boys with epilepsy achieved lowest scores, as did children with more severe seizure disorders. Across the groups a number of factors were associated with achievement levels: condition severity, children's attitudes towards their illness, and school adaptive functioning. The relationship between children's attitudes toward their illness and level of academic achievement has not been identified previously and is worthy of further study.

Psychosocial factors, rather than biological factors, may have a greater impact on the psychological functioning of the majority of children with epilepsy, particularly those with idiopathic epilepsy not associated with other neurological abnormalities. Psychosocial problems associated with epilepsy are often more handicapping than the seizures themselves, particularly if the seizures are controlled. Research shows that child and parent perceptions play a particularly important role (Curley, 1992), and such findings highlight the need for education of children and families about epilepsy, and for the provision of appropriate support in meeting the challenges associated with this disorder.

CONCLUSIONS

Many of the themes emerging from this review are likely to determine the direction of future research in the area of childhood epilepsy. A number of factors have been identified in the existing literature as having an important influence on the development of children with epilepsy. However, past research has been hampered by the complex interrelationships between these factors (listed in Table 9.5). The resulting methodological challenges are well illustrated by the research attempting to investigate the effects of AED therapy. It has been difficult to isolate medication effects from the impact of factors such as the underlying neurological abnormality, the seizures themselves, and the psychosocial difficulties associated with epilepsy. The issue is further complicated by the suggestion of a particular vulnerability in certain groups to negative AED effects, more common in children with severe neurological difficulties, and by the evidence for age-related effects associated with differential responses of the immature CNS. It appears that, for the majority of children with epilepsy, AED therapy is associated with few harmful effects. However, there is much more to be discovered about the effects of the individual AEDs, especially the newer varieties, the influence of more subtle effects, and the impact on vulnerable children, usually those with the most complex difficulties associated with their seizure disorder.

Although there has been an awareness that seizures are but one manifestation of diverse forms of brain dysfunction, there has been a tendency in previous studies to treat epilepsy as a unitary disorder. This approach is reflected in much of the psychological literature in this area. As individual seizure disorders are becoming better understood, with the ongoing refinement of the syndrome approach to classification of epilepsy, defining subgroups of children with more homogeneous characteristics may enable the factors influencing the psychological functioning of children to be more easily identified and understood.

Defining epilepsy-specific developmental factors will be an important key to a better understanding of the impact of epilepsy during childhood. Evidence is emerging that the onset of epilepsy, even in an already compromised brain, is associated with an additional burden for the child. The move towards earlier surgical interventions reflects the growing awareness of the detrimental impact of certain seizure disorders on the developmental process. Clearly there is an important role for neuropsychologists in evaluating the effectiveness of these interventions on long-term outcome for the child. It is likely that the development of laboratory techniques to study neuronal growth, together with animal models of epilepsy in the developing brain, will afford greater insights into the impact of epilepsy, and more specifically of epileptic activity, on the immature brain.

Much previous research has utilised highly selected samples of children, drawn from specialist epilepsy centres catering for patients with more complex disorders, including those who may be suitable for epilepsy surgery. These children represent a very small proportion of the total population of children with epilepsy. For this reason is important that future research also focuses on more representative samples of the population of children with clearly defined seizure disorders. Identifying the important factors influencing psychological functioning of children with epilepsy may be less methodologically challenging in groups of children with less, rather then more, complex seizure disorders.

Janet Lindsay and Christopher Ounsted (1987) authors of the important and unique longitudinal study of childhood-onset temporal lobe epilepsy begun in the 1940s, make the following observations:

> Epilepsy, especially when related to organic brain damage, is a long-lasting, if not lifelong condition, and one which affects all aspects of patients' lives. Therefore its study must also be pursued over the whole of a patient's life or at least a significant part of it, and must embrace all the consequences of the disorder, and not only the seizures themselves.
>
> This applies even more to the epilepsies of children because the whole development of personality and the very organisation of the brain may be profoundly affected by the presence of a cerebral lesion and of consequent seizures.

Despite such opinions, child studies remain relatively few in number in comparison with the total body of epilepsy research. Yet epilepsy is, in many respects, a disorder of childhood, with onset for the majority of adults with epilepsy occurring during their childhood years. Further, these areas represent an extremely fruitful area for future neuropsychological research, which has the opportunity to take advantage of the exciting advances being made in understanding specific epilepsy syndromes, in brain imaging, and in the genetics of epilepsy.

Epilepsy remains a poorly understood disorder by the wider community and as a result is still associated with considerable stigma. The importance of raising community awareness and of education of children, families, and those caring for children (teachers, community groups, government agencies, etc.) cannot be overestimated. Neuropsychologists are in a unique position in terms of their knowledge of brain–behaviour relationships to educate others about epilepsy. In Australia, the epilepsy associations in each state provide a range of services including support groups, social activities, educational seminars, and educational resources particularly relevant for children with epilepsy.

PART THREE

Neuropsychological practice within a developmental context

CHAPTER TEN

Child neuropsychological assessment: A conceptual framework

INTRODUCTION

Neuropsychological assessment is differentiated from more generic psychological evaluation, not so much by the test measures employed, but by the interpretation of the data resulting from those measures, in terms of knowledge of brain structure and function. The discipline is founded in the dual theoretical domains of the neurosciences and cognitive sciences. The practice of neuropsychology requires the integration of information across these disciplines, in as much as current knowledge allows. A sound theoretical basis, both with respect to neurological disorders and cognitive processes, is essential for a full neuropsychological evaluation and interpretation. Consider the situation where a child is referred for neuropsychological assessment of memory difficulties. To investigate these problems, the neuropsychologist might administer some memory tasks, for example, a word list learning test or a spatial learning measure. Results might demonstrate an impaired performance on the verbal memory task, with intact spatial memory. Without knowledge of brain–behaviour relationships, the neuropsychologist can make limited conclusions, and would possibly diagnose a verbal-specific memory deficit. However, if additional background history is available, indicating that the child suffers from intractable epilepsy, due to left-sided hippocampal sclerosis, then interpretation is based on behavioural findings plus an understanding that aspects of memory and learning are subsumed by the hippocampus and related cerebral structures. The resulting formulation may then conclude that the child is exhibiting verbal memory deficits consistent with documented cerebral pathology. More importantly, if there is a question of surgical treatment, as discussed in Chapter 9, it may be possible to relate verbal-specific memory deficits to radiological and neurological evidence of left-sided pathology, and intact right hippocampal function, and even to comment on likely prognosis.

The aim of this chapter is to consider the elements necessary for neuro-psychological evaluation, where the clinician is often required to integrate test data with medical information, to obtain an understanding of the child's presenting difficulties. As the previous illustration suggests, a working know-ledge of brain–behaviour relationships, as they relate to the developing brain, is essential, and has been addressed in previous chapters. Central to this chapter is a discussion of current models of neuropsychological assessment, with a focus on the capacity of each of these approaches to contribute to an understanding of the child. Assessment tools will also be described, with an emphasis on those cognitive domains most relevant to child neuro-psychology, for example, attention and information processing, memory and learning, and executive abilities. The process of assessment will be con-sidered, from the point of referral, examining data gathering, test administra-tion, formulation, and diagnosis. Finally, a clinical case will be described to illustrate the application of these various steps. As will be apparent from this discussion, we employ a hypothesis-testing model in our assessments, as described by Walsh (1978, 1985). Although such an approach is not uni-versally accepted, we would argue that it provides an effective framework for understanding the relationships among complex psychometric, qualitative, medical, and psychosocial information.

MULTIDISCIPLINARY LINKS

Current knowledge of central nervous system (CNS) structure and function remains far from complete, particularly during the developmental period. However, the last two decades have seen a dramatic increase in our under-standing of the impact of a range of developmental and acquired CNS disorders, as evidenced by the research reviewed in the previous chapters. Application of this knowledge has enhanced the quality of clinical practice in the paediatric domain. Neuropsychologists are now able to comment on the likely deficits associated with particular lesions and CNS conditions, and the possible impact these insults may have on development. It is possible to make predictions regarding outcome, and contribute to the formulation of appropriate management and rehabilitation strategies, based on findings from longitudinal and evaluation studies.

Although such neurobehavioural advances are crucial, it is equally important to utilise current models of cognitive development and function in constructing appropriate assessment techniques. Experimental cognitive psychology has assembled a rich foundation from which child neuropsychologists can draw, in order to better appreciate processes such as language, perception, attention, memory, and executive function. Such knowledge is central when interpreting test results, to facilitate an understanding of the child's cognitive processes, and avoid simply providing the child, family, and referring professional with a list of unrelated, uninterpreted test data. For example, if deficits are identified on "executive function" tests, a cognitive theoretical perspective will indicate the importance of evaluating the possible contributions of attention, working memory, and other lower-level cognitive functions to impaired performance. Contemporary models of working memory are particularly useful (e.g., Baddeley, 1990), describing components such as the phonological loop, visual sketch pad, and central executive, provide the clinician with a framework within which to analyse the independent and interacting contributions of auditory and visual processing, and the "central executive" for memory function, when interpreting performances on memory and learning tests.

For practice in adult neuropsychology, neurological and cognitive models are generally sufficient. In paediatric practice, the developmental perspective must also be considered. Several developmental neuropsychologists have emphasised important differences between adult and paediatric practice (Anderson, 1998; Fletcher & Taylor, 1984; Holmes-Bernstein & Waber, 1990; Taylor & Fletcher, 1990; Taylor & Schatschneider, 1992). First, in paediatric practice, many of the presenting disorders are congenital or perinatal (e.g., cerebral palsy, autism, spina bifida, birth complications, prematurity). In these conditions, the child has had no opportunity to experience the world and gain skills prior to CNS insult. Second, even in cases where brain insult is acquired during childhood, the vast majority of paediatric CNS disorders are generalised, causing diffuse brain pathology and dysfunction (e.g., traumatic brain injury, cerebral infection, hydrocephalus), with focal lesions such as tumours and vascular incidents less common. Both generalised and focal insults may interfere with ongoing CNS and cognitive development, causing different consequences from that seen following similar pathology within the adult brain. In consequence, it cannot be assumed that the same behavioural sequelae will result (Stoddart & Knights, 1986). A final difference lies in the interpretation of neuropsychological tests developed for adult practice. Fletcher and Taylor (1984) caution that it may be inappropriate to assume that these tests will measure the same brain–behaviour relationships in the child's brain as they do in the adult brain. Each of these issues highlights the importance of a thorough understanding of normal neural and cognitive development, if paediatric neuropsychologists are to interpret possible deviations exhibited by their patients.

Finally, the psychosocial context of the child is an important additional consideration. Although test results provide information relating to the child's cognitive status, this data needs to be interpreted with reference to the social and emotional context of the child. For example, a child evaluated in an unfamiliar hospital environment during inpatient admission may achieve quite different test results once he/she has settled back into the more secure home environment. Or, an adolescent who is unwilling to acknowledge his/her neurobehavioural problems may appear poorly motivated and perform uniformly badly in an effort to mask specific deficits. At a broader level, in formulating diagnoses and treatment plans, issues such as social history (e.g., depressed mother, frequent changes in schools, social interaction difficulties, history of abuse), access to resources (e.g., influenced by financial status, geographic factors, parental skills), and impact of family factors (e.g., marital problems, sibling conflict) need to be examined, not just with respect to test performance, but also in determining the likely aetiology of the presenting problems.

NEUROPSYCHOLOGICAL ASSESSMENT: PURPOSE AND PROCESS

Neuropsychological assessments have a number of primary goals. In some instances the aim is to provide information regarding the integrity of the CNS, which may then be used to inform medical diagnoses and treatment decisions. Alternatively, it may be that the pattern of neurobehavioural strengths and weaknesses is of particular interest, with this information utilised to gain a better understanding of the child's abilities, and to contribute to the establishment of appropriate rehabilitation and management interventions. Further objectives include monitoring of recovery or deterioration, and evaluating the impact of treatment interventions. For the paediatric neuropsychologist, the questions are most frequently directed towards gaining an understanding of the child's neurobehavioural profile for the purposes of remediation or rehabilitation: Where is the child in relation to their age peers, independent of neurological factors? What is the child's developmental trajectory? What can be done to reduce the gap between the child and his/her peers?

By and large, neuropsychological referrals represent a tertiary intervention, with most children referred having already undergone medical, sensory, speech, and educational evaluations. Primary links are with neurosciences, mental health, and education, although referrals may often derive from physical and language therapists, seeking consultation with respect to their observations of the child or their progress in therapy. Children seen for neuropsychological evaluation may be divided into a number of categories: (1) those with documented acquired CNS disorders, for example, traumatic brain injury, tumour, near drowning, cerebral infection, or toxicities, where it is important to describe neuropsychological profiles and monitor any changes over time; (2) those with developmental disorders affecting the CNS, for example, spina bifida, genetic disorders, cerebral palsy; (3) those with medical disorders that may impact on CNS functioning, for example, diabetes, phenylketonuria, cardiac disease; and (4) those with disorders of less clearly defined CNS involvement, for example, autism, attention deficit hyperactivity disorder, learning disability. In each instance, the neuropsychologist may work independently, or as part of a broader multidisciplinary team, to gain an understanding of the child and implement appropriate treatment plans.

A clinically relevant neuropsychological assessment considers all possible contributing factors for the child and his or her environment, and includes both qualitative and quantitative information. Background history and psychosocial context need to be documented, as well as developmental factors and current developmental age/stage of the child. The final interpretation incorporates this information, as well as qualitative observations and psychological assessment data. The challenge is to accurately identify the consistencies within these various data sets and, without overinterpretation, formulate diagnoses and treatment plans, as well as develop an understanding of the child, based on the integration of multiple sources of information.

Quantitative methods, such as standardised psychometric and neuropsychological measures, can provide information with respect to the "normality" of a child's cognitive status, and identify cognitive tasks or domains where the child exhibits particular strengths or weaknesses. They are less helpful in determining the aetiology of the presenting problem, or for understanding the real-life difficulties experienced by the child, because they are unable to measure attitude, motivation, or personality (Wilson, et al., 1997). Conversely, qualitative approaches are unable to inform the clinician with respect to the child's developmental level, and possible deviations from age expectations. They do facilitate the clinician's capacity to gain valuable insight into the nature of deficits displayed on multidetermined test procedures, with careful observation enabling differentiation between intact versus deficient skills. The limitations inherent in each of these approaches suggest that a compromise that includes aspects of both approaches may be most useful. Administering the appropriate standardised tests, while carefully observing the quality of a child's responses, may provide optimal understanding of the presenting problems.

Most measures employed in neuropsychological assessment derive from experimental psychology, cognitive psychology, and psychometric research. That is, the measures used are not unique to neuropsychological practice. Rather, it is the interpretation of the resultant data, within the context of knowledge of CNS structure and function, that distinguishes the neuropsychological assessment from more generic psychological methods. Perhaps because the available measures were not designed for use with brain-damaged populations, there are several problems that limit reliable and accurate diagnosis based on these techniques: (1) most tests used in paediatric practice were originally developed for adults, and may be of limited interest to children. For example, the Trail Making Test, which employs a "dot-to-dot" paradigm, with which children are familiar, is often disappointing, as accurate completion does not lead to the typical positive reinforcement, in the form of a recognisable picture; (2) many tests have used limited samples to develop age-based normative data, or have no age-based data at all, leading to difficulties in the distinction between normal versus pathological performance in the context of ongoing development; (3) as is the case for adults, neuropsychological tests are multidetermined, with a range of skills contributing to performance. Current approaches to measurement, utilising primarily summary or endpoint scores, do not allow for the microanalysis of individual skills that may be particularly relevant for diagnosis or localisation of dysfunction, or to the development of treatment programs; (4) as previously noted, adult models of brain–behaviour relationships and localisation of function may be inappropriate for children, particularly those with early lesions, where transfer or reorganisation of functions may occur. Clinicians need to be cautious in allocating traditional cerebral localisation principles to specific neuropsychological impairments for this reason; (5) many measures are designed to provide clear structure and direction for patients, thus masking the frequently encountered impairments in attention and executive function; (6) children are easily fatigued, with relatively limited capacity to tolerate extended assessment sessions. As a consequence, assessment often requires several separate sessions; (7) test measures are not sufficiently fine grained to address the issue of fluctuations or treatment-related changes in performance, which are commonly seen in disorders such as attention deficit hyperactivity disorder or epilepsy; and (8) diagnostic criteria for child-based CNS disorders are often ambiguous and difficult to apply within the developmental context. This is particularly true for many developmental conditions such as attention deficit hyperactivity disorder, autism, non-verbal learning disability, specific learning disability, and Asperger's syndrome, where there is substantial overlap in diagnostic criteria, resulting in poor diagnostic reliability.

Finally, the therapeutic role of neuropsychological assessment is often underplayed. As for psychological evaluation, a thorough and careful analysis, based on standardised testing and integrated with medical history and parental observations of the child, can provide an accurate explanation of the child's functional difficulties, resulting in acknowledgment, understanding, and support. Communication of assessment findings to child and family, in addition to other professionals involved with the child, can improve the family's attitude to the child's difficulties and facilitate appropriate management of these difficulties within the home environment and wider community.

These various difficulties may be related to the relative lag in development of paediatric assessment techniques and measures versus adult methods. However, a number of workers are now tackling the difficult problem of determining the boundaries and limitations of child neuropsychology assessment, as well as attempting to incorporate a developmental aspect to the process, currently lacking from our extensions of adult assessment techniques. The following sections provide a historical account of neuropsychological testing itself, and the models developed to incorporate developmental principles.

MODELS OF ASSESSMENT

The earliest forms of neuropsychological evaluation were crude by current standards. The task was often simply to determine whether signs of under-lying cerebral disorder were evident, and the measures used to do this were generally quite unsophisticated. Clinicians initially conceptualised brain damage in terms of poor performance on single, specific tests. For example, in paediatric practice, the Bender Gestalt Test (Bender, 1938) was traditionally employed and interpreted as a measure of both psychopathology and brain dysfunction. Poor performance on this task was thought to indicate under-lying cerebral dysfunction. The test involved copying a series of line drawings, with scoring procedures based on copy accuracy and quality of errors. Such a simplistic, unidimensional approach was quickly determined to be insuffi-cient to discern the complexities of brain dysfunction, particularly within a child population. From that time, more sophisticated procedures have been developed within adult practice, and child assessment techniques have tended to follow adult models closely.

As adult models have evolved, they have perhaps become more relevant to child-based practice. Rourke supports this suggestion, emphasising three stages in the development of neuropsychological assessment practices to date (Rourke et al., 1986). He describes the first stage as primarily directed towards the detection and localisation of brain lesions. He argues that this endeavour was largely irrelevant to child neuropsychology, due to our incomplete under-standing of the implications of early brain insult for functional organisation. This approach has also become somewhat redundant in adult practice, with advances in technology, and the availability of more accurate "localising tools" such as computed tomography (CT), magnetic resonance imaging (MRI), and position emission tomography (PET) techniques.

The second phase of development reflected an increased awareness of the functional implications of assessment data, with models focused on the iden-tification of patterns of neurobehavioural deficit, severity of deficit, and underlying components of impaired performance. This approach has extended the relevance of neuropsychological evaluation, particularly in children, where the clinician is frequently required to document the pattern of cognitive abilities for children who are experiencing functional difficulties in the absence of evidence of underlying neurological dysfunction, for example, learning disability and attention deficit hyperactivity disorder.

The third and most useful advance has been the development of an emphasis on the detection of cognitive strengths and weaknesses, not in isolation, but in relation to environmental demands. This progression stems from the move towards more practical applications for neuropsychological practice, and a need to relate test results to day-to-day performance more closely. Such an approach can be generalised across the developmental spectrum, as long as the dynamic, ever-changing nature of the child's environment is acknowledged. The development of more functional assessment batteries, such as the Rivermead Behavioural Memory Test for Children (Wilson, Ivani-Chalian, & Aldrich, 1991) and the Test of Everyday Attention for Children (Manly, Robertson, Anderson, & Nimmo-Smith, 1999), and research attempts to correlate test performances with daily activities show promise, enabling the neuropsychologist to better predict the child's level of function in daily life (Wilson et al., 1997).

Underpinning these advances in neuropsychological interpretation are the major assessment methods utilised in clinical practice. Although many practitioners and schools have developed unique approaches to assessment, these may be categorised as follows: fixed, eclectic, and qualitative batteries, process approaches, and functional evaluations.

Fixed batteries

Such approaches involve the standardised administration of an invariant set of test procedures (e.g., Halstead–Reitan Neuropsychological Test Battery [age range: 9–14 years], Reitan & Davison, 1974; Reitan–Indiana Neuropsychological Test Battery [age range: 5–8 years], Luria–Nebraska Neuropsychological Battery [age range: 8–12 years], Golden, 1986; Neuropsychological Investigation for Children (NEPSY, Korkman, Kirk, & Kemp, 1998 [age range: 3–12 years]). These batteries are usually comprehensive in terms of the range of cognitive domains assessed; however, the dominant characteristics of these tests generally reflect child extensions of adult batteries. They may be seen as particularly useful for the retrospective analysis of test data for research purposes. That is, all children will receive the same set of tests and thus individual children or patient groups can be readily compared. In addition, such approaches usually meet the necessary criteria for the provision of normative, age-related data.

With the exception of the NEPSY, these measures have been developed prior to the emergence of new knowledge in the paediatric area. Many do not incorporate adequate evaluation of processes now known to be impaired following childhood brain insult, including attention, information processing, memory, and executive function, placing greater emphasis on "posterior" or lower-order, domain-specific skills. Further, such approaches are time intensive, and do not acknowledge the child's more limited tolerance for extensive testing, or the financial restrictions placed on clinicians in the current economic environment. The NEPSY, although still relatively untested, represents a significant advance for paediatric neuropsychological assessment, being based on neuropsychology theory, incorporating measures of attention, executive function, and memory, in addition to being applicable to a wide age range.

Eclectic batteries

This classification refers to the use of idiosyncratic batteries developed by clinicians based on their personal theoretical perspective. Such batteries may not include traditional psychometric methods, but borrow from a variety of techniques, to answer questions of particular interest to the individual practitioner. For example, for a clinician who believes that executive functions do not develop until early adolescence, the choice of tests for evaluation of the young child would not include tasks that tap these skills. An eclectic battery approach is often appropriately employed in research paradigms, where the researcher may be more interested in testing a specific hypothesis with respect to the population under investigation than in gaining a full understanding of an individual child's neurobehavioural profile. Within a clinical context, use of eclectic batteries may lead to a failure to identify deficient skills, if measures tapping these skills are not included. Thus, whereas fixed batteries may be restricted due to their inflexibility, eclectic batteries may well be limited by idiosyncratic theoretical perspectives.

Qualitative batteries

In response to the problem that "scores do not reflect the performance in full" (Walsh, 1978), assessment models have gradually developed that systematically integrate observations made during testing with more formal psychometric data. Qualitative approaches are directed towards the identification of individual success and failure on particular tasks. Such techniques are less interested in determining the absolute level of performance in quantitative terms. Rather, they are focused on describing patterns of cognitive styles and the nature of deficits in relation to brain function (Lewandowski, 1985). The reliability of such approaches is particularly problematic in paediatric populations, due to complexities associated with developmental factors, individual

skills, problem solving, concept formation and reasoning, motor and psychomotor abilities. The tests employed by Rourke et al. (1983) are primarily derived from the Halstead–Reitan (Reitan & Davison, 1974) and Wechsler (1974) batteries.

Step 2 addresses the developmental tasks and real-life demands encountered by the child, including education and social interaction, and employment in the longer term. The fundamental requirements for successfully negotiating these tasks are considered, including maintaining attention, impulse control, and social skills, as well as more discrete abilities in the areas of literacy and numeracy. Children with cerebral disorders frequently experience difficulties attaining expected levels in these areas. With the background obtained with respect to medical factors and test performance, the clinician is able to contribute to the provision of practical interventions, both at home and at school, which may serve to minimise functional impairments. Rourke emphasises the needs for balance between supporting the child's learning in formal (educational) settings, while allowing sufficient time and energy for less formal learning (play, leisure).

Steps 3, 4, 5, and 6 focus on "treatment". Once the abilities and daily requirements of the child are established, appropriate interventions need to be formulated to meet daily demands. Rourke and colleagues argue that clinicians and carers need to develop a realistic view of the child's abilities and likely recovery/development, so that achievable goals may be generated and operationalised via treatment programmes. Interventions must be workable for the family unit, with frequency and intensity of therapies taking into account the range of family responsibilities, access to therapy, and the importance of maintaining a "normal" lifestyle. The final stage of the model, step 7, encourages ongoing review and evaluation of treatment plans. This phase of intervention, although often neglected or overlooked, is particularly important to determine whether the selected approach has had the predicted effect, and to examine whether the original treatment strategies continue to meet the needs of the developing child and his/her changing environmental demands.

Although much of Rourke's treatment-oriented model parallels adult practice, the emphasis on developmental factors, and the child's changing needs and environmental demands, provides a perspective previously lacking in child neuropsychology.

Holmes-Bernstein: A systemic approach to developmental neuropsychology

Some of the most significant advances in child neuropsychological practice have come from the work of Holmes-Bernstein, who has proposed an evaluation paradigm based on an integration of theoretical concepts from development, psychology, neuropsychology, and neuroscience. Holmes-Bernstein

(Holmes-Bernstein, 1999; Holmes-Bernstein & Waber, 1990) argues strongly that, in comparison to the static structure–function relationships emphasised in adult neuropsychology, child neuropsychology must acknowledge the dynamic interplay between the child and his/her environment, and the impact of that relationship both on biological and cognitive aspects of development.

Her "systemic" approach to developmental neuropsychology comprises two parallel strands: the "neuro" and the "psycho" dimensions. Within each of these domains they describe a series of essential elements: (1) developmental timetables, documenting the expected maturation of cerebral systems and cognitive abilities; (2) "processes", or approaches to intervention, either via alternative pathways or strategies; and (3) "context", or the role of experience and environment on both neurological and cognitive functions. The unique aspect of the model, however, is its description of structure, both neurological and cognitive. This author views the brain as having three discrete axes of influence, and emphasises the dynamic aspects of development along each of these axes. They describe a lateral or left/right, axis, an anterior/posterior axis, and a cortical/subcortical axis.

The left/right axis relates to the lateralisation of function across the cerebral hemispheres. The distinction here is the familiar one, between processing styles that are used to characterise the left "dominant" hemisphere and the right "non-dominant" hemisphere. The left hemisphere is traditionally seen as predominantly involved in language processing, employing an analytical, sequential mode. In contrast, the right hemisphere is argued to use a "holistic" processing style, more suited to spatial material. This axis has a well-documented role in developmental neuropsychology, and is cited in disorders such as learning disability and developmental language disorders (Geschwind & Galaburda, 1985; Witelson, 1976), where deviations in left hemisphere structure and function have frequently been documented.

The anterior/posterior axis has been defined more recently. The functions of anterior cerebral regions in children remain poorly understood. Anterior skills, loosely described in functional terms as "executive functions", have been largely neglected in child assessment based on the premise that these skills emerge late in childhood, consistent with frontal lobe maturation (Golden, 1981). As discussed in Chapter 3, executive functions may be defined as the ability to maintain an appropriate problem-solving set for the attainment of a future goal, and incorporate skills such as anticipation, goal establishment, planning, feedback, and monitoring. Posterior functions, which include reception, storage, and encoding of information, are in contrast to anterior functions directed towards the programming, regulation, and verification of activity (Luria, 1973).

The third axis refers to the cortical/subcortical dimension. In keeping with other theorists, Holmes-Bernstein and Waber (1990) argue that cortical functions subserve domain-specific higher-order functional systems, such as language and visual perception, whereas subcortical structures mediate more pervasive, non-specific functions such as attention, information processing, mood, and motivation.

Holmes-Bernstein also includes assessment and diagnostic procedures and intervention strategies, in the model, not dissimilar to those outlined by Rourke et al. (1983). In contrast, the brain–behaviour model they describe represents an attempt to provide a theoretical "developmental neuro-psychological" model within which clinicians can develop educated assessment approaches that are consistent with the neurological conditions and developmental levels of their patients.

NEUROPSYCHOLOGICAL ASSESSMENT TOOLS

Neuropsychologists employ an ever-increasing range of test measures in their assessments. In the paediatric area in particular, numerous new tests have become available in recent times, enabling child neuropsychologists to perform more valid and reliable evaluations. These newer tests have begun to address some of the problems inherent in the child neuropsychology field. Most include standardised administration and scoring criteria, and many have improved psychometric properties. The following discussion does not provide an exhaustive account of all neuropsychological measures employed in child assessment. In particular, commonly administered intellectual measures and language, visual and motor assessment techniques, listed in Tables 10.1–10.3, are not described in detail here. Many of these measures have been previously discussed in a variety of published texts (see Anastasi, 1988; Hynd, Snow, & Becker, 1986; Sattler, 1988; Tramontana & Hooper, 1988).

In keeping with the focus on acquired neurological disorders, the following description of child-based assessment will focus on skill areas that have received less emphasis in the general cognitive assessment literature, but which are commonly depressed in children with acquired CNS dysfunction, that is, the more fluid abilities of information-processing and executive functions. These areas of ability tend to be emphasised and developed more fully within the clinical neuropsychological context, and are less commonly assessed in more general psychological contexts. The assessment framework we will describe attempts to utilise elements from each of the developmental assessment models described earlier. Further, in addition to incorporating a developmental perspective to assessment, it advocates that assessment, interpretation, and diagnosis of childhood neuropsychological function should not occur within a theoretical vacuum. Recent theoretical advances in our understanding of brain structure and function, both in normal and dysfunctional situations, need to be integrated into assessment paradigms for best outcome. We argue that optimal assessment procedures emphasise the "dynamic" nature of cognitive skills during childhood, and employ an

TABLE 10.1

Intellectual tests commonly employed in neuropsychological assessments with children

Intellectual tests	Standard instructions	Age norms	Age range
Bailey Scales of Infant Development (Bailey, 1993)	Yes	Yes	0–42 months
Wechsler Preschool & Primary Scale of Intelligence—Revised (Wechsler, 1989)	Yes	Yes	3–7.3 years
Wechsler Intelligence Scale for Children—III (Wechsler, 1991)	Yes	Yes	6–16 years
Stanford Binet Fourth Edition (Thorndike et al., 1985)	Yes	Yes	2 years–adult
Kaufman Assessment Battery for Children (Kaufman & Kaufman, 1987)	Yes	Yes	2.6–12.6 years
McCarthy Scales of Children's Abilities (McCarthy, 1972)	Yes	Yes	2–8.6 years
NEPSY (Korkman et al., 1998)	Yes	Yes	3–12 years
Differential Ability Scales (Elliot, 1990)	Yes	Yes	2.6–17 years

TABLE 10.2
Components of neuropsychological assessment

Language tests	Standard instructions	Age norms	Age range
General			
Clinical Evaluation of Language Fundamentals—3 (Semel et al., 1995)	Yes	Yes	6+ years
Test of Language Competence (Wiig & Secord, 1989)	Yes	Yes	5–18 years
Expressive			
Expressive & Receptive One-Word Picture Vocabulary Test (Gardner, 1990)	Yes	Yes	2–11 years
Controlled Oral Word Association Test (Gaddes & Crocket, 1975; Anderson & Lajoie, 1996)	Yes	Yes	7–13 years
Boston Naming Test (Kaplan et al., 1983)	Yes	Yes	6–12 years
Rapid Automatised Naming Test (Denkla & Rudel, 1976)	Yes	No	–
Hundred Words Picture Naming Test (Fisher & Glenister, 1992)	Yes	Yes	4.6–11 years
Receptive			
Test of Auditory Comprehension of Language (Carrow-Woolfolk, 1985)	Yes	Yes	3–9 years
Peabody Picture Vocabulary Test (Dunn & Dunn, 1981)	Yes	Yes	2.5 years–adult
Children's Token Test (Di Simoni, 1978)	Yes	Yes	6–13 years
Test for the Reception of Grammar (Bishop, 1989)	Yes	Yes	4–12 years

TABLE 10.3

Visual tests commonly employed in neuropsychological assessments with children

Visual tests	Standard instructions	Age norms	Age range
Perceptual			
Facial Recognition Test (Benton et al., 1983)	Yes	Limited	–
Judgement of Line Orientation Test (Benton et al., 1983; Spreen & Gaddes, 1969)	Yes	Yes	6–12 years
Embedded Figures Test (Spreen & Benton, 1969; Witkin et al., 1971)	No	Limited	6–12 years
Gestalt Closure Test (Kaufman & Kaufman, 1987)	Yes	Yes	2.6–12.6 years
Hooper Visual Organisation Test (Hooper, 1983)	Yes	No	–
Constructional			
Test of 3-Dimensional Block Construction (Benton et al., 1983)			
Rey–Osterreith Complex Figure: copy (Anderson et al., 1996; Rey, 1941; Waber & Holmes, 1985)	Yes	Yes	6–12 years
	Yes	Yes	6+ years
Visuomotor			
Development of Visuomotor Integration (Beery, 1989)	Yes	Yes	2–14 years
Visuomotor Control (Bruininks, 1978)	Yes	Yes	4.6–14.6 years

363

information-processing framework to determine the nature of testing required, and the measures to be included.

A number of information-processing models are available within the literature, which hypothesise interactions among cognitive constructs such as attention, memory, learning, and executive function. The assessment techniques we will describe borrow from many of these models (Baddeley, 1990; Cowan, 1988; Goldman-Rakic, 1987; Luria, 1973; Mirsky et al., 1991; Posner & Peterson, 1990; Ruff & Rothbart, 1996; Shallice, 1982) in an attempt to generate a theoretically driven assessment approach. Each of these theories argues for a hierarchical, integrated system, where information is attended to, encoded, stored, and retrieved, with the efficiency of these processes influenced by the presence of a central executive. Figure 3.1, which was presented and discussed in detail earlier in the text, illustrates the basic processing components that may be included in a child-based neuropsychological evaluation.

Such an integrated "systems" approach suggests that, although there may be primary disruption to one component of the system, the resultant impact may be generalised, affecting the entire system. Further, the impact of deficits in the system for the child will not be static, but will also interfere with the acquisition of knowledge throughout childhood and later adulthood.

Clinical assessment of components of attention

Attention is a multidimensional construct that has proven difficult to operationalise, despite a large body of research focusing on its definition and measurement. Over the past several decades researchers have described various models of attention, with the most contemporary theorists arguing that attention is mediated via an integrated system, which incorporates a number of separate but interdependent components, including sustained attention, selective or focused attention, divided attention, search, and shifting attention, each of which is subsumed by a particular cerebral region (Mirsky et al., 1991; Posner & Peterson, 1990; Stuss et al., 1995). Most of these models describe broad representation of attention throughout the brain, with brain stem and reticular formation, as well as posterior and anterior cerebral regions all playing a role in efficient attentional function. Details of such models are described in Chapter 3. It is well documented that attentional skills develop through childhood, along with underlying cerebral structures, with individual components of attention having unique developmental trajectories (Cooley & Morris, 1990; Halperin, 1992; McKay et al., 1994; Manly et al., 1999; Posner & Rothbart, 1981). Thus it is important that any measure employed to tap these skills has appropriate age-related normative data available. Within the developmental context, a number of associated behaviours, also tapped by the majority of attentional tests, are frequently considered alongside attention (speed of processing, and response inhibition or impulsivity).

Although often omitted from clinical protocols, attention is increasingly recognised as a major casualty of childhood brain dysfunction. Attentional deficits have been documented in a variety of acquired disorders, including traumatic brain injury (Anderson & Pentland, 1998; Dennis et al., 1995; Kaufmann et al., 1993), epilepsy (Holdsworth & Whitmore, 1974), cranial irradiation therapy (V. Anderson, Godber, Anderson, Smibert, & Ekert, 1995; Brouwers et al., 1984), Tourette's syndrome (Lang et al., 1998), endocrine conditions (Northam et al., 1998; Rovet, 1995), hydrocephalus (Fletcher et al., 1995a), and in developmental disorders (Anderson & Stanley, 1992; Dennis, 1981; Rourke, 1989; Villela, Anderson, & Anderson, in press) and autism (Wing, 1981). Barkley (1988) notes that clinically significant attentional problems have been identified in 3–10% of school-aged children, establishing attention as a vital area to consider in assessment of children with documented or suspected brain pathology.

Approaches to the neuropsychological evaluation of attentional skills vary considerably. Table 10.4 lists a number of such measures that may be incorporated into the evaluation process. Some clinicians limit their attentional data to qualitative observations and rating scales completed by parents and/or teachers. Behavioural rating scales are commonly employed to enhance diagnosis of attentional problems. Like other forms of standardised assessment, they provide an indication of the child's behaviour relative to peers, and enable the clinician to determine the extent to which a child's behaviour is deviant. Although some scales are specifically designed to measure attention (for example, the ADHD Rating Scale: Barkley, 1990; Attention Deficit Disorders Evaluation Scale: McCarney, 1995; Rowe Behavioural Rating Inventory: Rowe & Rowe, 1993), others assess these behaviours in the broader context of overall behavioural functioning (Behavioral Assessment System for Children: Reynolds & Kamphaus, 1992: Child Behaviour Checklist: Achenbach, 1991; Conners Rating Scale: Conners, 1997; Personality Inventory for Children: Wirt, Lachar, Klinedinst, & Seat, 1977). One of the greatest advantages of these rating scales is that they provide data regarding the child's behaviour in a variety of settings. For example, each of the scales listed here has both parent and teacher versions, allowing for comparisons across settings. Collection of data from multiple sources enables the clinician to determine the pervasiveness of the presenting attention problems.

Empirical measures provide a range of methods to evaluate aspects of attention in the clinical setting. Traditionally, continuous performance paradigms (Rosvold et al., 1956) have been employed to assess sustained attention. On these tasks the child is required to detect a target from a series of non-targets presented on a computer screen. To accurately measure sustained attention, these tasks are typically long and boring for children, with a

TABLE 10.4
Attention and processing tests commonly employed in neuropsychological assessments with children

Measures	Standard instructions	Age norms	Age range
Continuous Performance Tests (CPT; TOVA, Gordon Diagnostic . . .)	Yes	Yes	Variable
Test of Everyday Attention for Children (Manly et al., 1999)	Yes	Yes	6–15 years
Contingency Naming Test (Taylor, 1988)	Yes	No	–
Underlining Test (Rourke & Gates, 1980)	Yes	Yes	5–15 years
Matching Familiar Figures Test (Cairns & Cammock, 1978)	Yes	No	–
Stroop Test (Golden, 1978)	Yes	Yes	7+ years
Wisconsin Card Sorting Test (Heaton, 1981; Chelune & Baer, 1986)	Yes	Yes	6–12 years
Trail Making Test (Reitan, 1969; Anderson, Lajoie, & Bell, 1995)	Yes	Yes	7–13 years
Paced Auditory Serial-Addition Test (Gronwall, 1977)	Several versions	Limited	–
Auditory Attention & Response Set (NEPSY: Korkman et al., 1997)	Yes	Yes	5–12 years
Visual Attention (NEPSY: Korkman et al., 1997)	Yes	Yes	3–12 years

sustained attention deficit being demonstrated where the child shows either (1) a difficulty in maintaining attention to the task throughout the duration of the test, as indicated by fluctuating responses; or (2) initial stable perform-ance followed by a deterioration, suggesting that the child's attention "span" has been exceeded. Although most traditional measures of sustained atten-tion are visually based, a number of auditory-based measures have emerged recently (e.g., the Auditory Continuous Performance Test: Keith, 1994; Codes, Test of Everyday Attention: Manly et al., 1999; Auditory Attention and Response Set, NEPSY, Korkman et al., 1997), and may enhance detec-tion of listening problems exhibited by many children with attentional and learning difficulties (Villela et al., in press).

Measures of selective or focused attention have been developed within both auditory and visual modalities. Such tasks require the child to extract salient information from background "noise". There are a number of com-monly employed measures that meet these criteria. Letter Cancellation (Tal-land, 1965), is one such test, where the child is presented with a page on which rows of letters are presented, and asked to cross through all Cs and Es in a given time period. Similarly, the Underlining Test (Rourke & Gates, 1980) involves underlining target symbols embedded in background noise. Within the auditory modality fewer measures are available. The Test of Everyday Attention for Children (age range 6–15 years: Manly et al., 1999) includes a range of both auditory and visual selective attention tasks. Auditory meas-ures are based on a tone-counting paradigm, where tones are presented at irregular intervals and children are directed to count the number of tones they hear. This task is then combined with background noise, so that the child needs to count the tones while a series of numbers are being vocalised. Visual subtests, Sky Search, and Map Mission are timed visual search tasks. In addition, the NEPSY (Korkman et al., 1997) includes a number of subtests tapping selective attention, specifically the Auditory Attention and Response Set and Visual Attention tasks.

Interpretation of performance on measures of selective attention is fre-quently contaminated by the simultaneous involvement of a range of other cognitive abilities. For example, selective attention measures are commonly designed to incorporate a timed component, where the child is either given a time limit to complete the task, or stimuli are presented on a timed basis. This leads to a confounding of selective attention and speed of processing skills. Measures capable of isolating these two aspects of processing are particularly helpful in discriminating specific attentional and speed of processing skills.

High-level attentional skills including divided attention (the capacity to work on two different activities simultaneously) and shifting attention (the ability to move flexibly from one dimension or approach to another) are less commonly evaluated in children. These skills mature relatively slowly, con-tinuing to improve through childhood and into adolescence. Interestingly, it is

TABLE 10.5

Memory tests commonly employed in neuropsychological assessments with children

Measures	Standard instructions	Age norms	Age range
General			
Wide Range Assessment of Memory and Learning (Sheslow & Adams, 1990)	Yes	Yes	5–17 years
Test of Memory and Learning (Reynolds & Bigler, 1993)	Yes	Yes	5–19 years
Children's Memory Scale (Cohen, 1997)	Yes	Yes	5–16 years
Rivermead Behavioural Memory Test for Children (Wilson et al., 1991)	Yes	Yes	5–11 years
Memory Index, McCarthy Scales of Children's Ability (McCarthy, 1972)	Yes	Yes	2–8.6 years
Memory Domain (NEPSY: Korkman et al., 1997)	Yes	Yes	3–12 years
Immediate memory/registration			
Digit Span (Wechsler, 1991; Anderson & Lajoie, 1996)	Yes	Yes	6+ years
Corsi blocks (Milner, 1971; Anderson & Lajoie, 1996)	Yes	Yes	7–13 years
Spatial Memory (Kaufman & Kaufman, 1987)	Yes	Yes	2.6–12.6 years
Story Recall (Christensen, 1979; Anderson & Lajoie, 1996)	Yes	Yes	7–13 years
Benton Visual Retention Test (Benton, 1982)	Yes	Yes	8+ years
New learning			
California Verbal Learning Test—Children's Version (Fridlund & Delis, 1994)	Yes	Yes	5–16 years
Rey Auditory–Verbal Learning Test (Rey, 1964; Forrester & Geffen, 1991; Anderson & Lajoie, 1996)	Yes	Yes	7–13 years
Spatial Learning (Lhermitte & Signoret, 1972; Anderson & Lajoie, 1996)	Yes	Yes	7–13 years
Rey–Osterreith Complex Figure: recall (Rey, 1941; Waber & Holmes, 1985; Anderson & Lajoie, 1996; Kolb & Whishaw, 1996)	Yes	Yes	6+ years

memory): and (3) learning paradigms, where the child is provided with several opportunities to learn new material (e.g., word learning lists, spatial learning arrays).

Information regarding modality specificity of memory functions, recognition versus retrieval skills, and the ability to formulate and implement strategies for learning are also important factors to consider, depending on the context of the assessment. For example, where a child with focal temporal seizures is being considered for epilepsy surgery, the evaluation may be directed to establishing the modality-specific aspects of the memory deficit. Where the question is more related to behavioural intervention, the task may be to identify the child's learning preferences and to develop compensatory strategies that utilise these preferences while bypassing areas of learning impairment.

Emergence of child-based assessments of executive function

A more recent advance in child neuropsychology assessment stems from an acknowledgement of the importance of executive functions and their gradual emergence during childhood (Welsh & Pennington, 1988; Welsh et al., 1991). The move to incorporate tasks that purport to measure these abilities into clinical and research protocols has strengthened during the 1990s, although the quality of such additions is still untested. Recent studies provide compelling evidence that these skills are assessable even during the preschool period, provided appropriate measures are employed. Given the vulnerability of executive functions to early brain damage (Mateer & Williams, 1991), and the importance of intact executive function to ongoing cognitive development (Dennis, 1989) and to the success of treatment and rehabilitation programmes, there is a need to devise valid and well-standardised assessment measures, specifically designed for children, and based on current understanding of the nature of both cerebral and cognitive development through childhood.

The assessment of executive functions is a topic that has received considerable attention in adult neuropsychology. Early localisationist models designated tests such as the Wisconsin Card Sorting Test (Heaton, 1981) or the Rey Complex Figure (Rey, 1941) as indicators of frontal lobe or executive function, based on poor performance by patients with frontal lobe pathology. Contemporary neuropsychological theory would argue that such an approach is too simplistic. The efficiency of executive skills, and also of frontal lobe functioning, is necessarily mediated by lower-order processes. It is important then to view executive functions in the context of these other functions, and to carefully evaluate assessment tools, considering the specific components of executive function they measure. In many cases this may be difficult to tease out, and often the traditionally quoted summary or "endpoint score" is not particularly sensitive to executive functions, as it commonly summarises performance on a variety of different cognitive components. Assessment and isolation of executive deficits may rely on administration of multiple tests, each focusing on specific aspects of function, and sequentially ruling out skills as deficient (Walsh, 1978). Alternatively, microanalysis of specific aspects of test performance may enable the isolation of executive abilities from lower-order cognitive skills (Anderson, 1998; V. Anderson, Anderson, Northam, et al., in press).

A number of authors comment on the problems of assessing executive function. In addition to being accessible only through tests that include lower-order functions, deficits in these skills are often difficult to detect within the clinical context, using standardised assessment tools. Typically the neuropsychological assessment is conducted in a well-structured clinic setting, where the examiner plans and initiates most of the evaluation. Lezak (1995) emphasises these factors, noting that deficits in executive function are rarely reflected in test scores, as the majority of assessment tools are also highly structured. Parker and Crawford (1992), in a review of assessment procedures claimed to measure executive functions, report "disappointingly few sensitive and reliable tests which the clinical neuropsychologist can depend upon" (p. 286). Others also comment on this, noting the problem of ensuring that the novelty required to assess these functions does not reduce the possibility of good test reliability (Rabbitt, 1997). When evaluating executive function, the clinician is often forced to rely on qualitative observation and informed judgement, as well as reports from family and social contexts.

To establish valid measures of executive function, it is essential to evaluate their capacity to measure the primary skills included in definitions of the concept: planning, problem solving, abstract thinking, concept formation, self-monitoring, and mental flexibility (Duncan, 1986; Luria, 1973; Neisser, 1967; Welsh & Pennington, 1988). Walsh (1978) argues that, in order to effectively tap these skills, tasks require several characteristics: novelty, complexity, and the need to integrate information. In support of Walsh's "formula", Shallice (1990) states that routinised tasks can be performed almost automatically, without reference to executive skills. Novel or complex tasks require the individual to develop new schemas, formulate new strategies, and monitor their effectiveness, thus activating executive skills.

The most widely accepted measures of executive function have been designed or borrowed from cognitive psychology, with these basic requirements in mind. One of the greatest problems, however, is the lack of consensus as to which of these measures are valid indicators of executive function. A review of a number of recent studies that have been designed to assess executive skills shows that individual researchers vary in their understanding of which tests provide the best measures of executive functions.

TABLE 10.6

Executive function tests commonly employed in neuropsychological assessments with children

Measures	Standard instructions	Age norms	Age range
Tower of London (Shallice, 1982; Krikorian et al., 1994; Anderson et al., 1996)	Yes	Yes	7–13 years
Porteus Mazes (Porteus, 1965)	Yes	No	–
Austin Maze Learning Test (Milner, 1965)	No	No	–
Controlled Oral Word Association Test (Gaddes & Crocket, 1975; Anderson, Lajoie, & Bell, 1995)	Yes	Yes	7–13 years
Twenty Questions Test (Denny & Denny, 1973; Levin et al., 1991)	Several versions	No	–
Wisconsin Card Sorting Test (Heaton, 1981; Chelune & Baer, 1986)	Yes	Yes	6–12 years
Children's Category Test (1992)	Yes	Yes	6–13 years
Matching Familiar Figures Test (Cairns & Cammock, 1978)	Yes	No	–
Concept Generation Test (Levine et al., 1995)	Yes	No	–
Trail Making Test (Reitan, 1969)	Yes	Yes	7–13 years
Rey–Osterreith Complex Figure: organisation score (Waber & Holmes, 1985; Anderson, Lajoie, & Bell, 1995)	Several versions	Yes	6–15 years
Attention/Executive Domain (NEPSY: Korkman et al., 1997)	Yes	Yes	3–12 years

Table 10.6 lists the tests included in a number of recent child-based studies, each of which employed multiple measures of executive functions. Some measures are more universally accepted than others. For example, in a review of studies employing measures of executive function we found that the Controlled Oral Word Association Test (Gaddes & Crockett, 1975), often described as a measure of abstraction or concept formation, was most frequently employed in both clinical and research contexts (Anderson, 1998). Similarly, the Wisconsin Card Sorting Test, variations of the Tower of London, the Rey Complex Figure, and Trail Making Test were also commonly included in batteries purported to tap executive skills in children. Details of each of these tests are provided in Table 10.6.

CHILD ASSESSMENT: PUTTING THEORY INTO PRACTICE

Despite the various limitations in research, theory and practice, the neuropsychologist has a unique contribution to make to the assessment, diagnosis, and treatment of childhood CNS dysfunction. The role of the neuropsychologist is to sample behaviour in a way that increases understanding of the underlying causes of these behaviours. Thus, although the diagnosis provides a label, the careful evaluation of the child's functional abilities provides information upon which treatment and management can be based. Access to standardised psychometric assessment tools enhances the neuropsychologist's capacity to evaluate a child's performance in comparison to age peers and to determine deviations from "normal", as well as to describe the child's cognitive strengths and weaknesses and their relationship to presenting problems. Training in the understanding of complex constructs such as information processing, attention, and executive function further enhances the neuropsychologist's ability to interpret test performances in a meaningful manner.

Paediatric neuropsychologists commonly receive referrals for the assessment of a variety of medical and neurological conditions. Most referrals simply require an opinion regarding the nature and severity of the child's problems. More sophisticated requests may seek a fine-grained evaluation of cognitive or learning skills or advice regarding appropriate treatment and management. Serial evaluations and "on–off" medication assessments, which evaluate functional abilities under standard conditions, may be particularly informative for families and physicians who need to make decisions regarding the course of the medical condition or the efficacy of treatments.

Regardless of the specific approach employed, clinical child neuropsychologists agree that it is important not to rely too heavily on any one source of information and data, but rather to collect material relating to a number of factors and then integrate this information in a meaningful way. One model for assessment suggests inclusion of a number of data sets that provide a wide range of information that can be integrated and interpreted. The clinician's task is to determine the consistencies within these data sets, which may lead to accurate diagnosis and interpretation of results. These stages are listed in Table 10.7 and may include: (1) background history; (2) behavioural observation, with data collected from multiple sources including parent, teacher, and clinician; (3) intellectual assessment; (4) evaluation of specific skills commonly impaired following brain insult, as evidenced by child-based research, including information-processing capacity, memory, learning, and executive function; (5) hypothesis testing, relating test profiles to task demands in problem areas; (6) formulation of a treatment plan based on assessment data; (7) feedback to child, parents and teachers; and (8) evaluation of intervention and effects of the condition and any treatments administered.

Background information

Details of the child's medical, developmental, educational, and social history provide a framework for understanding the context of presenting problems. For example, the nature and severity of any neurological disorder must be

TABLE 10.7
Components of neuropsychological assessment

Component	Assessment measure
A. *Nature of presenting problem*	Referral question
B. *Background history*	Parent interview
	Review of medical, school records
C. *Qualitative data*	
Direct observation	Observation of child's behaviour, preferably in a variety of settings including clinic, school, home
Parent/teacher observation	Behaviour Rating Scales
D. *Quantitative data*	IQ test (e.g., WISC-III)
Intellectual evaluation	Attention and information processing
Evaluation of specific skills	Memory and learning
	Executive function
	Academic abilities
Functional evaluation	Behaviour/personality
	Adaptive behaviour
	Integration of multiple data sources
E. *Formulation/diagnosis*	Feedback interview with parent and child
F. *Feedback/treatment*	Feedback to referral source
	School consultation
	Follow-up with child, family, school
G. *Evaluation of intervention*	On/off treatment evaluations

established. Certainly it would be reasonable to expect a different neuro-psychological profile for a child with a mild traumatic brain injury, associated with minimal complications, from one with a more severe injury, associated with prolonged coma and multiple neurological signs. Similarly, a child with uncomplicated bacterial meningitis may be expected to have few neuropsychological impairments, whereas the child with postinfection complications such as hearing deficits, and epilepsy, may be expected to exhibit definitive neurobehavioural signs. A well-controlled metabolic condition (e.g., phenylketonuria) may be less likely to result in deficits than a poorly controlled condition. Thus, knowing the nature of the medical disorder is not sufficient; it is important to be aware of the details of the illness and recovery course, and the likelihood of residual underlying brain damage. Access to radiological data, including EEG, single-photon emission computed tomography (SPECT), CT, and MRI scans, is valuable, although the limitations of such methods must be acknowledged. Similarly, knowledge of medications and their possible side effects will also enhance diagnosis.

Developmental history is also relevant. A history of specific language delay, for example, may provide additional evidence of the nature of a learning disability. Lack of evidence of developmental delay may support the diagnosis of an acquired condition, and enable the clinician to comment on loss of function associated with pathology. History of disrupted education may raise the possibility that an educational deficit is not necessarily cognitively based, but perhaps due to poor or interrupted schooling experience. For example, the child with a chronic illness may have had frequent absences from school, thus contributing to educational impairment.

Psychosocial factors will also impact on both current levels of functioning, and general development. Knowledge of family structure, family medical and developmental histories provides a general context within which the child can be evaluated. Qualitative material regarding family dynamics, recent family disruptions, attitude to the child's problems, the child's role within the family, the family's perception of the child, and their capacity to provide for the child' needs will inform the clinician with respect to possible psychosocial contributions to presentation, as well as realistic goals for intervention.

Behavioural observations

Direct observations constitute an important aspect of assessment. At the extreme, standardised psychometric assessment measures may be seen as providing the clinician with a structured and standard opportunity to sample behaviour. Qualitative observations may enrich assessment on many levels. At the basic level, the clinician will be able to establish the child's motivation and investment in testing, and identify any anxiety present, as a gauge to determining the validity of results. More specifically, language functions, attention, persistence to task, ability to develop strategies, evidence of impulsivity, inflexibility, and perseveration may all be detected, with the possibility of following these areas up later with standardised tests.

Behaviour rating scales are commonly employed to quantify these observations and facilitate diagnosis. Like other forms of standardised assessment, they provide an indication of the child's personality, emotional functioning, and behaviour relative to age expectations, and enable the clinician to determine the extent to which a child's behaviour is deviant. There are a number of scales that have been specifically designed to measure a range of behavioural characteristics simultaneously, in the context of overall behavioural functioning (Behavioral Assessment System for Children: Reynolds & Kamphaus, 1992; Child Behaviour Checklist: Achenbach, 1991; Conners Rating Scale: Conners, 1997; Personality Inventory for Children: Wirt et al., 1977); others address specific aspects of behaviour commonly associated with CNS dysfunction such as attentional abilities and adaptive and executive functions (Vineland Adaptive Behaviour Scales: Sparrow, Balla, & Cicchetti, 1984; Behavioral Rating Inventory of Executive Function: Gioa, Isquith, Hoffhines, & Guy, 1999). A number of these measures and their respective age ranges are listed in Table 10.8.

Neuropsychological assessment

The administration of formal psychological tests is the primary focus of the evaluation process. Given the limitations of available tests and the difficulty of reliable detection of abnormal performance in children, it is important to include well-normed measures as an initial step. For example, administration of a standard IQ test such as the Stanford Binet (4th edition) or the appropriate Wechsler Intelligence Scale provides essential information with respect to the child's overall level of ability, which can then be employed to determine whether a poor test performance is a reflection of a specific cognitive deficit or an indicator of more globally low levels of cognitive ability. Each of these measures provides a breakdown of skills that may also provide useful material. A discussion of the specific neuropsychological interpretation of these measures is beyond the scope of this chapter, and readers are directed to the relevant texts that cover these topics (see Kaufman, 1979; Sattler, 1988).

Neuropsychological assessment cannot be limited to intellectual evaluation for several reasons. First, standardised test procedures are based largely on multidetermined activities, and generally fail to directly address functional abilities such as attention, information processing, or executive function. Observed patterns of performance commonly require follow-up to determine the specific nature of underlying deficits. Second, the assessment needs to be relevant to the problem, and intellectual evaluation in isolation may not address many aspects of functioning that are relevant to CNS function.

TABLE 10.8

Assessment of associated functions: Academic, behavioural, and psychosocial

Ability area	Tests	Standard instructions	Age norms	Age range
Academic	Wide Range Achievement Test (Jastak & Wilkinson, 1994)	Yes	Yes	5+ years
	Peabody Individual Assessment Test (Markwardt, 1989)	Yes	Yes	5–17 years
	Wechsler Individual Achievement Test (Wechsler, 1993)	Yes	Yes	5–19 years
	Woodcock Reading Mastery Tests (Woodcock & Mather, 1989)	Yes	Yes	
	Neale Analysis of Reading Ability—Revised (Neale, 1988)	Yes	Yes	6–12 years
Adaptive ability	Vineland Adaptive Behavior Scales (Sparrow et al., 1984)	Yes	Yes	0–12 years
Behaviour/personality	Child Behaviour Checklist (Achenbach, 1991)	Yes	Yes	2–18 years
	Rowe Behavioural Rating Inventory (Rowe & Rowe, 1993)	Yes	Yes	5–12 years
	Conners Behavioural Rating Scales (Conners, 1997)	Yes	Yes	3–17 years
	Children's Depression Scale (Lang & Tisher, 1983)	Yes	Yes	9–16 years
	Personality Inventory for Children (Wirt et al., 1977)	Yes	Yes	6–16 years
	Behavior Assessment System for Children (Reynolds & Kamphaus, 1992)	Yes	Yes	4–18 years
	Coopersmith Self-Concept (Coopersmith, 1984)	Yes	Yes	8–12 years
Family functioning	General Heath Questionnaire (Goldberg, 1978)	Yes	N/A	N/A
	Parenting Stress Index (Abidin, 1995)	Yes	N/A	N/A
	Family Assessment Device (Miller et al., 1985)	Yes	N/A	N/A
	Family Environment Scale (Moos & Moos, 1986)	Yes	N/A	N/A
	Family Burdens Questionnaire (Taylor et al., 1995)	Yes	N/A	N/A

Third, because IQ is frequently observed to be within the average range for children with CNS disorders, IQ tests may be an insensitive indicator of common but subtle neuropsychological dysfunction. Additional tests, focusing on the presenting problems, or established patterns of deficit identified for specific forms of CNS dysfunction, may then be employed to test hypotheses derived from knowledge of the presenting disorder, contextual information, qualitative observations, and IQ data.

Based on a hypothesis testing model (Anderson & Gilandis, 1994; Saling, 1994; Walsh, 1978), the tests chosen at this second stage of evaluation need to take account of the pattern of cognitive strengths and weaknesses exhibited by the child on standardised measures, and the way that this ability profile might interact with the demands placed on the child in home and school environments. As discussed previously, and detailed in Tables 10.1–10.6, such measures may focus on a range of neurobehavioural skills, including language, visual abilities, attention and processing, memory, and executive function. Assessment tools need to reflect a cohesive theory of neuro-psychological development and dysfunction, and encompass the ever-growing knowledge base in the field. More and more information is becoming available on the typical deficits exhibited in association with particular pathologies and syndromes, and this data may be usefully employed to direct assessment procedures.

Evaluation of functional abilities, such as behaviour, educational skills and adaptive abilities, may also be required, depending upon the nature of the referral and the context of the clinician. These measures will inform the neuropsychologist of the child's ability to translate neurobehavioural skills into the real-world context. They may often provide the clearest evidence of impairment, reflecting the child's difficulties in managing independently within a dynamic environment, where multiple activities may be occurring at once, and where there may be minimal supervision. Table 10.8 lists measures commonly employed to document these skills.

Interpretation

Collating these various information sources is the final and most important aspect of evaluation. The aim is to achieve a formulation that is reliable and accurate. As previously noted, the multidimensional nature of many psychological and neuropsychological measures makes it difficult to identify a specific deficit on the basis of a single test performance. Thus reliable and objective interpretations are achieved by administering standardised and valid test measures, utilising the psychometric information provided by these measures, and adding this data to the background material and qualitative data obtained via the assessment process and through other sources. For example, to diagnose a specific deficit in sustained attention, the clinician may use as supporting evidence a background history of inability to maintain attention on an activity, or a description of difficulties completing tasks without supervision. An observed difficulty in sustaining attention in the test situation, added to poor performances on formal tests tapping these skills, such as the Continuous Performance Test, would be expected. In contrast, other tests should be performed at age-appropriate levels. The validity of neuropsychological findings may then be examined by comparing this data with the functional deficits reported by the child and family. Taking the example of a sustained attention deficit once again, the functional features of such a problem might include difficulties completing work at school, or inability to maintain concentration on a television programme or video game, with other skills intact.

A further example of this process is demonstrated in the case of a child presenting for assessment of cognitive deficits following a traumatic brain injury. Assessment results may indicate moderate to severe information-processing deficits, and significantly reduced speed of processing, typical of the pattern of impairment following traumatic brain injury. However, the medical data may suggest that the child's injury was mild, with no loss of consciousness, no post-traumatic amnesia, and no abnormalities on MRI scan. Clearly these two sources of information are contradictory, with the mild nature of the injury not consistent with the severity of documented impairments. Additional information provided by home and school, suggesting delayed early development, including poor articulation and reduced fine-motor skills, as well as poor development of academic skills, will provide vital data to indicate that the child was experiencing a developmental delay prior to injury, which may have been exacerbated by the injury, but is not consistent with the nature of the traumatic brain injury alone.

Formulation, feedback, and evaluation of intervention strategies

Although direct and appropriate intervention is the ultimate aim of neuropsychological evaluation, a parallel benefit may also be achieved, if the clinician is able to impart his or her understanding of the child's difficulties to the child, family, and teacher. It is not uncommon in child disorders for there to be considerable confusion and distress over the child's difficulties. This may be true for both home and school environments, with the problem often increased by a lack of understanding of the underlying deficits and their manifestations in the child's day-to-day activities. In many instances the child is seen as disruptive or uncooperative by both parents and teachers. The child may also experience difficulties coming to terms with secondary social and academic failures, particularly where there is a lack of recognition and support for his or her problems. The wealth of information available from neuropsychological evaluation can be used constructively to improve the understanding of those working and living with the child.

When providing feedback, families and children will frequently validate clinical findings by offering their own examples of the described deficits in everyday life. For example, an adolescent boy who had recently been diagnosed as suffering from attention deficit hyperactivity disorder recounted his experience of the classroom environment throughout his school life by stating that "the teacher just goes on and on until I feel like I'm in the middle of the ocean with waves washing over me". This boy's parents were then able to re-evaluate their observations of their son's poor study skills, including his short bursts of effort punctuated by frequent interruptions. They could relate these behaviours to difficulties in sustaining attention, rather than a simple lack of motivation. When reviewed 6 months later, following implementation of some classroom strategies aimed at slowing the flow of information, the boy was able to state that he felt "more in control" of his environment. His parents reported that they were encouraging shorter homework sessions, with more frequent breaks, with the result that family conflict was reduced and the boy had fewer outbursts of frustration and aggression. In this child's case, no other specialist intervention was instituted, but positive changes had occurred, based primarily on a better understanding of the child's pattern of attentional strengths and weaknesses.

Once the child's pattern of abilities has been identified and interpreted, the next step is to use this information to devise appropriate interventions. This is a difficult task, for which there is little in the way of theoretical guidance. Research addressing links between diagnosis and treatment is scarce and evaluation studies are rare. Regardless of the particular approach taken to intervention, it is critical to evaluate the effects of treatment over time, to determine its usefulness and to document developmental changes in the child that may indicate that modifications to the initial programme are necessary. Neuropsychologists have an important contribution to make in this area, particularly in reference to the supposedly measurable effects of intervention.

CASE ILLUSTRATION: PETER

The following case illustration is provided to demonstrate the process of neuropsychological assessment we have described earlier, from initial interview, through formal evaluation and feedback, to follow-up, with particular emphasis on the neuropsychological data and its relationship to the presenting symptoms, and the usefulness of integrating these data sources when considering appropriate intervention strategies.

Peter is a 13-year-old boy who was referred for neuropsychological evaluation of chronic learning difficulties. The referral was initiated by a psychiatrist who was assessing some recently developed behavioural difficulties,

relative difficulties on Coding and Symbol Search subtests, suggesting that some visuomotor or psychomotor processing difficulty was present. Qualitative analysis of Peter's functional impairment, that is, his spelling problem (Figure 10.2), adds a further dimension to his profile, illustrating the nature of his difficulties. Peter tended to use phonetic strategies, and so often his spelling was decipherable. He had difficulty with unfamiliar words and often misplaced letters within a word. He also had trouble reviewing an incorrect word and, although he was aware that the word was spelt incorrectly, he was unable to correct it. In isolation, neither of these performances clarify the specific nature of Peter's problems. What they do show is the significant discrepancy between his spelling abilities and his above-average performance on intellectual assessment.

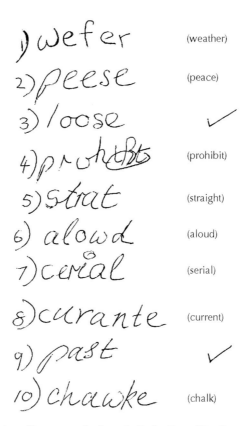

1) wefer (weather)

2) peese (peace)

3) loose ✓

4) prohtbts (prohibit)

5) strat (straight)

6) alowd (aloud)

7) cerial (serial)

8) curante (current)

9) past ✓

10) chawke (chalk)

Figure 10.2. Peter's spelling test results from the Boder Test of Reading and Spelling Abilities (Boder, 1973). Peter's errors suggest that he utilises a phonetic approach to spelling, with poorer visual skills.

Hypothesis testing

Further testing was conducted to gain a better understanding of why Peter's learning problems may have arisen. Based on results from the intellectual assessment, it appeared that linguistic and visual abilities were intact, but as the intellectual test used does not specifically address relevant skills such as registration and retention of information and executive function, these areas needed to be investigated. The remainder of the evaluation was directed to gaining more information in these domains. Peter's test results are outlined below.

Memory assessment
(from *Neuropsychological Assessment of the School-aged Child*, Anderson, Lajoie, & Bell, 1995)

Immediate memory/registration:
Digit span: Forwards = 6 (mean = 6.5, SD = 1.2)
                 Backwards = 4
Block Span: Forwards = 3 (mean = 5.8, SD = 1.0)

New learning:
Story Recall: Story A = 9 (mean = 13.5, SD = 3.3)
                Story B = 16 (mean = 17.4, SD = 3.4)
                Sequence of recall was very poor

Rev Auditory–Verbal Learning Test:

Trial	*1*	*2*	*3*	*4*	*5*	*RECALL A*	*RECOGNITION*
Correct	7	8	13	14	15	15	15
Age norms	7	10	11	12	12	14	14

Rey Complex Figure (see Figure 9.3)
Copy: 29/36 (mean = 31.4, SD = 2.9), but very piecemeal
             organisation
Recall: 27/36 (mean = 19.7, SD = 6.1)

Other neuropsychological measures

Developmental Test of Visuomotor Integration:
Age Equivalent = 13 years 7 months

Trail Making Test:
Trials A = time = 14 s (mean = 15.7, SD = 9.1)   errors = 0
Trials B = time = 84 s (mean = 30.6, SD = 11.6)   errors = 5

Controlled Oral Word Association Test:
 F = 16 (mean = 9.9, SD = 3.3)
 A = 7 (mean = 7.8, SD = 3.3)
 S = 12 (mean = 11.3, SD = 3.5)

Interpretation and formulation

Examining the pattern of results achieved through neuropsychological assessment, several trends emerge. First, Peter demonstrated a number of cognitive strengths. His results on tasks of language function, visuomotor ability, visual perception, and new learning were all age appropriate. He also achieved adequate results on simple tasks, tapping visual constructional skills and visual analysis. New learning appeared intact. Such an array of intact abilities suggests that neuropsychological strength approaches, employing these stronger cognitive skill areas to compensate for weaker skills, may be beneficial for Peter.

Deficient performance was observed on Block Span, Trails B, Digits Backwards, copy of Rey Complex Figure, Processing Speed Index from WISC-III (Coding and Symbol Search), and on spelling tasks. These tasks each have in common a visual component, requiring registration, sequencing, organisation, or manipulation of visual material. Although Peter's actual scores on some of these tasks appeared adequate, they were depressed in comparison to his other advanced abilities. Further, the qualitative difficulties he experienced suggested that he needed to implement compensatory strategies to achieve these age-appropriate results.

Peter's copy of the Rey Complex Figure provides an excellent example of this. On this task Peter scored within the average range, but analysis of his copy indicated that he went about it in a most disorganised, piecemeal way, as illustrated in Figure 10.3. Peter began his copy in the top left corner, completed that quadrant of the figure and then went to the quadrant below. Overall his approach was extremely disjointed and piecemeal. He often forgot small details of individual elements, and needed to return to them at a later stage. Interestingly, when asked to copy the figure on a second occasion he used a more organised approach, suggesting that with additional opportunity he was able to devise an efficient strategy. Similarly, on more difficult items on both the Visuomotor Integration Test and Block Design task, Peter showed no indication that he was able to perceive the "gestalt" of the stimulus. Rather he divided these tasks into a number of steps. The difficulties he experienced on tasks such as Block Span and Digits Backwards were also interesting. Although Peter was able to hold information in mind, when it required some manipulation (e.g., reversing the order of a string of numbers), he experienced difficulties, suggesting problems with parallel processing. These problems may be relevant to spelling difficulties. If one considers the skills necessary for adequate spelling, visual sequencing and visual organisation are important. Inspection of Peter's spelling suggests that he prefers to employ phonic decoding strategies, with little evidence of any visual representation of words in his productions. Where phonetic decoding is difficult, such as for phonetically irregular words, Peter often makes errors in sequencing his

Copy sequence

1. ▬▬▬
2. ─────
3. ·········
4. ■ ■ ■ ●
5. ─ ─ · ─ ⌐

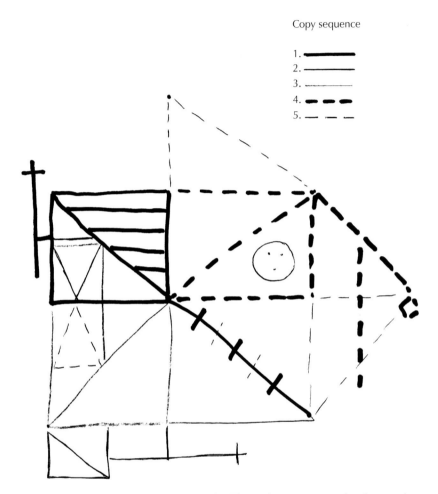

Figure 10.3. Peter's copy of the Rey Complex Figure. Accuracy scores for the copy is age appropriate, but the copy is poorly organised, reflecting a piecemeal approach.

letters. Thus there is some consistency between neuropsychological and educational patterns for Peter.

In contrast to these deficiencies, Peter performed well above age expectations on the Picture Arrangement subtest, suggesting that he was able to sequence and organise material that was verbalisable, but experienced more difficulty organising and sequencing visual material.

Peter's case emphasises the need to look carefully at qualitative as well as quantitative aspects of test performance. For Peter, his IQ scores give little information regarding his learning difficulties. Even his poor Coding score might be easily dismissed by attributing it to anxiety and fatigue. In contrast, qualitative observation of the surprising difficulties Peter experienced when performing complex visual tasks, such as Block Design, provided some evidence to support a cognitively based learning disability. Even then, the exploration for Peter needed to be fairly extensive. Looking retrospectively at Peter's Rey Complex Figure, for example, may have provided little information to aid diagnosis. However, watching his approach to the task showed that he experienced difficulties managing the complex visual material provided. These observations, coupled with slowness and sequencing difficulties on Coding, Block Span, and Trails B, suggest a specific difficulty in visual sequencing and visual organisational skills that relate to Peter's learning problems, and in particular to his pattern of spelling difficulties.

Follow-up and treatment

In the feedback sessions with Peter and his parents these interpretations were discussed and general strategies for minimising his difficulties were suggested. These strategies (e.g., provision of extra time for written work, verbal presentation of information wherever possible, breaking complex tasks down into a series of logical steps, use of word processing and spellcheck facilities, taping class notes for later transcription) were also discussed with Peter's teachers, who enthusiastically implemented them over the following months. Review 6 months later, and again 12 months later, showed a steady improvement in Peter's grades at school and in his attitude to study. These improvements were accompanied by improved affect, and there was no evidence of depression at follow-up sessions.

FROM ASSESSMENT TO INTERVENTION

In general, neuropsychologically oriented interventions within the child context are reported infrequently. Perusal of the increasing number of child neuropsychology texts identifies a lack of focus on this area, possibly due to the difficulties in initiating, maintaining, and evaluating such activities. Further, there are very few rehabilitation facilities specifically designed for the treatment of children with acquired CNS disorders, in contrast to the large industry directed towards rehabilitation in adults. Possibly, one of the primary reasons for this difference is the commonly held perception that children will recover better within the familiarity and security of their family environment. As a consequence, following CNS insult, children are discharged home to the care of their parents as soon as possible. Discharge usually occurs as soon as the child is medically stable, and the parents are sufficiently informed regarding care requirements for the child. Although intensive rehabilitation may continue to occur on an outpatient basis in the acute stages post-insult, this diminishes as the child is well enough to return to school. Reintegration into the school environment is seen as an important step in the recovery process, and is initially aimed at enhancing socialisation and adjustment, even before the child is ready to benefit from the educational curriculum. Thus, the school becomes a de facto "rehabilitation" provider, often despite any previous expertise in working with children with neurological impairments. The nature and degree of support will then depend on the resources of the school and its staff, their attitude to accommodating children with special needs, and the quality of liaison with rehabilitation staff. In optimal situations, the school, family, and rehabilitation staff work together, via regular school meetings and less formal contact, in an attempt to provide an appropriate context and educational programme for the child.

The neuropsychologist may take on a number of roles in such situations. Possibly the most specific task is the communication of medical and assessment data in a manner appropriate and useful for the school context. Rourke (1986) describes a model for such a process, suggesting that relevant factors for consideration include: (1) the types of skills impaired; (2) the number of skills impaired; (3) the degree of impairment; (4) the child's capacity for adaptation; and (5) the quality of intact abilities. These factors then need to be integrated with the demands of the child's environment, both academic and social. Although this model is primarily presented from a cognitive perspective, it may also be extended to incorporate social and behavioural features of the child's presentation, enhancing its utility.

The neuropsychologist needs to inform teachers of the child's neurobehavioural strengths and weaknesses and the way these might be displayed in the classroom or playground. As previously discussed, common issues for the child with an acquired CNS disorder may include attention and learning difficulties, slowed speed of processing, impulsivity, or executive deficits. From a behavioural perspective symptoms such as fatigue, irritability, poor impulse control, and adjustment problems may also be present. Each of these problems will impede efficient functioning within the school environment. Impairments in such functions may cause the child to exhibit a range of symptoms including vagueness and distractibility, impulsivity, difficulties listening to and acting on instructions, inability to commence or complete work without assistance and supervision, poor organisation and reasoning, inability to complete work within given time frames, and social difficulties. Without detailed knowledge of the child, teachers may interpret such behaviours in terms of laziness or poor motivation, and respond accordingly. However, with appropriate evidence, the classroom environment and teacher expectations may be modified to accommodate the child's needs, leading to a more understanding and supportive situation.

The neuropsychologist may also contribute to the development and evaluation of educational and behavioural programmes, using the knowledge gained from assessment, and combining this with the skills of educational

TABLE 11.2
Test results pre- and post-lobectomy for Emma

Test measure	Pre-lobectomy	1 month post-lobectomy	6 months post-lobectomy
General intelligence			
VIQ	79*		85*
PIQ	106		110
FSIQ	91		95
Language			
WISC Vocabulary (scaled score)	7*	4*	8
WISC Similarities (scaled score)	6*	5*	8
COWAT (total words)	21*	9*	20*
COWAT intrusions	–	4*	–
Non-verbal			
Picture Completion (scaled score)	11	–	13
Block Design (scaled score)	12	8	11
Object Assembly (scaled score)	13	–	13
Memory			
Digit Span (scaled score)	8	4*	9
RAVLT (total words)	49	27*	37*
Story Recall (raw score)	27	8*	8*
Spatial Learning (trials)	2	4*	2
CFR copy (raw score)	34	28*	35
CFR recall (raw score)	15	11*	17
Processing speed			
Coding (scaled score)	9	4*	8

* Denotes performance greater than or equal to one standard deviation below the mean, based on age-normed data.

COWAT, Controlled Oral Word Association Test; RAVLT, Rey Auditory–Verbal Learning Test; CFR: Complex Figure of Rey; VIQ, verbal IQ; PIQ, performance IQ; FSIQ, full-scale IQ.

This data represents a subset of the test results from assessments with Emma. Note that the first two evaluations were conducted with the WISC-III and the third with the WAIS-R.

showed average capacity for immediate registration of material (e.g., Digit Span), low average retention for verbal material (e.g., RAVLT, Story Recall), and age-appropriate performance on non-verbal memory tasks (Spatial Learning, CFR recall).

These results were considered consistent with documented left hemisphere pathology, although a clearly lateralised memory deficit was not suggested. Emma then underwent sodium amytal ablation, with her left hemisphere anaesthetised to simulate the effects of surgery. Results from that procedure showed that, although Emma had been unable to retain verbal material, her non-verbal memory was intact, suggesting that her intact right hemisphere had some capacity for learning.

Post-surgery neuropsychological assessments

Although Emma was seen frequently during the few weeks following surgery, no formal evaluation was conducted until just prior to discharge at 1 month post-surgery. In the intervening weeks Emma had experienced a number of complications, including wound infection, severe dysphasia, and associated anxiety and depression. In conversation she was tearful and anxious, and exhibited significant word-finding problems. It appeared that, although there was a functional aspect to her presentation, Emma was experiencing significant language difficulties. These lessened over the month post-surgery, and at 1 month assessment Emma was bright and cheerful, although still mildly dysfluent.

As is illustrated in Table 11.2, Emma's performance at this time was globally depressed. Language skills, non-verbal abilities, and memory functions were all well below age-appropriate levels. Qualitatively, Emma's attention was poor, and there was evidence of psychomotor slowing. This pattern of results probably reflects the generalised cerebral trauma associated with temporal lobe surgery, as well as the specific effects related to removal of temporal lobe tissue. At this time it was difficult to determine the residual consequences of surgery, and it was considered necessary to remain in regular contact with the family to monitor Emma's progress, and to assist with return to school.

Emma was assessed again 6 months post-surgery. In the intervening months Emma had no recurrence of her seizures, although she remained on anticonvulsant medication. She had returned to school and reported that she was managing a restricted curriculum adequately.

Test results at this time appeared more consistent with expectations, and Emma no longer exhibited the global difficulties that were present immediately post-surgery. In particular, non-verbal skills had returned to pre-surgery levels, with memory for non-verbal information intact. Measures of verbal intelligence were also at pre-surgery levels, and there were no residual signs of language dysfluency. Verbal learning remained depressed, with word list learning and story recall continuing to fall more than two standard deviations below age expectations, and representing a significant deterioration from pre-surgery levels. Such a pattern is consistent with removal of left temporal lobe tissue, which has been documented to play an important role in verbal encoding and memory.

Interventions and outcome

These findings were discussed in detail with Emma and her parents, with suggestions to minimise their impact wherever possible. In keeping with a compensatory approach to intervention, strategies were focused on adapting

Emma's environment to her needs. For example, Emma was encouraged to use a diary to record important information rather than relying on her memory. Her family was counselled to write down instructions wherever possible, using calenders and organisers and keeping a message pad beside the phone. At school, Emma's teachers were asked to provide written notes and reference materials, and to ensure that Emma was encouraged to seek clarification, and had ample opportunity for revision. Her workload was reduced, so that she did fewer subjects than her peers, and spent additional time revising her work. These approaches were generally successful, and Emma has gone on to complete tertiary education.

Although Emma experienced some difficulty adapting to her decreased memory function post-surgery, she had greater trouble coping with social and emotional changes. During a family interview conducted 6 months after her surgery, Emma described not feeling "special any more" once she no longer experienced seizures, and being scared about whether she could deal with life without the "excuse" of her epilepsy. She reported being a different person after surgery. At a superficial level, her hair was shaved, and she had a large, unsightly scar. Her conversation was slow, which made her feel self-conscious. She felt embarrassed when she was with people, and didn't know whether to talk about her surgery or not. In the months following surgery, her particular friendship group, which had been nurturing and supportive previously, lost interest in her and Emma gradually became more isolated and withdrawn. She spent most of her time alone in her room. Even her parents were less attentive. Now that they were not so worried about her suffering a seizure they went out more, and focused less on her well-being.

By 12 months post-surgery Emma had little social contact and had become angry and depressed, and her parents were becoming increasingly concerned. At this point Emma returned for review and she and her family were referred to family therapy, which continued over the next 12 months. Review 2 years post-surgery revealed that Emma continued to be seizure free and was in the process of reducing her anticonvulsant medication. Her neuropsychological profile was largely unchanged from the six-month evaluation, and she had negotiated a successful return to a full academic programme. Emotional and social functioning had also improved. Emma had regained much of her confidence and established a new friendship group. She was able to talk to her friends more freely, and felt that she was able to cope with being "normal".

Summary

As is frequently the case in childhood brain disorders, Emma's problems were multidimensional and illustrate the wide range of consequences that may occur. In such instances, the child neuropsychologist may be required to take on a number of roles. In the case of temporal lobe surgery, the assessment role is central to diagnosis and management initially, and later to the documentation of residual deficits. The unique knowledge of the neuropsychologist is also central for specific procedures such as the sodium amytal ablation and related memory assessment. However, the neuropsychologist's knowledge of the possible cognitive repercussions and recovery processes in such a condition indicate a further, more long-term counselling and therapeutic responsibility, which may continue for many years. Educational liaison, documentation of cognitive recovery, and monitoring of psychosocial adjustment may all be managed within a neuropsychological context.

CASE 2: MIGRATIONAL DISORDERS: SUBCORTICAL BAND HETEROTOPIA

The condition

Band heterotopia or "double cortex" is a neuromigrational disorder, caused by an interruption of proliferation and migration of neuroblasts during months three to five of gestation, and leading to migrational arrest. It results in a symmetrical subcortical neuronal band. MRI images demonstrate a thick layer of subcortical tissue similar to that of grey matter, separated from the cortex by a thin layer of white matter. The overlying cortex may be abnormal, characterised by agyria or macrogyria, or it may be normal. Cerebral atrophy manifested by enlarged lateral ventricles and central sulci may also be evident. The disorder is most common in girls, suggesting a genetic cause (Barkovich et al., 1994; Ianetti et al., 1993), but there is some suggestion that the disorder is more severe in boys, and generally incompatible with life. A number of case reports suggest that patients with subcortical band heterotopia suffer from mental retardation and behaviour problems; however, few reports describe any formal testing. Most cases of double cortex are referred to clinical services for investigation of seizure disorders, rather than intellectual impairment (Dobyns et al., 1996; Ianetti et al., 1993; Kirham & Ebbing, 1994). It is likely that, prior to advances in structural brain imaging, many cases of double cortex may have gone undiagnosed, being classified as developmental disorders of unknown origin.

The child

Nina is a 9-year-old girl who was referred to an outpatient neuropsychology clinic for evaluation following diagnosis of subcortical band heterotopia. She had initially presented for neurological investigation at age 8 years 11 months with recent onset of seizures characterised by head and arm movements to the right and right-sided arm movements. Prior to that time her parents describe an uneventful medical history, although Mrs K. reports that her pregnancy with Nina was preceded by four miscarriages. Nina was reported to attain her developmental milestones within normal limits, although towards the slower end of expectations. Her parents note adequate progress at school, although Nina is slow to complete tasks, and quite shy socially.

Her EEG showed prominent epileptic activity in the occipital and posterior–temporal regions bilaterally, and she was prescribed anticonvulsant medication. Despite this treatment Nina's seizures remain poorly controlled. Nina's MRI scan is illustrated in Figure 11.1, showing the typical pattern of thickened cortex on both hemispheres, with the presence of a mantle of white/grey matter, a thin band of white matter and a further band of grey

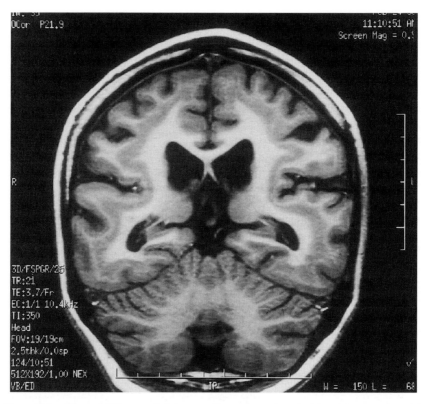

Figure 11.1. Nina's MRI scan. Axial scans, illustrating subcortical band heterotopia, with typical pattern of thickened cortex bilaterally, with evidence of abnormal white/grey matter, then further white matter, then more grey matter. This pattern is mainly seen in the frontal lobes, and to a lesser degree in both superior and inferior parietal lobes. Ventricles, basal ganglia, and posterior fossa appear normal.

matter beneath. There is also evidence of agyria and pachygyria, with abnormalities most marked in the frontal regions.

Nina is the older child in an intact family unit. She has a younger sister who shows normal development. Nina's parents are of European extraction, and emigrated to Australia prior to the birth of their children. Both parents speak good English, and English is the primary language spoken at home. Nina spent 1 year in kindergarten, and was reported to show expected progress during that time, although she did not mix well with other children. She is now in Grade 3 at school, and educational evaluation indicates that reading and spelling skills are age appropriate, with basic maths concepts also intact. At initial interview Nina's family had no real concerns regarding her educational progress, and there was no history of educational intervention prior to her assessment. They did observe that she often failed to follow through on instructions, and found it difficult to learn new skills (e.g., bicycle riding, card games).

The neuropsychological evaluation

Nina presented as a quiet child who was initially difficult to engage. She lacked confidence in novel or unfamiliar environments, and was easily overwhelmed in such situations. Despite this she was motivated to do well, and showed good task persistence. As the assessment progressed, Nina relaxed and began to enjoy the test activities. Qualitatively, the most dramatic feature of Nina's performance was her slowed processing. This was true for both motor and speech production. During assessment Nina often failed to provide a response within the required time constraints, leading to reduced overall scores. She required a great deal of time to grasp new instructions, and was very slow to communicate her ideas in conversation.

As illustrated in Table 11.3, test results demonstrated that Nina's general intellectual functioning was below age expectations. Verbal scores fell within the low average and non-verbal abilities were in the mentally deficient range. She did exhibit some relative strengths in verbal knowledge (general knowledge, word knowledge, arithmetic concepts), with below average scores for more abstract or complex language-based tasks. On the Performance scale of the WISC-III Nina's responses were extremely slow, with her low scores reflecting a frequent failure to complete tasks within time limits. When additional time was provided, Nina was often able to complete tasks accurately.

Assessment of attention identified this was a significant area of weakness for Nina, with selective attention, divided attention, and speed of processing outside normal limits. There were some fluctuations in memory skills, with Nina's verbal recall being particularly reduced. In contrast, visual learning skills were age appropriate, and Nina exhibited a capacity to learn new material where repetition was provided.

TABLE 11.3
Neuropsychological data for Nina (aged 9 years)

A. General intelligence (WISC-III)

Information	8	Picture Completion	8
Similarities	6	Coding	5
Arithmetic	9	Picture Arrangement	2
Vocabulary	8	Block Design	2
Comprehension	5	Object Assembly	5
Digit Span	6	Symbol Search	5
Verbal IQ	84	Performance IQ	66

Full-scale IQ = 73

B. Attention (Test of Everyday Attention for Children)

Selective attention	Sky Search (time)	$217 (x = 76 \pm 22)$
Processing speed	Sky Search Motor (time)	$46 (x = 20 \pm 18)$
Divided attention	Sky Search Dual (time)	$183 (x = 82 \pm 18)$
	Score Dual (correct)	$9/20 (x = 17 \pm 2)$

C. Psychomotor skills

Developmental Test of Visuomotor Integration (age equivalent)	7.0 years

D. Memory (Wide Range Assessment of Memory and Learning)

Verbal Scale (scaled scores)	Story Memory	5
	Sentence Memory	5
	Number/letter Memory	3
Visual Scale (scaled scores)	Picture Memory	19
		(many false positives)
	Design Memory	7
	Finger Windows	8
Learning Scale (scaled scores)	Verbal Learning	8
	Visual Learning	10

E. Executive skills

(i)	COWAT	Total Words	9 (stanine = 2)
(ii)	Trail Making Test	Part A	59 s, 1 error (standard score = 2)
		Part B	226 s, 4 errors (standard score = 2)
(iii)	CFR	Copy/Recall	<1st centile (see Figure 10.2)
(iv)	Tower of London	Total	Standard score <65
		Failed	$5 (x = 9 \pm 3)$

Not surprisingly, measures of executive skills were globally depressed, with planning, problem solving, abstraction, and mental flexibility all reduced. Figure 11.2 provides a graphic example of Nina's difficulties in organising complex material, with her attempt to copy the Rey Complex Figure being unscorable, with no evidence of a strategic, planned approach. To emphasise her slowed output, Nina, took 10 min to complete this drawing. Similar deficits were noted on other executive tasks, where Nina made perseverative errors, failed to follow rules, and commenced tasks impulsively, before identifying a strategy.

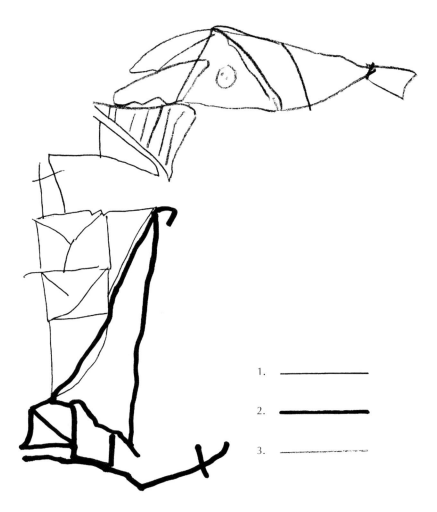

Figure 11.2.   Nina's production of the Rey Complex Figure, suggesting significant impairments in skills required to perform this task, including motor functioning, non-verbal processing, and organisational abilities.

Interpretation of qualitative and quantitative findings from assessment suggest that, while Nina exhibited a range of reduced skills, her primary impairment was one of psychomotor slowing. This problem restricted Nina's capacity to grasp and consolidate new knowledge, to communicate effectively with her environment and to provide motor responses that might accurately indicate her level of ability. These difficulties may be seen as consistent with her condition of band heterotopia, where white matter within the brain is abnormally structured, and information flow likely to be interrupted as a result. The more "executive" type deficits detected are more difficult to interpret. It may be that these are directly related to the migrational disorder, and pathology within anterior cerebral regions. Equally, taking a systemic approach, executive deficits may result from the failure of lower-order systems to process information effectively and transfer it to anterior regions for subsequent action. Regardless of the basic mechanism, assessment suggests that Nina will require support in situations where she is required to work under time constraints or to deal with novel or complex information.

Interventions and recommendations

Results from neuropsychological evaluation were considered to be inconsistent with parental reports of good school progress. It was thought that the parents' lack of experience with the school system, and some language difficulties, may have impeded communication between the family and school. Permission was sought to make contact with Nina's school to clarify these inconsistencies, and to provide support if needed. Consultation with the school revealed that Nina struggled within the classroom and had great difficulty following instructions and completing her work. Her class teacher felt that Nina failed to benefit from much of the instruction provided in the classroom, and was very worried about her progress. She noted that Nina had required large amounts of additional instruction over her school years to provide her with the revision necessary to acquire new skills. Further discussion with Nina's previous teachers suggested that Nina was falling further behind her classmates with time, as class activities became more complex, and better writing skills were expected. There were also concerns regarding social skills, and Nina was noted to have few friends, finding it difficult to keep up with age peers both in the playground and in conversation.

A school meeting was arranged with parents and teachers, to formulate an educational plan to support Nina's difficulties. It was considered that educational progress should be a primary aim. A number of initial steps were agreed on the basis of the meeting. First, the school would apply for financial aid to provide one-to-one support for Nina within the classroom for several hours each day. This would allow the much needed repetition and revision to enhance learning. Training in computer skills was also considered to be a priority. At a classroom level other compensatory strategies were to be trialled, including the use of a scribe or dictaphone, provision of written notes and instructions, and the availability of extra time to complete tasks. Nina was to be excused from some classes (e.g., second language classes) to allow extra time to complete essential tasks and go over class work. The impact of these interventions has yet to be evaluated; however, the involvement of Nina's parents in this process has been helpful, and they have been able to utilise some of the suggested strategies at home to minimise Nina's previous difficulties with following instructions and learning new skills.

Summary

Nina's rare disorder, diagnosed through advances in structural imaging, provides an opportunity to examine the behavioural consequences of neurodevelopmental abnormalities that may have previously gone undetected. The importance of collating data from standardised test procedures in teasing out the primary causes of Nina's functional difficulties is evident, as is the need for thorough assessment. The relevance of cognitive strengths, as well as weaknesses, is emphasised in situations where the neuropsychologist is required to translate assessment data into applied situations and provide suggestions to enhance development.

CASE 3: CEREBRAL TUMOUR

The condition

David was diagnosed with a left frontoparietal glioma at age 12 years. Gliomas, which are a relatively common form of tumour, arise from the glial cells that form the connective tissue of the brain. They range from relatively benign to highly malignant. As Lezak (1995) notes, tumours interfere with brain functioning in a number of ways: (1) destruction of brain tissue via either invasion or replacement; (2) increasing intracranial pressure and oedema, resulting in displacement of brain structures; (3) inducing seizures; and (4) secreting hormones that alter body function. Treatment for tumours generally involves a combination of chemotherapy, radiation therapy, and surgery, with specific interventions dependent on the nature of the lesion.

The functional impairments associated with a tumour may include focal deficits, reflecting the site of the lesion, as well as more global problems as a consequence of processes such as oedema. The degree of impairment may be related to the growth rate of the tumour. For example, many developmental tumours occurring in childhood are very slow growing, and the brain is able to accommodate the gradual expansion of the lesion, with cerebral functions displaced to adjacent healthy brain tissue, so that deficits may be quite subtle. When a tumour grows rapidly, it is more likely that functions are lost. In many patients the first symptoms of tumour include headache and seizures, with focal neurological and neuropsychological signs evident further along in the course of the illness.

TABLE 11.4

Neuropsychological assessment results for David 1½, 3, and 3½ years post-treatment

Test measure		Test 1 (1½ years post)	Test 2 (3 years post)	Test 3 (3½ years post)
Age (years/months)		13 years 6 months	15 years	15 years 6 months
General intelligence				
VIQ:	Information	14	–	12
	Similarities	13	10[a]	9[a]
	Arithmetic	10	4*[a]	4*[a]
	Vocabulary	15	13	13
	Digit Span	14	–	7[a]
PIQ:	Picture Completion	12	14	–
	Coding	4*	2*	2*
	Picture Arrangement	8	8	9
	Block Design	11	9	10
	Object Assembly	8	9	9
Executive function				
COWAT (total words)		34	15*[a]	10*[a]
COWAT intrusions		–	2	6[a]
Colour Form Sorting (categories)		7	3*[a]	2*[a]
Maze completion (trials)		16	30*[a]	30+*[a]
CFR copy (raw score)		36	32	34
Memory				
CFR recall (raw score)		20	11*[a]	26
RAVLT (total words)		50	35*[a]	34*[a]
Story Recall (raw score)		34	25*[a]	18*[a]
Spatial Learning (standard score)		9	9	9

* Denotes performance greater than or equal to one standard deviation below the mean, based on age-normed data.

[a] Denotes decrease of greater than or equal to one standard deviation from Test 1.

Neuropsychological assessment results showed some marked discrepancies from previous testing. David had maintained his average levels of ability in non-verbal areas, including visual perception, learning capacity, and constructional skills. Fine-motor skills and processing speed continued to be impaired but had remained relatively stable over time. In contrast, only well-learned verbal knowledge (general knowledge, word knowledge) remained intact. Higher-order language skills, including verbal reasoning, fluency, and abstract thought, showed marked deterioration. Verbal learning ability was also markedly reduced, for both simple and complex material. David exhibited profound difficulties on arithmetic tasks. Although he was able to perform simple, one-step addition and subtraction calculations, he was incapable of sequencing or manipulating mathematical information in order to solve problems.

Interventions and outcome

These results provided clear evidence that David had experienced significant functional deterioration since the previous evaluation, in keeping with his mother's observations and his school difficulties. Although this deterioration was represented by reduced test performance, there were also new symptoms of emotional, social, and academic dysfunction. It was considered that some of David's difficulties on testing may have resulted from his high levels of anxiety and impulsivity during testing. However, his pattern of deficits (high-level language, arithmetic, memory, maze completion) was consistent with previous diagnosis of left frontoparietal pathology, and given his history such findings were of great concern. David was referred to his neurosurgeon for urgent review, and subsequent MRI scan demonstrated recurrence of tumour, again in the area of the left frontotemporal region. Further neuro-surgery was conducted to remove the tumour, and although this was success-ful, neuropsychological review 6 months later indicated little change in neuropsychological function (see Table 11.4).

David showed no additional physical or cognitive deficits post-surgery, and no further radiation therapy was conducted. Not surprisingly, David was severely depressed over the following months, describing realistic fears for his life, and a lack of interest in becoming involved with any academic or leisure activities. He spent most of his time in his room, and did not return to school for several months. During this period David was referred for individual psychological counselling in order to help him work through his fears. Unfortunately this was of limited value, possibly due to his lack of invest-ment, and difficulties with retaining information and dealing with conceptual issues. Later, family therapy was instituted, with greater success. David's par-ents were able to use these sessions well and draw on suggested strategies to support David at a practical level.

No academic intervention was commenced until David had returned to school and gained some of his strength and confidence, and re-established social networks. At that time, David's curriculum was modified to exclude mathematics and related topics, with David focusing to a greater degree on areas where he experienced least difficulty (e.g., art, English, humanities). He used his free time to work with his tutor, who provided a structured approach to study as well as the opportunity for revision. David continued in the main-stream school system with this extra support for another year, but was unable to cope at senior levels. He has recently left school. He is currently unemployed and receiving an invalid pension.

Summary

David's case demonstrates the diagnostic and monitoring roles often required in child neuropsychology, where knowledge of brain–behaviour relationships can direct interpretation of test data. For David, the changes in test performance over time were dramatic and consistent with the location of the original tumour, and alerted the clinician to the likelihood of tumour recurrence without reference to additional information. Where more subtle changes in neuropsychological function are present, contextual data from family and school may also be helpful for interpreting the possibility of underlying brain changes. However, as frequently observed, the interaction between organic, cognitive, and psychosocial factors is complex, and needs to be carefully considered. Although for David the most likely explanation for his difficulties was clear, the presence of emotional difficulties in reaction to such life-threatening illness may sometimes mask important cognitive indicators.

CASE 4: HEAD INJURY IN THE CONTEXT OF DEVELOPMENTAL DELAY

The condition

As discussed in detail in Chapter 5, childhood traumatic brain injury (TBI) has a variable outcome depending upon a range of injury and non-injury factors, including the nature and severity of injury, age at injury, pre-injury child and family characteristics, psychosocial context, and access to appropriate resources. For mild to moderate TBI, outcome is considered to be relatively good, and characterised by an initial recovery period during which reduced attention and slowed speed of processing are the most commonly described sequelae. The child is often said to achieve pre-injury levels within the first 12 months post-injury. Such claims are difficult to evaluate in very young children such as Tim, where no objective pre-injury school or work history is available. The lack of pre-injury data leads to difficulties accurately gauging the relative contributions of pre-injury abilities and TBI to neuropsychological presentation. In such cases family report is relied upon to a large extent, and this may be problematic where litigation is an issue.

Although contentious, it is argued that children sustaining TBI are not representative of the normal population, and may be more likely to have premorbid developmental and behavioural problems and come from a lower socioeconomic background. For Tim a number of these risk factors were evident. His age, 5 years, placed him at increased risk of sequelae from TBI. He had a documented history of behavioural difficulties, including impulsivity, overactivity, and inattention. His parents were both unemployed at the time of his accident, despite having previously stable employment histories. There were marital difficulties, and Tim's siblings also exhibited some behavioural difficulties. Observation suggested that the family unit was dis-organised, with parents exhibiting high stress levels, evident in their inability to manage the children or day-to-day responsibilities.

The child

Tim was admitted to hospital following an accident where he was knocked from his bicycle and dragged 25 m along the road. He suffered multiple trauma including a closed head injury with skull fracture in the right parietal region, fractured right tibia and fibia, and facial abrasions, most severe on the right side of his face, and requiring grafting. Determining injury severity is often difficult in young children, particularly where early surgical interven-tion is required, as was the case for Tim, who underwent plastic surgery for his facial abrasions. Medical records suggest a brief period of unconscious-ness at the scene of the accident and Tim was described as agitated and crying by the time he reached hospital some 10 min later. He is reported to have remained quiet but confused for several days, although this may have been due to the effects of medication required for severe pain associated with his injuries. CT scan was essentially normal, with a question regarding mild cerebral oedema; however, no neurosurgical intervention was required and no neurological abnormalities were detected, indicating a TBI of mild/moderate severity.

Tim was an inpatient for approximately 4 weeks, primarily due to his facial injuries. He required no cognitive rehabilitation, although he was involved in physiotherapy during his admission, for treatment of his physical injuries. During these sessions Tim was observed to have trouble following simple instructions and was easily confused. Social difficulties were also identified. In particular, it was noted that Tim and his siblings often exhibited episodes of uncontrolled behaviour, and that Mrs K. had few skills to manage these episodes. In this context, Mr K.'s failure to visit was also considered of con-cern. As a result the family were referred to the neuropsychologist attached to the neurosurgical unit for assessment prior to Tim's discharge. At the same time the family was referred for family assessment and therapy.

Tim presented as a friendly young boy, who was wearing a face mask for protection of his newly grafted facial tissue. He attended initial sessions with his mother and two brothers aged 8 and 3 years. During these sessions the boys were boisterous, active, and loud in their play. There were many instances of conflict between them. Mrs K. failed to intervene on any occa-sion, instead allowing the clinician to step in and structure the situation. Tim's mother appeared listless and overwhelmed. She described little support from her husband who was busy seeking employment. She noted that Tim's hospitalisation had been stressful, and that she had no time to get things done. She also commented that she was not going to attend family sessions and that they were an added burden. Tim's mother often arrived late or failed to attend subsequent sessions, appearing tired and harassed. It was very difficult to gain a cohesive background history from her during these sessions, as she tended to lose her train of conversation easily when responding to specific questions.

Over several sessions, both in the acute phase and after Tim had been discharged, Mrs K. reported that Tim had no previous medical problems and was healthy at the time of his injury. She identified no premorbid developmental difficulties, and noted that Tim had no interventions, and had completed kindergarten successfully the previous year. Specific questioning, however, revealed that Tim's language skills may have been delayed. Tim was not speaking in sentences until his kindergarten year, and Mrs K. described his speech as immature and difficult to understand. She also stated that he had difficulty following instructions. Similarly, his fine-motor skills had been slow to develop, and he was not writing or holding scissors before his accident. Mrs K.'s main concern regarding pre-injury function was with respect to behaviour, and she thought that Tim had always been very active, with a short attention span, and a tendency to be impulsive. She reported that she had discussed these difficulties with her local doctor on several occasions. When questioned about changes post-injury, Mrs K. commented on increased behavioural difficulties, but gave no indication that language or fine-motor skills had deteriorated.

Tim was in his first year of school at the time of the accident. Not unexpectedly, he had acquired few literacy skills, although number skills were noted to be quite strong. His teacher frequently complained about his disruptive behaviour in class. Over the next 3 years Tim was assessed a number of times. Complaints were consistent over this time period and included poor attention, immature language, failure to acquire literacy skills, and behavioural difficulties.

The neuropsychological evaluation

Tim was seen for neuropsychological evaluation on three separate occasions, initially 1 month post-injury (aged 5 years 5 months), and then 12 months and 2½ years post-injury. Test results for each testing are presented in Table 11.5.

Initial assessment (1 month post-injury)

Tim was aged 5 years 5 months at the time of this assessment, which was conducted over a number of short sessions, due to Tim's difficulties sustaining attention and limited interest in test activities. Tim presented as an active, friendly young child. Although he was not particularly motivated by test

TABLE 11.5

Neuropsychological test results for Tim at 1 month, 12 months, and 2½ years post-injury

Test measure		Test 1 (1 month post)	Test 2 (12 months post)	Test 3 (2½ years post)
Age		5 years 6 months	6 years 5 months	8 years
General intelligence (WPPSI-R/WISC-III)				
VIQ:	Information	8		3*
	Similarities	6*	6*	4*
	Arithmetic	9	9	8
	Vocabulary	6*	4*	6*
	Comprehension	4*	5*	10
	Digit Span/Sentences	6*	4*	6*
PIQ:	Picture Completion	10		9
	Geometric Design/	6*		–
	Picture Arrangement	–		10
	Block Design	12		13
	Object Assembly	13		16
	Coding/Animal Pegs	10		13
	Verbal IQ	74*	73*	77*
	Performance IQ	101	–	114
Language				
PPVT-R	Age equivalent	3.6 years*	4.2 years*	5.7 years*
TROG	Age equivalent	3.0 years*	3.5 years*	4.0 years*
Visual skills				
Gestalt Closure Test[a]	Age equivalent	5.0 years	6.5 years	8.6 years
VMI	Age equivalent	4.1 years	4.6 years	6.2 years
Memory				
Spatial Memory[a]	Age equivalent	6.8 years	7.6 years	10.3 years
Spatial Learning[c]	Age equivalent	7.0 years	8.0 years	10.0 years
Verbal Memory I[b]	Age equivalent	3.0 years*	3.0 years*	4.0 years*
Verbal Memory II[b]	Age equivalent	4.0 years	5.0 years	7.6 years
Numerical Memory[b]	Age equivalent	3.0 years*	–	–

[a] From Kaufman Ability Battery for Children.

[b] From McCarthy Scales of Children's Abilities.

[c] From Neuropsychological Assessment of the School-aged Child.

PPVT-R, Peabody Picture Vocabulary Test—Revised; TROG, Test for the Reception of Grammar; VMI, Developmental Test of Visuomotor Integration.

* Denotes one or more standard deviations or 2 years or more below expectations.

procedures, he participated adequately and was generally able to grasp test instructions. Tim's expressive language was immature and sometimes difficult to understand. He was impulsive and fidgety, particularly towards the end of test sessions.

Assessment results indicated that Tim had inconsistent abilities, with age-appropriate non-verbal skills, and verbal skills within the "borderline" range, suggesting significant language difficulties. Language difficulties were global and included comprehension, expression, verbal knowledge, and verbal memory. Tim's test results indicated a language delay of approximately 2 years, on average, with performances falling within the 3- to 4-year-old age band. He also demonstrated a less severe impairment in fine-motor and visuomotor abilities, with these skills depressed by 1–2 years. In contrast, non-verbal skills were average to slightly above average. Visual perception, constructional ability, and visual memory were all areas of relative strength for Tim. Arithmetic skills were age appropriate.

At that time speech pathology assessment was recommended, and Tim had regular contact with the hospital for ongoing medical treatment. In the intervening months, Tim's mother was in frequent contact, as he failed to make progress at school and his behavioural difficulties increased. The neuropsychologist's role shifted to management. Speech assessment confirmed language delay, and audiological assessment was arranged and identified central auditory processing problems. Parenting sessions were conducted, in conjunction with a family therapist, to address Tim's mother's difficulties in this area and provide her with management strategies. School liaison was frequent, and documentation was required to support application for special educational support for Tim.

Twelve-month review assessment (age 6 years 5 months)

An incomplete review assessment was conducted, due to the family's failure to attend several sessions. Mrs K. reported ongoing concerns with concentration, behaviour, and school progress. She indicated a lack of confidence in the school's ability to help Tim, despite access to individual intervention for several hours each day. Tim's pattern of performance on testing was consistent with previous results, demonstrating continued language difficulties and reduced verbal memory. At that point contact with the family was lost for several years.

Two-and-a-half-year review (age 8 years)

Some 18 months later Mrs K. re-contacted the clinic, requesting neuropsychological review, in association with a medicolegal claim. On this occasion Tim presented as more contained and attentive. He was able to maintain attention throughout an hour-long test session without distraction or restlessness. Qualitatively, expressive language skills remained depressed and Tim had difficulty formulating his thoughts into words.

Neuropsychological assessment results are outlined in Table 11.5, and indicate ongoing strengths in non-verbal abilities, with Tim's performance IQ now in the high average range. The 13-point increase in performance IQ from acute assessment may simply reflect a practice effect, although it could also indicate general recovery of function, with recovery of attention and speed of processing over time since injury. Visual memory capacity, too, had maintained its above average levels. Language skills, however, remained depressed. Verbal IQ continued to fall well below age expectations, with expression, comprehension, and verbal memory all impaired. Literacy skills were still below age expectations but had shown some progress, and Tim was now able to sound and recognise a small group of simple words. Writing skills were limited by ongoing, mild motor incoordination.

At 2½ years post-injury it was likely that Tim's recovery was now largely complete and that his resultant neuropsychological profile reflected stable functioning. Interpretation of findings suggested that Tim's primary needs were in the domains of language and education, where he was likely to require ongoing support. His improved cooperation and attentional capacity indicated that he may be ready to take maximum advantage of any interventions available to him. At this point, a mixture of approaches was considered appropriate. First, Tim's severe linguistic and educational problems required intensive remediation. To achieve this, regular speech therapy and educational intervention were recommended. However, a more compensatory model was also adopted, and it was suggested that approaches to intervention should take into account Tim's strong non-verbal abilities as a means of compensating for some of his weaknesses. For example, visual/written presentation of material to be learned would utilise non-verbal memory capacity. For practical situations this was operationalised as "showing rather than telling" Tim about new tasks. In the context of reading and spelling, an initial emphasis on sight vocabulary and recognition of familiar syllables was encouraged to increase Tim's word range. Familiarity with word-processing skills was also identified as a useful goal, again employing non-verbal strengths to minimise the impact of psychomotor difficulties.

Interventions and outcome

Differential diagnosis

The availability of longitudinal data on this child enables some clarification of the relative contribution of TBI and developmental factors. It appears that Tim did exhibit developmental weaknesses prior to his accident, with symptoms of attention deficit hyperactivity disorder and specific language delay from his early history. It is unlikely that the mild/moderate nature of his TBI could account for the immediate and severe language difficulties observed in the acute stages of recovery, particularly when his parents failed to report any significant change in these skills. Further, failure to observe any recovery of these skills suggests that effects of TBI cannot fully explain Tim's neuropsychological profile. As is often seen in children with premorbid problems, Tim's developmental difficulties may have rendered him particularly vulnerable to the impact of TBI, possibly exacerbating his pre-injury difficulties, or slowing down his rate of development. Certainly there is some evidence from serial testing that Tim is failing to make the expected developmental gains in linguistic abilities.

Tim's pattern of non-verbal ability also provides some suggestion for a dual aetiology, where both developmental and acquired factors are acting. Increase in performance IQ from acute to 30-month assessment may reflect a return to high average skill in the long term, with the initial results reflecting the typical slowed processing and attentional difficulties seen in the acute stages post-TBI. Improvements in non-verbal memory capacity over and above developmental expectations are also consistent with this interpretation, suggesting that a "TBI" factor may have caused a global dampening of Tim's skills acutely.

Interaction between child and family factors

With the past history of family stress and difficulties following through with therapeutic interventions, it was initially thought unlikely that recommendations derived from the assessment would be taken up. However, at a routine review 12 months later it was found that Tim had made substantial gains. Since the previous evaluation the family situation had altered in a number of aspects. First, Mr K. was now employed, and earning a salary sufficient to afford private school education for his children. Marital problems had subsided and Tim's parents had been involved in further counselling to help their management of the three boys. Both Mr and Mrs K. appeared happier and more in control of their lives. Tim was now in Grade 3 and attending a private school, where he had been provided with an individual programme and substantial educational intervention. He was also attending speech therapy on a regular basis. Mrs K. reported being pleased with Tim's progress, and felt that his school had been successful in helping him acquire academic skills. Tim's teachers were also pleased with his development, and although Tim continued to be active and disruptive at times, these behaviours were less frequent. The school had tried the various educational strategies suggested with some success, and Tim's teacher had modified these to suit her classroom and Tim's needs. There were regular meetings arranged for parents and teachers to discuss recent problems and progress, enhancing and structuring communication between home and school.

For Tim, it appears that family factors were of central importance to his good outcome. While his family were stressed they were unable to cater for his needs and problems were evident in home, school, and family contexts. Once these family difficulties diminished, Mr and Mrs K. were able to identify problems that required action, both at a family level and for Tim individually. Availability of adequate financial and emotional resources enabled his parents to provide input that Tim was then able to utilise successfully, leading to a positive outcome.

Summary

Although sometimes not requested, the task of differential diagnosis is often required in the evaluation process. It is well known that many CNS disorders have associated risk factors such as low socioeconomic status and pre-existing behavioural and learning difficulties. Where such risk factors are present, they need to be taken into consideration when determining the relative contributions of developmental, psychosocial, and acquired conditions. Such factors may influence treatment suggestions and may also have serious consequences for litigation in the case of injury.

An additional issue illustrated in this case is the importance of the family context to outcome. Despite the availability of resources, Tim's family were initially unable to utilise these due to family difficulties, leading to ongoing problems in a range of contexts. As family stresses diminished, Tim's family was then able to access appropriate resources independently, with the resultant improvement in Tim's level of functioning.

CASE 5: EARLY HEMISPHERECTOMY FOR TREATMENT OF INTRACTABLE EPILEPSY

The condition

Hemispherectomy is a radical form of neurosurgery, usually performed for the treatment of intractable epilepsy. It involves removal of the cortical mantle, unilaterally, to prevent the spread of epileptic activity from the affected cerebral hemisphere to the non-damaged hemisphere. In adults such surgery has been shown to have devastating consequences, including dense hemiplegia and, when the left hemisphere is removed, severe, persisting aphasia. These impairments show minimal improvement with time. When such surgery is conducted in young children, particularly between birth and 1 year of age, clinical evidence suggests better outcome. For example, following left-sided hemispherectomy, children less than 1 have been observed to demonstrate language recovery and less severe motor disability than seen in adults. Such good recovery has been argued to reflect cerebral plasticity within the child's brain, where language functions subsumed by the damaged hemisphere are transferred to the intact right hemisphere, with surprisingly little loss of function. Recent research indicates that, as the child develops, symptoms of language impairment may emerge, and intellectual abilities may be globally depressed due to crowding within the limited healthy tissue. To date, reports suggest that such deficits may be relatively subtle, affecting higher-order language skills and functional abilities that rely on these skills (e.g., conceptual thought, literacy skills).

The child

Jamie, aged 4 years 1 month, was referred to a private neuropsychology clinic by his paediatrician, for cognitive evaluation and advice regarding future educational needs prior to school entry. Jamie's medical history is complex. He was born at 24 weeks gestation following a previously uneventful pregnancy. He had some early phototherapy, but otherwise progressed well until about 6 weeks of age, when his parents noted that he was not looking to the right. Paediatric evaluation at the time also detected some problems and further investigations were performed, including CT scan, ultrasound, and EEG. Infantile spasms were diagnosed, with Jamie experiencing up to 30 fits per day in the ensuing months, despite high doses of anticonvulsant medication. As a consequence of these intractable seizures Jamie underwent left hemispherectomy at 9 months of age, involving total removal of cortical tissue within the left hemisphere. His pre- and post-surgery scans showed evidence of left middle cerebral artery occlusion estimated to have occurred during pregnancy. Post-surgery brain scans are presented in Figure 11.3, illustrating resection of the left hemisphere, with only a small area of the frontal lobe remaining. The surgery was successful and since that time Jamie has had no seizures, with motor and language development accelerating as well. Residual effects of surgery include reduced mobility of the right leg and minimal function of the right hand. Despite these problems, Jamie walked independently at 2 years of age, and language development was only slightly delayed.

At the time of assessment Jamie was attending kindergarten, where he was observed to have problems in the following areas: (1) limited sustained attention, particularly when participating in listening activities. In contrast, he was reported to be able to watch television and videos with less distractibility; (2) poor memory, particularly for multiple instructions; (3) unusual language, including frequent meaningless statements, and tangential and inappropriate conversation; and (4) significant behavioural difficulties including disinhibition, aggression, tantrums, and obsessive-compulsive type rituals. Mrs R. also noted that it was difficult to reason with Jamie.

Jamie received intervention from occupational therapy, speech therapy and physiotherapy services on a regular basis following his surgery. He attended a regular kindergarten, and his parents planned for him to attend mainstream school. They intended to use the results from the assessment to support their application for additional teacher support when Jamie commenced school.

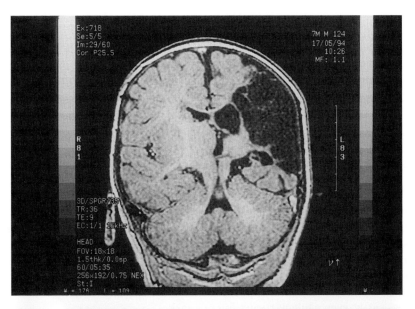

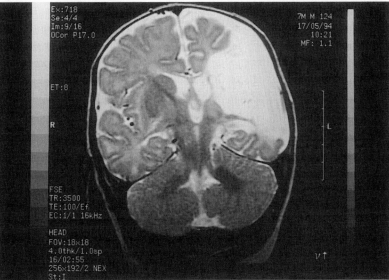

Figure 11.3. Jamie's post-surgery MRI scans illustrating removal of substantial tissue within the left hemisphere, with only a small residual component of the frontal lobe remaining. The right hemisphere has expanded to fill some of the available space, with an extradural hygroma filling the remainder of the area.

Jamie is the third of four children in an intact family unit. His siblings are all healthy and developing well. His father has a tertiary education and works as an accountant. Mrs R. completed secondary school and is currently involved in home duties. They described Jamie as a sociable boy who makes friends easily. They were concerned that these friendships were sometimes indiscriminate, and that Jamie had no fear of approaching strangers.

The neuropsychological evaluation

Jamie presented as a pleasant, friendly boy who readily engaged in test activities. He was cooperative and motivated throughout, although limited attention sometimes detracted from his ability to complete test activities. Qualitatively, Jamie was sometimes impulsive, responding before thinking, but could be directed to think tasks through more carefully. Jamie's right-sided weakness restricted his capacity to perform motor tasks such as drawing, writing, or constructional activities. Jamie's understanding of task requirements fluctuated. On some occasions his understanding was excellent, whereas at other times it was poorer, with Jamie seeming to "forget" instructions easily, even while participating in a task.

On the Weschler Primary and Preschool Intelligence Scale—Revised Jamie performed within the "low average" range, indicating that overall cognitive abilities were just below age expectations. Verbal and Performance IQs were relatively consistent. However, there were significant fluctuations across individual skills, with subtest scores ranging from 10 (Object Assembly, Information, Vocabulary) to 1 (Animal Pegs). A full list of test scores is provided in Table 11.6.

Jamie's language skills were generally within the average to low average range. Language comprehension was age appropriate on testing, although in general conversation it was observed that he sometimes had difficulty understanding specific sentence structures. For example, when asked a question beginning with "Why?" Jamie was often unable to respond accurately; however, when the question was rephrased he could cope better. Expressive language was intact, and Jamie exhibited age-appropriate word knowledge and general knowledge. Verbal reasoning and abstract thought were slightly reduced, consistent with Mrs R.'s reports of poor reasoning skills.

Jamie performed consistently within the average range on tasks of visuospatial ability. Visual perception, visual analysis, and visual constructional abilities were age appropriate, despite his inability to use his right hand to support these activities. Where motor skills were the focus of the task, for example, writing or drawing, Jamie's performance was poorer, to a large extent due to his difficulties using his right hand.

As previously noted, Jamie had difficulty maintaining attention over time, particularly on auditory–verbal activities, showing evidence of distractibility

TABLE 11.6
Test data for Jamie (aged 4 years 1 month)

A. General intelligence (WPPSI-R)			
Information	10	Object Assembly	10
Similarities	6*	Geometric Design	5
Arithmetic	5*	Block Design	8
Vocabulary	10	Mazes	–
Comprehension	7*	Picture Completion	8
Sentences	9	Animal Pegs	1

Verbal IQ   = 85
Performance IQ = 83
Full-scale IQ   = 82

B.   Language skills

Peabody Picture Vocabulary Test—Revised (age equivalent)	3.6 years
Test for the Reception of Grammar (age equivalent)	4.6 years
Expressive One Word Picture Vocab. Test (age equivalent)	4.0 years

C.   Spatial/Psychomotor skills

Gestalt Closure Test[a] (age equivalent)	3.3 years
Developmental Test of Visuomotor Integration (age equivalent)	2.11 years

D.   Memory skills

McCarthy Memory Scale:	Verbal memory I (age equivalent)	4.0 years
	Verbal Memory II (age equivalent)	4.6 years
	Num. Memory I (age equivalent)	3.6 years
Spatial Memory[a] (age equivalent)		6.0 years
Spatial Learning[b] (age equivalent)		6.0 years

[a] From Kaufman Ability Battery for Children.
[b] From Neuropsychological Assessment of the School-aged Child.
* Denotes score is one or more standard deviations or 2 years or more below expectations.

and difficulty persisting on long or open-ended tasks. Jamie often repeated questions and seemingly forgot instructions, also suggesting difficulties maintaining attention and registering new material. His ability to learn and retain information was age appropriate for auditory–verbal material and slightly advanced for non-verbal information. Jamie showed that he could benefit from repetition and revision of information and instructions, with learning improving when such opportunities were available.

Intervention and recommendations

Jamie was 4 years of age at the time of testing. Despite history of premature birth, cerebral infarction, infantile spasms, and subsequent left hemispherectomy, Jamie has acquired basic language skills, non-verbal abilities, and mobility, and is able to function independently in a normal preschool environment.

Neuropsychological evaluation indicated that Jamie had average to low average abilities on a range of cognitive and information-processing activities, including verbal knowledge, visuospatial processing, and simple learning capacity. Jamie did exhibit mild to moderate difficulties in the following areas: (1) *attentional problems*, which reduced his ability to maintain attention and persist on tasks, which, in turn, compromised new learning capacity. Such a limitation in information-processing skills will place Jamie at risk within a classroom environment, where he may miss or misinterpret information or instructions that are presented aurally. To minimise these difficulties Jamie should be seated close to his teacher, so intervening distractions are minimised. Instructions provided in short sentences, with pauses for processing time will improve Jamie's ability to take in information. He should be encouraged to seek clarification when he is unsure of information. Structuring material (e.g., via a story or familiar theme), a familiar routine to the provision of new material, and presentation in small amounts will also help Jamie maintain attention to task; (2) *motor difficulties*, exacerbated by Jamie's right hand impairment, limited his capacity to participate on written tasks or other fine-motor activities requiring both hands. Appropriate compensatory aids will be essential to support his full participation in class. For example, once Jamie has acquired literacy skills, use of a word processor will be beneficial. Prior to that he may require access to a touch screen or a scribe when written output is required; and (3) *subtle verbal reasoning/abstract thinking difficulties*, suggesting that Jamie may need additional instruction and explanation of complex information, including social and day-to-day situations.

At a more general level, it was strongly recommended that all current therapy services be continued when Jamie commences school, and that additional educational support be available at school, to compensate for significant attentional and motor difficulties. Review assessment was suggested following school commencement.

Summary

Jamie provides a good example of an instance where medical parameters are clear and treatment has been successful. He is being well managed both by his paediatrician and by his family, and the neuropsychologist was asked to complete a well-defined task: documentation of cognitive abilities, and appropriate action regarding school resources. Jamie's neuropsychological profile, which includes a number of intact skills, suggests a range of possibilities for intervention and compensatory strategies.

From a theoretical perspective, Jamie's current level of ability provides indirect support for the notion of cerebral plasticity, with evidence that he has been able to develop basic language skills without language cortex. It might be predicted that Jamie will encounter more difficulties as he moves through childhood and is required to develop high-level language skills and executive abilities. Ongoing review of his progress will be of interest from a theoretical perspective, but may also be critical clinically, to ensure early identification and intervention for emerging problems.

CASE 6: NON-VERBAL LEARNING DISABILITY: A LONGITUDINAL PERSPECTIVE

The condition

The syndrome of non-verbal learning disability (NVLD; Rourke, 1988, 1989) has been described in detail in Chapter 1. NVLD is thought to be associated with subcortical pathology within the white matter of the brain, resulting from cerebral insult perinatally or early in childhood. This early damage is argued to impact on the right hemisphere primarily, due to its reliance on the interconnections of the subcortex. The core features include: (1) bilateral tactile-perceptual and psychomotor deficits; (2) impaired visual recognition and discrimination and visuospatial organisational deficiencies; (3) difficulties processing novel information. Associated problems can include poor visual attention and memory, subtle language problems, difficulties learning complex or novel information, as well as higher-order cognitive deficits, arithmetic and writing difficulties, and socioemotional problems, such as anxiety and depression. In contrast, intact function is usually demonstrated in the following domains: simple motor skills, auditory perception, rote learning, selective and sustained attention for auditory–verbal information, basic expressive and receptive language, word reading, and spelling.

Recent research suggests ongoing difficulties for children with NVLD, with increasing academic failure and social difficulties through childhood and into adolescence. In contrast to children with more obvious language impairments, children with NVLD may not present for investigation until quite late in childhood. Initial presentation may be due to social and emotional difficulties, rather than cognitive problems.

The child

Jenny is a 14-year-old girl who presents for neuropsychological review and assistance with diagnosis of her ongoing developmental difficulties. Jenny was previously referred for neuropsychological evaluation in late 1988, aged 5 years, by her paediatrician, who noted that she was experiencing some learning and behavioural difficulties. Interview with her parents at that time revealed a largely normal medical history, with the exception of some fetal distress at birth (Apgar score = 7/10), and severe colic (requiring medication) during the neonatal period. Her general health was noted to be good, with hearing and vision intact. Paediatric examination revealed no abnormalities. Developmental milestones were achieved within expectations, and Jenny was reported to develop expressive language quite early. In contrast, Mrs H. reported that gross and fine-motor skills were established more slowly, and Jenny did not crawl until about 12 months of age. Jenny's parents were first concerned during her kindergarten year, when she was observed to have some social difficulties, despite being quite outgoing. These problems continued when Jenny commenced school, and she also experienced problems learning within the classroom, particularly in the area of mathematics.

Since first evaluation Jenny has had a number of interventions. Initially she underwent a period of individual psychotherapy, which the family discontinued as they felt it was not helping Jenny. A later assessment suggested that Jenny was exhibiting features of attention deficit hyperactivity disorder (ADHD), and she commenced on medication for this condition at age 11 years. Her parents and teachers felt that this was beneficial, but noted ongoing difficulties with task persistence, distractibility, and comprehension. In 1994, Jenny had paediatric review which supported the ADHD diagnosis and recommended continued medication. Despite these interventions, Jenny continued to exhibit behavioural and learning problems. Just prior to her second neuropsychological evaluation, in response to the development of some unusual behaviours, Jenny was admitted to an inpatient psychiatric facility to determine if she was suffering from a psychotic illness. Symptoms reported at that time included inflexible thought processes and some obsessive-compulsive behaviours, including a constant sensation that people were watching her. These people included TV stars, as well as school colleagues. Jenny described feeling a need to dress in the dark as a result. However she did not report particular fear or anxiety in these situations. Rather, she noted that she felt some pressure from peers for her to be "cool". Some obsessive-compulsive behaviours were also present, including a need to lock doors, and a difficulty shifting from one activity to another. Jenny also had, and continues to have, great difficulty settling to sleep at night. As a result she is difficult to wake, and sometimes unable to get organised to get to school. A number of medications have been trialled (Melliril, antidepressants) to manage these problems, with no clear benefit.

Following discharge from the psychiatric unit, Jenny commenced at a new school, where she received additional support in educational areas. She was able to keep up with school work, but experienced difficulties on complex tasks such as projects, where she had problems initiating new activities and developing a logical plan. Jenny's mother had been able to provide support for Jenny on such tasks.

Jenny is the oldest of three children in an intact family unit. She has a sister, Amy, with whom she experiences some relational difficulties, and a brother, Jonathan, to whom she relates better. There is a family history of psychiatric illness. Jenny's father reported considerable tension and conflict within the family associated with the poor relationship between Amy and Jenny, and with Jenny's difficult, uncooperative behaviours.

At age 14 years Jenny re-presented for neuropsychological assessment. On this occasion the referral originated from her family doctor, who noted that Jenny was experiencing depressive symptoms, as well as ongoing behavioural and learning difficulties. Concurrent neurological evaluation revealed no abnormalities. Interview with Jenny and her father identified ongoing social difficulties. Mr H. noted that Jenny found it easier to relate to adults than to her peers. Jenny described difficulties with mathematics, and other school-based activities such as essay writing and projects. She felt that her skills were stronger in language areas. Her father added that Jenny found rote-learning tasks relatively simple, but had more problems with activities that required planning and reasoning.

The neuropsychological evaluation

As previously noted, Jenny was seen for neuropsychological evaluation on two occasions, with a 9-year interval, providing an opportunity to follow the development of her pattern of abilities from early childhood into ado-lescence. While the referral question was similar on both occasions, the mag-nitude of her problems appeared to have increased over time, despite her access to a variety of treatments. At age 5 years, Jenny was assessed as func-tioning within the average range on tests of intellectual ability, with intact language abilities, and some specific problems in the areas of visual and auditory information processing. Later psychometric assessment (age 14 years) indicated that Jenny had not maintained expected intellectual devel-opment, with test results falling at the lower end of the "borderline" range. Interestingly, the pattern of cognitive ability remained relatively stable, with best performance for language tasks, poor information processing, and add-itional difficulties in tasks requiring non-verbal abilities. These test results were consistent with Jenny's ongoing functional difficulties in cognitive, academic, and affective areas.

Initial assessment (aged 5 years 9 months)

Jenny presented as a shy child whose confidence increased with time. During assessment, she spoke quietly and offered little spontaneous conversation. She tended to respond slowly, reflecting a cautious, careful approach to test activities. She was generally cooperative with testing, but experienced some problems on more complex and conceptually demanding tasks.

On the Weschler Primary and Preschool Scale—Revised (WPPSI-R),

Jenny performed within the average range, achieving a full-scale IQ of 105 (verbal IQ = 112; performance IQ = 96). Analysis of subtest scores revealed a relatively consistent pattern, as indicated in Table 11.7. The McCarthy Scales of Children's Abilities were also administered, and Jenny's General Cognitive Index was slightly lower than expected from the WPPSI-R, falling at 93, with poorer scores for memory and motor activities.

It was concluded that Jenny was exhibiting overall intact intellectual abilities, with age-appropriate linguistic abilities, including expression, comprehension, and abstraction. Qualitatively, there was no evidence of attentional difficulties and Jenny was able to sustain attention, without distraction, throughout test sessions. Non-verbal abilities were seen to be less well developed. In particular, visual perception and visuomotor abilities were below age expectations, and Jenny appeared disorganised and lacking in confidence on such activities. There were also some concerns regarding memory and learning capacity. Although Jenny's immediate memory appeared to be intact, she exhibited difficulties on recall tasks that required her to encode and retain material. When combined with symptoms of social difficulty, these features were thought to be consistent with a diagnosis of non-verbal learning disability, and a range of educational and social strategies were suggested to minimise Jenny's difficulties, with a particular focus on school function.

TABLE 11.7
Cognitive data for Jenny from initial assessment, aged 4 years 9 months, and review, at 14 years 4 months

Test measure		Test 1	Test 2
General intelligence	VIQ	112	88
(WPPSI-R/WISC-III)	PIQ	96	72
	FSIQ	105	78
	Information	9	9
	Similarities	14	9
	Arithmetic	11	7
	Vocabulary	13	8
	Comprehension	13	6
	Sentences/Digit Span	10	7
	Picture Completion	9	1
	Animal Pegs/Coding	9	6
	Geom. Design/Pict. Arr	9	4
	Block Design	10	8
	Mazes/Object Assembly	8	8
McCarthy Scales	General Cognitive Index	93	
	Verbal Scale	50	
	Perceptuo/Perf. Scale	45	
	Quantitative Scale	52	
	Motor Scale	42	
	Memory Scale	39	

Review assessment (aged 14 years 4 months)

At follow-up assessment, Jenny presented as a quiet, passive adolescent who appeared willing to participate in initial interview. Although she did not offer any spontaneous conversation, she did respond easily when questions were directed to her. During our test sessions Jenny was constantly concerned that she do well, and appeared quite anxious throughout. As a result, her test response times were quite slow, reflecting her hesitancy. Her approach to test activities suggested very poor self-esteem and a lack of confidence.

Results from intellectual evaluation are presented in Table 11.7. A comparison with previous results indicated that Jenny had failed to meet developmental expectations, and that her cognitive abilities were now well below average, with particular difficulties in social comprehension, visual perceptual skills, visual memory, and visuomotor coordination. Basic language skills were intact, with expressive and receptive skills age appropriate. General knowledge, word knowledge, and literacy skills were intact. Similarly, sustained attention was good, and Jenny was task oriented throughout the assessment, with no evidence of distractibility. Verbal learning capacity was age appropriate, as noted in Table 11.8 and Jenny was able to register, store, and retain language-based material well.

TABLE 11.8
Neuropsychological test data from review assessment for Jenny
(aged 14 years 4 months)

A. Educational skills		
Wide Range Achievement Test—3	Reading (Standard Score)	106
	Spelling (Standard Score)	122
	Arithmetic (Standard Score)	80
B. Psychomotor skills		
Developmental Test of Visuomotor Integration (age equivalent)		9.0 years
C. Memory (Wide Range Assessment of Memory and Learning)		
Verbal Scale (scaled scores)	Story Memory	11
	Sentence Memory	7
Visual Scale (scaled scores)	Picture Memory	4
	Design Memory	7
Learning Scale (scaled scores)	Verbal Learning	12
	Visual Learning	6
D. Executive skills		
(i) COWAT	Total Words	15 (standard score = 2)
(iii) CFR	Copy	35 ($x = 31.4 \pm 2.9$)
	Organisation	1 ($x = 3.4 \pm 0.9$)
	Recall	13 ($x = 19.7 \pm 6.1$)
(iv) Tower of London	Total	Standard score = 75
	Failed attempts	12 ($x = 7.6 \pm 3.4$)

Jenny performed inconsistently on tasks tapping visual or non-verbal abilities. Visual perceptual skills were reduced, but she was able to perform constructional tasks well. When required to integrate or sequence non-verbal information, Jenny exhibited significant difficulties. On these tasks she appeared unable to develop a plan of action to deal with the presented material. She was anxious and easily overwhelmed in such situations. In addition, processing and retention of non-verbal information were markedly reduced.

Educational assessment revealed a pattern of intact literacy skills, with significant difficulties in mathematics, as reported by her parents. These problems were evident on tasks of written and mental arithmetic.

For tasks of executive function, difficulties were also identified. Although Jenny's copy score on the Rey Complex Figure was good, her organisation was piecemeal (see Figure 11.4), interfering with her capacity for efficient recall. Similarly, on the Tower of London test, Jenny's overall score was low, due to impulsive and inaccurate responses and a slowed completion rate, further supporting the presence of reduced planning and problem-solving skills. Executive dysfunction was also observed on language-based tasks. For the Controlled Oral Word Association Test, Jenny's word generation was poor, and she was unable to follow the rules of the task. Similarly, on tasks tapping mental flexibility (e.g., the Contingency Naming Test), Jenny had difficulty following the test's rules consistently, and was unable to switch rules efficiently.

Diagnosis and recommendations

Jenny is a 14-year-old girl, with a history of mild but persistent developmental difficulties, of unknown aetiology. Although Jenny exhibited many intact cognitive abilities (e.g., language, attention, verbal memory, literacy skills), she displayed a pattern of mild to moderate problems, involving (1) the processing, retention, and interpretation of non-verbal information and (2) executive functions, including organisation, problem solving, and mental flexibility. Jenny's cognitive profile, and her decline in cognitive ability through childhood, is consistent with a diagnosis of NVLD, which is characterised by difficulties in mathematics, problem solving, visual learning, integration of complex material, and social processing and judgement. Observed decreases in Jenny's IQ scores may reflect problems in skills that emerge during childhood. For example, executive functions, which are yet to be acquired in a 5-year-old child, are not well represented in standard IQ tests for that age group, and impairments in these skills may have gone undetected at initial assessment. However, by adolescence such skills have become established, and may be readily assessed via neuropsychological tests such as the Tower of London or Rey Complex Figure, as well as by components of standard IQ tests that require organisation and problem-solving capabilities.

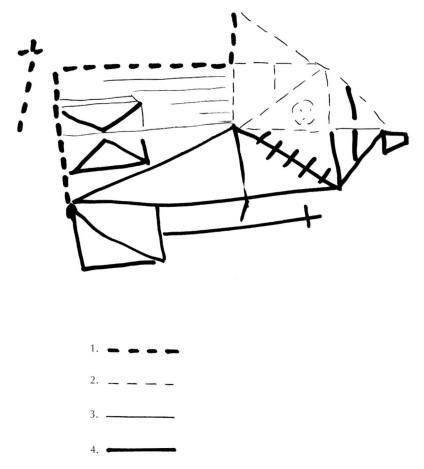

Figure 11.4. Jenny's attempt at copying the Rey Complex Figure. Although her production scores well in terms of accuracy, her organisation is poor and below age expectations, indicating an ineffective, piecemeal approach to the task.

Jenny's pattern of difficulties with executive tasks and non-verbal information may interfere with her day-to-day functioning in a range of areas. For example, social interactions require the integration of a sequence of non-verbal cues, in addition to any verbal information. Jenny may experience problems interpreting these cues, and so may not accurately "read" the emotions or intentions of those around her. As a result she may respond inappropriately, in a way that inhibits her interactions. Jenny has developed some strategies to deal with these problems. Although these are useful, they mean her response time is slow and stilted. Further intervention to develop and practise such strategies may be helpful.

Jenny's weaknesses will also impact on educational development. For example, in subjects such as mathematics or science, which require high levels of problem solving and abstract thought, she may experience problems, particularly where subject matter is complex. At a more general level, large or complex tasks may also be problematic. Jenny will need help on tasks such as projects or essays, in breaking down the project into a series of manageable steps. Further, the subtle inferences and abstract ideas presented in novels or movies may be difficult for Jenny to grasp without discussion and some provision of "verbal labels" by her parents and teachers.

To minimise Jenny's difficulties it is important that her language-based strengths are utilised wherever possible, both socially and educationally. For example, when Jenny has difficulties in a social situation, it may be helpful to discuss whatever occurred, providing verbal labels for specific behaviours and responses. Experiential group situations will be difficult for Jenny. For educational tasks, such as projects or essays, Jenny would benefit from help to break tasks down into small components.

Summary

The opportunity for long-term follow-up in this case has provided useful insight for understanding the consequences of disorders such as NVLD and the abnormal development that may occur in such conditions. Further, Jenny's dramatic decline on neuropsychological assessment measures demonstrates the difficulties involved in predicting future outcomes for children presenting with developmental disabilities. On the basis of Jenny's initial evaluation, it appeared that her cognitive difficulties were relatively mild and quite specific, and it may have been predicted that she would function adequately with access to appropriate intervention. However, conclusive prognoses are problematic in young children, where many skills are emerging and developing, and assessment techniques are not sufficiently sensitive to measure these processes. It is likely that Jenny's initial evaluation failed to tap into executive functions, which may have been in the early acquisition stages at that time. Although her poorer results at follow-up may suggest some form of cognitive deterioration, it could also be argued that Jenny's lack of expected development over time is due to executive deficits that interfere with efficient acquisition of new skills and knowledge, causing a flat developmental trajectory. This pattern of declining IQ scores, in association with behavioural and social difficulties, has been observed in a number of children with NVLD followed over time in our clinic, and is consistent with some of the recent research conducted with this group (Rourke & Fuerst, 1991).

CASE 7: ATTENTION DEFICIT HYPERACTIVITY DISORDER

The condition

ADHD refers to a complex of symptoms including inattentiveness, hyperactivity, and impulsivity. Diagnosis requires that these symptoms are detected within the preschool years, that they are inconsistent with the child's developmental age, and that they are of clinical significance in the child's day-to-day life. The incidence of ADHD is cited at around 8–10% of the school-aged population and affects boys most commonly. The causes of ADHD are likely to be variable, and there is growing evidence that the disorder is actually an umbrella diagnosis, encompassing a range of developmental conditions. Current research suggests that ADHD is due to some form of brain dysfunction, with possible mechanisms including genetic factors, neurotransmitter abnormalities, structural anomalies, and cerebral immaturity. Interestingly, children with diagnosed cerebral pathology, for example epilepsy and TBI, frequently present with neuropsychological profiles not dissimilar to those demonstrated by children with ADHD, supporting the involvement of the CNS in the disorder (Anderson, 1997a).

Some studies have implicated specific cerebral regions and systems in ADHD. In particular, a number of researchers have identified the frontal regions, and particularly the right hemisphere, demonstrating abnormalities in structural and functional brain imaging in these areas in both adults and children with ADHD. Behavioural research is consistent with such suggestions, documenting impulsivity and disinhibition as primary features of the disorder. However, diagnosis is rarely simple, and many children with ADHD present with a number of co-morbid difficulties, including learning difficulties and conduct disorder. It is often difficult to determine which of these diagnoses is primary, and which are as a result of others. To further complicate the picture, associated family dysfunction is also common.

The most popular treatment modality is medication, with stimulants commonly employed to reduce symptoms of overactivity and inattention. Research suggests that such interventions are successful in terms of reducing difficult behaviours, but there is limited evidence of any broader effects in terms of improved school performance or social skills. Others argue for a multi-modal approach to therapy, where medication is combined with educational, behavioural, or family interventions, depending on the individual needs of the child.

In the case of ADHD, the neuropsychologist may contribute in a range of ways. In contrast to children with acquired disorders, referrals frequently originate from paediatricians, schools, and parents. Common requests include confirmation of diagnosis, description of cognitive profile, recommendations for treatment, liaison/counselling with school and family, and monitoring of treatment effects. There is often little medical information, and the clinician may need to collate data from multiple sources to understand the cause and nature of the child's problems. It is generally accepted that, although standardised psychometric test measures (e.g., IQ tests) may help describe a child's cognitive abilities, they are of limited use in diagnosing ADHD or in measuring treatment effects, due to a lack of sensitivity and specificity. Tasks designed specifically to tap attention and speed of processing (continuous performance paradigms, Test of Everyday Attention for Children) show greater promise, being able to differentiate individual components of attention. However, the individual context and the low levels of distraction present in the test situation may mask the ADHD child's difficulties, providing sufficient structure for him or her to maintain attention and persist on tasks. This artificial environment may give an inaccurate indication of the child's functional difficulties and it may be necessary to obtain information from other sources, particularly the parent and teacher, rather than simply relying on test results.

The child

William was referred to a private neuropsychology clinic by his paediatrician, who requested clarification of William's cognitive abilities. The referral noted a history of food allergies and slow growth, high activity levels, and poor concentration. No further medical or diagnostic information was available, and William was not receiving any treatment at the time of referral.

William attended an initial interview with his mother, who described a range of severe behavioural difficulties, which were evident within the session. She noted that William had always been hyperactive. As a baby he had slept very little, and required her constant attention. When he became mobile she was unable to leave him unsupervised. At 12 months of age he was never still. As he reached toddlerhood he would climb over furniture, onto tables or pull wires from electrical appliances, resisting attempts to impose more reasonable behaviour. He showed no fears and did not seem to understand the consequences of his actions. He was unable to sit and watch television, and shifted rapidly from one activity to another. Mrs S. related that she was unable to take him shopping as he was constantly moving and would usually get lost. She stopped visiting her friends because she could not manage William's behaviour and this caused mounting tension and conflict within the family.

Mrs S. reported that her husband found William's behaviour difficult too. As a result he tended to spend less and less time with his son, leaving much of the responsibility for William's management to her. Over time, Mrs S. found that William's behaviour was best when his environment was clearly structured and his day followed a regular routine. During the preschool years this tended to mean that William and she spent their days at home, alone, together. They rarely went out, and even family holidays became too difficult.

At the time of the original referral William was aged 8 years and in Grade 1 at school. He attended the local primary school and was in a small class of Prep and Grade 1 children. Mrs S. noted that one of the reasons for referral was to provide information and support to William's school, who were finding him increasingly difficult to manage. Although William was thought to be a bright child he was unable to sit still in class and was constantly disruptive. His teachers did not complain that he was oppositional or defiant, but described an inability to conform to classroom expectations. William was also struggling with literacy skills and was unable to complete tasks unless closely supervised by his teacher.

The neuropsychological evaluation

William was seen for neuropsychological evaluation on two occasions, once at age 8 and again at age 10 years 9 months. On the second occasion assessments were performed on and off medication in an attempt to measure any treatment effects. Review was sought by Mrs S. to evaluate William's progress in the intervening years, during which time a number of interventions had been successfully implemented.

Initial assessment (8 years)

William presented as extremely active and inattentive. He was unable to sit at a desk for more than a few minutes at a time, and was easily distracted by items on the desk or by environmental noises. He required close supervision and encouragement to complete tasks, and exhibited greatest difficulty on listening activities. Despite these limitations William was generally cooperative and well motivated.

Test results are provided in Table 11.9. They indicated that William was functioning within the high average range in terms of intellectual ability, with Full-scale IQ = 116, Verbal IQ = 109, and Performance IQ = 120. With the exception of a strong score for general knowledge, William's language skills were consistently age appropriate. Qualitatively, he found it difficult to maintain attention when required to provide a verbal response, often losing track of his response in mid-sentence, or having difficulty retrieving appropriate words in conversation. William also found it hard to follow instructions, and was restricted to single-step tasks before he required repetition. Verbal memory was severely restricted and on the Rey Auditory–Verbal Learning Test (15-word list); William recalled only 3 words on the initial trial, and then 3, 5, 4, and 5 words on subsequent trials, indicating no real retention of information over time, and no capacity to organise the material for efficient learning.

TABLE 11.9
Neuropsychological data for William from initial assessment, aged 8 years, and following treatment, at 10 years 9 months

Test measure		Pre-treatment (8 years)	Post-treatment (10.9 years)
General intelligence	VIQ	109	128*
(WISC-III)	PIQ	120	128
	FSIQ	116	131*
	Information	14	13
	Similarities	10	15*
	Arithmetic	10	17*
	Vocabulary	11	14*
	Comprehension	11	15*
	Digit Span	9	9
	Picture Completion	12	15*
	Coding	9	11
	Picture Arrangement	15	15
	Block Design	15	15
	Object Assembly	13	13
Motor skills			
VMI	Age equivalent	7.9 years	10.6 years
Upper Limb Speed [a]	Age equivalent	7.11 years	10.9 years
Executive function			
CFR—copy [c]	Total (std score)	3	8*
COWAT [c]	Total words (std score)	2	7*
Memory/Attention			
Spatial Memory [b]	Age equivalent	7.9 years	10.6 years
RAVLT [c]	Total words (std score)	2	8*
Story Recall [c]	Total recall (std score)	3	7*
Trail Making A [c]	Time taken (std score)	6	7
Trail Making B [c]	Time taken (std score)	4	6
Block Span [c]	No correct (std score)	5	5
Digit Span [c]	No correct (std score)	4	5
Contingency Naming [c]	Time (std score)	2	6*
	Errors/corrections (std score)	3	6*

*Denotes change of one or more standard deviations or 3 years between pre- and post-treatment results.
[a] From Bruininks–Oseretsky Test of Motor Proficiency.
[b] From Kaufman Ability Battery for Children.
[c] From Neuropsychological Assessment of the School-aged Child.

On a story recall task, William retained only the last few phrases of two stories, failing to comprehend the overall gist in each case.

Non-verbal skills were better, with most Performance Scale subtests being scored at above average levels. William was able to maintain his attention to visual material and benefited from the brief structured nature of test items.

Although not at such advanced levels, motor skills were also intact, with visuomotor control and psychomotor speed age appropriate. Spatial memory and learning skills were within the average range; however, measures of sustained and selective attention were severely reduced and William was particularly inefficient on these tasks, making a number of careless errors. These inefficiencies were also reflected in William's performance on tests tapping executive skills. William performed poorly on tasks requiring planning and organisational skills, abstract thought, and mental flexibility. On such tasks he demonstrated poor self-monitoring, an inability to benefit from external feedback, and limited insight into his difficulties.

Functionally, William's educational skills were inconsistent. Simple arithmetic skills were age appropriate, but William remained at a preschool level in the areas of reading and spelling. Analysis of errors, using the Boder Test of Reading and Spelling Patterns (Boder, 1973), suggested that William had a dysphonetic profile, with limited phonic decoding strategies and better sight vocabulary. William was also experiencing social difficulties, with his peers becoming frustrated with his short attention span and unwillingness to participate in games and activities. In addition, William often exhibited impulsive behaviour, being unable to wait his turn or think through the consequences of his actions.

William appeared to exhibit the hallmark behavioural features of ADHD. Testing and background data indicated evidence of inattention, hyperactivity, and impulsivity, as well as specific weakness in sustained and selective attention and aspects of executive function. It appeared that these problems were developmental in nature, having been identified in very early childhood and continuing unremittingly since then. The degree of the problems was severe, and was interfering with William's ability to meet his intellectual potential. Further, his difficulties were limiting his capacity to function normally in a range of contexts, but particularly at home and at school. The neuropsychologist's task in this case was to discuss assessment results with William's family and to communicate findings and opinions regarding treatment to William's paediatrician for his consideration. This was done, and there was no further contact with the family for several years.

Interventions and outcome

The results from review evaluation will be discussed in the context of "intervention and outcome", as they provide a measure of the effectiveness of a range of interventions that occurred following initial evaluation. As is frequently the case in treatment evaluation, it was impossible to link changes in function to a single cause, as there were a number of factors that may have contributed to William's post-treatment outcome.

As previously noted, Mrs S. sought review to document changes in

William's abilities since his previous evaluation. She and her husband recounted a number of changes over the intervening period. First, William had commenced stimulant medication some time after the original evaluation. This appeared to reduce his restless, disruptive behaviour, and Mrs S. noted that she thought he was able to concentrate for longer when taking his medication. However, family and educational difficulties continued. At the family level, William and his father still had a distant relationship, and Mrs S. described being resentful of her husband's lack of support and involvement in William's difficulties. On the suggestion of their paediatrician the family commenced family therapy, and continued this for several years. They found this helpful, first in re-establishing the father–son relationship, and also for working on management strategies. They also noted that the intervention enabled them to see William as a person, rather than a problem, for the first time. Their therapist became involved at a school level, working to establish consistent discipline and boundaries at home and at school. Again, this was successful, and William's parents and teachers were able to support each other to help him. Finally, seeing his improved behaviour, William's school implemented an educational intervention aimed at improving William's literacy skills. This quickly showed benefits, and William was reading at age level within 6 months.

Assessment results serve to emphasise the positive outcome described by William's parents. William was initially seen 1 hour after taking his medication. Qualitatively, William presented as a more contained boy. He was able to attend adequately to test activities, to maintain attention throughout a 1-hour test session, and persist well, even on listening tasks. Even when seen 1 week later, without the benefit of medication, William's attentional abilities appeared age appropriate.

Assessment results showed that William had made excellent progress in verbal abilities, with verbal knowledge and more conceptual skills showing improvements well in excess of developmental expectations on second testing. Similarly, previously impaired verbal learning skills were now above average. Executive functions had also improved and were now consistent with his superior intellectual abilities. Non-verbal abilities remained advanced, with measures of perception, construction, and analysis all above age expectations. Motor skills showed relatively stable development over time.

With respect to attentional skills, improvements were also evident, having increased from well below age expectations to within the average range. This was evident on measures of sustained attention, as well as in the areas of selective attention and mental flexibility. Attentional and memory skills were reassessed 1 week later, with William abstaining from medication for 48 hours. Although no differences were detected for memory measures, there were some changes on attentional tasks. In particular it was observed that, on timed tasks, William's completion time was consistently slower on all tasks for the "on-medication" assessment. In contrast, William exhibited better cognitive efficiency on medication, giving fewer impulsive responses and making fewer errors. An example of William's performances on and off medication for the four trials of the Contingency Naming Test are provided in Figure 11.5; as previously described, this task involves increasing demands on attentional processes, beginning with two simple naming tasks and then moving to a more complex level where the child is required to provide responses on the basis of an increasing number of conflicting rules. It appeared that, for

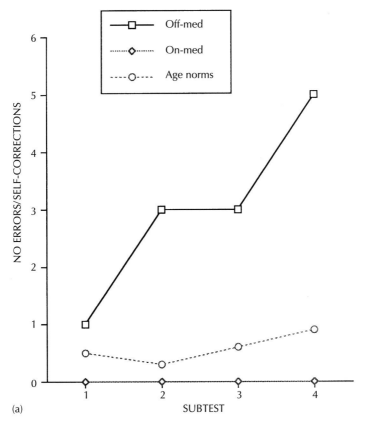

(a)

Figure 11.5 (a). William's on- and off-medication performances on the Contingency Naming Test. His results show (a) improved accuracy, but (b—*see over*) slower completion time when on medication, suggesting that medication effects are associated with a trade-off between speed and accuracy.

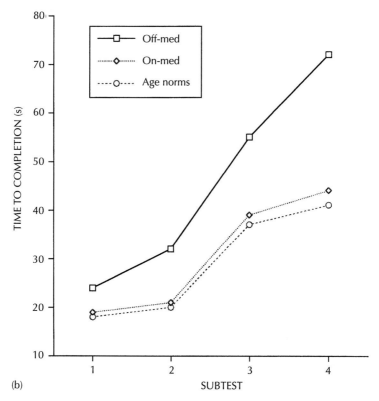

(b)

Figure 11.5 (b).

William, there was a treatment-based trade-off between speed and accuracy; however, given his intact processing speed, he was able to afford a slightly slower performance rate to achieve more accurate results.

William clearly exhibited excellent outcome in a broad range of domains, following appropriate and multi-modal intervention, with improvements in neuropsychological skills possibly of least importance. The simultaneous implementation of a number of therapies makes it difficult to determine if one was especially beneficial, or if there was a synergistic effect, maximising the impact of each approach. The likely impact of the normal developmental process is also worthy of consideration, with evidence of substantial increases in memory capacity through childhood. Although William's progress exceeded such expectations, maturation may have played a minor role. The dramatic nature of William's progress is emphasised by evidence that, in cases of severe ADHD, lack of appropriate intervention may be associated with deterioration over time, with a compounding of attentional, social, and learning difficulties leading to co-morbid learning disability and conduct disorder as children move towards adolescence.

Summary

For William the neuropsychologist's role was relatively minor in the context of the course of his disorder, simply providing a piece of diagnostic data to help complete the overall picture, and later to provide objective information regarding both short-term effects of medication and more long-term impact of the total treatment intervention. Although difficult to unravel in the context of the range of presenting problems (attention, behaviour, education, family), multiple information sources available to the neuropsychologist (natural history of disorder, test findings) indicated that William's primary difficulty may have been in the area of attention, with other problems developing as a consequence.

CASE 8: SEVERE MEMORY DEFICIT ASSOCIATED WITH ANOXIA

The condition

Hypoxia refers to oxygen deprivation within the brain, associated drop in cerebral perfusion pressure and compensatory dilation of blood vessels. When perfusion pressure is severely depressed, ischaemic injury may occur within a few minutes, with sites of predilection including border zones between major arteries of supply, as well as parts of the hippocampus and the cerebellum (Adams & Victor, 1993). Hypoxic episodes usually occur as a result of respiratory or cardiac failure. When hypoxia is severe it can result in permanent brain damage. Muramoto, Kuru, Sugishita, and Toyokura (1979) have reported severe bilateral hippocampal atrophy in a patient who suffered a post-anaesthesia accident resulting in respiratory difficulties. On cognitive testing this patient was noted to be amnesic. Review of the neuro-psychological literature suggests that memory and learning difficulties commonly occur following a hypoxic episode, with other cognitive symptoms including visual deficits and executive dysfunction. Lezak (1995) also reports social problems, including reduced spontaneity and self-care, as well as impulsive and disinhibited behaviours.

The child

Daniel was initially referred for urgent neuropsychological evaluation following a neurological consultation that revealed a severe memory impairment, with onset 2 months previously, associated with a surgical procedure. It was reported that, following a routine appendectomy at his local hospital, Daniel failed to recover from the anaesthetic, and it was thought that he suffered a period of oxygen deprivation (duration undocumented). He was then transferred to a tertiary centre, and admitted to intensive care. He remained unconscious and required respiratory support for a period of 24 hours. Investigations revealed that Daniel lacked an enzyme, pseudocholinesterase. As a result, the antidote that is administered to reverse the effects of muscle relaxants used during the anaesthetic were ineffective. Thus the effects of the drugs continued for several days post-surgery.

Once Daniel regained consciousness he was observed to be confused and disoriented. He exhibited poor motor coordination and balance and had significant memory loss, particularly for recent events. Neurological and radiological investigations at that time revealed no abnormalities; Daniel was discharged home and outpatient review was organised. At follow-up Mr and Mrs M. reported that Daniel was experiencing a range of problems. Memory difficulties were of particular concern. They reported that Daniel was unable to find his way around the house, and needed to be directed to his room. He frequently got lost on his way home from school, and he had no recall of his illness or the time following surgery, although he had good recall for earlier events. His father described Daniel as a different child. He was previously a placid, easy-going boy but was now temperamental and aggressive. Mr M. noted that he was unable to physically control Daniel when he became aggressive, and was afraid for the safety of the rest of the family in these situations. He noted that Daniel had limited insight into his behaviour, and blamed his parents for his problems. His sleep patterns were erratic, and he woke frequently during the night. He had developed a pattern of overeating, apparently unaware of when he had finished his last meal, and was gaining weight as a result. He was unable to participate in many former leisure activities, such as cricket, without becoming confused and disorganised. Upon return to school, he was unable to function within the classroom or find his way around the school independently. He required an integration aid to be with him during classes, to provide structure and routine. Without this input, Daniel's behaviour was noted to deteriorate. His teachers also reported a severe reduction in learning ability and basic skills.

In the weeks post-surgery, the family had increasing difficulties coping with Daniel's behaviour, and attended the local hospital and doctor on a number of occasions. After 2 months, which included an episode where Daniel attacked his father with a knife, Daniel was referred for neurological assessment. Neurological examination was normal, as was MRI scan. EEG showed some evidence of generalised seizure activity, and severe memory deficits were noted. The neurologist concluded that Daniel's problems were related to hypoxic brain damage, occurring in the post-surgical period. He further hypothesised that Daniel may have sustained damage to the hippocampal structures, not evident on MRI scan, which was causing his current memory and behavioural difficulties.

Interview with Daniel's parents revealed that, prior to his surgery, he had been in good health, with no significant medical history. His early development was unremarkable and he was noted to be an average student. He had just completed his first year of high school. He is the middle of three children in an intact family unit, and was said to have good social skills, with a large group of friends. There was no history of behavioural problems, and Daniel enjoyed a number of leisure activities including a range of sports, and was captain of his cricket team.

The neuropsychological evaluation

Daniel was seen for neuropsychological evaluation 2 months post-surgery, aged 13 years 4 months. He continued to be reviewed on a regular basis over a number of years. On these occasions the focus was on management of his ongoing memory impairment, and full neuropsychological review was not conducted until 3 years post-insult.

Initial neuropsychological evaluation

Daniel presented as a stockily built boy, who was friendly and cooperative throughout assessment. He was alert and well oriented, but appeared frustrated and perplexed when he was unable to recall information, and tired quickly in test sessions. He showed a tendency to respond impulsively and needed encouragement to reconsider such responses. When asked about recent events he showed no recall. On subsequent sessions he showed no recognition of the neuropsychologist. Even after he had been attending the clinic for several years he was unable to find his way to the test room or recall the clinician's name. Daniel did appear frustrated by his situation, and often asked when he was going to get better.

Neuropsychological testing suggested that Daniel was generally functioning below age level. Intellectual assessment indicated that Daniel's cognitive abilities fell towards the low end of the "low average" range. Analysis of his cognitive profile showed better skills in the language domain, with expressive and receptive language intact. Daniel was able to participate in conversation, although he tended to repeat his comments. Verbal knowledge including general knowledge and word knowledge was intact, showing maintenance of previously learned information. Visual abilities including visual perception, analysis, and constructional skills were low average, and subtests tapping attentional skills were below age expectations. On the basis of his parents' reports of good school progress, it is likely that this level of performance reflects some deterioration in function from pre-surgery levels.

Daniel's memory performance was particularly concerning. As shown in Table 11.10, Daniel exhibited global memory and learning deficits. Immediate memory capacity was reduced, and although Daniel could hold small amounts of material in mind he was unable to retain information over time. This was particularly evident on the delayed recall trial of Story Recall, where he was unable to remember even hearing a story. Similarly, for the Rey Complex Figure (Figure 11.6), although Daniel took great care with his copy and utilised good organisational strategies, his recall was severely impoverished.

TABLE 11.10
Results of Daniel's neuropsychological assessment

Test measure		Acute (13.4 years)	Chronic (16.11 years)
General intelligence	VIQ	88	–
(WISC-III)	PIQ	74	–
	FSIQ	80	–
	Information	10	8
	Similarities	9	9
	Arithmetic	6	–
	Vocabulary	8	6
	Comprehension	8	–
	Digit Span	6	6
	Picture Completion	7	7
	Coding	7	5
	Picture Arrangement	6	–
	Block Design	8	6
	Object Assembly	3	–
Memory/Attention	Spatial Learning (trials)	discontinued at 10 trials	–
	RAVLT (T1–T5)	1,5,5,4,5	5,8,5,5,6
	Total (stanine)	1	1
	Recognition (correct)	10	6
	Stories (stanine)	1	1
	Stories: Delay (stanine)	1	1
	WRAML: Vis. Learn. (ss)	4	3
	Verb. Learn. (ss)	4	4
	Sentences (ss)	4	9
	Stories (ss)	3	2
	CFR: copy (stanine)	3	3
	Organisation (stanine)	4	4
	Recall (stanine)	1	1

COPY

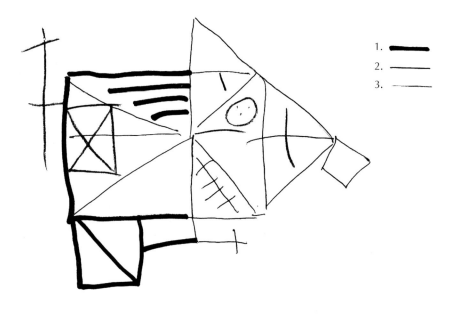

1. ■■■
2. ──
3. ──

RECALL

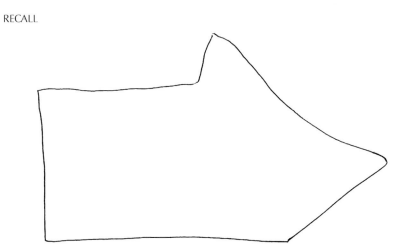

Figure 11.6. Daniel's copy and recall of the Rey Complex Figure, indicating age-appropriate copying capacity and adequate organisational ability (as denoted by the copy sequence listed on the right of the copy), but severely reduced memory capacity.

The severity of Daniel's impairments was consistent with family and school reports, and suggested that Daniel would experience significant difficulties in everyday life. It was considered essential that Daniel have regular, ongoing support in a number of domains including educational, social, and emotional. Specifically, special education intervention and family and individual counselling were recommended. In addition, a range of strategies and compensatory approaches were suggested, for example: (1) provision of a clearly structured and routine environment, both at home and at school; (2) access to individual support within the classroom, and opportunity for revision of classroom materials; (3) reduction of school programme; (4) provision of written notes and textbooks; (5) training in use of diary and related external memory aids. These strategies were implemented by the school, and monitored via regular school visits from the clinician.

Despite substantial input, Daniel's difficulties continued, largely unchanged, over the following years. He was reported to cope well within the structure of the school environment, although academic progress was limited. In contrast, severe behavioural problems were evident at home, with Daniel frequently aggressive and abusive to family members. Counselling did not appear to help, and Daniel appeared unable to control his aggressive outbursts.

Review evaluation

Daniel underwent a full neuropsychological review at age 16 years 11 months, more than 3½ years post-surgery. He attended the session with his father. Although he had attended at 3-monthly intervals since his initial assessment, Daniel still became confused in the clinic environment. He did show some recognition of the tester. Interview with Daniel and his father indicated that he was coping well at school, and was participating in a modified programme, which included a reduced number of subjects, and an emphasis on applied areas such as woodwork and typing. He continued to receive individual support at school. Daniel no longer used his diary as a memory aid, but had developed a number of alternative strategies to facilitate his recall. He and his father both felt that there had been little, if any, improvement in basic memory skills, but that Daniel was more able to compensate for his difficulties. Mr M. also reported that although Daniel's severe behavioural problems had continued for a long period, they had now subsided. He continued to attend individual counselling sessions, which he stated were helpful and allowed him to discuss the frustrations of his condition.

As shown in Table 11.10, neuropsychological assessment results were similar to those achieved during the acute stages of recovery, suggesting that Daniel has severe residual impairments. His memory function continued to be severely and globally impaired, with little evidence of learning capacity, even where repetition and structure are provided. The functional improvements noted by Daniel and his father may represent improved utilisation and formulation of compensatory aids. Visual skills and linguistic abilities had remained stable, although there was a slight reduction in verbal knowledge, which was likely to be due to Daniel's reduced learning capacity.

Diagnosis and interventions

Daniel's neuropsychological profile is consistent with the initial hypothesis of hypoxic brain damage, where the hippocampus and surrounding structures are vulnerable to damage. Daniel's global memory impairment, and particularly his pattern of "recent forgetting", suggests dysfunction within hippocampal structures bilaterally, and his stable deficits indicate that this damage is likely to be permanent. Behavioural features, including problems with eating and sleeping patterns and with impulse control, are also in keeping with damage to mesial structures, and suggest an organic basis for these problems. No doubt additional adjustment problems will have exacerbated these problems, resulting in the severe problems that Daniel experienced in the initial phases of recovery.

As a result of these difficulties, Daniel has experienced slowed academic progress, reducing his opportunities for future study and employment. Although he is well supported in his school environment, Daniel will face significant problems when attempting to find employment. His memory deficits will eliminate a large number of possible careers, and he will require a great deal of support to familiarise himself with any work context, and additional input to learn the job requirements. It is unclear whether he will be able to be fully independent in adulthood, and he may require support in areas such as financial and domestic management. Daniel's improved behavioural function will enhance his capacity to maintain social contacts and broaden his circle of friends, which had diminished in the months and years post-surgery. It may also indicate that Daniel has begun to accept his difficulties and work to overcome them.

Summary

Hypoxia in childhood is a relatively uncommon occurrence, as is acquired amnesic syndrome. The severity of Daniel's problem and its manifestation in daily life created a significant challenge for Daniel and those working with him. Daniel's plight emphasised the lack of established programmes and interventions available for treatment of childhood disorders, and Daniel was unable to access any cohesive multidisciplinary rehabilitation facilities, as such agencies are frequently unable to cater for the needs of a child. Rather, Daniel received "rehabilitation" in his normal environment, with educators and clinicians trialling a variety of approaches with him in an attempt to achieve recovery. Although such an approach was piecemeal at best, Daniel's motivation and his family support were strong and lasting, allowing him to take maximum advantage of any services available.

The contrast between Daniel's lack of improvement on neuropsychological tests and his somewhat surprising capacity to cope at a functional level is worthy of comment, and may reflect the "substitution" model of recovery, which stresses use of intact skills to compensate for deficit areas. Daniel infers such a process himself when he describes the strategies he has developed to minimise his memory difficulties. The fact that neuropsychological measures may not detect such "recovery" emphasises the importance of collecting data from multiple sources when conducting an evaluation.

CONCLUSIONS

The cases described in the preceding pages illustrate the broad scope of the clinical role in child neuropsychology. They emphasise the importance of employing a developmental model when assessing children and attempting to predict outcome from CNS insult. The utility of review and follow-up, both for the clinician and for the patient, is also clear, with longitudinal data providing the opportunity to monitor development and recovery, as well as to follow the natural history of CNS dysfunction through the various transitions of childhood.

The multidimensional nature of problems experienced by families and children with CNS dysfunction indicates the range of skills required by the clinician. Although knowledge of neurobehavioural functioning is clearly the keystone of clinical practice for the child neuropsychologist, there is also a need for some understanding of the implications of test findings for day-to-day life. If clinical neuropsychologists are to be useful, and make a difference to their patients' quality of life, they must be able to inform and evaluate subsequent educational interventions. Skills for managing and treating the various behavioural and family problems that commonly arise following CNS insults are also necessary. The capacity to provide these skills ensures that a neuropsychological evaluation is a therapeutic intervention, not simply an assessment.

Concluding comments

Paediatric neuropsychology has grown enormously over the past two decades, and is now established as a specific focus within the broader discipline of neuropsychology. Such advances are reflected in the increased profile of the field. Today there are specific professional journals dedicated to the study and discussion of brain dysfunction in children. At an international level, paediatric neuropsychology is identified as a core topic at professional and clinical meetings and conferences. Specialised child neuropsychology training programmes, emphasising the principles of both child development and neuropsychology, are now offered in many countries. As paediatric neuropsychology has continued to flourish, its potential to contribute to the understanding of child health and outcome from disease has become better recognised, and the importance of supporting further advances in the field is illustrated by growing research opportunities. Looking to the future, it is a field wide open for further exploration, with many exciting and important challenges both at the clinical and empirical levels.

The ongoing development of paediatric neuropsychology reflects a number of interacting factors. Recent advances in medical knowledge, including the capacity for more accurate diagnosis and improved treatment options, have led to lower mortality rates for many childhood central nervous system (CNS) disorders, for example, cerebral infections, cancers, metabolic disorders, and spina bifida. Now, large numbers of children who suffered such conditions survive, with long-term quality of life issues becoming of interest. Clinical observations have identified a range of subtle, and more severe,

449

residual impairments in these survivors as they move through childhood into adolescence and adulthood. Research endeavours have been successful in documenting outcomes for many of these children, and providing better information for professionals and families regarding appropriate interventions and future prognosis.

With time, it has become clear that adult-based neuropsychological principles, such as functional localisation or recovery trajectories, do not adequately explain outcome from childhood CNS insult. The dynamic nature of physiological and cognitive development during childhood creates an everchanging interplay as the child moves to maturity. Where this developmental process is interrupted by dysfunction or insult, anomalies may occur, both at the level of brain structure and function, and in cognition. To understand the impact of pathology within the developing brain it is necessary to incorporate principles of neural and cognitive development. Documented instances of cerebral plasticity, as illustrated by children who have undergone hemispherectomy but maintained a surprising level of cognitive function, provide a dramatic contrast to the poorer outcome exhibited by adults following similar interventions. Alternatively, a lesion that may cause specific cerebral and cognitive impairment in an adult, for example, a frontal lobe tumour, may result in a more generalised pattern of deficit in a young child. Disruption to higher-order skills, thought to be subsumed by frontal regions, may interfere with the young child's capacity to interact with the environment in an adaptive manner. Further, these higher-order skills, which are immature in early childhood, may fail to develop adequately due to permanent cerebral damage in the area. Even within the child population, varying outcomes may be observed depending on the age or developmental stage at which the child sustains CNS insult. Such examples emphasise the need for specific developmental models that take into account stages of cerebral and cognitive development.

In response to observations of unexpected outcome in children with brain insult, a number of developmental models have emerged. These models have benefited from expanding interdisciplinary links, for example those that relate stages of brain development to cognitive maturation, providing interesting parallels to support previously hypothetical theories. As previously discussed, such models have provided a much needed theoretical framework for clinical practice. Their focus on specific developmental principles, both biological and cognitive, illustrates the complex and dynamic nature of childhood CNS disorder. Although quite varied in emphasis, they each describe changing patterns of symptoms and impairments, as children move through developmental milestones, and need to interact adaptively with their particular environment. Interestingly, although many current research findings can be accommodated within these models, this is not universally true, suggesting that there is a need for ongoing formulation and interpretation. A range of child-specific issues need to be incorporated in future models: age/developmental stage at insult, nature of insult (focal/generalised), time since insult, limitations to plasticity, potential for environmental (family, school, community) influence.

Although research and theoretical advances have been steady, clinical tools have been slower to emerge. It has long been accepted that adult-based assessment techniques are inadequate for use in child populations. Although there are well-established concerns regarding the interpretation of such measures using adult models, there is a range of more practical problems with such tools. Adult test procedures are frequently unappealing to children, both in terms of test materials and content. The absence of developmentally appropriate instructions and normative data has made interpretation of results difficult, and largely subjective. Similarly, tests employed in standard child psychology practice are often insufficient to detect the specific nature of deficits resulting from childhood brain insult. In response to these frustrating limitations, a number of child-specific neuropsychological measures have recently been published. Such measures focus on abilities of particular relevance to the paediatric neuropsychologist, including attention, memory, and learning, and executive function as well as more traditional cognitive skills. They include bright, interesting stimulus material, take into account the relatively short attention span of the child, and provide solid normative information. Such advances increase confidence in test results, allowing more reliable diagnosis and interpretation.

Paediatric neuropsychology, thus, is an ever-growing and exciting field. Over recent years it has gradually established a solid foundation, and generated a framework within which ongoing theoretical, empirical, and clinical progress can occur. It is important to evaluate where we are now, to define the future challenges, and to postulate how these may be achieved.

WHERE ARE WE NOW? STATE OF THE ART

Empirical knowledge

To date we have established some understanding of brain–behaviour relationships within the developing brain. Through study of specific childhood disorders, such as traumatic brain injury, epilepsy, and cancers, we now know that the dose–response relationship observed with respect to degree of cerebral insult is similar for adults and children. More severe brain damage, or more serious medical complications, result in greater cognitive impairment and poorer functional outcome. Throughout this text there have been many research studies that have illustrated this relationship and emphasised its consistency. Severe traumatic brain injury results in significant physical and neuropsychological impairment. Acute complications in meningitis and encephalitis, such as seizures or hydrocephalus (which are indicative of under-lying brain dysfunction) are associated with significant deficits. Delayed treatment of metabolic disorders, such as phenylketonuria or hypothyroidism (reflecting a longer period of cerebral toxicity), results in intellectual dis-ability. Prognosis for less serious brain insults remains more poorly defined, and may be determined by a range of factors, biological, developmental, and environmental.

In keeping with adult models, we also know that different mechanisms and sites of brain damage result in unique patterns of neuropsychological impairment. As described in Chapter 5, traumatic brain injury and its associ-ated shearing injuries, which impact selectively on frontal regions, lead to problems with attention, speed of processing, and adaptive abilities. In con-trast, the generalised but transient impact of cerebral infection or metabolic disturbance may be more subtle, having mild effects on cognitive efficiency, evident in the more dynamic skills such as memory and attention. Impair-ments associated with focal cerebral pathology, such as mesial temporal sclerosis, may reflect the particular function subsumed by the damaged area, causing specific memory deficits.

Awareness of the importance of developmental factors for ultimate out-come for children with CNS insult has also increased. Although there are still many uncertainties, we know that the child's age at insult will influence out-come, although not consistently. Earlier age at insult is associated with poorer outcome where the insult is generalised, but better outcome where the insult is focal, and where there is an opportunity for reorganisation within the brain. Developmental stage is also critical. Skills that have been acquired prior to insult are less vulnerable than those that are yet to be established. For example, the child who has learned to read before sustaining a traumatic brain injury usually retains these skills. However, a child injured prior to school entry will have great difficulty acquiring such abilities. Further, chil-dren who sustain insult early in life often appear to "recover " quite well initially, but over time age-appropriate skills (e.g., executive functions) fail to emerge normally, resulting in a pattern of increasing functional impairment.

Recent research evidence suggests that environmental and psychosocial factors may play a central role, both in normal development and outcome following brain insult. Studies examining cerebral development note differ-ences associated with enriched versus impoverished environments in young animals. Behavioural research describes a relationship between child and family functioning and severity of insult, with psychosocial factors having the capacity to enhance or inhibit potential recovery. Others have examined social disadvantage and reduced access to rehabilitation resources, identify-ing these as associated with poor long-term outcome. However, such research is in its infancy, and the full extent and relative importance of external influ-ences on recovery following brain insult are still to be determined.

Theoretical models

Parallel with research knowledge, a number of theoretical principles have been established and incorporated into paediatric neuropsychology models over recent years. Neurodevelopmental theory informs us that the brain is in a rapid state of development through childhood, and that damage pre- or postnatally has the capacity to interrupt and change the course of development irreversibly. Such change will be reflected in the geography of the brain in terms of its functional localisation. We know that the young brain has some capacity for plasticity and transfer of function, leading to better outcome than might be expected.

Theories of cognitive development are also well established, describing ongoing maturation of cognitive skills through childhood, with different developmental trajectories associated with specific abilities. Theorists describe both sequential and parallel developmental processes, with the maturation of higher-order skills such as reasoning and problem solving dependent on, but also feeding into, adequate development of lower-order abilities. Such concepts provide a basis for understanding the normal versus deviant abilities of children who have sustained brain insult.

These neurological and cognitive concepts have been incorporated into the most influential models of paediatric neuropsychology—those described by Byron Rourke and Maureen Dennis. These theorists have provided us with frameworks for understanding and even predicting the sometimes unexpected outcomes seen in children who have sustained brain insult. Both emphasise the importance of timing of insult in the context of either neurological or cognitive development. They also refer to the ongoing impact of CNS insult through childhood, describing the gradual emergence of both cognitive and social disturbances through childhood and into adolescence. Interestingly, although the various concepts espoused in each model can be readily seen in various child populations, enhancing their appeal, both have proven difficult to test empirically. Further, neither has attempted to address the dimension of psychosocial impact on long-term outcome, possibly omitting an important and informative prognostic factor.

Clinical practice

Our clinical knowledge base is largely dependent upon what we have learned through research and the development of theoretical models. We know that cognitive skills develop through childhood and into adolescence. As a consequence, we need access to techniques that can plot this development and identify deviations from normal. Only in recent years have such measures become available, providing a solid foundation for the "testing" component of clinical practice. Further, research and clinical observation have shown that "IQ" tests, and in particular summary IQ scores, are frequently insensitive to the symptoms common to childhood CNS disorders, particularly acquired conditions. It is now clear that appropriate assessment needs to include measures of attention, memory, and learning, psychomotor skills, and executive function. Inclusion of "functional" measures of educational and behavioural abilities can provide further information and validation of neuropsychological findings.

Longitudinal studies and clinical follow-up have illustrated that children sustaining brain insult require long-term support and intervention. As children pass through each developmental milestone new crises can occur, usually indicated by functional deficits such as behavioural disturbance or poor school performance. Routine follow-up has the potential to maintain contact with children and families, facilitating access during difficult times and resulting in timely intervention.

Largely through clinical observation, there is growing awareness of the importance of the family and the psychosocial environment for children with brain insult. Children are dependent on their family/school for appropriate care and support. Children with problems at a psychosocial level may need particular care and attention, as they may be at greatest risk for ongoing problems.

WHAT WE DON'T KNOW: FUTURE DIRECTIONS

As knowledge in paediatric neuropsychology has advanced, it has become increasingly clear that outcome from childhood cerebral insult is determined by a wide range of interacting factors. To gain a better understanding of the process of recovery and eventual outcome, it is essential to take account of these factors. Our knowledge is still in its infancy, and there are many challenges for the future. We have chosen to focus on a small number of such challenges that we see as critical to the continued development of theoretical and research endeavours in the field, and to the application of this knowledge via clinical practice.

Natural history of childhood CNS conditions

Although we have amassed an extensive literature describing the consequences of cerebral insult during childhood, much of this data reflects studies that are both retrospective and cross-sectional in design. There is a need for prospective, longitudinal studies that have the capacity to follow children from the time of insult through various developmental transitions into adolescence and adulthood. These studies need to be multifactorial, enabling a better grasp of the interplay between biological, cognitive, developmental, and psychosocial factors as well as an increased understanding of the relative contribution of each to long-term outcome. This information is often available anecdoctally, through long-term clinical follow-up, but well-designed empirical research is lacking.

Evaluation of cognitive skills and their development

Although the developmental literature provides us with considerable information with respect to cognitive development, such information is also cross-sectional in nature. There is little empirical data regarding changes over time in cognitive skills. With regard to standard assessment techniques, few are applicable throughout childhood and comparisons across tests are often problematic. For example, when following a child from infancy into adolescence, it may be necessary to employ numerous test measures, even to document summary intellectual levels. The Bayley Scales of Infant Development may be used up to age 3½, but then it is necessary to employ a different measure, such as the NEPSY, the McCarthy Scales of Children's Abilities or the Wechsler Preschool and Primary Intelligence Scale. Once children reach school age another measure may need to be substituted (e.g., Wechsler Intelligence Scale for Children). Results across these measures are not easily compared, leading to difficulties establishing the stability of cognitive abilities over time. Even within standardised measures of cognitive ability (e.g., IQ tests), psychometric properties are imperfect, with fluctuations in scores often attributable to test factors rather than to the child's performance. Longitudinal studies mapping development of cognitive skills through childhood would provide valuable information for paediatric neuropsychologists who need to identify "real" as opposed to test-dependent changes in children's abilities over time.

Understanding developmental factors

At present our knowledge of developmental factors that impact on children with brain insult is limited. In particular, given its established contribution to outcome, the relationship between "age at insult" and recovery is worthy of further study. However, this endeavour is limited due to the imperfect relationship between chronological age and developmental level. Generally, it is not the actual age of the child but the skill level that they have attained that is of interest. Chronological age provides, at best, an approximate indicator. In children, where development is rapid and trajectories vary considerably, errors of measurement may have a significant impact on results. Future studies may attempt to address this problem, utilising pre-insult indicators of developmental levels and grouping children according to these variables rather than chronological age alone.

Advances in both structural and functional imaging techniques provide exciting opportunities for understanding other developmental concepts such as cerebral plasticity. The ability to map functional brain activity using non-invasive techniques has the potential to provide direct evidence of reorganisation of cerebral function following early brain insult, and to inform clinicians regarding appropriate intervention. However, before such methods can be applied clinically it is essential to collect data on the localisation and lateralisation of cognitive functions in unimpaired children. It is possible that cerebral activation patterns in children may be quite different from those observed in the mature brain and, further, that throughout childhood these patterns might continue to change as functions are acquired and become better established.

Research design

In order to recruit patient samples of sufficient size and diversity, it may be useful to move away from the traditional "disorder-based" designs employed to date. These research paradigms have been essential in establishing an understanding of the sequelae of specific cerebral conditions. It may be that alternative models are necessary to address more theoretical issues, such as the "age at insult" question described earlier. Studies that stratify age or developmental stage at time of insult, regardless of the specific condition, may identify patterns of impairment that have not been apparent to date. For example, in keeping with notions of critical periods, children with moderate/severe brain damage (traumatic brain injury, cerebral infection, tumour) prior to 3 years of age might all exhibit language problems, whereas children with injuries sustained from 4 to 5 years might exhibit visuospatial or psychomotor deficits. Alternatively, to improve our knowledge of brain–behaviour relationships and localisation of function in children, it may be useful to adopt adult models that compare cognitive skills in relation to lesion location. Thus studies that focus on specific pathology locations, for example temporal or frontal lobe pathology, may detect patterns of performance that provide insight into the specific functions of these areas in childhood which we have been unable to identify from disorder-based designs.

Intervention and treatment

The implementation of efficacious intervention and treatment models is of critical importance to children and families, and perhaps to the survival of paediatric neuropsychology. Unfortunately, this area of clinical practice remains poorly established. Although a large number of child neuropsychologists do perform various therapies and treatments—parents/teachers would not accept anything less—these interventions are largely undescribed and inadequately evaluated. This area constitutes a major challenge both now and in the future. Evaluation of childhood interventions is fraught with problems. There are a range of confounding variables: premorbid ability levels and behavioural skills, family resources and environment, willingness to participate in therapies, geographical limitations (neuropsychologists most often work in city hospitals/clinics and are not particularly accessible to families). Assessment of the impact of intensive therapies is often complicated by the possible confounding effects of parallel school programmes. The implementation of such programmes may be difficult due to a lack of personnel or financial resources. Further, as children are less commonly retained in hospitals or inpatient rehabilitation programmes, with the main aim being return to the family environment, it is often impractical to establish such therapy regimes.

Although such problems must be acknowledged, it is also important to recognise that, with children who are rapidly developing skills and knowledge, there may be a greater opportunity for appropriate intervention to make a significant contribution to future outcome. Research and theoretical advances have established a solid basis from which appropriate and informed intervention models may be generated, which focus on skills relevant to children with brain insult. The time seems right to apply this knowledge. Rourke, in his practical approach to intervention, stresses that neuropsychological treatment models need to begin with goals that are achievable, taking into account the child's level of function, physical stamina, and attention span, as well as the commitment of the family and their capacity to follow through with any intervention.

Where resources are available, this may involve implementation of regular and intensive theory-driven therapy programmes in attention, memory, and learning, or executive abilities. It may also involve a more "functional" or compensatory approach, where the child's environment (both physical and social) is modified to meet his or her needs in the best possible way. Irrespective of the approach employed, it is important to document the utility and outcome from such interventions in a rigorous and scientific manner that takes into account the complexities of child development and psychosocial factors.

References

Aarts, J.H.P., Binnie, C.D., Smith, A.M., & Wilkins, A.J. (1984). Selective cognitive impairment during focal and generalised epileptiform EEG activity. *Brain*, *107*, 293–308.

Abidin, R. (1995). *Parenting Stress Index manual* (3rd ed.). Charlottesville, VA: Pediatric Psychology Press.

Achenbach, T.M. (1991). *Manual for the Child Behaviour Checklist and Revised Child Behaviour Profile*. Burlington, VT: Department of Psychiatry, University of Vermont.

Ack, M., Miller, I., & Weil, W. (1961). Intelligence of children with diabetes mellitus. *Pediatrics*, *28*, 764–770.

Ackerly, S.S., & Benton, A.L. (1948). Report of a case of bilateral frontal lobe defect. *Association for Research on Nervous and Mental Disorders*, *27*, 479–504.

Adams, J.H., Mitchell, D.E., Graham, D.I., & Doyle, D. (1977). Diffuse brain damage of the immediate impact type. *Brain*, *100*, 489–502.

Adams, W.G., Deaver, K.A., Cochi, S.L., Plikaytis, B.D., Zell, E.R., Broome, C.V., & Wenger, J.D. (1993). Decline of childhood *Haemophilus influenzae* type b (Hib) disease in the Hib vaccine era. *Journal of the American Medical Association*, *269*, 221–226.

Aicardi, J. (1986). *Epilepsy in children*. New York: Raven Press.

Aicardi, J. (1994). *Epilepsy in children* (2nd ed.). New York: Raven Press.

Aicardi, J. (1996). Lennox–Gastaut syndrome. In S. Wallace (Ed.), *Epilepsy in children* (pp. 249–261). London: Chapman & Hall Medical.

Alajouanine, T., & Lhermitte, F. (1965). Acquired aphasia in children. *Brain*, *88*, 653–662.

Aldenkamp, A.P., Alperts, W.C.J., Blennow, G., Elmqvist, D., Heijbel, J., Nilsson, H.L., Sandstedt, P., Tonnby, B., Wåhlander, L., & Wosse, E. (1993). Withdrawal of antiepileptic medication in children—effects on cognitive function: The multicentre Holmfrid study. *Neurology*, *43*, 41–50.

Aldenkamp, A.P., Alperts, W.C.J., Sandstedt, P., Blennow, G., Elmqvist., D., Heijbel, J., Nilsson, H.L., Tonnby, B., Wåhlander, L., & Wosse. E. (1998). Antiepileptic drug-related cognitive complaints in seizure free children with epilepsy before and after drug discontinuation. *Epilepsia*, *39*(10), 1070–1074.

Altman, J., & Bayer, S. (1993). Are new neurons formed in the brain of adult mammals? In C. Cuello (Ed.), *Restorative neurology: Vol. 6. Neuronal cell death and repair* (pp. 203–225). Amsterdam: Elsevier.

Amacher, A.L. (1988). *Pediatric head injuries*. St Louis, MO: Warren H. Green.

Aminoff, M.J. (Ed.) (1992). *Electrodiagnosis in clinical neurology, 3rd ed.* New York: Churchill Livingstone.

Anastasi, A. (1988). *Psychological testing* (6th ed.). New York: Macmillan.

Anderson, D., Bundlie, S., & Rockswold, G. (1984). Multimodality evoked potentials in closed head trauma. *Archives of Neurology, 41,* 369–374.

Anderson, D., Harvey, A., Anderson, V., Kean, M., Jacobs, R., Abbott, D., Saling, M., & Jackson, G. (2000). *Differential language activation demonstrated by functional magnetic resonance imaging in twins discordant for a left frontal tumour.* Manuscript submitted for publication.

Anderson, E., & Spain, B. (1977). *The child with spina bifida.* London: Oxford University Press.

Anderson, P., Anderson, V., & Garth, J. (in press). Complex Figure Organizational Strategy Score. *The Clinical Neuropsychologist.*

Anderson, P., Anderson, V., Grimwood, K., Nolan, T., Catroppa, C., & Keir, E. (1997). Neuropsychological consequences of bacterial meningitis: A prospective study. *Journal of the International Neuropsychological Society, 3,* 47–48.

Anderson, P., Anderson, V., & Lajoie, G. (1996). The Tower of London Test: Validation and standardization for pediatric populations. *The Clincal Neuropsychologist, 10,* 54–65.

Anderson, S., Classey, J., Conde, F., Lunde, J., & Lewis, D. (1995). Synchronous development of pyramidal neurondendritic spines and parvalbumin-immunoreactive chandelier neuron axon terminals in layer III of monkey prefrontal cortex. *Neuroscience, 67,* 7–22.

Anderson, V. (1988). Recovery of function in children: The myth of cerebral plasticity. In M. Matheson & H. Newman (Eds.), *Proceedings from the 13th annual Brain Impairment Conference* (pp. 223–247). Sydney: Academic Press.

Anderson, V. (1997a). Attention deficit/hyperactivity disorder: Current neuropsychological perspectives. In J. Bailey & D. Rice (Eds.). *Attention deficit/hyperactivity disorder* (pp. 19–48). Sydney: AASE.

Anderson, V. (1997b). Brain plasticity during development. In G. Jackson, M. Saling, & S. Berkovic (Eds.), *Third annual epilepsy retreat: Neuropsychology and neuroimaging.* Marysville, Australia.

Anderson, V. (1998). Assessing executive functions in children: Biological, physiological, and developmental considerations. *Neuropsychological Rehabilitation, 8,* 319–350.

Anderson, V., Anderson, P., Northam, E., Jacobs, J., & Catroppa, C. (in press). Development of executive functions through late childhood and adolescence: An Australian sample. *Developmental Neuropsychology.*

Anderson, V., Bond, L., Catroppa, C., Grimwood, K., Keir, E., & Nolan, T. (1997). Childhood bacterial meningitis: Impact of age at illness and medical complications on long term outcome. *Journal of the International Neuropsychological Society, 3,* 147–158.

Anderson, V., & Buffery, A.W.H. (1982). Personality change after head injuries in children. In *Proceedings of the seventh annual Brain Impairment Conference* (pp. 360–375). ASSBI: Melbourne.

Anderson, V., Catroppa, C., Morse, S., Haritou, F., & Rosenfeld, J. (2000). Recovery of intellectual ability following TBI in childhood: Impact of injury severity and age at injury. *Pediatric Neurosurgery, 32,* 282–290.

Anderson, V., Fenwick, T., Manly, T., & Robertson, I. (1998). Attentional skills following traumatic brain injury in childhood: A componential analysis. *Brain Injury, 12,* 937–949.

Anderson, V., & Gilandis, A. (1994). Neuropsychological assessment of learning disabilities. In S. Touyez, D. Byrne, & A. Gilandis (Eds.), *Neuropsychology in clinical practice* (pp. 128–161). New York: Harcourt Brace Jovanich.

Anderson, V., Godber, T., Anderson, D., Smibert, E., & Ekert, H. (1995). Specific attention deficits following cranial irradiation therapy for the treatment of childhood leukaemia. *Journal of the International Neuropsychological Society*, *2*, 33.

Anderson, V., Godber, T., Smibert, E., & Ekert, H. (1997). Neurobehavioral sequelae from cranial irradiation and chemotherapy in children: An analysis of risk factors. *Pediatric Rehabilitation*, *1*, 63–76.

Anderson, V., Godber, T., Smibert, E., Weiskop, S., & Ekert, H. (2000). Impairments of attention following treatment with cranial irradiation and chemotherapy in young children. *British Journal of Cancer*, *82*, 255–262.

Anderson, V., Harvey, A.S., Anderson, D., & Kean, M. (1999). Functional magnetic resonance imaging in children: A tool to understand cerebral plasticity? Proceedings of the Fifth Annual Austin Epilepsy Retreat, Castlemaine, Australia.

Anderson, V., & Lajoie, G. (1996). Development of memory and learning skills in school-aged children: A neuropsychological perspective. *Applied Neuropsychology*, *3/4*, 128–129.

Anderson, V., Lajoie, G., & Bell, R. (1995). *Neuropsychological assessment of the school-aged child*. Melbourne: University of Melbourne.

Anderson, V., Leaper, P.M., & Judd, K. (1987). Bacterial meningitis in childhood: Neuropsychological sequelae. In G.R. Gates (Ed.), *Developmental neuropsychology* (pp. 153–168). [Proceedings from the 12th annual Brain Impairment Conference.] Armidale, NSW, Australia: ASSBI.

Anderson, V., & Moore, C. (1995). Age at injury as a predictor of outcome following pediatric head injury. *Child Neuropsychology*, *1*, 187–202.

Anderson, V., Morse, S.A., Klug, G., Catroppa, C., Haritou, F., Rosenfeld., J., & Pentland, L. (1997). Predicting recovery from head injury in school-aged children: A prospective analysis. *Journal of the International Neuropsychological Society*, *3*, 568–580.

Anderson, V., & Pentland, L. (1998). Residual attention deficits following childhood head injury. *Neuropsychological Rehabilitation*, *8*, 283–300.

Anderson, V., Smibert, E., Ekert, H., & Godber, T. (1994). Intellectual, educational and behavioral sequelae following cranial irradiation and chemotherapy. *Archives of Disease in Childhood*, *70*, 476–483.

Anderson, V., & Stanley, G.S. (1992). Ability profiles of learning disabled children. *Australian Psychologist*, *27*, 48–51.

Anderson, V., & Taylor, H.G. (1999). Meningitis. In K.O. Yeates, M.D. Ris, & H.G. Taylor (Eds.), *Pediatric neuropsychology: Research, theory and practice* (pp. 117–148). New York: Guilford Press.

Annegers, J.F. (1983). The epidemiology of head trauma in children. In K. Shapiro (Ed.), *Pediatric head trauma* (pp. 1–10). Mount Kisco, NY: Futura.

Aram, D. (1988). Language sequelae of unilateral brain lesions in children. In F. Plum (Ed.), *Language, communication, and the brain* (pp. 171–197). New York: Raven Press.

Aram, D. & Eisele, J. (1994). Intellectual stability in children with unilateral brain lesions. *Neuropsychologia*, *32*, 85–95.

Aram, D., & Ekelman, B. (1986). Cognitive profiles of children with early onset unilateral lesions. *Developmental Neuropsychology*, *2*, 155–172.

Asarnow, R.F., Satz, P., Light, R., Lewis, R., & Neumann, E. (1991). Behavior problems and adaptive functioning in children with mild and severe closed head injury. *Journal of Pediatric Psychology*, *16*, 543–555.

Asarnow, R.F., Satz, P., Light, R., Zaucha, K., Lewis, R., & McCleary, C. (1995). The UCLA study of mild head injury in children and adolescents. In S.H. Broman & M.E. Michel (Eds.), *Traumatic head injury in children* (pp. 117–146). New York: Oxford University Press.

Atkinson, J., Barlow, H.B., & Braddick, O.J. (1982). The development of sensory systems and their modification by experience. In H.B. Barlow & J. Mollon (Eds.), *The senses* (pp. 448–467). Cambridge, UK: Cambridge University Press.

Atkinson, R.C., & Shiffrin, R.M. (1968). Human memory: A proposed system and its control processes. In K.W. Spence (Ed.), *The psychology of learning and motivation: Advances in research and theory* (Vol. 2, pp. 89–195). New York: Academic Press.

August, G.J., & Garfinkel, B.D. (1990). Comorbity of ADHD and reading disability among clinic-referred children. *Journal of Abnormal Child Psychology, 18,* 29–45.

Austin, J.K., Huberty, T.J., Huster, G.A., & Dunn, D.W. (1998). Academic achievement in children with epilepsy and asthma. *Developmental Medicine and Child Neurology, 40,* 248–255.

Austin, J.K., Risinger, M.W., & Beckett, L.A. (1992). Correlates of behaviour problems in children with epilepsy. *Epilepsia, 33*(6), 1115–1122.

Aylward, G. (1997). *Infant and early childhood neuropsychology.* New York: Plenum Press.

Azen, C., Koch, R.R., Friedman, E.G., Berlow, S., Coledale, J., Krause, W., Metalline, R., McCabe, E., O'Flynn, M., Peterson, R., Rouse, B., Scott, C.R., Sigman, B., Valle, D., & Warner, R. (1991). Intellectual development in 12-year-old children treated for phenylketonuria. *American Journal of the Disabled Child, 145,* 35–39.

Azen, C., Koch, R., Friedman, E., Wenz, E., & Fishler, K. (1996). Summary of findings from the United States collaborative study of children treated for phenylketonuria. *European Journal of Pediatrics, 155,* S29–S32.

Bachevalier, J., & Mishkin, M. (1984). An early and a late developing system for learning and retention in infant monkeys. *Behavioral Neuroscience, 98,* 770–778.

Baddeley, A. (1986). *Working memory.* Oxford: Oxford University Press.

Baddeley, A. (1990). *Human memory: Theory and practice.* London: Lawrence Erlbaum Associates Ltd.

Bailey, N. (1993). *Manual for the Bayley Scales of Infant Development* (2nd ed.). New York: Psychological Corporation.

Bakay Pragay, E., Mirsky, A.F., Fullerton, B.C., Oshima, H.I., & Arnold, S.W. (1975). Effect of electrical stimulation of the brain on visually controlled (attentive) behaviour in the *Macaca mulatta. Experimental Neurology, 49,* 203–220.

Bakay Pragay, E., Mirsky, A.F., & Nakamura, R.K. (1987). Attention-related unit activity in the frontal association cortex during a go/no go discrimination task. *Experimental Neurology, 96,* 481–500.

Baker, A., Moulton, R., MacMillan, V., & Sheddon, P. (1993). Excitatory amino acid in cerebrospinal fluid following traumatic brain injury in humans. *Journal of Neurosurgery, 79,* 369–372.

Baker, R.C., Kummer, A.W., Schultz, J.R., Ho, M., & Gonzalez del Rey, J. (1996). Neurodevelopmental outcome of infants with viral meningitis in the first three months of life. *Clinical Pediatrics,* 295–301.

Bakker, K., Anderson, V., Morse, S. Catroppa, C., Haritou, F., & Klug, G. (2000). Attention in preschool head injury. *Pediatric Rehabilitation, 3,* 149–158.

Ballantyne, A., Scarvie, K., & Trauner, D. (1992). IQ patterns in children with early-onset focal barin lesions. *Journal of Clinical and Experimental Neuropsychology, 14,* 115.

Banich, M., Cohen-Levine, S., Kim, H., & Huttenlocher, P. (1990). The effects of developmental factors on IQ in hemiplegic children. *Neuropsychologia, 28*(a), 35–47.

Baraff, L.J., Lee, S.I., & Schriger, D.L. (1993). Outcomes of bacterial meningitis in children: A meta-analysis. *Pediatric Infectious Diseases, 12,* 389–394.

Barbarotto, R., Capitani, E., & Laiacona, M. (1996). Naming deficit in herpes simplex encephalitis. *Acta Neurologica Scandanavica, 93,* 272–280.

Barbas, H. (1992). Architecture and cortical connections of the prefrontal cortex in the rhesus monkey. In P. Chauvel & A. Delgado-Esceuta (Eds.), *Advances in neurology* (pp. 91–115). New York: Raven Press.

Barclay, A., & Walton, O. (1988). Phenylketonuria: Implications of initial serum phenylalanine levels on cognitive development. *Psychological Reports, 63,* 135–142.

Barkley, R. (1988). Attention. In M.G. Tramontana & S.R. Hooper (Eds.), *Assessment issues in child neuropsychology* (pp. 145–176). New York: Plenum.

Barkley, R. (1990). *Attention deficit/hyperactivity disorder: A handbook for diagnosis and treatment* (2nd ed.). New York: Guilford Press.

Barkovich, A., Guerrini, R., Battaglia, G., Kalifa, G., N'Guyen, T., Parmeggiani, A., Santucci, M., Giovardi-Rossi, P., Granata, T., & D'Incerti, L. (1994). Band heterotopia: Correlation of outcome with magnetic resonance parameters. *Annals of Neurology*, *36*, 609–617.

Barkovich, A., Kjos, B., Jackson, D., & Norman, D. (1988). Neural maturation of the neonatal and infant brain: MR imaging at 1.5 T. *Neuroradiology*, *166*, 173–180.

Barkovich, A., Kuzniecky, R., Dobyns, W., Jackson, G., Becker, L., & Evrard, P. (1996). A classification scheme for malformations of cortical development. *Neuropediatrics*, *27*, 59–63.

Barnes, M., & Dennis, M. (1992). Reading in children and adolescents after early onset hydrocephalus and in normally developing age peers: Phonological analysis, word recognition, and passage comprehension skills. *Journal of Pediatric Psychology*, *17*, 445–466.

Barnes, M., & Dennis, M. (1998). Discourse after early onset hydrocephalus: Core deficits in children of average intelligence. *Brain and Language*, *61*, 309–334.

Barnes, M., Dennis, M., & Wilkinson, M. (1999). Reading after closed head injury in childhood: Effects on accuracy, fluency, and comprehension. *Developmental Neuropsychology*, *15*, 1–24.

Baron, I.S., Fennell, E.B., & Voeller, K. (1996). *Pediatric neuropsychology in the medical setting*. New York: Oxford University Press.

Baron, I.S., & Goldberger, E. (1993). Neuropsychological disturbances of hydrocephalic children with implications for special education and rehabilitation. *Neuropsychological Rehabilitation*, *3*, 389–410.

Basser, L. (1962). Hemiplegia of early onset and the faculty of speech with special reference to the effects of hemispherectomy. *Brain*, *85*, 427–460.

Bauman, M., & Kemper, T. (1982). Morphological and histoanatomic observations of the brain in untreated human phenylketonuria. *Acta Neuropathologica (Berl.)*, *58*, 55–63.

Bawden, H.N., Knights, R.M., & Winogron, H.W. (1985). Speeded performance following head injury in children. *Journal of Clinical and Experimental Neuropsychology*, *7*, 39–54.

Baxendale, S.A., van Paesschen, W., Thompson, P.J., Connelly, A., Duncan, J.S., Harkness, W.F., & Shorvon, S.D. (1998). *Epilepsia*, *39*(2), 158–166.

Bear, D.M., & Fedio, P. (1977). Quantitative analysis of interictal behaviour in temporal lobe epilepsy. *Archives of Neurology*, *34*, 54–67.

Beardsworth, E.D., & Zaidel, D.W. (1994). Memory for faces in epileptic children before and after brain surgery. *Journal of Clinical and Experimental Neuropsychology*, *16*(4), 589–596.

Becker, L., Armstrong, D., Chan, F., & Wood, M. (1984). Dendritic development in human occipital cortical neurons. *Developmental Brain Research*, *13*, 117–124.

Becker, M.G., Isaac, W., & Hynd, G. (1987). Neuropsychological development of non-verbal behaviors attributed to the frontal lobes. *Developmental Neuropsychology*, *3*, 275–298.

Beers, S. (1992). Cognitive effects of mild head injury in children and adolescents. *Neuropsychology Review*, *3*, 281–319.

Beery, K.E. (1989). *Revised administration, scoring and teaching manual for the Developmental Test of Visuo-motor Integration*. Cleveland, OH: Modern Curriculum Press.

Begali, V. (1992). *Head injury in children and adolescents* (2nd ed.). Brandon, VT: Clinical Psychology Publishing Company.

Bell, M.A., & Fox, N.A. (1992). The relations between frontal brain electrical activity and cognitive development during infancy. *Child Development*, *63*, 1142–1163.

Bendersky, M., & Lewis, M. (1994). Environmental risk, biological risk, and developmental outcome. *Developmental Psychology*, *30*, 484–494.

Benes, F., Turtle, M., Khan, Y., & Farol, P. (1994). Myelination of a key relay zone in the hippocampal formation occurs in the human being during childhood, adolescence and adulthood. *Archives of General Psychiatry*, *51*, 477–484.

Bennet-Levy, J., & Stores, G. (1984). The nature of cognitive dysfunction in school-children with epilepsy. *Acta Neurologica Scandinavica, 69*(Suppl. 99), 79–82.

Benton, A.L. (1982). *Benton Visual Retention Test* (5th ed.). San Antonio, TX: Psychological Corporation.

Benton, A.L., Hamsher, K., Varney, N.R., & Spreen, O. (1983). *Contributions of neuropsychological assessment: A clinical manual*. New York: Oxford University.

Berger, M.S., Pitts, L.H., Lovely, M., Edwards, M.S., & Bartkowsky, H.M. (1985). Outcome from severe head injury in children and adolescents. *Journal of Neurosurgery*, *62*, 194–195.

Berger-Gross, P., & Shackelford, M. (1985). Closed-head injury in children: Neuropsychological and scholastic outcomes. *Perceptual and Motor Skills*, *61*, 254.

Bergman, I., Painter, M.J., Wald, E.R., Chiponis, D., Holland, A.L., & Taylor, H.G. (1987). Outcome of children with enteroviral meningitis during the first year of life. *Journal of Pediatrics*, *110*, 705–709.

Berker, E., Goldstein, G., Lorber, J., Priestley, B., & Smith, A. (1992). Reciprocal neurological developments of twins discordant for hydrocephalus. *Developmental Medicine and Child Neurology*, *34*, 623–632.

Berkovic, S.F. (1998). Genetics of epilepsy: Where are we now? In S.F. Berkovic & G.D. Jackson (Eds.), *Fourth annual Epilepsy Retreat (Proceedings)*. Melbourne: Austin-Repatriation Medical Centre.

Berkovic, S.F., & Scheffer, I.E. (1998). Febrile seizures: Genetics and relationship to other epilepsy syndromes. *Current Opinion in Neurology*, *11*, 129–134.

Berney, J., Favier, J., & Froidevaux, A. (1994a). Pediatric head trauma: Influence of age and sex: I. Epidemiology. *Child's Nervous System*, *10*, 509–516.

Berney, J., Froidevaux, A., & Favier, J. (1994b). Pediatric head trauma: Influence of age and sex: II. Biochemical and anatomo-clinical observations. *Child's Nervous System*, *10*, 517–523.

Berry, H.K., O'Grady, D.J., Perlmutter, L.J., & Bofinger, M.K. (1979). Intellectual development and academic achievement of children treated early for phenylketonuria. *Developmental Medicine and Child Neurology*, *21*, 311–320.

Bessman, S. (1985). Stress: Its pathophysiology in diabetic failure. In F. Lifshitz (Ed.), *Pediatric endocrinology* (Vol. 3, pp. 437–449). New York: Marcel Dekker.

Bick, U., Ullrich, K., Stober, U., Moller, H., Schuierer, G., Ludolph, A.C., Oberwittler, C., Weglage, J., & Wendel, U. (1993). White matter abnormalities in patients with treated hyperphenylalaninaemia: Magnetic resonance relaxometry and proton spectroscopy findings. *European Journal of Pediatrics*, *152*, 1012–1020.

Bier, J., Morales, Y., Liebling, J., Geddes, L., & Kim, E. (1997). Medical and social factors associated with cognitive outcome in individuals with myelomeningocele. *Developmental Medicine and Child Neurology*, *39*, 263–266.

Biessels, G., Kappelle, A., Bravenboer, B., Erkelens, D., & Gispen, W. (1994). Cerebral function in diabetes mellitus. *Diabetelogia*, *37*, 643–650.

Bijur, P.E., & Haslam, M. (1995). Cognitive, behavioral, and motoric sequelae of mild head injury in a national birth cohort. In S.H. Broman & M.E. Michel (Eds.), *Traumatic head injury in children* (pp. 147–165). New York: Oxford University Press.

Billard, C., Autret, A., Lucas, B., Degiovanni, E., Gillet, P., Santini, J.J., & de Toffol, B. (1990). Are frequent spike–waves during non-REM sleep in relation with an acquired neuropsychological deficit in epileptic children? *Neurophysiologie Clinique*, *20*, 439–453.

Billard, C., Santini, J.J., Gillet, P., Nargeot, M.C., & Adrien, J.L. (1985). Long-term prognosis of hydrocephalus with reference to 77 children. *Pediatric Neuroscience*, *12*, 219–225.

Binnie, C.D., & Marston, D. (1992). Cognitive correlates of interictal discharges. *Epilepsia*, *33*(Suppl. 6), S11–S17.

Bishop, D. (1985). Age of onset and outcome in "acquired aphasia with convulsive disorder" (Landau Kleffner syndrome). *Developmental Medicine and Child Neurology, 27,* 705–712.

Bishop, D. (1989). *Test for the Reception of Grammar.* Cambridge, UK: Medical Research Council, Chapel Press.

Bjorgaas, M., Gimse, R., Vik, T., & Sand, T. (1997). Cognitive function in Type 1 diabetic children with and without episodes of severe hypoglycaemia. *Acta Paediatrica, 86,* 148–153.

Bjorkland, A., & Stenevi, U. (1971). Growth of central catacholamine neurons into mesencephalon. *Brain Research, 31,* 1–20.

Bjorklund, D.F. (1989). *Children's thinking: Developmental function and individual differences.* Pacific Grove, CA: Brooks/Cole.

Black, P., Jeffries, J., Blumer, D., Wellner, A., & Walker, A. (1969). The post-traumatic syndrome in children. In A. Walker, W. Caveness, M. Critchley, & C. Charles (Eds.), *The late effects of head injury* (pp. 142–149). Springfield, IL: Thomas.

Blakemore, C. (1974). Development of functional connections in the mammalian visual system. *British Medical Bulletin, 30,* 152–157.

Blakemore, C., & Van Slayters, R. (1975). Innate and environmental factors in the development of the kitten's visual cortex. *Journal of Physiology, 248,* 663–716.

Blatter, D., Bigler, E., Gale, S., Johnson, S., Anderson, C., Burnett, B., et al. (1995). Quantitative volumetric analysis of brain MR: Normative data base spanning five decades of life. *American Journal of Neuroradiology, 16,* 241–251.

Bohnert, A., Parker, J., & Warschausky, S. (1997). Friendship and social adjustment following traumatic brain injury: An exploratory investigation. *Developmental Neuropsychology, 13,* 477–486.

Boll, T. (1983). Minor head injury in children: Out of sight but not out of mind. *Journal of Clinical Child Psychology, 12,* 74–80.

Bolter, J.F. (1986). Epilepsy in children. In J.E. Obrzut & G.W. Hynd (Eds.), *Child neuropsychology: Vol. 2. Clinical practice* (pp. 59–81). Orlando, FL: Academic Press.

Borchgrevik, H.M. (1989). Cerbral processes underlying neuropsychological and neuromotor impairment in children with ADD/MBD. In T. Sagvolden & T. Archer (Eds.), *Attention deficit disorder: Clinical and basic research* (pp. 105–130). Hove, UK: Lawrence Erlbaum Associates Ltd.

Bourgeois, B.F.D. (1996a). Antiepileptic drugs. In S. Wallace (Ed.), *Epilepsy in children* (pp. 535–552). London: Chapman & Hall Medical.

Bourgeois, B.F.D. (1996b). Behavioural and social therapies. In S. Wallace (Ed.), *Epilepsy in children* (pp. 557–559). London: Chapman & Hall Medical.

Bourgeois, B.F.D. (1996c). Diets. In S. Wallace (Ed.), *Epilepsy in children* (pp. 553–555). London: Chapman & Hall Medical.

Bourgeois, B.F.D. (1998). Antiepileptic drugs, learning and behaviour in childhood epilepsy. *Epilepsia, 39*(9), 913–921.

Bourgeois, B.F.D., Prensky, A.L., Palkes, H.S., Talent, B.K., & Busch, S.G. (1983). Intelligence in epilepsy: A prospective study in children. *Annals of Neurology, 14,* 438–444.

Breslau, N. (1985). Psychiatric disorder in children with physical disability. *Journal of the American Academy of Child Psychiatry, 24,* 87–94.

Breslau, N. (1990). Does brain dysfunction increase children's vulnerability to environmental stress? *Archives of General Psychiatry, 47,* 15–20.

Brierley, J. (1981). Brain damage due to hypoglycaemia. In V. Marks & F. Rose (Eds.), *Hypoglycaemia* (pp. 213–240). London: Blackwell Scientific.

Brink, J., Imbus, C., & Woo-Sam, J. (1980). Physical recovery after closed head trauma in children and adolescents. *Journal of Pediatrics, 97,* 721–727.

Broadbent, D.E. (1958). *Perception and communication.* London: Pergamon Press.

Broca, P. (1861). Remarques sur le siège de la faculté du language articule: suivies d'une observation d'aphemie (perte de la parole). *Bulletin de la Sociétée d'Anatomique, 6,* 330–357.

Broca, P. (1865). Sur le siège de la faculté du language articule. *Bulletin de la Société d'Anthropologie, 6,* 377–393.

Brodal, P. (1992). *The central nervous system: Structure and function.* New York: Oxford University Press.

Brooks, P. (Ed.). (1985). *The injured child.* Austin, TX: University of Texas Press.

Brookshire, B.L., Fletcher, J.M., Bohan, T.P., Landry, S.H., Davidson, K.C., & Francis, D.J. (1995a). Specific language deficiencies in children with early onset hydrocephalus. *Child Neuropsychology, 1,* 106–117.

Brookshire, B.L., Fletcher, J.M., Bohan, T.P., Landry, S.H., Davidson, K.C., & Francis, D.J. (1995b). Verbal and nonverbal skills discrepancies in children with hydrocephalus: A five year longitudinal follow-up. *Journal of Pediatric Psychology, 20,* 785–800.

Brouwers, P., & Poplack, D. (1990). Memory and learning sequelae in long-term survivors of acute lymphoblastic leukaemia: Association with attention deficit. *American Journal of Pediatric Hematology/Oncology, 12,* 171–184.

Brouwers, P., Riccardi, R., Poplack, D., & Fedio, P. (1984). Attentional deficits in long-term survivors of childhood acute lymphoblastic leukemia. *Journal of Clinical Neuropsychology, 6,* 325–336.

Brown, A., & Scott, M. (1971). Recognition memory for pictures in preschool children. *Journal of Experimental Child Psychology, 11,* 401–412.

Brown, G. (1938). The development of diabetic children, with special reference to mental and personality comparisons. *Child Development, 9,* 175–183.

Brown, G., Chadwick, O., Shaffer, D., Rutter, M., & Traub, M. (1981). A prospective study of children with head injuries: II. Psychiatric sequelae. *Psychological Medicine, 11*(1), 49–62.

Bruce, D.A., Raphaely, R.C., Goldberg, A.I., Zimmerman, R.A., Bilaniuk., L.T., Schut, L., & Kuhl, D.E. (1979). Pathophysiology, treatment and outcome following severe head injury in children. *Child's Brain, 2,* 174–191.

Bruce, D.A., Schut, L., Bruno, L.A., Wood, J.H., & Sutton, L.N. (1978). Outcome following severe head injury in children. *Journal of Neurosurgery, 48,* 679–688.

Bruininks, R.H. (1978). *Bruininks–Oseretsky Test of Motor Proficiency.* Circle Pines, MN: American Guidance Service.

Brunner, R.L., Berch, D.B., & Berry, H. (1987). Phenylketonuria and complex spatial visualization: An analysis of information processing. *Developmental Medicine and Child Neurology, 29,* 460–468.

Brunner, R.L., Jordan, M.K., & Berry, H.K. (1983). Early-treated phenylketonuria: Neuropsychologic consequences. *Journal of Pediatrics, 102,* 102–131.

Bryan, D. (1994). Neural tube defects. In M.J. Robinson & D.M. Roberton (Eds.), *Practical paediatrics* (pp. 476–482). Melbourne: Churchill Livingstone.

Bureau, M., Cordova, S., Dravet, C., et al. (1990). Epilepsie avec pointes-ondes continues dans le sommeil lent (POCS): Evolution à moyen et à la long terme. *Epilepsies, 2,* 89–94.

Burgard, P., Armbruster, M., Schmidt, E., & Rupp, A. (1994). Psychopathology of patients treated early for phenylketonuria: Results of the German collaborative study of phenylketonuria. *Acta Paediatrica Suppl., 407,* 108–110.

Burgard, P., Schmidt, E., Rupp, A., Schneider, W., & Bremer, H.J. (1996). Intellectual development of the patients of the German collaborative study of children treated for phenylketonuria. *European Journal of Pediatrics, 155,* S33–S38.

Butler, K., Rourke, B., Feurst, D., & Fisk, J. (1997). A typology of psychosocial functioning in pediatric closed head injury. *Child Neuropsychology, 3,* 98–133.

Byrne, K., Abbedata, I., & Brooks, R. (1990). The language of children with spina bifida and hydrocephalus: Meeting task demands and mastering syntax. *Journal of Speech and Hearing Disorders*, *55*, 118–123.

Cabalaska, B., Durzynska, N., Borzymonwska, J., Zorska, K., Kaslacz-Folga, A., & Bozkowa, K. (1977). Termination of dietary treatment of phenylketonuria. *European Journal of Pediatrics*, *126*, 253–262.

Caeser, P. (1993). Old and new facts about perinatal brain development. *Journal of Child Psychology and Psychiatry*, *34*, 101–109.

Caeser, P., & Lagae, L. (1991). Age specific approach to neurological assessment in the first year of life. *Acta Pediatrica Japonica*, *33*, 125–138.

Cairns, E., & Cammock, T. (1978). Development of a more reliable version of the "Matching Familiar Figures Test". *Developmental Psychology*, *14*, 555–560.

Camfield, C., Camfield, P., Smith, B., Gordon, K., & Dooley, J. (1993). Biologic factors as predictors of social outcome of epilepsy in intellectually normal children: A population-based study. *Journal of Pediatrics*, *122*(6), 869–873.

Camfield, C., Caplan, S., Doyle, A., Shapiro, S.H., Cummings, C., & Camfield, P.R. (1979). Side effects of phenobarbital in toddlers: Behavioural and cognitive aspects. *Journal of Pediatrics*, *95*, 361.

Camfield, P.R. (1997). Recurrent seizures in the developing brain are not harmful. *Epilepsia*, *38*(6), 735–737.

Camfield, P.R., Gates, R., Ronen, G., Camfield, C., Ferguson, M.A., & MacDonald, G.W. (1984). Comparison of cognitive ability, personality profile, and school success in epileptic children with pure right versus left temporal lobe EEG foci. *Annals of Neurology*, *15*, 122–126.

Campbell, T.F., & Dollaghan, C.A. (1990). Expressive language recovery in severely brain-injured children and adolescents. *Journal of Speech and Hearing Disorders*, *55*, 567–581.

Cannon, W., & Rosenbleuth, A. (1949). *The supersensitivity of denervated structures*. New York: Macmillan.

Caplan, R. (1998). Epilepsy syndromes. In C. Coffey & R. Brumback (Eds.), *Textbook of pediatric neuropsychiatry* (pp. 977–1010). Washington: Blackwell Science.

Caplan, R., Curtis, S., Chugani, H.T., & Vinters, H.V. (1996). Pediatric Rasmussen encephalitis: Social communication, language, PET, and pathology before and after hemispherectomy. *Brain and Cognition*, *32*, 45–66.

Capone, G. (1996). Human brain development. In A. Capute & P. Accardo (Eds.), *Developmental disabilities in infancy and childhood: Vol. 1. Neurodevelopmental diagnosis and treatment* (2nd ed., pp. 25–75). Baltimore: Paul H. Brookes.

Carlton-Ford, S., Miller, R., Nealeigh, N., & Sanchez, N. (1997). The effects of perceived stigma and psychological over-control on the behavioural problems of children with epilepsy. *Seizure*, *6*, 383–391.

Carrow-Woolfolk, E. (1985). *Examiner's manual: Test for Auditory Comprehension of Language—Revised*. Allen, TX: DLM Teaching Resources.

Case, R. (1985). *Intellectual development: A systematic reinterpretation*. New York: Academic Press.

Case, R. (Ed.). (1992). *The mind's staircase: Exploring the conceptual underpinnings of children's thought and knowledge*. Hillsdale, NJ: Lawrence Erlbaum Associates Inc.

Casey, B., Gordon, C., Mannheim, G., & Rumsey, J. (1993). Dysfunctional attention in autistic savants. *Journal of Clinical and Experimental Neuropsychology*, *15*, 933–946.

Casey, J., Rourke, B., & Picard, E. (1991). Syndrome of non-verbal learning disabilities: Age differences in neuropsychological, academic and socioemotional functioning. *Developmental Psychopathology*, *3*, 329–345.

Catroppa, C. & Anderson, V. (1999). Attentional skills in the acute phase following pediatric traumatic brain injury. *Child Neuropsychology*, *5*, 251–264.

Catroppa, C., Anderson, V., & Stargatt, R. (1999). A prospective study of the recovery of attention following pediatric head injury. *Journal of the International Neuropsychological Society, 5*, 48–57.

Catroppa, V., & Anderson, V. (2000). Recovery of educational skills following pediatric head injury. *Pediatric Rehabilitation, 3*, 167–176.

Catroppa, C. & Anderson, V. (2001). Recovery of memory skills in the first year following TBI in childhood. *Manuscript submitted for publication.*

Cattelani, R., Lombardi, F., Brianti, R., & Mazzuchi, A. (1998). Traumatic brain injury in childhood: Intellectual, behavioral and social outcome into adulthood. *Brain Injury, 12*, 283–296.

Ceci, S., & Liker, J. (1986). A day at the races: The study of IQ, expertise, and cognitive complexity. *Journal of Experimental psychology: General, 115*, 225–266.

Cermak, L.S., & O'Connor, M. (1983). The anterograde and retrograde retrieval ability of a patient with amnesia due to encephalitis. *Neuropsychologia, 21*, 213–234.

Chadwick, O., Rutter, M., Brown, G., Shaffer, D., & Traub, M. (1981a). A prospective study of children with head injuries: II. Cognitive sequelae. *Psychological Medicine, 11*, 49–61.

Chadwick, O., Rutter, M., Shaffer, D., & Shrout, P. (1981b). A prospective study of children with head injuries: IV. Specific cognitive deficits. *Journal of Clinical Neuropsychology, 2*, 101–120.

Chalmers, J., Risk, M., Kean, D.M., Grant, R., Ashworth, B., & Campbell, I. (1991). Severe amnesia after hypoglycemia. *Diabetes Care, 14*, 922–925.

Chaplin, D., Deitz, J., & Jaffe, K. (1993). Motor performance in children after traumatic brain injury. *Archives of Physical Medicine and Rehabilitation, 74*, 161–164.

Chapman, S. (1995). Discourse as an outcome measure in pediatric head-injured populations. In S.H. Broman & M.E. Michel (Eds.), *Traumatic head injury in children* (pp. 95–116). New York: Oxford University Press.

Chapman, S., Levin, H., Wanek, A., Weyrauch, J., & Kufera, J. (1998). Discourse after closed head injury in young children: Relationship of age to outcome. *Brain and Language, 61*, 420–449.

Charney, E. (1992). Neural tube defects: Spina bifida and myelomeningocele. In M. Batshaw & Y. Perret (Eds.), *Children with disabilities: A medical primer* (3rd ed., pp. 471–488). Baltimore: Paul H. Brookes.

Chelune, G.J., & Baer, R.A. (1986). Developmental norms for the Wisconsin Card Sorting Test. *Journal of Clinical and Experimental Neuropsychology, 8*, 219–228.

Cherry, J.D. (1992). Aseptic meningitis and viral meningitis. In R.D. Feigin & J.D. Cherry (Eds.), *Textbook of pediatric infectious diseases* (3rd ed., Vol. 1, pp. 439–445). Philadelphia: W.B. Saunders.

Chiron, C., Raynaud, C., Maziere, B., Zilbovicius, M., Laflamme, L., Masure, M., Dulac, O., Bourguignon, M., & Syrota, A. (1992). Changes in regional cerebral blood flow during brain maturation in children and adolescents. *Journal of Nuclear Medicine, 33*, 696–703.

Choi, D. (1988). Glutamate neurotoxicity and diseases of the nervous system. *Neuron, 1*, 623–634.

Choux, M. (1986). Incidence, diagnosis and management of skull fractures. In A.J. Raimondi, M. Choux, & C. DiRocco (Eds.), *Head injuries in the new born and infant* (pp. 163–182). New York: Springer.

Christensen, A. (1979). *Luria's neuropsychological investigation.* Munksgaard: Schmidts Bogtrykkeri Vojens.

Chugani, H.T. (1994). Development of regional brain glucose metabolism in relation to behavior and plasticity. In G. Dawson & K. Fischer (Eds.), *Human behavior and the developing brain* (pp. 153–175). New York: Guilford Press.

Chugani, H.T., Phelps, M.E., & Mazziotta, J.C. (1987). Positron emission tomography study of human brain functional development. *Annals of Neurology, 22*, 287–297.

Clarke, J.T., Gates, R.D., Hogan, S.E., Barrett, M., & MacDonald, G.W. (1987). Neuro-psychological studies in adolescents with phenylketonuria returned to phenylalanine-restricted diets. *American Journal of Mental Retardation, 92*, 255–262.

Cleary, M.A., Walter, J.H., Wraith, J.E., & Jenkins, J.P. (1995). Magnetic resonance imaging in phenylketonuria: Reversal of cerebral white matter change. *Journal of Pediatrics, 127*, 251–255.

Close, H., Davies, A.G., Price, D.A., & Goodyer, E.M. (1986). Emotional difficulties in diabetes mellitus. *Archives of Disease in Childhood, 61*, 337–340.

Cochrane, H.C., Marson, A.G., Baker G.A., & Chadwick, D.W. (1998). Neuropsychological outcomes in randomised controlled trials of antiepileptic drugs: A systematic review of methodology and reporting standards. *Epilepsia, 39*(10), 1088–1097.

Cohen, M. (1992). Auditory/verbal and visual/spatial memory in children with complex partial epilepsy of temporal lobe origin. *Brain and Cognition, 20*, 315–326.

Cohen, M. (1997). *Children's Memory Scale*. San Antonio, TX: Psychological Corporation.

Cohen-Levine, S. (1993). Effects of unilateral lesions: Changes over the course of development. In G. Turkewitz & D. Devenny (Eds.), *Developmental time and timing*. Hove, UK: Lawrence Erlbaum Associates Ltd.

Cole, M., Frankel, F., & Sharp, D. (1971). Development of free recall learning in children. *Developmental Psychology, 4*, 109–123.

Collings, J.A. (1990). Psychosocial well-being and epilepsy: An empirical study. *Epilepsia, 31*(4), 418–426.

Columbo, M., & Gross, C. (1994). Responses of inferior temporal cortex and hippocampal neurones during delayed matching to sample in monkeys (*Macaca fascicularis*). *Behavioral Neuroscience, 108*, 443–455.

Commission on Classification and Terminology of the International League Against Epilepsy (1981). Proposal for revised clinical and electroencephalographic classification of epileptic seizures. *Epilepsia, 22*, 489–501.

Commission on Classification and Terminology of the International League Against Epilepsy (1989). Proposal for the revised classification of epilepsies and epileptic syndromes. *Epilepsia, 30*, 389–399.

Condor, A., Anderson, V., & Saling, M. (1996). Do reading disabled children have planning problems? *Developmental Neuropsychology, 11*, 485–502.

Connell, H., & McConnel, T. (1981). Psychiatric sequelae in children treated operatively for hydrocephalus in infancy. *Developmental Medicine and Child Neurology, 23*, 505–517.

Conners, C. (1997) *Conners Rating Scales*. Wilmington, DE: Jastak.

Cooley, E.L., & Morris, R.D. (1990). Attention in children: A neuropsychologically-based model for assessment. *Developmental Neuropsychology, 6*, 239–274.

Coopersmith, S. (1984). *Self-Esteem Inventories*. Palo Alto, CA: Consulting Psychologists Press.

Coster, W.H., Haley, S., & Baryza, M. (1994). Functional performance of young children after traumatic brain injury: A six month follow-up study. *American Journal of Occupational Therapy, 48*, 211–218.

Coulombe, P., & Ruel, J. (1983). Mechanisms of action of thyroid hormones. In J.H. Dussault & P. Walker (Eds.), *Congenital hypothyroidism* (pp. 37–61). New York: Dekker.

Counsell, C.E., Taylor, R., Whittle, I.R. (1994). Focal necrotising herpes simplex encephalitis: A report of two cases with good clinical and neuropsychological outcomes. *Journal of Neurology, Neurosurgery, and Psychiatry, 57*, 1115–1117.

Courville, C.B. (1945). *Pathology and the nervous system*. Mountain View, CA: Pacific Press.

Cousens, P., Ungerer, J.A., Crawford, J.A., & Stevens, M.M. (1991). Cognitive effects of childhood leukemia therapy: A case for four specific deficits. *Journal of Pediatric Psychology, 16*, 475–488.

Cowan, N. (1988). Evolving conceptions of memory storage, selective attention and their mutual constraints within the human information processing system. *Psychological Bulletin, 104*, 163–191.

Cowan, N. (1995). *Attention and memory: An integrated framework*. New York: Oxford University Press.

Cowan, N. (1997). The development of working memory. In N. Cowan (Ed.), *The development of memory in childhood* (pp. 163–199). Hove, UK: Psychology Press.

Cowan, W.M. (1979). The development of the brain. *Scientific American, 241*, 116.

Cowan, W., Fawcett, J., O'Leary, D., & Stanfield, B. (1984). Regressive events in neurogenesis. *Science, 225*, 1258–1265.

Craft, A.W., Shaw D.A., & Cartlidge, N.E. (1972). Head injuries in children. *British Medical Journal, 4*, 200–203.

Craft, S., Gourovitch, M.L., Dowton, S.B., Swanson, J.M., & Bonforte, S. (1992). Lateralised deficits in visual attention in males with developmental dopamine depletion. *Neuropsychologia, 30*, 341–351.

Culatta, B., & Egolf, D. (1980). Perceptual and linguistic performance of spina bifida–hydrocephalic children. *Spina Bifida Therapy, 1*, 235–247.

Cull, C., & Wyke, M. (1984). Memory function of children with spina bifida and shunted hydrocephalus. *Developmental Medicine and Child Neurology, 26*, 177–183.

Cummings, J. (1993). Frontal–subcortical circuits and human behavior. *Archives of Neurology, 50*, 873–880.

Curley, A.D. (1992). Behavioural disturbance in children with seizures. In M.G. Tramontana & S.R. Hooper (Eds.), *Advances in child neuropsychology* (Vol. 1, pp. 109–136). New York: Springer.

Curtiss, S. (1981). Feral children. In J. Wortis (Ed.), *Mental retardation and developmental disabilities* (pp. 129–161). New York: Brunner/Mazel.

Dalby, P.R., & Obrzut, J.E. (1991). Epidemiologic characteristics and sequelae of closed head-injured children and adolescents: A review. *Developmental Neuropsychology, 7*, 35–68.

D'Alessandro, P., Piccirilli, M., Tiacci, C., Ibba, A., Maiotti, M., Sciarma, T., & Testa, A. (1990). Neuropsychological features of benign partial epilepsy in children. *Italian Journal of Neurological Science, 11*, 265–269.

Dall'Oglio, A., Bates, E., Volterra, V., Di Capua, M., & Pezzini, G. (1994). Early cognition, communication and language in children with focal brain injury. *Developmental Medicine and Child Neurology, 36*, 1076–1098.

Damasio, A.R., Tranel, D., & Damasio, H. (1989). Amnesia caused by herpes simplex encephalitis, infarctions in basal forebrain, Alzheimer's disease and anoxia/ischemia. In F. Boller & J. Grafman (Eds.), *Handbook of neuropsychology* (pp. 149–166). New York: Elsevier Science.

Daniels, D., Miller, J., Billings, A.G., & Moos, R.H. (1986). Psychosocial functioning of siblings of children with rheumatic disease. *Journal of Pediatrics, 109*, 379–383.

Davies, P.A., & Rudd, R.T. (1994). *Neonatal meningitis* (Clinics in Developmental Medicine No. 132). London: Cambridge University Press.

Deary, I., Langan, S., Graham, K., Hepburn, D., & Frier, B. (1992). Recurrent severe hypoglycemia, intelligence, and speed of information processing. *Intelligence, 16*, 337–359.

Dejgaard, A., Gade, A., Larsson, H., Balle, V., Parving, A., & Parving, H. (1991). Evidence for diabetic encephalopathy. *Diabetic Medicine, 8*, 162–167.

Dekaban, A.S., & Sadowsky, D. (1978). Changes in brain weights during the span of human life: Relation of brain weights to body heights and body weights. *Annals of Neurology, 4*, 345–356.

Del Bigio, M.R. (1993). Neuropathological changes caused by hydrocephalus. *Acta Neuropathologica, 85*, 573–585.

Delis, D., Kramer, J., Kaplan, E., & Ober, B.A. (1991). *California Verbal Learning Test Manual: Children's version*. San Antonio, TX: Psychological Corporation.

Dempster, F. (1981). Memory span: Sources of individual and developmental differences. *Psychological Bulletin*, *89*, 63–100.

Dempster, F.N. (1991). Inhibitory processes: A neglected dimension of intelligence. *Intelligence*, *15*, 157–173.

Denckla, M.B., & Rudel, R.G. (1976). Rapid "automatized" naming (R.A.N.): Dyslexia differentiated from other learning disabilities. *Neuropsychologia*, *14*, 471–479.

Dennis, M. (1980). Capacity and strategy for syntactic comprehension after left or right hemidecortication. *Brain and Language*, *10*, 287–317.

Dennis, M. (1981). Language in a congenitally acallosal brain. *Brain and Language*, *12*, 33–53.

Dennis, M. (1985). Intelligence scores after early brain injury: I. Predicting IQ scores from medical variables. *Journal of Clinical and Experimental Neuropsychology*, *7*, 526–554.

Dennis, M. (1989). Language and the young damaged brain. In T. Boll & B.K. Bryant (Eds.), *Clinical neuropsychology and brain function: Research, measurement and practice* (pp. 85–124). Washington: American Psychological Association.

Dennis, M. (1999). Childhood medical disorders and cognitive impairment: Biological risk, time, development, and reserve. In K. Yeates, D. Ris, & H. Taylor (Eds.), *Pediatric neuropsychology: Research, theory and practice* (pp. 3–22). New York: Guilford Press.

Dennis, M., & Barnes, M. (1990). Knowing the meaning, getting the point, bridging the gap, and carrying the message: Aspects of of discourse following closed head injury in childhood and adolescence. *Brain and Language*, *39*, 428–446.

Dennis, M., & Barnes, M.A. (1993). Oral discourse after early onset hydrocephalus: Linguistic ambiguity, figurative language, speech acts, and script-based inferences. *Journal of Pediatric Psychology*, *18*, 639–652.

Dennis, M., & Barnes, M. (1994a). Developmental aspects of neuropsychology: Childhood. In D.W. Zaidel (Ed.), *Neuropsychology* (pp. 221–246). New York: Academic Press.

Dennis, M., & Barnes, M.A. (1994b). Neuropsychologic function in same-sex twins discordant for perinatal brain damage. *Developmental and Behavioral Pediatrics*, *15*, 124–130.

Dennis, M., Barnes, M.A., Donnelly, R.E., Wilkinson, M., & Humphreys, R.P. (1996). Appraising and managing knowledge: Metacognitive skills after childhood head injury. *Developmental Neuropsychology*, *12*, 77–103.

Dennis, M., Fitz, C.R., Netley, C.T., Sugar, J., Harwood-Nash, C.F., Hendrick, E.B., Hoffman, H.J., & Humphreys, R.P. (1981). The intelligence of hydrocephalic children. *Archives of Neurology*, *38*, 607–661.

Dennis, M., Hendrick, E.B., Hoffman, H.J., & Humphreys, R.P. (1987). The language of hydrocephalic children. *Journal of Clinical and Experimental Neuropsychology*, *9*, 593–621.

Dennis, M., Jacennik, B., & Barnes, M. (1993). The content of narrative discourse in children and adolescents with early-onset hydrocephalus and in normally-developing peers. *Brain and Language*, *46*, 129–165.

Dennis, M., & Whitaker, H. (1976). Language acquisition following hemidecortication: Linguistic superiority of the left over the right hemisphere. *Brain and Language*, *3*, 404–433.

Dennis, M., Wilkinson, M., Koski, L., & Humphreys, R.P. (1995). Attention deficits in the long term after childhood head injury. In S. Broman & M.E. Michel (Eds.), *Traumatic head injury in children* (pp. 165–187). New York: Oxford University Press.

Denny, D.R., & Denny, N.W. (1973). The use of classification for problem solving: A comparison of middle and old age. *Developmental Psychology*, *9*, 275–278.

Deonna, T. (1996). Epilepsies with cognitive symptomatology. In S. Wallace (Ed.), *Epilepsy in children* (pp. 315–322). London: Chapman & Hall Medical.

Derksen-Lubsen, G., & Verkerk, P. (1996). Neuropsychologic development in early treated congenital hypothyroidism: Analysis of literature data. *Pediatric Research*, *39*, 561–574.

de Sonneville, L., Schmidt, E., Michel, U., & Batzler, U. (1990). Preliminary neuropsychological test results. *European Journal of Pediatrics*, *149*(Suppl. 1), 39–43.

de Sonneville, L., Schmidt, E., & Michel, U. (1989). Information processing in early-treated PKU. *Journal of Clinical and Experimental Neuropsychology, 11*, 362.

Devinsky, O. (1995). Cognitive and behavioural effects of antiepileptic drugs. *Epilepsia, 36*(Suppl. 2), S46–S65.

Devinsky, O., Perrine, K., Llinas, R., Luciano, D., & Dogali, M. (1993). Anterior temporal language areas in patients with early onset of temporal lobe epilepsy. *Annals of Neurology, 34*, 727–732.

DeVos, K., Wyllie, E., Geckler, C., Kotagal, P., & Comair, Y. (1995). Language dominance in patients with early childhood tumors near left hemisphere language areas. *Neurology, 45*, 349–356.

Di Simoni, F.G. (1978). *The Token Test for Children*. Boston: Teaching Resources.

Diabetes Control and Complications Trial Research Group (DCCT). (1994). A screening algorithm to identify clinically significant changes in neuropsychological functions in the Diabetes Control and Complications Trial. DCCT Research Group. *Journal of Clinical and Experimental Neuropsychology, 16*, 303–316.

Diamond, A. (1985). Development of the ability to use recall to guide action, as indicated by infants' performance on AB. *Child Development, 56*, 868–883.

Diamond, A. (1988). Differences between adult and infant cognition: Is the crucial variable presence or absence of language? In L. Weiskrantz (Ed.), *Thought without language* (pp. 337–370). New York: Oxford University Press.

Diamond, A. (1990). The development of neural bases of memory function as indexed by the AB and delayed response tasks in human infants and rhesus monkeys. In A. Diamond (Ed.), *The development of neural bases of higher cortical function* (pp. 267–317). New York: New York Academy of Science Press.

Diamond, A. (1994). Phenylalanine levels of 6–10 mg/dl may not be as benign as once thought. *Acta Paediatrica Suppl., 407*, 89–91.

Diamond, A. (1995). Evidence of robust recognition memory early in life even when assessed by reaching behaviour. *Journal of Experimental Child Psychology, 49*, 419–474.

Diamond, A., & Doar, B. (1989). The performance of human infants on a measure of frontal cortex function: The delayed response task. *Developmental Psychology, 22*, 271–294.

Diamond, A., & Goldman-Rakic, P. (1985). Evidence for involvement of prefrontal cortex in cognitive changes during the first year of life: Comparison of human infants and rhesus monkeys on a detour task with transparent barrier. *Neurosciences Abstracts (Pt. II), 11*, 832.

Diamond, A., & Goldman-Rakic, P. (1989). Comparison of human infants and rhesus monkeys on Piaget's AB task: Evidence for dependence on dorsolateral prefrontal cortex. *Experimental Brain Research, 74*, 24–40.

Diamond, A., & Herzberg, C. (1996). Impaired sensitivity to visual contrast in children treated early and continuously for phenylketonuria. *Brain, 119*, 523–538.

Dirks, J., & Neisser, U. (1977). Memory for objects in real scenes: The development of recognition and recall. *Journal of Experimental Child Psychology, 23*, 315–328.

Dise, J.E., & Lohr, M.E., (1998). Examination of deficits in conceptual reasoning abilities associated with spina bifida. *American Journal of Physical and Medical Rehabilitation, 77*, 247–251.

Dobyns, W., Andermann, F., Czasapansky-Beilman, D., Dabeau, F., Dulac, O., Guerrini, R., Hirsh, B., Ledbetter, D., Lee, N., Motte, J., Pinard, J.-M., Radtke, R., Ross, M., Tampiere, D., Walsh, C., & Truwit, C. (1996). X-linked malformations of neuronal migration. *Neurology, 47*, 331–339.

Dodrill, C.B. (1992a). Interictal cognitive aspects of epilepsy aspects of epilepsy. *Epilepsia, 33*(Suppl. 6), S7–S10.

Dodrill, C.B. (1992b). Problems in the assessment of cognitive effects of antiepileptic drugs. *Epilepsia, 33*(Suppl. 6), S29–S32.

Dodrill, C.B., & Clemmons, D. (1984). Use of neuropsychological tests to identify high school students with epilepsy who later demonstrate inadequate performances in life. *Journal of Consulting and Clinical Psychology, 52*, 520–527.

Dodrill, C.B., & Troupin, A.S. (1977). Psychotropic effects of carbamazepine in epilepsy: A double blind comparison with phenytoin. *Neurology, 27*, 1023–1028.

Dodrill, C.B., & Troupin, A.S. (1991). Neuropsychological effects of carbamazepine and phenytoin: A reanalysis. *Neurology, 41*, 141–143.

Donders, J. (1992). Premorbid behavioral and psychosocial adjustment of children with traumatic brain injury. *Journal of Abnormal Child Psychology, 20*, 233–246.

Donders, J. (1994). Academic placemnt after traumatic brain injury. *Journal of School Psychology, 32*, 53–65.

Donders, J., Canady, A., & Rourke, B. (1990). Psychometric intelligence after infantile hydrocephalus. *Child's Nervous System, 6*, 148–154.

Donders, J., Rourke, B., & Canady, A. (1991). Neuropsychological functioning of hydrocephalic children. *Journal of Clinical and Experimental Neuropsychology, 13*, 607–613.

Donders, J., Rourke, B., & Canady, A. (1992). Emotional adjustment of children with hydrocephalus and of their parents. *Journal of Child Neurology, 7*, 375–380.

Dorman, J., O'Leary, L., & Koehler, A. (1995). Epidemiology of childhood diabetes. In C. Kelnar (Ed.), *Childhood and adolescent diabetes* (Vol. 1, pp. 139–159). London: Chapman & Hall.

Duchowny, M. (1996). Identification of surgical candidates and timing of operation: An overview. In E. Wyllie (Ed.), *The treatment of epilepsy: Principles and practice* (2nd ed., pp. 967–975). Baltimore: Williams & Wilkins.

Duchowny, M., & Harvey, A.S. (1996). Pediatric epilepsy syndromes: An update and critical review. *Epilepsia, 37*(Suppl. 1), S26–S40.

Duchowny, M., Jaakar, P., Resnick, T., Harvey, A.S., Alvarez, L. Dean, P., Gilman, J., Yaylali, I., Morrison, G., Prats, A., Altman, N., Birchanaky, S., & Bruce, J. (1998). Epilepsy surgery in the first three years of life. *Epilepsia, 39*(7), 737–743.

Duchowny, M., Jayakar, P., Harvey, A.S., Altman, N., Resnick, T., & Levin, B. (1996). Language cortex representation: Effects of developmental versus acquired pathology. *Annals of Neurology, 40*, 91–98.

Duckrow, R., Beard, D., & Brennan, R. (1987). Regional cerebral blood flow decreases during chronic and acute hyperglycemia. *Stroke, 18*, 52–58.

Dulac, O., & Kaminska, A. (1997). Use of lamotrogine in Lennox Gastaux and related epilepsy syndromes. *Journal of Child Neurology, 12*(Suppl. 1), 523–528.

Dulac, O., Plouin, P., & Jambaque, I. (1993). Predicting favourable outcome in ideopathic West syndrome. *Epilepsia, 34*, 747–756.

Duncan, C. (1988). Application of event-related brain potentials to the analysis of interictal attention in absence epilepsy. In M. Myslobodsky & A. Mirsky (Eds.), *Elements of petit mal epilepsy* (pp. 341–364). New York: Peter Lang.

Duncan, J. (1986). Disorganization of behavior after frontal lobe damage. *Cognitive Neuropsychology, 3*, 271–290.

Dunn, D.W., Austin, J.K., & Huster, G.A. (1997). Behaviour problems in children with new-onset epilepsy. *Seizure, 6*, 283–287.

Dunn, L.M., & Dunn, L.M. (1981). *Peabody Picture Vocabulary Test—Revised.* Circle Pines, MN: American Guidance Service.

Earnest, M.P., Goolishian, H.A., Calverlay, J.R., Hayes, R.O., & Hill, R. (1971). Neurologic, intellectual, and psychologic sequelae following western encephalitis: A follow-up study of 35 cases. *Neurology, 21*, 969–974.

Eckenhoff, M., & Rakic, P. (1991). A quantitative analysis of synaptogenesis in the molecular layer of the dentate gyrus in the rhesus monkey. *Developmental Brain Research, 564*, 129–135.

Gastaut, H. (1973). *Dictionary of epilepsy: Part 1. Definitions.* Geneva: World Health Organization.

Gazzaniga, M. (Ed.). (1995). *The cognitive neurosciences.* Cambridge, MA: MIT Press.

Genton, P., Bureau, M., Dravet, C., & Roger, J. (1996). Less common epileptic syndromes. In E. Wyllie (Ed.), *The treatment of epilepsy: Principles and practice* (pp. 584–591). Baltimore: Williams & Wilkins.

Genton, P., & Guerrini, R. (1993). What differentiates Landau Kleffner syndrome from the syndrome of continuous spikes and waves during slow sleep (letter)? *Archives of Neurology, 50,* 1008–1009.

Gentry, L., Godersky, J., & Thompson, B. (1988). MR imaging of head trauma: Review of the distribution and radiographic features of traumatic lesions. *Archives of Neurology, 44,* 194–198.

Geschwind, N., & Galaburda, A. (1985). Cerebral lateralisation: Biological mechanisms, associations and pathology: I. A hypothesis and a program for research. *Archives of Neurology, 42,* 521–552.

Geschwind, N., & Levitsky, W. (1968). Human brain: Left-right asymmetries in temporal speech region. *Science, 161,* 186–187.

Gioa, G., Isquith, P., Hoffhines, V., & Guy, S. (1999). Examining the clinical utility of the Behavioral Rating Inventory of Executive Functions. *Journal of the International Neuropsychological Society, 5,* 117.

Gibson, K.R. (1991). Myelination and behavioral development: A comparative perspective on questions of neoteny, altriciality, and intelligence. In K.R. Gibson & A.C. Petersen (Eds.), *Brain maturation and cognitive development: Comparative and cross-cultural perspectives* (pp. 29–64). New York: Aldine De Gruter.

Giedd, J., Castellanos, F., Rajapaske, J., Vaituzis, A., & Rapaport, J. (1997). Sexual dimorphism in the developing human brain. *Progress in Neuro-psychopharmacology and Biological Psychiatry, 21,* 1185–1201.

Giedd, J., Snell, J., Lange, N., Rajapaske, J., Casey, B., Kozuch, P., et al. (1996). Quantitative magnetic resonance imaging of human brain development: Ages 4–18. *Cerebral Cortex, 6,* 551–560.

Giffin, F.D., Clarke, J.T., & d'Entremont, D.M. (1980). Effect of dietary phenylalanine restriction on visual attention span in mentally retarded subjects with phenylketonuria. *Canadian Journal of Neurological Sciences, 7,* 127–131.

Gillberg, C. (1995). *Clinical child neuropsychiatry.* Cambridge, UK: Cambridge University Press.

Gillberg, C., & Hagberg, B. (1998). Neurometabolic disease. In C. Coffey & R. Brumback (Eds.), *Textbook of pediatric neuropsychiatry* (pp. 913–938). Washington: Blackwell Science.

Giordani, B., Berent, S., Sackellares, C., Rourke, D., Seidenberg, M., O'Leary, D.S., Dreifuss, F.E., & Boll, T.J. (1985). Intelligence test performance of patients with partial and generalised seizures. *Epilepsia, 26*(1), 37–42.

Glauser, T. (1997). Preliminary observations on topiramate in pediatric epilepsies. *Epilepsia, 38*(Suppl. 1), S37–S41.

Glorieux, G., Dussault, J., & Van Vliet, G. (1992). Intellectual development at 12 years of children with congenital hypothyroidism diagnosed by neo-natal screening. *Journal of Pediatrics, 121,* 581–584.

Glorieux, J., Dussault, M.D., Letarte, J., Guyda, H., & Morissette, J. (1983). Preliminary results on the mental development of hypothyroid infants detected by the Quebec Screening Progam. *Journal of Pediatrics, 102,* 19–22.

Glorieux, J., Dussault, M.D., Morissette, J., Desjardins, M., Letarte, J., & Guyda, M.D. (1985). Follow-up at ages 5 and 7 years on mental development in children with hypothyroidism detected by Quebec Screening Program. *Journal of Pediatrics, 107,* 913–918.

Glosser, G., Cole, L.C., French, J.A., Saykin, A.J., & Sperling, M.R. (1997). Predictors of intellectual performance in adults with intractable temporal lobe epilepsy. *Journal of the International Neuropsychological Society*, *3*, 252–259.

Glosser, G., & Goodglass, H. (1990). Disorders in executive control functions among aphasic and other brain-damaged patients. *Journal of Clinical and Experimental Neuropsychology*, *12*(4), 485–501.

Goldberg, D. (1978). *Manual of the General Health Questionnaire*. Windsor: Nfer-Nelson.

Goldberg, E., & Costa, L. (1981). Hemisphere differences in the acquisition and use of descriptive systems. *Brain and Language*, *14*, 144–173.

Golden, C.J. (1978). *Stroop Color and Word Test*. Chicago, IL: Stoelting.

Golden, C.J. (1981). The Luria–Nebraska Children's Battery: Theory and formulation. In G.W. Hynd & J.E. Obrzut (Eds.), *Neuropsychological assessment of the school-aged child* (pp. 277–302). New York: Grune & Stratton.

Golden, M.P., Ingersoll, G.M., Brack, C.J., Russell, B.A., Wright, J.C., & Huberty, T.J. (1989). Longitudinal relationship of asymptomatic hypoglycemia to cognitive function in IDDM. *Diabetes Care*, *12*, 89–93.

Goldman-Rakic, P.S. (1986). Circuitry of the frontal cortex and the regulation of behavior by representational knowledge. In F. Plum & V. Mountcastle (Eds.), *Handbook of physiology—revised* (pp. 373–417). Bethesda, MD: American Physiological Society.

Goldman-Rakic, P.S. (1987). Development of cortical circuitry and cognitive function. *Child Development*, *58*, 601–622.

Goldman-Rakic, P.S., Bourgeois, J., & Rakic, P. (1997). Synaptic substrate of cognitive development: Life-span analysis of synaptogenesis in the prefrontal cortex of the nonhuman primate. In N. Krasnegor, G. Lyon, & P.S. Goldman-Rakic (Eds.), *Development of the prefrontal cortex: Evolution, neurology, and behaviour* (pp. 9–26). Baltimore: Brookes.

Goldstein, F.C., & Levin, H.S. (1985). Intellectual and academic outcome in children and adolescents: Research and empirical findings. *Developmental Neuropsychology*, *1*, 195–214.

Goldstein, F.C., & Levin, H.S. (1987). Epidemiology of pediatric closed head injury: Incidence, clinical characteristics and risk factors. *Journal of Learning Disabilities*, *20*, 518–525.

Goldstein, L.H. (1997). Effectiveness of psychological interventions for people with poorly controlled epilepsy. *Journal of Neurology, Neurosurgery and Psychiatry*, *63*, 137–142.

Gordon, B., Selnes, O.A., Hart, J., Hanley, D.F., & Whitly, R.J. (1990). Long-term cognitive sequelae of acyclovir-treated herpes simplex encephalitis. *Archives of Neurology*, *47*, 646–647.

Gordon, E. (1994). Brain imaging measures in cognition: An emerging multidisciplinary field. In S. Touyz, D. Byrne, & A. Gialandis (Eds.), *Neuropsychology in clinical practice* (pp. 61–78). Sydney: Academic Press.

Goswami, U. (1998). *Cognition in children*. Hove, UK: Psychology Press.

Gottschalk, B., Richman, R.A., & Lewandowski, L. (1994). Subtle speech and motor deficits of children with congenital hypothyroidism treated early. *Developmental Medicine and Child Neurology*, *36*, 216–220.

Gourovitch, M.L., Craft, S., Dowton, S.B., Ambrose, P., & Sparta, S. (1994). Interhemispheric transfer in children with early-treated phenylketonuria. *Journal of Clinical and Experimental Psychology*, *16*, 393–404.

Graham, D., Ford, I, Adams, J., Doyle, D., Lawrence, A., McLellan, D., & Ng, H. (1989). Fatal head injury in children. *Clinical Pathology*, *42*, 18.

Greenough, W., Black, J., & Wallace, C. (1987). Experience and brain development. *Child Development*, *58*, 539–559.

Greenough, W., Juraska, J., & Volkmar, R. (1979). Maze training effects on dendritic branching of neurons in the rat motor-sensory forelimb cortex. *Behavioral and Neural Biology*, *44*, 301–314.

Greenspan, A., & MacKenzie, E. (1994). Functional outcome after pediatric head injury. *Pediatrics*, *94*, 425–432.

Griffiths, P., Paterson, L., & Harvie, A. (1995). Neuropsychological effects of subsequent exposure to phenylalanine in adolescents and young adults with early-treated phenylketonuria. *Journal of Intellectual Disability Research*, *39*, 365–372.

Grimwood, K., Anderson, P., Anderson, V.A., Nolan, T., & Tan, L. (2000). Twelve-year outcomes following bacterial meningitis: Further evidence for persisting effects. *Archives of Disease in Childhood*, *83*, 111–116.

Grimwood, K., Anderson, V.A., Bond, L., Catroppa, C., Hore, R.L., & Keir, E.H. (1995). Adverse outcomes of bacterial meningitis in school-age survivors. *Pediatrics*, *95*, 646–656.

Grimwood, K., Nolan, T., Bond, L., Anderson, V., Catroppa, C., & Keir, E. (1996). Risk factors for advers outcomes of bacterial meningitis. *Journal of Pediatric Child Health*, *32*, 457–462.

Grishaw, W., West, H., & Smith, B. (1939). Juvenile diabetes mellitus. *Archives of Internal Medicine*, *64*, 787–799.

Groher, M. (1977). Language and memory disorders after closed head injury. *Journal of Speech and Hearing Research*, *20*, 212–230.

Gronwall, D. (1977). Paced auditory serial-addition task: A measure of recovery from concussion. *Perceptual and Motor Skills*, *44*, 367–373.

Gronwall, D., Wrightson, P., & McGinn, V. (1997). Effects of mild head injury during the preschool years. *Journal of the International Neuropsychological Society*, *6*, 592–597.

Gross, P.T., Berlow, S., Schuett, V.E., & Fariello, R. (1981). EEG in phenylketonuria: Attempt to establish clinical importance of EEG changes. *Archives of Neurology*, *38*, 122–126.

Gruneberg, F., & Pond, D.A. (1957). Conduct disorders in epileptic children. *Journal of Neurology, Neurosurgery and Psychiatry*, *20*, 65–68.

Gulbrandsen, G.B. (1984). Neuropsychological sequelae of light head injury in older children six months after trauma. *Journal of Clinical Neuropsychology*, *6*, 257–268.

Hagberg, B. (1962). The sequelae of spontaneously arrested hydrocephalus. *Developmental Medicine and Child Neurology*, *4*, 583–587.

Hagen, J.W., Barclay, C.R., Anderson, B.J., Feeman, D.J., Segal, S., Bacon, G., & Goldstein, G.W. (1990). Intellective functioning and strategy use in children with insulin-dependent diabetes mellitus. *Child Development*, *61*, 1714–1727.

Hale, S. (1989). A global developmental trend in cognitive processing speed. *Child Development*, *61*, 653–663.

Hale, S., Bronik, M.D., & Fry, A.F. (1997). Verbal and spatial working memory in school-age children: Developmental differences in susceptibility to interference. *Developmental Psychology*, *33*, 364–371.

Hallett, T., & Proctor, A. (1996). Maturation of the central nervous system as related to communication and cognitive development. *Infants and Young Children*, *8*, 1–15.

Halperin, J.M. (1992). The clinical assessment of attention. *International Journal of Neuroscience*, *58*, 171–182.

Halperin, J.M., Healey, J.M., Zeitchik, E., Ludman, W.L., & Weinstein, L. (1989). Developmental aspects of linguistic and mnestic abilities in normal children. *Journal of Clinical and Experimental Neuropsychology*, *11*, 518–528.

Halstead, W. (1947). *Brain and intelligence*. Chicago: University of Chicago Press.

Hanlon, H., Thatcher, R., & Cline, M. (1999). Gender differences in the development of EEG coherence in normal children. *Developmental Neuropsychology*, *16*, 479–506.

Hanson, C.L., Hengeller, S.W., & Burghen, G.A. (1987). Model of associations between psychosocial variables and health-outcome measures of adolescents with IDDM. *Diabetes Care*, *10*, 313–318.

Hanson, C.L., Hengeller, S.W., Harris, M.A., Burghen, G.A., & Moore, M. (1989). Family system variables and the health status of adolescents with insulin-dependent diabetes mellitus. *Health Psychology, 8*, 239–253.

Hara, H. (1989). Sustained attention in mentally normal children with convulsive disorders. In J. Susuki, M. Seino, Y. Fukuyama, & S. Komai (Eds.), *Art and science of epilepsy* (pp. 123–126). Amsterdam: Elsevier Science.

Harik, S., & LaManna, J. (1988). Vascular perfusion and blood–brain glucose transport in acute and chronic hyperglycemia. *Journal of Neurochemistry, 51*, 1924–1929.

Haritou, F., Ong, K., Morse, S., Anderson, V., Catroppa, C., Rosenfeld, J., Klug, G., & Bucolo, C. (1997). A syntactic and pragmatic analysis of the conversational speech of young head injured children. In J. Ponsford, P. Snow, & V. Anderson. (Eds.), *International perspective in traumatic brain injury* (pp. 187–190). Melbourne: Academic Press.

Harris, E., Schuerholz, L., Singer, H., Reader, M., Brown, J., Cox, C., Mohr, J., Chase, G., & Denckla, M. (1995). Executive function in children with Tourette's syndrome and/or attention deficit hyperactivity disorder. *Journal of the International Neuropsychological Society, 1*, 511–516.

Harvey, A.S. (1999). The role of febrile convulsions in mesial temporal sclerosis. In H. Lüders & P. Kotagal (Eds.), *The epilepsies: Etiologies and prevention* (pp. 125–131). New York: Academic Press.

Harvey, A.S., Anderson, V., Kean, M., Anderson, D., Abbot, D., Saling, M., & Jackson, G. (1997). Functional MRI of language cortex in children with brain lesions. In G. Jackson, M. Saling, & S. Berkovic (Eds.), *Proceedings: Third annual epilepsy retreat: Neuropsychology and neuroimaging*. Marysville, Australia.

Harvey, A.S., Berkovic, S.F., Wrennall, J.A., & Hopkins, I.J. (1997). Temporal lobe epilepsy in childhood: Clinical, EEG, and neuroimaging findings and syndrome classification in a cohort with new-onset seizures. *Neurology, 49*, 960–968.

Harvey, A.S., Scheffer, I., Hayllar, S., Leventer, R., Jackson, G., & Berkovic, S.F. (1998). Genetic and acquired factors in the aetiology of cortical malformations. In S.F. Berkovic & G.D. Jackson (Eds.), *Proceedings: Fourth annual epilepsy retreat*. Marysville, Australia.

Haumont, D., Dorchy, H., & Pelc, S. (1979). EEG abnormalities in diabetic children. *Clinical Pediatrics, 18*, 750–753.

Hauser, E., Strohmayer, C., Seidl, R., Birnbacher, R., Lischka, A., & Schober, E. (1995). Quantitative EEG in young diabetics. *Journal of Child Neurology, 10*, 330–334.

Hauser, P., Zametkin, A.J., Martinez, P., Vitielo, B., Matochick, J., Mixson, J., & Weintraub, B. (1993). Attention deficit–hyperactivity disorder in people with generalised resistance to thyroid hormone. *New England Journal of Medicine, 328*, 997–1001.

Hayes, H.R., & Jackson, R.H. (1989). The incidence and prevention of head injuries. In D.A. Johnson, D. Uttley, & M.A. Wyke (Eds.), *Children's head injury: Who cares?* (pp. 183–193). London: Taylor & Francis.

Heaton, R.K. (1981). *Wisconsin Card Sorting Test (WCST)*. Odessa, FL: Psychological Assessment Resources.

Hebb, D.O. (1942). The effects of early and late injury upon test scores, and the nature of normal adult intelligence. *Proceedings of the American Philosophical Society, 85*, 275–292.

Hebb, D.O. (1949). *The organization of behaviour*. New York: McGraw-Hill.

Hecaen, H. (1976). Acquired aphasia in children and the ontogenesis of hemispheric functional specialization. *Brain and Language, 3*, 114–134.

Heilman, K., Voeller, K., & Nadeau, S. (1991). A possible pathophysiologic substrate of attention deficit hyperactivity disorder. *Journal of Child Neurology, 6*(Suppl.), 76–81.

Heiss, W., Kessler, J., Thiel, A., Ghaemi, M., & Karbe, H. (1999). Differential capacity of left and right hemispheric areas for compensation of poststroke aphasia. *Annals of Neurology, 45*, 430–438.

Hendy, J., & Anderson, V. (1994). Development, pathology and the frontal lobes. *Journal of the International Neuropsychological Society*, *1*, 199.

Henry, L.A., & Millar, S. (1993). Why does memory span improve with age: A review of the evidence for two current hypotheses. *European Journal of Cognitive Psychology*, *5*, 241–287.

Hermann, B.P. (1982). Neuropsychological functioning and psychopathology in children with epilepsy. *Epilepsia*, *23*, 545–554.

Hermann, B.P., Seidenberg, M., Haltiner, A., & Wyler, A.R. (1992). Adequacy of language function and verbal memory performance in unilateral temporal lobe epilepsy. *Cortex*, *28*, 423–433.

Hermann, B.P., Seidenberg, M., Haltiner, A., & Wyler, A.R. (1995). Relationship of age of onset, chronological age and adequacy of postoperative performance to verbal memory change after anterior temporal lobectomy. *Epilepsia*, *36*, 137–145.

Hermann, B.P., Seidenberg, M., Schoenfield, J., & Davies, K. (1997). Neuropsychological characteristics of the syndrome of mesial temporal lobe epilepsy. *Archives of Neurology*, *54*, 369–376.

Hermann, B.P., & Whitman, S. (1984). Behavioural and personality correlates of epilepsy: A review, methodological critique and conceptual model. *Psychological Bulletin*, *95*, 451–497.

Hermann, B.P., & Whitman, S. (1986). Psychopathology in epilepsy: A multietiologic model. In B.P. Hermann & S. Whitman (Eds.), *Psychopathology in epilepsy: Social dimensions* (pp. 5–37). New York: Oxford University Press.

Hermann, B.P., Whitman, S., & Dell, J. (1989). Correlates of behaviour problems and social competence in children with epilepsy, aged 6–11. In B.P. Hermann & M. Seidenberg (Eds.), *Childhood epilepsies: Neuropsychological, psychosocial and intervention aspects* (pp. 143–157). Chichester, UK: Wiley.

Hermann, B.P., Whitman, S., Hughes, J.R., Melyn, M.M., & Dell, J. (1988). Multietiological determinants of psychopathology and social competence in children with epilepsy. *Epilepsy Research*, *2*, 51–60.

Hershey, T., Craft, S., Bhargava, N., & White, N. (1997). Memory and insulin dependent diabetes mellitus (IDDM): Effects of chidhood onset and severe hypoglycemia. *Journal of the International Neuropsychological Society*, *3*, 509–520

Hertz-Pannier, L., Gaillard, W., Mott, S., Cuenod, C., Bookheimer, S., Weinstein, S., et al. (1997). Noninvasive assessment of language dominance in children and adolescents with functional MRI. *Neurology*, *48*, 1003–1012.

Heyerdahl, S., Kase, B.F., & Lie, S.O. (1991). Intellectual development in children with congenital hypothyroidism in relation to recommended thyroxine treatment. *Journal of Pediatrics*, *118*, 850–857.

Heywood, C.A., & Canavan, A. (1987). Developmental neuopsychological correlates of language. In W. Yule & M. Rutter (Eds.), *Language development and disorders* (Clinics in developmental medicine No. 101–102, pp. 146–158). London: MacKeith/Blackwell.

Hoare, P. (1984). The development of psychiatric disorder among schoolchildren with epilepsy. *Developmental Medicine and Child Neurology*, *26*, 3–13.

Hoare, P., & Curley, S. (1991). Psychosocial adjustment of children with chronic epilepsy and their families. *Developmental Medicine and Child Neurology*, *33*, 201–215.

Hoffman, R.G. (1981). Selective cognitive deficits in myelomeningocele children. *Dissertation Abstracts International*, *41*, 4264B.

Hoffman, R.G., Speelman, D.J., Hinnen, D.A., Conley, K.L., Guthrie, R.A., & Knapp, R.K. (1989). Changes in cortical functioning with acute hypoglycemia and hyperglycemia in Type 1 diabetes. *Diabetes Care*, *6*, 180–185.

Hokkanen, L., Pontiainen, E., Valanne, L., Saknen, O., Iivanainen, H., & Launes, T. (1996). Cognitive impairment after acute encephalitis: Comparion of herpes simplex and other aetiologies. *Journal of Neurology, Neurosurgery, and Psychiatry*, *61*, 478–484.

Holdsworth, L., & Whitmore, K. (1974). A study of children with epilepsy attending ordinary schools: 1. Seizure patterns, progress and behaviour in schools. *Developmental Medicine and Child Neurology, 16*, 746–758.

Holland, B., Haas, D., Brant-Zawadski, M., & Newton, T. (1986). MRI of normal brain maturation. *American Journal of Neuroradiology, 7*, 201–208.

Holler, K.A., Fennell, E.B., Crosson, B., Boggs, S.R., & Mickle, J.P. (1995). Neuropsychological and adaptive functioning in younger versus older children shunted for early hydrocephalus. *Child Neuropsychology, 1*, 63–73.

Holloway, M., Bye, A., & Moran, K. (1994). Non-accidental head injury in children. *Medical Journal of Australia, 160*, 786–789.

Holmes, C.S. (1990). Neuropsychological sequelae of acute and chronic blood glucose disruption in adults with insulin-dependent diabetes. In C.S. Holmes (Ed.), *Neuropsychological and behavioural aspects of diabetes* (pp. 122–154). New York: Springer.

Holmes, C.S., Dunlap, W.P., Chen, R.S., & Cornwell, J.M. (1992). Gender differences in the learning status of diabetic children. *Journal of Consulting and Clinical Psychology, 60*, 698–704.

Holmes, C.S., Koepke, K.M., & Thompson, R.G. (1986). Simple versus complex performance impairments at three blood glucose levels. *Psychoneuroendocrinology, 11*, 353–357.

Holmes, C.S., & Richman, L.C. (1985). Cognitive profiles of children with insulin-dependent diabetes. *Journal of Developmental and Behavioral Pediatrics, 6*, 323–326.

Holmes, G.L. (1997). Epilepsy in the developing brain: Lessons from the laboratory and clinic. *Epilepsia, 38*(1), 12–30.

Holmes, M.D., Dodrill, C.B., Wilkus, R.J. Ojemann, L.M., & Ojemann, G.A. (1998). Is partial epilepsy progressive? Ten-year follow-up of EEG and neuropsychological changes in adults with partial seizures. *Epilepsia, 39*(11), 1189–1193.

Holmes-Bernstein, J. (1999). Developmental neuropsychological assessment. In K.O. Yeates, M.D. Ris, & H.G. Taylor (Eds.), *Pediatric neuropsychology: Research, theory and practice* (pp. 405–438). New York: Guilford Press.

Holmes-Bernstein, J., & Waber, D.P. (1990). Developmental neuropsychological assessment: The systemic approach. In A.A. Boulton, G.B. Baker, & M. Hiscock (Eds.), *Neuromethods: Vol. 17. Neuropsychology* (pp. 311–371). Clifton, NJ: Humana Press.

Holtzman, N.A., Kronmal, R.A., Van Doorninck, W., Azen, C., & Koch, R. (1986). Effect of age at loss of dietary control on intellectual performance and behavior of children with phenylketonuria. *New England Journal of Medicine, 314*, 593–598.

Honavar, M., Janota, I., & Polkey, C.E. (1992). Rasmussen's encephalitis in surgery for epilepsy. *Developmental Medicine and Child Neurology, 34*, 3–14.

Hooper, H. (1983). *Hooper Visual Organization Test Manual*. Los Angeles: Psychological Services.

Horn, D.G., Lorch, E.P., Lorch, R.F., & Culatta, B. (1985). Distractibility and vocabulary deficits in children with spina bifida and hydrocephalus. *Developmental Medicine and Child Neurology, 27*, 713–720.

Horowitz, I., Costeff, H., Sadan, N., Abraham, E., Geyer, S., & Najenson, T. (1983). Childhood head injuries in Israel: Epidemiology and outcome. *International Rehabilitation Medicine, 5*, 32–36.

Horowitz, S.J., Boxerbaum, B., & O'Bell, J. (1980). Cerebral herniation in bacterial meningitis in childhood. *Annals of Neurology, 7*, 534–528.

Hough, B., Wysocki, T., & Linscheid, T. (1994). Intellectual, behavioral and social-cognitive sequelae of severe hypoglycemia in early childhood, middle childhood and adolescence. *Diabetes, 43*(Suppl.), 129A.

House, E., Pansky, B., & Siegel, A. (1979). *A systematic approach to neuroscience*. New York: McGraw-Hill.

Hoving, K., Spencer, T., Robb, K., & Schulte D. (1978). Developmental changes in visual information processing. In P.A. Ornstein (Ed.), *Memory development in children*, Hillsdale, NJ: Lawrence Erlbaum Associates Inc.

Howard, L., & Polich, J. (1985). P300 latency and memory span development. *Developmental Psychology, 21*, 283–289.

Hrachovy, R., Glaze, D., & Frost, J. (1991). A retrospective study of spontaneous remission and long-term outcome in patients with infantile spasms. *Epilepsia, 32*, 212–214.

Huberty, T.J., Austin, J.K., Risinger, M.W., & McNelis, A.M. (1992). Relationship between selected seizure variables in children with epilepsy to performance on school-administered achievement tests. *Journal of Epilepsy, 5*, 10–16.

Hudspeth, W., & Pribram, K. (1990). Stages of brain and cognitive maturation. *Journal of Educational Psychology, 82*, 881–884.

Hulme, C., Thomson, N., Muir, C., & Lawrence, A. (1984). Speech rate and the development of short-term memory span. *Journal of Experimental Child Psychology, 38*, 241–253.

Hunt, G., & Holmes, A. (1976). Factors relating to intelligence in treated cases of spina bifida cystica. *American Journal of Diseases of Children, 130*, 823–827.

Hurley, A., Laatsch, L., & Dorman, C. (1983). Comparison of spina bifida hydrocephalic patients and matched controls on neuropsychological tests. *Zeitschrift für Kinderchirurgie, 38*(Suppl. 2), 116–118.

Huttenlocher, P.R. (1974). Dendritic development in neocortex of children with mental defect and infantile spasm. *Neurology, 24*, 203–210.

Huttenlocher, P.R. (1979). Synaptic density in human frontal cortex: Developmental changes and effects of aging. *Brain Research, Amsterdam, 163*, 195–205.

Huttenlocher, P.R. (1990). Morphometric study of human cerebral cortex development. *Neuropsychologia, 28*, 517–527.

Huttenlocher, P.R. (1994). Synaptogenesis in human cerebral cortex. In G. Dawson & K. Fischer (Eds.), *Human behaviour and the developing brain* (pp. 137–152). New York: Guilford Press.

Huttenlocher, P.R. (1996). Morphometric study of human cerebral cortex development. In M. Johnson (Ed.), *Brain development and cognition: A reader* (pp. 112–124). Cambridge, MA: Blackwell.

Huttenlocher, P.R., & Dabholkar, A. (1997). Developmental anatomy of prefrontal cortex. In N. Krasnegor, G. Lyon, & P.S. Goldman-Rakic (Eds.), *Development of the prefrontal cortex: Evolution, neurology, and behaviour* (pp. 69–84). Baltimore: Brookes.

Huttenlocher, P.R., & de Courten, C. (1987). The development of synapses in striate cortex of man. *Human Neurobiology, 6*, 1–9.

Huttenlocher, P.R., de Courten, C., Garey, L., & Van der Loos, H. (1982). Synaptogenesis in human cerebral cortex: Evidence for synapse elimination during normal development. *Neuroscience Letters, 33*, 247–252.

Hynd, G.W., Snow, J., & Becker, M.G. (1986). Neuropsychological assessment in clinical child psychology. In B.B. Lahey & A.E. Kazden (Eds.), *Advances in clinical child psychology* (Vol. 9, pp. 35–86). New York: Plenum Press.

Hynd, G.W., & Willis, W.G. (1988) *Pediatric neuropsychology*. New York: Grune & Stratton.

Ianetti, P., Ranucci, U., Basile, L., Spalice, A., DiBiasi, C., Trasimen, G., & Gualdi, G. (1993). Neuronal migration disorders: Diffuse cortical dysplasia or the "double cortex" syndrome. *Acta Paediatrie, 82*, 501–503.

Ilicki, A., & Larsson, A. (1991). Psychological development at 7 years of age in children with congenital hypothyroidism: Timing and dosage of initial treatment. *Acta Paediatrica Scandinavia, 80*, 199–204.

Jacobs, B., & Scheibel, A. (1993). A quantitative dendritic analysis of Wernicke's area in humans: I. Life-span changes. *Journal of Comparative Neurology, 327*, 97–111.

Jacobs, R., Anderson, V., & Harvey, S. (1997). Concept generation and temporal judgement as measures of executive function in children: Examination of developmental trends. *Journal of the International Neuropsychological Society*, *3*, 212.

Jacobs, R., Anderson, V., & Harvey, S. (1998). *Executive functions in children with focal frontal brain injuries*. Paper presented at the Australian annual meeting of the College of Clinical Neuropsychologists, Lorne.

Jacobs, R., Anderson, V., & Harvey, A.S. (in press) When one is simple enough: Neuropsychological profile of a girl with double cortex. *Developmental Medicine and Child Neurology*.

Jacobs, R., Northam, E., & Anderson, V. (in press). Cognitive outcome in children with myelomeningocele and perinatal hydrocephalus: A longitudinal perspective. *Journal of Physical and Developmental Disabilities*.

Jadavji, T., Biggar, W.D., Gold, R., & Prober, C.G. (1986). Sequelae of acute bacterial meningitis in children treated for seven days. *Pediatrics*, *78*, 21–25.

Jaffe, K.M., Fay, G.C., Polissar, N.L., Martin, K.M., Shurtlef, H.A., Rivara, J.B., & Winn, R. (1992). Severity of pediatric traumatic brain injury and neurobehavioral outcome: A cohort study. *Archives of Physical Medicine and Rehabilitation*, *73*, 540–547.

Jaffe, K.M., Fay, G.C., Polissar, N.L., Martin, K.M., Shurtlef, H.A., Rivara, J.B., & Winn, R. (1993). Severity of pediatric traumatic brain injury and neurobehavioral recovery at one year: A cohort study. *Archives of Physical Medicine and Rehabilitation*, *74*, 587–595.

Jaffe, K.M., Polissar, N.L., Fay, G.C., & Liao, S. (1995). Recovery trends over three years following pediatric traumatic brain injury. *Archives of Physical Medicine and Rehabilitation*, *76*, 17–26.

Jambaquè, I., Dellatolas, G., Dulac, O., Ponsot, G., & Signoret, J.-L. (1993). Verbal and visual memory impairment in children with epilepsy. *Neuropsychologia*, *31*(12), 1321–1337.

Jannoun, L.. & Chessels, J.M. (1987). Long-term psychological effects of childhood leukemia and its treatment. *Pediatrc Hematology and Oncology*, *4*, 293–308.

Jastak, S., & Wilkinson, G. (1994). *Wide Range Achievement Test—Third version*. Wilmington, DE: Jastak.

Jennett, B. (1976). Assessment of the severity of head injury. *Journal of Neurology, Neurosurgery, and Psychiatry*, *39*, 647–655.

Jennett, B. (1979). Post-traumatic epilepsy. *Advances in Neurology*, *22*, 137–147.

Jennett, B., Teasdale, G., Galbraith, S., Pickard, J., Grant, H., Braakman, R., Avezaat, C., Maas, A., Minderhoud, J., Vecht, C., Heiden, J., Small, R., Caton, W., & Kurtz, T. (1977). Severe head injuries in three countries. *Journal of Neurology, Neurosurgery, and Psychiatry*, *40*, 291–298.

Jensen, P.B. (1987). Psychological aspects of myelomeningocele: A longitudinal study. *Scandanavian Journal of Psychology*, *28*, 313–321.

Jernigan, T.L., & Tallal, P. (1990). Late childhood changes in brain morphology observable with MRI. *Developmental Medicine and Child Neurology*, *32*, 379–385.

Jernigan, T.L., Trauner, D.A., Hesselink, J.R., & Tallal, P.A. (1991). Maturation of human cerebrum observed in vivo during adolescence. *Brain*, *114*, 2037–2049.

Johnson, D. (1992). Head injured children and education: A need for greater delineation and understanding. *British Journal of Educational Psychology*, *62*, 404–409.

Johnson, M. (Ed.). (1996). *Brain development and cognition: A reader*. Oxford, UK: Blackwell.

Johnson, M. (1997). *Developmental cognitive neuroscience*. Oxford, UK: Blackwell.

Johnson, S. (1995). Insulin-dependent diabetes mellitus in childhood. In M. Roberts (Ed.), *Handbook of pediatric psychology* (2nd ed., pp. 263–285). New York: Guilford Press.

Kail, R. (1986). Sources of age differences in speed of processing. *Child Development*, *57*, 969–987.

Kail, R. (1988). Developmental processes for speeds of cognitive processes. *Journal of Experimental Child Psychology*, *45*, 339–364.

Kandel, E. (1985). Cellular mechanisms of learning and the biological basis of individuality. In E. Kandel & J.H. Schwartz (Eds.), *Principles of neural science* (2nd ed., pp. 816–844). New York: Elsevier.

Kandel, E., Schwartz, T., & Jessell, T. (1991). *Principles of neural science* (3rd ed.). New York: Elsevier.

Kanner, L. (1960). Do behavioral symptoms always indicate psychopathology? *Journal of Child Psychology and Psychiatry, 1,* 17–25.

Kaplan, E. (1989). A process approach to neuropsychological assessment. In T. Boll & B. Bryant (Eds.), *Clinical neuropsychology and brain function: Research, measurement and practice.* Washington: Amerian Psychological Association.

Kaplan, E., Fein, D., Morris, R., & Delis, D. (1991). *WAIS-R as a neuropsychological instrument.* San Antonio, TX: Psychological Corporation.

Kaplan, E., Goodglass, H., & Weintraub, S. (1983). *The Boston Naming Test.* Philadelphia: Lea & Febiger.

Kapur, N., Barker, S., Burrows, E.H., Ellison, D., Brice, J., Illis, L.S., Scholey, K., Colbourn, C., Wilson, B., & Loates, M. (1994). Herpes simplex encephalitis: Longterm magnetic resonance imaging and neuropsychological profile. *Journal of Neurology, Neurosurgery, and Psychiatry, 57,* 1334–1342.

Kasteleijn-Nolst Trenité, D.A. (1996). Cognitive aspects. In S. Wallace (Ed.), *Epilepsy in children* (pp. 581–599). London: Chapman & Hall Medical.

Kasteleijn-Nolst Trenité, D.G.A., Bakker, D.J., Binnie, C.D., Buerman, A., & van Raaij, M. (1988). Psychological effects of sub-clinical epileptiform EEG discharges: Scholastic skills. *Epilepsy Research, 2,* 111–116.

Kasteleijn-Nolst Trenité, D.G.A., Siebelink, B.N., Berends, S.G.C., van Strien, J.W., & Meinardi, H. (1990b). Lateralised effects of sub-clinical epileptiform EEG discharges on scholastic performance in children. *Epilepsia, 31*(16), 740–746.

Kasteleijn-Nolst Trenité, D.G.A., Smit, A.M., Velis, D.N., Willemse, J., & van Emde Boas, W. (1990a). On-line detection of transient neuropsychological disturbances during EEG discharges in children with epilepsy. *Developmental Medicine and Child Neurology, 32,* 46–50.

Kaufmann, A. (1975). Factor analysis of the WISC-R at eleven age levels between $6\frac{1}{2}$ and $16\frac{1}{2}$ years. *Journal of Consulting and Clinical Psychology, 43,* 135–147.

Kaufman, A.S. (1979). *Intelligent testing with the WISC–R.* New York: Wiley.

Kaufman, A.S., & Kaufman, N.L. (1983). *Kaufman Assessment Battery for Children.* Circle Pines, MN: American Guidance Service.

Kaufman, A.S., & Kaufman, N.L. (1987). *The Kaufman Assessment Battery for Children: Interpretive manual.* Circle Pines, MN: American Guidance Services.

Kaufmann, P., Fletcher, J., Levin, H., Miner, M., & Ewing-Cobbs, L. (1993). Attention disturbance after pediatric closed head injury. *Journal of Child Neurology, 8,* 348–353.

Kazak, A.E. (1987). Families with disabled children: Stress and social networks in three samples. *Journal of Abnormal Child Psychology, 15,* 137–146.

Kazak, A.E., Reber, M., & Snitzer, L. (1988). Childhood chronic disease and family functioning: A study in phenylketonuria. *Pediatrics, 81,* 224–230.

Keith, R. (1994). *Auditory Continuous Performance Test.* San Antonio, TX: Psychological Corporation.

Kennard, M.A. (1936). Age and other factors in motor recovery from precentral lesions in monkeys. *American Journal of Physiology, 115,* 138–146.

Kennard, M.A. (1940). Relation of age to motor impairment in man and in subhuman primates. *Archives of Neurology and Psychiatry, 44,* 377–397.

Kennedy, C., Sakurada, O., Shinohara, M., & Miyaoka, M. (1982). Local cerebral glucose utilization in the newborn macaque monkey. *Annals of Neurology, 12,* 333–340.

Kennedy, C.R., Duffy, S.W., Smith, R., & Robinson, R.O. (1987). Clinical predictors of outcome in encephalitis. *Archives of Disease in Childhood, 62*, 1156–1162.

Kiefel, J., Guy, S., Yeates, K., Loss, N., & Enrile, B. (1997). Constructional and figural memory skills in children with myelomeningocele and shunted hydrocephalus. *Journal of the International Neuropsychological Society, 3*, 20.

Killackey, H. (1990). Neocortical expansion: An attempt towards relating phylogeny and ontogeny. *Journal of Cognitive Neuroscience, 2*, 1–17.

Kilp, T., Antilla, M., Kallio, M., & Peltola, H. (1993). Length of pre-diagnostic history related to the course and sequelae of childhood bacterial meningitis. *Journal of Pediatric Infectious Diseases, 12*, 184–188.

Kinney, H.C., Brody, B.A., Kloman, A.S., & Gilles, F.H. (1988). Sequence of central nervous system myelination in human infancy: II. Patterns of myelination in autopsied infants. *Journal of Neuropathology and Experimental Neurology, 47*, 217–234.

Kinsbourne, M. (1996). Models of consciousness: Serial and parallel in the brain. In M. Gazzaniga (Ed.), *The cognitive neurosciences* (pp. 1321–1330). Cambridge, MA: MIT Press.

Kinsella, G., Prior, M., Sawyer, M., Murtagh, D., Eisenmajer, R., Anderson, V., Bryan, D., & Klug, G. (1995). Neuropsychological deficit and academic performance in children and adolescents following traumatic brain injury. *Journal of Pediatric Psychology, 20*, 753–767.

Kinsella, G., Prior, M., Sawyer, M., Ong, B., Murtagh, D., Eisenmajer, R., Bryan, D., Anderson, V., & Klug, G. (1997). Predictors and indicators of academic outcome in children 2 years following traumatic head injury. *Journal of the International Neuropsychological Society, 3*, 608–616.

Kinsman, S.L., Vining, E.P.G., Quaksey, S.A., Mellits, D., & Freeman, J.M. (1992). Efficacy of the ketogenic diet for intractable seizure disorders: Review of 58 cases. *Epilepsia, 33*, 1132–1136.

Kirham, F., & Ebbing, A. (1994). Case summary: Kate. *Seizure, 3*(Suppl. A), 33–36.

Kirk, U. (1985). Hemispheric contributions to the development of graphic skills. In C. Best (Ed.), *Hemispheric function and collaboration in the child.* (pp. 193–228). New York: Academic Press.

Klein, J.O., Feigin, R.D., & McCracken, G.H. (1986). Report of the task force on diagnosis and management of meningitis. *Pediatrics, 78*(Suppl.), 959–982.

Klemp, S.B., & La Greca, A.M. (1987). Adolescents with IDDM: The role of family cohesion and conflict. *Diabetes, 36*, 18A.

Klin, A., Sparrow, S., Volkmar, F., Cicchetti, D., & Rourke, B. (1995). Asperger syndrome. In B. Rourke (Ed.), *Syndrome of non-verbal learning disabilities* (pp. 93–119). New York: Guilford Press.

Klinberg, T., Viadya, C., Gabrieli, J., Moseley, M., & Hedehus, M. (1999). Myelination and organisation of the frontal white matter in children: A diffusion tensor MRI study. *NeuroReport, 10*, 2817–2821.

Klonoff, H. (1971). Head injuries in children: Predisposing factors, accident conditions, accident proneness and sequelae. *American Journal of Public Health, 61*, 2405–2417.

Klonoff, H., Clark, C., & Klonoff, P. (1995). Outcome of head injuries from childhood to adulthood: A twenty-three year follow-up study. In S.H. Broman & M.E. Michel (Eds.), *Traumatic head injury in children* (pp. 219–234). New York: Oxford University Press.

Klonoff, H., Low, M.D., & Clark, C. (1977). Head injuries in children: A prospective five year follow-up. *Journal of Neurology, Neurosurgery, and Psychiatry, 40*, 1211–1219.

Klonoff, H., & Paris, R. (1974). Immediate, short-term and residual effects of acute head injuries in children: Neuropsychological and neurological correlates. In R.M. Reitan & L.A. Davison (Eds.), *Clinical neuropsychology: Current status and applications* (pp. 179–210). New York: Wiley.

Kløve, H. (1963). Clinical neuropsychology. In F. Forster (Ed.), *The medical clinics of North America*. New York: Saunders.

Kløve, H., & Matthews, C.G. (1974). Neuropsychological studies of patients with epilepsy. In R.M. Reitan & L.A. Davidson (Eds.), *Clinical neuropsychology: Current status and applications* (pp. 237–263). New York: Wiley.

Klug, G. (1994). The child with the large head. In M.J. Robinson & D.M. Roberton (Eds.), *Practical paediatrics* (pp. 467–475). Melbourne: Churchill Livingstone.

Koch, R., Azen, C., Friedman, E.G., & Williamson, M.L. (1984). Paired comparisons between early treated PKU children and their matched sibling controls on intelligence and school achievement test results at eight years of age. *Journal of Inherited Metabolic Disease, 7*, 86–90.

Kokkonen, J., Kokkonen, E.-R., Saukkonen, A.-L., & Pennanen, P. (1997). Psychosocial outcome of young adults with epilepsy in childhood. *Journal of Neurology, Neurosurgery and Psychiatry, 62*, 265–268.

Kolb, B. (1995). *Brain plasticity and behavior*. Hillsdale, NJ: Lawrence Erlbaum Associates Inc.

Kolb, B., & Fantie, B. (1989). Development of the child's brain and behavior. In C. Reynolds & E. Fletcher-Janzen (Eds.), *Handbook of clinical child neuropsychology* (pp. 17–39). New York: Plenum.

Kolb, B., Forgie, M., Gibb, R., Gorny, G., & Rowntree, S. (1998). Age, experience and the changing brain. *Neuroscience Biobehavioral Review, 22*, 143–159.

Kolb, B., & Gibb, R. (1999). Neuroplasticity and recovery of function after brain injury. In D. Stuss, G. Winocur, & I. Robertson (Eds.), *Cognitive neurorehabilitation* (pp. 9–25). New York: Cambridge University Press.

Kolb, B., & Stewart, J. (1991). Sex-related differences in dendritic branching of cells in the prefrontal cortex of rats. *Journal of Neuroendocrinology, 3*, 95–99.

Kolb, B., & Wishaw, Q. (1996). *Fundamentals of human neuropsychology* (4th ed.). New York: W.H. Freeman.

Koo, B., Hwang, P., & Logan, W. (1993). Infantile spasms: Outcomes and prognostic factors of cryptogenic and symptomatic groups. *Neurology, 43*, 2322–2327.

Kooistra, L., Laane, C., Vulsma, T., Schellekens, J. M., van der Meere, J., & Kalverboer, A.F. (1994). Motor and cognitive development in children with congenital hypothyroidism: A long-term evaluation of the effects of neonatal treatment. *Journal of Pediatrics, 124*, 903–909.

Koopmans, R.A., Li, D.K., Grochowski, E., Cutler, P.J., & Paty, D.W. (1989). Benign versus chronic progressive multiple sclerosis: Magnetic resonance imaging features. *Annals of Neurology, 25*, 74–81.

Korinthenberg, R., Ullrich, K., & Fullenkemper, F. (1988). Evoked potentials and electro-encephalography in adolescents with phenylketonuria. *Neuropediatrics, 19*, 175–178.

Korkman, M., Kirk, U., & Kemp, S. (1998). *Manual for the NEPSY*. San Antonio, TX: Psychological Corporation.

Koskiniemi, M., Donner, M., & Pettay, O. (1983). Clinical appearance and outcome in mumps encephalitis in children. *Acta Paediatrica Scandanavia, 72*, 603–609.

Kovacs, M., Goldston, D., & Iyengar, S. (1992). Intellectual development and academic performance of children with insulin-dependent diabetes: A longitudinal study. *Developmental Psychology, 28*, 676–684.

Kovacs, M., Ryan, C., & Obrosky, D. (1994). Verbal intellectual and verbal memory performance of youths with childhood-onset insulin-dependent diabetes mellitus. *Journal of Pediatric Psychology, 19*, 475–483.

Kraus, J.F. (1995). Epidemiological features of brain injury in children. In S.H. Broman & M.E. Michel (Eds.), *Traumatic head injury in children* (pp. 117–146). New York: Oxford University Press.

Kraus, J.F., Fife, D., Cox, P., Ramstein, K., & Conroy, C. (1986). Incidence, severity, and external causes of pediatric brain injury. *American Journal of Epidemiology*, *119*, 186–201.

Krause, W.L., Halminski, M., McDonald, L., Dembure, P., Salvo, R., Freides, D., & Elsas, L.J. (1985). Biochemical and neuropsychological effects of elevated plasma phenylalanine in patients with treated phenylketonuria: A model for the study of phenylalanine and brain function in man. *Journal of Clinical Investigation*, *75*, 40–48.

Kresky, B., Buchbinder, S., & Greenberg, I. (1962). The incidence of neurologic residua in children after recovery from bacterial meningitis. *Archives of Pediatrics*, *79*, 63–71.

Kriel, R.L., Krach, L.E., & Panser, L.A. (1989). Closed head injury: Comparisons of children younger and older than six years of age. *Pediatric Neurology*, *5*, 296–300.

Krikorian, R., Bartok, J., & Gay, N. (1994). Tower of London procedure: A standard method and developmental data. *Journal of Clinical and Experimental Neuropsychology*, *16*, 840–850.

Krishnamoorthy, K., Shannon, D., DeLong, G., Todres, I., & Davis, K. (1979). Neurologic sequelae in the survivors of neonatal intraventricular haemorrhage. *Pediatrics*, *64*, 233–237.

Krugman, S., Katz, S., & Gershon, A., et al. (1992). *Infectious diseases of children*. St Louis, MO: Mosby Year Book.

Krynauw, R.A. (1950). Infantile hemiplegia treated by removing one cerebral hemisphere. *Journal of Neurology, Neurosurgery, and Psychiatry*, *13*, 243–267.

Kubany, A., Danowski, T., & Moses, C. (1956). The personality and intelligence of diabetics. *Diabetes*, *5*, 462–467.

Kuzniecky, R. (1994). Magnetic resonance imaging in developmental disorders of the cerebral cortex. *Epilepsia*, *35*(Suppl. 6), S44–S56.

Laiacona, M., Capitani, E., & Barbarotto, R. (1993). Perceptual and associative knowledge in category specific impairment of semantic memory: A study of two cases. *Cortex*, *29*, 727–740.

Landry, S., Chapiesky, L., Fletcher, J., & Denson, S. (1988). Three year outcomes for low birthweight infants: Differential effects of early medical complications. *Journal of Pediatric Psychology*, *13*, 317–327.

Landry, S., Fletcher, J., Zarling, C., Chapiesky, L., Francis, D., & Denson, S. (1984). Differential outcomes associated with early medical complications in premature infants. *Journal of Pediatric Psychology*, *9*, 385–401.

Landry, S., Jordan, T., & Fletcher, J. (1994). Developmental outcomes for children with spina bifida. In M. Tramontana & S. Hooper (Eds.), *Advances in child neuropsychology* (pp. 85–118). New York: Springer.

Lane, D.M., & Pearson, D.A. (1982). The development of selective attention. *Merrill-Palmer Quarterly*, *28*, 317–337.

Lang, M., & Tisher, M. (1983). *Children's Depression Scale*. Melbourne: ACER.

Lang, W., Athanasopoulous, O., & Anderson, V. (1998). Do attentional profiles vary across developmental disorders? *Journal of the International Neuropsychological Society*, *4*, 221.

Langan, S.J., Deary, I.J., Hepburn, D.A., & Frier, B.M. (1991). Cumulative cognitive impairment following recurrent severe hypoglycaemia in adult patients with insulin-treated diabetes mellitus. *Diabetologia*, *34*, 337–344.

Lange-Cosack, H., Wider, B., Schlesner, H.J., Grumme, T., & Kubicki, S. (1979). Prognosis of brain injuries in young children (one until five years of age). *Neuropaediatrie*, *10*, 105–127.

Lashley, K. (1929). *Brain mechanisms and intelligence*. Chicago: University of Chicago Press.

Laurence, K.M. (1969). Neurological and intellectual sequelae of hydrocephalus. *Archives of Neurology*, *20*, 73–81.

Laurence, S., & Stein, D. (1978). Recovery after brain damage and the concept of localisation of function. In S. Finger (Ed.), *Recovery from brain damage* (pp. 369–407). New York: Plenum Press.

Laurent, B., Allegri, R.F., Thomas-Anterion, C., Foyatier, N., Naegelle-Faure, B., & Pellat, J.

(1991). Long term neuropsychological follow-up in patients with herpes simplex encephalitis and predominantly left-sided lesions. *Behavioural Neurology, 4*, 211–224.

Lavigne, J., & Faier-Routman, J. (1992). Psychological adjustment to pediatric physical disorders: A meta-analytic review. *Journal of Pediatric Psychology, 17*, 133–157.

Lavigne, J., Nolan, D., & McLone, D. (1988). Temperament, coping, and psychological adjustment in young children with myelomeningocele. *Journal of Pediatric Psychology, 13*, 363–378.

Lebel, M.H., Hoyt, M.J., Waagner, D.C., Rollins, N.K., Finitzo, T., & McCracken, G.H., Jr. (1989). Magnetic resonance imaging and dexamethasone therapy for bacterial meningitis. *American Journal of Diseases of Childhood, 143*, 301–306.

Legido, A., Tonyes, L., Carter, D., Schoemaker, A., Di George, A., & Grover, W. (1993). Treatment variables and intellectual outcome in children with classic phenylketonuria: A single-center based study. *Clinical Pediatrics, 32*, 417–425.

Lehr, E. (1990). *Psychological management of traumatic brain injuries in children and adolescents.* Rockville, MD: Aspen.

Lenneberg, E.H. (1967). *Biological foundations of language.* New York: Wiley.

Lennox W.G. (1942). Brain injury, drugs and environment as causes of mental decay in epilepsy. *American Journal of Psychiatry, 99*, 174–180.

Lesser, B., & Kaplan, P. (1994). Long-term monitoring with digital technology for epilepsy. *Journal of Child Neurology, 9*(Suppl.), S64–70.

Lester, M., & Fishbein, D. (1989). Nutrition and childhood neuropsychological disorders. In C. Reynolds & E. Fletcher-Jonger (Eds.), *Handbook of clinical child neuropsychology* (pp. 291–335). New York: Plenum Press.

Leventer, R., Phelan, E., Coleman, L., Kean, M., Jackson, G., & Harvey, A. (1999). Clinical and imaging features of cortical malformations in childhood. *Neurology, 53*, 715–722.

Levin, H.S., Aldrich, E.F., Saydjari, C., Eisenberg, H.M., Foulkes, M.A., Bellefleur, M., Leurssen, T.G., Jane, J.A., Marmarou, A., Marshall, L.F., & Young, H.F. (1992). Severe head injury in children: Experience of the traumatic coma bank. *Neurosurgery, 31*, 435–444.

Levin, H., Amparco, E., Eisenberg, J., Williams, D., High, W., McArdle, C., & Weiner, R. (1987). Magnetic resonance imaging and computerised tomography in relation to the neurobehavioral sequelae of mild and moderate head injuries. *Journal of Neurosurgery, 66*, 706–713.

Levin, H.S., Culhane, K.A., Hartmann, J., Evankovich, K., Mattson, A.J., Harward, H., Ringholz, G., Ewing-Cobbs, L., & Fletcher, J.M. (1991). Developmental changes in performance on tests of purported frontal lobe functioning. *Developmental Neuropsychology, 7*, 377–395.

Levin, H., Culhane, K., Mendelsohn, D., Lilly, M., Bruce, D., Fletcher, J., Chapman, S., Harward, H., & Eisenberg, H. (1993). Cognition in relation to magnetic resonance imaging in head-injured children and adolescents. *Archives of Neurology, 50*, 897–905.

Levin, H., & Eisenberg, H. (1979). Neuropsychological impairment after closed head injury in children and adolescents. *Journal of Pediatric Psychology, 4*, 389–402.

Levin, H., Eisenberg, H., Wigg, N., & Kobayashi, K. (1982). Memory and intellectual ability after head injury in children and adolescents. *Neurosurgery, 11*, 668–673.

Levin, H., Grafman, J., & Eisenberg, H. (1987). *Neurobehavioral recovery from head injury.* New York: Oxford University Press.

Levin, H.S., High, W., Ewing-Cobbs, L., Fletcher, J.M., Eisenberg, H.M., Miner, M., & Goldstein, F. (1988). Memory functioning during the first year after closed head injury in children and adolescents. *Neurosurgery, 22*, 17–34.

Levin, H., Mendelsohn, D., Lilly, M., Fletcher, J., Culhane, K., Chapman, S., Harward, H., Kusnerik, L., Bruce, D., & Eisenberg, H. (1994). Tower of London performance in relation to magnetic resonance imaging following closed head injury in children. *Neuropsychology, 8*, 171–179.

Levin, H., Song, J., Scheibel, R., Fletcher, J., Harward, H., Lilly, M., & Goldstein, F. (1997).

Concept formation and problem solving following closed head injury in children. *Journal of the International Neuropsychological Society, 3,* 598–607.

Levine, B., Stuss, D.T., & Milberg, W.P. (1995). Concept generation: Validation of a test of executive functioning in a normal aging population. *Journal of Clinical and Experimental Neuropsychology, 17,* 740–758.

Levy, H.L., & Waisbren, S.E. (1994). PKU in adolescents: Rationale and psychosocial factors in diet continuation. *Acta Paediatrica Suppl., 407,* 92–97.

Lezak, M. (1995). *Neuropsychological assessment* (3rd ed.). New York: Oxford University Press.

Lhermitte, J., & Signoret, J.L. (1972). Analyse neuropsychologique et différenciation des syndromes amnesique. *Revue Neurologique, 74,* 20–38.

Lichty, W., & Klachko, D. (1985). Memory in Type 1 diabetics. *Diabetes, 35*(Suppl.), 19A.

Lidow, M., & Goldman-Rakic, P.S. (1991). Synchronised overproduction of neurotransmitter receptors in diverse regions of the primate cerebral cortex. *Proceedings of the National Academy of Science, 88,* 10218–10221.

Lidsky, A., Robson, T., & Chandra, P. (1985). Regional mapping of the human phenylalanine hydroxylase gene and the PKU locus on chromosome 12. *Proceedings of the National Academy of Science USA, 82,* 9221–6225.

Lindsay, J., & Ounstead, C. (1987). Temporal lobe epilepsy: A biographical study 1948–1986. In J. Aicardi (Ed.), *Epilepsy in children* (2nd ed.). New York: Raven Press.

Lishman, W.A. (1978). *Organic psychiatry.* Oxford: Blackwell Scientific.

Lockman, L. (1989). Absence, myoclonic and atonic seizures. *Pediatric Clinics of North America, 36,* 331–341.

Lois, C., & Alvarez-Buylla, A. (1994). Long distance neuronal migration in the adult mammalian brain. *Science, 264,* 1145–1148.

Lollar, D.J. (1990). Learning patterns among spina bifida children. *Zeitschrift für Kinderchirurgie, 45*(Suppl. 1), 39.

Long, C.G., & Moore, J.R. (1979). Parental expectations for their epileptic children. *Journal of Child Psychology and Psychiatry, 20,* 299–312.

Lonton, A. (1976). Hand preference in children with myelomeningocele and hydrocephalus. *Developmental Medicine and Child Neurology, 18*(Suppl. 37), 143–149.

Lonton, A. (1977). Location of the myelomeningocele and its relationship to subsequent physical and intellectual abilities in children with myelomeningocele associated with hydrocephalus. *Zeitschrift für Kinderchirurgie, 22,* 510–519.

Lonton, A. (1979). The relationship betweem intellectual skills and the computerised axial tomograms of children with spina bifida and hydrocephalus. *Zeitschrift für Kinderchirurgie, 28,* 368–374.

Lorber, J. (1968). The results of early treatment of extreme hydrocephalus. *Developmental Medicine and Child Neurology Suppl., 16,* 21–30.

Lortie, A., Chiron, C., Mumford, J., & Dulac, O. (1993). The potential for increasing seizure frequency, relapse and appearance of new seizures types with vigabatrin. *Neurology, 43*(Suppl. 5), S25–S27.

Loss, N., Yeates, K.O., & Enrile, B.G. (1998). Attention in children with myelomeningocele. *Child Neuropsychology, 4,* 7–20.

Lou, H.C. (1994). Dopamine precursors and brain function in phenylalanine hydroylase deficiency. *Acta Paediatrica Suppl., 407,* 86–88.

Lou, H.C., Guttler, G., Lykelund, C., Bruhn, P., & Niederwieser, A. (1985). Decreased vigilance and neurotransmitter synthesis after discontinuation of dietary treatment of phenylketonuria in adolescents. *European Journal of Pediatrics, 144,* 17–20.

Lowe, T.L., Tanaka, K., Seashore, M.R., Young, J.G., & Cohen, D.J. (1980). Detection of phenylketonuria in autistic and psychotic children. *Journal of the American Medical Association, 243,* 126–128.

Luciana, M., & Nelson, C. (1998). The functional emergence of pre-frontally guided working memory systems in four-to-eight year old children. *Neuropsychologia, 30,* 273–293.

Luria, A.R. (1963). *Restoration of function after brain injury.* New York: Macmillan.

Luria, A.R. (1973). *The working brain.* New York: Basic Books.

McCall, A.L. & Figlewicz, D.P. (1997). How does diabetes mellitus produce brain dysfunction? *Diabetes Spectrum, 10,* 25–32.

McCallum, J.E., & Turbeville, D. (1994). Cost and outcome in a series of shunted premature infants with intraventricular haemorrhage. *Pediatric Neurosurgery, 20,* 63–67.

McCarney, S. (1995). *The Attention Deficit Disorders Evaluation Scale—Revised.* Columbia, MO: Hawthorne Educational Services.

McCarthy, D. (1972). *McCarthy Scales of Children's Abilities.* New York: Psychological Corporation.

McCarthy, R.A., Evans, J.J., & Hodges, J.R. (1996). Topographic amnesia: Spatial memory disorder, perceptual dysfunction, or category specific semantic memory impairmnent. *Journal of Neurology, Neurosurgery, and Psychiatry, 60,* 318–325.

McCarthy, R.A., & Warrington, E.K. (1990). *Cognitive neuropsychology: A clinical introduction.* New York: Academic Press.

McCombe, P.A., McLaughlin, D.B., Chalk, J.B., Brown, N.N., McGill, G.G., & Pender, M.P. (1992). Spasticity and white mater abnormalities in adult phenylketonuria. *Journal of Neurology, Neurosurgery, and Psychiatry, 55,* 359–361.

McCrimmon, R.J., Deary, I.J., Huntly, B.J., MacLeod, K.J., & Frier, B.M. (1996). Visual information processing during controlled hypoglycaemia in humans. *Brain, 119,* 1277–1287.

McCullough, D., & Balzer-Martin, L. (1982). Current prognosis in overt neonatal hydrocephalus. *Journal of Neurosurgery, 57,* 378–383.

McIntyre, P., Jepson, R., Leeder, S., & Irwig, I. (1993). The outcome of childhood *Haemophilus influenzae* meningitis: A population based study. *Medical Journal of Australia, 159,* 766–772.

McKay, K.E., Halperin, J.M., Schwartz, S.T., & Sharma, V. (1994). Developmental analysis of three aspects of information processing: Sustained attention, selective attention, and response organization. *Developmental Neuropsychology, 10,* 121–132.

McKean, C.M. (1972). The effects of high phenylanaline concentrations on serotonin and catecholamine metabolism in the human brain. *Brain Research, 47,* 469–476.

McKendall, R. (1989). Herpes simplex. In P.J. Vinken, G.W. Bruyn, & H. Klawans (Eds.), *Handbook of clinical neurology* (Vol. 56, pp. 207–227). Amsterdam: Elsevier.

McKinney, B., & Peterson, R.A. (1987). Predictors of stress in parents of developmentally disabled children. *Journal of Pediatric Psychology, 12,* 133–150.

McLachlan, R.S., Girvin, J.P., Blume, W.T., & Reichman, H. (1993). Rasmussen's chronic encephalitis in adults. *Archives of Neurology, 50,* 269–274.

McLone, D., Czyzewski, D., Raimondi, A., et al. (1982). Central nervous system infections as a limiting factor in intelligence of children with myelomeningocele. *Pediatrics, 70,* 338–342

McMenemin, J.B., & Volpe, J.J. (1984). Bacterial meningitis in infancy: Effects of intracranial pressure and cerebral blood flow velocity. *Neurology, 34,* 500–504.

McMillan, T.M., Powell, G.E., Janota, I., & Polkey, C.E. (1987). Relationships between neuropathology and cognitive functioning in temporal lobectomy patients. *Journal of Neurology, Neurosurgery and Psychiatry, 50,* 167–176.

Mabbott, D.J., & Smith, M.L. (1998). Memory functioning in children with temporal lobectomies. *Epilepsia, 39*(Suppl. 6), 252 [abstract].

Madeline Foundation (1995). *Hydrocephalus: A Handbook for Parents and Patients.* Sydney, Australia: Madeline Foundation.

Maddison, D., & Raphael, B. (1971). Social and psychological consequences of chronic disease in childhood. *Medical Journal of Australia, 2,* 1265–1270.

Maguire, E., Frackowiak, R., & Frith, C. (1996). Learning to find your way: A role for the human hippocampal formation. *Proceedings of the Royal Society of London, 263*, 1715–1750.

Maher, J., & McLachlan, R.S. (1995). Febrile convulsions: Is seizure duration the most important aspect of temporal lobe epilepsy, *Brain, 118*, 1521–1528.

Mahoney, W., D'souza, B., Haller, J., Rogers, M., Epstein, M., & Freeman, J. (1983). Long-term outcome of children with severe head trauma and prolonged coma. *Pediatrics, 71*, 756–762.

Manly, T., Robertson, I., Anderson, V., & Nimmo-Smith, I. (1999). *Test of Everyday Attention for Children*. Cambridge, UK: Thames Valley Test Company.

Mapstone, T., Rekate, H., Nulsen, F., Dixon, M., Glaser, N., & Jaffe, M. (1984). Relationship of CSF shunting and IQ in children with myelomeningocele: A retrospective analysis. *Child's Brain, 11*, 112–118.

Markwardt, F.C. (1989). *Peabody Individual Achievement Test—Revised. PIAT Manual*. Circle Pines, MN: American Guidance Service.

Martin, R.C., Haut, M.W., Goeta-Kreisler, K., & Blumenthal, D. (1996). Neuropsychological functioning in a patient with pareneoplastic limbic encephalitis. *Journal of the International Neuropsychological Society, 2*, 460–466.

Mateer, C.A. (1990). Cognitive and behavioral sequalae of face and forehead injury in childhood. *Journal of Clinical and Experimental Neuropsychology, 12*, 95.

Mateer, C.A., & Williams, D. (1991) Effects of frontal lobe injury in childhood. *Developmental Neuropsychology, 7*, 69–86.

Matsumoto, T., Takahashi, S., Sato, A., Imaizumi, M., Higano, S., Sakamoto, K., Asakawa, H., & Tada, K. (1995). Leukoencephalopathy in childhood hematopic neoplasm caused by moderate-dose methotrexate and prophylactic cranial radiotherapy: An MR analysis. *International Journal of Radiation Oncology and Biological Physics, 32*, 913–918.

Matthews, W.S., Barbas, G., & Ferrari, M. (1983). Achievement and school behaviour among children with epilepsy. *Psychology in the Schools, 20*, 10–12.

Mauss-Clum, N., & Ryan, M. (1981). Brain injury and the family. *Journal of Neurosurgical Nursing, 13*, 165–169.

Max, J., Smith, W., Sato, Y., Mattheis, P., Castillo, C., Lindgren, S., Robin, D., & Stierwalt, J. (1997a). Predictors of family functioning following traumatic brain injury in children and adolescents. *Journal of the Academy of Child and Adolescent Psychiatry, 37*, 83–90.

Max, J., Smith, W., Sato, Y., Mattheis, P., Castillo, C., Lindgren, S., Robin, D., & Stierwalt, J. (1997b). Traumatic brain injury in children and adolescents: Psychiatric disorders in the first three months. *Journal of the Academy of Child and Adolescent Psychiatry, 36*, 94–102.

Maytal, J., Shinnar, S., Moshé, S.L., & Alvarez, L.A. (1989). Low morbidity and mortality of status epilepticus in children. *Pediatrics, 83*(3), 323–331.

Mazzocco, M., Nord, A., Van Doorninck, W., Greene, C., Kovar, G., & Pennington, B. (1994). Cognitive development among children with early-treated phenylketonuria. *Developmental Neuropsychology, 10*, 133–151.

Meador, K.J. (1998). The effects of antiepileptic drugs and seizures on the unborn child: Implications for treatment of the mother. *Epilepsia, 39*(Suppl. 6), 133.

Meador, K.L., & Baker, G.A. (1997). Behavioural and cognitive side effects of lamotrigine. *Journal of Child Neurology, 12*(Suppl. 1), S44–S47.

Meador, K.J., Loring, D.W., Allen, M.E., Zamrini, E.Y., Moore, E.E., Abney, O.L., & King, D.W. (1991). Comparative cognitive effects of carbamazepine and phenytoin in healthy adults. *Neurology, 41*, 1537–1540.

Menkes, J.H. (1990). *Textbook of child neurology* (4th ed.). Philadelphia: Lea & Febinger.

Mertsola, J., Kennedy, W.A., Waagner, D., Saez-Llorens, X., Olsen, K., Hansen, E.J., & McCracken, G.H. (1991). Endotoxin concentrations in cerebrospinal fluid correlated with clinical severity and neurological outcome of *Haemophilus influenzae* type b meningitis. *American Journal of Disease in Childhood, 145*, 1099–1103.

Mesulam, M. (1985). Attention, confusional states and neglect. In M.M. Mesulam (Ed.), *Principles of behavioural neurology* (pp. 125–168). Philadelphia: F.A. Davis.

Michaud, L.J., Rivara, F.P., Grady, M.S., & Reay, D.T. (1992). Predictors of survival and severe disability after severe brain injury in children. *Neurosurgery, 31*, 254–264.

Mikati, M.A., Holmes, G.L., Chronopoulos, A., Hyde, P., Thurber, S., Gatt, A., Liu, Z., Werner, S., & Stafstrom, C.E. (1994). Phenobarbital therapy modifies seizure related brain injury in the developing brain. *Annals of Neurology, 36*, 425–433.

Miller, I., Bishop, D., Epstein, N., & Keitner, G. (1985). The McMaster Family Assessment Devise: Reliability and validity. *Journal of Marital and Family Therapy, 11*, 345–356.

Miller, J.D. (1991). Pathophysiology and management of head injury. *Neuropsychology, 5*, 235–261.

Miller, P.H., & Weiss, M.G. (1981). Children's attentional allocation, understanding of attention, and performance on the incidental learning task. *Child Development, 52*, 1183–1190.

Milner, B. (1958). Psychological defects produced by temporal lobe excision. *Research Publications/Association for Research in Nervous and Mental Disease, 36*, 244–257.

Milner, B. (1965). Visually-guided maze learning in man: Effects of bilateral hippocampal, bilateral frontal and unilateral cerebral lesions. *Neuropsychologia, 3*, 317–338.

Milner, B. (1967). Brain mechanisms suggested by studies of the temporal lobes. In C.H. Milikan & F.L. Darley (Eds.), *Brain mechanisms underlying speech and language* (pp. 122–131). New York: Grune & Stratton.

Milner, B. (1971). Interhemispheric differences in localization of psychological processes in man. *British Medical Bulletin, 27*, 272–277.

Milner, B. (1974). Hemispheric specialization: Scope and limits. In F. Schmitt & F. Worden (Eds.), *The neurosciences: Third study program* (pp. 75–89). Boston: MIT Press.

Mirsky, A. (1989). Information processing in petit mal epilepsy. In B. Hermann & M. Seidenberg (Eds.), *Childhood epilepsies: Neuropsychological, psychosocial and intervention aspects* (pp. 51–80). New York: Wiley.

Mirsky, A. (1996). Disorders of attention: A neuropsychological perspective. In G. Lyon & N. Krasnegor (Eds.), *Attention, memory and executive function* (pp. 71–96). Baltimore: Paul H. Brookes.

Mirsky, A.F., Anthony, B.J., Duncan, C.C., Ahearn, M.B., & Kellam, S.G. (1991). Analysis of the elements of attention: A neuropsychological approach. *Neuropsychology Review, 2*, 109–145.

Mishkin, M., Malamut, B., & Bachevalier, J. (1984). Memories and habits: Two neural systems. In G. Lynch, J. McGaugh, & N. Weinberger (Eds.), *Neurobiology of memory and learning* (pp. 65–77). New York: Guilford Press.

Mitchell, W.G., Scheier, L.M., & Baker, S.A. (1994). Psychosocial, behavioural and medical outcomes in children with epilepsy: A developmental risk factor model using longitudinal data. *Pediatrics, 94*(4), 471–477.

Mitchell, W.G., Zhou, Y., Chavez, J.M., & Guzman, B.L. (1992). Reaction time, attention and impulsivity in epilepsy. *Pediatric Neurology, 8*, 19–24.

Mittl, R., Grossman, R., Hiehle, J., Hurst, R., Kauder, D., Gennarelli, T., & Alburger, G. (1994). Prevalence of MR evidence of diffuse axonal injury in patients with mild head injury and normal CT findings. *American Journal of Neuroradiology, 15*, 1583–1589.

Mizrahi, E.M. (1996). Seizures in the neonate. In S. Wallace (Ed.), *Epilepsy in children* (pp. 167–183). London: Chapman & Hall Medical.

Mogford, K., & Bishop, D. (1993). Language development in exceptional circumstances. In D. Bishop & K. Mogford, K. (Eds), *Language development in exceptional circumstances* (pp. 10–28). Hove, UK: Lawrence Erlbaum Associates Ltd.

Molfese, D., & Molfese, V. (1980). Cortical responses of preterm infants to phonetic and non-phonetic speech stimuli. *Developmental Psychology, 16,* 574–581.

Molliver, M.E., Kostovic, I., & Van der Loos, H. (1973). The development of synapses in cerebral cortex in the human fetus. *Brain Research, 50,* 403–407.

Mooradian, A. (1988). Diabetic complications of the central nervous system. *Endocrine Reviews, 9,* 346–356.

Moos, R.H., & Moos, B.S. (1986). *Family Environment Scale.* Palo Alto, CA: Consulting Psychologists Press.

Morikawa, T., Seino, N., Osawa, T., et al. (1985). Five children with continuous spike waves during sleep. In R. Dravet & M. Bureau (Eds.), *Epileptic syndromes in infancy, childhood and adolescence* (pp. 205–212). London: John Libbey Eurotext.

Moshé, S.L., Koszer, S., Wolf, S.M., & Cornblath, M. (1996). Developmental aspects of epileptogenesis. In E. Wyllie (Ed.), *The treatment of epilepsy: Principles and practice* (2nd ed., pp. 139–150). Baltimore: Williams & Wilkins.

Moyes, C. (1980). Epidemiology of serious head injuries in childhood. *Child Care, Health, and Development, 6,* 1–9.

Mulder, H.C., & Suurmeijer, T.P. (1977). Families with a child with epilepsy: A sociological contribution. *Journal of Biosocial Science, 9,* 13–24.

Muller, R., Rothermel, R., Behan, M., Muzik, O., Mangner, T., & Chugani, H. (1998). Differential patterns of language and motor reorganisation following early left hemisphere lesions. *Archives of Neurology, 55,* 1113–1119.

Muller, R., Rothermel, R., Behen, M., Muzik., O., Mangner, T., & Chugani, H. (1999). Language localisation in patients with early and late left hemisphere lesion: A PET study. *Neuropsychologia, 37,* 545–557.

Munk, H. (1881). Ueber die funktion der grosshirnrinde. *Gesammelte aus den Jahren 1877–80.* Berlin: Hirschwald.

Muramoto, O., Kuru, Y., Sugishita, M., & Toyokura, Y. (1979). Pure memory loss with hippocampal lesions: A pneumoencephalographic study. *Archives of Neurology, 36,* 54–56.

Murch, R., & Cohen, L. (1989). Relationships among life stress, perceived family environment, and the psychological disorders of spina bifida adolescents. *Journal of Pediatric Psychology, 14,* 149–175.

Murphy, G., Hulse, J.A., Jackson, D., Tyrer, P., Glossop, J., Smith, I., & Grant, D. (1986). Early treated hypothyroidism: Development at 3 years. *Archives of Disease in Childhood, 61,* 761–765.

Murray, R., Shum, D., & McFarland, K. (1992) Attentional deficits in head-injured children: An information processing analysis. *Brain and Cognition, 18,* 99–115.

Naughten, E.R., Kiely, B., Saul, I., & Murphy, D. (1987). Phenylketonuria: Outcome and problems in a "diet-for-life" clinic. *European Journal of Pediatrics, 146*(Suppl. 1), A23–A24.

Neale, M. (1988). *Neale analysis of reading ability—revised.* London: Macmillan.

Nedd, K., Sfakianakis, G., Ganz, W., Urriccho, B., Vernberg, D., Villanueva, P., Jabir, A., Bartlett, J., & Keena, J. (1993). 99m Tc-HMPAQ SPECT of the brain in mild to moderate traumatic brain injury patients: Compared with CT—a prospective study. *Brain Injury, 7,* 469–479.

Neisser, U. (1967). *Cognitive psychology.* New York: Appleton-Century-Crofts.

Nelson, C. (1995). The ontogeny of human memory: A cognitive neuroscience perspective. *Developmental Psychology, 31,* 723–735.

Nester, M.J. (1996). Use of a brief assessment examination in a study of subacute sclerosing panencephalitis. *Journal of Child Neurology, 11,* 173–180.

Neville, H. (1993). Neurobiology of cognitive and language processing: Effects of early experience. In M. Johnson (Ed.), *Brain development and cognition* (pp. 427–447). Oxford, UK: Blackwell.

New England Congenital Hypothyroidism Collaborative. (1985). Neonatal hypothyroidism screening: Status of patients at 6 years of age. *Journal of Pediatrics, 107*, 915–918.

New England Congenital Hypothyroidism Collaborative. (1990). Elementary school performance of children with congenital hypothyroidism. *Journal of Pediatrics, 116*, 27–32.

New England Congenital Hypothyroidism Collaborative. (1994). Correlation of cognitive test scores and adequacy of treatment in adolescents with congenital hypothyroidism. *Journal of Pediatrics, 124*, 383–387.

Newton, M., Greenwood, R., Britton, K., Charlesworth, M., Nimmon, C., Carroll, M., & Dolke, G. (1992). A study comparing SPECT with CT and MRI after closed head injury. *Journal of Neurology, Neurosurgery, and Psychiatry, 55*, 92–94.

Nielsen, H.H. (1980). A longitudinal study of the psychological aspects of myelomeningocele. *Scandanavian Journal of Psychology, 21*, 45–54.

North, B. (1984). *Jamieson's first notebook of head injury* (3rd ed.). London: Butterworths.

Northam, E. (1998). Neuropsychological function. In G.A. Werther & J.M. Court (Eds.), *Diabetes and the adolescent* (pp. 71–83). Melbourne: Miranova.

Northam, E., Anderson, P., Werther, G., Adler, R., & Andrewes, D. (1995). Neuropsychological complications of insulin dependent diabetes in children. *Child Neuropsychology, 1*, 74–87.

Northam, E., Anderson, P., Werther, G., Adler, R., & Warne, G. (1996). Psychosocial and family functioning in children with insulin-dependent diabetes at diagnosis and one year later. *Journal of Pediatric Psychology, 21*, 699–717.

Northam, E., Anderson, P., Werther, G., Warne, G., Adler, R., & Andrewes, D. (1998). Neuropsychological complications of insulin dependent diabetes in children two years after disease onset. *Diabetes Care, 21*, 379–384.

Northam, E., Anderson, P., Werther, G., Warne, G., & Andrewes, D. (1999) Predictors of change in the neuropsychological profiles of children two years after disease onset. *Diabetes Care, 22*, 1438–1444.

Novack, T., Dillon, M., & Jackson, W. (1996). Neurochemical mechanisms in brain injury and treatment: A review. *Journal of Clinical and Experimental Neuropsychology, 18*, 685–706.

Nowakowski, R. (1996). Basic concepts of CNS development. In M. Johnson (Ed.), *Brain development and cognition: A reader* (pp. 54–92). Cambridge, MA: Blackwell.

Oddy, M. (1993). Head injury during childhood. *Neuropsychological Rehabilitation, 3*, 301–320.

O'Donohoe, N.V. (1994). *Epilepsies of childhood* (3rd ed.). Oxford: Butterworth-Heinemann.

Ohtahara, S., & Ohtsuki, Y. (1996). Early epileptic encephalopathies. In S. Wallace (Ed.), *Epilepsy in childhood* (pp. 201–208). London: Chapman & Hall Medical.

Ohtahara, S., Ohtsuka, Y., & Yoshinaga, H. (1988). Lennox Gastaux syndrome: Etiological considerations. In E. Niedermeyer & R. Degen (Eds.), *The Lennox Gastaux syndrome* (pp. 47–63). New York: Liss.

O'Leary, D. (1989). Do cortical areas emerge from a protocortex? *Trends in the Neurosciences, 12*, 400–406.

O'Leary, D.S., Lovell, M.R., Sackellares, J.C., Berent, S., Giordani, B., Seidenberg, M., & Boll, T.J. (1983). *Journal of Nervous and Mental Disease, 171*(10), 624–629.

Ommaya, A., & Gennarelli, T. (1974). Cerebral concussion and traumatic unconsciousness: Correlation of experimental and clinical observations on blunt head injuries. *Brain, 97*, 633–654.

O'Neil, M.E., & Douglas, V.I. (1991). Study strategies and story recall in attention deficit disorder and reading disability. *Journal of Abnormal Child Psychology, 19*, 671–692.

Ong, L., Chandran, V., & Zasmani, S. (1998). Outcome of closed head injury in Malaysian children: Neurocognitive and behavioural sequelae. *Journal of Paediatric and Child Health, 34*, 363–368.

Orzhekhovskaya, N.S. (1981). Fronto-striatal relationships in primate ontogeny. *Neuroscience and Behavioral Physiology, 11*, 379–385.

Ounstead, C., Lindsey, J.T., & Norman, R.M. (1966). *Biological factors in temporal lobe epilepsy* (Clinics in Developmental Medicine No. 22). London: Heinemann Medical Books.

Overmann, W., Bachevalier, J., Sewell, F., & Drew, J. (1993). A comparison of children's performance on two recognition memory tasks: Delayed nonmatch-to-sample vs visual paired comparison. *Developmental Psychobiology, 26*, 345–357.

Oxbury, J., & Oxbury, S.M. (1989). Neuropsychology: Memory and hippocampal pathology. In E.G. Reynolds & M.R. Trimble (Eds.), *The bridge between neurology and psychiatry* (pp. 135–150). Edinburgh: Churchill Livingstone.

Oxbury, S.M., Creswell, P.H., Oxbury, S.M., & Adams, C.B.T. (1996). Neuropsychological outcome after temporal lobe epilepsy surgery in children under 16 years: 5 years follow-up. *Epilepsia, 37*(Suppl. 5), 183.

Paakko, E., Vainionpaa, L., Lanning, M., Laitinen, J., & Pyhtinen, J. (1992). White matter changes in children treated for acute lymphoblastic leukemia. *Cancer, 70*, 2728–2733.

Palmini, A., Gambardella, A., Andermann, F., Dubeau, F., da Costa, J.C., Olivier, A., Tampieri, D., Gloor, P., Quesney, F., Andermann, E., Paglioli, E., Paglioli-Neto, E., Coutinho, L., Leblanc, R., & Kim, H.-I. (1995). Intrinsic epileptogenicity of human dysplastic cortex as suggested by corticography and surgical results. *Annals of Neurology, 37*, 476–487.

Pang, D. (1985). Pathophysiologic correlates of neurobehavioral syndromes following closed head injury. In M. Ylvisaker (Ed.), *Head injury rehabilitation: Children and adolescents* (pp. 3–70). London: Taylor & Francis.

Papalia, D., & Olds, S. (1992). *Human development* (5th ed.). New York: McGraw-Hill.

Papero, P., Prigatano, G., Snyder, H., & Johnson, D. (1993). Children's adaptive behavioural competence after head injury. *Neuropsychological Rehabilitation, 3*, 321–340.

Paris, S.G., & Lindauer, B.K. (1976). The role of inference in children's comprehension and memory for sentences. *Cognitive Psychology, 8*, 217–227.

Parker, D.M., & Crawford, J.R. (1992). Assessment of frontal lobe dysfunction. In J.R. Crawford, D.M. Parker, & W.W. McKinlay (Eds.), *A handbook of neuropsychological assessment* (pp. 267–294). Hove, UK: Lawrence Erlbaum Associates Ltd.

Parmalee, A., & Sigman, M. (1983). Perinatal brain devlopment and behaviour. In M. Haith & J. Campos (Eds.), *Infancy and the biology of development: Vol. 2. Handbook of child psychology* (pp. 95–155). New York: Oxford University Press.

Pascual-Leone, J. (1970). A mathematical model for transition in Piaget's developmental stages. *Acta Psychologica, 32*, 301–345.

Pascual-Leone, J. (1987). Organismic processes for Neo-Piagetian theories: A dialectical causal account of cognitive development. *International Journal of Psychology, 22*, 531–570.

Passler, M.A., Isaac, W., & Hynd, G.W. (1985). Neuropsychological development of behavior attributed to frontal lobe functioning in children *Developmental Neuropsychology, 1*, 349–370.

Pearson, K.D., Gean-Marton, A.D., Levy, H.L., & Davis, K.R. (1990). Phenylketonuria: MR imaging of the brain with clinical correlation. *Radiology, 177*, 437–440.

Pellock, J.M. (1997). Overview of lamotrigine and the new antiepileptic drugs: The challenge. *Journal of Child Neurology, 12*(Suppl. 1), S48–S52.

Peltola, H., Kilpi, T., & Antilla, M. (1992). Rapid disappearance of *Haemophilus influenzae* type b meningitis after routine childhood immunizations with conjugate vaccines. *Lancet, 340*, 592–594.

Pennington, B. (1997). Dimensions of executive functions in normal and abnormal development. In N. Krasnegor, G. Lyon, & P.S. Goldman-Rakic (Eds.), *Development of the prefrontal cortex: Evolution, neurology, and behaviour* (pp. 265–282). Baltimore: Brookes.

Pennington, B.F., van Doorninck, W.J., McCabe, L.L., & McCabe, E.R. (1985). Neuropsychological deficits in early treated phenylketonuric children. *American Journal of Mental Deficiency, 89*, 467–474.

Pentland, L., Anderson, V.A., & Wrennall, J. (1997). Bacterial meningitis: Implications of age at illness for language development. *Journal of the International Neuropsychological Society, 3*, 213.

Pentland, L., Anderson, V., & Wrennall, J. (2000). Bacterial meningitis: Implications of age at illness for language development. *Child Neuropsychology, 6*, 87–100.

Pentland, L., Todd, J.A., & Anderson, V. (1998). The impact of head injury severity on planning ability in adolescence: A functional analysis. *Neuropsychological Rehabilitation, 8*, 301–317.

Perez, E., Davidoff, V., Desplan, P., et al. (1993). Mental and behavioral deterioration of children with epilepsy and CSWS: Acquired epileptic frontal syndrome. *Developmental Medicine and Child Neurology, 35*, 661–674.

Perrott, S.B., Taylor, H.G., & Montes, J.L. (1991). Neuropsychological sequelae, familial stress, and environmental adaptation following pediatric head injury. *Developmental Neuropsychology, 7*, 69–86.

Pfefferbaum, A., Mathalon, D., Sullivan, E., Rawles, J., Zipursky, R., & Lim, K. (1994). A quantitative magnetic resonance imaging study of changes in brain morphology from infancy to late adulthood. *Archives of Neurology, 34*, 227–234.

Piaget, J. (1963). *The origins of intelligence in children.* New York: W.W. Norton.

Piccirilli, M., D'Alessandro, P., Sciama, T., Cantoni, C. Dioguardi, M.S., Giuglietti, M., Ibba, A., & Tiacci, C. (1994). Attention problems in epilepsy: Possible significance of the epileptogenic focus. *Epilepsia, 35*(5), 1091–1096.

Pietrini, V., Nertempi, P., Vaglia, A., Revello, H., Pinna, V., & Ferro-Milone, F. (1988). Recovery from herpes simplex encephalitis: Selective impairment of specific semantic categories with radiological correlation. *Journal of Neurology, Neurosurgery, and Psychiatry, 51*, 1284–1293.

Pietz, J., Benninger, C., Schmidt, H., Scheffner, D., & Bickel, H. (1988). Long-term development of intelligence (IQ) and EEG in 34 children with phenylketonuria treated early. *European Journal of Pediatrics, 147*, 361–367.

Pietz, J., Schmidt, E., Matthis, P., Kobialka, B., Kutscha, A., & de Sonneville, L. (1993). EEGs in phenylketonuria: I. Follow-up to adulthood. II. Short-term diet-related changes in EEGs and cognitive function. *Developmental Medicine and Child Neurology, 35*, 54–64.

Polissar, N., Fay, G., Jaffe, K., Liao, S., Martin, K., Shurtleff, H., Rivara, J., & Winn, H. (1994). Mild pediatric traumatic brain injury: Adjusting significance levels for multiple comparisons. *Brain Injury, 8*, 249–264.

Polkey, C.E. (1996). Surgical treatment of epilepsy in children. In S. Wallace (Ed.), *Epilepsy in children* (pp. 561–579). London: Chapman & Hall Medical.

Pomeroy, S.I., Holmes, S.J., Dodge, P.R., & Feigin, R.D. (1990). Seizures and other neurological sequelae of bacterial meningitis in children. *New England Journal of Medicine, 323*, 1651–1657.

Pond, D. (1974). Epilepsy and personality disorders. In P. Vinken & G. Bruhn (Eds.), *Handbook of clinical neurology* (Vol. 15, pp. 576–592). Amsterdam: North-Holland.

Ponsford, J., & Kinsella, G. (1992). Attentional deficits following closed head injury. *Journal of Clinical and Experimental Neuropsychology, 14*, 822–838.

Ponsford, J., Sloan, S., & Snow, P. (1995). *Traumatic brain injury: Rehabilitation for everyday adaptive living.* Hove, UK: Lawrence Erlbaum Associates Ltd.

Ponsford, J., Willmott, C., Rothwell, A., Cameron, P., Kelly, A., Ayton, G., Curran, C., & Nelms, R. (1997). Cognitive and behavioural outcome following mild traumatic brain injury in children. *Journal of the International Neuropsychological Society, 3*, 225.

Porterfield, S.P., & Hendrich, C.E. (1993). The role of thyroid hormones in prenatal and neonatal neurological development: Current perspectives. *Endocrine Reviews, 14*, 94–104.

Porteus, S.D. (1965). *Porteus maze test: Fifty years' application.* New York: Psychological Corporation.

Posner, M. (1978). *Chronometric explorations of mind*. Hillsdale, NJ: Lawrence Erlbaum Associates Ltd.

Posner, M., & Petersen, S.E. (1990). The attention system of the human brain. *Annual Review in Neuroscience*, *15*, 25–42.

Posner, M., & Rothbart, M. (1981). The development of attentional mechanisms. In J.H. Flowers (Ed.), *Nebraska Symposium on Motivatiroscience*, *15*, 25–42.

Pozzessere, G., Valle, E., de Crignis, C., Cordischi, V., Fattapposta, F., Rizzo, P., Pietravalle, P., Cristina, G., Monaro, S., & Di Mario, U. (1991). Abnormalities of cognitive functions in IDDM revealed by P300 event-related potentials: Comparison with short latency evoked potential and psychometric tests. *Diabetes*, *40*, 952–958.

Pramming, S., Thorsteinsson, B., Theilgaard, A., Pinner, E., & Binder, C. (1986). Cognitive function during hypoglycaemia in type 1 diabetes mellitus. *British Medical Journal*, *292*, 647–650.

Prigatano, G.P., O'Brien, K., & Klonoff, P.S. (1993). Neuropsychological rehabilitation of young adults who suffer brain injury in childhood: Clinical observations. *Neuropsychological Rehabilitation*, *3*, 411–414.

Prigatano, G.P., Zeiner, H.K., Pollay, M., & Kaplan, R.J. (1983). Neuropsychological functioning in children with shunted uncomplicated hydrocephalus. *Child's Brain*, *10*, 112–120.

Prior, M., Kinsella, G., Sawyer, M., Bryan, D., & Anderson, V. (1994). Cognitive and psychosocial outcomes after head injury in childhood. *Australian Psychologist*, *29*, 116–123.

Prior, M., & Hoffman, W. (1990). Neuropsychological testing of autistic children through an exploration of frontal lobe tests. *Journal of Autism and Developmental Disorders*, *20*, 581–590.

Pueschel, S.M., Fogelson-Doyle, L., Kammerer, B., & Matsumiya, Y. (1983). Neurophysiological, psychological and nutritional investigations during discontinuation of the phenylalanine-restricted diet in children with classic phenylketonuria. *Journal of Mental Deficiency Research*, *27*, 61–67.

Purpura, D. (1975). Normal and aberrant neuronal development in the cerebral cortex of human fetus and young infant. In N.A. Buchwald & M. Brazier (Eds.), *Brain mechanisms of mental retardation* (pp. 141–169). New York: Academic Press.

Quadliarello, V., & Scheld, W.M. (1992). Bacterial meningitis: Pathogenesis, pathophysiology, and progress. *New England Journal of Medicine*, *327*, 864–872.

Quattrocchi, K., Prasad, P., Willits, N., & Wagner, F. (1991). Quantification of midline shift as a predictor of poor outcome following head injury. *Surgical Neurology*, *35*, 183–188.

Quesney, L., Constain, M., & Rasmussen, T. (1992). Seizures from dorsolateral frontal lobe. *Advances in Neurology*, *57*, 233–243.

Rabbitt, P. (1997). Introduction: Methodologies and models in the study of executive function. In P. Rabbitt (Ed.), *Methodology of frontal and executive function* (pp. 11–38). Hove, UK: Psychology Press.

Rabinowicz, T. (1976). Morphological features of the developing brain. In M.A.B. Brazier & F. Coceani (Eds.), *Brain dysfunction in infantile febrile convulsions* (pp. 1–23). New York: Raven.

Radetsky, M. (1992). Duration of symptoms and outcome in bacterial meningitis: An analysis of causation and the implications of a delay in diagnosis. *Pediatric Infectious Diseases Journal*, *11*, 694–698.

Raimondi, A. (1994). A unifying theory for the definition and classification of spina bifida. *Child's Nervous System*, *10*, 2–12.

Raimondi, A., & Hirschauer, J. (1984). Head injury in the infant and toddler. *Child's Brain*, *11*, 12–35.

Raimondi, A.J., & Soare, P. (1974). Intellectual development in shunted hydrocephalic children. *American Journal of Diseases in Children*, *127*, 664–671.

Rakic, P. (1975). Timing of major ontogenetic events in the visual cortex of the rhesus monkey.

In N. Buchwald & N. Brazier (Eds.), *Brain mechanisms in mental retardation* (pp. 3–40). New York: Academic Press.

Rakic, P. (1988). Specification of cerebral cortical areas. *Science, 241,* 170–176.

Rakic, P. (1995). Corticogenesis in human and nonhuman primates. In M. Gazzaniga (Ed.), *The cognitive neurosciences* (pp. 127–145). Cambridge, MA: MIT Press.

Rakic, P., Bourgeois, J.-P., Eckenhoff, M., Zecevic, N., & Goldman-Rakic, P. (1986). Concurrent overproduction of synapses in diverse regions of the primate cerebral cortex. *Science, 232,* 232–235.

Rankur, J., Aram, D., & Horowitz, S. (1980). *A comparison of right and left hemiplegic children's language ability.* Unpublished paper presented at the International Neuropsychological Society Meeting, San Francisco.

Ransom, B.R., & Elmore, J.G. (1991). Effects of antiepileptic drugs on the developing central nervous system. In D. Smith, D. Treiman, & M. Trimble (Eds.), *Advances in neurology* (Vol. 55, pp. 225–237). New York: Raven.

Rantala, H., Uhari, M., Uhari, M., Saukkonen, A., & Sorri, M. (1991). Outcome after childhood encephalitis. *Developmental Medicine and Child Neurology, 33,* 858–867.

Rasmussen, T. (1978). Further observations on the syndrome of chronic encephalitis and epilepsy. *Applied Neurophysiology, 41,* 1–12.

Rasmussen, T., & Milner, B. (1977). The role of early left-brain injury in determining lateralisation. *Annals of the New York Academy of Science, 299,* 255–269.

Ray, C.L., Mirsky, A.F., & Bakay Pragay, E. (1982). Functional analysis of attention-related unit activity in the reticular formation of the monkey. *Experimental Neurology, 77,* 544–562.

Rayport, S. (1992). Cellular and molecular biology of the neuron. In S. Yudofsky & R. Hales (Eds.), *The American Psychiatric Press textbook of neuropsychiatry* (2nd ed., pp. 3–28). Washington: American Psychiatric Press.

Reich, J.N., Kaspar, C., Puczynski, M.S., Puczynski, S., Cleland, J., Dell'Angela, K., & Emanuele, M. (1990). Effect of a hypoglycemic episode on neuropsychological functioning in diabetic children. *Journal of Clinical and Experimental Neuropsychology, 12,* 613–626.

Reilly, P., Simpson, D., Sprod, R., & Thomas, L. (1988). Assessing the conscious level of infants and young children: A pediatric version of the Glasgow Coma Scale. *Child's Nervous System, 4,* 30–33.

Reiss, A., Abrams, M., Singer, H., Ross, J., & Denckla, M. (1996). Brain development, gender and IQ in children: A volumetric imaging study. *Brain, 119,* 1763–1774.

Reitan, R.M. (1969). *Manual for administration of neuropsychological test batteries for adults and children.* Indianapolis, IN: Author.

Reitan, R.M., & Davison, L.A. (Eds.). (1974). *Clinical neuropsychology: Current status and applications.* Washington: Winston.

Rey, A. (1941). L'examine psychologique dans les cas d'encephalopathie traumatique. *Archives de Psychologique, 28,* 286–240.

Rey, A. (1964). *L'examen clinique en psychologie.* Paris: Press Universitaire de France.

Reynolds, C., & Bigler, E. (1993). *Test of memory and learning: Examiner's manual.* New York: Psychological Assessment Resources.

Reynolds, C., & Kamphaus, R. (1992). *Behavior assessment system for children.* Circle Pines, MN: Amerian Guidance Service.

Reynolds, R., Burri, R., Mahal, S., & Herschkowitz, N. (1992). Disturbed myelinogenesis and recovery in hyperphenylalaninemia in rats: An immunohistochemical study. *Experimental Neurology, 115, 347–367.*

Richens, A. (1996). Pharmacology and pharmacokinetics of antiepileptic drugs. In S. Wallace (Ed.), *Epilepsy in children* (pp. 513–531). London: Chapman & Hall Medical.

Rickards, A. L. (1993). *Prediction of developmental problems in children of very low birth-weight and normal birth-weight.* Unpublished doctoral dissertation. University of Melbourne, Australia.

Rickards, A., Coakley, J., Francis, I., Armstrong, S., Medson, H., & Connelly, J. (1989). Results of follow-up at five years in a group of hypothyroid Australian children detected by newborn screening. In F. Delange, D.A. Fisher, & D. Glineor (Eds.), *Research in congenital hypothyroidism* (p. 341). London: Plenum Press.

Ris, M.D., Williams, S.E., Hunt, M.M., Berry, H.K., & Leslie, N. (1994). Early-treated phenylketonuria: Adult neuropsychologic outcome. *Journal of Pediatrics, 124,* 388–392.

Risser, A.H., & Edgell, D. (1988). Neuropsychology of the developing brain: Implications for neuropsychological assessment. In M.G. Tramontana & S.R. Hooper (Eds.), *Assessment issues in child neuropsychology* (pp. 41–60). New York: Plenum.

Ritchie, K. (1981). Research note: Interaction in the families of epileptic children. *Journal of Child Psychology and Psychiatry, 22,* 65–71.

Riva, D., & Cassaniga, L. (1986). Late effect of unilateral brain lesions before and after the first year of life. *Neuropsychologia, 24,* 423–428.

Riva, D., Milani, N., Giorgi C., Pantaleoni C., Zorzi C., & Devoti, M. (1994). Intelligence outcome in children with shunted hydrocephalus of different etiology. *Child's Nervous System, 10,* 70–73.

Rivara, J.B, Jaffe, K.M., Fay, G.C., Polissar, N.L., Martin, K.M., Shurtleff, H.A., & Liao, S. (1993). Family functioning and injury severity as predictors of child functioning one year following traumatic brain injury. *Archives of Physical Medicine and Rehabilitation, 74,* 1047–1055.

Rivara, J.B., Jaffe, K.M., Polissar, N.L, Fay, G.C., Martin, K.M., Shurtleff, H.A., & Liao, S. (1994). Family functioning and children's academic performance and behavior problems in the year following traumatic brain injury. *Archives of Physical Medicine and Rehabilitation, 75,* 368–379.

Roberts, A. (1969). *Brain damage in boxers.* London: Pitman.

Roberts, M., Manshad, F., Bushnell, D., & Hines, M. (1995). Neurobehavioural dysfunction following mild traumatic brain injury in childhood: A case report with positive findings on positron emission tomography (PET). *Brain Injury, 9,* 427–436.

Robertson, I. (1999). The rehabilitation of attention. In D. Stuss, G. Winocur, & I. Robertson (Eds.), *Cognitive neurorehabilitation* (pp. 302–313). New York: Cambridge University Press.

Rodin, E.A., Schmaltz, S., & Twitty, G. (1986). Intellectual functions of patients with childhood epilepsy. *Developmental Medicine and Child Neurology, 28,* 25–33.

Rorabaugh, M.L., Berlin, L.E., Heldrich, F., Roberts, K., Rosenberg, L.A., Dorin, T., & Modlin, J.F. (1993). Aseptic meningitis in infants younger than two years of age: Acute illness and neurologic complications. *Pediatrics, 92,* 206–211.

Rosvold, H., Mirsky, A., Sarason, I., Bransome, E., & Beck, L. (1956). A continuous performance test of brain damage. *Journal of Consulting Psychology, 20,* 343–350.

Rothi, L., & Horner, J. (1983). Restitution and substitution: Two theories of recovery with application to neurobehavioral treatment. *Journal of Clinical Neuropsychology, 3,* 73–81.

Rourke, B.P. (1987). Syndrome of non-verbal learning disabilities: The final common pathway of white matter disease/dysfunction. *The Clinical Neuropsychologist, 1,* 209–234.

Rourke, B.P. (1988). The syndrome of nonverbal learning disabilities: Developmental manifestations of neurological disease, disorder, and dysfunction. *The Clinical Neuropsychologist, 2,* 292–330.

Rourke, B.P. (1989). *Nonverbal learning disabilities.* New York: Guilford Press.

Rourke, B.P. (Ed.). (1995). *Syndrome of non-verbal learning disabilities.* New York: Guilford Press.

Rourke, B.P., Bakker, D.J., Fisk, J.L., & Strang, J.D. (1983). *Child neuropsychology: An introduction to theory, research, and clinical practice.* New York: Guilford Press.

Rourke, B.P., Fisk, J.L., & Strang, J.D. (1986). *Neuropsychological assessment of children: A treatment oriented approach.* New York: Guilford Press.

Rourke, B.P., & Fuerst, D.R. (1991). *Learning disabilities and psychosocial functioning.* New York: Guilford Press.

Rourke, B.P., & Gates, R. (1980). *Underlining Test: Preliminary norms.* Windsor, Ontario: Authors.

Rovee-Collier, C., & Gerhardstein, P. (1997). The development of infant memory. In N. Cowan (Ed.), *The development of memory in childhood* (pp. 5–40). Hove, UK: Psychology Press.

Rovet, J. (1995). Congenital hyperthyroidism. In B. Rourke (Ed.), *Syndrome of nonverbal learning disabilities* (pp. 255–281). New York: Guilford Press.

Rovet, J., & Alvarez, M. (1996). Thyroid hormone and attention in school-age children with congenital hypothyroidism. *Journal of Child Psychology and Psychiatry, 37,* 579–585.

Rovet, J., Czuchta, D., & Ehrlich, R. (1990). Intellectual characteristics of diabetic children at diagnosis and one year later. *Journal of Pediatric Psychology, 15,* 775–788.

Rovet, J.F., & Ehrlich, R.M. (1988). Effect of temperament on metabolic control in children with diabetes mellitus. *Diabetes Care, 11,* 77–82.

Rovet, J.F., & Ehrlich, R.M. (1995). Long-term effects of L-thyroxine therapy for congenital hypothyroidism. *Journal of Pediatrics, 126,* 386–386.

Rovet, J., Ehrlich, R., & Hoppe, M. (1987). Intellectual deficits associated with early onset of insulin-dependent diabetes mellitus in children. *Diabetes Care, 10,* 510–515.

Rovet, J., Ehrlich, R., & Hoppe, M. (1988). Specific intellectual deficits in children with early onset diabetes mellitus. *Child Development, 59,* 226–234.

Rovet, J.F., Ehrlich, R.M., & Sorbara, D.L. (1987). Intellectual outcome in children with fetal hypothyroidism. *Journal of Pediatrics, 110,* 700–704.

Rovet, J.F., Ehrlich R.M., & Sorbara, D.L. (1989). The effect of thyroid hormone on temperament in infants with congenital hypothyroidism detected by newborn screening. *Journal of Pediatrics, 114,* 63–69.

Rovet, J.F., Ehrlich, R.M., & Sorbara, D.L. (1992). Neurodevelopment in infants and preschool children with congenital hypothyroidism: Etiological and treatment factors affecting outcome. *Journal of Pediatric Psychology, 17,* 187–213.

Rowe, K.S., & Rowe, K.J. (1993). *The RBRI Users Manual: Parent and teacher administered inventories for the assessment of child externalizing behaviours, for use in educational and epidemiological research.* Department of Paediatrics, University of Melbourne.

Rowley, G., & Fielding, K. (1991). Reliability and accuracy of the Glasgow Coma Scale with experienced and inexperienced raters. *Lancet, 337,* 535–538.

Rubenstein, C.L., Varni, J.W., & Katz, E.R. (1990). Cognitive functioning in long-term survivors of childhood leukemia: A prospective analysis. *Developmental and Behavioral Pediatrics, 11,* 301–305.

Rubin, R., Hochwald, G., Tiell, M., Liwnicz, B., & Epstein, F. (1975). Reconstitution of the cerebral cortical mantle in shunt-corrected hydrocephalus. *Developmental Medicine and Child Neurology, 17,* 151–156.

Ruff, H., & Rothbart, M. (1996). *Attention in early development: Themes and variations.* New York: Oxford University Press.

Ruijs, M., Gabreels, F., & Thijssen, H. (1994). The utility of electroencephalography and cerebral computed tomography in children with mild and moderately severe closed head injuries. *Neuropediatrics, 25,* 73–77.

Ruijs, M., Keyser, A., & Gabreels, F. (1992). Assessment of post-traumatic amnesia in young children. *Developmental Medicine and Child Neurology, 34,* 885–892.

Russell, W. (1971). *The traumatic amnesias.* Oxford: Oxford University Press.

Rutter, M., Chadwick, O., & Shaffer, D. (1983). Head injury. In M. Rutter (Ed.), *Developmental neuropsychiatry* (pp. 83–111). New York: Guilford Press.

Rutter, M., Graham, P., & Yule, W. (1970). *A neuropsychiatric study in childhood.* Philadelphia: Lippincott.

Ryan, C. (1988). Neurobehavioral complications of type 1 diabetes in childhood. *Diabetes Care, 11*, 86–93.

Ryan, C. (1990). Neuropsychological consequences and correlates of diabetes in childhood. In C. Holmes (Ed.), *Neuropsychological and behavioural aspects of diabetes* (pp. 58–84). New York: Springer.

Ryan, C., Atchison, J., Puczynski, S., Puczynski, M., Arslanian, S., & Becker D. (1990). Mild hypoglycemia associated with a deterioration of mental efficiency in children with insulin-dependent diabetes mellitus. *Journal of Pediatrics, 117*, 32–38.

Ryan, C., Vega, A., & Drash, A. (1985). Cognitive deficits in adolescents who developed diabetes early in life. *Pediatrics, 75*, 921–927.

Ryan, C., Williams, T., Orchard, T., & Finegold, D. (1992). Psychomotor slowing is associated with distal symmetrical polyneuropathy in adults with diabetes mellitus. *Diabetes, 41*, 107–113.

Ryan, C., Williams, T., Orchard, T., & Finegold D. (1993). Cognitive dysfunction in adults with type 1 (insulin-dependent) diabetes mellitus of long duration: Effects of recurrent hypoglycaemia and other chronic complications. *Diabetelogia, 36*, 329–334.

Saling, M. (1994). Neuropsychology beyond 2000: The failure of diagnostic expertise. In S. Touyz, D. Byrne, & A. Gilandis (Eds.), *Neuropsychology in clinical practice* (pp. 3–14). Sydney: Academic Press.

Saling, M.M., Berkovic, S.F., O'Shea, M.F., Kalnins, R.M., Darby, D.G., & Bladin, P.F. (1993). Lateralisation of verbal memory and unilateral hippocampal sclerosis: Evidence of task-specific effects. *Journal of Clinical and Experimental Neuropsychology, 15*(4), 608–618.

Sameroff, A. (1983). Developmental systems: Contexts and evolution. In P.H. Mussen (Ed.), *Handbook of child psychology: Vol. 1. History, theory and methods* (pp. 237–294). New York: Wiley.

Sander, J.W.A.S. (1998). New drugs for epilepsy. *Current Opinion in Neurology, 11*, 141–148.

Sartori, G., Job, R., Miozzo, M., Zago, S., & Marchiori G. (1993). Category-specific form-knowledge deficit in a patient with herpes simplex virus encephalitis. *Journal of Clinical and Experimental Neuropsychology, 15*, 280–299.

Sattler, J.M. (1988). *Assessment of children* (3rd ed.). San Diego: Jerome M. Sattler.

Satz, P., & Bullard-Bates, C. (1981). Acquired aphasia in children. In M.T. Sarno (Ed.), *Acquired aphasia* (pp. 399–426). New York: Academic Press.

Saykin, A.J., Gur, R.C., Sussman, N.M., O'Connor, M.J., & Gur, R.E. (1989). Memory deficits before and after temporal lobectomy: Effect of laterality and age of onset. *Brain and Cognition, 9*, 191–200.

Scambler, G., & Hopkins, A. (1990). Generating a model of epileptic stigma: The role of qualitative analysis. *Social Science and Medicine, 30*, 1187–1194.

Schaad, U., Suter, S., Gianella-Borradori, A., Pfenninger, J., Auckanthaler, R., Bernath, O., Cheseaux, J., & Wedgewood, J. (1990). A comparison of cetriaxone and cefuroxime for the treatment of bacterial meningitis in children. *New England Journal of Medicine, 322*, 141–147.

Scheffer, I.E., Phillips, H.A., O'Brien, C.E., Saling, M.M., Wrennall, J.A., Wallace, R.H., Mulley, J.C., & Berkovic, S.J. (1998). Familial partial epilepsy with variable foci: A new partial epilepsy syndrome with suggestion of linkage to chromosome 2. *Annals of Neurology, 44*(6), 890–899.

Scherer, L. (1995). Diagnostic imaging in pediatric trauma. *Seminars in Pediatric Surgery, 4*, 100–108.

Schlumberger, E., & Dulac, O. (1994). A simple, effective and well tolerated treatment regime for West syndrome. *Developmental Medicine and Child Neurology, 36*, 863–872.

Schmechel, D., & Rakic, P. (1979). A Golgi study of radial glial cells in developing monkey telencephalon: Morphogenesis and transformation into astrocytes. *Anatomy and Embryology, 156*, 115–152.

Schmidt, E., Rupp, A., Burgard, P., Pietz, J., Weglage, J., & de Sonneville, L. (1994). Sustained attention in adult phenylketonuria: The influence of the concurrent phenylalanine blood level. *Journal of Clinical and Experimental Neuropsychology, 16*, 681–688.

Schmidt, H., Mahle, M., Michel, U., & Pietz, J. (1987). Continuation vs discontinuation of low-phenylalanine diet in PKU adolescents. *European Journal of Pediatrics, 1987*(Suppl. 1), A17–A19.

Schneider, G. (1979). Is it really better to have your brain lesion early? A revision of the Kennard principle. *Neuropsychologia, 17*, 557–583.

Schuchat, A., Robinson, K., Wenger, J., Harrison, L., Farley, M., Reingold, A., Lefkowitz, L., & Perkins, B. (1997). Bacterial meningitis in the United States in 1995. Active Surveillance Team. *New England Journal of Medicine, 337*, 970–976.

Schwartz, M. (1997). Organization and development of callosal connectivity in prefrontal cortex. In N. Krasnegor, G. Lyon, & P.S. Goldman-Rakic (Eds.), *Development of the prefrontal cortex: Evolution, neurology, and behaviour* (pp. 49–68). Baltimore: Brookes.

Scott, M.A., Davidson, K.C., Fletcher, J.K., Brookshire, B.L., Handry, S.H., Bohan, T.C., & Francis, D.J. (1998). Memory functions in children with early hydrocephalus. *Neuropsychology, 12*, 578–589.

Scott, R.C., & Neville, B. (1998). Developmental perspectives on epilepsy. *Current Opinion in Neurology, 11*(2), 115–118.

Seashore, M.R., Friedman, E., Novelly, R.A., & Bapat, V. (1985). Loss of intellectual function in children with phenylketonuria after relaxation of dietary phenylalanine restriction. *Pediatrics, 75*, 226–232.

Seidel, U., Chadwick, O., & Rutter, M. (1975). Psychological disorders in crippled children: A comparative study of children with and without brain damage. *Developmental Medicine and Child Neurology, 17*, 563–573.

Seidenberg, M. (1989). Academic achievement and school performance of children with epilepsy. In B.P. Hermann & M. Seidenberg (Eds.), *Childhood epilepsies: Neuropsychological, psychosocial and intervention aspects* (pp. 105–118). Chichester, UK: Wiley.

Seidenberg, M., Beck, N., Geisser, M., Giordani, J., Sackellares, C., Berent, S., Dreifuss, F.E., & Boll, T.J. (1986). Academic achievement in children with epilepsy. *Epilepsia, 27*(6), 753–759.

Seidenberg, M., Hermann, B., Schoenfeld, J., Davies, K., Wyler, A., & Dohan, C. (1997). Reorganisation of verbal memory function in early onset temporal lobe epilepsy. *Brain and Cognition, 35*, 132–148.

Seidl, R., Birnbacher, R., Hauser, E., Bernert, G., Freilinger, M., & Schober, E. (1996). Brain-stem auditory evoked potentials and visually evoked potentials in young patients with IDDM. *Diabetes Care, 19*, 1220–1224.

Sell, S. (1983). Long-term sequelae of bacterial meningitis in children. *Pediatric Infectious Diseases, 2*, 90–93.

Sell, S. (1987). *Haemophilus influenzae* type b meningitis: Manifestations and long term sequelae. *Pediatric Infectious Diseases, 6*, 775–778.

Sell, S., Webb, W.W., Pate, J.E., & Doyne, E.O. (1972). Psychological sequelae to bacterial meningitis: Two controlled studies. *Pediatrics, 49*, 212–217.

Sellal, F., Fontaine, S.F., Van Der Linden, M., Rainville, C., & Labrecque, R. (1996). To be or not to be at home? A neuropsychological approach to delusion for place. *Journal of Clinical and Experimental Neuropsychology, 18*, 234–248.

Sells, C.J., Carpenter, R.L., & Ray, C.G. (1975). Sequelae of central nervous system enterovirus infections. *New England Journal of Medicine, 293*, 1–4.

Selwa, L.M., Berent, S., Giordani, B., Henry, T.H., Buchtel, H.A., & Ross, D.A. (1994). Serial cognitive testing in temporal lobe epilepsy: Longitudinal changes with medical and surgical therapies. *Epilepsia, 35*(4), 743–749.

Selzer S.C., Lindgren, S.D., & Blackman, J. (1992). Long-term neuropsychological outcome of high risk infants with intracranial haemorrhage. *Journal of Pediatric Psychology, 17*, 407–422.

Semel, E., Wiig, E., & Secord, W. (1995). *Clinical Evaluation of Language Fundamentals* (3rd ed.). San Antonio, TX: Psychological Corporation.

Seymoure, R., & Juraska, J. (1992). Sex differences in cortical thickness and the dendritic tree in the monocular and binocular subfields of the rat cortex at weaning age. *Developmental Brain Research, 69*, 185–189.

Shaffer, J., Wolfe, L., Friedrich, W., Shurtleff, H., Shurtleff, D., & Fay, G. (1985). Cognitive and achievement status of children with myelomeningocele. *Journal of Pediatric Psychology, 10*, 325–335.

Shaffer, J., Wolfe, L., Friedrich, W., Shurtleff, H., Shurtleff, D., & Fay, G. (1986). Developmental expectations: Intelligence and fine motor skills. In D. Shurtleff (Ed.), *Myelodysplasias and exstophies: Significance, prevention and treatment* (pp. 359–372). New York: Grune & Stratton.

Shallice, T. (1982). Specific impairments of planning. *Philosophical Transcripts of the Royal Society of London, 298*, 199–209.

Shallice, T. (1990). *From neuropsychology to mental structure*. New York: Cambridge University Press.

Shapiro, J. (1983). Family reactions and coping strategies in response to the physically ill or handicapped child. *Social Science Medicine, 17*, 913–931.

Sharma, M., & Sharma, A. (1994). Mode, presentation, CT findings and outcome of pediatric head injury. *Indian Pediatrics, 31*, 733–739.

Sharples, P., Stuart, A., Matthews, D., & Eyre, J. (1995). Cerebral blood flow and metabolism in children with severe head injury: Part I. Relation to age, Glasgow Coma Score, outcome, intracranial pressure, and time after injury. *Journal of Neurology, Neurosurgery, and Psychiatry, 58*, 145–152.

Shaywitz, B., Shaywitz, S., Pugh, K., Constable, R., Skudlarski, P., Fulbright, R., et al. (1995). Sex differences in the functional organization of the brain for language. *Nature, 373*, 607–609.

Shepherd, G.M. (1994). *Neurobiology* (3rd ed.). New York: Oxford University Press.

Shepp, B.E., Barrett, S.E., & Kolbet, L.I. (1987). The development of selective attention: Holistic perception versus resource allocation. *Journal of Experimental Child Psychology, 43*, 159–180.

Sheslow, D., & Adams, W. (1990). *Wide Range Assessment of Memory and Learning: Administration manual*. Wilmington, DE: Jastak.

Shirley, H., & Greer, I. (1940). Environmental and personality problems in the treatment of diabetic children. *Journal of Pediatrics, 16*, 775–781.

Shores, A.E. (1989). Comparison of the Westmead PTA Scale and the Glasgow Coma Scale of predictors of neuropsychological outcome following extremely severe blunt head injury. *Journal of Neurology, Neurosurgery, and Psychiatry, 52*, 126–127.

Shrier, L., Schopps, J., & Feigin, R. (1996). Bacterial and fungal infections of the central nervous system. In B. Berg (Ed.), *Principles of child neurology* (pp. 749–783). New York: McGraw-Hill.

Shulman, S., Fisch, R.O., Zempel, C.E., Gadish, O., & Chang, P. (1991). Children with phenylketonuria: The interface of family and child functioning. *Developmental and Behavioral Pediatrics, 12*, 315–321.

Shum, D.K., McFarland, K.A., Bain, J.D., & Humphreys, M.S. (1990). The effects of closed head injury upon attentional processes: An information processing stage analysis. *Journal of Clinical and Experimental Neuropsychology, 12*, 247–264.

Shurtleff, D., Foltz, E., & Loeser, J. (1973). Hydrocephalus: A definition of its progression and relationship to intellectual function, diagnosis and complications. *American Journal of Diseases of Children, 125*, 688–693.

Siebelink, B.M, Bakker, D.J., Binnie, C.D., & Kasteleijn-Nolst Trenité, D.G.A. (1988). Psychological effects of subclinical epileptiform EEG discharges in children: II. General intelligence tests. *Epilepsy Research, 2*, 117–121.

Siegler, R. (1991). *Children's thinking.* Englewood Cliffs, NJ: Prentice-Hall.

Silink, M. (1994). Childhood diabetes and hypoglycaemia. In M.J. Robinson & D. Roberton (Eds.), *Practical paediatrics* (3rd ed., pp. 533–540). Melbourne: Churchill Livingstone.

Simon, H.A. (1974). How big is a chunk? *Science, 183*, 482–488.

Simonds, J., Goldstein, D., Walker, B., & Rawlings, S. (1981). The relationship between psychosocial factors and blood glucose regulation in insulin-dependent diabetic adolescents. *Diabetes Care, 4*, 610–615.

Simons, W.F., Fuggle, P.W., Grant, D.B., & Smith, I. (1994). Intellectual development at 10 years in early treated congenital hypothyroidism. *Archives of Disease in Childhood, 71*, 232–234.

Smibert, E., Anderson, V., Godber, T., & Ekert, H. (1996). Risk factors for intellectual and educational sequelae of cranial irradiation in childhood acute lymphoblastic leukemia. *British Journal of Cancer, 73*, 825–833.

Smith, A. (1981). On the organization, disorganization and reorganization of language and other brain functions. In Y. Lebrun & O. Zangwill (Eds.), *Lateralization of language in the child.* Lisse, The Netherland: Swets & Zeitlinger.

Smith, A., & Sugar, C. (1975). Development of above normal language and intelligence 21 years after left hemispherectomy. *Neurology, 25*, 813–818.

Smith, D.B., Craft, B.R., Collins, J.F., Mattson, R.H., & Cramer, J.A. (1986). VA Cooperative Study Group 118. Behavioural characteristics of epilepsy patients compared with normal controls. *Epilepsia, 27*, 760–768.

Smith, D.B., Mattson, R.H., Cramer, J.A., Collins, J.F., Novelly, R.A., & Craft, B. (1987). Results of a nationwide Veterans Administration cooperative study comparing the toxicity of carbamazepine, phenobarbital, phenytoin and primadone. *Epilepsia, 28*(Suppl. 3), S50–S58.

Smith, I., & Beasley, M.G. (1989). Intelligence and behaviour in children with early treated phenylketonuria. *European Journal of Clinical Nutrition, 43*, 1–5.

Smith, I., Beasley, M.G., & Ades, A.E. (1991). Intelligence and quality of dietary treatment in phenylketonuria. *Archives of Disease in Childhood, 66*, 311–316.

Snoek, J., Jennett, B., Adams, D., Graham, D., & Doyle, D. (1979). Computerised tomography after recent head injury in patients without acute intracranial haematoma. *Journal of Neurology, Neurosurgery, and Psychiatry, 42*, 215–225.

Snow, J.H., Prince, M., Souheaver, G., Ashcraft, E., Stefans, V., & Edmonds, J. (1994). Neuropsychological patterns of adolescents and young adults with spina bifida. *Archives of Clinical Neuropsychology, 9*, 277–287.

Snyder, R.D., Stovring, I., Cushing, A.H., Davis, L.E., & Hardy, T.L. (1981). Cerebral infarction in childhood bacterial meningitis. *Journal of Neurology, Neurosurgery and Psychiatry, 44*, 581–585.

Soare, P., & Raimondi, J. (1977). Intellectual and perceptual-motor characteristics of treated myelomeningocele children. *American Journal of Diseases of Children, 131*, 199–204.

Soltesz, G., & Acsadi, G. (1989). Associations between diabetes, severe hypoglycaemia and electroencephalographic abnormalities. *Archives of Disease in Childhood, 64*, 992–996.

Sowell, E., & Jernigan, T. (1998). Further MRI evidence of late brain maturation: Limbic volume increases and changes asymmetries during childhood and adolescence. *Developmental Neuropsychology*, *14*, 599–618.

Spain, B. (1974). Verbal and performance ability in preschool children with spina bifida. *Developmental Medicine and Child Neurology*, *16*, 773–780.

Sparrow, S., Balla, D.A., & Cicchetti, D.V. (1984). *Vineland Adaptive Behavior Scales: Interview edition: Survey form manual.* Circle Pines, MN: American Guidance Services.

Spinelli, D., Jensen H., & Di Prisco, G. (1980). Early experience effect on dendritic branching in normally reared kittens. *Experimental Neurology*, *68*, 1–11.

Spreen, O., & Gaddes, W. (1969). Developmental norms for 15 neuropsychological tests age 6 to 15. *Cortex*, *5*, 171–191.

Spreen, O., & Strauss, E. (1991). *A compendium of neuropsychological tests.* New York: Oxford University Press.

Sproles, E.T., Azerrad, J., Williamson, C., & Merrill, R.E. (1969). Meingitis due to *Haemophilus influenzae*: Long term sequelae. *Pediatrics*, *75*, 782–788.

Squire, L., & Zola-Morgan, S. (1991). The medial temporal lobe memory system. *Science*, *253*, 1380–1386.

St James-Roberts, I. (1979). Neurological plasticity, recovery from brain insult, and child development. *Advances in Child Development and Behavior*, *14*, 253–319.

Stalings, G., Ewing-Cobbs, L., Francis, D., & Fletcher, J. (1996). Prediction of academic placement after pediatric head injury using neurological, demographic and neuropsychological variables. *Journal of the International Neuropsychological Society* [Chicago abstracts].

Stanford, L.D., Chelune, G.J., & Wyllie, E. (1998). Neuropsychological functioning of children with hippocampal sclerosis. *Epilepsia*, *39*(Suppl. 6), 249 [abstract].

Stark, R., & McGregor, K. (1997). Follow-up study of a right- and a left-hemispherectomised child: Implications for localisation and impairment of language in children. *Brain and Language*, *60*, 222–242.

Stauder, J., Molenaar, P., & van der Molen, M. (1999). Brain activity and cognitive transition during childhood: A longitudinal event-related potential study. *Child Neuropsychology*, *5*, 41–59.

Staudt, M., Schropp, C., Staudt, F., Obletter, N., Bise, K., & Breit, A. (1993). Myelination of the brain in MRI: A staging system. *Pediatric Radiology*, *23*, 169–176.

Steen, R., Ogg, R., & Reddick, W. (1997). Age-related changes in the pediatric brain: Quantitative MR evidence of maturational changes during adolescence. *American Journal of Neuroradiology*, *18*, 819–828.

Stein, S., & Spettell, C. (1995). Delayed and progressive brain injury in children and adolescents with head trauma. *Pediatric Neurosurgery*, *23*, 299–304.

Stein, S., Spettell, C., Young, G., & Ross, S. (1993). Delayed and progressive brain injury in closed-head trauma: Radiological demonstration. *Neurosurgery*, *32*, 25–31.

Sternberg, S. (1975). Memory scanning: New findings and current controversies. *Quarterly Journal of Experimental Pychology*, *27*, 1–32.

Stewart, J., & Kolb, B. (1994). Dendritic branching in cortical pyramidal cells in response to ovariectomy in adult female rats: Suppression by neonatal exposure to testosterone. *Brain Research*, *654*, 149–154.

Stoddart, C., & Knights, R.M. (1986). Neuropsychological assessment of children: Alternative approaches. In J.E. Obrzut & G.W. Hynd (Eds.), *Child neuropsychology: Vol. 2. Clinical practice* (pp. 229–244). San Diego, CA: Academic Press.

Stores, G. (1978). School-children with epilepsy at risk for learning and behaviour problems. *Developmental Medicine and Child Neurology*, *20*, 502–508.

Stores, G. (1980). Children with epilepsy: Psychosocial aspects. In B.P. Hermann (Ed.), *A multidisciplinary handbook of epilepsy* (pp. 224–242), Springfield: Thomas.

Stores, G., & Hart, J. (1976). Reading skills of children with generalised or focal epilepsy attending ordinary school. *Developmental Medicine and Child Neurology, 18*, 703–716.

Stovring, J., & Snyder, R. (1980). Computed tomography in childhood bacterial meningitis. *Journal of Pediatrics, 96*, 820–823.

Strauss, E., Loring, D., Chelune, G., Hunter, M., Hermann, B., Perrine, K., Westerveld, M., Trenerry, M., & Barr, W. (1995). Predicting cognitive impairment in epilepsy: Findings from the Bozeman Epilepsy Consortium. *Journal of Clinical and Experimental Neuropsychology, 17*, 909–917.

Strauss, E., Wada, J., & Hunter, M. (1992). Sex-related differences in the cognitive consequences of early left-hemisphere lesions. *Journal of Clinical and Experimental Neuropsychology, 14*, 738–748.

Sturniolo, M.G., & Galletti, F. (1994). Idiopathic epilepsy and school achievement. *Archives of Disease in Childhood, 70*, 424–428.

Stuss, D., & Benson, F. (1987). The frontal lobes and control of cognition and memory. In E. Perecman (Ed.), *The frontal lobes revisited* (pp. 141–158). New York: IRBN Press.

Stuss, D.T. (1992). Biological and psychological development of executive functions. *Brain and Cognition, 20*, 8–23.

Stuss, D.T., Binns, M., Carruth, F., Brandys, C., Moulton, R., Levine, B., Snow, W., & Schwartz, M. (1999). The TBI acute recovery period: Post-traumatic amnesia or post-traumatic confusional state? *Journal of Neurosurgery, 90*, 635–643.

Stuss, D.T., Shallice, T., Alexander, M., & Picton, T. (1995). A multidisciplinary approach to anterior attentional functions. *Annals of the New York Academy of Science, 769*, 191–211.

Stuss, D.T., Stethem, L.L, Hugenholtz, H., Picton, T., Pivik, J., & Richard, M.T. (1989). Reaction time after head injury: Fatigue, divided and focussed attention, and consistency of performance. *Journal of Neurology, Neurosurgery, and Psychiatry, 52*, 742–748.

Swanson, H., Cooney, J., & Brock, S. (1993). The influence of working memory and classification ability on children's word problem solution. *Journal of Experiemntal Child Psychology, 55*, 374–395.

Swisher, L.P., & Pinsker, E.J. (1971). The language characteristics of hyperverbal, hydrocephalic children. *Developmental Medicine and Child Neurology, 13*, 746–755.

Szabó, C.A., Wyllie, E., Standford, L.D., Geckler, C. Kotagal, P., Comair, Y.G., & Thornton, A.E. (1998). Neuropsychological effect of temporal lobe resection in preadolescent children with epilepsy. *Epilepsia, 39*(8), 814–819.

Takala, A.K., & Clements, D.A. (1992). Socioeconomic risk factors for invasive *Haemophilus influenzae* type b disease. *Journal of Infectious Diseases, 165*(Suppl. 1), S11–S15.

Talland, G.A. (1965). *Deranged memory*. New York: Academic Press.

Tallroth, G., Ryding, E., & Agardh, C. (1992). Regional cerebral blood flow in normal man during insulin-induced hypoglycemia and in the recovery period following glucose infusion. *Metabolism, 41*, 717–721.

Tassinari, C., Bureau, M., Dravet, C., et al. (1982). Electrical status epilepticus during sleep in children (ESES). In M. Sterman, M. Shouse, & P. Passouant (Eds.), *Sleep and epilepsy* (pp. 465–479). New York: Academic Press.

Taylor, H.G. (1984). Early brain injury and cognitive development. In C. Almli & S. Finger (Eds.), *Early brain damage: Research orientations and clinical observations* (pp. 325–345). New York: Academic Press.

Taylor, H.G. (1988). Learning disabilities. In E. Mash (Ed.), *Behavioral assessments of childhood disorders* (2nd ed, pp. 402–405). New York: Guilford Press.

Taylor, H.G., & Alden, J. (1997). Age-related differences in outcomes following childhood brain insults: An introduction and overview. *Journal of the International Neuropsychological Society, 3*, 555–567.

Taylor, H.G., Barry, C.T., & Schatscheider, C. (1993). School-age consequences of *Haemophilus influenzae* Type B meningitis. *Journal of Clinical Child Psychology, 22*, 196–206.

Taylor, H.G., Drotar, D., Wade, S., Yeates, K., Stancin, T., & Klein, S. (1995). Recovery from traumatic brain injury in children: The importance of the family. In S.H. Broman & M.E. Michel (Eds.), *Traumatic head injury in children* (pp. 188–218). New York: Oxford University Press.

Taylor, H.G., & Fletcher, J.M. (1990). Neuropsychological assessment in children. In G. Goldstein & M. Herson (Eds.), *Handbook of psychological assessment* (2nd ed., pp. 228–255). New York: Pergamon Press.

Taylor, H.G., Hack, M., & Klein, N. (1998). Attention deficits in children with <750 gm birthweight. *Child Neuropsychology, 4*, 21–34.

Taylor, H.G., Michaels, R.H., Mazur, P.M., Bauer, R.E., & Liden, C.B. (1984). Intellectual, neuropsychological, and achievement outcomes in children six to eight years after recovery from *Haemophilus influenzae* meningitis. *Pediatrics, 74*, 198–205.

Taylor, H.G., Mills, H.L., Ciampi, A., Gerber, R., Watters, G., Gold, R., MacDonald, N., & Michael, R.H. (1990). The sequelae of *Haemophilus influenzae* meningitis in school-age children. *New England Journal of Medicine, 323*, 1657–1663.

Taylor, H.G., & Schatsneider, C. (1992). Child neuropsychology assessment: A test of basic assumptions. *The Clinical Neuropsychologist, 6*, 259–275.

Taylor, H.G., Schatsneider, C., Petrill, S., Barry, C.T., & Owens, C. (1996). Executive dysfunction in children with early brain disease: Outcomes post-*Haemophilus influenzae* meningitis. *Developmental Neuropsychology, 12*, 35–51.

Taylor, H.G., & Schatsneider, C., & Rich, D. (1992). Sequelae of *Haemophilus influenzae* meningitis: Implications for the study of brain disease and development. In M.G. Tramontana & S.R. Hooper (Eds.), *Advances in child neuropsychology* (Vol. 1, pp. 50–108). New York: Springer.

Teasdale, G., & Jennett, B. (1974). Assessment of coma and impaired consciousness. *Lancet, 2*, 81–84.

Tejani, A., Dobias, B., & Sambursky, J. (1982). Long term prognosis after *H. influenzae* meningitis: Prospective evaluation. *Developmental Medicine and Child Neurology, 24*, 338–343.

Temple, C. (1997). *Developmental cognitive neuropsychology*. Hove, UK: Psychology Press.

Ternard, C., Go, V., Gerich, J., & Haymond, M. (1982). Endocrine pancreatic response in children with onset of insulin-requiring diabetes before age 3 and after age 5. *Pediatrics, 101*, 36–39.

Teuber, M.L. (1962). Behaviour after cerebral lesions in children. *Developmental Medicine and Child Neurology, 4*, 3–20.

Tew, B. (1979). The "cocktail party syndrome" in children with hydrocephalus and spina bifida. *British Journal of Disorders of Communication, 14*, 89–101.

Tew, B., & Laurence, K. (1975). The effects of hydrocephalus on intelligence, visual perception and school attainment. *Developmental Medicine and Child Neurology, 17*, 129–134.

Tew, B., & Laurence, K. (1979). The clinical and psychological characteristics of children with "cocktail party syndrome". *Zeitschrift für Kinderchirurgie, 28*, 360–367.

Tew, B., & Laurence, K. (1983). The relationship between spina bifida children's intelligence scores on school entry and at school leaving: A preliminary report. *Child: Care, Health and Development, 9*, 13–17

Tew, B., Laurence, K., & Richards, A. (1980). Inattention among children with hydrocephalus and spina bifida. *Zeitschrift für Kinderchirurgie, 31*, 381–385.

Tew, B., Payne, H., & Laurence, K. (1974). Must a family with a handicapped child be a handicapped family? *Developmental Medicine and Child Neurology, 16*(Suppl. 32), 95–98.

Thatcher, R.W. (1991). Maturation of the human frontal lobes: Physiological evidence for staging. *Developmental Neuropsychology, 7*, 397–419.

Thatcher, R.W. (1992). Cyclical cortical reorganization during early childhood. *Brain and Cognition, 20*, 24–50.

Thatcher, R.W. (1997). Human frontal lobe development: A theory of cyclical cortical reorganization. In N. Krasnegor, G. Lyon, & P.S. Goldman-Rakic (Eds.), *Development of the prefrontal cortex: Evolution, neurology, and behaviour* (pp. 85–116). Baltimore: Brookes.

Thomas, V.H., & Hopkins, I.J. (1984). Arteriographic demonstrations of vascular lesions in the study of neurologic deficit in advanced *Haemophilus influenzae* meningitis. *Developmental Medicine and Child Neurology, 14*, 783–787.

Thompson, A.J., Smith, I., Brenton, D., Youl, B.D., Rylance, G., Davidson, D.C., Kendall, B., & Lees, A.J. (1990). Neurological deterioration in young adults with phenylketonuria. *Lancet, 336*, 602–605.

Thompson, G. (1994). Inborn errors of metabolism. In M.J. Robinson & D. Roberton (Eds.), *Practical paediatrics* (3rd ed., pp. 54–61). Melbourne: Churchill Livingstone.

Thompson, N.M., Fletcher, J.M., Chapieski, L., Landry, S.H., Miner, M.E., & Bixby, J. (1991). Cognitive and motor abilities in preschool hydrocephalics. *Journal of Clinical and Experimental Neuropsychology, 13*, 245–258.

Thompson, N.M., Fletcher, J.M., & Levin, H.S. (1982). Hydrocephalic infants: Developmental assessment and computerised tomography. *Child's Brain, 9*, 400–410.

Thompson, N.M., Francis, D.J., Stuebing, K.K., Fletcher, J.M, Ewing-Cobbs, L., Miner, M.E., Levin, H.S., & Eisenberg, H.M. (1994). Motor, visuo-spatial, and somatosensory skills after closed head injury in children and adolescents: A study of change. *Neuropsychology, 8*, 333–342.

Thompson, P.J., & Trimble, M.R. (1982). Comparative effects of anticonvulsant drugs on cognitive functioning. *British Journal of Clinical Practice, 18*(Suppl.), 154–156.

Thompson, R.J., Kronenberger, W.G., Johnson, D.F., & Whiting, K. (1989). The role of CNS functioning and family functioning, behavioural problems of children with myelodysplasia. *Developmental and Behavioural Pediatrics, 10*, 242–248.

Thomsen, I.V. (1975). Evaluation of outcome of aphasia in patients with severe closed head trauma. *Journal of Neurology, Neurosurgery, and Psychiatry, 47*, 260–268.

Thorndike, R., Hagan, E., & Sattler, J. (1985). *The Stanford Binet Intelligence Scale* (4th ed.) New York: Psychological Corporation.

Thulborn, K. (1998). High field clinical functional magnetic resonance imaging: Applications in stroke and epilepsy. *Third Australian symposium on functional brain mapping*, Melbourne, Australia.

Tiffin, J. (1968). *Purdue Pegboard examiner's manual*. Rosemont, IL: London House.

Tillotson, S.L., Fuggle, P.W., Smith, I., Ades, A.E., & Grant, D.B. (1994). Relation between biochemical severity and intelligence in early treated congenital hypothyroidism: A threshold effect. *British Medical Journal, 309*, 440–445.

Timmermans, S.R., & Christensen, B. (1991). The measurement of attention deficits in TBI children and adolescents. *Cognitive Rehabilitation*, 26–31.

Timmings, P., & Richens, A. (1992). Lamotrogine as an add-on drug in the management of Lennox Gastaux syndrome. *European Neurology, 32*, 305–307.

Todd, J.A., Anderson, V.A., & Lawrence, J.A. (1996). Planning skills in head injured adolescents and their peers. *Neuropsychological Rehabilitation, 6*, 81–99.

Toltzis, P. (1995). Infective encephalitis. In H.B. Jenson, R.S. Baltimore, R.I. Markowitz, & A.B. West (Eds.), *Pediatric infectious diseases*. Norwalk, CN: Appleton & Lange.

Tompkins, C.A., Holland, A.L., Ratcliff, G., Costello, A., Leahy, L., & Cowell, V. (1990). Predicting cognitive recovery from closed head injury in children and adolescents. *Brain and Cognition, 13*, 86–97.

Tramontana, M.G., & Hooper, S.R. (Eds.). (1988). *Assessment issues in child neuropsychology*. New York: Plenum.

Trenerry, M.R., Loring, D.W., Petersen, R.C., & Shargrough, F.W. (1996). The Wada Test. In E. Wyllie (Ed.), *The treatment of epilepsy: Principles and practice* (2nd ed., pp. 1000–1005). Baltimore: Williams & Wikins.

Trimble, M.R., & Corbett, J.A. (1980). Anticonvulsant drugs and cognitive function. In J.A. Wada & J.K. Penry (Eds.), *Advances in epileptology: The X International Symposium*. New York: Raven Press.

Tuchmann-Duplessis, H., Auroux, M., & Haegel, P. (1975). *Illustrated human embryology: Vol. 3. Nervous system and endocrine glands*. Paris: Mason.

Uemura, E., & Hartmann, H.A. (1978). RNA content and volume of nerve cell bodies in human brain: I. Prefrontal cortex in aging normal and demented patients. *Journal of Neuropathology and Experimental Neurology, 37*, 487–496.

Ullrich, K., Moller, H., Weglage, J., Schuierer, G., Bick, U., Ludolph, A., Hahn-Ullrich, H., Funders, B., & Koch, H.-G. (1994). White matter abnormalities in phenylketonuria: Results of magnetic resonance measurements. *Acta Paediatrica Suppl., 407*, 78–82.

Ungerstedt, U. (1971). Post-synaptic supersensitivity after 6-hydroxydopamine induced degeneration of the nigro-striatal dopamine system. *Acta Psychologica Scandanavica Suppl., 367*, 69–93.

Upton, D., & Thompson, P.J. (1997). Age of onset and neuropsychological function in frontal lobe epilepsy. *Epilepsia, 36*(10), 1103–1113.

Valk, J., & Van der Knap, M.S. (1992). Toxic encephalopathy. *American Journal of Neuroradiation, 13*, 747–760.

Van der Knapp, M., Valk, J., Bakker, C., Schoonfeld, M., Faberm J., et al. (1991). Myelination as an expression of the functional maturity of the brain. *Developmental Medicine and Child Neurology, 33*, 849–857.

Van der Schot, L.W., Doesburg, W.H., & Sengers, R.C. (1994). The phenylalanine response curve in relation to growth and mental development in the first years of life. *Acta Paediatrica Suppl., 407*, 68–69

van Zomeren, A., & Brouwer, W. (1994). *Clinical neuropsychology of attention*. New York: Oxford University Press.

Vargha-Khadem, F., Isaacs, E., Papaleloudi, H., Polkey, C., & Wilson, J. (1991). Development of language in six hemispherectomized patients. *Brain, 114*, 473–495.

Vargha-Khadem, F., Isaacs, E., Papaleloudi, H., Polkey, C., & Wilson, J. (1992). Development of intelligence and memory in children with hemiplegic cerebral palsy. *Brain, 115*, 315–329.

Vargha-Khadem, F., O'Gorman, A., & Watters, G. (1985). Aphasia and handedness in relation to hemispheric side, age at injury and severity of cerebral lesion during childhood. *Brain, 108*, 677–696.

Varney, N.R., Campbell, D., & Roberts, R.J. (1994). Long-term neuropsychological sequelae of fever associated with amnesia. *Archives of Clinical Neuropsychology, 9*, 347–352.

Verity, C.M., Ross, E.M., & Golding, J. (1993). Outcome of childhood status epilepticus and lengthy febrile convulsions: findings of a national cohort study. *British Medical Journal, 307*, 225–228.

Vermeulen, J., & Aldenkamp, A.P. (1995). Cognitive side effects of chronic antiepileptic drug treatment: A review of 25 years research. *Epilepsy Research, 22*, 65–95.

Vermeulen, J., Kortstee, S.W.A.T., Alpherts, W.C.J., & Aldenkamp, A.P. (1994). Cognitive performance in learning disabled children with and without epilepsy. *Seizure, 3*(1), 13–21.

Viberg, M., Blennow, G., & Polski, B. (1987). Epilepsy in adolescence: Implications for the development of personality. *Epilepsia, 28*(5), 542–546.

Villasana, D., Butler, I.J., Williams, J.C., & Roongta, S.M. (1989). Neurological deterioration in adult phenylketonuria. *Journal of Inherited Metabolic Diseases, 12*, 451–457.

Villella, S., Anderson, V., & Anderson, J. (in press). Sustained and selective attention in children with attention deficit/hyperactivity disorder and learning disabilities. *Clinical Neuro-psychological Assessment*.

Vining, P.G., Freeman, J.M., Brandt, J., Carson, B.S., & Uematsu, S. (1993). Progressive uni-lateral encephalopathy of childhood (Rasmussen's syndrome): A reappraisal. *Epilepsia, 34*, 639–650.

Vlassara, H., Brownlee, M., & Cerami, A. (1983). Excessive nonenzymatic glycosylation of peripheral and central nervous system myelin components in diabetic rats. *Diabetes, 32*, 670–674.

Vlieger, R., Sadikoglu, S., & Van Eijndhoven, J. (1980). Visual evoked potentials, audio evoked potentials, and EEG in shunted hydrocephalic children. *Neuropediatrics, 12*, 55–61.

Volpe, J.L. (1989). Intraventricular hemorrhage in the premature infant—current concepts: Part 1. *Annals of Neurology, 25*, 3–11.

Von Monokow, C. (1914). *Die lokalisation in der grosshirnrinde und der abbau der funktion durch korticale herde*. Wiesbaden: Bergman.

Waaland, P., & Kreutzer, J. (1988). Family response to childhood traumatic brain injury. *Journal of Head Trauma Rehabilitation, 3*, 51–63.

Waber, D.P., & Holmes, J.M. (1985). Assessing children's copy productions of the Rey–Osterreith Complex Figure. *Journal of Clinical and Experimental Neuropsychology, 7*, 264–280.

Waber, D., Tarbell, N., Fairclough, D., Atmore, K., Castro, R., Isquith, R., Lussier, F., Romero, I., Carpenter, P., Schiller, M., & Sallan, S.E. (1995). Cognitive sequelae of treatment in childhood acute lymphoblastic leukemia: Cranial radiation requires an accomplice. *Journal of Clinical Oncology, 13*, 2490–2496.

Wada, J., Clark, R., & Hamm, A. (1975). Cerebral hemispheric asymmetry in humans. *Archives of Neurology, 32*, 239–246.

Wade, S., Taylor, H.G., Drotar, D., Stancin, T., & Yeates, K.O. (1996). Childhood traumatic brain injury: Initial impact on the family. *Journal of Learning Disabilities, 29*, 652–661.

Wainwright-Sharp, J., & Bryson, S. (1993). Visual orienting deficits in high functioning people with autism. *Journal of Autism and Developmental Disorders, 23*, 1–13.

Waisbren, S.E., Mahon, B.E., Schnell, R.R., & Levy, H.L. (1987). Predictors of intelligence quotient and intelligence quotient change in persons treated for phenylketonuria early in life. *Pediatrics, 79*, 351–355.

Waisbren, S.E., Brown, M.J., de Sonneville, L.M., & Levy, H.L. (1994). Review of neuro-psychological functioning in treated phenylketonuria: An information processing approach. *Acta Paediatrica Suppl., 407*, 98–103.

Wald, E.R., Bergman, I., Taylor, H.G., Chiponis, D., Porter, C., & Kubek, K. (1986). Long-term outcome of Group B streptococcal meningitis. *Pediatrics, 77*, 217–221.

Walker, M., Mayer, T., Storrs, B., & Hylton, P. (1985). Pediatric head injury: Factors which influence outcome. In P. Chapman (Ed.), *Concepts in pediatric neurosurgery* (Vol. 6, pp. 84–97). Basel: Karger.

Wallace, R.H., Berkovic, S.F., Howell, R.A., Sutherland, G.R., & Mulley, J.C. (1996). Suggestion of a major gene for familial febrile convulsions mappings to 8q 13–21. *Journal of Medical Genetics, 33*, 308–312.

Wallace, R.H., Wang, D.W., Singh, R., Scheffer, I.E., George, A.L., Phillips, H.A., Saar, K., Reis, A., Johnson, E.W., Sutherland, G.R., Berkovic, S.F., & Mulley, J.C. (1998). Febrile seizures and generalised epilepsy associated with a mutation in the Na$^+$-channel β1 subunit gene SCN1B. *Nature Genetics, 19*, 366–370.

Wallander, J.L., & Thompson, R.J., Jr. (1995). Psychosocial adjustment of children with chronic physical conditions. In M.C. Roberts (Ed.), *Handbook of pediatric psychology* (2nd ed., pp. 124–141). New York: Grune & Stratton.

Wallander, J., Varni, J., Babini, L., Banis, H.T., & Wilcox (1989). Disability parameters, chronic strain, and adaptation of physically handiapped children and their mothers. *Journal of Pediatric Psychology, 14*, 23–42.

Walsh, K.W. (1978). *Neuropsychology: A clinical approach.* New York: Churchill Livingstone.

Walsh, K.W. (1985). *Understanding brain damage.* New York: Churchill Livingstone.

Wansart, W. (1990). Learning to solve a problem: A microanalysis of the solution strategies of children with learning disabilities. *Journal of Learning Disabilities, 23*, 164–170.

Ward, J.J., Margolis, H.S., Lum, M.K., Fraser, D.W., Bender, T.R., & Anderson, P. (1981). *Haemophilus influenzae* disease in Alaskan eskimos: Characteristics of a population with an unusual incidence of invasive disease. *Lancet, 1*, 1281–1284.

Warrington, E.K., & Shallice, T. (1984). Category specific semantic impairments. *Brain, 107*, 829–854.

Wasterlain, C.G. (1997). Recurrent seizures in the developing brain are harmful, *Epilepsia, 38*(6), 728–734.

Watanabe, K. (1996). Benign partial epilepsies. In S. Wallace (Ed.), *Epilepsy in childhood* (pp. 293–313). London: Chapman & Hall Medical.

Weber, B. (1989). Pathophysiology of diabetes mellitus. In C. Brook (Ed.), *Clinical paediatric endocrinology* (pp. 555–598). London: Blackwell Scientific.

Weber, G., Siragusa, V., Rondanina, G.F., Cerai, L.M., Mora, S., Colombino, J., Medaglini, S., Lia, C., Locatelli, T., Comi, G., & Chiumello, G. (1995). Neurophysiologic studies and cognitive function in congenital hypothyroid children. *Pediatric Research, 37*, 736–740.

Wechsler, D. (1974). *Manual for the Wechsler Scale of Children's Intelligence—Revised.* New York: Psychological Corporation.

Wechsler, D. (1989). *Manual for the Wechsler Preschool and Primary Scale of Intelligence—Revised.* San Antonio, TX: Psychological Corporation.

Wechsler, D. (1991). *Manual for the Wechsler Scale of Children's Intelligence—III.* San Antonio, TX: Psychological Corporation.

Wechsler, D. (1993). *Manual for the Wechsler Individual Achievement Test.* San Antonio, TX: Psychological Corporation.

Weglage, J., Funders, B., Ullrich, K., Rupp. A., & Schmidt, E. (1996). Psychosocial aspects in phenylketonuria. *European Journal of Pediatrics, 155*, S101–104.

Weil, M., & Levin, M. (1995). Infections of the nervous system. In J. Menkes (Ed.), *Textbook of child neurology* (pp. 379–509). Baltimore: Williams & Wilkins.

Weiland, S.K., Pless, I.B., & Roghmann, K.J. (1992). Chronic illness and mental health problems in pediatric practice: Results from a survey of primary care providers. *Pediatrics, 89*, 445–449.

Weinberger, D. (1987). Implications of normal brain development for the pathogenesis of schizophrenia. *Archives of General Psychiatry, 44*, 660–669.

Weissberg-Benchell, J., & Glasgow, A. (1997). The role of temperament in children with insulin-dependent diabetes mellitus. *Journal of Pediatric Psychology, 22*, 795–809.

Welch, K., & Lorenzo, A. (1991). Pathology of hydrocephalus. In C. Bannister & B. Tew (Eds.), *Current concepts in spina bifida and hydrocephalus* (pp. 55–82). New York: Cambridge University Press.

Welsh, M.C. (1996). A prefrontal dysfunction model of early-treated phenylketonuria. *European Journal of Pediatrics, 155*, 587–589.

Welsh, M.C., & Pennington, B.F. (1988). Assessing frontal lobe functioning in children: Views from developmental psychology. *Developmental Neuropsychology, 4*, 199–230.

Welsh, M.C., Pennington, B.F., & Groisser, D.B. (1991). A normative-developmental study of executive function: A window on prefrontal function in children. *Developmental Neuropsychology, 7*, 131–149.

Welsh, M.C., Pennington, B.F., Ozonoff, S., Rouse, B., & McCabe, E.R. (1990). Neuropsychology of early-treated phenylketonuria: Specific executive function deficits. *Child Development, 61*, 1697–1713.

Werther, G. (1994). Thyroid disorders in children. In M.J. Robinson & D. Roberton (Eds.), *Practical paediatrics* (3rd ed., pp. 520–526). Melbourne: Churchill Livingstone.

Wertlieb, D., Hauser, S., & Jacobson, A. (1986). Adaptation to diabetes: Behavior symptoms and family context. *Journal of Pediatric Psychology*, *11*, 463–479.

Westerveld, M., Zawacki, T., Spencer, S.S., Sass, K.J., Sass, A.T., & Spencer, D.D. (1993). Epilepsy surgery in children and adolescents: Cognitive outcome. *Epilepsia*, *34*(Suppl. 6), 36.

Whitley, R. (1990). Viral encephalitis. *New England Journal of Medicine*, *323*, 242–250.

Whitley, R., & Lakeman, F. (1995). Herpes simplex infections of the central nervous system: Therapeutic and diagnostic considerations. *Clinical Infectious Diseases*, *20*, 414–420.

Whitman, S., Hermann, B.P., Black, R.B., & Chhabria, S. (1982). Psychopathology and seizure type in children with epilepsy. *Psychological Medicine*, *12*, 843–853.

Wiig, E., & Secord, W. (1989). *Test of Language Competence—expanded edition: Administration manual level 1 and level 2*. San Antonio, TX: Psychological Corporation.

Wilkinson, G.S. (1993). *Wide Range Achievement Test—Revision 3*. Wilmington, DE: Jastak.

Williams, D., & Mateer, C. (1992). Developmental impact of frontal lobe injury in middle childhood. *Brain and Cognition*, *20*, 96–204.

Williams, J., Bates, S., Griebel, M.L., Lange, B., Mancias, P., Pihoker, C.M., & Dykman, R. (1998a). Does short-term antiepileptic drug treatment in children result in cognitive or behavioural changes? *Epilepsia*, *39*(10), 1064–1069.

Williams, J., Griebel, M.L., & Dykman, R.A. (1998b). Neuropsychological patterns in pediatric epilepsy. *Seizure*, *7*, 223–228.

Williams, J., Sharp, G., Lange, B., Bates, S., Griebel, M., Spence, G.T., & Thomas, P. (1996). The effects of seizure type, level of seizure control, and antiepileptic drugs on memory and attention skills in children with epilepsy. *Developmental Neuropsychology*, *12*, 241–253.

Williamson, M.L., Koch, R., Azen, C., & Chang, C. (1981). Correlates of intelligence test results in treated phenylketonuric children. *Paediatrics*, *68*, 161–167.

Williamson, P. (1992). Frontal lobe seizures: Problems of diagnosis and classification. *Advances in Neurology*, *57*, 289–309.

Willmott, C., Anderson, V., & Anderson, P. (2000) Attention following pediatric head injury: A developmental perspective. *Developmental Neuropsychology*, *17*, 361–379.

Willoughby, R., & Hoffman, R. (1979). Cognitive and perceptual impairments in children with spina bifida: A look at the evidence. *Spina Bifida Therapy*, *2*, 127–134.

Wills, K. (1993). Neuropsychological functioning in children with spina bifida and/or hydrocephalus. *Journal of clinical Child Psychology*, *22*, 247–265.

Wills, K., Holmbeck, G.N., Dillon, K., & McLone, D.G. (1990). Intelligence and achievement in children with myelomeningocele. *Journal of Pediatric Psychology*, *15*, 161–176.

Wilson, B.A., Baddeley, A.D., & Kapur, N. (1995). Dense amnesia in a professional musician following herpes simplex virus encephalitis. *Journal of Clinical and Experimental Neuropsychology*, *17*, 668–681.

Wilson, B.A., Evans, J., Alderman, N., Burgess, P., & Emslie, H. (1997). Behavioural assessment of the dysexecutive syndrome. In P. Rabbitt (Ed.), *Methodology of frontal and executive function* (pp. 239–248). Hove, UK: Psychology Press.

Wilson, B.A., Ivani-Chalian, R., & Aldrich, F. (1991). *The Rivermead Behavioural Memory Test for Children Aged 5 to 10 Years*. Cambridge, UK: Thames Valley Test Company.

Wilson, H., & Haltalin, K. (1975). Ampicillin in *Haemophilus influenzae* meningitis. *American Journal of the Disabled Child*, *129*, 208–215.

Wilson, J., Wiedmann, K., Hadley, D., Condon, B., Teasdale, G., & Brooks, D. (1988). Early and late magnetic resonance imaging and neuropsychological outcome after head injury. *Journal of Neurology, Neurosurgery, and Psychiatry*, *51*, 391–396.

Wing, S. (1981). Asperger's syndrome: A clinical account. *Psychological Medicine*, *11*, 115–130.

Winogron, H.W., Knights, R.M., & Bawden, H.N. (1984). Neuropsychological deficits following head injury in children. *Journal of Clinical Neuropsychology*, *6*, 269–286.

Wirt, R., Lachar, D., Klinedinst, J., & Seat, P. (1977). *Multidimensional description of child personality: A manual for the Personality Inventory for Children*. Los Angeles, CA: Western Psychology Services.

Witelson, S. (1976). Sex and the single hemisphere: Specialization of the right hemisphere for spatial processing. *Science*, *193*, 425–427.

Witelson, S., Glezen, H., & Kigar, D. (1995). Woman have greater density of neurons in posterior temporal cortex. *Journal of Neurosciences*, *15*, 3418–3428.

Witelson, S., & Pallie, W. (1973). Left hemisphere specialization language in the newborn: Neuroanatomical evidence of asymmetry, *Brain*, *96*, 641–646.

Witkin, H., Oltman, P., Raskin, E., & Karp, S. (1971). *Children's Embedded Figures Test—manual*. Palo Alto, CA: Consulting Psychologists Press.

Wolf, R.L., Ivnik, R.J., Hirshorn, K.A., Sharborough, F.W., Casino, G.D., & Marsh, W.R. (1993). Neurocognitive efficiency following left temporal lobectomy: Standard versus limited resection. *Journal of Neursurgery*, *79*, 76–83.

Wolf, S.M., Forsythe, A., Stunden, A.A., Friedman, R., & Diamond, H. (1981). Long-term effect of phenobarbital on cognitive function in children with febrile convulsions. *Pediatrics*, *68*(6), 820–823.

Wolters, C.A., Yu, S.L., Hagen, J.W., & Kail, R. (1996). Short-term memory and strategy use in children with insulin-dependent diabetes mellitus. *Journal of Consulting and Clinical Psychology*, *64*, 1397–1405.

Wood, K.M., & Richman, L.C. (1988). Developmental trends within memory deficient reading disability groups. *Developmental Neuropsychology*, *4*, 261–274.

Woodcock, R., & Mather, N. (1989). *Woodcock–Johnson Tests of Achievement: Examiner's manual*. Allen Park, TX: DLM Teaching Services.

Woods, B. (1980). The restricted effects of right hemisphere lesions after age one: Wechsler test data. *Neuropsychologia*, *18*, 65–70.

Woods, B., & Carey, S. (1979). Language deficits after apparent recovery from childhood aphasia. *Annals of Neurology*, *6*, 405–409.

Wrennall, J., & Hopkins, I. (1989). Neuropsychological and psychosocial outcome of temporal lobectomy in children. In V. Anderson & M. Bailey, (Eds.), *Theory and function bridging the gap: Proceedings of the 14th annual Brain Impairment Conference*. Melbourne: ASSBI.

Wrennall, J., Pentland, L., & Harvey, A.S. (1998). *The impact of temporal lobe epilepsy during childhood: A five year follow-up*. Paper presented at the Australian annual meeting of the College of Clinical Neuropsychologists, Lorne.

Wright, M., & Nolan, T. (1994). Impact of cyanotic heart disease on school performance. *Archives of Disease in Childhood*, *71*, 64–70.

Wrightson, P., McGinn, V., & Gronwall, D. (1995). Mild head injury in preschool children: Evidence that it can be associated with persisting cognitive defect. *Journal of Neurology, Neurosurgery, and Psychiatry*, *59*, 375–380.

Wyllie, E. (1996). *The treatment of epilepsy: Principles and practice* (2nd ed.). Baltimore: Williams & Wilkins.

Wyllie, E., & Lüders, H. (1996a). Classification of seizures. In E. Wyllie (Ed.), *The treatment of epilepsy: Principles and practice* (2nd ed., pp 355–363). Baltimore: Williams & Wilkins.

Wyllie, E., & Lüders, H. (1996b). Classification of the epilepsies. In E. Wyllie (Ed.), *The treatment of epilepsy: Principles and practice* (2nd ed., pp. 364–375). Baltimore: Williams & Wilkins.

Wysocki, T., Huxtable, K., Linscheid, R., & Wayne, W. (1989). Adjustment to diabetes mellitus in preschoolers and their mothers. *Diabetes Care*, *12*, 524–529.

Yamatogi, Y., & Ohtahara, S. (1981). Age-dependent epileptic encephalopathy: A longitudinal study. *Folia Psychiatrica et Neurologica Japonica, 35*, 321–332.

Yakovlev, P.I. (1962). Morphological criteria of growth and maturation of the nervous system in man. *Research Publications Association for Research in Nervous and Mental Disease, 39*, 3–46.

Yakovlev, P.I., & Lecours, A.R. (1967). The myelogenetic cycles of regional maturation of the brain. In A. Minkiniwski (Ed.), *Regional development of the brain in early life* (pp. 3–10). Oxford: Blackwell.

Yeates, K. (1999). Closed-head injury. In K.O. Yeates, M.D. Ris, & H.G. Taylor (Eds.), *Pediatric neuropsychology: Research, theory and practice* (pp. 192–218). New York: Guilford Press.

Yeates, K., Blumstein, E., Patterson, C.M., & Delis, D.C. (1995). Verbal memory and learning following pediatric closed head injury. *Journal of the International Neuropsychological Society, 1*, 78–87.

Yeates, K., & Bornstein, R. (1994). Attention deficit disorder and neuropsychological functioning in children with Tourette's syndrome. *Neuropsychology, 8*, 65–74.

Yeates, K., Enrile, B., & Loss, N. (1998). Spina bifida and hydrocephalus. In E. Coffey & R. Brumback (Eds.), *Texbook of pediatric neuropsychiatry* (pp. 1141–1165). Washington: Blackwell Science.

Yeates, K., Enrile, B., Loss, N., Blumenstein, E., & Delis, D. (1995). Verbal learning and memory in children with myelomeningocele. *Journal of Pediatric Psychology, 20*, 801–815.

Yeates, K., Taylor, H.G., Drotar, D., Wade, S., Stancin, T., & Klein, S. (1997) Pre-injury environment as a determinant of recovery from traumatic brain injuries in school-aged children. *Journal of the International Neuropsychological Society, 3*, 617–630.

Ylivasaker, M. (Ed.). (1985). *Head injury rehabilitation: Children, and adolescents.* London: Taylor & Francis.

Yoneda, Y., Mori, E., Yamashita, H., & Yamadori, A. (1994). MRI volumetry of medial temporal lobe structures in amnesia following herpes simplex encephalitis. *European Neurology, 34*, 243–252.

Young, H., Nulsen, F., Weiss, M., & Thomas, P. (1973). The relationship of intelligence and cerebral mantle in treated infantile hydrocephalus. *Pediatrics, 52*, 54–60.

Zangwill, O.L. (1946). Some qualitative observations on verbal memory in cases of cerebral lesion. *British Journal of Psychology, 37*, 8–19.

Zeiner, H., & Prigatano, G. (1982). Information processing deficits in hydrocephalic and letter reversal children. *Neuropsychologia, 20*, 483–490

Zeiner, H., Prigatano, G., Pollay, M., Briscoe, C., & Smith, R. (1985). Ocular motility, visual acuity and dysfunction of neuropsychological impairment in children with shunted uncomplicated hydrocephalus. *Child's Nervous System, 1*, 115–122.

Zentner, J., Steidele, S., Kowalik, A. Hufnagel, A., Ostertun, B., Wolf, H.K., Lendt, W.M., & Elger C.E. (1995). Surgical treatment of temporal lobe epilepsy in children. *Epilepsia, 36*(Suppl. 3), 23.

Zola-Morgan, S., & Squire, L.R. (1993). Neuroanatomy of memory. *Annual Review of Science, 16*, 547–563.

Author index

Subject index